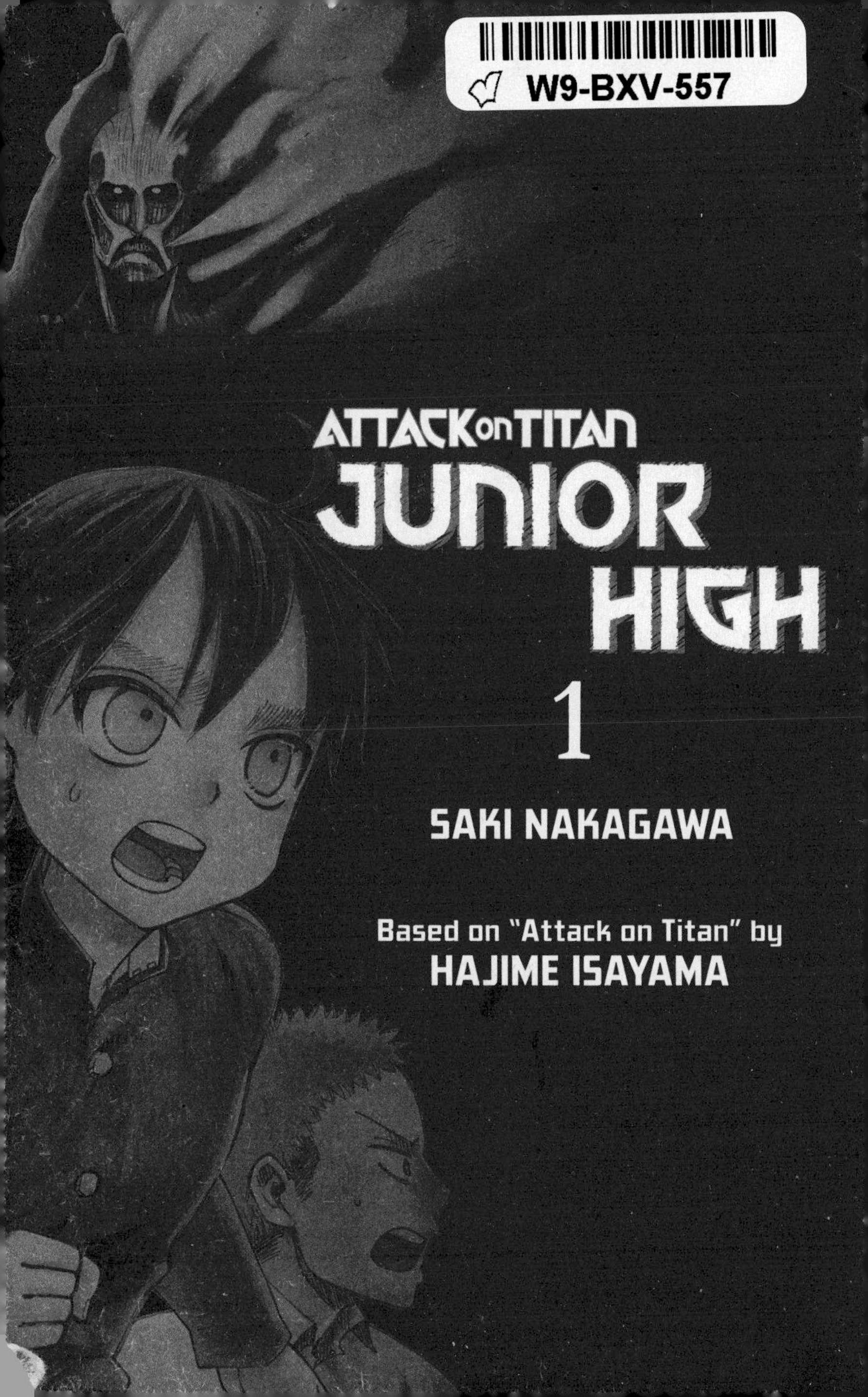

ATTACK on TITAN JUNIOR HIGH

1

SAKI NAKAGAWA

Based on "Attack on Titan" by

HAJIME ISAYAMA

Contents

SCHEDULE FOR WEDNESDAY, APRIL 9

EREN

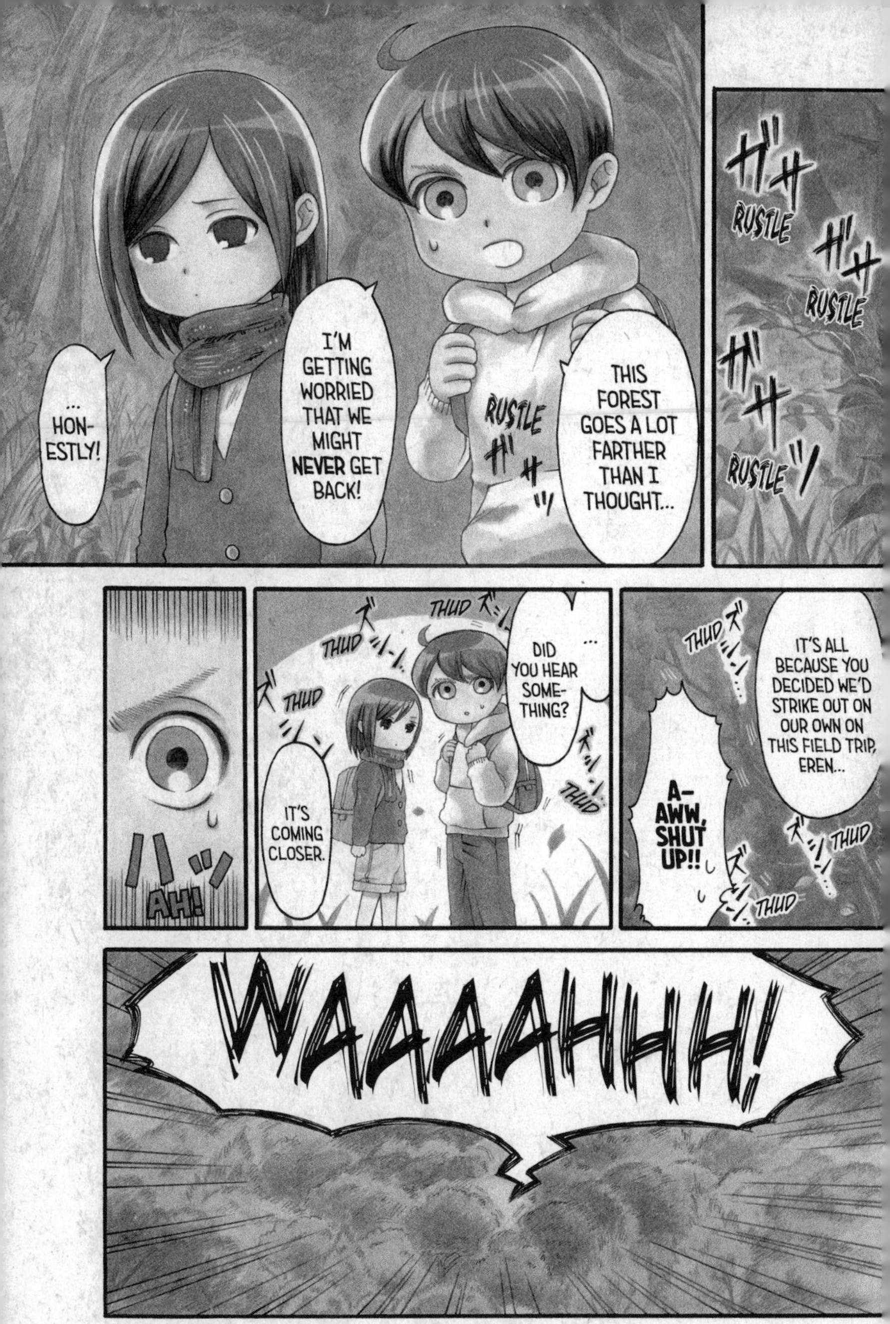
RUSTLE
RUSTLE
RUSTLE
THIS FOREST GOES A LOT FARTHER THAN I THOUGHT...
RUSTLE
I'M GETTING WORRIED THAT WE MIGHT NEVER GET BACK!
... HONESTLY!
IT'S ALL BECAUSE YOU DECIDED WE'D STRIKE OUT ON OUR OWN ON THIS FIELD TRIP, EREN...
THUD
A-AWW, SHUT UP!!
THUD
THUD
... DID YOU HEAR SOMETHING?
THUD
THUD
THUD
THUD
IT'S COMING CLOSER.
AH!
WAAAAHHH!

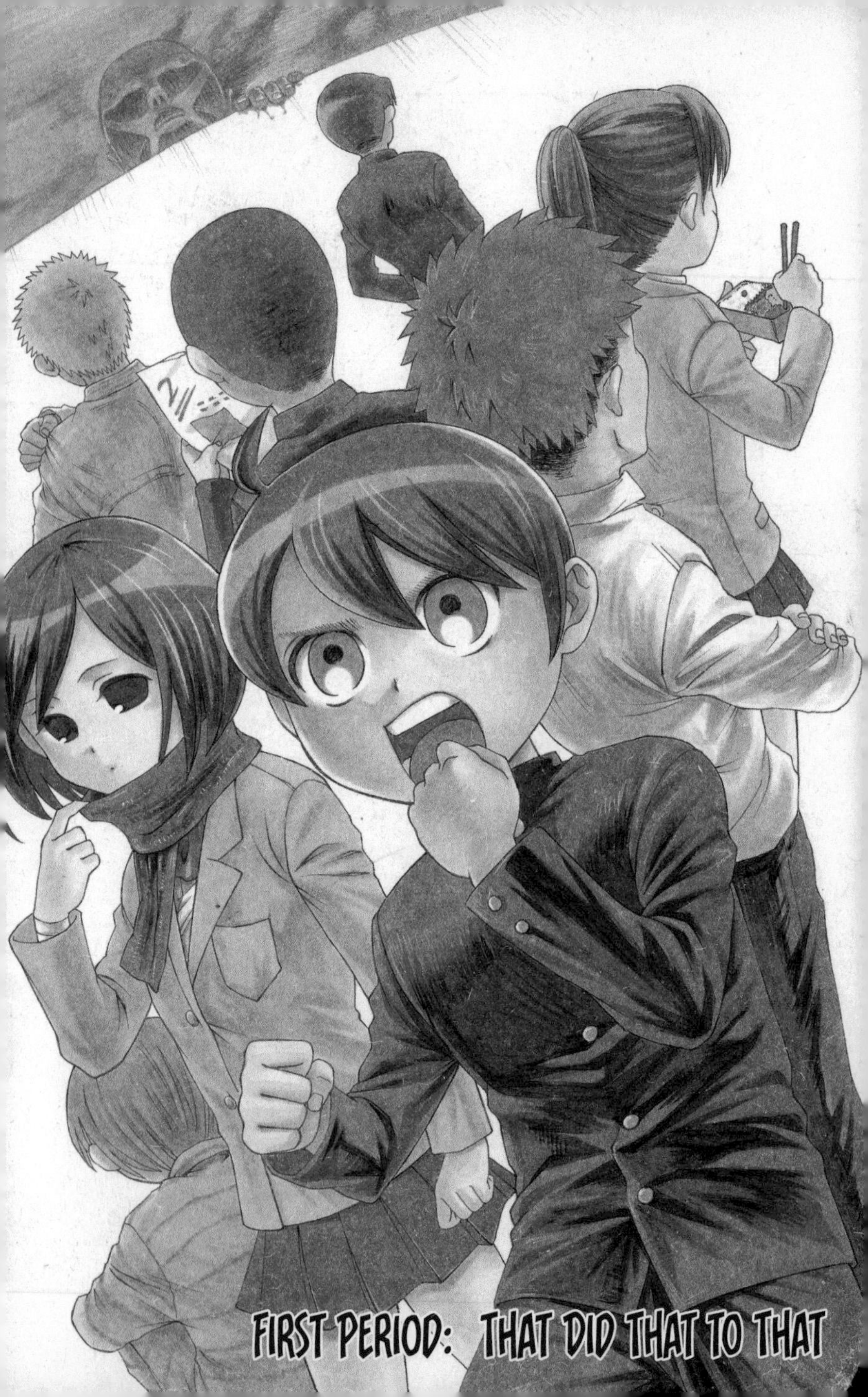

FIRST PERIOD: THAT DID THAT TO THAT

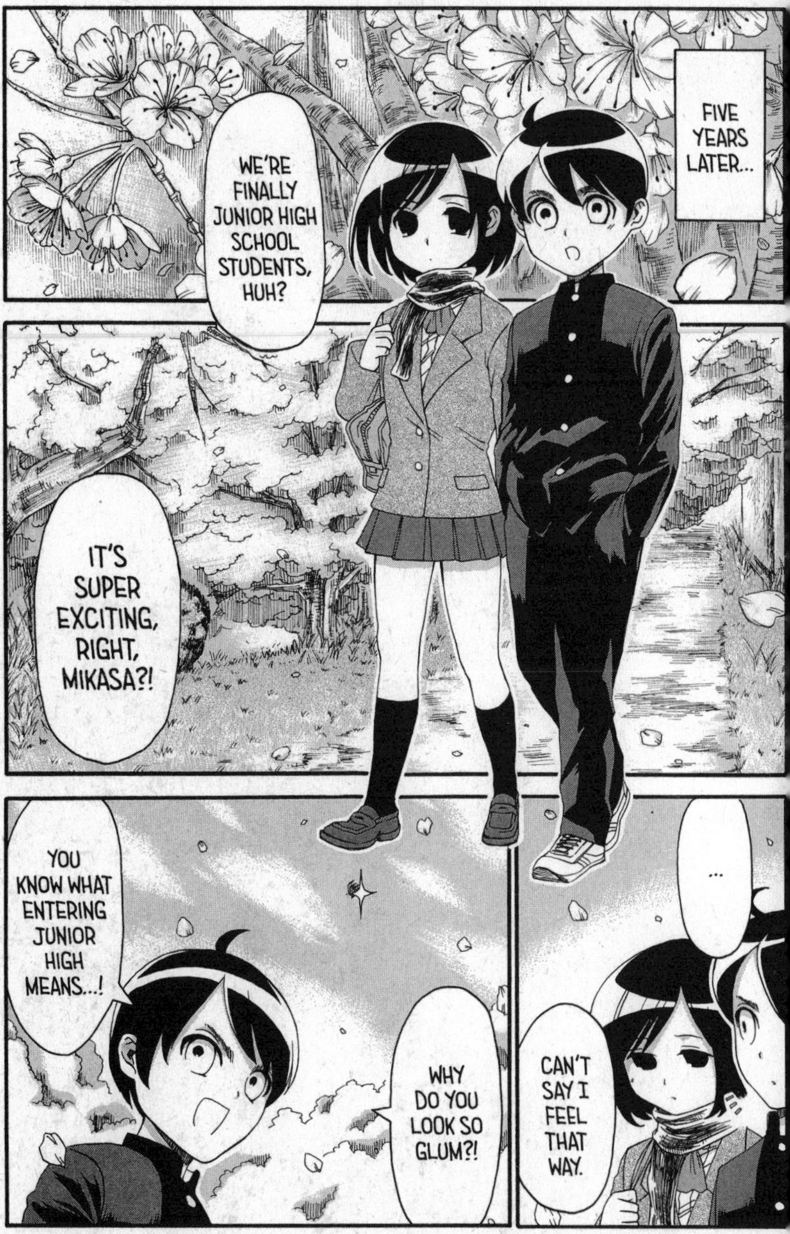
FIVE YEARS LATER...
WE'RE FINALLY JUNIOR HIGH SCHOOL STUDENTS, HUH?
IT'S SUPER EXCITING, RIGHT, MIKASA?!
...
CAN'T SAY I FEEL THAT WAY.
WHY DO YOU LOOK SO GLUM?!
YOU KNOW WHAT ENTERING JUNIOR HIGH MEANS...!

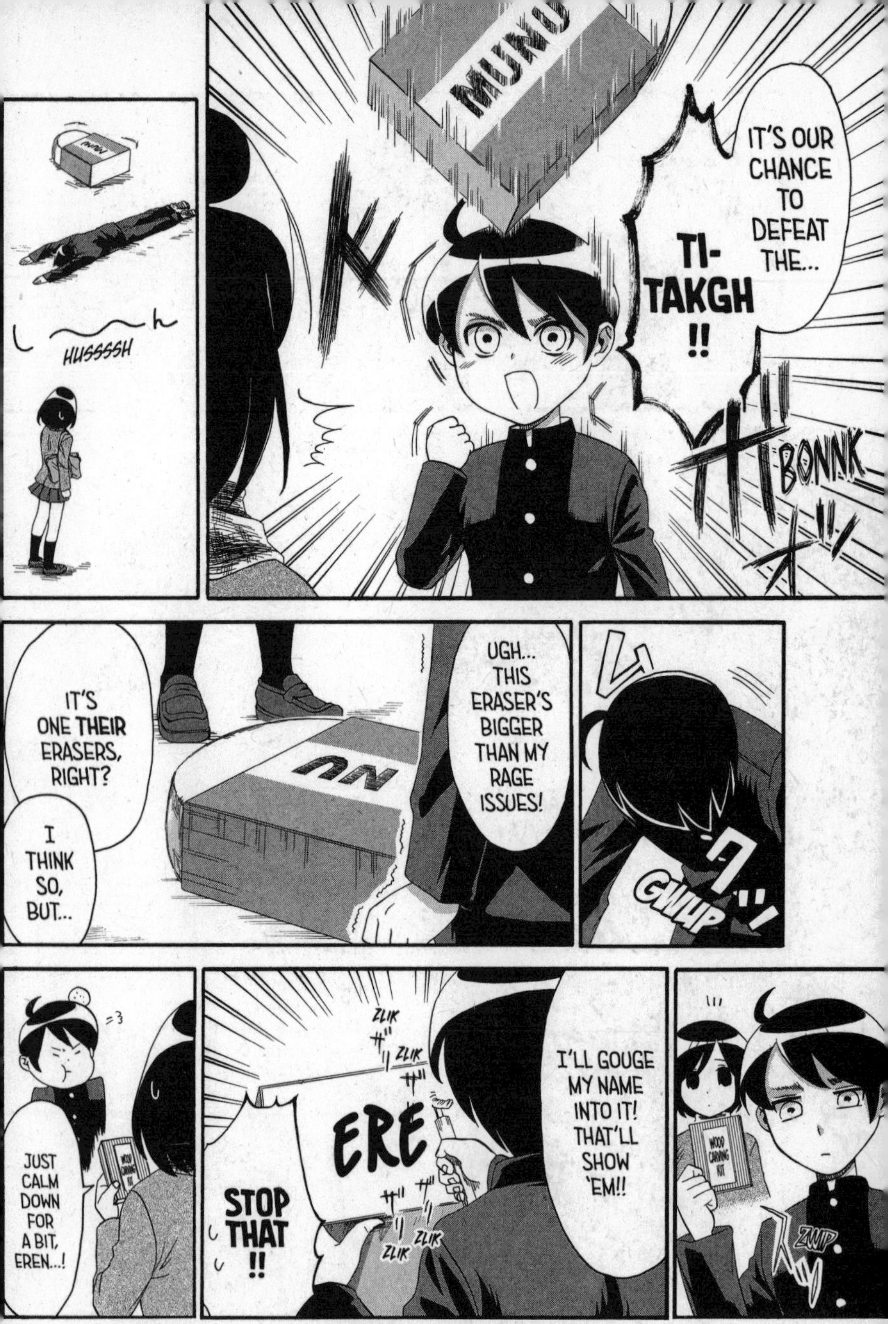
MUNU
IT'S OUR CHANCE TO DEFEAT THE...
TI-TAKGH!!
BONNK
HUSSSSH
GWUP
UGH... THIS ERASER'S BIGGER THAN MY RAGE ISSUES!
NU
IT'S ONE THEIR ERASERS, RIGHT?
I THINK SO, BUT...
WOOD CARVING KIT
ZWIP
I'LL GOUGE MY NAME INTO IT! THAT'LL SHOW 'EM!!
ZLIK
ZLIK
ERE
ZLIK
ZLIK
STOP THAT!!
JUST CALM DOWN FOR A BIT, EREN...!

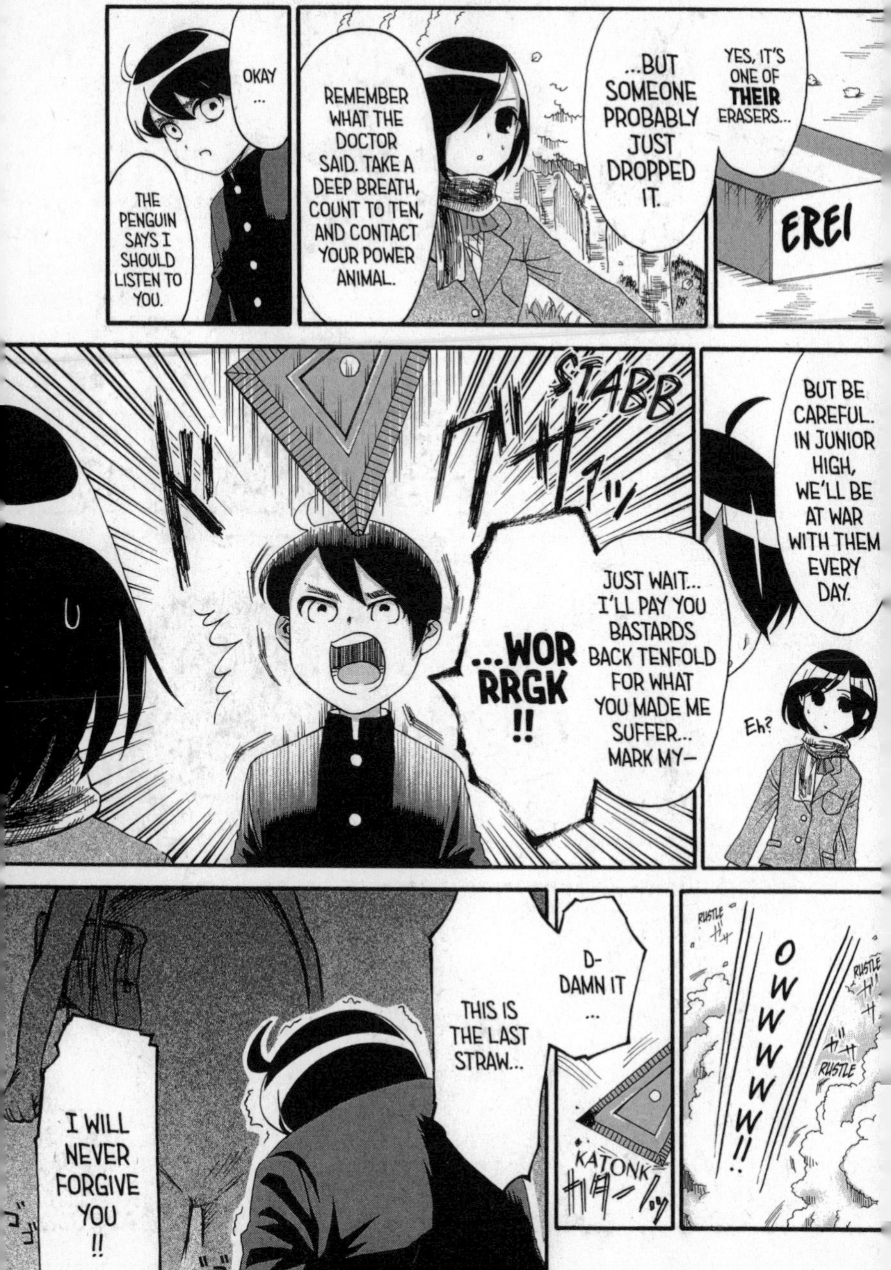
YES, IT'S ONE OF THEIR ERASERS...
EREI
...BUT SOMEONE PROBABLY JUST DROPPED IT.
REMEMBER WHAT THE DOCTOR SAID. TAKE A DEEP BREATH, COUNT TO TEN, AND CONTACT YOUR POWER ANIMAL.
OKAY ...
THE PENGUIN SAYS I SHOULD LISTEN TO YOU.
BUT BE CAREFUL. IN JUNIOR HIGH, WE'LL BE AT WAR WITH THEM EVERY DAY.
Eh?
STABB
JUST WAIT... I'LL PAY YOU BASTARDS BACK TENFOLD FOR WHAT YOU MADE ME SUFFER... MARK MY—
...WORRRGK !!
RUSTLE
OWWWWWWW!!
RUSTLE
RUSTLE
D-DAMN IT ...
KATONK
THIS IS THE LAST STRAW...
I WILL NEVER FORGIVE YOU !!
RUMMBLE

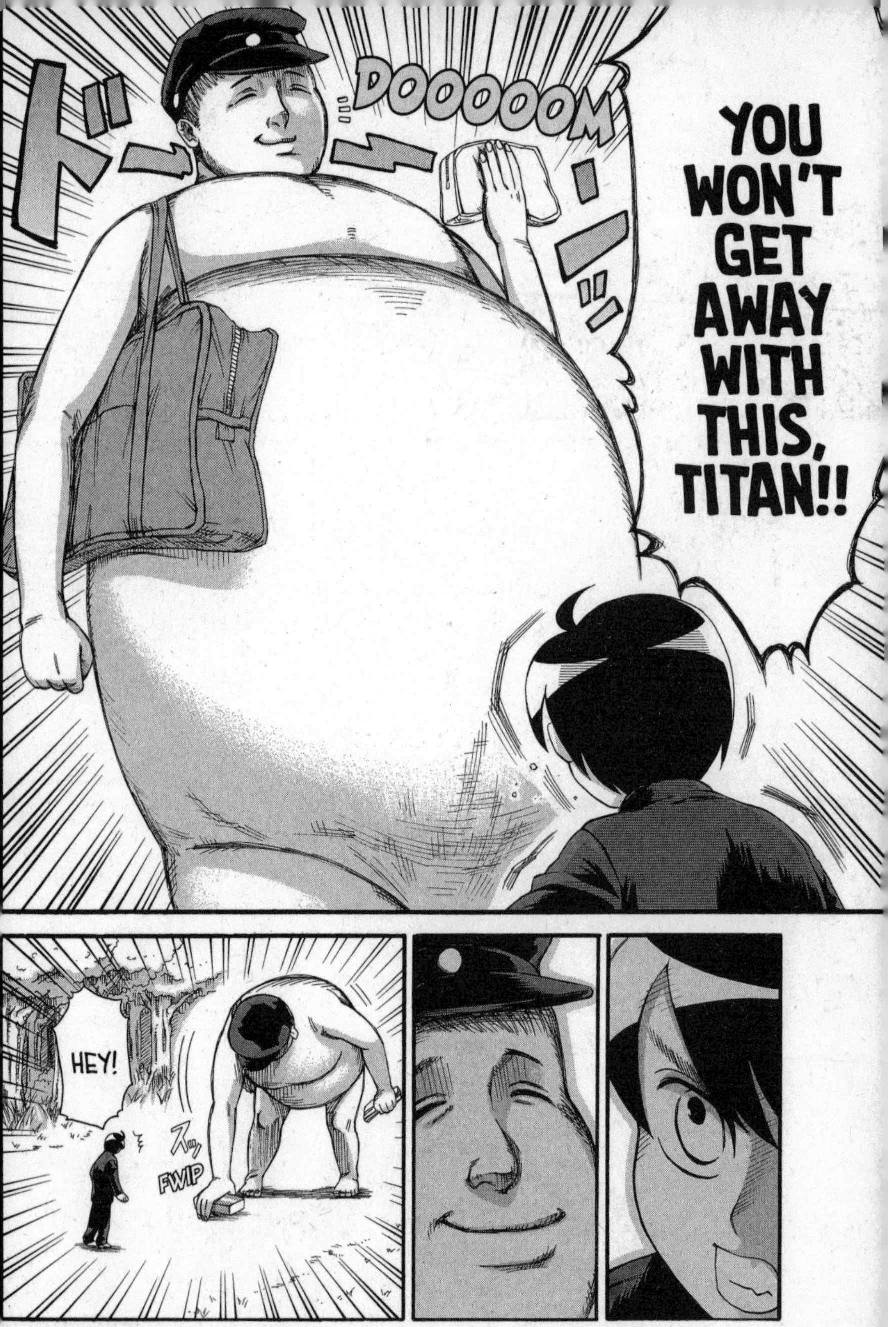
DOOOOOM
YOU WON'T GET AWAY WITH THIS, TITAN!!
HEY!
スッ
FWIP

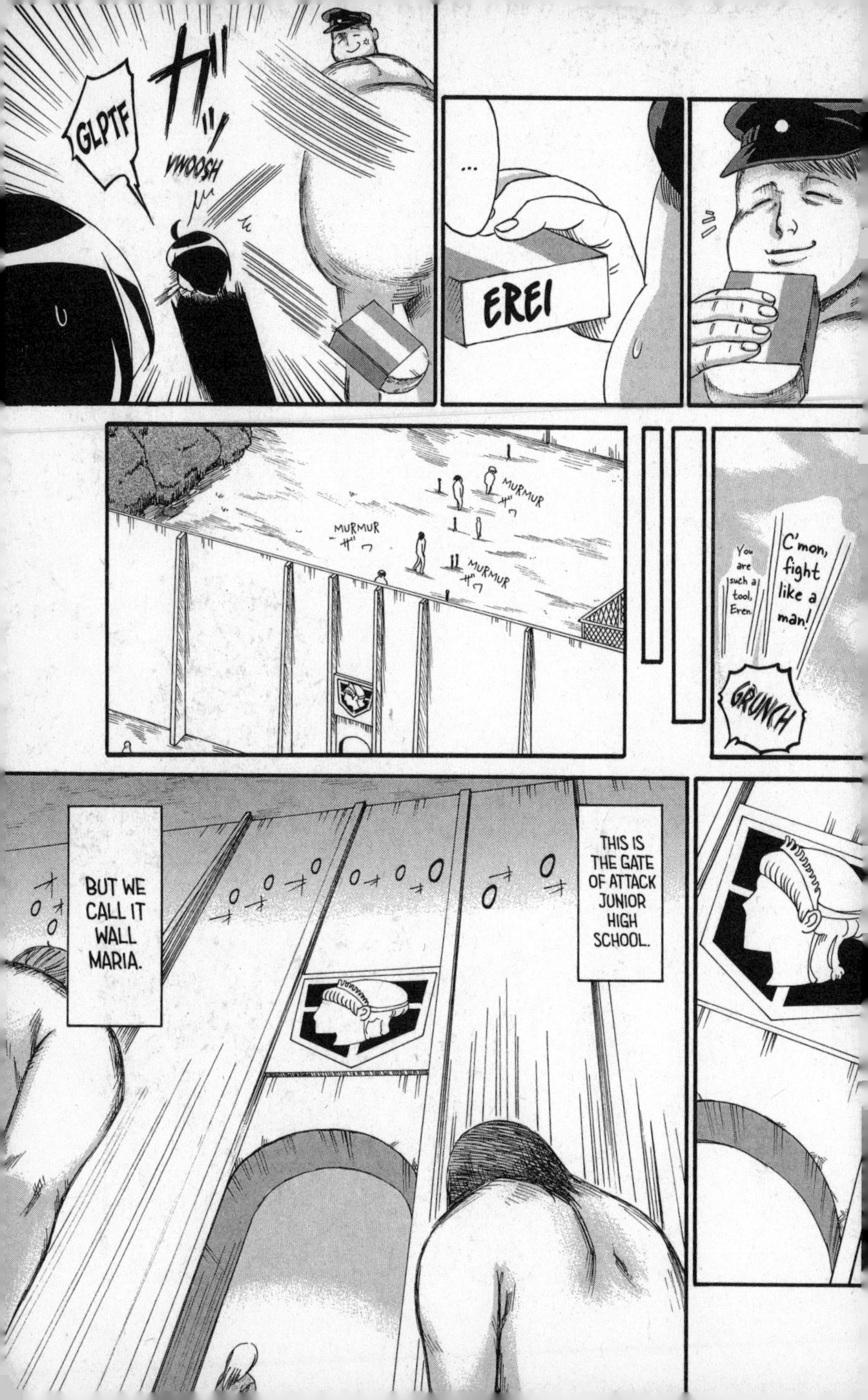
...
EREI
GLPTF
VWOOSH
C'mon, fight like a man!
You are such a tool, Eren.
GRUNCH
MURMUR
MURMUR
MURMUR
THIS IS THE GATE OF ATTACK JUNIOR HIGH SCHOOL.
BUT WE CALL IT WALL MARIA.

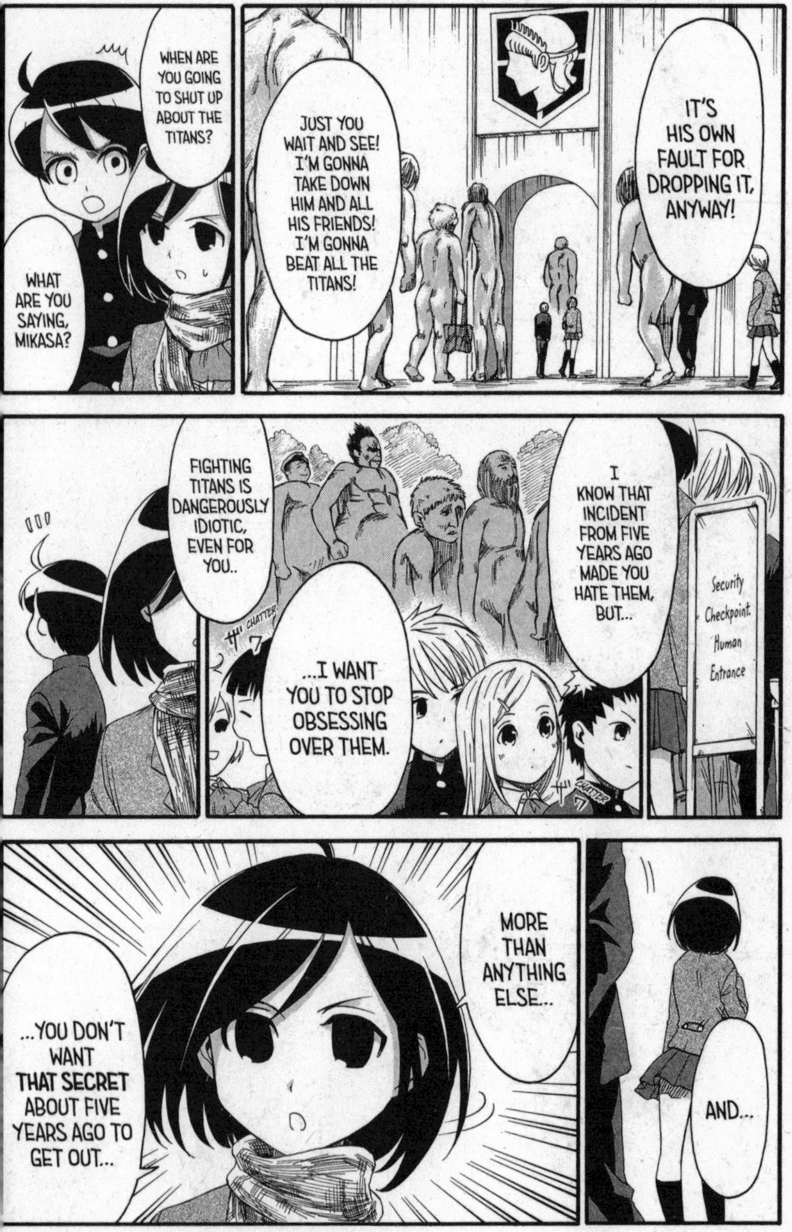
IT'S HIS OWN FAULT FOR DROPPING IT, ANYWAY!
JUST YOU WAIT AND SEE! I'M GONNA TAKE DOWN HIM AND ALL HIS FRIENDS! I'M GONNA BEAT ALL THE TITANS!
WHEN ARE YOU GOING TO SHUT UP ABOUT THE TITANS?
WHAT ARE YOU SAYING, MIKASA?
Security Checkpoint Human Entrance
I KNOW THAT INCIDENT FROM FIVE YEARS AGO MADE YOU HATE THEM, BUT...
CHATTER
...I WANT YOU TO STOP OBSESSING OVER THEM.
CHATTER
FIGHTING TITANS IS DANGEROUSLY IDIOTIC, EVEN FOR YOU..
AND...
MORE THAN ANYTHING ELSE...
...YOU DON'T WANT THAT SECRET ABOUT FIVE YEARS AGO TO GET OUT...

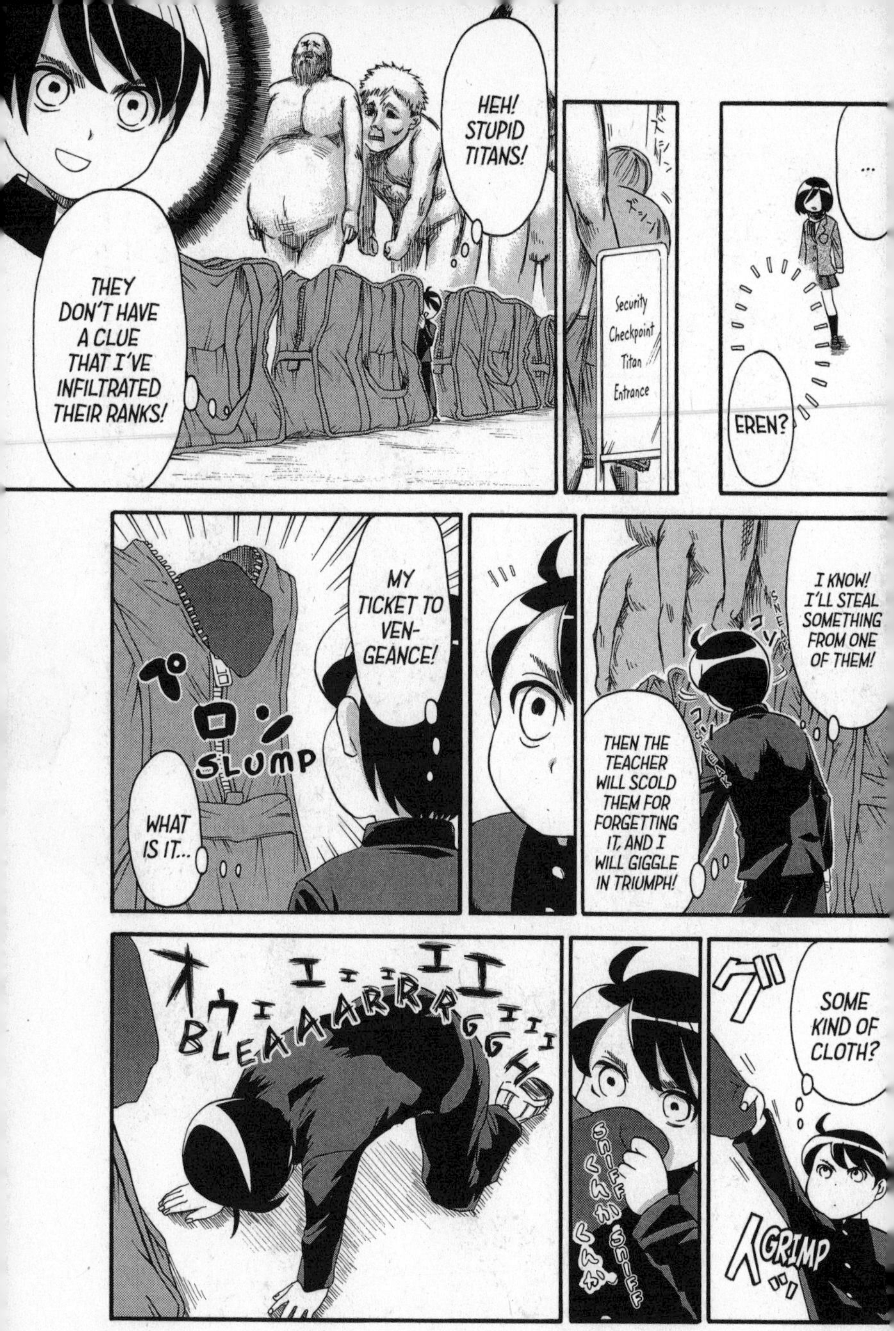
...
EREN?
Security Checkpoint Titan Entrance
HEH! STUPID TITANS!
THEY DON'T HAVE A CLUE THAT I'VE INFILTRATED THEIR RANKS!
I KNOW! I'LL STEAL SOMETHING FROM ONE OF THEM!
SNEAK
THEN THE TEACHER WILL SCOLD THEM FOR FORGETTING IT, AND I WILL GIGGLE IN TRIUMPH!
SNEAK
MY TICKET TO VEN-GEANCE!
SLUMP
WHAT IS IT...
SOME KIND OF CLOTH?
GRIMP
SNIFF SNIFF
BLEAAARRRGGH

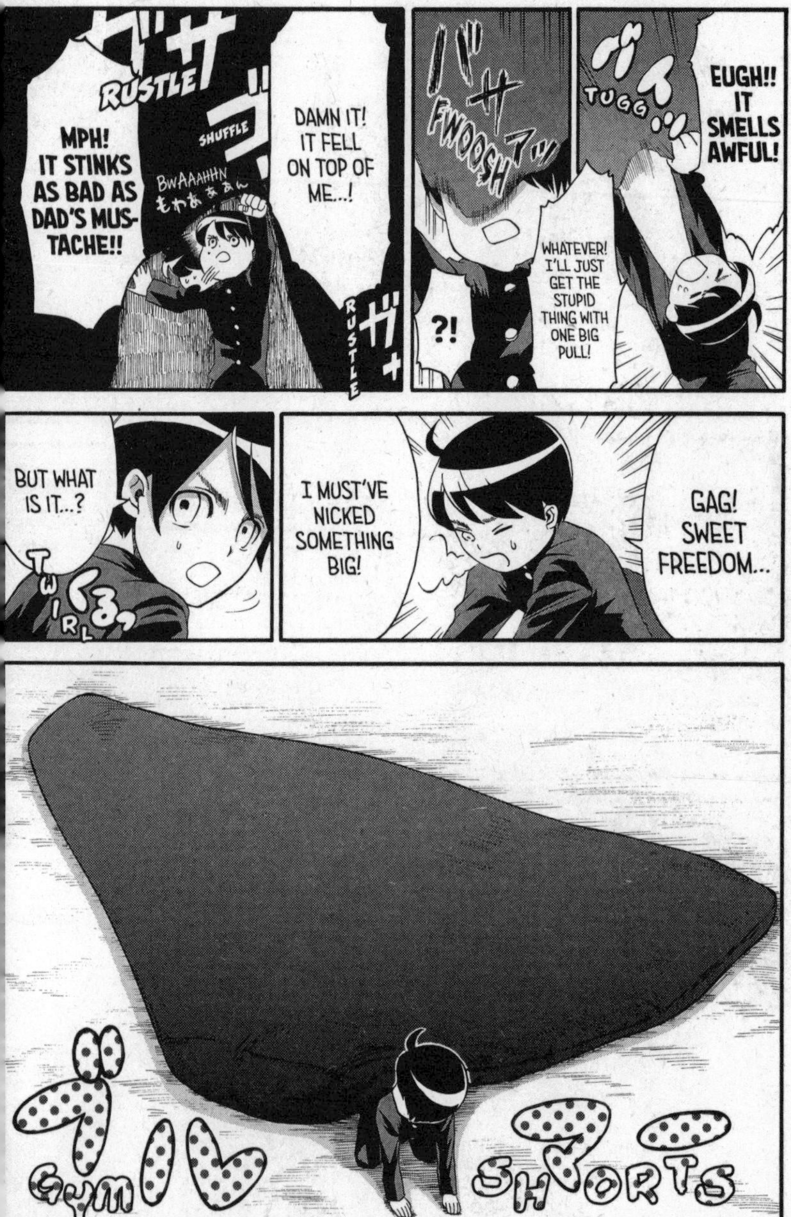
EUGH!! IT SMELLS AWFUL!
TUGG
WHATEVER! I'LL JUST GET THE STUPID THING WITH ONE BIG PULL!
FWOOSH
?!
DAMN IT! IT FELL ON TOP OF ME...!
RUSTLE
SHUFFLE
MPH! IT STINKS AS BAD AS DAD'S MUS-TACHE!!
BWAAAHHN
もわあぁあん
RUSTLE
GAG! SWEET FREEDOM...
I MUST'VE NICKED SOMETHING BIG!
BUT WHAT IS IT...?
TWIRL
SHORTS
GYM

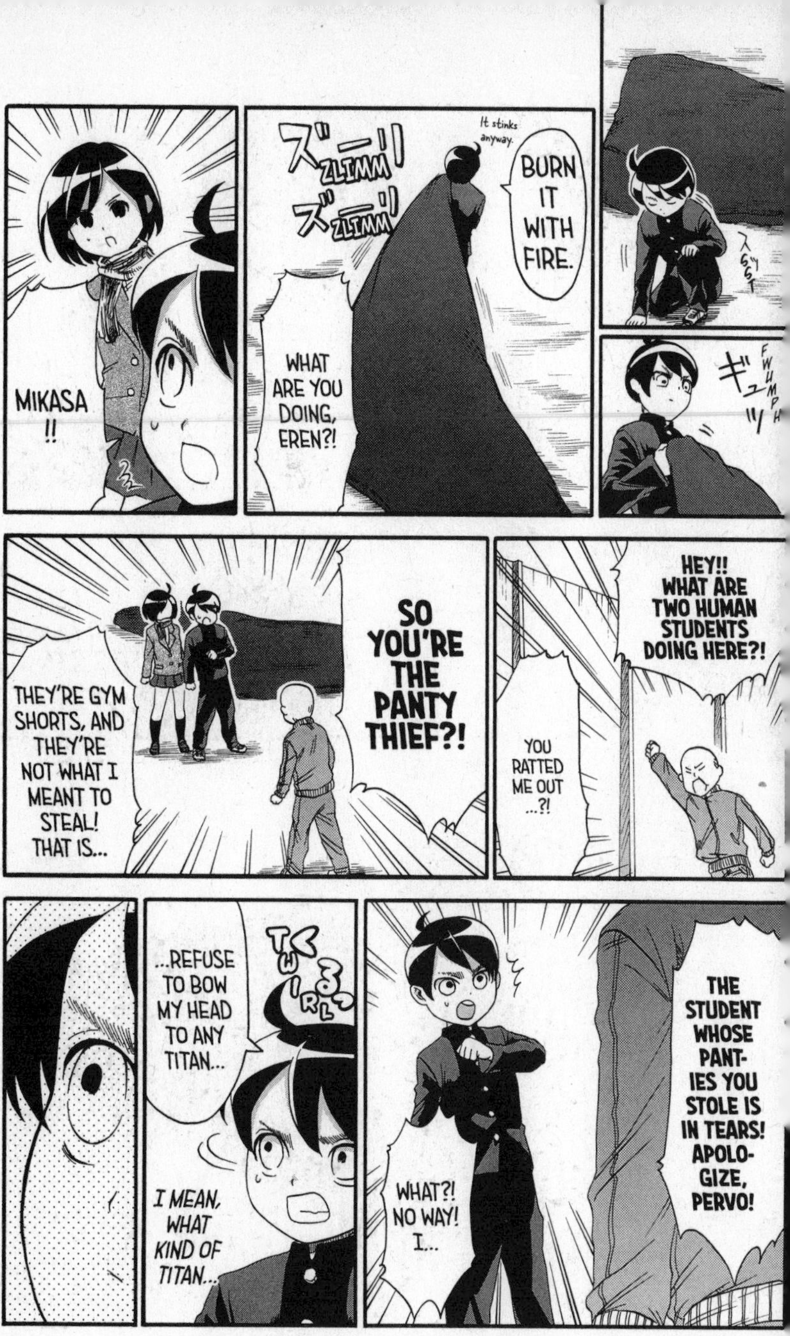
ギュッ
FWUMPH
ズーーリ
ZLIMM
ズーーリ
ZLIMM
It stinks anyway.
BURN IT WITH FIRE.
WHAT ARE YOU DOING, EREN?!
MIKASA !!
HEY!! WHAT ARE TWO HUMAN STUDENTS DOING HERE?!
YOU RATTED ME OUT ...?!
SO YOU'RE THE PANTY THIEF?!
THEY'RE GYM SHORTS, AND THEY'RE NOT WHAT I MEANT TO STEAL! THAT IS...
THE STUDENT WHOSE PANT-IES YOU STOLE IS IN TEARS! APOLO-GIZE, PERVO!
WHAT?! NO WAY! I...
くるっ
THWIRL
...REFUSE TO BOW MY HEAD TO ANY TITAN...
I MEAN, WHAT KIND OF TITAN...

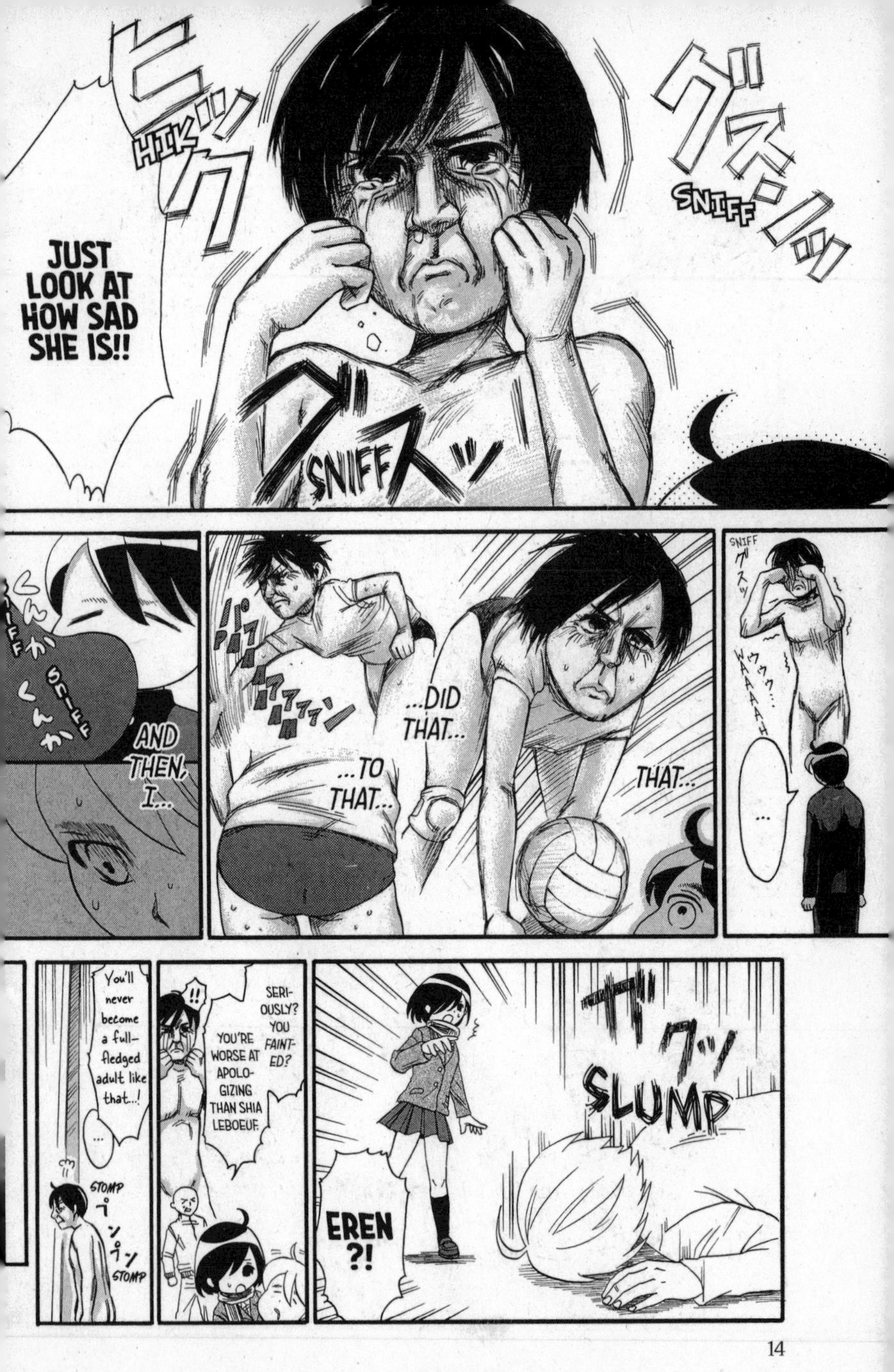
HIK
SNIFF
JUST LOOK AT HOW SAD SHE IS!!
SNIFF
SNIFF
WAAAAH
...
THAT...
...DID THAT...
...TO THAT...
SNIFF
SNIFF
AND THEN, I...
SLUMP
EREN?!
SERIOUSLY? YOU FAINTED?
YOU'RE WORSE AT APOLOGIZING THAN SHIA LEBOEUF.
!!
You'll never become a full-fledged adult like that...!
...
STOMP
STOMP

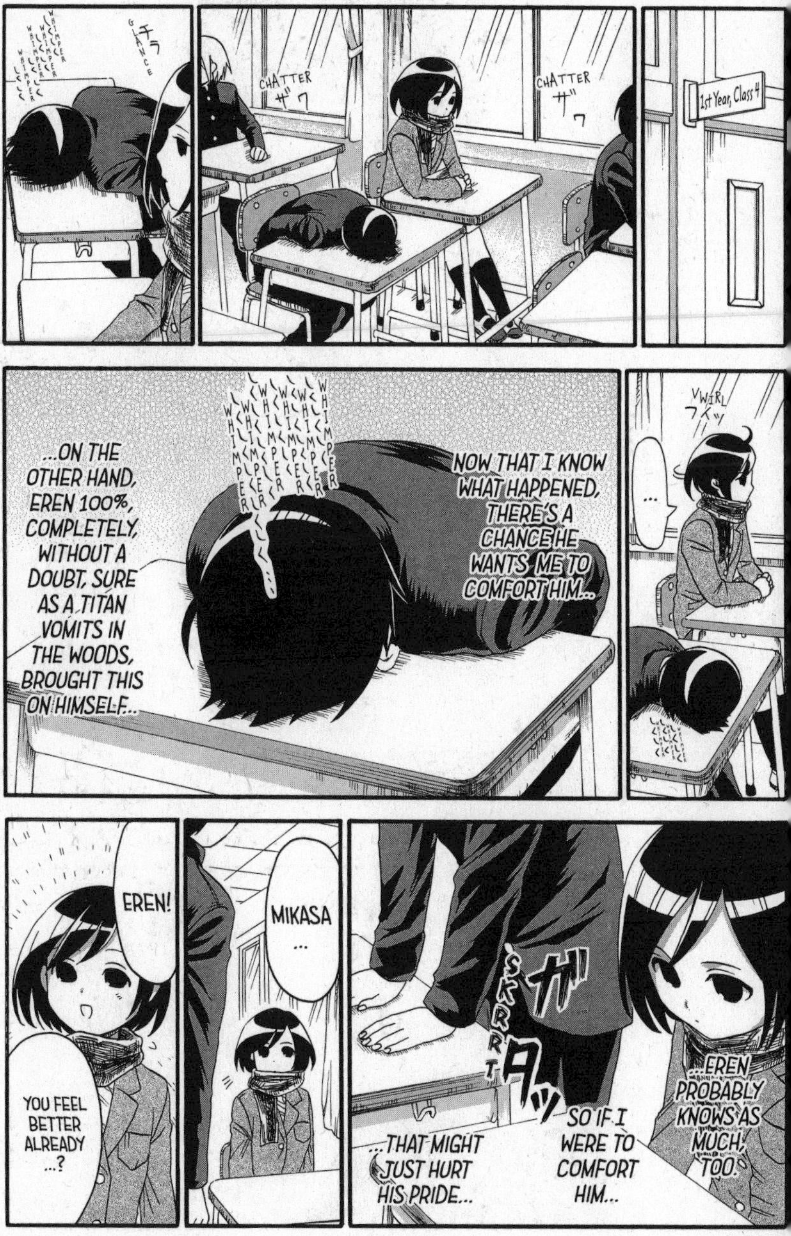
1st Year, Class 4
CHATTER
ザワ
CHATTER
ザワ
GLANCE
チラ
WHIMPER
VWIRL
フイッ
...
NOW THAT I KNOW WHAT HAPPENED, THERE'S A CHANCE HE WANTS ME TO COMFORT HIM...
WHIMPER
...ON THE OTHER HAND, EREN 100%, COMPLETELY, WITHOUT A DOUBT, SURE AS A TITAN VOMITS IN THE WOODS, BROUGHT THIS ON HIMSELF...
EREN PROBABLY KNOWS AS MUCH, TOO.
SO IF I WERE TO COMFORT HIM...
...THAT MIGHT JUST HURT HIS PRIDE...
SKRRRT
ガタッ
MIKASA ...
EREN!
YOU FEEL BETTER ALREADY ...?

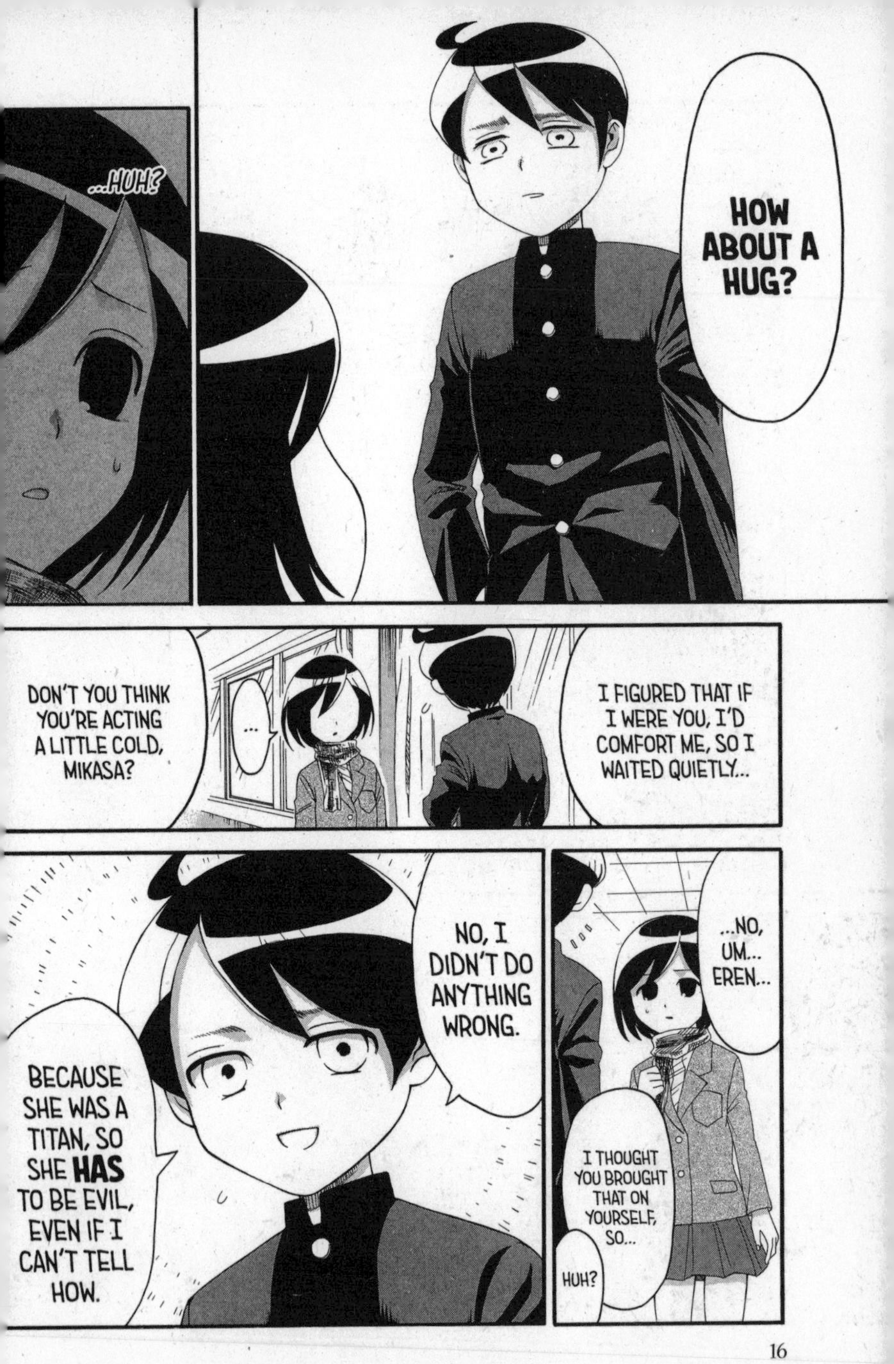
HOW ABOUT A HUG?
...HUH?
I FIGURED THAT IF I WERE YOU, I'D COMFORT ME, SO I WAITED QUIETLY...
...
DON'T YOU THINK YOU'RE ACTING A LITTLE COLD, MIKASA?
...NO, UM... EREN...
I THOUGHT YOU BROUGHT THAT ON YOURSELF, SO...
HUH?
NO, I DIDN'T DO ANYTHING WRONG.
BECAUSE SHE WAS A TITAN, SO SHE **HAS** TO BE EVIL, EVEN IF I CAN'T TELL HOW.

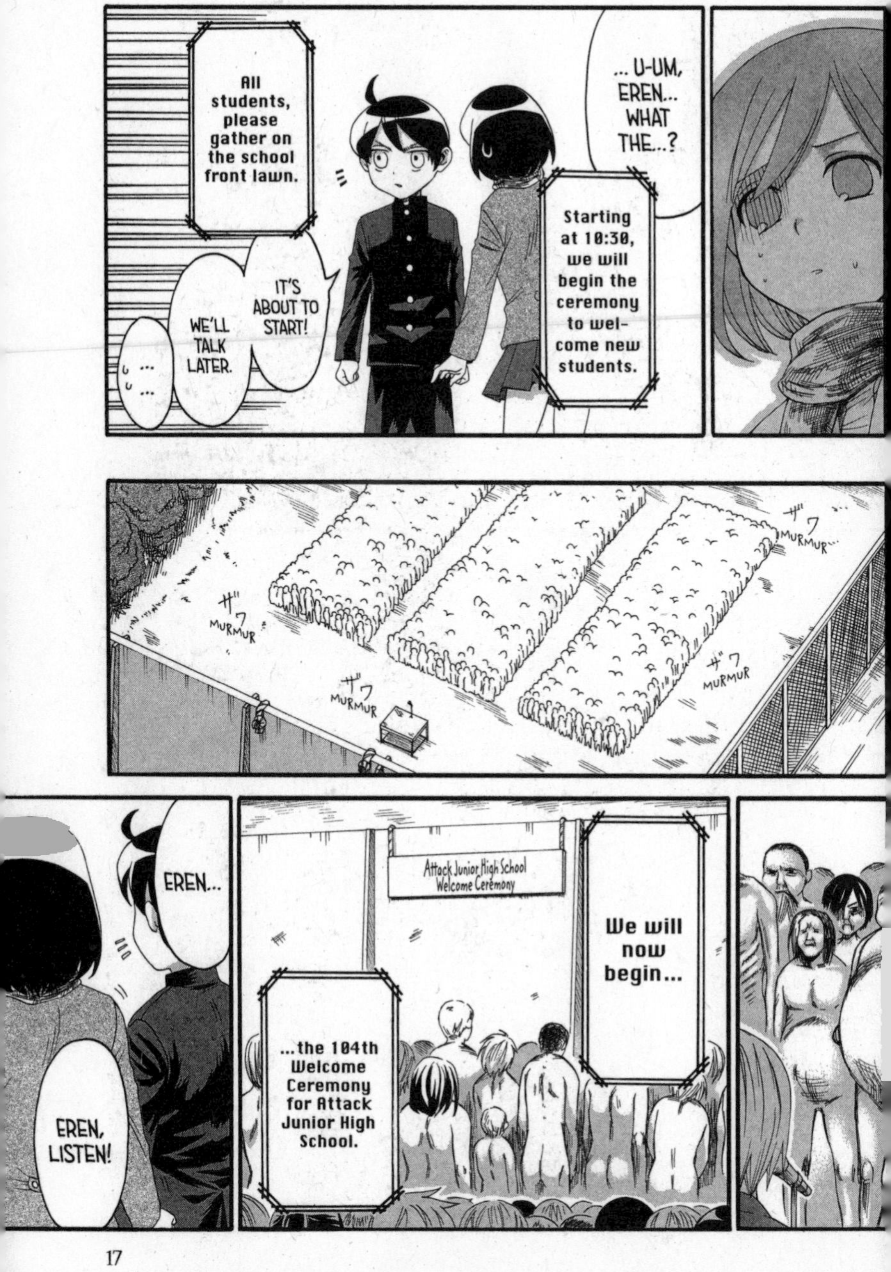
... U-UM, EREN... WHAT THE...?
Starting at 10:30, we will begin the ceremony to welcome new students.
All students, please gather on the school front lawn.
IT'S ABOUT TO START!
WE'LL TALK LATER.
... ...
ザワ MURMUR...
ザワ MURMUR
ザワ MURMUR
ザワ MURMUR
We will now begin...
Attack Junior High School Welcome Ceremony
...the 104th Welcome Ceremony for Attack Junior High School.
EREN...
EREN, LISTEN!

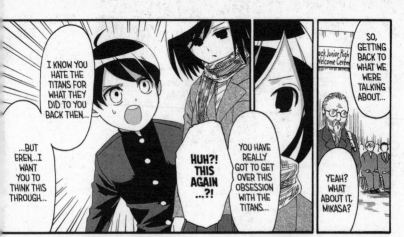

ack Junior High
Welcome Cerem
SO, GETTING BACK TO WHAT WE WERE TALKING ABOUT...
YEAH? WHAT ABOUT IT, MIKASA?
YOU HAVE REALLY GOT TO GET OVER THIS OBSESSION WITH THE TITANS...
HUH?! THIS AGAIN ...?!
I KNOW YOU HATE THE TITANS FOR WHAT THEY DID TO YOU BACK THEN...
...BUT EREN...I WANT YOU TO THINK THIS THROUGH...
YOU MAY NOT HAVE HEARD OF IT...
...BUT THERE'S THIS THING CALLED COMMON SENSE.
FOR EX-AMPLE ...
...YOU APOLOGIZE WHEN YOU'RE BEING A TOOL TO SOMEONE, EVEN IF IT'S A TITAN.
MIKASA ...
I'M SORRY, BUT THAT'S NOT THE POINT...
No, I think it is ...
EVEN I WISH I COULD...
...STOP FIXATING ON THE TITANS.
BUT... BUT EVEN SO, I...

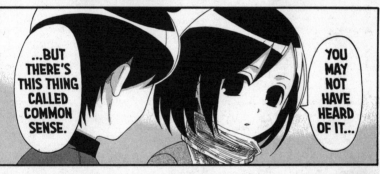

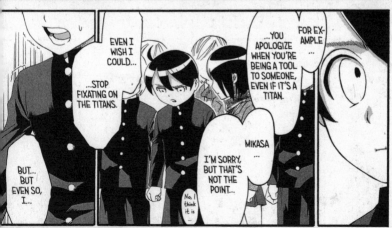

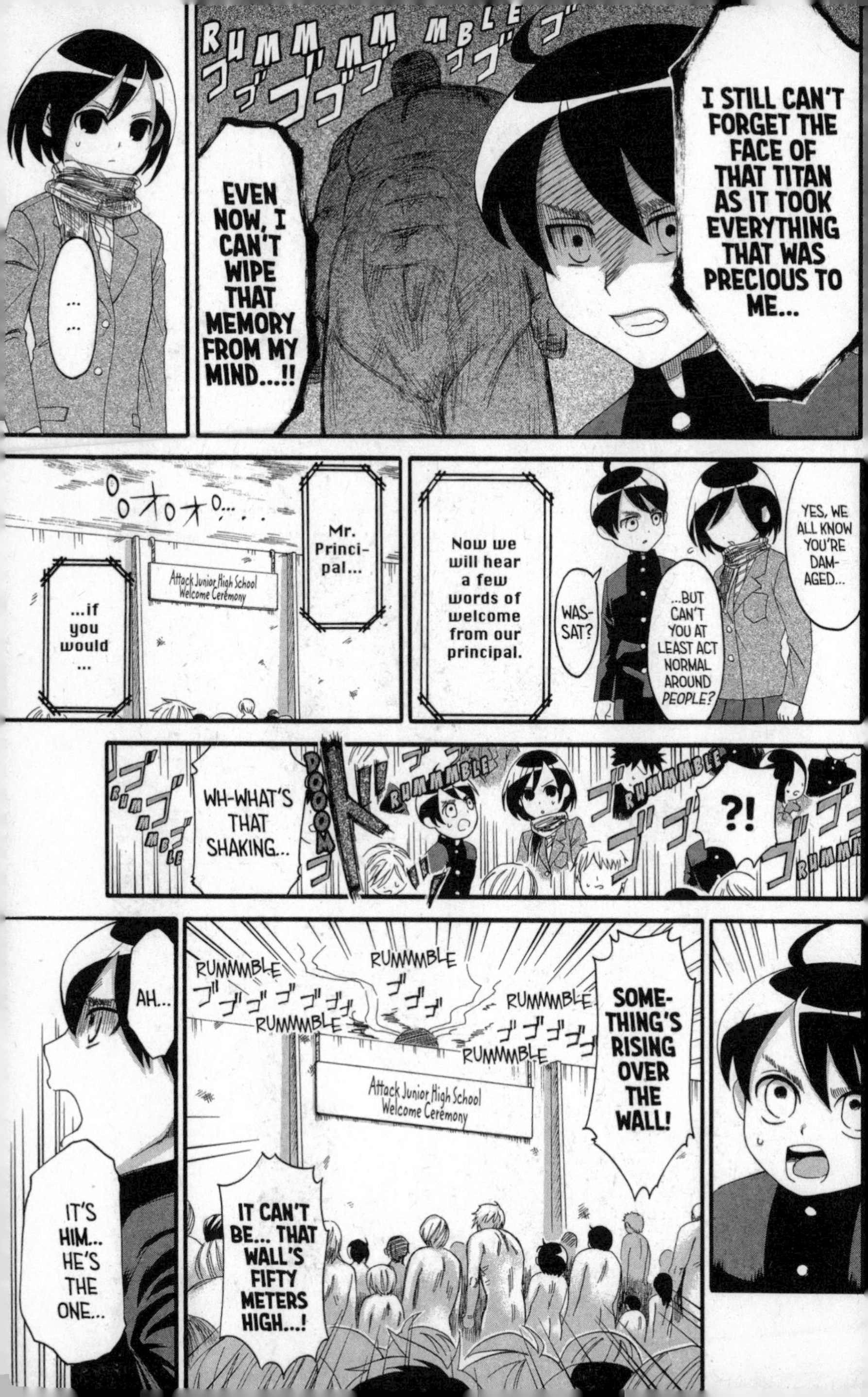
RUMMM MMMBLE
I STILL CAN'T FORGET THE FACE OF THAT TITAN AS IT TOOK EVERYTHING THAT WAS PRECIOUS TO ME...
EVEN NOW, I CAN'T WIPE THAT MEMORY FROM MY MIND...!!
...
...
YES, WE ALL KNOW YOU'RE DAMAGED...
...BUT CAN'T YOU AT LEAST ACT NORMAL AROUND PEOPLE?
WAS-SAT?
Now we will hear a few words of welcome from our principal.
Mr. Principal...
Attack Junior High School Welcome Ceremony
...if you would...
?!
RUMMMMBLE
RUMMMMBLE
DOOOM
WH-WHAT'S THAT SHAKING...
RUMMBLE
SOME-THING'S RISING OVER THE WALL!
RUMMMBLE
RUMMMBLE
RUMMMBLE
RUMMMBLE
RUMMMBLE
Attack Junior High School Welcome Ceremony
IT CAN'T BE... THAT WALL'S FIFTY METERS HIGH...!
AH...
IT'S HIM... HE'S THE ONE...

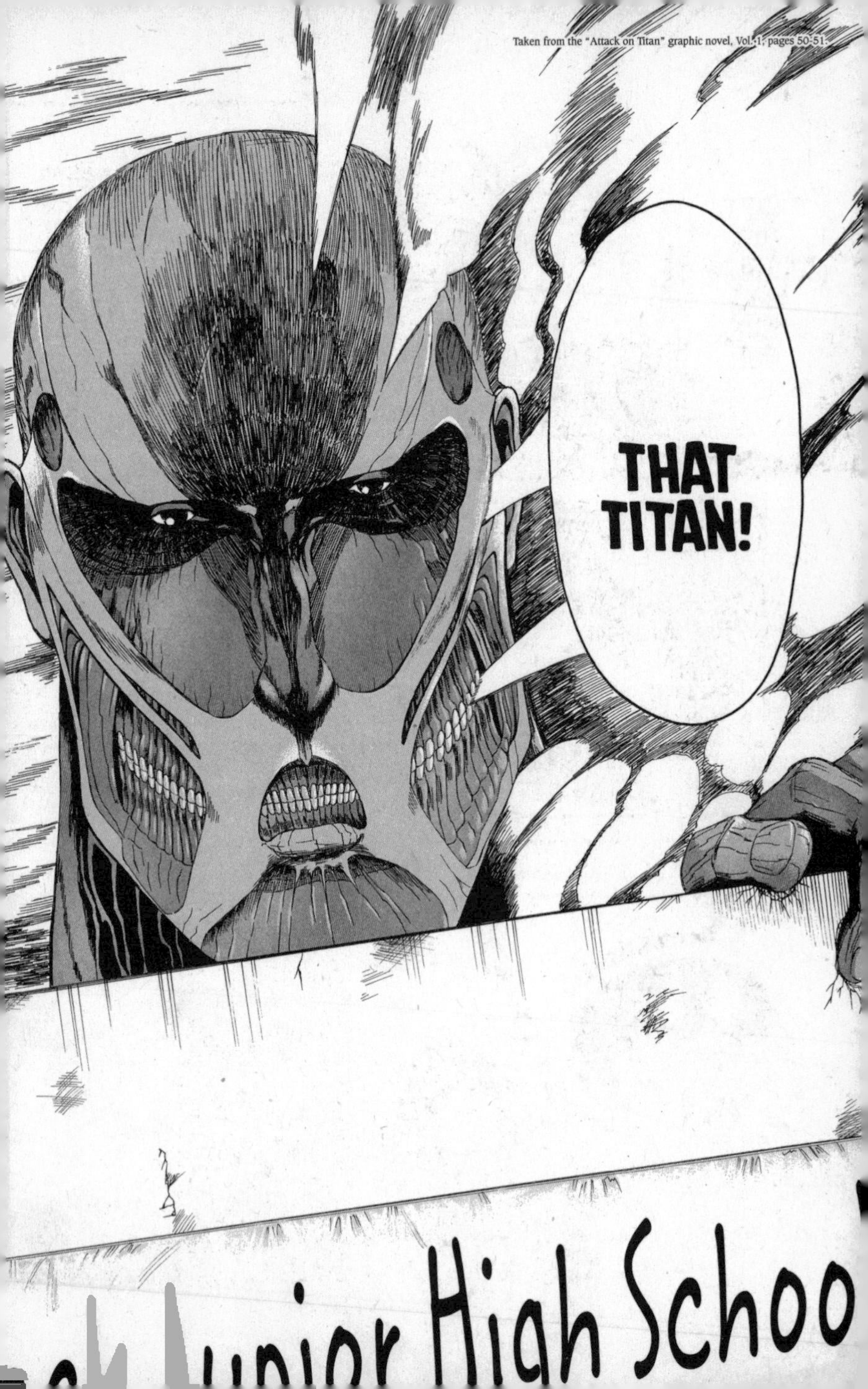
THAT TITAN!
Junior High Schoo
Taken from the "Attack on Titan" graphic novel, Vol. 1, pages 50-51.

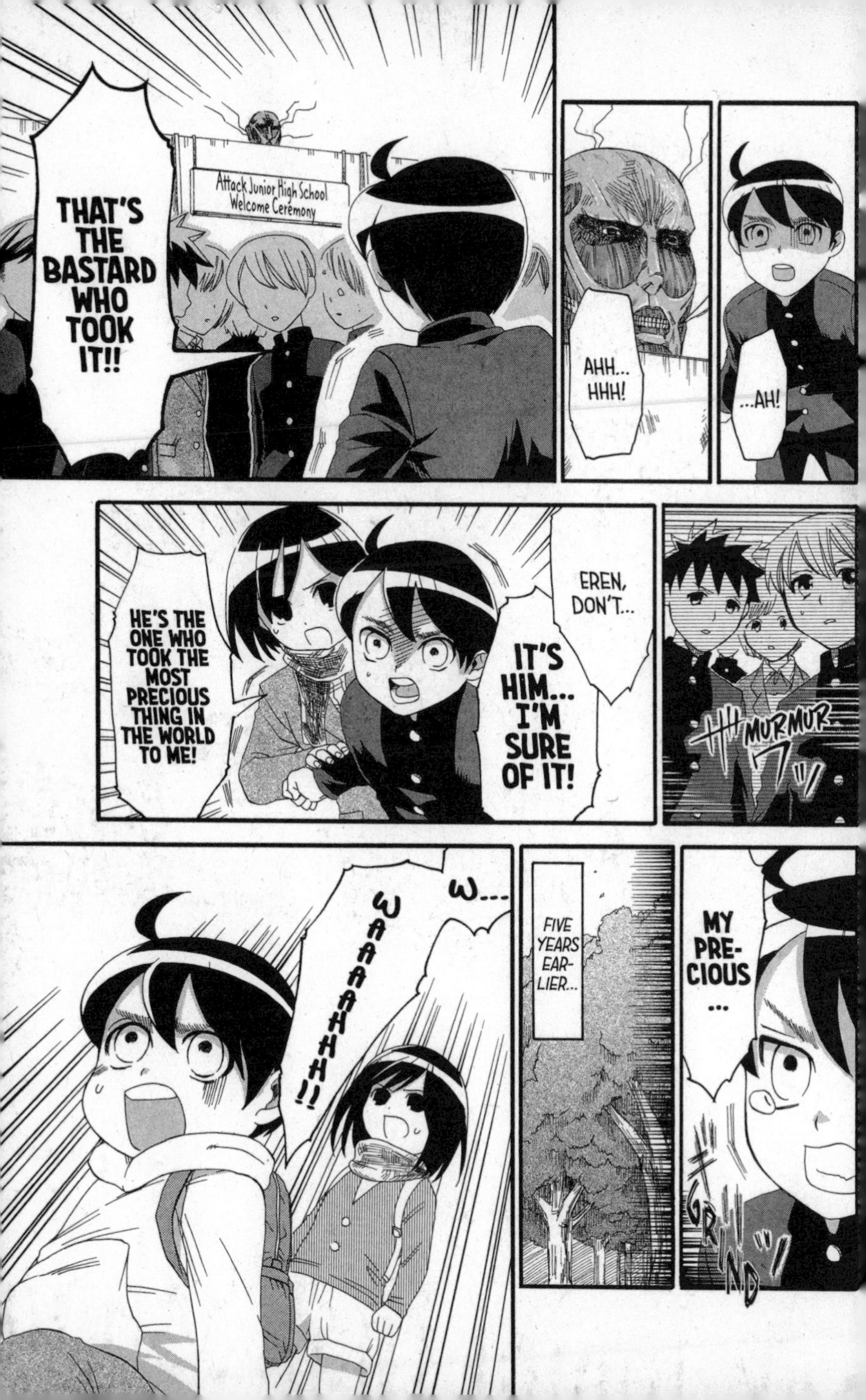
...AH!
AHH... HHH!
Attack Junior High School Welcome Ceremony
THAT'S THE BASTARD WHO TOOK IT!!
MURMUR
EREN, DON'T...
IT'S HIM... I'M SURE OF IT!
HE'S THE ONE WHO TOOK THE MOST PRECIOUS THING IN THE WORLD TO ME!
MY PRE-CIOUS...
GRIND
FIVE YEARS EAR-LIER...
W...
WAAAAAHHHH!!

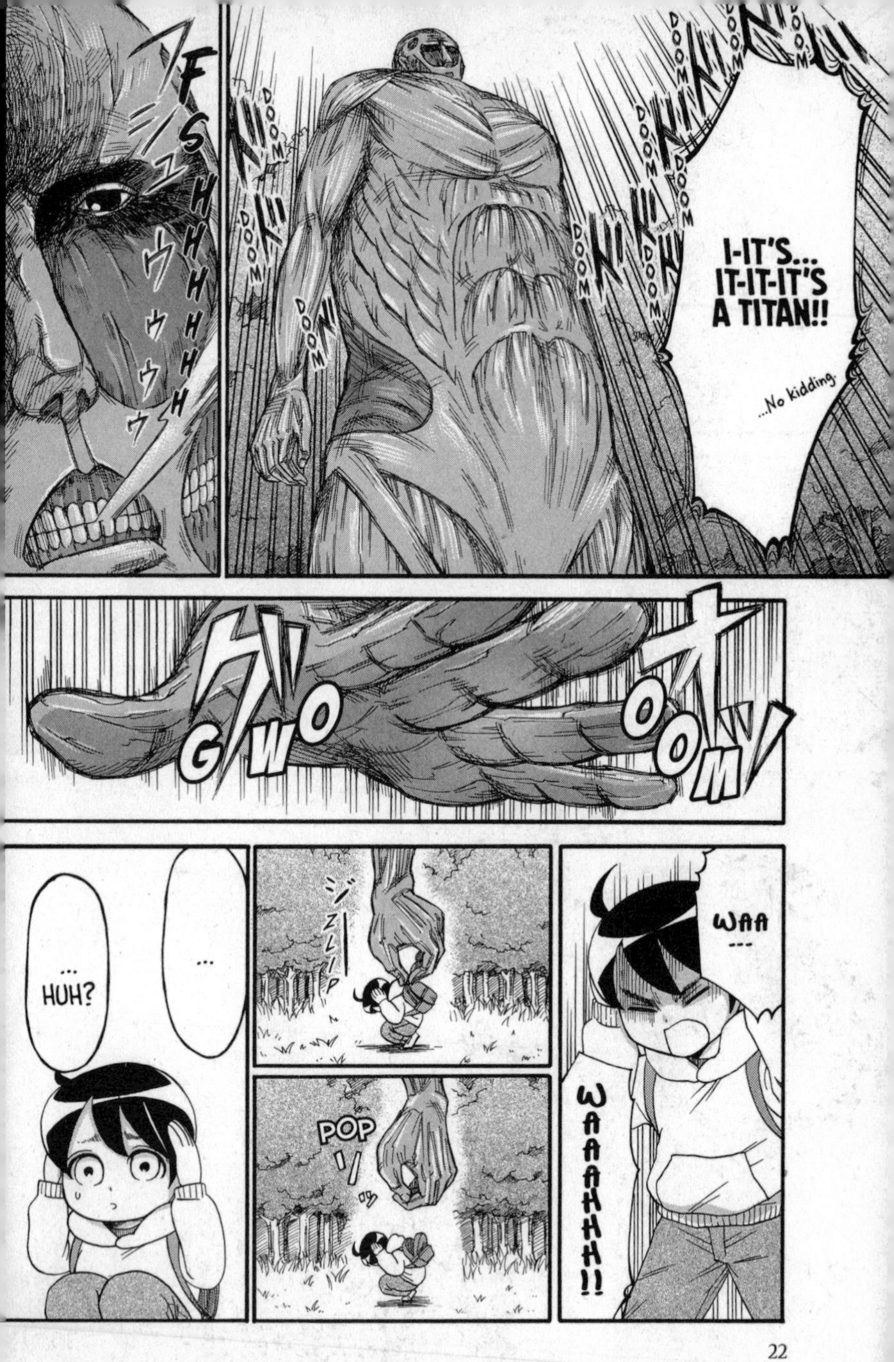
DOOM
DOOM
DOOM
DOOM
DOOM
DOOM
DOOM
DOOM
DOOM
I-IT'S... IT-IT-IT'S A TITAN!!
...No kidding.
FSHHHHHHHH
GWOOOM
WAA---
WAAAAAHHH!!
ZZLIP
POP
...
... HUH?

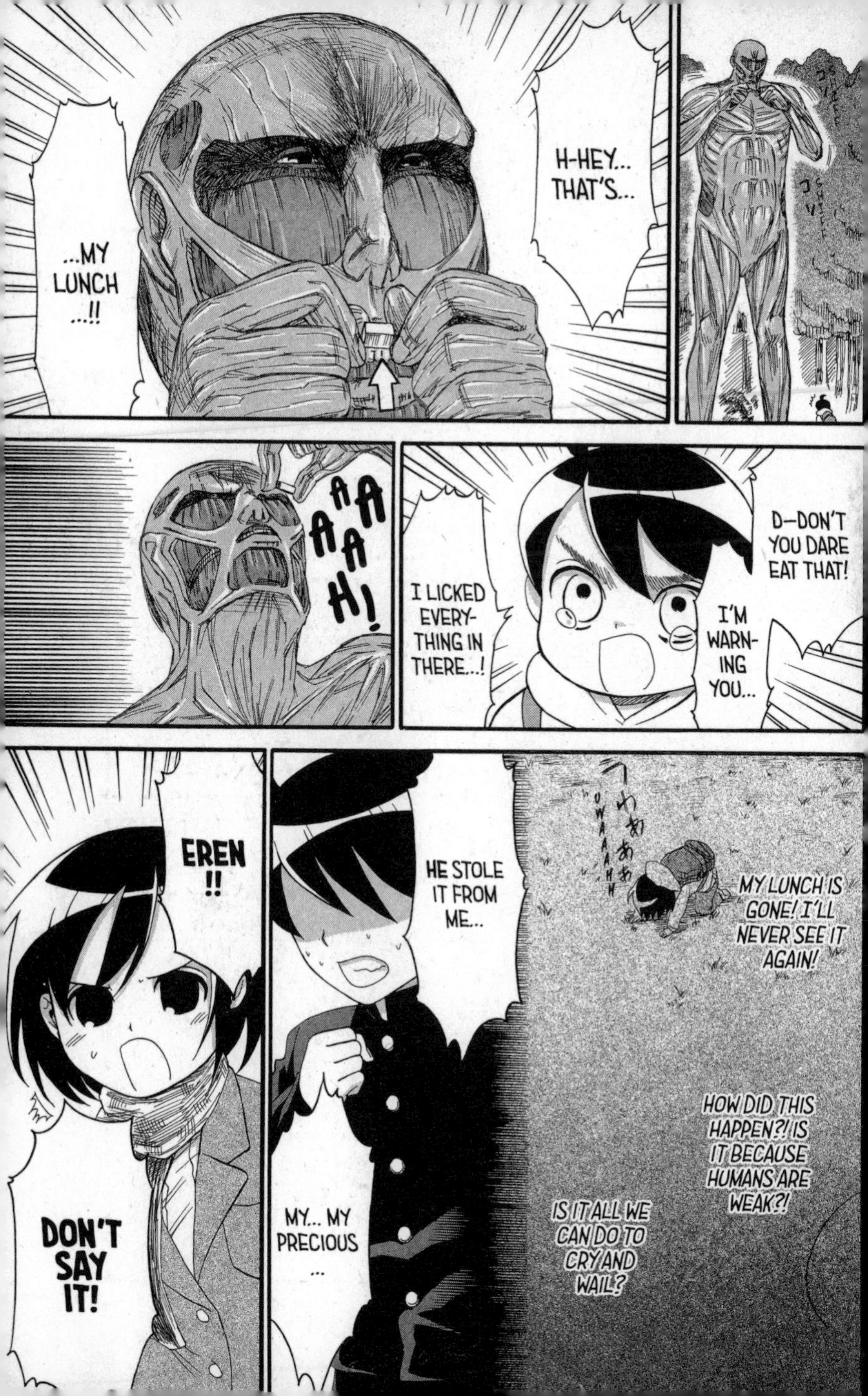
H-HEY... THAT'S...
...MY LUNCH ...!!
D—DON'T YOU DARE EAT THAT!
I'M WARNING YOU...
I LICKED EVERYTHING IN THERE...!
AAAAH!
UWAAAAHH
MY LUNCH IS GONE! I'LL NEVER SEE IT AGAIN!
HOW DID THIS HAPPEN?! IS IT BECAUSE HUMANS ARE WEAK?!
IS IT ALL WE CAN DO TO CRY AND WAIL?
HE STOLE IT FROM ME...
MY... MY PRECIOUS ...
EREN !!
DON'T SAY IT!

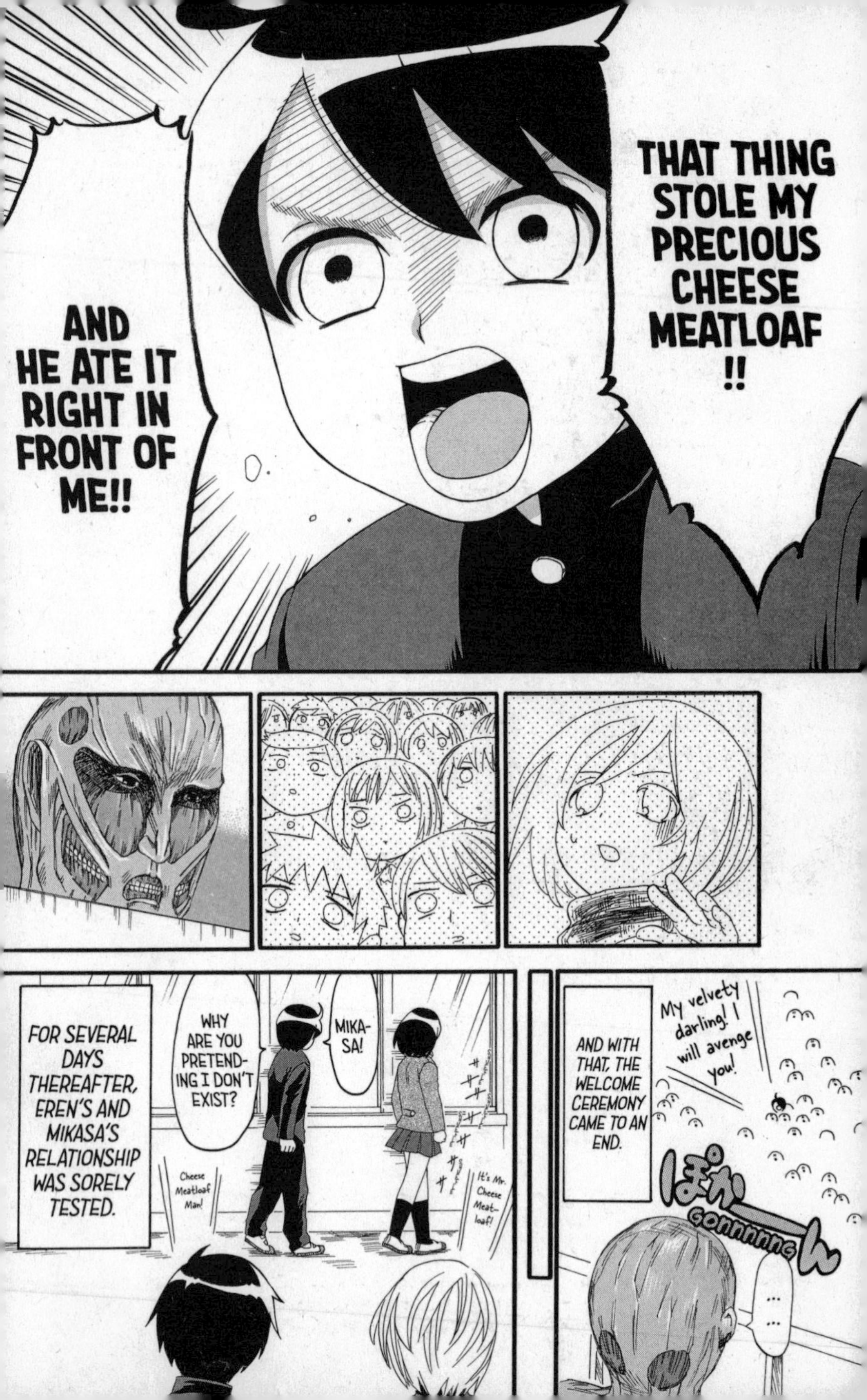
THAT THING STOLE MY PRECIOUS CHEESE MEATLOAF !!
AND HE ATE IT RIGHT IN FRONT OF ME!!
AND WITH THAT, THE WELCOME CEREMONY CAME TO AN END.
My velvety darling! I will avenge you!
GONNNNNNG
... ...
MIKA-SA!
WHY ARE YOU PRETEND-ING I DON'T EXIST?
FOR SEVERAL DAYS THEREAFTER, EREN'S AND MIKASA'S RELATIONSHIP WAS SORELY TESTED.
It's Mr. Cheese Meat-loaf!
Cheese Meatloaf Man!

SPOT THE LOUDMOUTH! (CAN YOU FIND EREN?)

ANSWER ON PAGE 43.

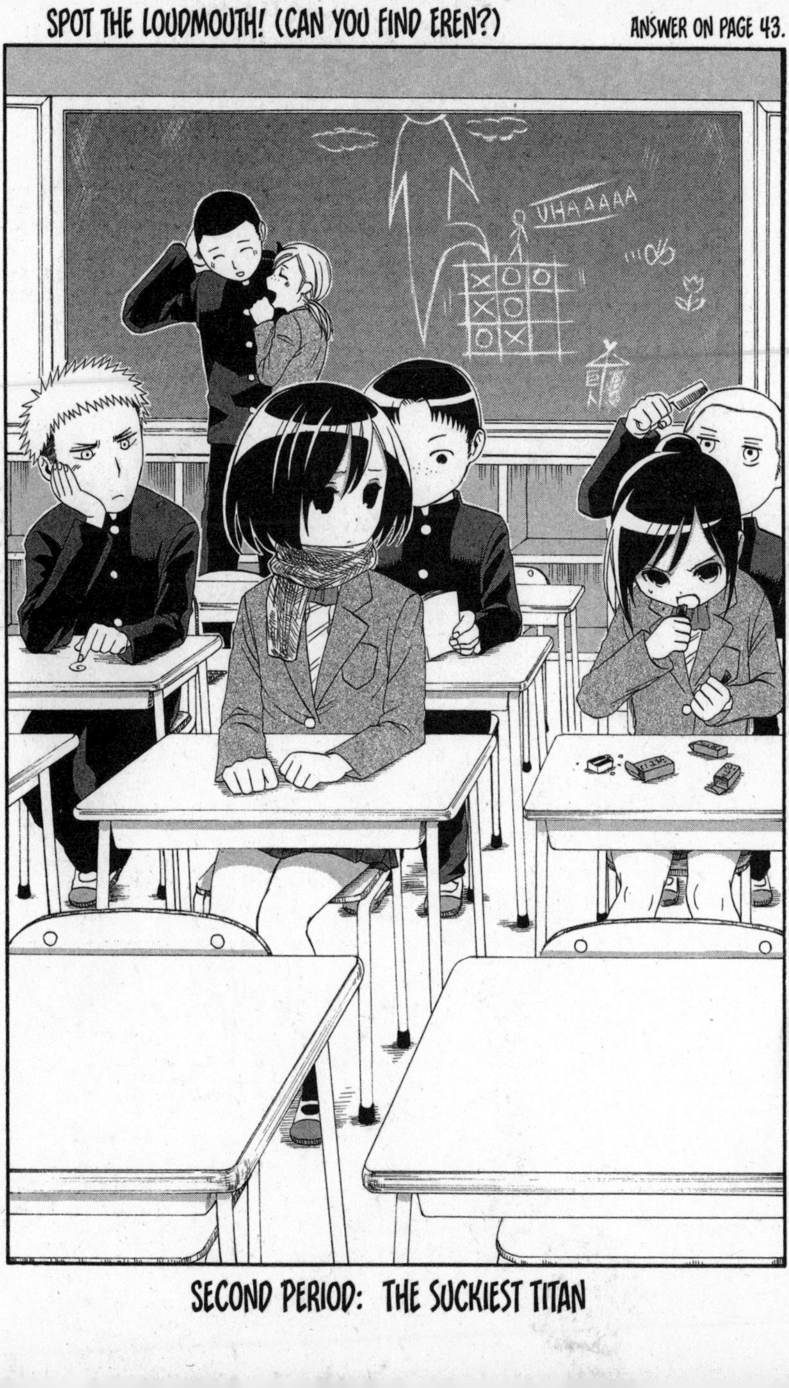
UHAAAAA

SECOND PERIOD: THE SUCKIEST TITAN

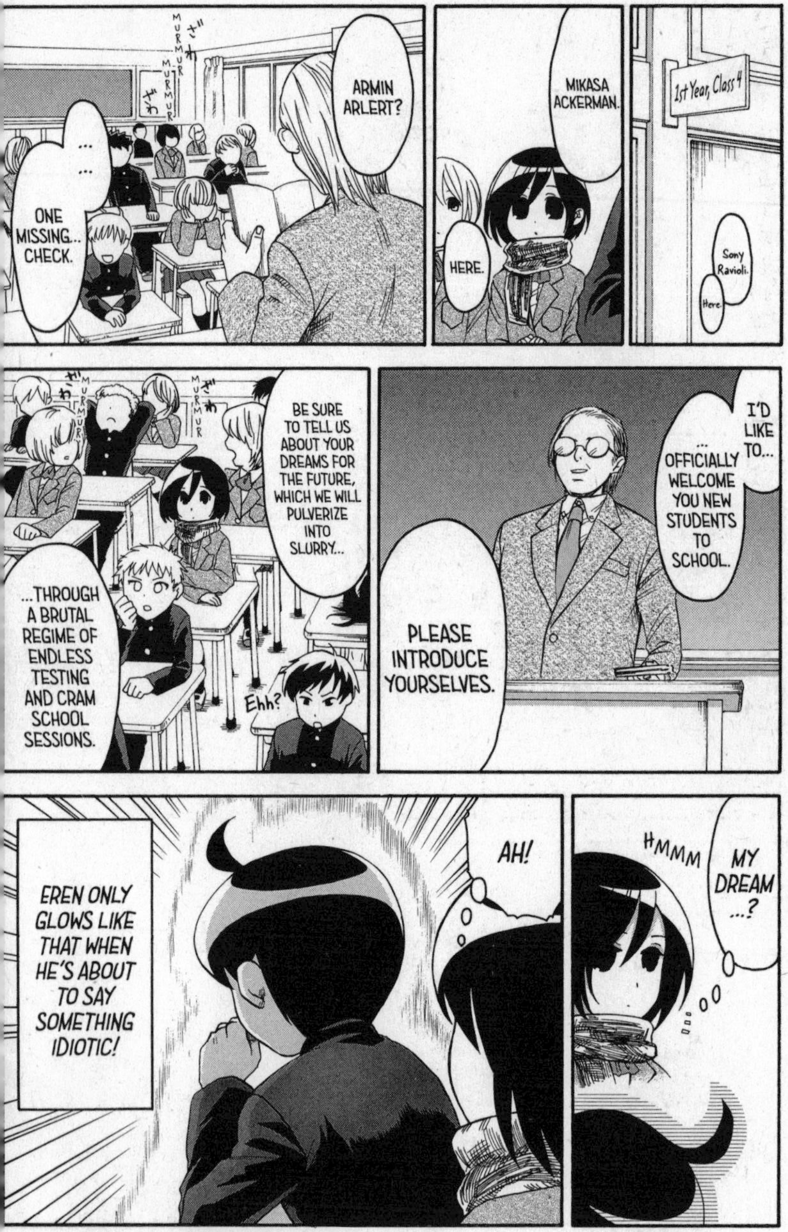
1st Year, Class 4
Sony Ravioli.
Here.
MIKASA ACKERMAN.
HERE.
ARMIN ARLERT?
MURMUR
MURMUR
……
ONE MISSING... CHECK.
I'D LIKE TO...
...OFFICIALLY WELCOME YOU NEW STUDENTS TO SCHOOL.
PLEASE INTRODUCE YOURSELVES.
BE SURE TO TELL US ABOUT YOUR DREAMS FOR THE FUTURE, WHICH WE WILL PULVERIZE INTO SLURRY...
MURMUR
MURMUR
...THROUGH A BRUTAL REGIME OF ENDLESS TESTING AND CRAM SCHOOL SESSIONS.
Ehh?
MY DREAM ...?
HMMM
AH!
EREN ONLY GLOWS LIKE THAT WHEN HE'S ABOUT TO SAY SOMETHING IDIOTIC!

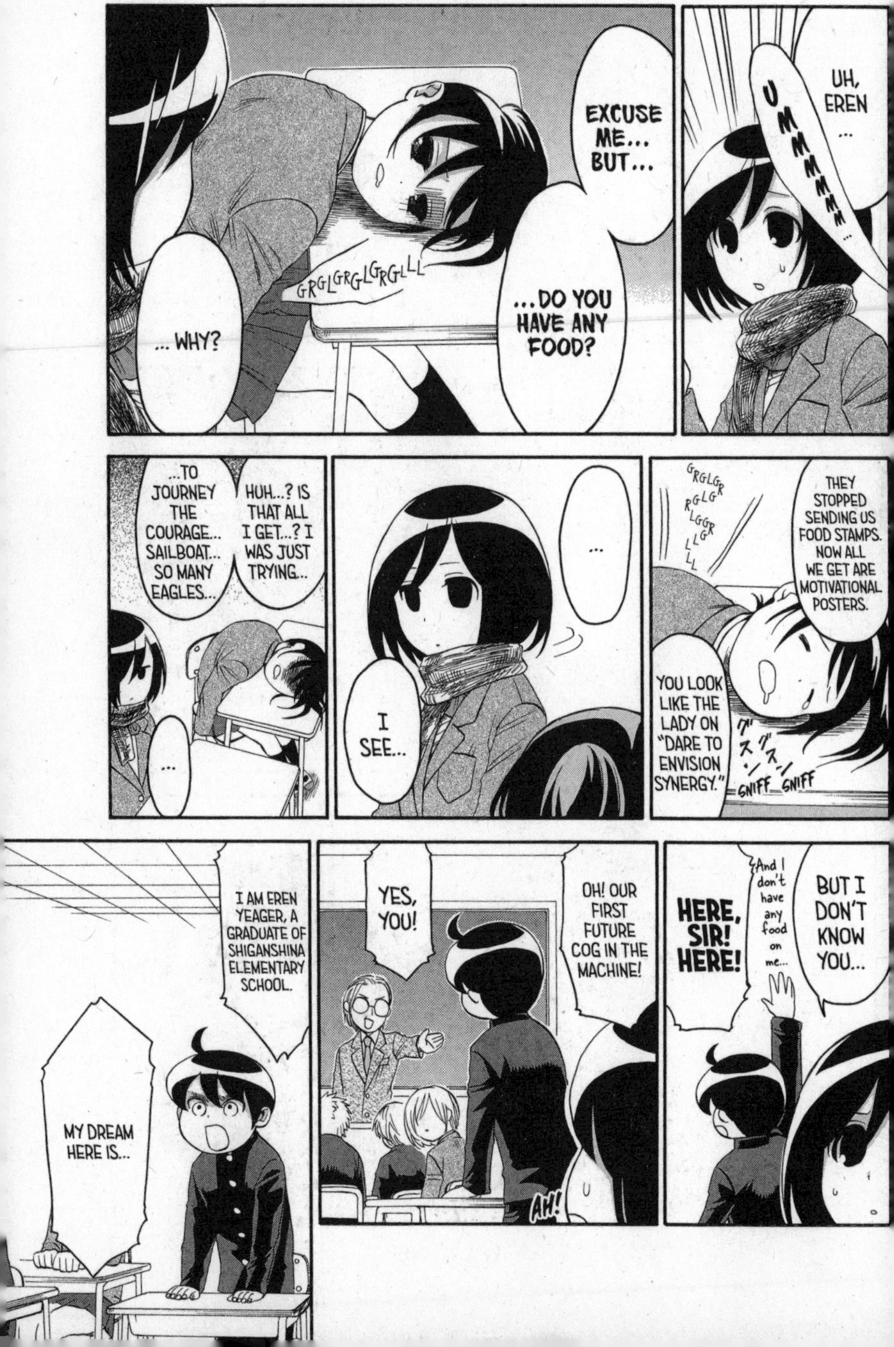
UH, EREN ...
UMMMMMMM...
EXCUSE ME... BUT...
...DO YOU HAVE ANY FOOD?
GRGLGRGLGRGLLL
... WHY?
THEY STOPPED SENDING US FOOD STAMPS. NOW ALL WE GET ARE MOTIVATIONAL POSTERS.
YOU LOOK LIKE THE LADY ON "DARE TO ENVISION SYNERGY."
SNIFF SNIFF
...
I SEE...
HUH...? IS THAT ALL I GET...? I WAS JUST TRYING...
...TO JOURNEY THE COURAGE... SAILBOAT... SO MANY EAGLES...
...
BUT I DON'T KNOW YOU...
And I don't have any food on me...
HERE, SIR! HERE!
OH! OUR FIRST FUTURE COG IN THE MACHINE!
YES, YOU!
AH!
I AM EREN YEAGER, A GRADUATE OF SHIGANSHINA ELEMENTARY SCHOOL.
MY DREAM HERE IS...

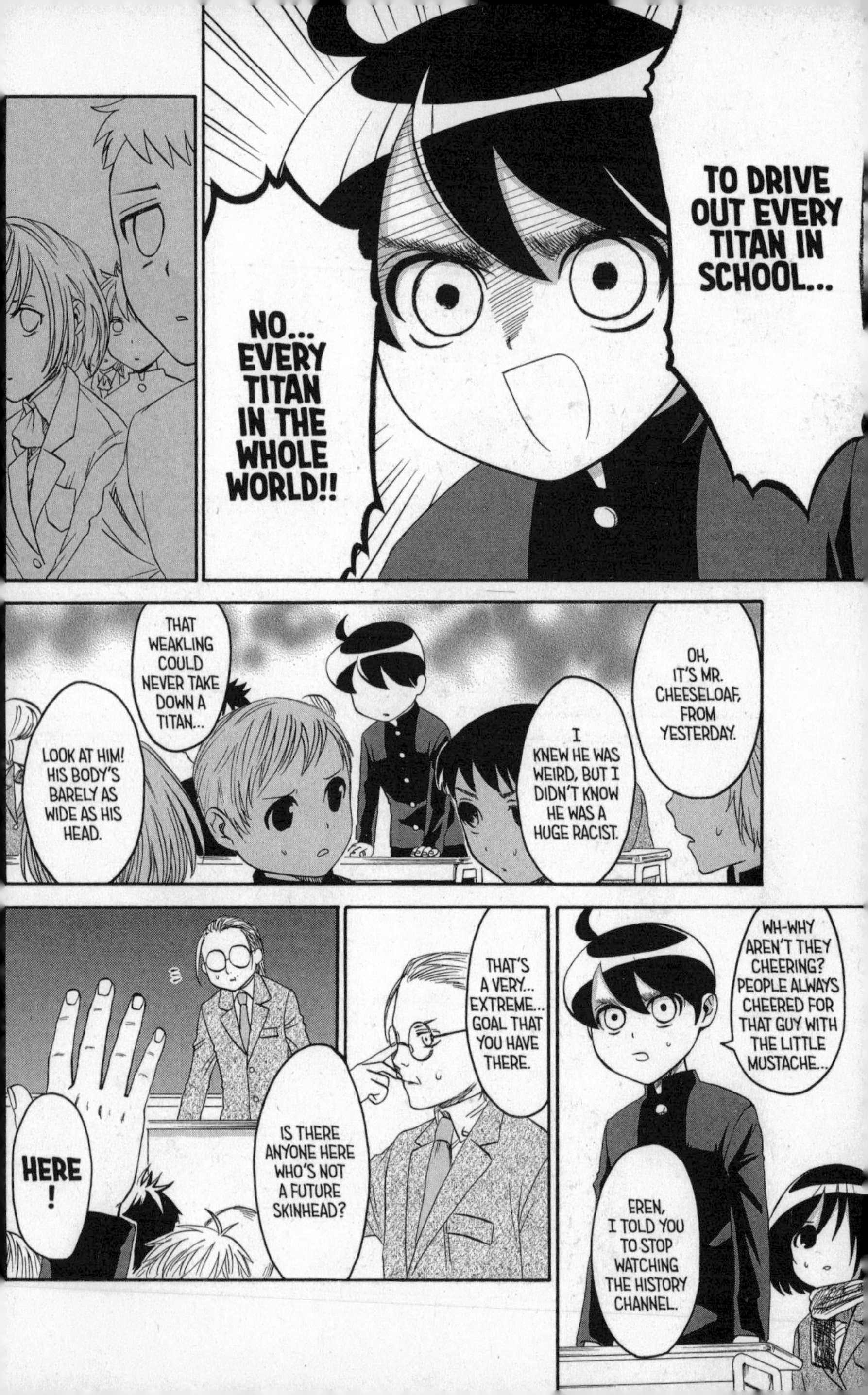
TO DRIVE OUT EVERY TITAN IN SCHOOL...
NO... EVERY TITAN IN THE WHOLE WORLD!!
OH, IT'S MR. CHEESELOAF, FROM YESTERDAY.
I KNEW HE WAS WEIRD, BUT I DIDN'T KNOW HE WAS A HUGE RACIST.
THAT WEAKLING COULD NEVER TAKE DOWN A TITAN...
LOOK AT HIM! HIS BODY'S BARELY AS WIDE AS HIS HEAD.
WH-WHY AREN'T THEY CHEERING? PEOPLE ALWAYS CHEERED FOR THAT GUY WITH THE LITTLE MUSTACHE...
EREN, I TOLD YOU TO STOP WATCHING THE HISTORY CHANNEL.
THAT'S A VERY... EXTREME... GOAL THAT YOU HAVE THERE.
IS THERE ANYONE HERE WHO'S NOT A FUTURE SKINHEAD?
HERE!

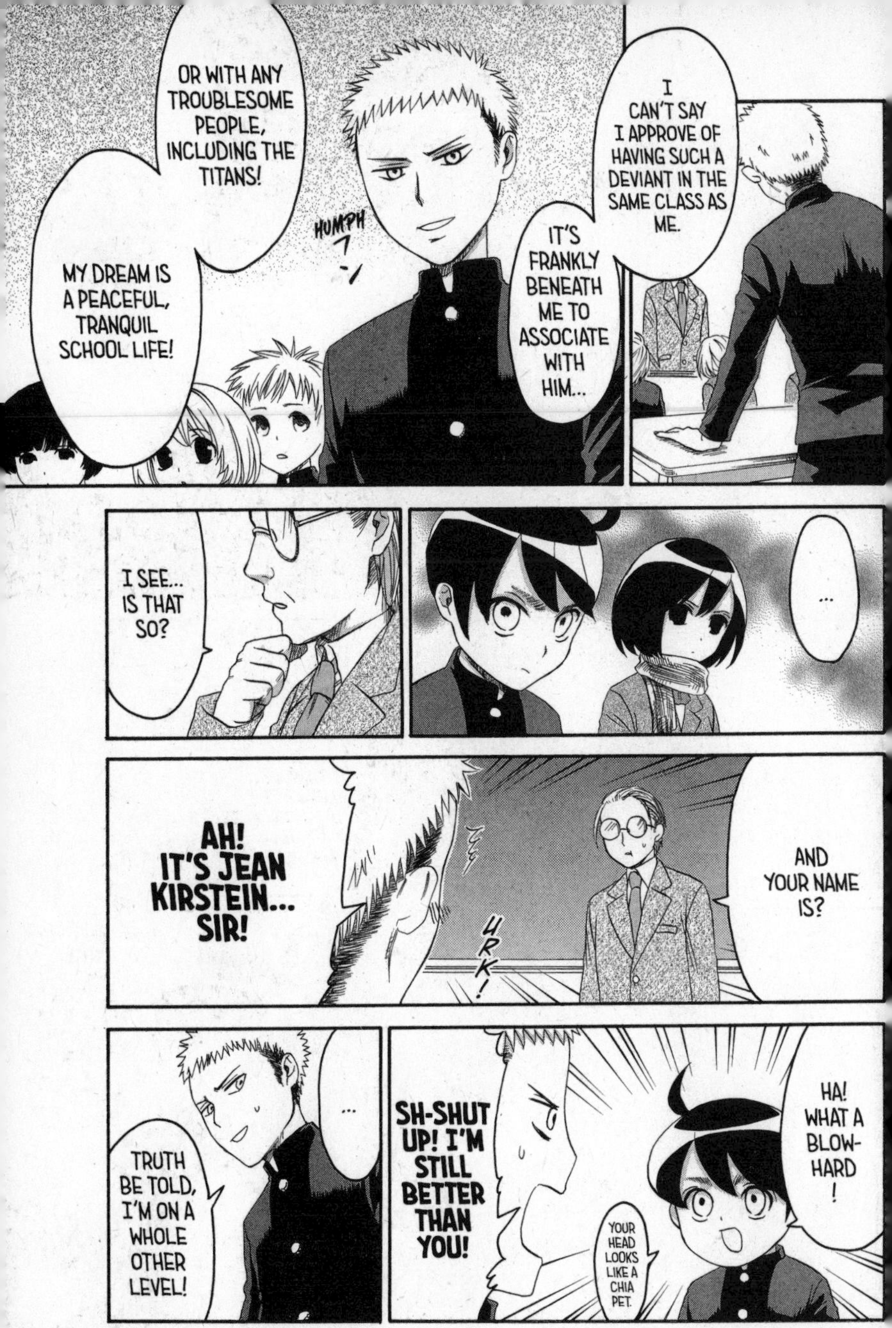
I CAN'T SAY I APPROVE OF HAVING SUCH A DEVIANT IN THE SAME CLASS AS ME.
IT'S FRANKLY BENEATH ME TO ASSOCIATE WITH HIM...
HUMPH
OR WITH ANY TROUBLESOME PEOPLE, INCLUDING THE TITANS!
MY DREAM IS A PEACEFUL, TRANQUIL SCHOOL LIFE!
...
I SEE... IS THAT SO?
AND YOUR NAME IS?
URK!
AH! IT'S JEAN KIRSTEIN... SIR!
HA! WHAT A BLOW-HARD!
YOUR HEAD LOOKS LIKE A CHIA PET.
SH-SHUT UP! I'M STILL BETTER THAN YOU!
...
TRUTH BE TOLD, I'M ON A WHOLE OTHER LEVEL!

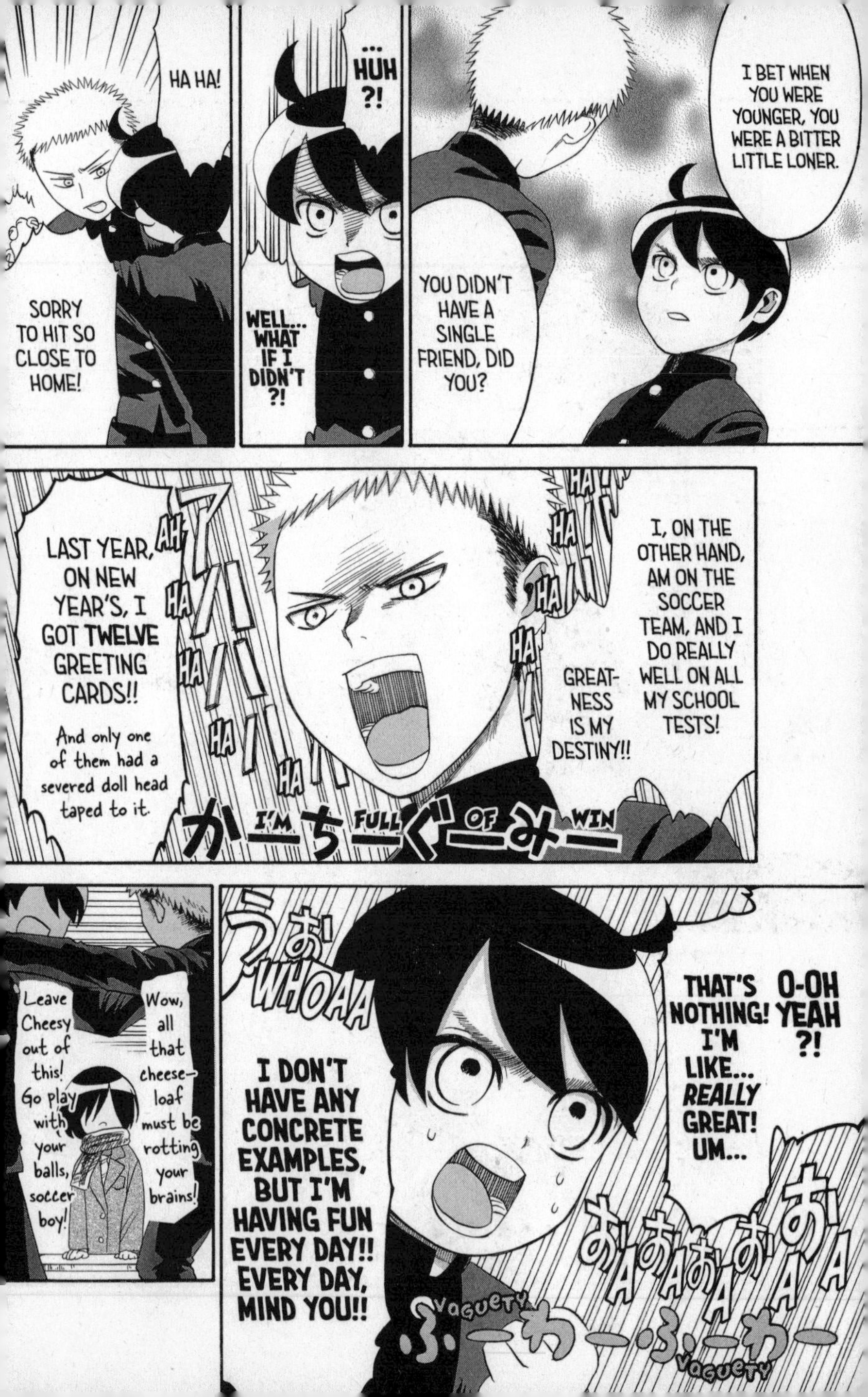
I BET WHEN YOU WERE YOUNGER, YOU WERE A BITTER LITTLE LONER.
YOU DIDN'T HAVE A SINGLE FRIEND, DID YOU?
... HUH ?!
WELL... WHAT IF I DIDN'T ?!
HA HA!
SORRY TO HIT SO CLOSE TO HOME!
I, ON THE OTHER HAND, AM ON THE SOCCER TEAM, AND I DO REALLY WELL ON ALL MY SCHOOL TESTS!
GREAT-NESS IS MY DESTINY!!
HA HA HA HA HA
AH HA HA HA HA HA
LAST YEAR, ON NEW YEAR'S, I GOT TWELVE GREETING CARDS!!
And only one of them had a severed doll head taped to it.
かーちーぐーみー
I'M FULL OF WIN
O-OH YEAH ?!
THAT'S NOTHING! I'M LIKE... REALLY GREAT! UM...
おおおおお
AAAAA
I DON'T HAVE ANY CONCRETE EXAMPLES, BUT I'M HAVING FUN EVERY DAY!! EVERY DAY, MIND YOU!!
うお
WHOAA
ふ.ーわーふ.ーわー
VAGUETY VAGUETY
Wow, all that cheese-loaf must be rotting your brains!
Leave Cheesy out of this! Go play with your balls, soccer boy!

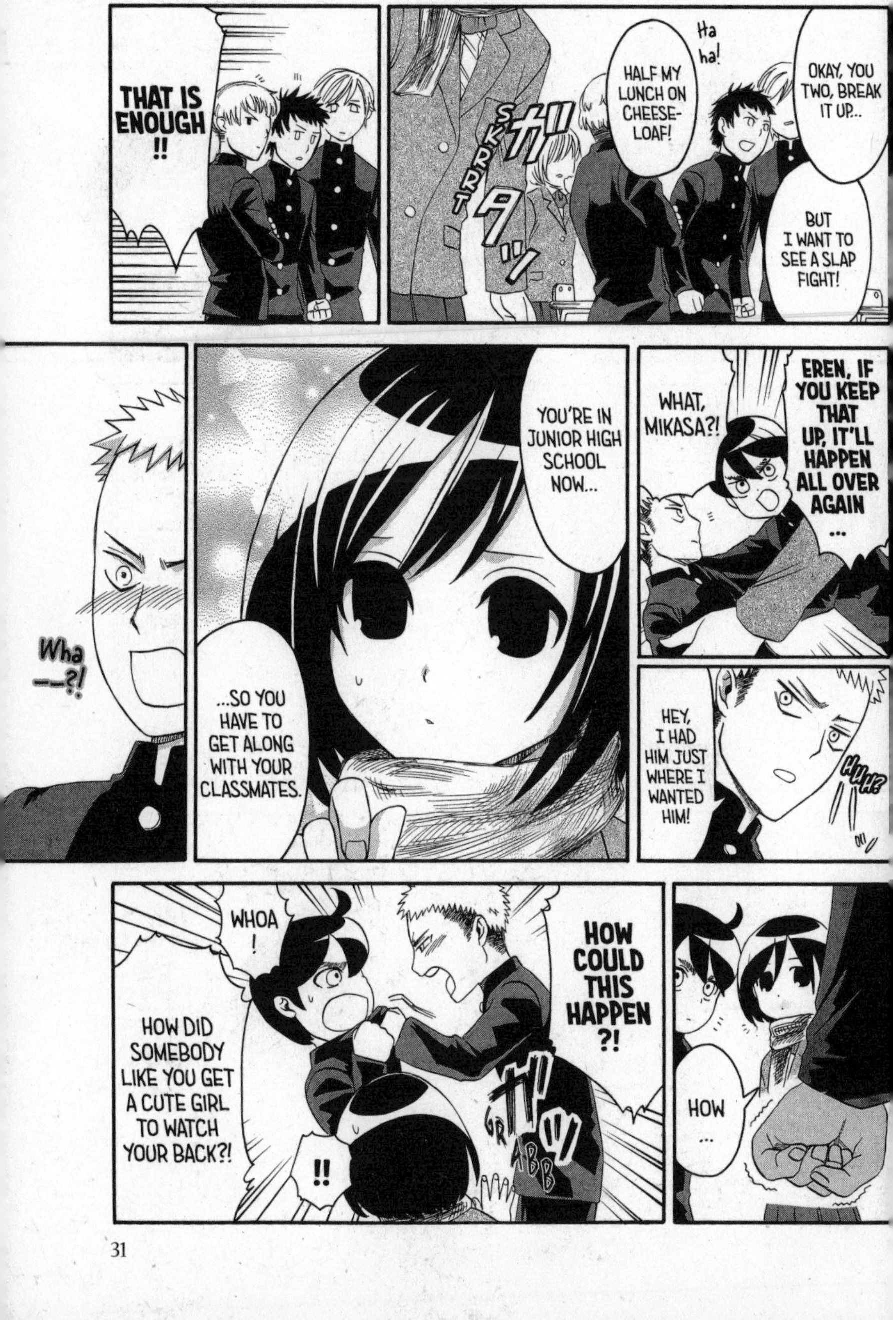
OKAY, YOU TWO, BREAK IT UP...
BUT I WANT TO SEE A SLAP FIGHT!
Ha ha!
HALF MY LUNCH ON CHEESE-LOAF!
SKRRRT
THAT IS ENOUGH !!
EREN, IF YOU KEEP THAT UP, IT'LL HAPPEN ALL OVER AGAIN ...
WHAT, MIKASA?!
HUH?
HEY, I HAD HIM JUST WHERE I WANTED HIM!
YOU'RE IN JUNIOR HIGH SCHOOL NOW...
...SO YOU HAVE TO GET ALONG WITH YOUR CLASSMATES.
Wha—?!
HOW ...
HOW COULD THIS HAPPEN ?!
WHOA !
HOW DID SOMEBODY LIKE YOU GET A CUTE GIRL TO WATCH YOUR BACK?!
GRABB
!!

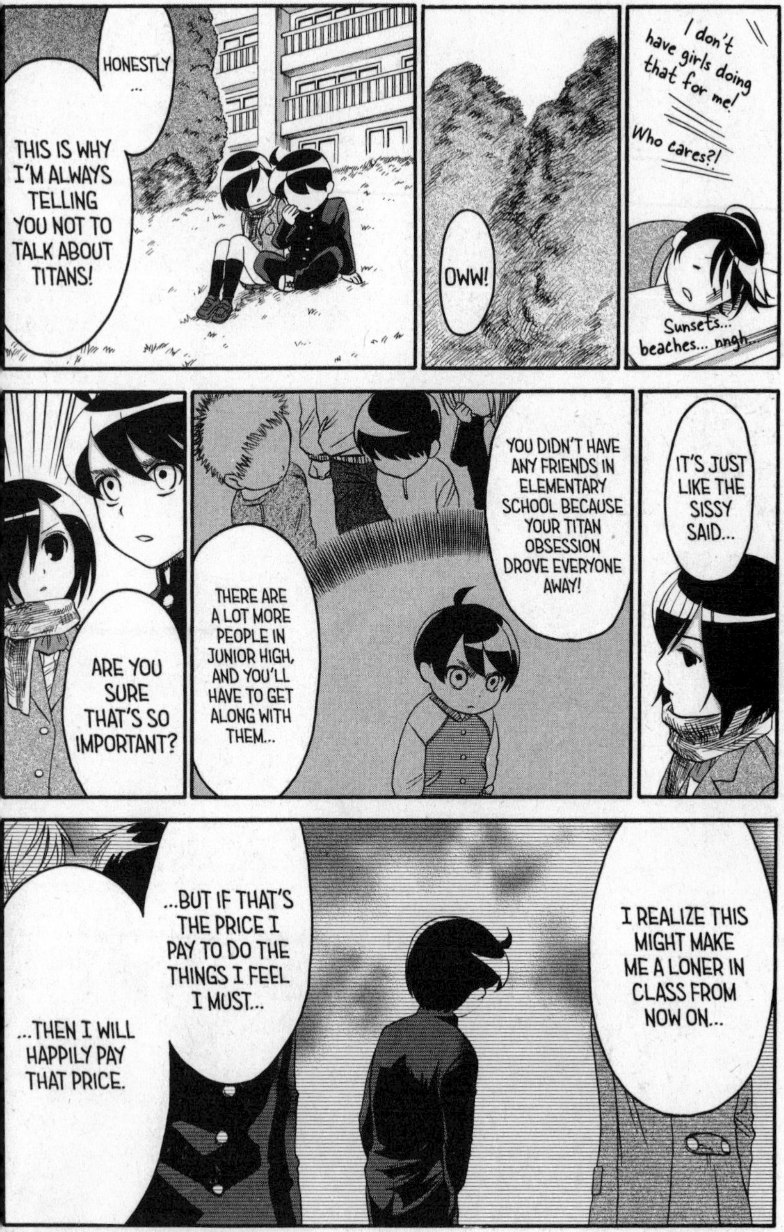
I don't have girls doing that for me!
Who cares?!
Sunsets... beaches... nngh...
OWW!
HONESTLY...
THIS IS WHY I'M ALWAYS TELLING YOU NOT TO TALK ABOUT TITANS!
IT'S JUST LIKE THE SISSY SAID...
YOU DIDN'T HAVE ANY FRIENDS IN ELEMENTARY SCHOOL BECAUSE YOUR TITAN OBSESSION DROVE EVERYONE AWAY!
THERE ARE A LOT MORE PEOPLE IN JUNIOR HIGH, AND YOU'LL HAVE TO GET ALONG WITH THEM...
ARE YOU SURE THAT'S SO IMPORTANT?
I REALIZE THIS MIGHT MAKE ME A LONER IN CLASS FROM NOW ON...
...BUT IF THAT'S THE PRICE I PAY TO DO THE THINGS I FEEL I MUST...
...THEN I WILL HAPPILY PAY THAT PRICE.

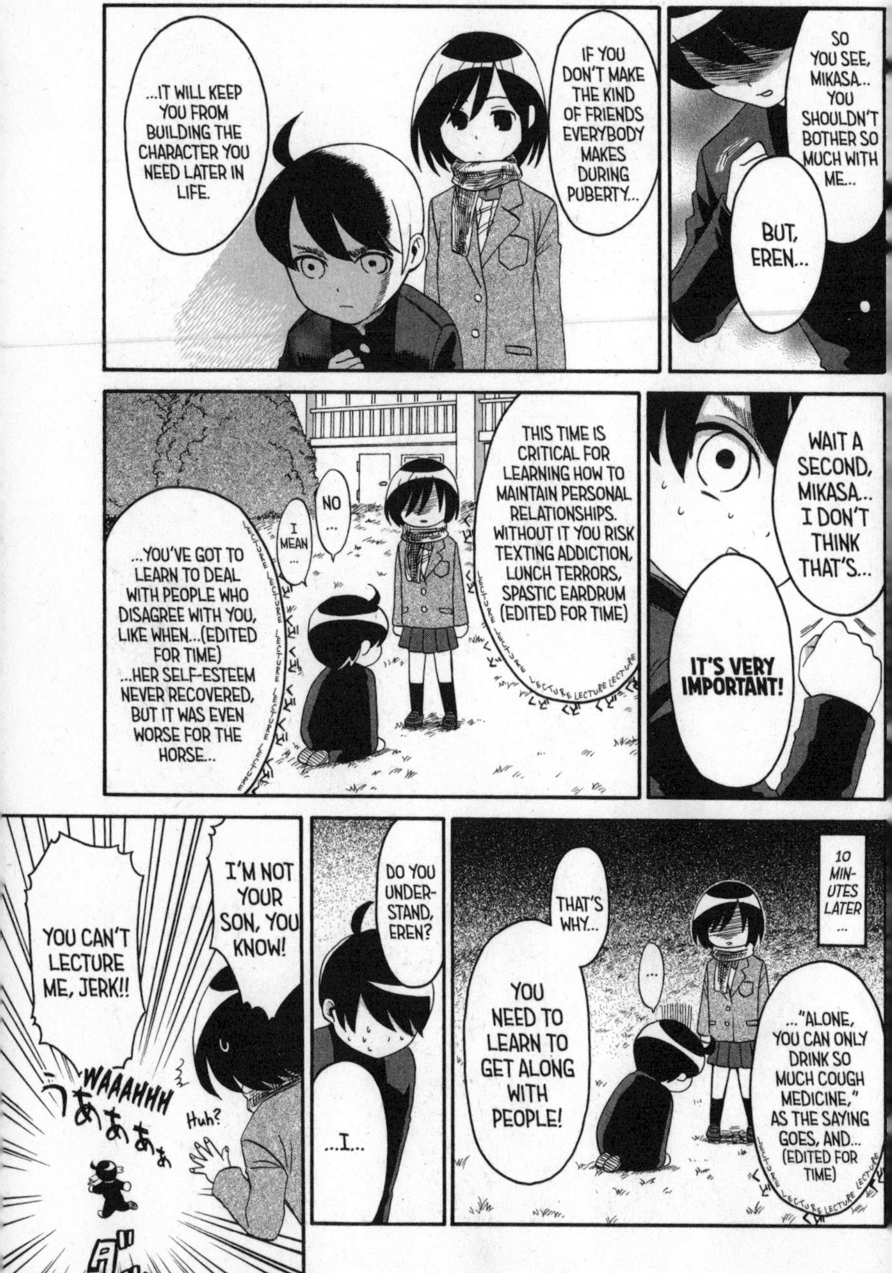
SO YOU SEE, MIKASA... YOU SHOULDN'T BOTHER SO MUCH WITH ME...
BUT, EREN...
IF YOU DON'T MAKE THE KIND OF FRIENDS EVERYBODY MAKES DURING PUBERTY...
...IT WILL KEEP YOU FROM BUILDING THE CHARACTER YOU NEED LATER IN LIFE.
WAIT A SECOND, MIKASA... I DON'T THINK THAT'S...
IT'S VERY IMPORTANT!
THIS TIME IS CRITICAL FOR LEARNING HOW TO MAINTAIN PERSONAL RELATIONSHIPS. WITHOUT IT YOU RISK TEXTING ADDICTION, LUNCH TERRORS, SPASTIC EARDRUM (EDITED FOR TIME)
NO ...
I MEAN ...
...YOU'VE GOT TO LEARN TO DEAL WITH PEOPLE WHO DISAGREE WITH YOU, LIKE WHEN...(EDITED FOR TIME) ...HER SELF-ESTEEM NEVER RECOVERED, BUT IT WAS EVEN WORSE FOR THE HORSE...
10 MINUTES LATER ...
..."ALONE, YOU CAN ONLY DRINK SO MUCH COUGH MEDICINE," AS THE SAYING GOES, AND... (EDITED FOR TIME)
THAT'S WHY...
YOU NEED TO LEARN TO GET ALONG WITH PEOPLE!
...
DO YOU UNDERSTAND, EREN?
...I...
I'M NOT YOUR SON, YOU KNOW!
YOU CAN'T LECTURE ME, JERK!!
Huh?
WAAAHHH
DASH

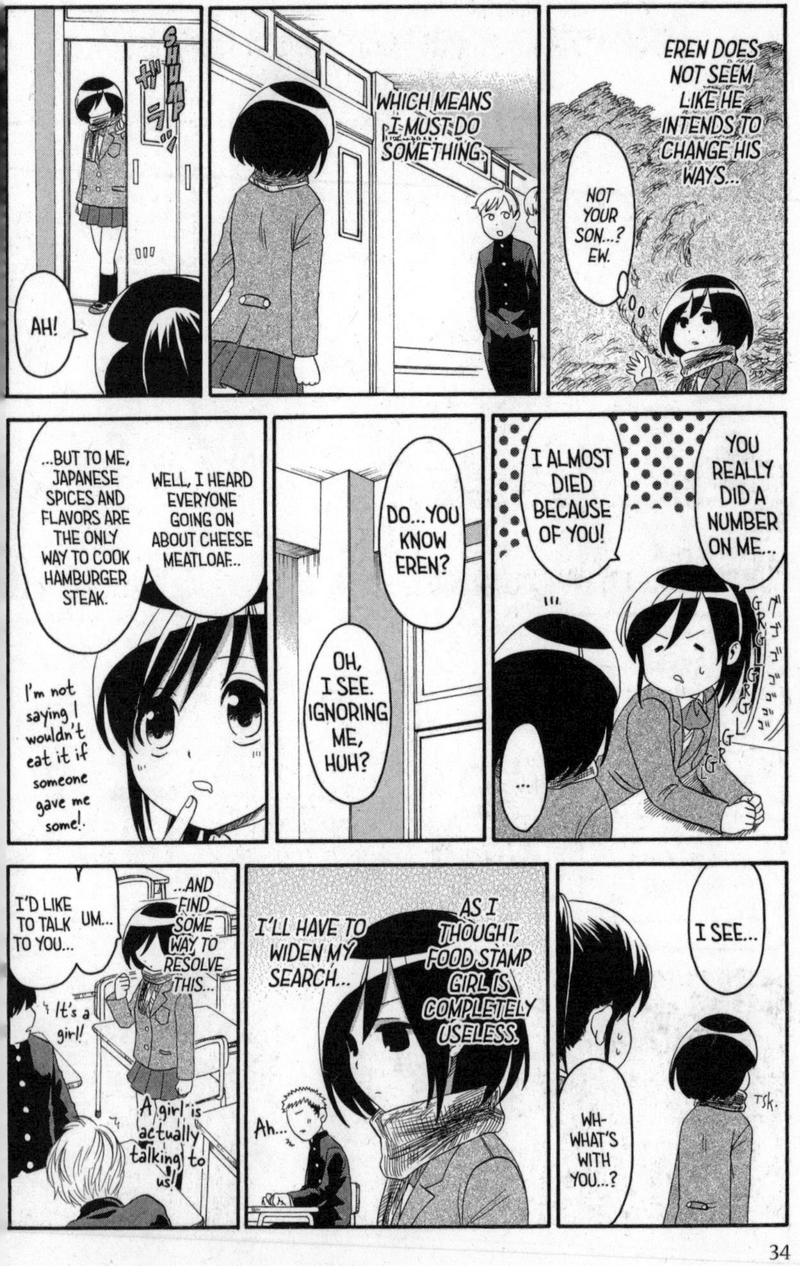
EREN DOES NOT SEEM LIKE HE INTENDS TO CHANGE HIS WAYS...
NOT YOUR SON...? EW.
WHICH MEANS I MUST DO SOMETHING.
SHUMP
AH!
YOU REALLY DID A NUMBER ON ME...
I ALMOST DIED BECAUSE OF YOU!
...
DO...YOU KNOW EREN?
OH, I SEE. IGNORING ME, HUH?
WELL, I HEARD EVERYONE GOING ON ABOUT CHEESE MEATLOAF...
...BUT TO ME, JAPANESE SPICES AND FLAVORS ARE THE ONLY WAY TO COOK HAMBURGER STEAK.
I'm not saying I wouldn't eat it if someone gave me some!.
I SEE...
WH-WHAT'S WITH YOU...?
Tsk.
AS I THOUGHT, FOOD STAMP GIRL IS COMPLETELY USELESS.
I'LL HAVE TO WIDEN MY SEARCH...
Ah...
...AND FIND SOME WAY TO RESOLVE THIS...
UM...
I'D LIKE TO TALK TO YOU...
It's a girl!
A girl is actually talking to us!

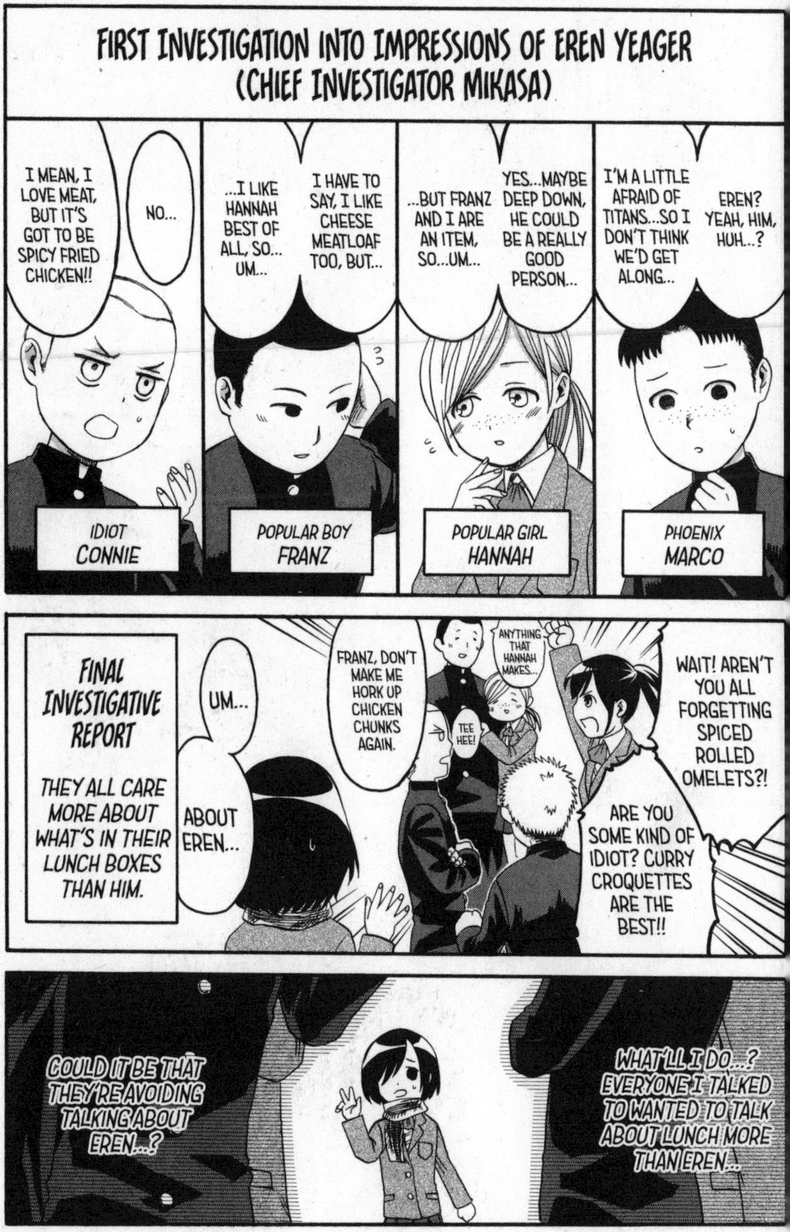

FIRST INVESTIGATION INTO IMPRESSIONS OF EREN YEAGER
(CHIEF INVESTIGATOR MIKASA)
EREN? YEAH, HIM, HUH...?
I'M A LITTLE AFRAID OF TITANS...SO I DON'T THINK WE'D GET ALONG...
PHOENIX MARCO
YES...MAYBE DEEP DOWN, HE COULD BE A REALLY GOOD PERSON...
...BUT FRANZ AND I ARE AN ITEM, SO...UM...
POPULAR GIRL HANNAH
I HAVE TO SAY, I LIKE CHEESE MEATLOAF TOO, BUT...
...I LIKE HANNAH BEST OF ALL, SO... UM...
POPULAR BOY FRANZ
NO...
I MEAN, I LOVE MEAT, BUT IT'S GOT TO BE SPICY FRIED CHICKEN!!
IDIOT CONNIE
WAIT! AREN'T YOU ALL FORGETTING SPICED ROLLED OMELETS?!
ANYTHING THAT HANNAH MAKES...
TEE HEE!
FRANZ, DON'T MAKE ME HORK UP CHICKEN CHUNKS AGAIN.
ARE YOU SOME KIND OF IDIOT? CURRY CROQUETTES ARE THE BEST!!
UM...
ABOUT EREN...
FINAL INVESTIGATIVE REPORT
THEY ALL CARE MORE ABOUT WHAT'S IN THEIR LUNCH BOXES THAN HIM.
WHAT'LL I DO...? EVERYONE I TALKED TO WANTED TO TALK ABOUT LUNCH MORE THAN EREN...
COULD IT BE THAT THEY'RE AVOIDING TALKING ABOUT EREN...?

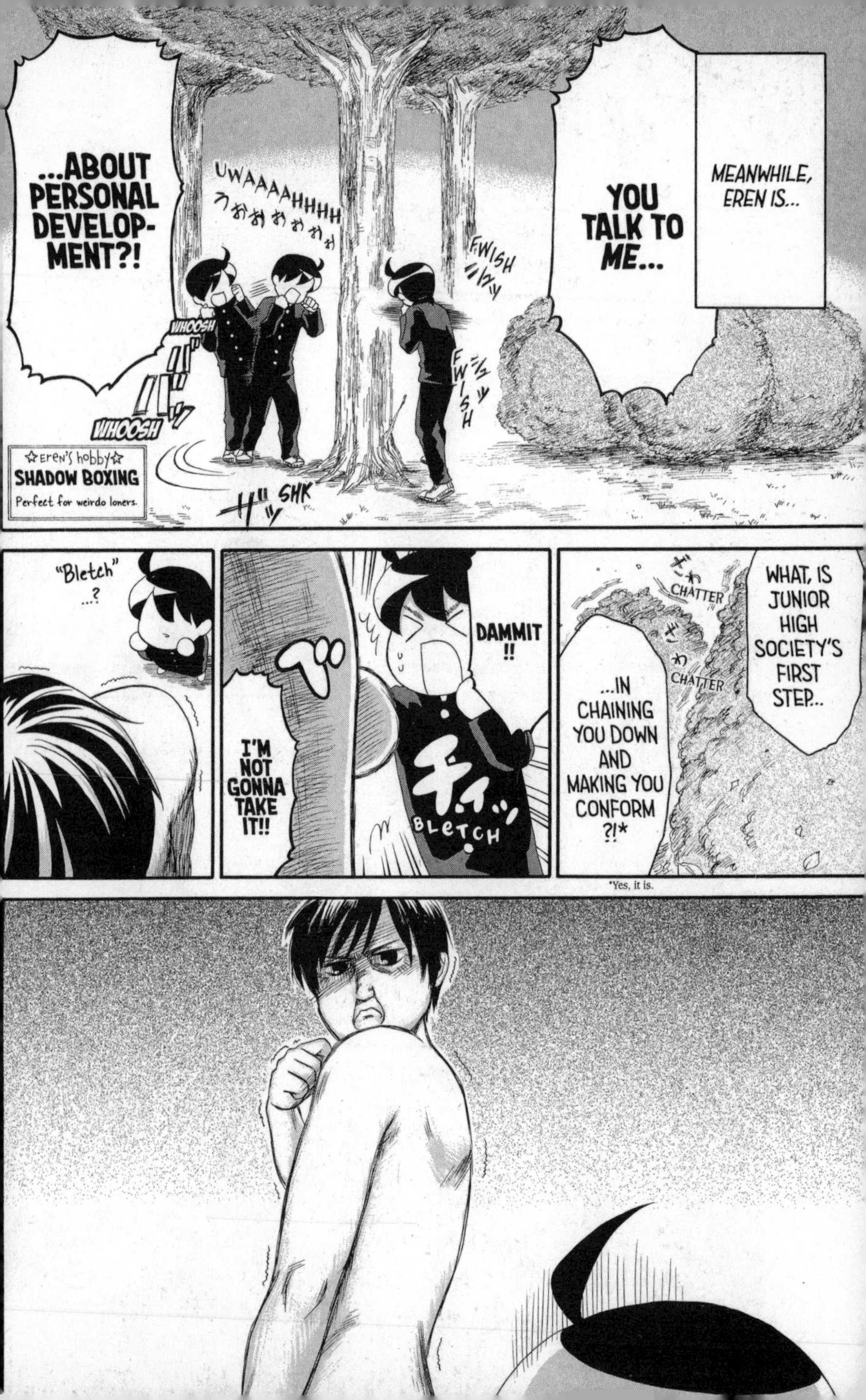
MEANWHILE, EREN IS...
YOU TALK TO ME...
UWAAAAHHHH
FWISH
FWISH
...ABOUT PERSONAL DEVELOP-MENT?!
WHOOSH
WHOOSH
☆Eren's hobby☆
SHADOW BOXING
Perfect for weirdo loners.
SHK
WHAT, IS JUNIOR HIGH SOCIETY'S FIRST STEP...
CHATTER
CHATTER
...IN CHAINING YOU DOWN AND MAKING YOU CONFORM?!*
DAMMIT!!
I'M NOT GONNA TAKE IT!!
BLETCH
"Bletch" ...?
*Yes, it is.

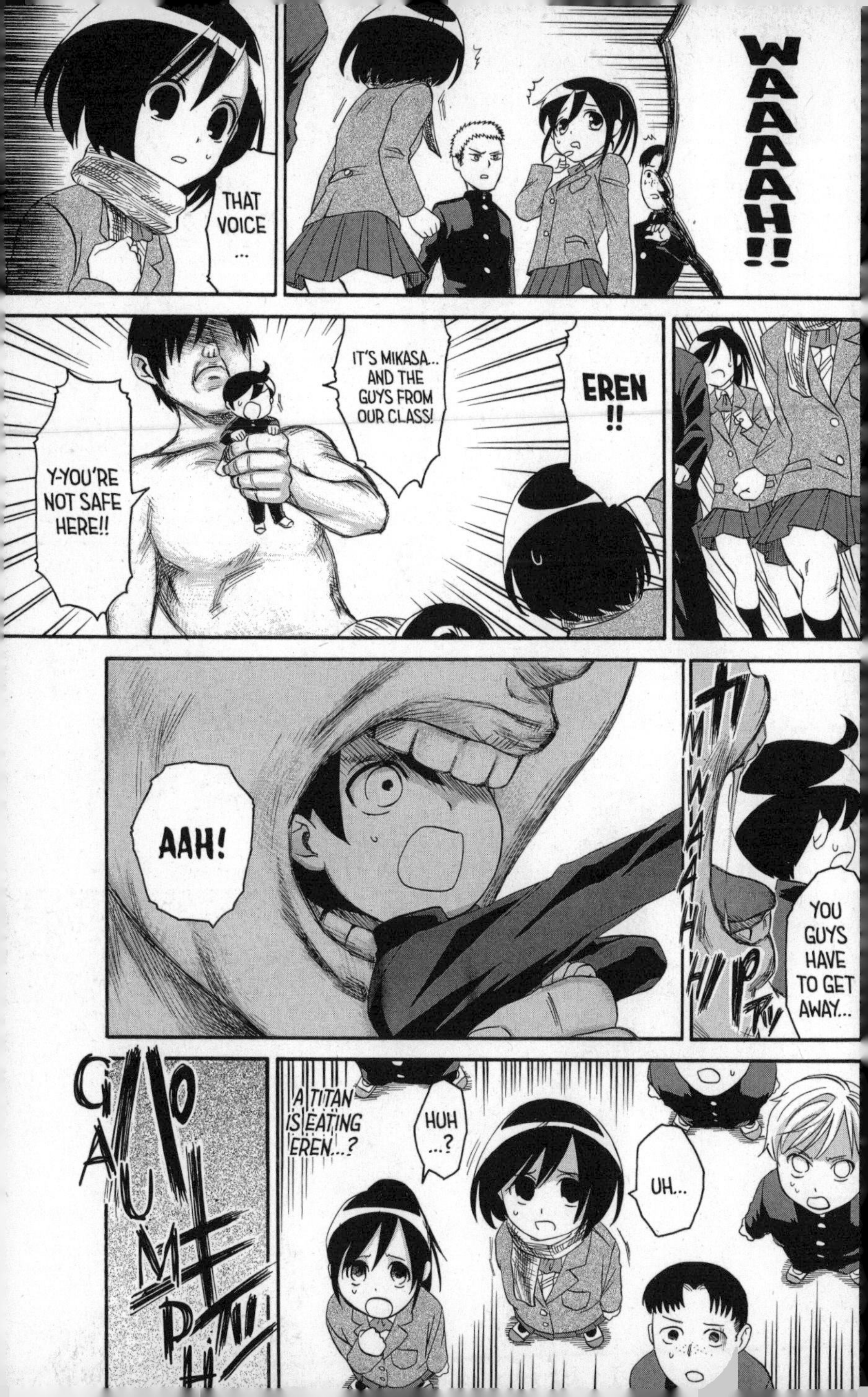
WAAAAH!!
THAT VOICE ...
EREN !!
IT'S MIKASA... AND THE GUYS FROM OUR CLASS!
Y-YOU'RE NOT SAFE HERE!!
YOU GUYS HAVE TO GET AWAY...
AAH!
UH...
HUH ...?
A TITAN IS EATING EREN...?
GAUMPH

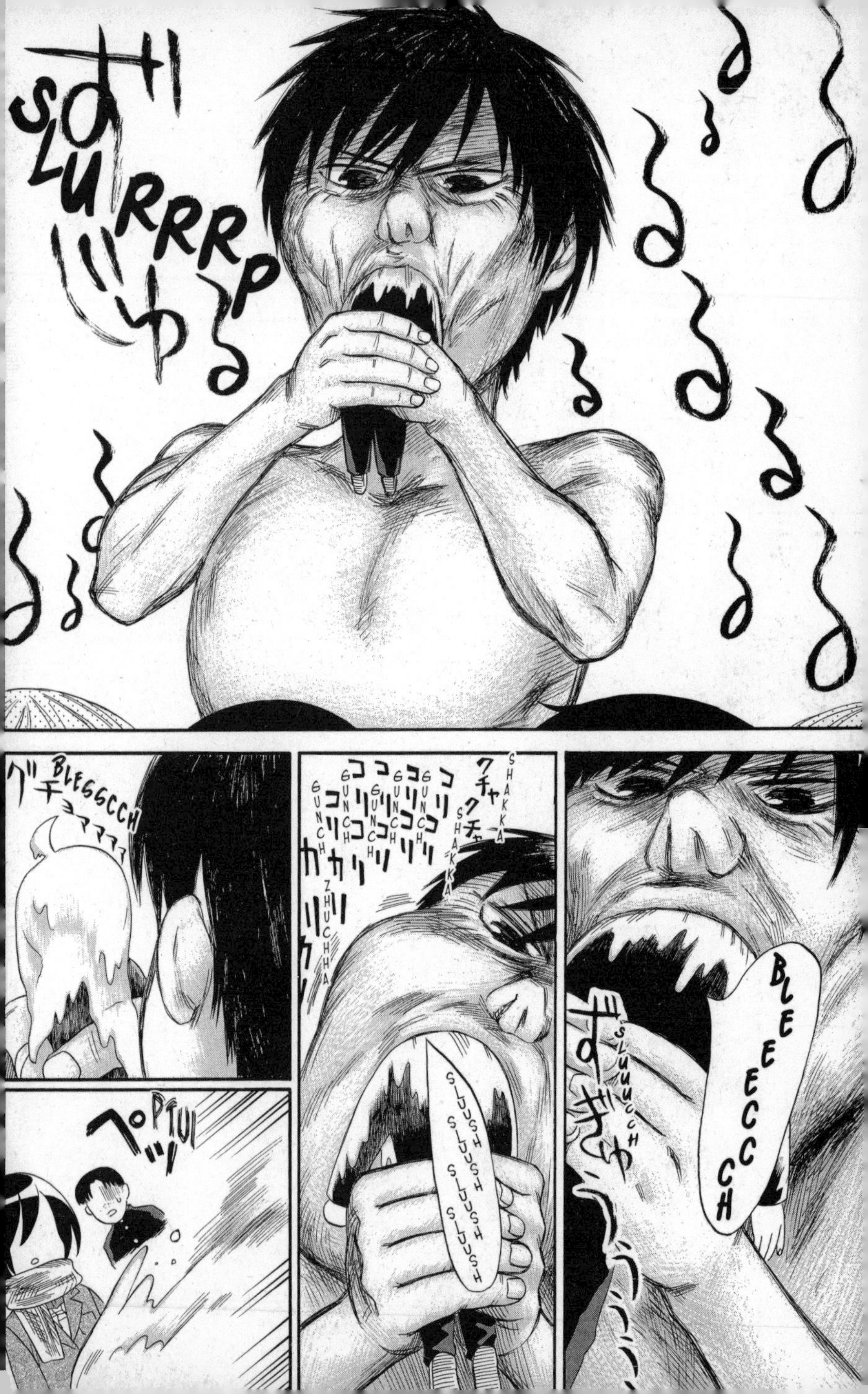

SLURRRP
BLEEECCCH
SLUUUCCH
SHAKKA SHAKKA
GUNCH GUNCH GUNCH GUNCH
ZHUCHHA
SLUUSH SLUUSH SLUUSH SLUUSH
BLESSCCH
PTUI

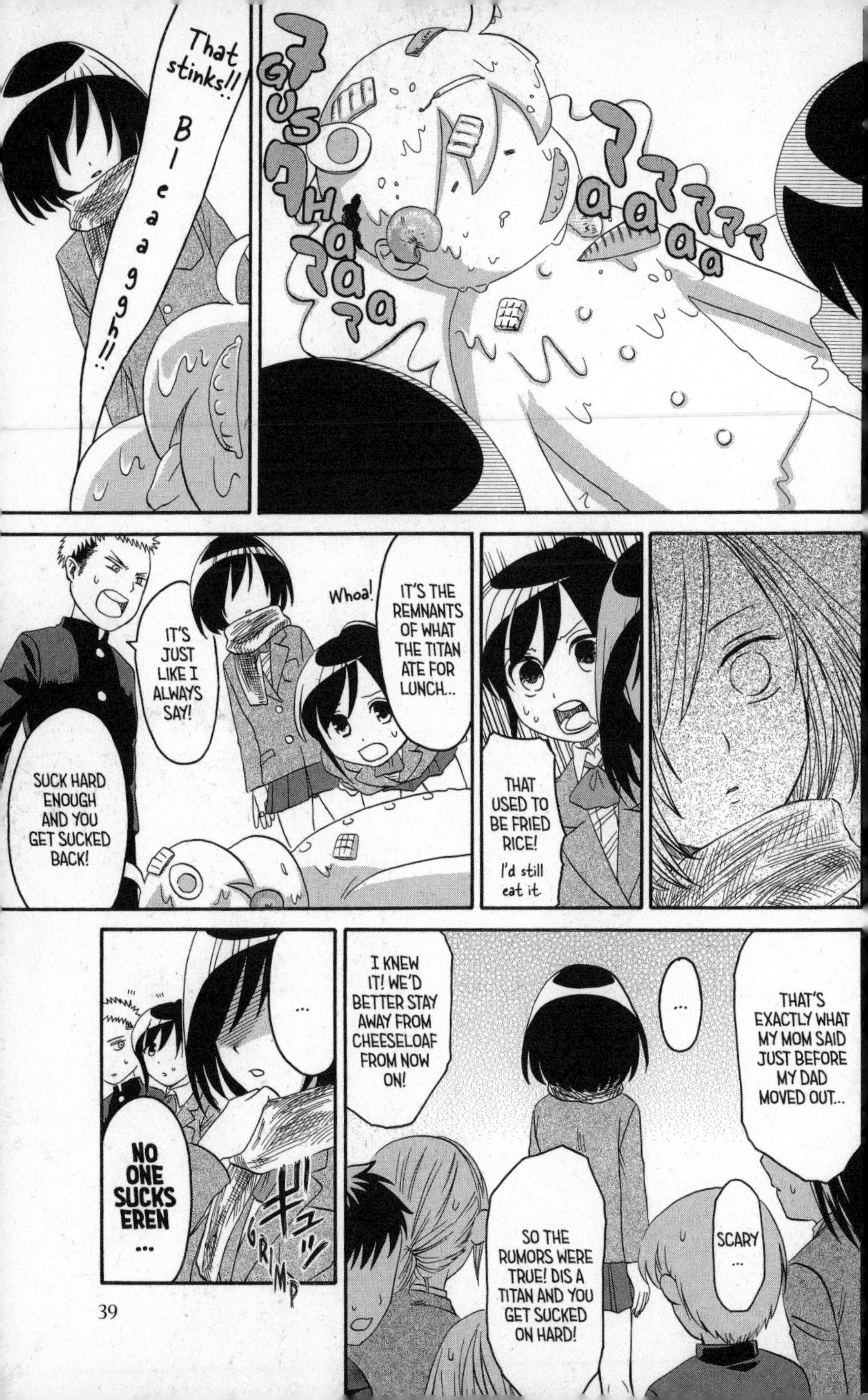
GUSHaaaa
aaaaa
That stinks!!
Bleaagggh!!
THAT USED TO BE FRIED RICE!
I'd still eat it.
Whoa!
IT'S THE REMNANTS OF WHAT THE TITAN ATE FOR LUNCH...
IT'S JUST LIKE I ALWAYS SAY!
SUCK HARD ENOUGH AND YOU GET SUCKED BACK!
THAT'S EXACTLY WHAT MY MOM SAID JUST BEFORE MY DAD MOVED OUT...
...
I KNEW IT! WE'D BETTER STAY AWAY FROM CHEESELOAF FROM NOW ON!
SCARY ...
SO THE RUMORS WERE TRUE! DIS A TITAN AND YOU GET SUCKED ON HARD!
...
NO ONE SUCKS EREN ...
GRIMP

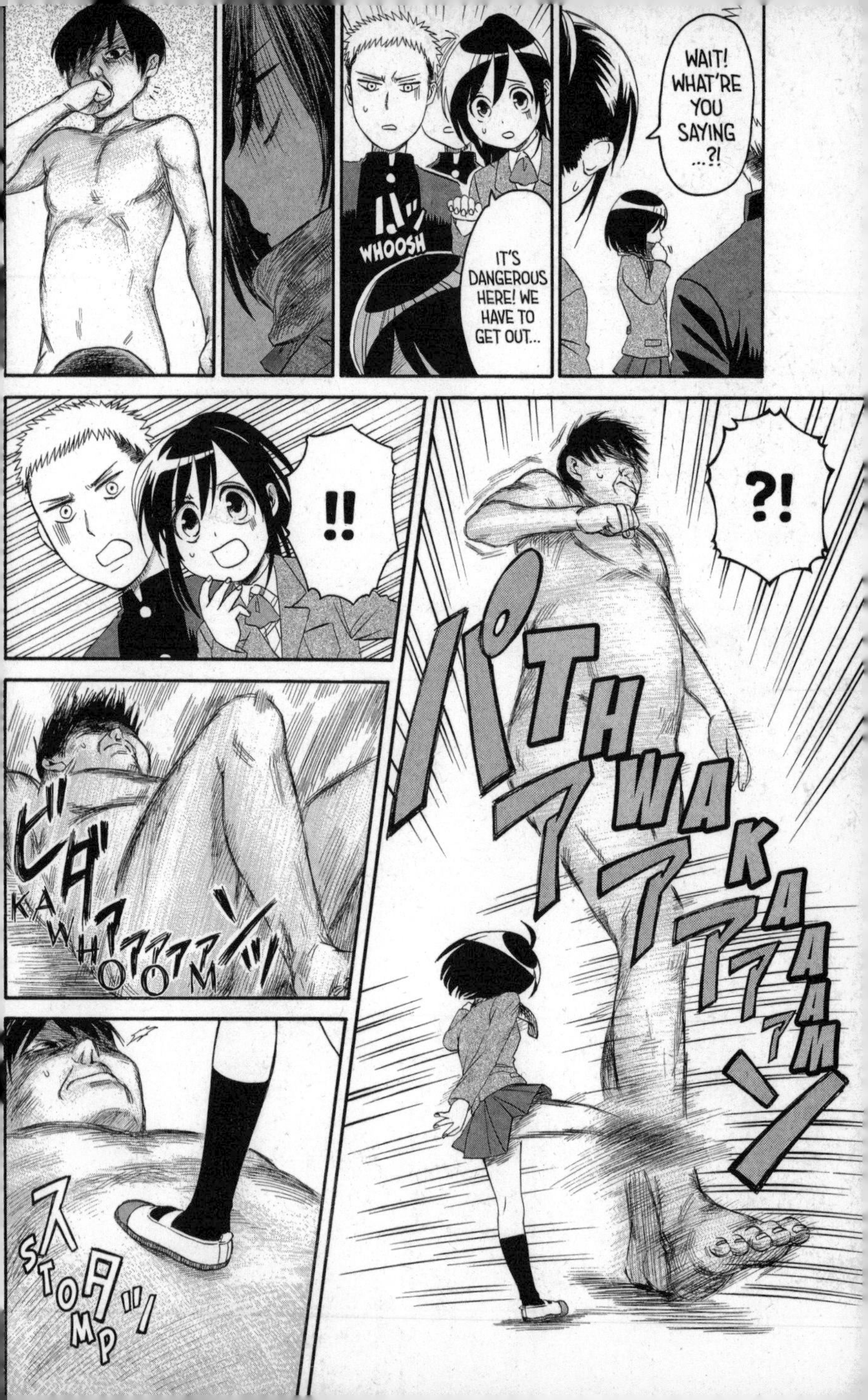
WAIT! WHAT'RE YOU SAYING ...?!
WHOOSH
IT'S DANGEROUS HERE! WE HAVE TO GET OUT...
?!
THWAKAAAAM
!!
KAWHOOOM
STOMP

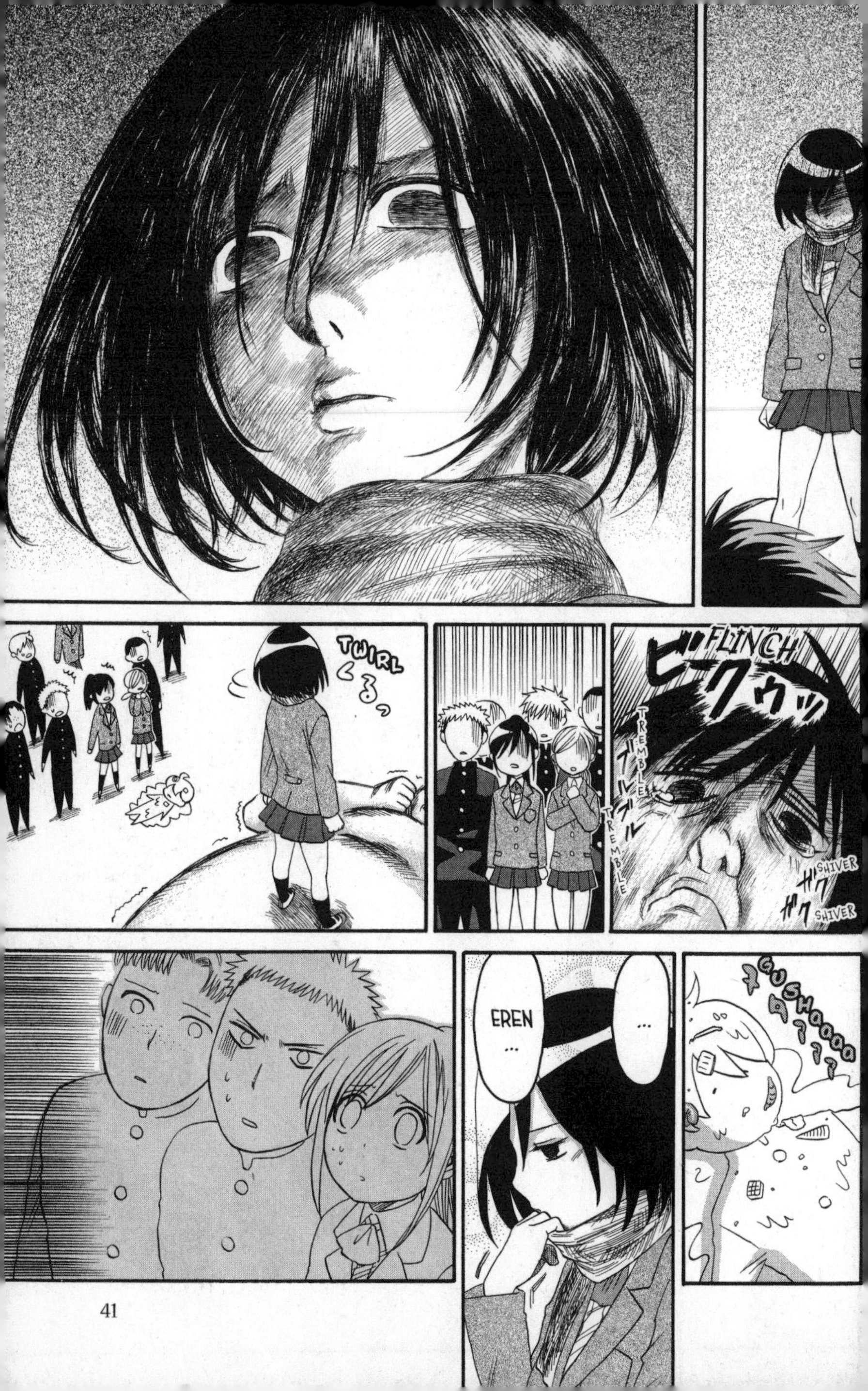
FLINCH
TREMBLE
TREMBLE
SHIVER
SHIVER
TWIRL
GUSHOOOOA
...
EREN
...

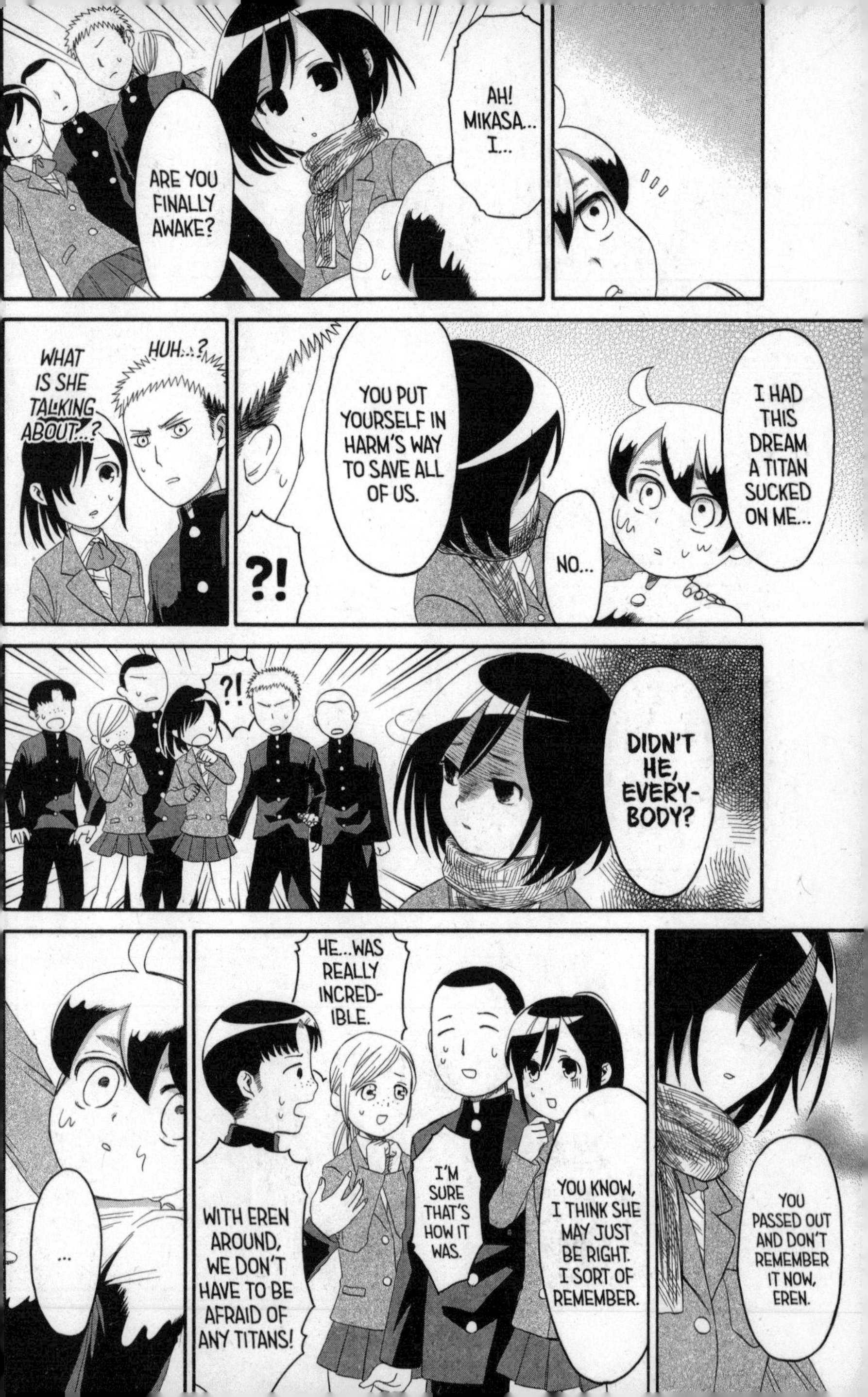
AH! MIKASA... I...
ARE YOU FINALLY AWAKE?
I HAD THIS DREAM A TITAN SUCKED ON ME...
NO...
YOU PUT YOURSELF IN HARM'S WAY TO SAVE ALL OF US.
?!
HUH...?
WHAT IS SHE TALKING ABOUT...?
DIDN'T HE, EVERYBODY?
?!
YOU PASSED OUT AND DON'T REMEMBER IT NOW, EREN.
YOU KNOW, I THINK SHE MAY JUST BE RIGHT. I SORT OF REMEMBER.
I'M SURE THAT'S HOW IT WAS.
HE...WAS REALLY INCREDIBLE.
WITH EREN AROUND, WE DON'T HAVE TO BE AFRAID OF ANY TITANS!
...

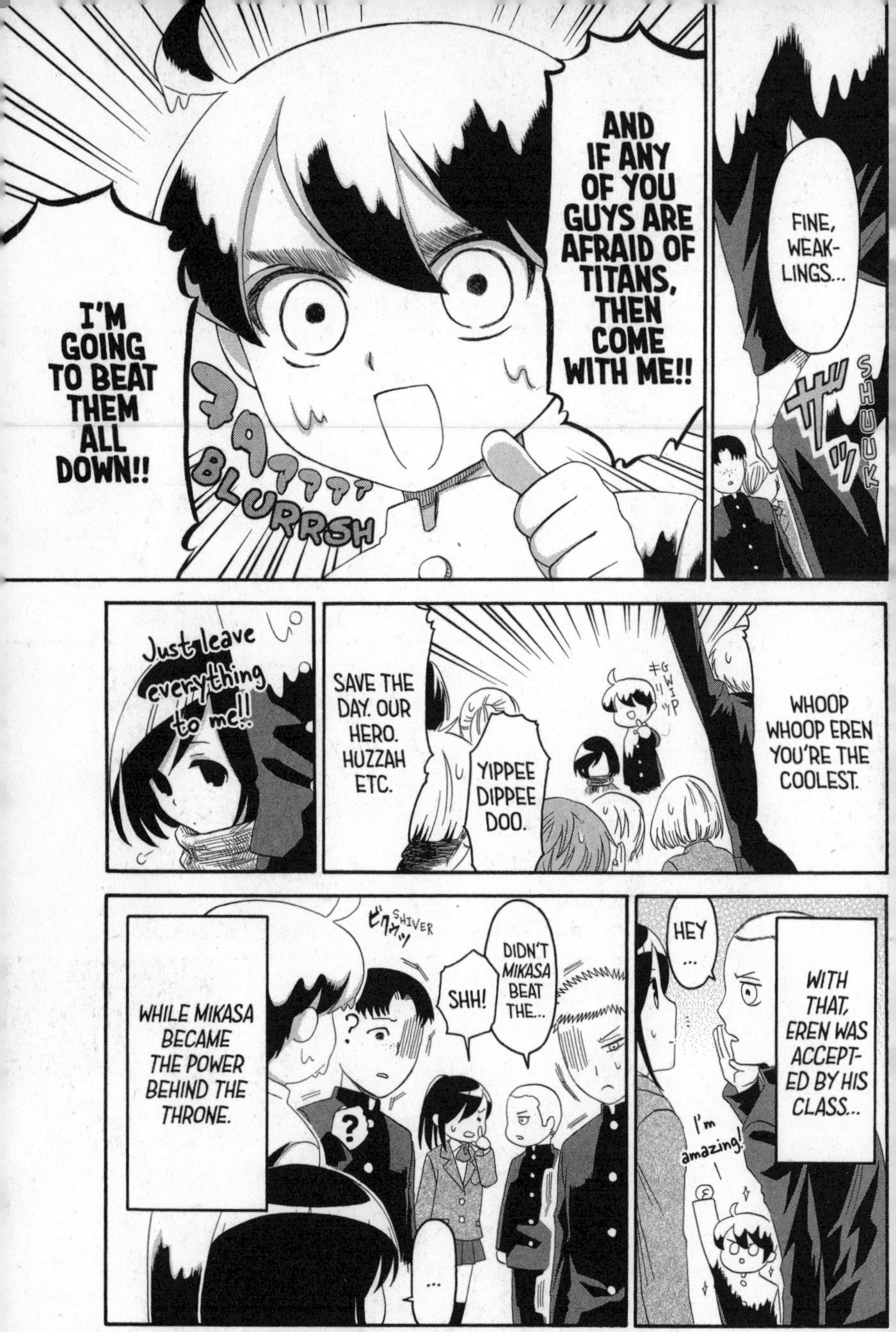
FINE, WEAKLINGS...
SHUCK
AND IF ANY OF YOU GUYS ARE AFRAID OF TITANS, THEN COME WITH ME!!
I'M GOING TO BEAT THEM ALL DOWN!!
BLURRSH
WHOOP WHOOP EREN YOU'RE THE COOLEST.
GWIP
YIPPEE DIPPEE DOO.
SAVE THE DAY. OUR HERO. HUZZAH ETC.
Just leave everything to me!!
WITH THAT, EREN WAS ACCEPTED BY HIS CLASS...
HEY ...
I'm amazing!
DIDN'T MIKASA BEAT THE...
SHIVER
SHH!
WHILE MIKASA BECAME THE POWER BEHIND THE THRONE.
...

The answer to the question on page 25 is: He's between Franz and Hannah!

TO CELEBRATE "TITAN JUNIOR HIGH" GOING ON SALE!

HAJIME ISAYAMA × SAKI NAKAGAWA

TALK ABOUT TITAN! 1

TELL US HOW YOU TWO MET.

ISAYAMA: ACTUALLY, WE BOTH WENT TO THE SAME DESIGN GRADUATE SCHOOL IN KYUSHU.

NAKAGAWA: HE GRADUATED BEFORE I DID.

I: I WENT TO VISIT MY OLD ALMA MATER AT ONE POINT, AND THAT'S WHERE I FIRST MET NAKAGAWA.

N: I REMEMBER THAT I ALSO HAD AN EDITOR FROM WEEKLY SHONEN MAGAZINE, (F-KAWA-SAN), AND WE TALKED ABOUT OUR EDITORS.

I: I HAD ALSO MET F-KAWA-SAN, AND WHAT I REMEMBER MOST IS NAKAGAWA-SAN SAYING HOW THERE WAS A BIG DIFFERENCE BETWEEN F-KAWA-SAN ON THE PHONE AND F-KAWA-SAN IN PERSON.

N: D-DID I REALLY SAY SOMETHING LIKE THAT? (LAUGHS)

HOW DID "TITAN JUNIOR HIGH" GET STARTED?

I: ONE OF THE EDITORS ASKED THE BESSATSU SHONEN MAGAZINE EDITOR IF THERE COULD BE A SPIN-OFF MANGA. A FOUR-PANEL STRIP WAS A POSSIBILITY.

N: F-KAWA-SAN SAID THAT I SHOULD ENTER INTO AN "ATTACK ON TITAN" SPIN-OFF COMPETITION.

I: I HEAR THEY CHOSE NAKAGAWA-SAN FROM A BUNCH OF DIFFERENT ENTRIES.

N: I WAS PRETTY UNSURE WHEN I WAS SELECTED. I WAS LIKE, "ARE YOU SURE?"

I: IS THAT RIGHT?

N: STILL, I WAS AN "ATTACK ON TITAN" FAN MYSELF, SO I WENT INTO IT WITH A LOT OF RESPECT.

I: IT'S TRUE THAT AFTER THE MANGA ARTIST WAS SELECTED, I SUGGESTED THAT WE DO SOMETHING LIKE "BLAME ACADEMY."

N: RIGHT! AND I WENT OUT AND BOUGHT IT! I REMEMBER THINKING, SO ISAYAMA-SENSEI IS A "BLAME" FAN TOO!

I: I KNOW WE'RE OFF TOPIC, BUT YEAH. I'M A HUGE NIHEI-SENSEI FAN!

CONTINUED ON P. 84.

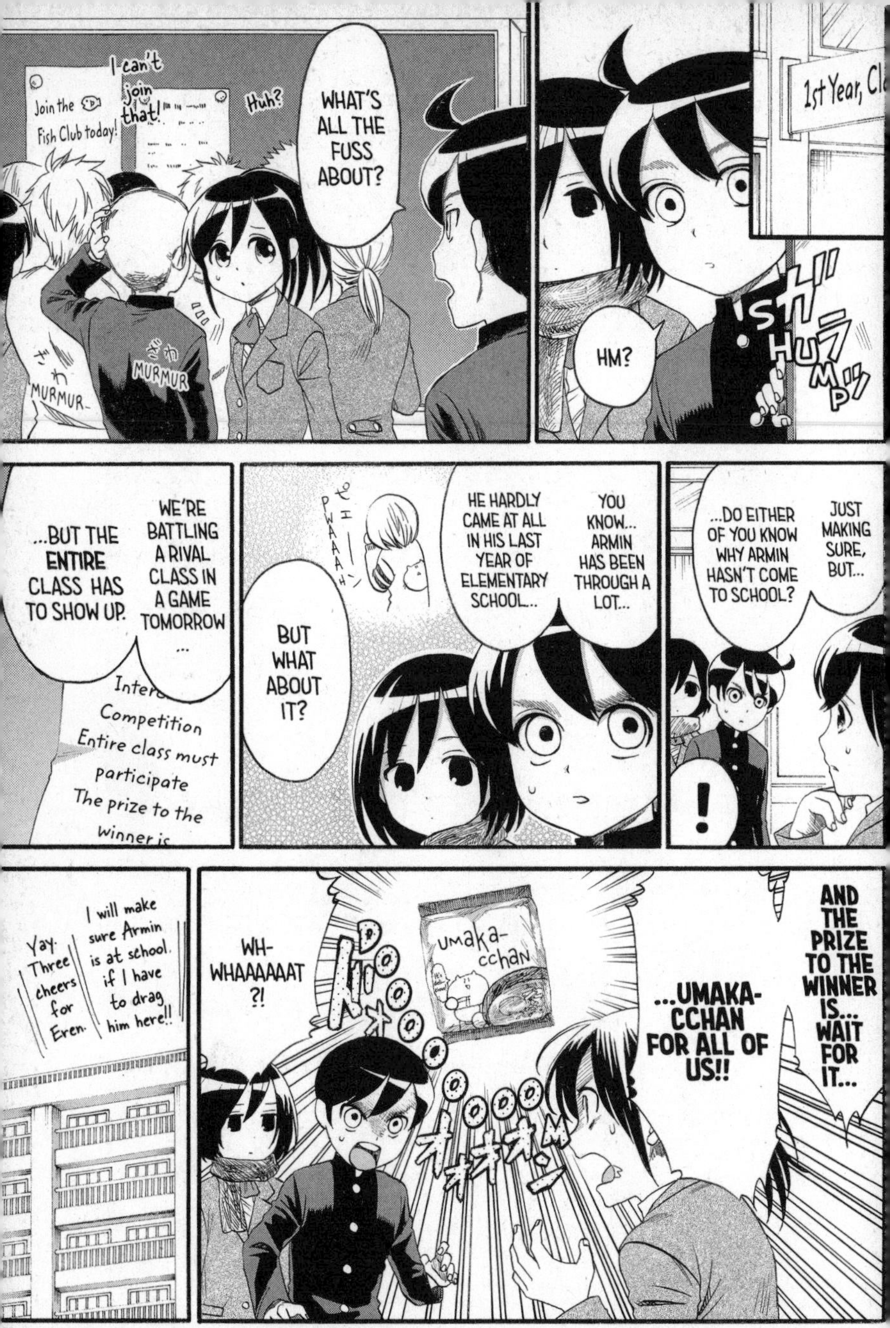

1st Year, Cl
HM?
WHAT'S ALL THE FUSS ABOUT?
Huh?
I can't join that!
Join the Fish Club today!
MURMUR
MURMUR
JUST MAKING SURE, BUT...
...DO EITHER OF YOU KNOW WHY ARMIN HASN'T COME TO SCHOOL?
!
YOU KNOW... ARMIN HAS BEEN THROUGH A LOT...
HE HARDLY CAME AT ALL IN HIS LAST YEAR OF ELEMENTARY SCHOOL...
PWAAAH
BUT WHAT ABOUT IT?
WE'RE BATTLING A RIVAL CLASS IN A GAME TOMORROW...
...BUT THE ENTIRE CLASS HAS TO SHOW UP.
Competition
Entire class must participate
The prize to the winner is
AND THE PRIZE TO THE WINNER IS... WAIT FOR IT...
...UMAKA-CCHAN FOR ALL OF US!!
Umaka-cchan
WH-WHAAAAAAT?!
I will make sure Armin is at school if I have to drag him here!!
Yay. Three cheers for Eren.

This ramen is the pride and joy of everyone living in the Kyushu region. Of course that includes Isayama-sensei and Nakagawa-sensei, who both come from Kyushu. Pity their poor existence, because they now live in Tokyo, where it can hardly be found anywhere. And it doesn't even need to be said that Eren and all the gang are slaves to their desire for Umaka-cchan.

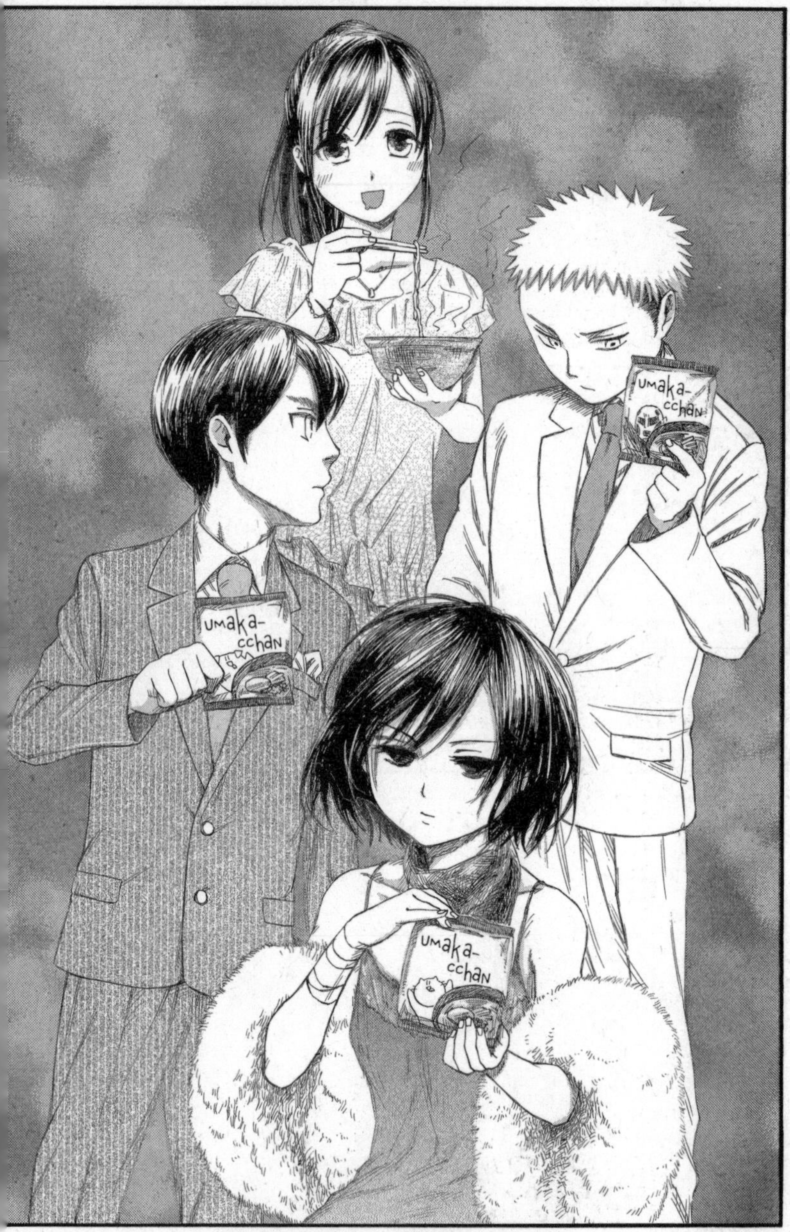
UMAKA-CCHAN
UMAKA-CCHAN
UMAKA-CCHAN

THIRD PERIOD: GRANDPA ARLERT

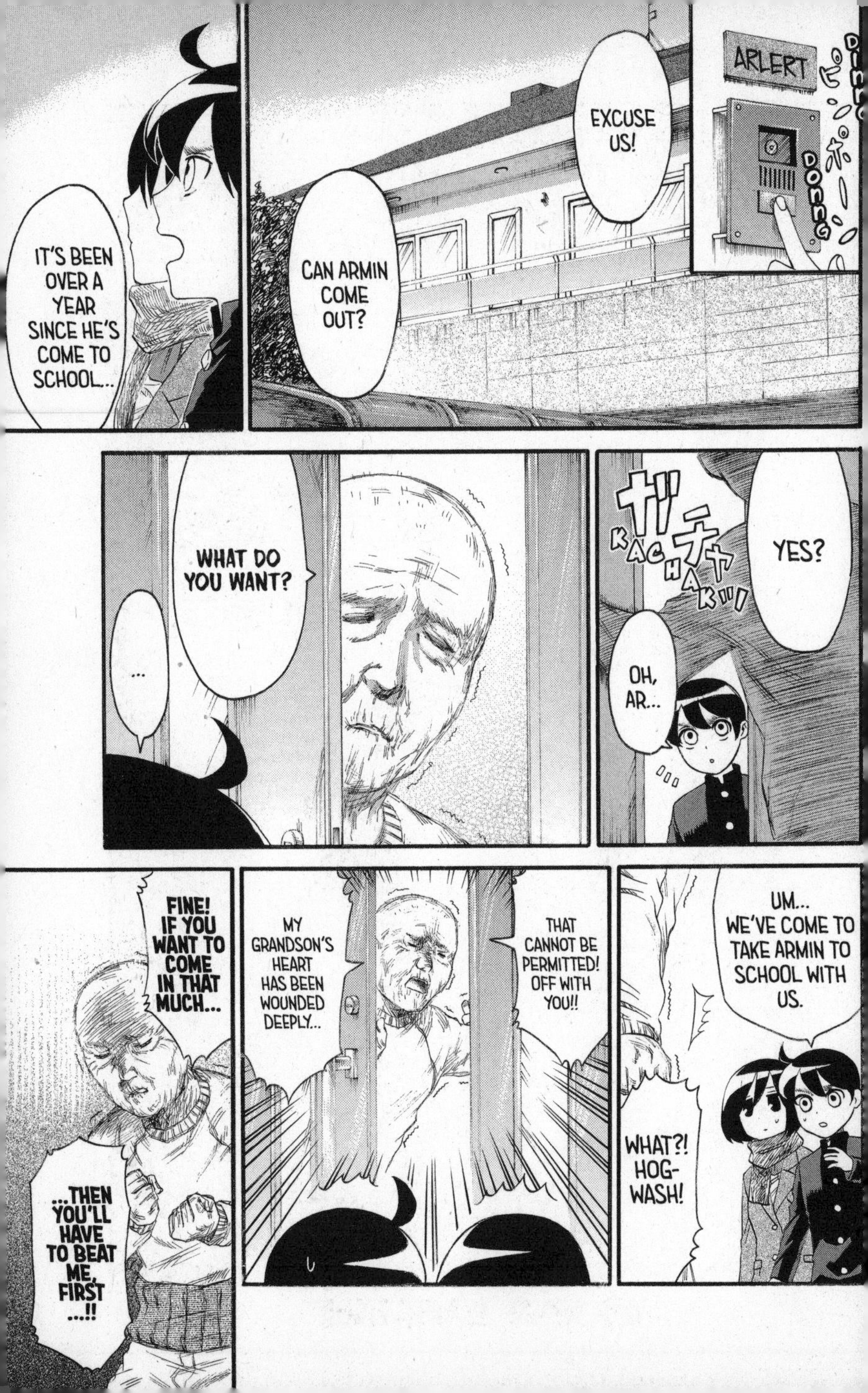
ARLERT
DONG
EXCUSE US!
CAN ARMIN COME OUT?
IT'S BEEN OVER A YEAR SINCE HE'S COME TO SCHOOL...
KACHAK!!
YES?
OH, AR...
WHAT DO YOU WANT?
...
UM... WE'VE COME TO TAKE ARMIN TO SCHOOL WITH US.
WHAT?! HOG-WASH!
THAT CANNOT BE PERMITTED! OFF WITH YOU!!
MY GRANDSON'S HEART HAS BEEN WOUNDED DEEPLY...
FINE! IF YOU WANT TO COME IN THAT MUCH...
...THEN YOU'LL HAVE TO BEAT ME, FIRST ...!!

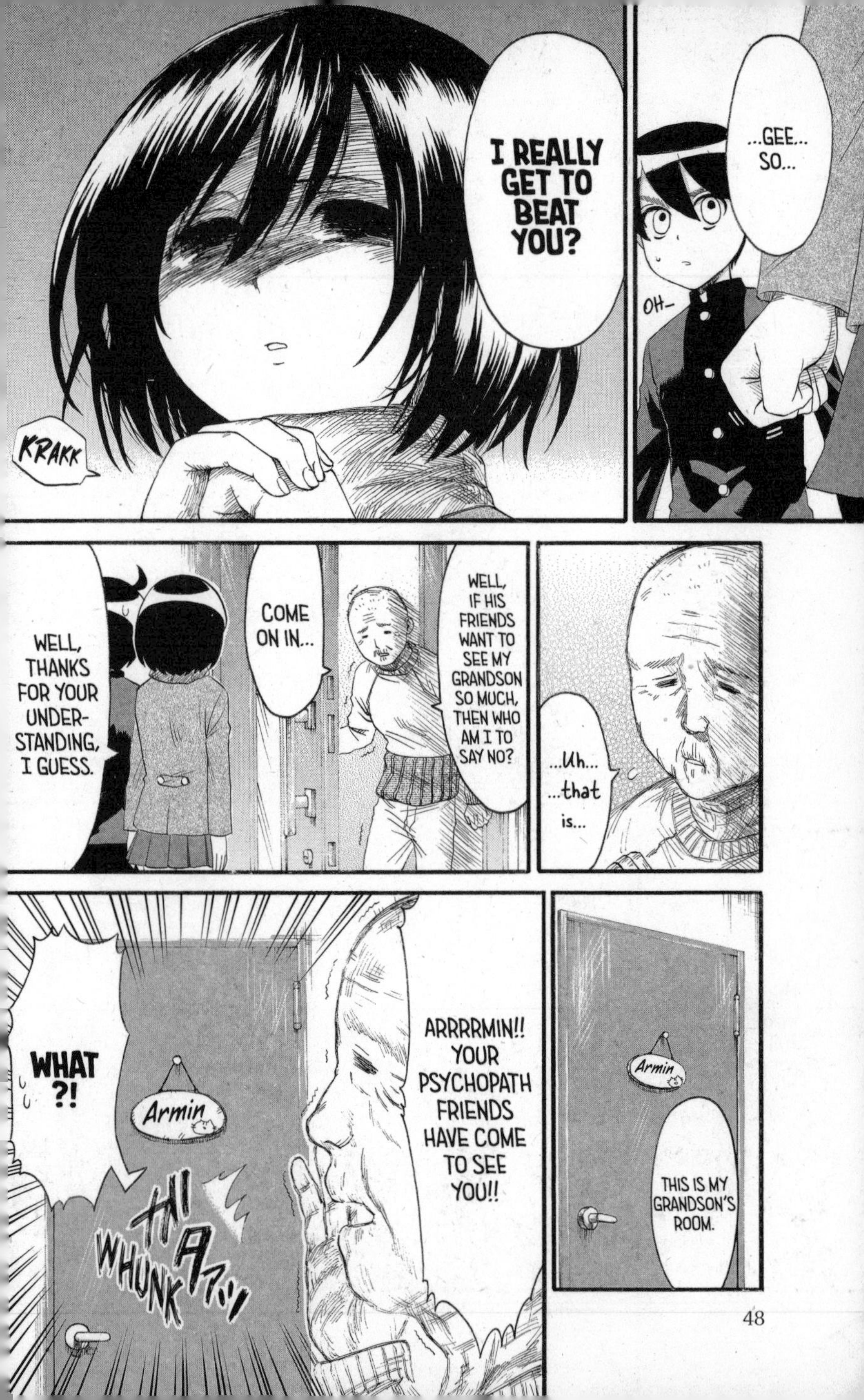
...GEE... SO...
OH–
I REALLY GET TO BEAT YOU?
KRAKK
...Uh... ...that is...
WELL, IF HIS FRIENDS WANT TO SEE MY GRANDSON SO MUCH, THEN WHO AM I TO SAY NO?
COME ON IN...
WELL, THANKS FOR YOUR UNDER-STANDING, I GUESS.
Armin
THIS IS MY GRANDSON'S ROOM.
ARRRRMIN!! YOUR PSYCHOPATH FRIENDS HAVE COME TO SEE YOU!!
Armin
WHAT?!
WHUNK

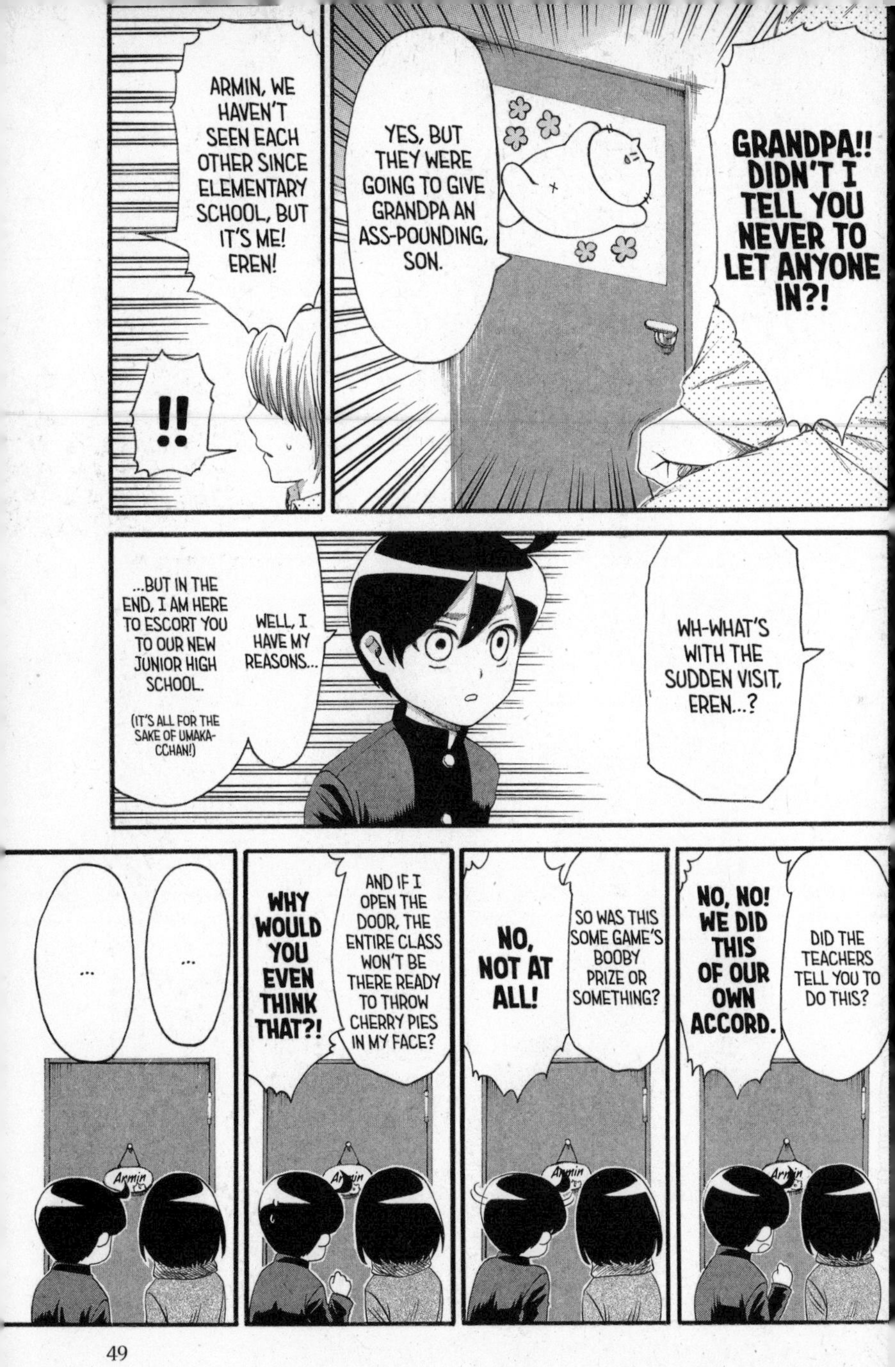
GRANDPA!! DIDN'T I TELL YOU NEVER TO LET ANYONE IN?!
YES, BUT THEY WERE GOING TO GIVE GRANDPA AN ASS-POUNDING, SON.
ARMIN, WE HAVEN'T SEEN EACH OTHER SINCE ELEMENTARY SCHOOL, BUT IT'S ME! EREN!
!!
WH-WHAT'S WITH THE SUDDEN VISIT, EREN...?
WELL, I HAVE MY REASONS...
...BUT IN THE END, I AM HERE TO ESCORT YOU TO OUR NEW JUNIOR HIGH SCHOOL.
(IT'S ALL FOR THE SAKE OF UMAKA-CCHAN!)
DID THE TEACHERS TELL YOU TO DO THIS?
NO, NO! WE DID THIS OF OUR OWN ACCORD.
SO WAS THIS SOME GAME'S BOOBY PRIZE OR SOMETHING?
NO, NOT AT ALL!
AND IF I OPEN THE DOOR, THE ENTIRE CLASS WON'T BE THERE READY TO THROW CHERRY PIES IN MY FACE?
WHY WOULD YOU EVEN THINK THAT?!
...
...

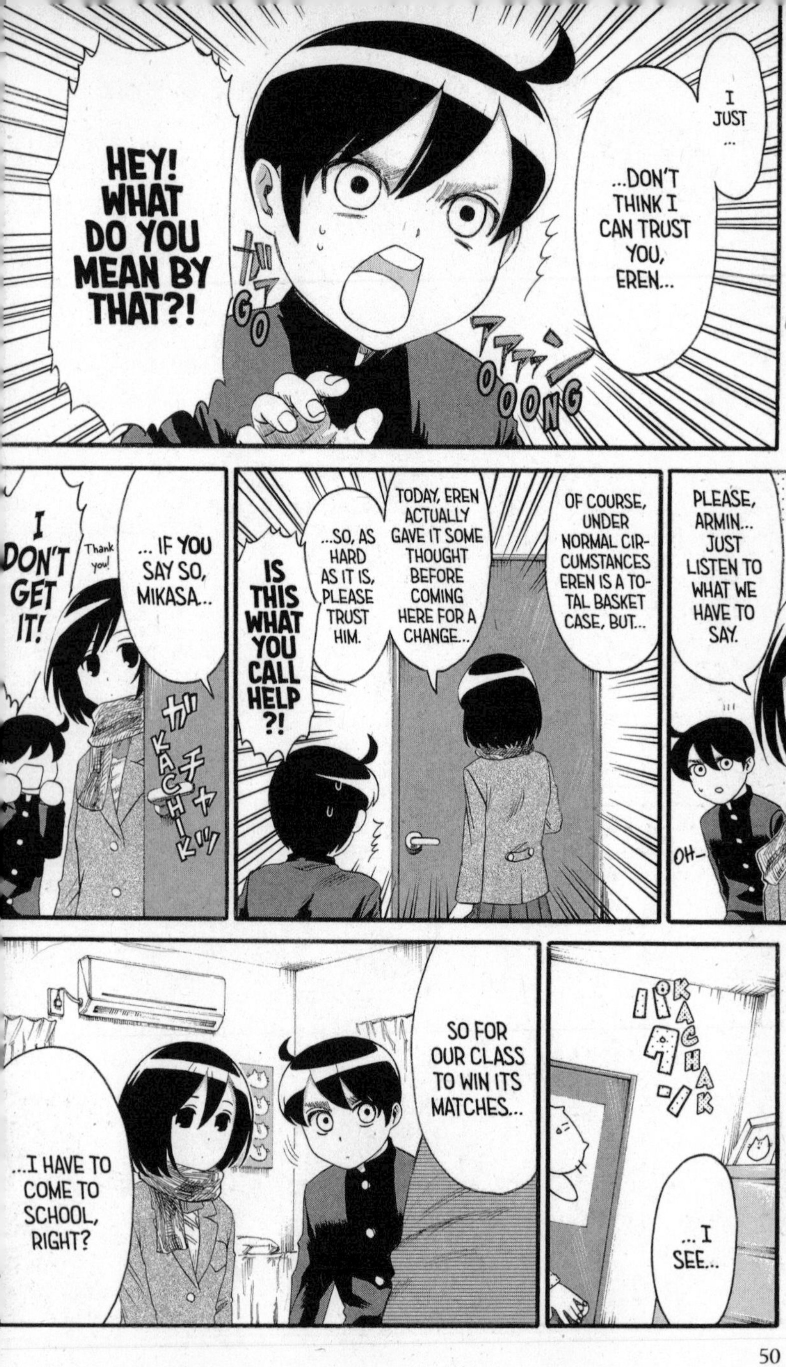
I JUST ...
...DON'T THINK I CAN TRUST YOU, EREN...
GOOOONG
GO
HEY! WHAT DO YOU MEAN BY THAT?!
PLEASE, ARMIN... JUST LISTEN TO WHAT WE HAVE TO SAY.
OH–
OF COURSE, UNDER NORMAL CIR- CUMSTANCES EREN IS A TO- TAL BASKET CASE, BUT...
TODAY, EREN ACTUALLY GAVE IT SOME THOUGHT BEFORE COMING HERE FOR A CHANGE...
...SO, AS HARD AS IT IS, PLEASE TRUST HIM.
IS THIS WHAT YOU CALL HELP?!
... IF YOU SAY SO, MIKASA...
KACHIK
Thank you!
I DON'T GET IT!
KACHAK
... I SEE...
SO FOR OUR CLASS TO WIN ITS MATCHES...
...I HAVE TO COME TO SCHOOL, RIGHT?

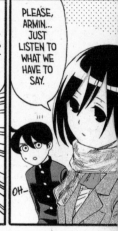

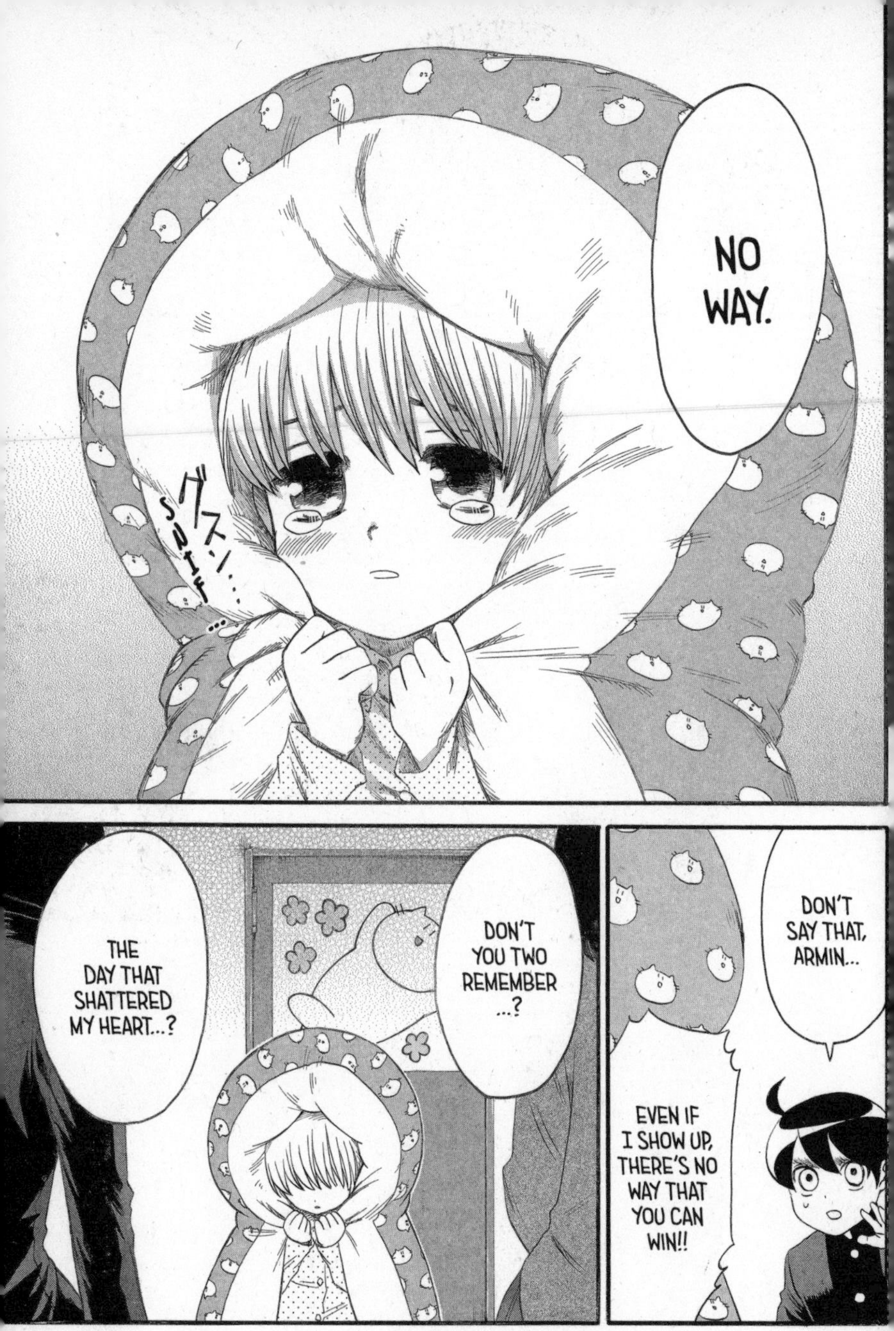
NO WAY.
グスン…
SNIFF...
DON'T SAY THAT, ARMIN...
EVEN IF I SHOW UP, THERE'S NO WAY THAT YOU CAN WIN!!
DON'T YOU TWO REMEMBER ...?
THE DAY THAT SHATTERED MY HEART...?

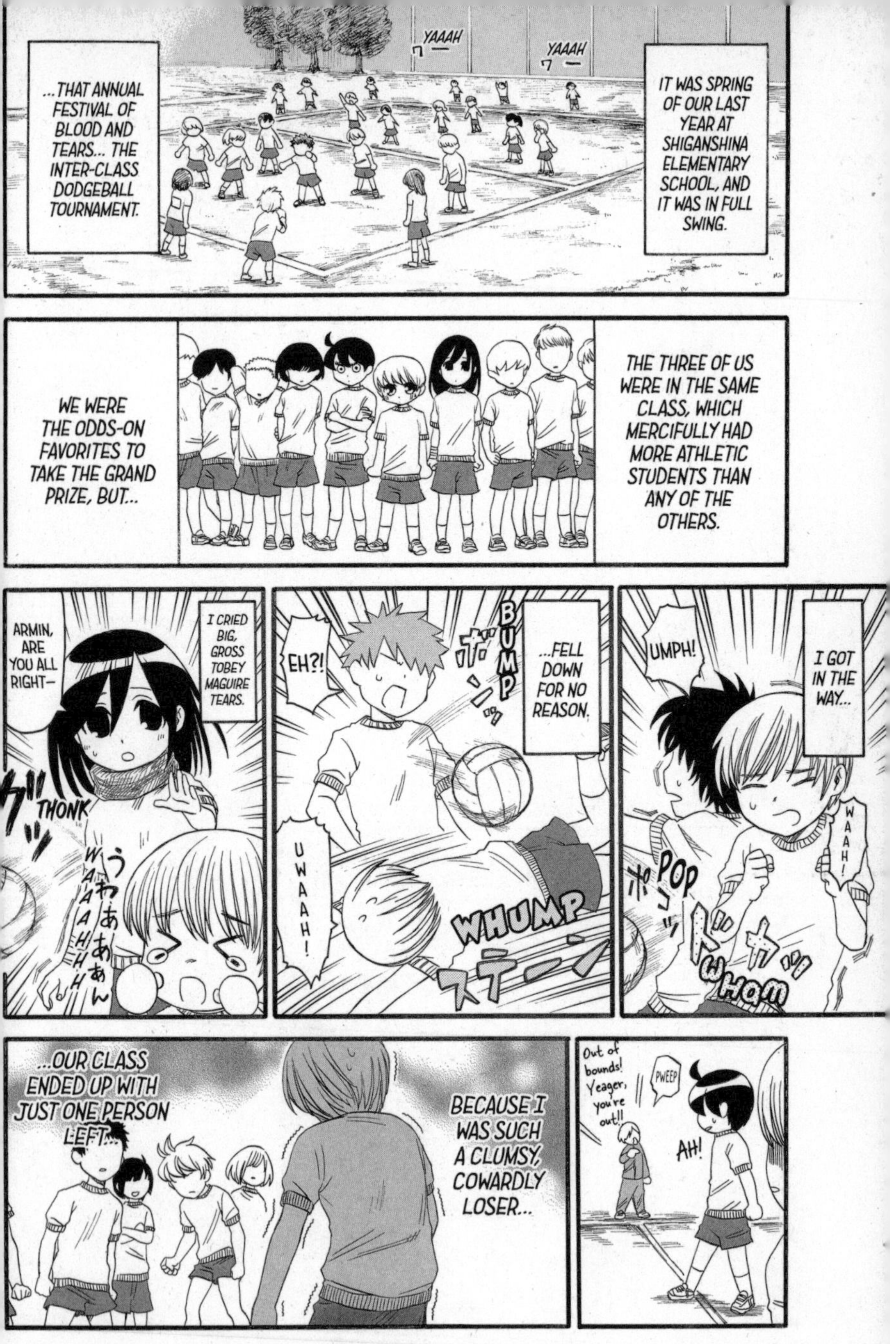
IT WAS SPRING OF OUR LAST YEAR AT SHIGANSHINA ELEMENTARY SCHOOL, AND IT WAS IN FULL SWING.
YAAAH
YAAAH
...THAT ANNUAL FESTIVAL OF BLOOD AND TEARS... THE INTER-CLASS DODGEBALL TOURNAMENT.
THE THREE OF US WERE IN THE SAME CLASS, WHICH MERCIFULLY HAD MORE ATHLETIC STUDENTS THAN ANY OF THE OTHERS.
WE WERE THE ODDS-ON FAVORITES TO TAKE THE GRAND PRIZE, BUT...
I GOT IN THE WAY...
UMPH!
WAAAH!
POP
WHAM
...FELL DOWN FOR NO REASON.
BUMP
EH?!
UWAAAH!
WHUMP
I CRIED BIG, GROSS TOBEY MAGUIRE TEARS.
ARMIN, ARE YOU ALL RIGHT—
THONK
WAAAHHH
PWEEP
Out of bounds! Yeager, you're out!!
AH!
BECAUSE I WAS SUCH A CLUMSY, COWARDLY LOSER...
...OUR CLASS ENDED UP WITH JUST ONE PERSON LEFT...

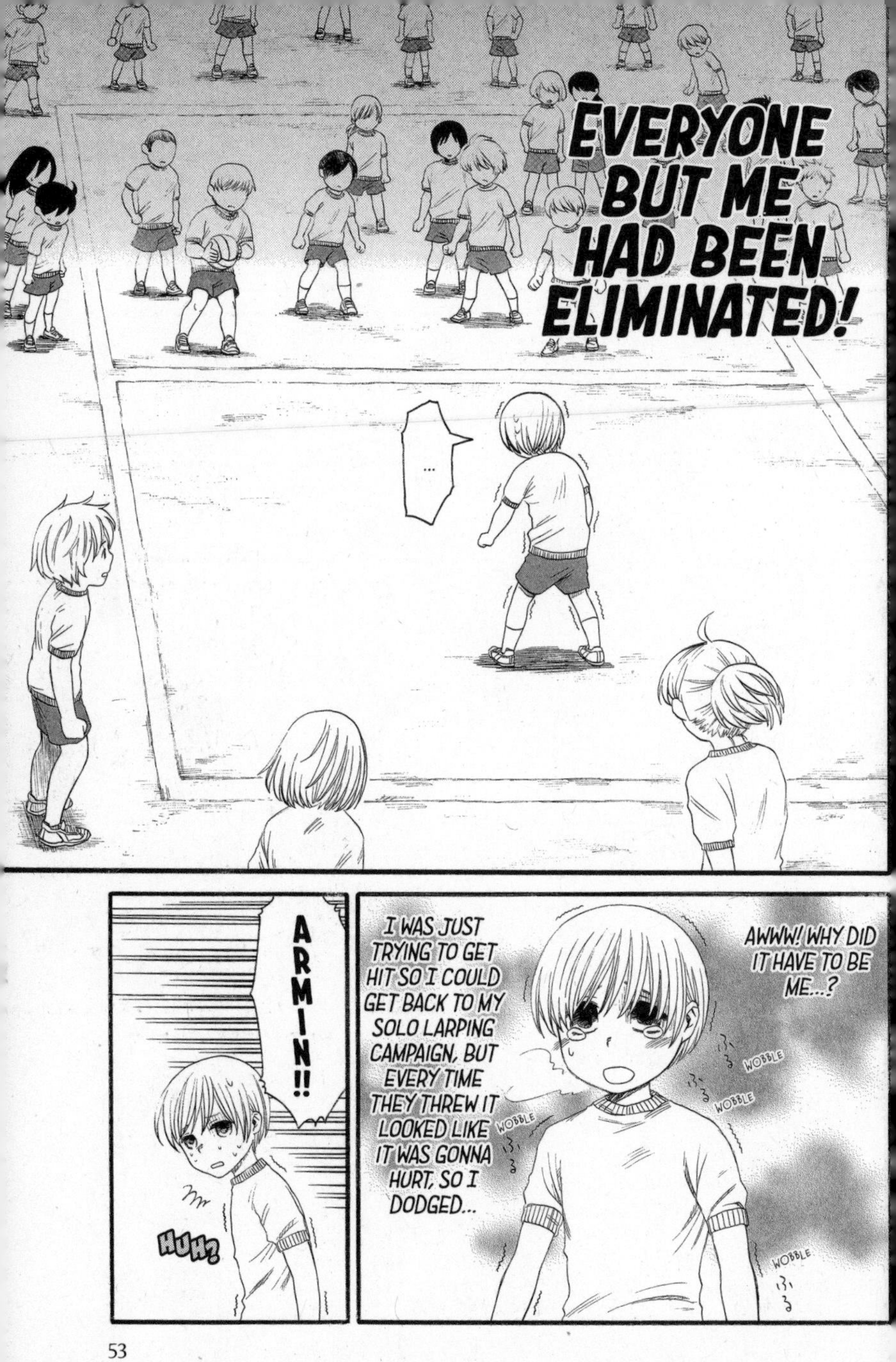
EVERYONE BUT ME HAD BEEN ELIMINATED!
...
AWWW! WHY DID IT HAVE TO BE ME...?
WOBBLE
WOBBLE
WOBBLE
WOBBLE
I WAS JUST TRYING TO GET HIT SO I COULD GET BACK TO MY SOLO LARPING CAMPAIGN, BUT EVERY TIME THEY THREW IT LOOKED LIKE IT WAS GONNA HURT, SO I DODGED...
ARMIN!!
HUH?

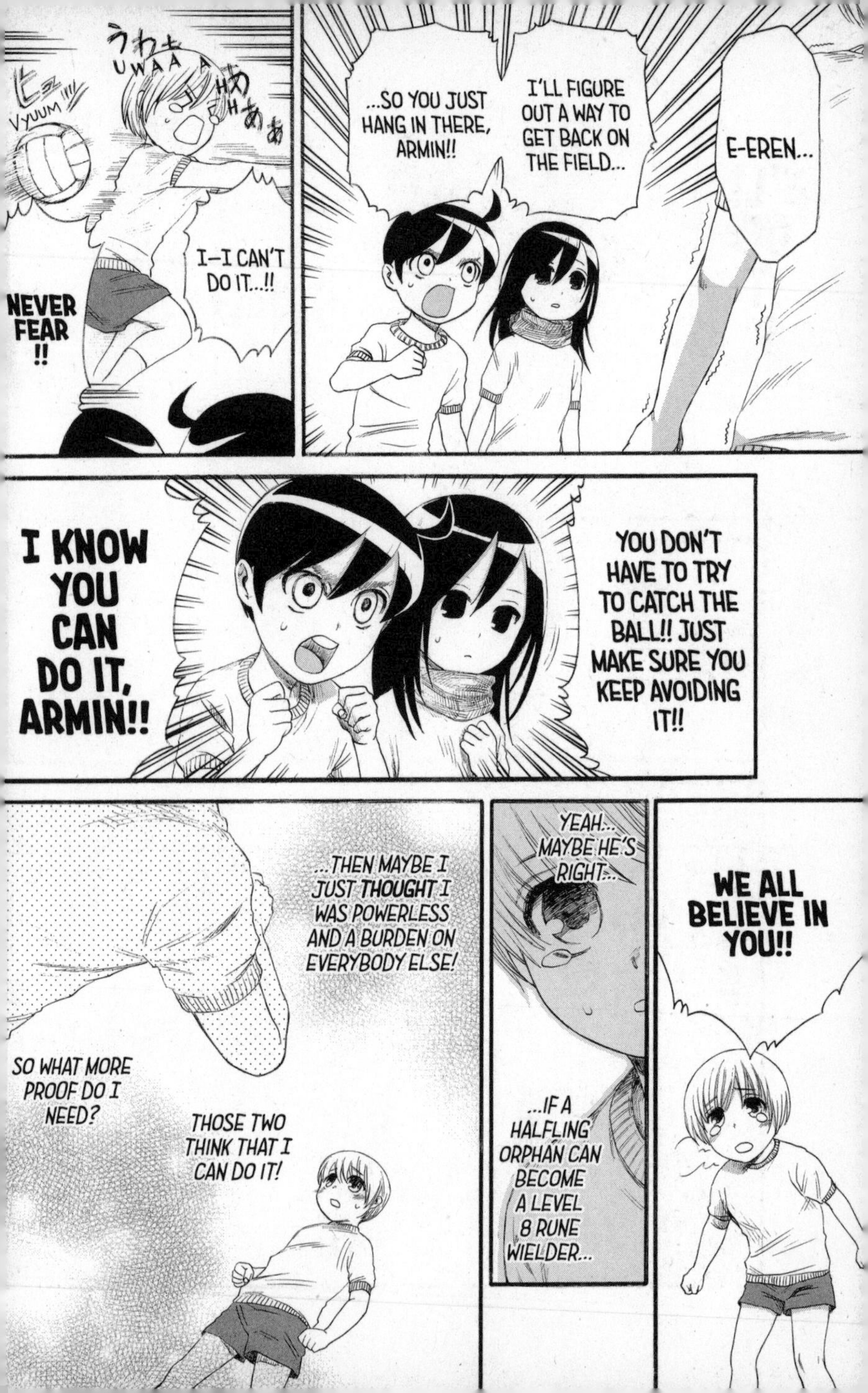
E-EREN...
I'LL FIGURE OUT A WAY TO GET BACK ON THE FIELD...
...SO YOU JUST HANG IN THERE, ARMIN!!
UWAAAAHH
VYUUM!!!
I-I CAN'T DO IT...!!
NEVER FEAR!!
YOU DON'T HAVE TO TRY TO CATCH THE BALL!! JUST MAKE SURE YOU KEEP AVOIDING IT!!
I KNOW YOU CAN DO IT, ARMIN!!
WE ALL BELIEVE IN YOU!!
YEAH... MAYBE HE'S RIGHT...
...IF A HALFLING ORPHAN CAN BECOME A LEVEL 8 RUNE WIELDER...
...THEN MAYBE I JUST THOUGHT I WAS POWERLESS AND A BURDEN ON EVERYBODY ELSE!
SO WHAT MORE PROOF DO I NEED?
THOSE TWO THINK THAT I CAN DO IT!

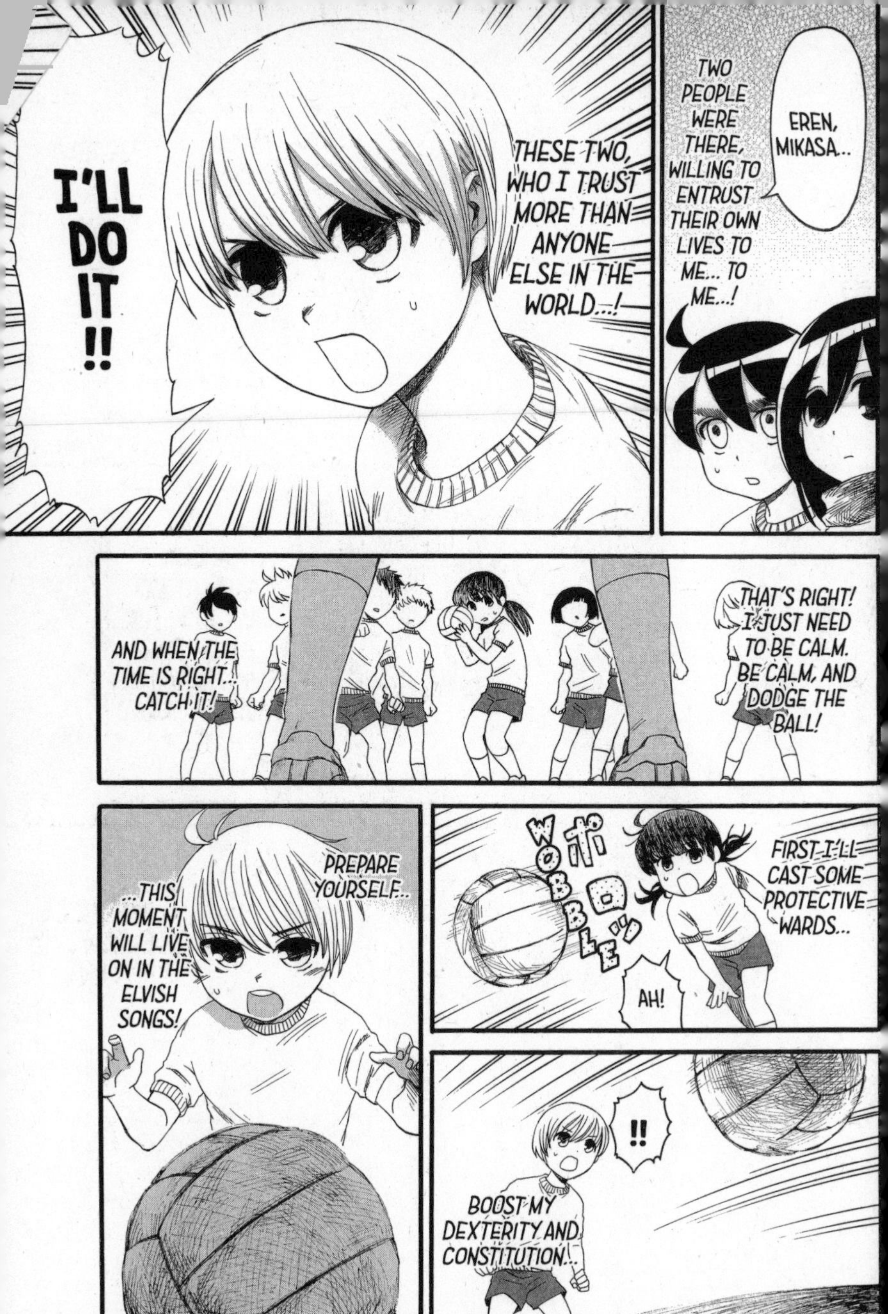
EREN, MIKASA...
TWO PEOPLE WERE THERE, WILLING TO ENTRUST THEIR OWN LIVES TO ME... TO ME...!
THESE TWO, WHO I TRUST MORE THAN ANYONE ELSE IN THE WORLD...!
I'LL DO IT!!
THAT'S RIGHT! I JUST NEED TO BE CALM. BE CALM, AND DODGE THE BALL!
AND WHEN THE TIME IS RIGHT... CATCH IT!
FIRST I'LL CAST SOME PROTECTIVE WARDS...
WOBBLE
AH!
!!
BOOST MY DEXTERITY AND CONSTITUTION...
PREPARE YOURSELF...
...THIS MOMENT WILL LIVE ON IN THE ELVISH SONGS!

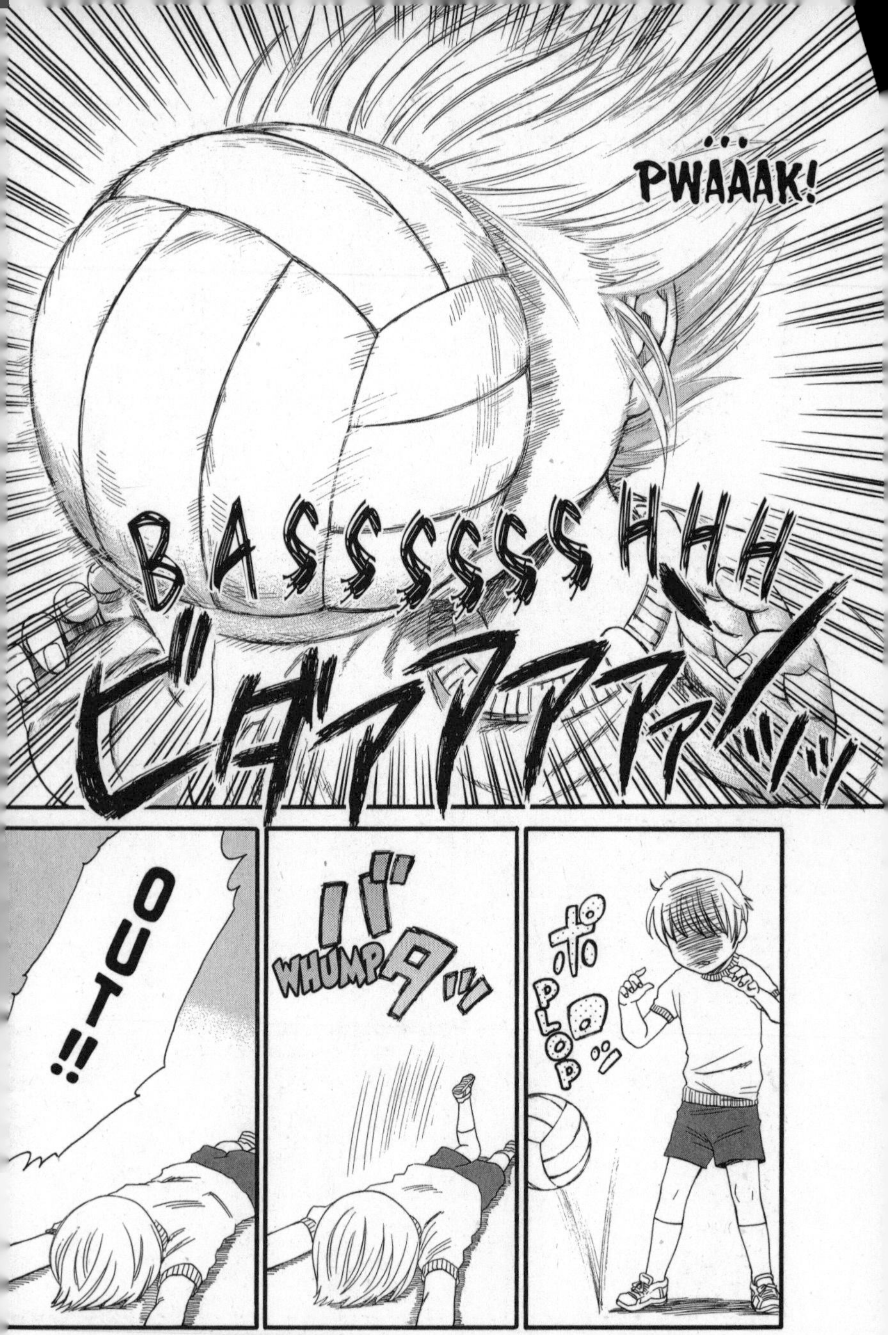

...PWAAAK!
BASSSSSHHH
PLOP
WHUMP
OUT!!

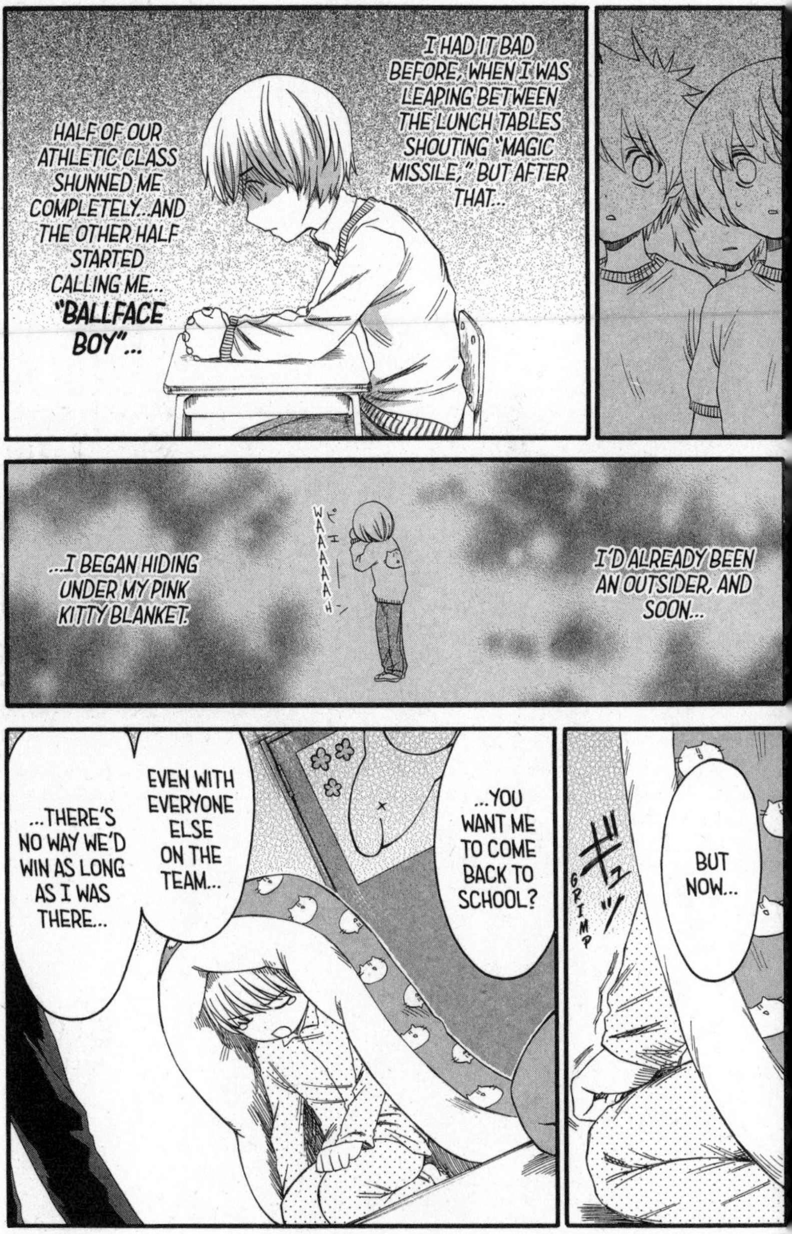
I HAD IT BAD BEFORE, WHEN I WAS LEAPING BETWEEN THE LUNCH TABLES SHOUTING "MAGIC MISSILE," BUT AFTER THAT...
HALF OF OUR ATHLETIC CLASS SHUNNED ME COMPLETELY...AND THE OTHER HALF STARTED CALLING ME... "BALLFACE BOY"...
I'D ALREADY BEEN AN OUTSIDER, AND SOON...
WAAAAAAH
...I BEGAN HIDING UNDER MY PINK KITTY BLANKET.
BUT NOW...
GRIMP
...YOU WANT ME TO COME BACK TO SCHOOL?
EVEN WITH EVERYONE ELSE ON THE TEAM...
...THERE'S NO WAY WE'D WIN AS LONG AS I WAS THERE...

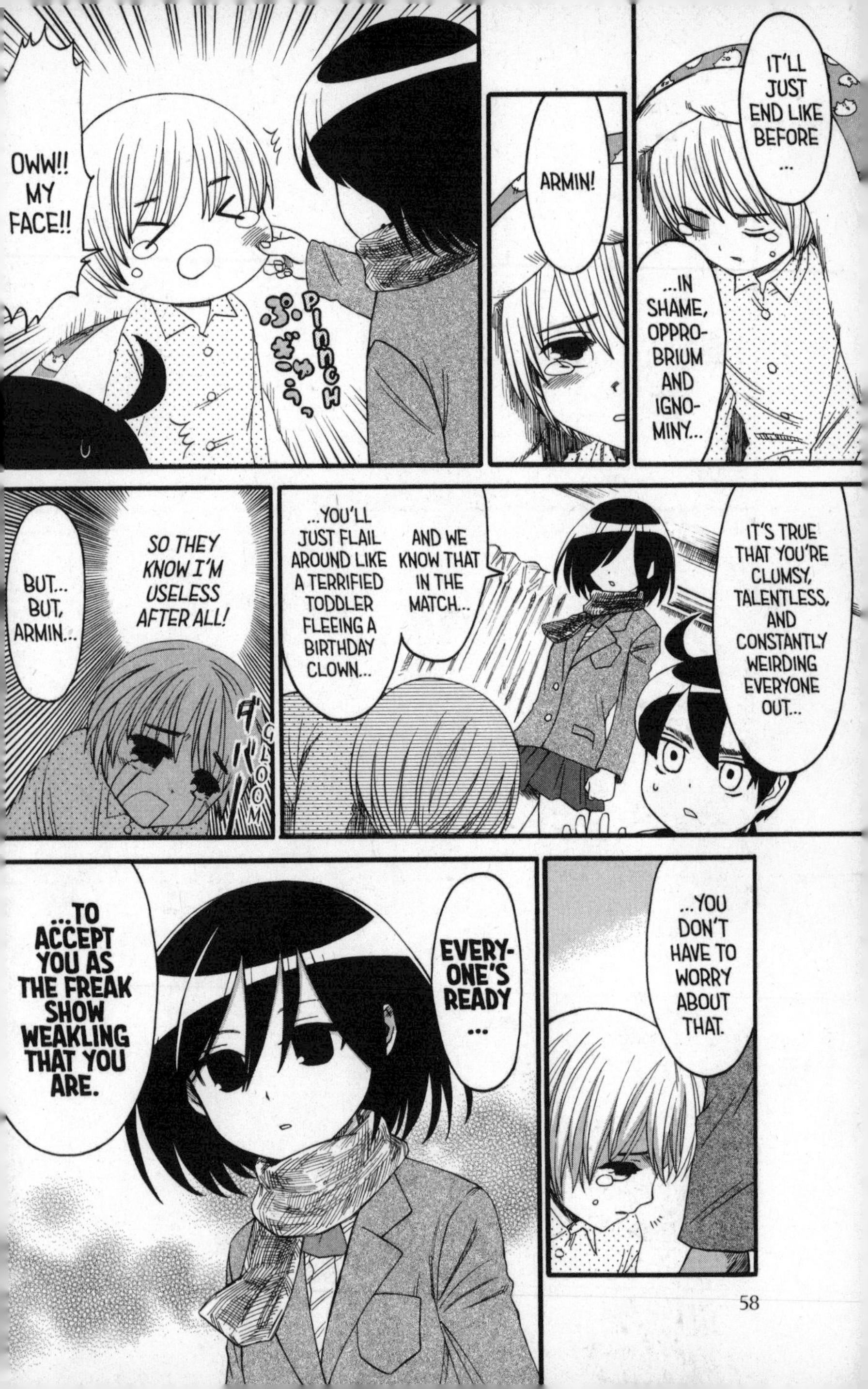
IT'LL JUST END LIKE BEFORE ...
...IN SHAME, OPPROBRIUM AND IGNOMINY...
ARMIN!
OWW!! MY FACE!!
ぷぎゅっ
PINNCH
IT'S TRUE THAT YOU'RE CLUMSY, TALENTLESS, AND CONSTANTLY WEIRDING EVERYONE OUT...
AND WE KNOW THAT IN THE MATCH...
...YOU'LL JUST FLAIL AROUND LIKE A TERRIFIED TODDLER FLEEING A BIRTHDAY CLOWN...
SO THEY KNOW I'M USELESS AFTER ALL!
BUT... BUT, ARMIN...
GLOOM
...YOU DON'T HAVE TO WORRY ABOUT THAT.
EVERYONE'S READY ...
...TO ACCEPT YOU AS THE FREAK SHOW WEAKLING THAT YOU ARE.

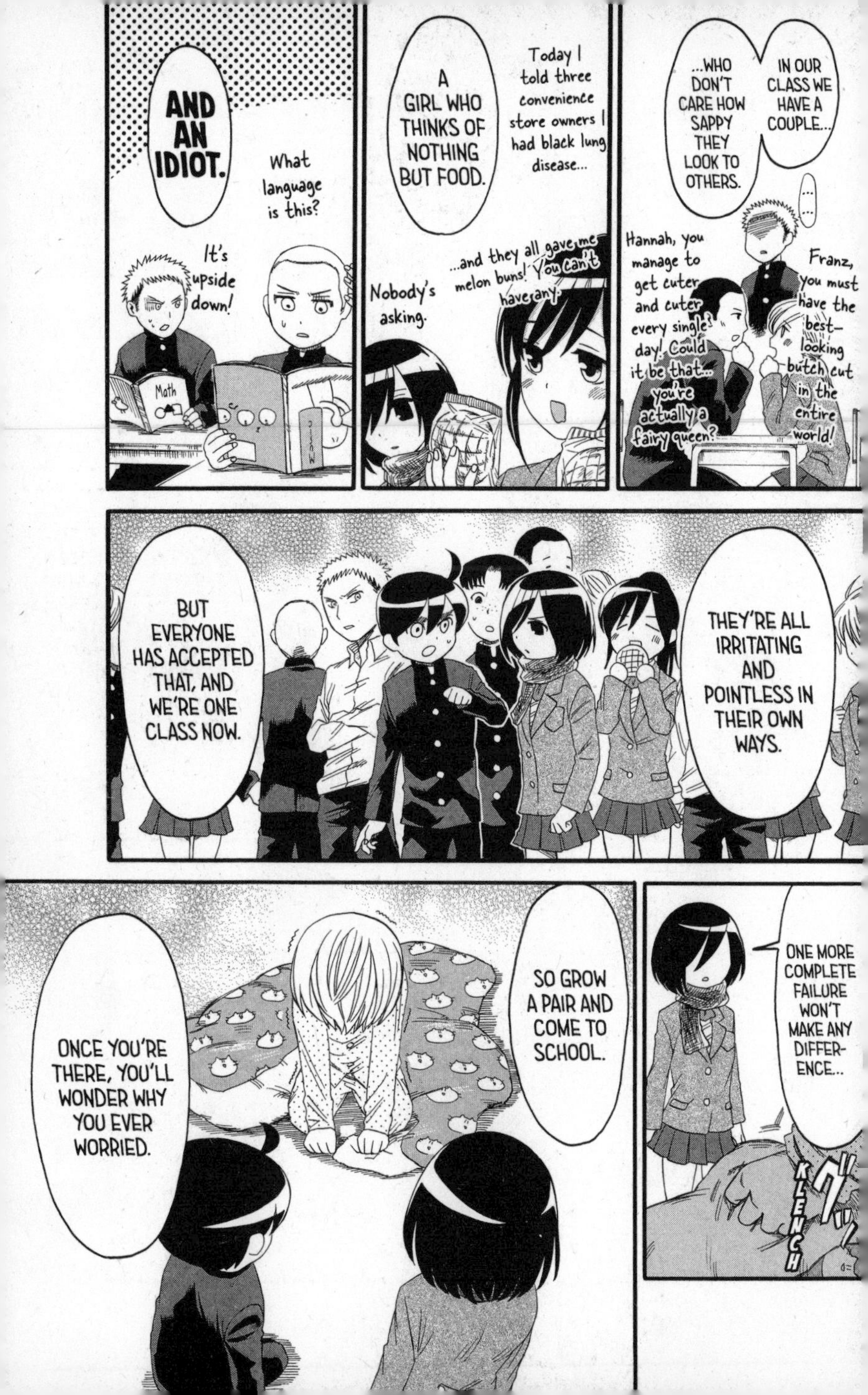
IN OUR CLASS WE HAVE A COUPLE...
...WHO DON'T CARE HOW SAPPY THEY LOOK TO OTHERS.
...
Franz, you must have the best-looking butch cut in the entire world!
Hannah, you manage to get cuter and cuter every single day! Could it be that... you're actually a fairy queen?
A GIRL WHO THINKS OF NOTHING BUT FOOD.
Today I told three convenience store owners I had black lung disease...
...and they all gave me melon buns! You can't have any.
Nobody's asking.
AND AN IDIOT.
What language is this?
It's upside down!
Math
THEY'RE ALL IRRITATING AND POINTLESS IN THEIR OWN WAYS.
BUT EVERYONE HAS ACCEPTED THAT, AND WE'RE ONE CLASS NOW.
ONE MORE COMPLETE FAILURE WON'T MAKE ANY DIFFER-ENCE...
KLENCH
SO GROW A PAIR AND COME TO SCHOOL.
ONCE YOU'RE THERE, YOU'LL WONDER WHY YOU EVER WORRIED.

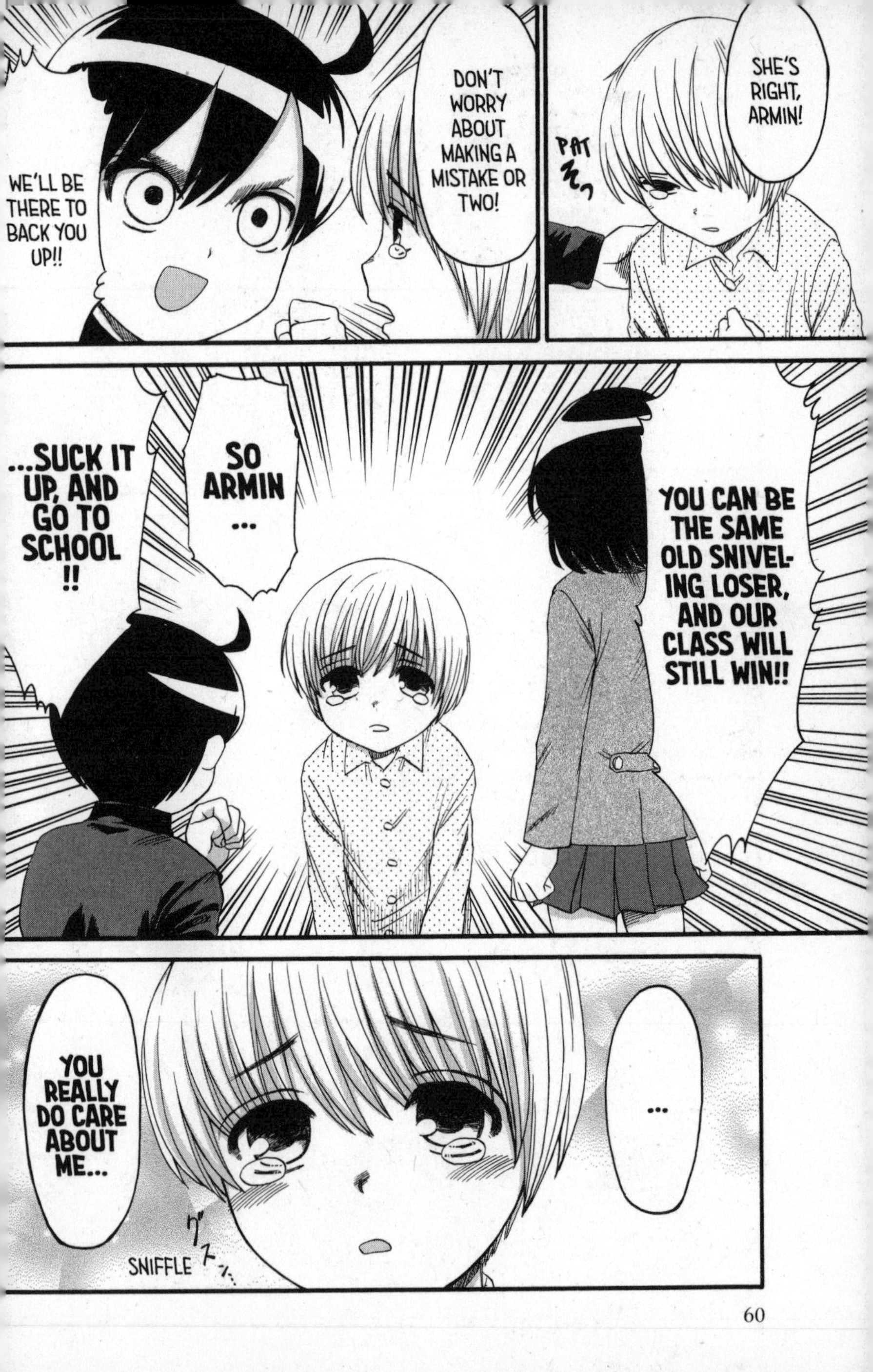
SHE'S RIGHT, ARMIN!
PAT
DON'T WORRY ABOUT MAKING A MISTAKE OR TWO!
WE'LL BE THERE TO BACK YOU UP!!
YOU CAN BE THE SAME OLD SNIVEL-ING LOSER, AND OUR CLASS WILL STILL WIN!!
SO ARMIN...
...SUCK IT UP, AND GO TO SCHOOL!!
...
YOU REALLY DO CARE ABOUT ME...
SNIFFLE

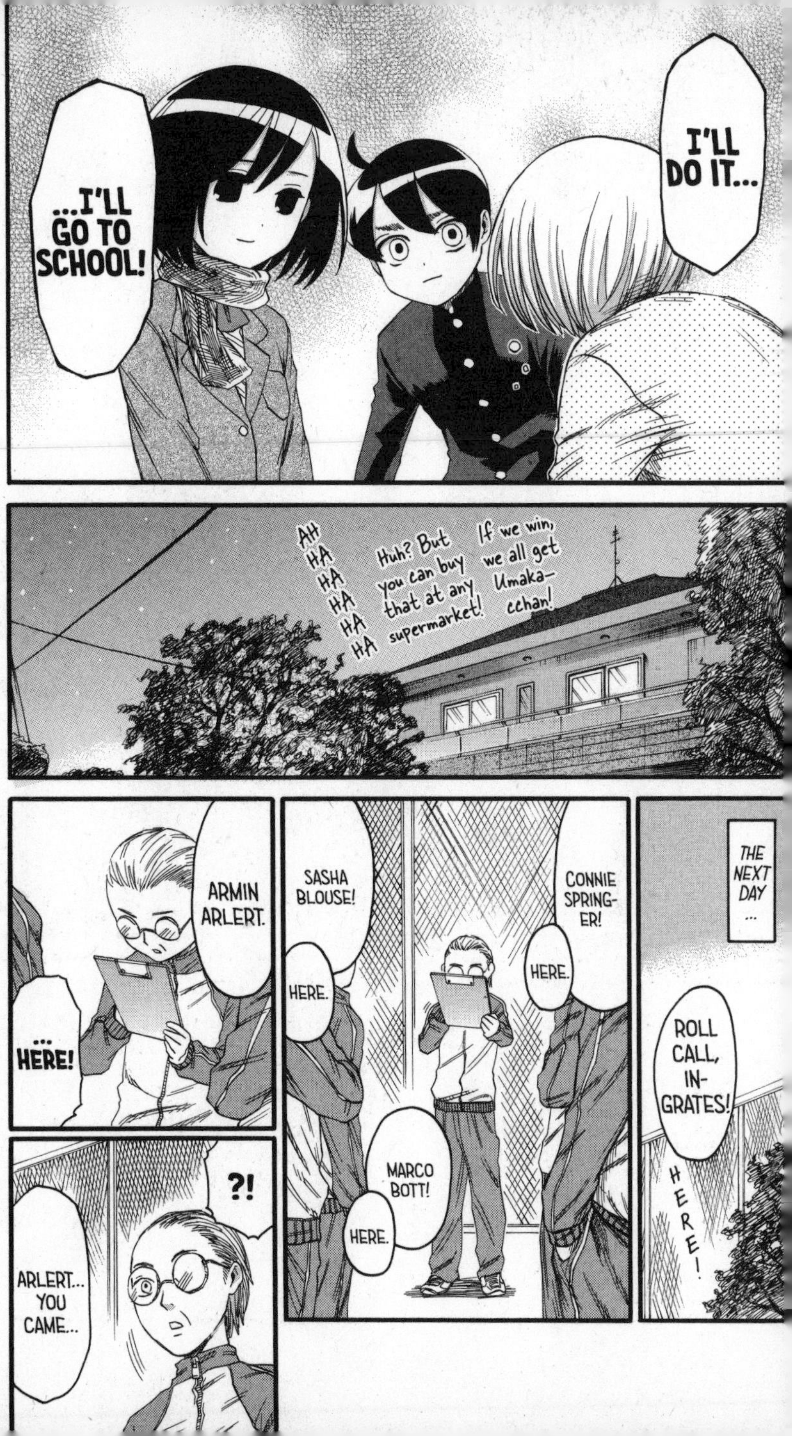
I'LL DO IT...
...I'LL GO TO SCHOOL!
If we win, we all get Umaka-cchan!
Huh? But you can buy that at any supermarket!
AH HA HA HA HA HA
THE NEXT DAY ...
ROLL CALL, INGRATES!
HERE!
CONNIE SPRINGER!
HERE.
SASHA BLOUSE!
HERE.
MARCO BOTT!
HERE.
ARMIN ARLERT.
... HERE!
?!
ARLERT... YOU CAME...

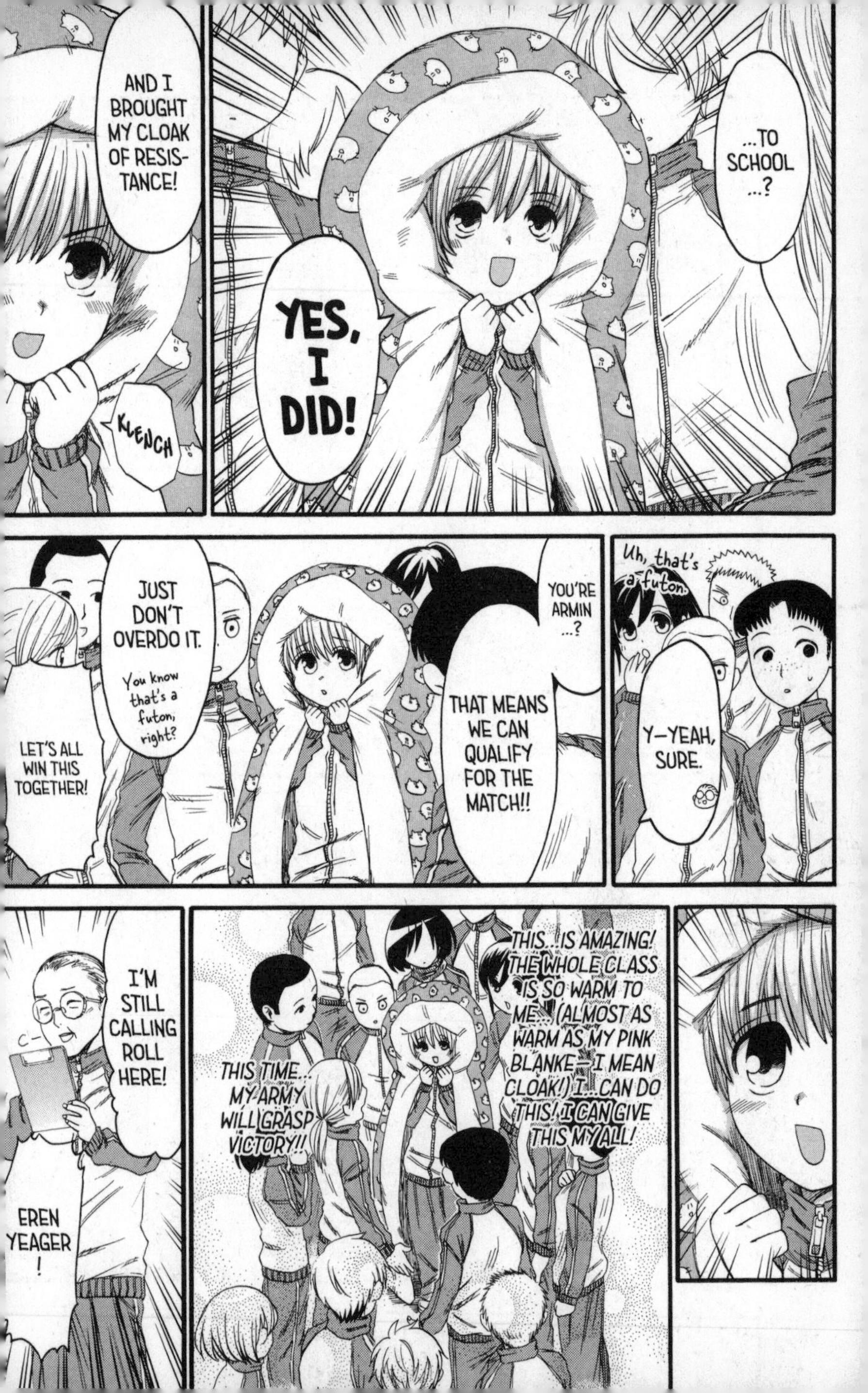
...TO SCHOOL ...?
YES, I DID!
AND I BROUGHT MY CLOAK OF RESISTANCE!
KLENCH
Uh, that's a futon.
Y—YEAH, SURE.
YOU'RE ARMIN ...?
THAT MEANS WE CAN QUALIFY FOR THE MATCH!!
JUST DON'T OVERDO IT.
You know that's a futon, right?
LET'S ALL WIN THIS TOGETHER!
THIS... IS AMAZING! THE WHOLE CLASS IS SO WARM TO ME... (ALMOST AS WARM AS MY PINK BLANKE— I MEAN CLOAK!) I... CAN DO THIS! I CAN GIVE THIS MY ALL!
THIS TIME... MY ARMY WILL GRASP VICTORY!!
I'M STILL CALLING ROLL HERE!
C—
EREN YEAGER !

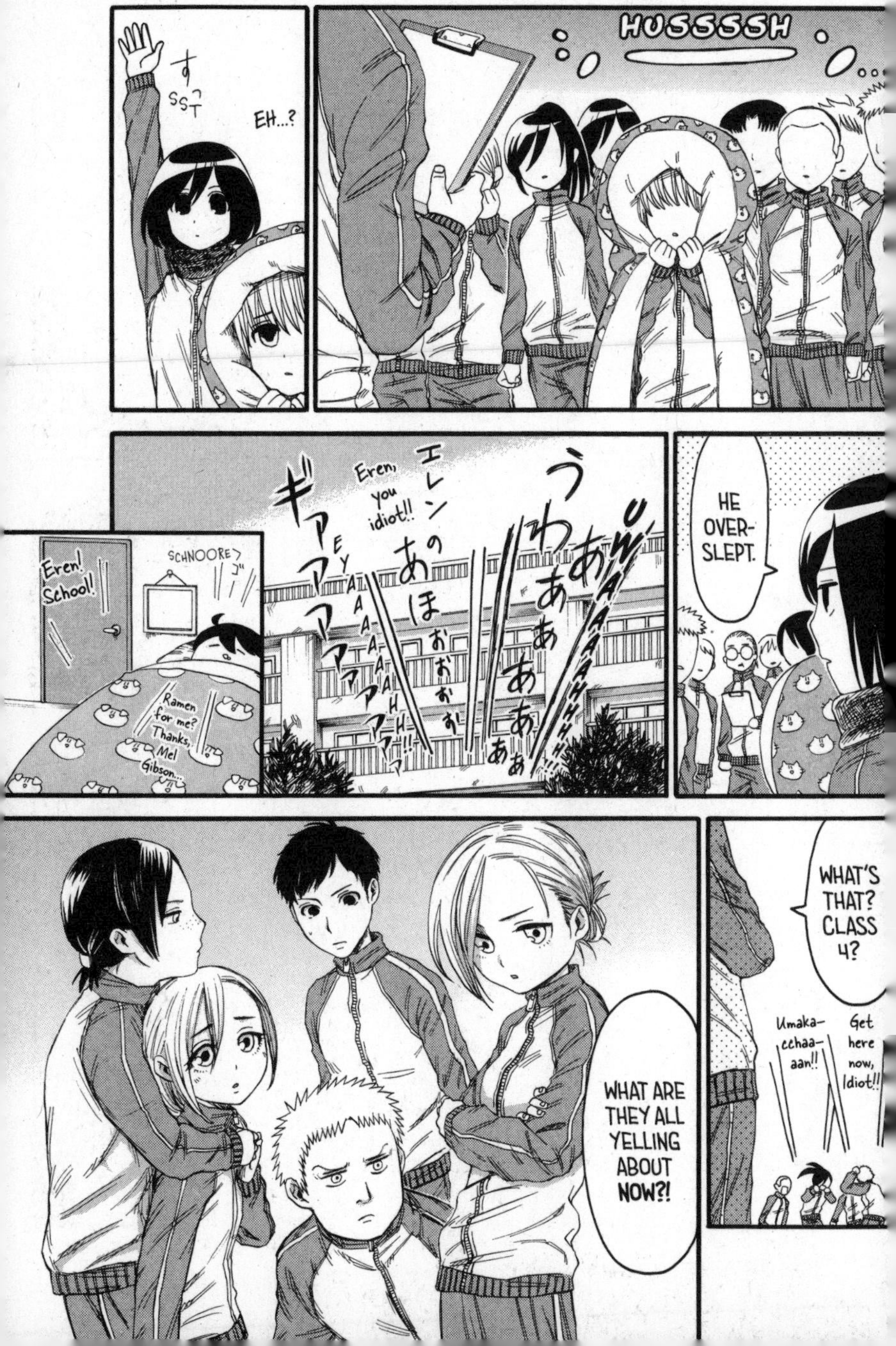
HUSSSSH
すっ
SST
EH...?
HE OVER-SLEPT.
うわあああああああ
UWAAAAAAHHHHH!!
エレンのあほおおおお
Eren, you idiot!!
ギアアアア
EYAAAAAAAH!!
Eren! School!
SCHNOORE
ゴ
Ramen for me? Thanks, Mel Gibson...
WHAT'S THAT? CLASS 4?
Get here now, Idiot!!
Umaka-echaa-aan!!
WHAT ARE THEY ALL YELLING ABOUT NOW?!

TITAN JR. HIGH BONUS THEATER 1

WHAT'S WITH THE DARNED FUTON QUILT?!

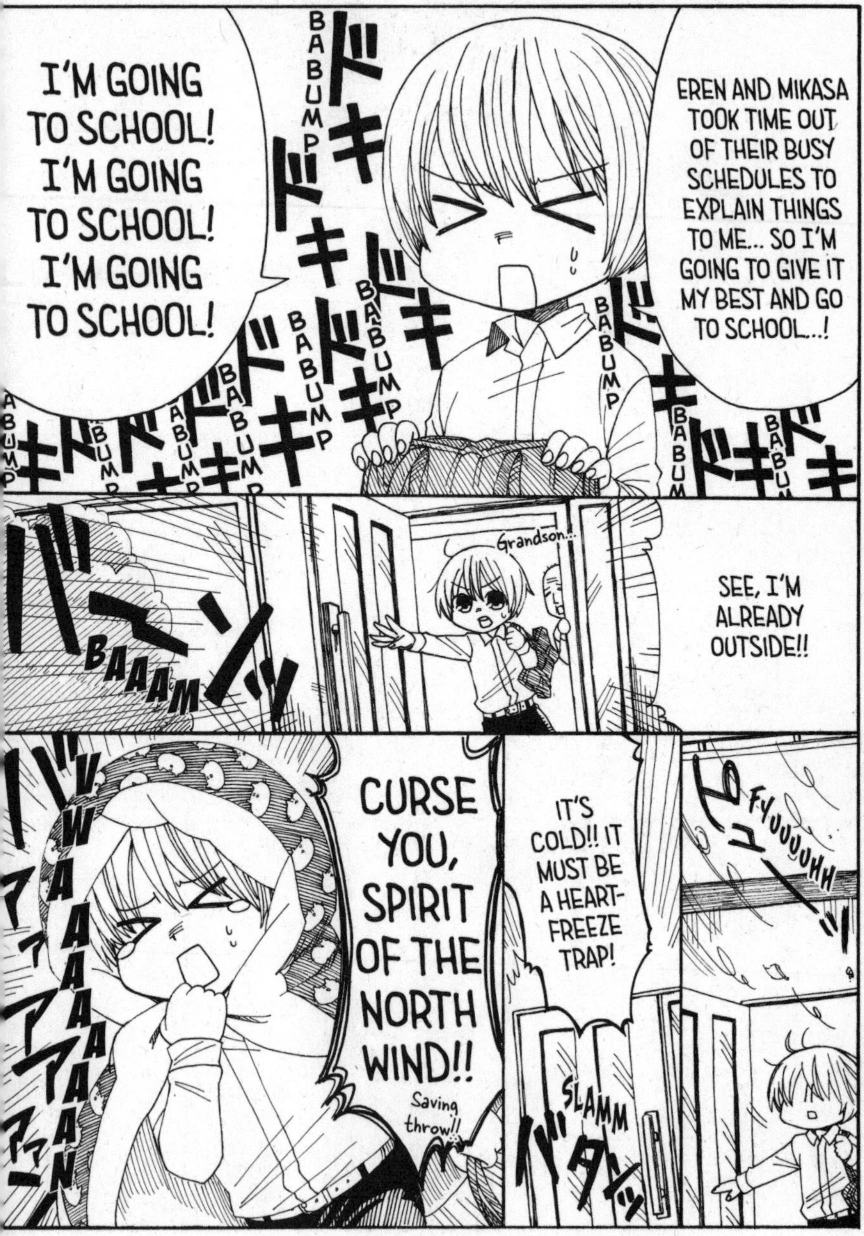

EREN AND MIKASA TOOK TIME OUT OF THEIR BUSY SCHEDULES TO EXPLAIN THINGS TO ME... SO I'M GOING TO GIVE IT MY BEST AND GO TO SCHOOL...!
BABUMP
I'M GOING TO SCHOOL! I'M GOING TO SCHOOL! I'M GOING TO SCHOOL!
BABUMP
SEE, I'M ALREADY OUTSIDE!!
Grandson...
BAAAM
FYUUUUUHH
IT'S COLD!! IT MUST BE A HEART-FREEZE TRAP!
SLAMM
CURSE YOU, SPIRIT OF THE NORTH WIND!!
Saving throw!!
VWAAAAAAAAAN

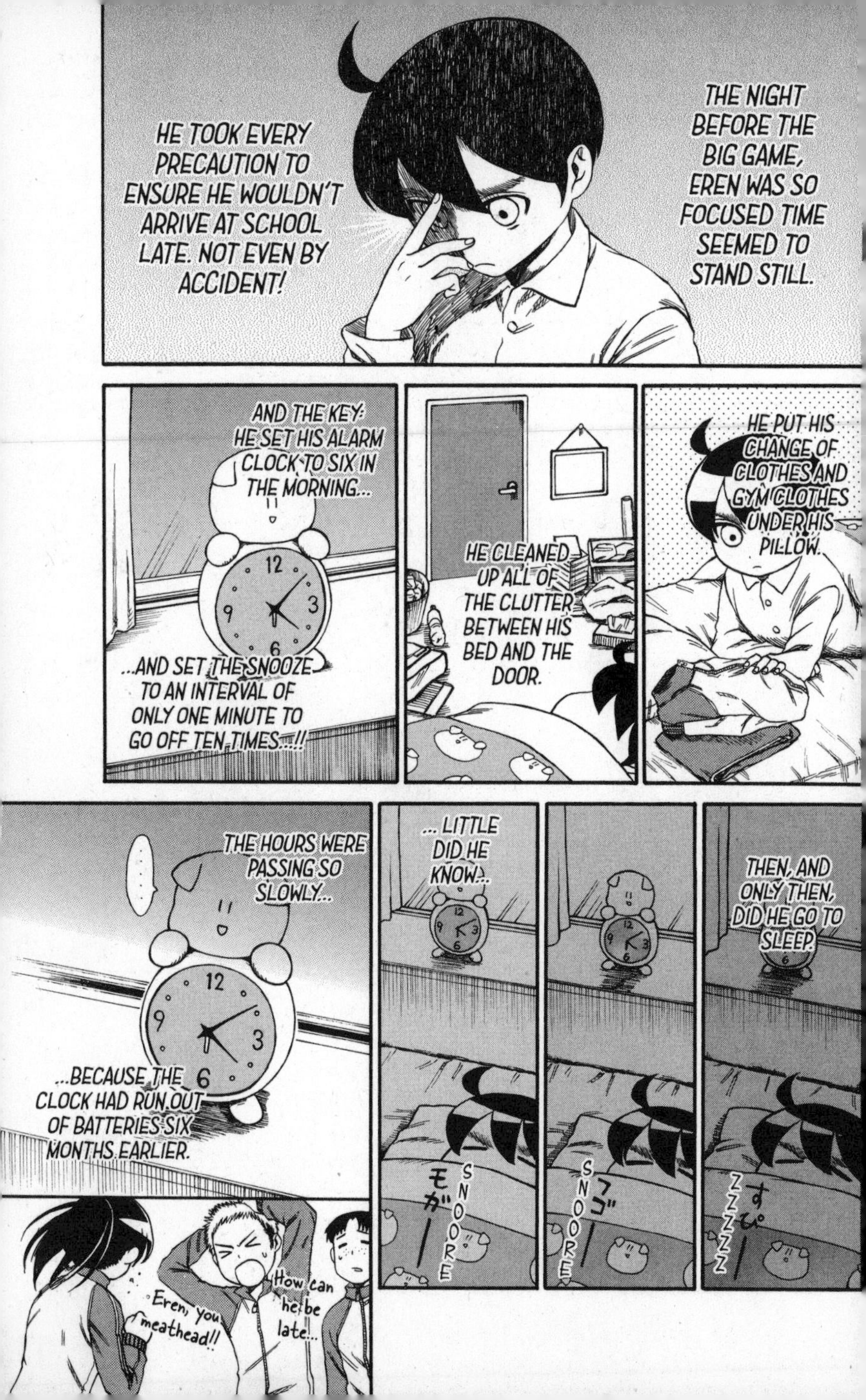
THE NIGHT BEFORE THE BIG GAME, EREN WAS SO FOCUSED TIME SEEMED TO STAND STILL.
HE TOOK EVERY PRECAUTION TO ENSURE HE WOULDN'T ARRIVE AT SCHOOL LATE. NOT EVEN BY ACCIDENT!
HE PUT HIS CHANGE OF CLOTHES AND GYM CLOTHES UNDER HIS PILLOW.
HE CLEANED UP ALL OF THE CLUTTER BETWEEN HIS BED AND THE DOOR.
AND THE KEY: HE SET HIS ALARM CLOCK TO SIX IN THE MORNING...
...AND SET THE SNOOZE TO AN INTERVAL OF ONLY ONE MINUTE TO GO OFF TEN TIMES...!!
THEN, AND ONLY THEN, DID HE GO TO SLEEP.
ZZZZZ
すぴー
SNOORE
フゴー
... LITTLE DID HE KNOW...
SNOORE
モガー
THE HOURS WERE PASSING SO SLOWLY...
...
...BECAUSE THE CLOCK HAD RUN OUT OF BATTERIES SIX MONTHS EARLIER.
How can he be late...
Eren, you meathead!!

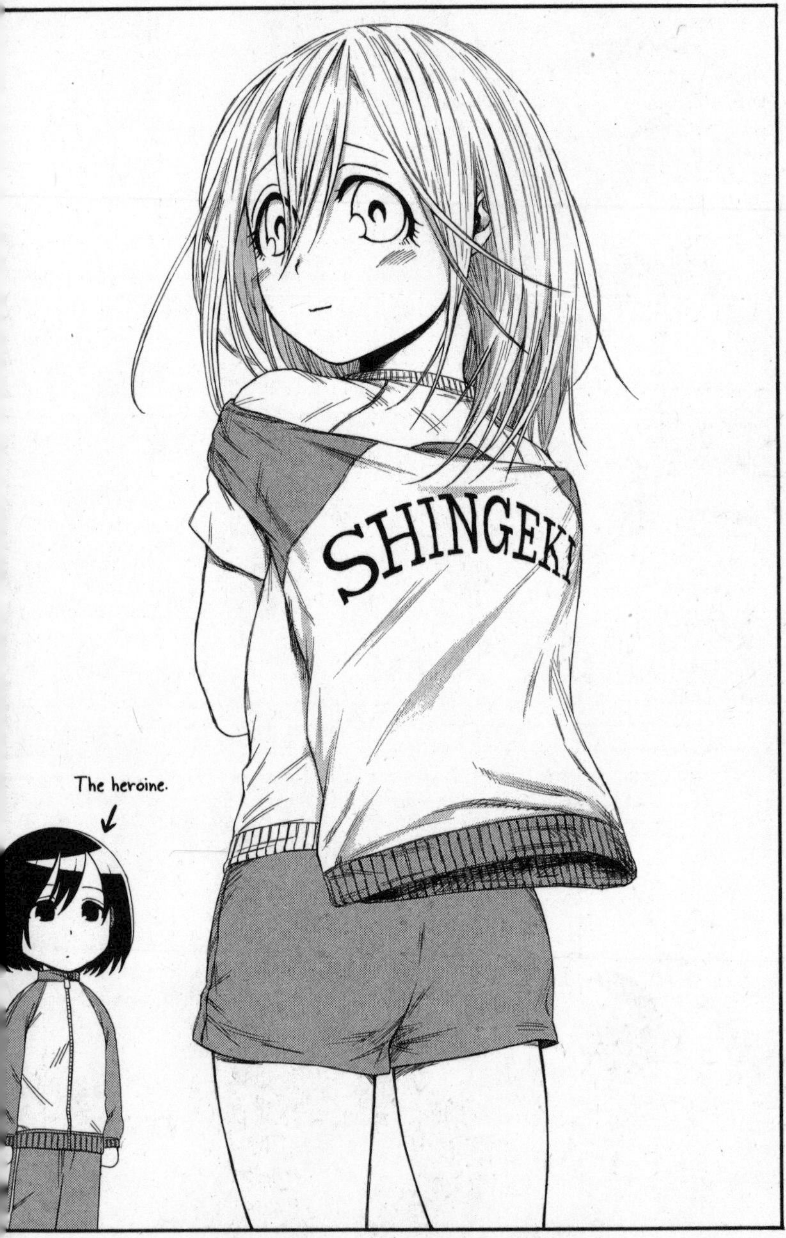
SHINGEKI
The heroine.

FOURTH PERIOD: THE ALARM CLOCK TRAP

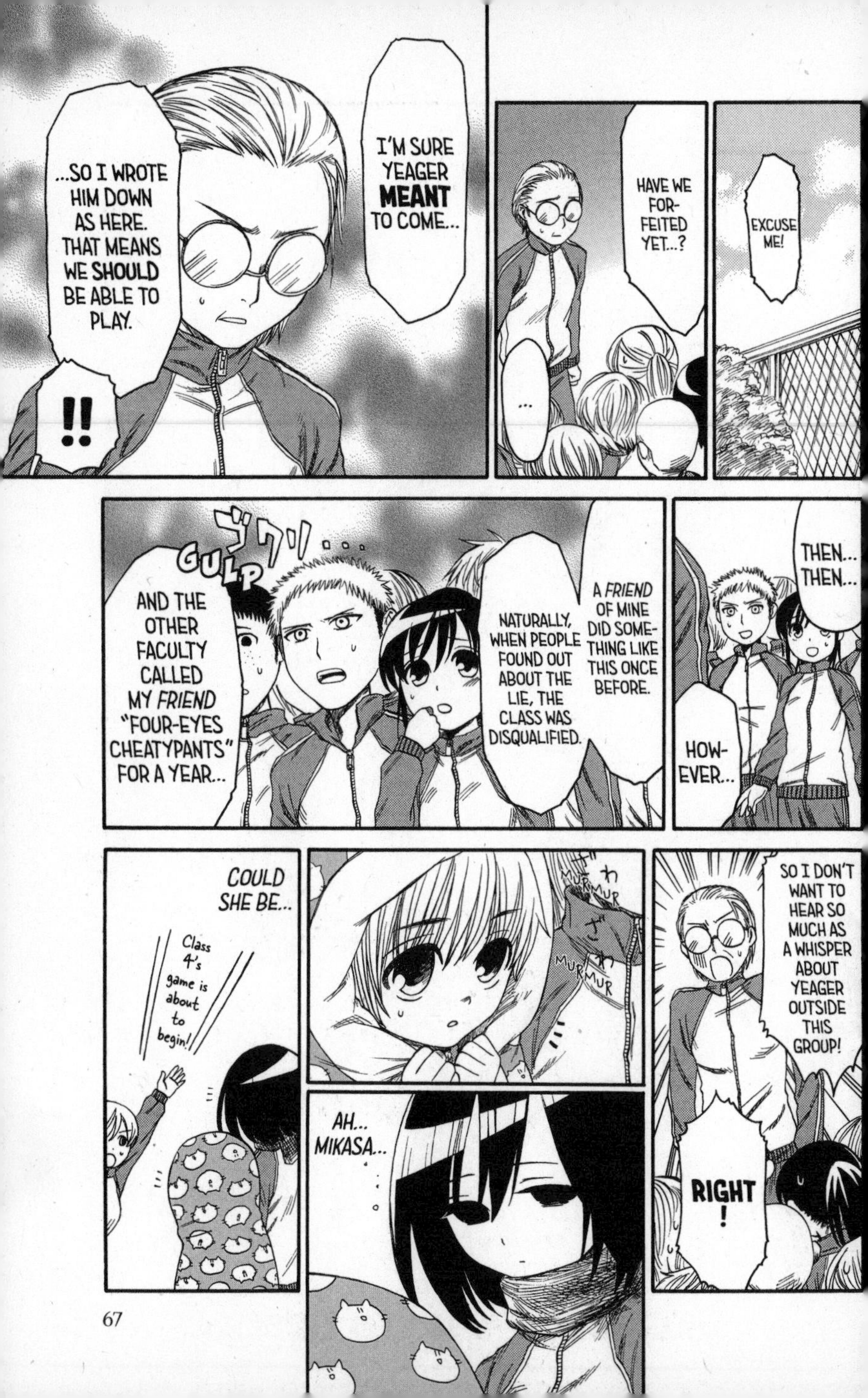
EXCUSE ME!
HAVE WE FOR-FEITED YET...?
...
I'M SURE YEAGER **MEANT** TO COME...
...SO I WROTE HIM DOWN AS HERE. THAT MEANS WE **SHOULD** BE ABLE TO PLAY.
!!
THEN... THEN...
HOW-EVER...
A *FRIEND* OF MINE DID SOME-THING LIKE THIS ONCE BEFORE.
NATURALLY, WHEN PEOPLE FOUND OUT ABOUT THE LIE, THE CLASS WAS DISQUALIFIED.
GULP
AND THE OTHER FACULTY CALLED MY *FRIEND* "FOUR-EYES CHEATYPANTS" FOR A YEAR...
SO I DON'T WANT TO HEAR SO MUCH AS A WHISPER ABOUT YEAGER OUTSIDE THIS GROUP!
RIGHT!
MURMUR
MURMUR
AH... MIKASA...
COULD SHE BE...
Class 4's game is about to begin!

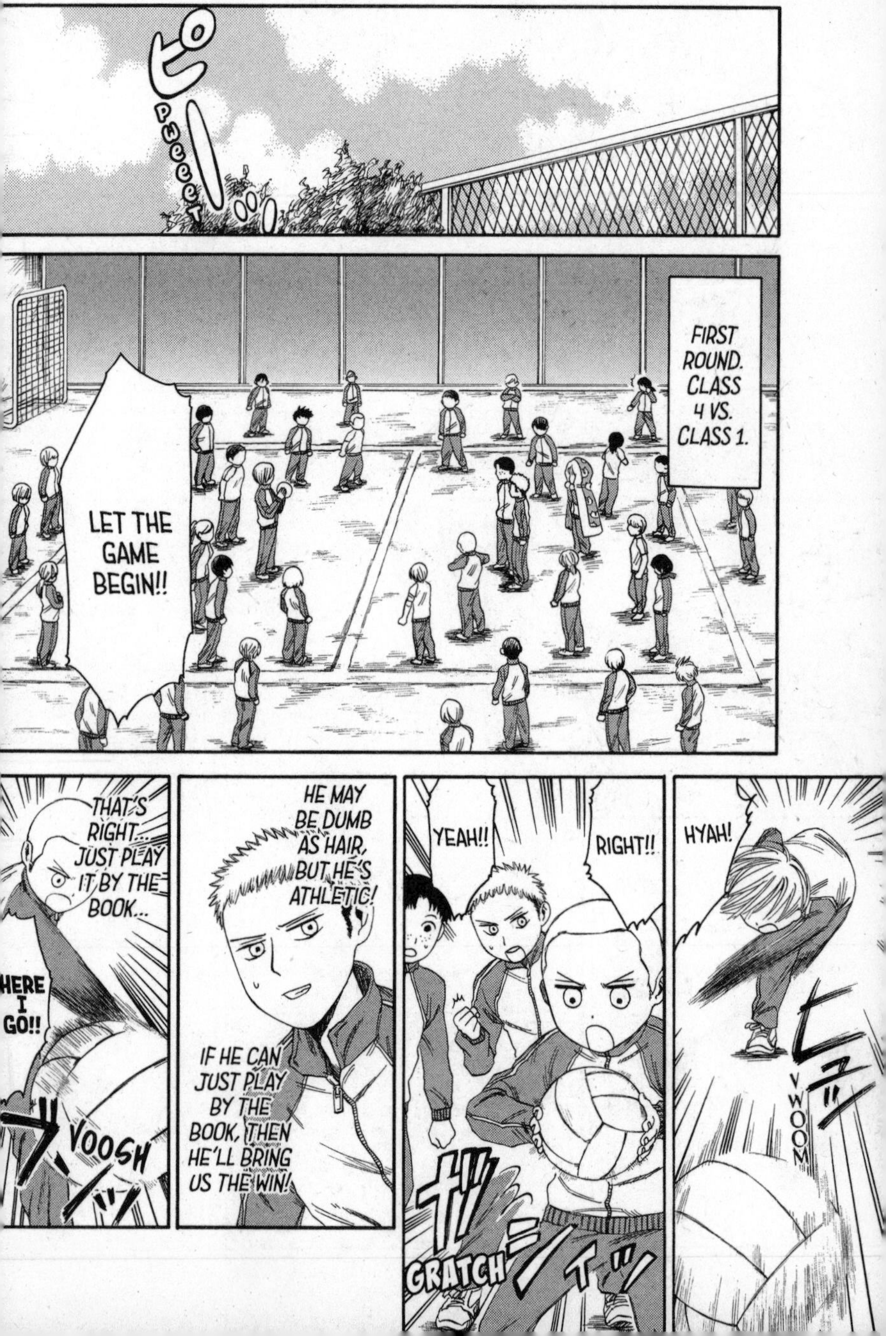
PWEEEET
FIRST ROUND. CLASS 4 VS. CLASS 1.
LET THE GAME BEGIN!!
HYAH!
VWOOM
RIGHT!!
YEAH!!
GRATCH
HE MAY BE DUMB AS HAIR, BUT HE'S ATHLETIC!
IF HE CAN JUST PLAY BY THE BOOK, THEN HE'LL BRING US THE WIN!
THAT'S RIGHT... JUST PLAY IT BY THE BOOK...
HERE I GO!!
VOOSH

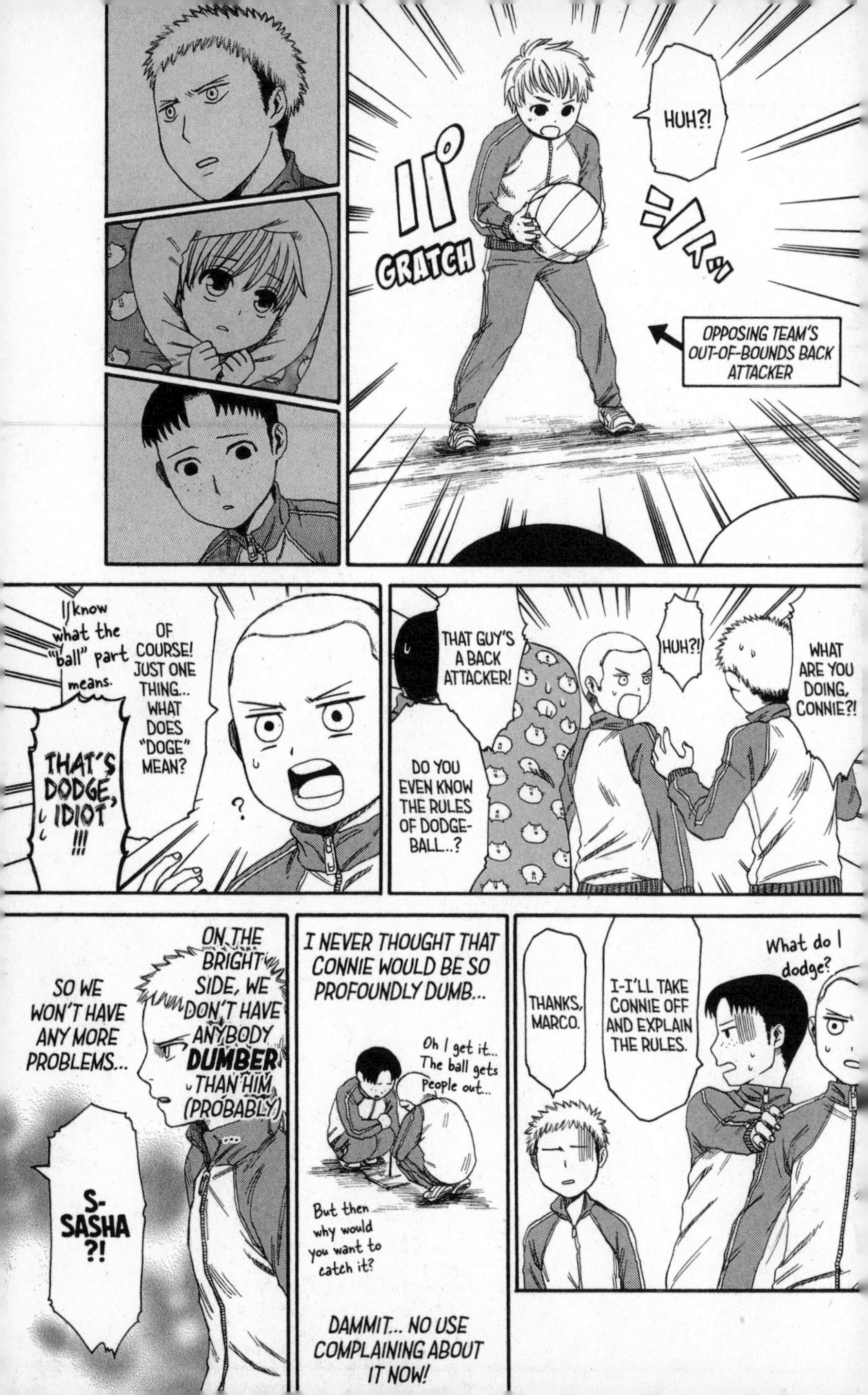
HUH?!
GRATCH
OPPOSING TEAM'S OUT-OF-BOUNDS BACK ATTACKER
WHAT ARE YOU DOING, CONNIE?!
HUH?!
THAT GUY'S A BACK ATTACKER!
DO YOU EVEN KNOW THE RULES OF DODGE-BALL...?
OF COURSE! JUST ONE THING... WHAT DOES "DOGE" MEAN?
I know what the "ball" part means.
THAT'S DODGE, IDIOT!!!
What do I dodge?
I-I'LL TAKE CONNIE OFF AND EXPLAIN THE RULES.
THANKS, MARCO.
I NEVER THOUGHT THAT CONNIE WOULD BE SO PROFOUNDLY DUMB...
Oh I get it... The ball gets people out...
But then why would you want to catch it?
DAMMIT... NO USE COMPLAINING ABOUT IT NOW!
ON THE BRIGHT SIDE, WE DON'T HAVE ANYBODY DUMBER THAN HIM (PROBABLY)
SO WE WON'T HAVE ANY MORE PROBLEMS...
S-SASHA?!

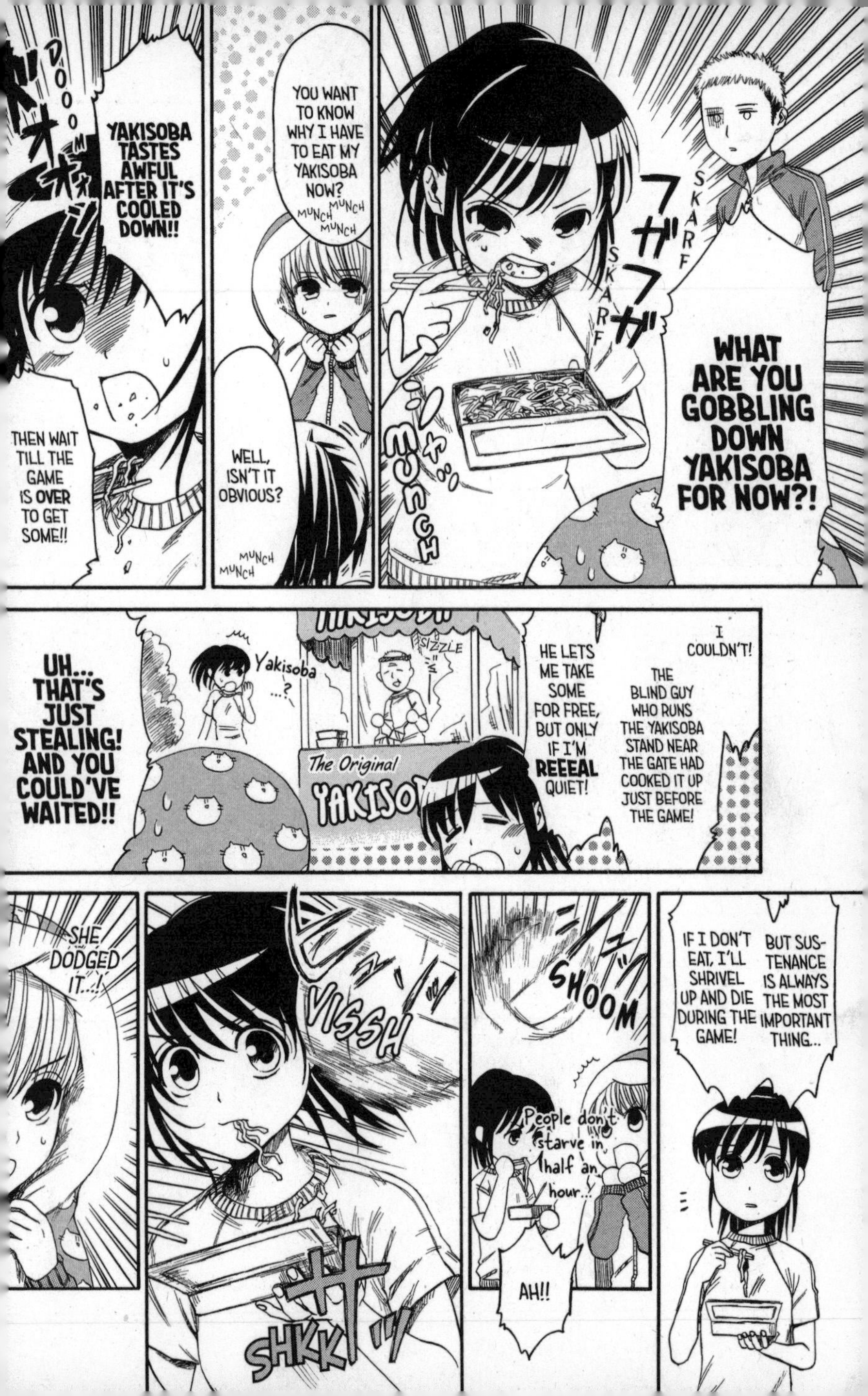
WHAT ARE YOU GOBBLING DOWN YAKISOBA FOR NOW?!
SKARF
SKARF
MUNCH
YOU WANT TO KNOW WHY I HAVE TO EAT MY YAKISOBA NOW?
MUNCH MUNCH MUNCH MUNCH
WELL, ISN'T IT OBVIOUS?
MUNCH MUNCH
DOOOOM
YAKISOBA TASTES AWFUL AFTER IT'S COOLED DOWN!!
THEN WAIT TILL THE GAME IS OVER TO GET SOME!!
I COULDN'T!
THE BLIND GUY WHO RUNS THE YAKISOBA STAND NEAR THE GATE HAD COOKED IT UP JUST BEFORE THE GAME!
HE LETS ME TAKE SOME FOR FREE, BUT ONLY IF I'M REEEAL QUIET!
SIZZLE
The Original YAKISOB
Yakisoba ...?
UH... THAT'S JUST STEALING! AND YOU COULD'VE WAITED!!
BUT SUS- TENANCE IS ALWAYS THE MOST IMPORTANT THING...
IF I DON'T EAT, I'LL SHRIVEL UP AND DIE DURING THE GAME!
SHOOM
People don't starve in half an hour...
AH!!
VISSH
SHKK
SHE DODGED IT...!

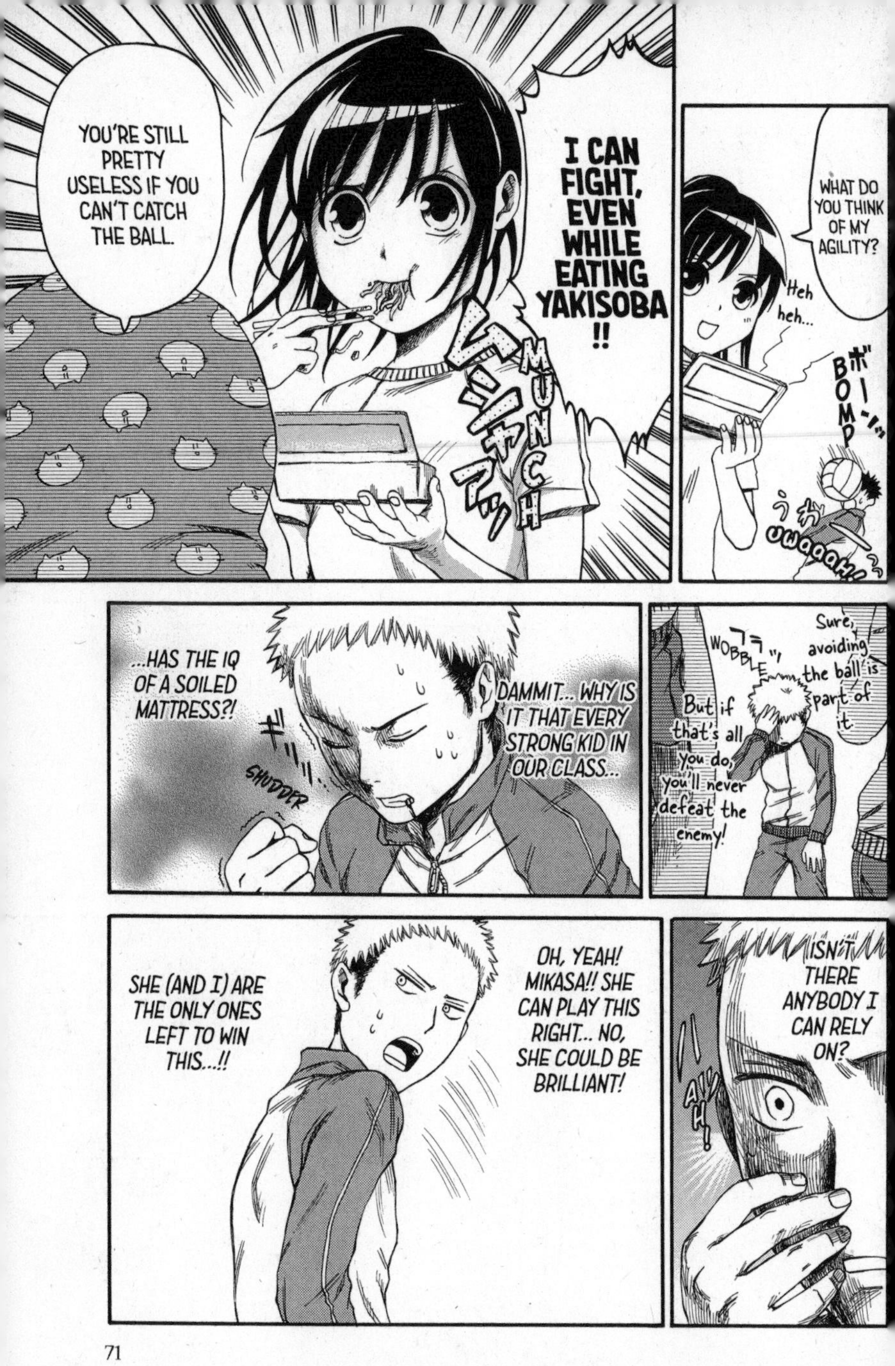
WHAT DO YOU THINK OF MY AGILITY?
Heh heh...
BOMP
UWAAAAH!
I CAN FIGHT, EVEN WHILE EATING YAKISOBA!!
MUNCH
YOU'RE STILL PRETTY USELESS IF YOU CAN'T CATCH THE BALL.
Sure, avoiding the ball is part of it.
WOBBLE
But if that's all you do, you'll never defeat the enemy!
DAMMIT... WHY IS IT THAT EVERY STRONG KID IN OUR CLASS...
SHUDDER
...HAS THE IQ OF A SOILED MATTRESS?!
ISN'T THERE ANYBODY I CAN RELY ON?
AH!
OH, YEAH! MIKASA!! SHE CAN PLAY THIS RIGHT... NO, SHE COULD BE BRILLIANT!
SHE (AND I) ARE THE ONLY ONES LEFT TO WIN THIS...!!

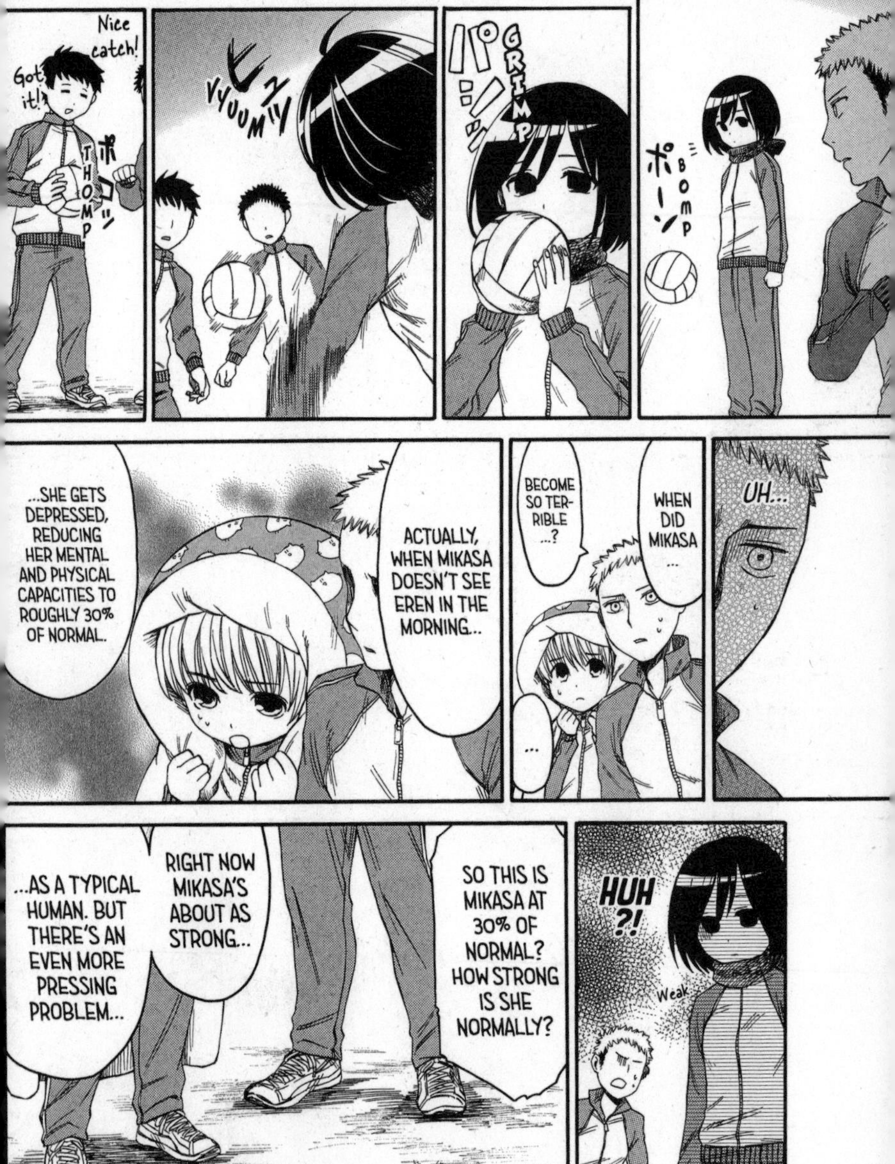
BOMP
GRIMP
VYUUM
Nice catch!
Got it!
THOMP
UH...
WHEN DID MIKASA...
BECOME SO TERRIBLE...?
...
ACTUALLY, WHEN MIKASA DOESN'T SEE EREN IN THE MORNING...
...SHE GETS DEPRESSED, REDUCING HER MENTAL AND PHYSICAL CAPACITIES TO ROUGHLY 30% OF NORMAL.
HUH?!
Weak
SO THIS IS MIKASA AT 30% OF NORMAL? HOW STRONG IS SHE NORMALLY?
RIGHT NOW MIKASA'S ABOUT AS STRONG...
...AS A TYPICAL HUMAN. BUT THERE'S AN EVEN MORE PRESSING PROBLEM...

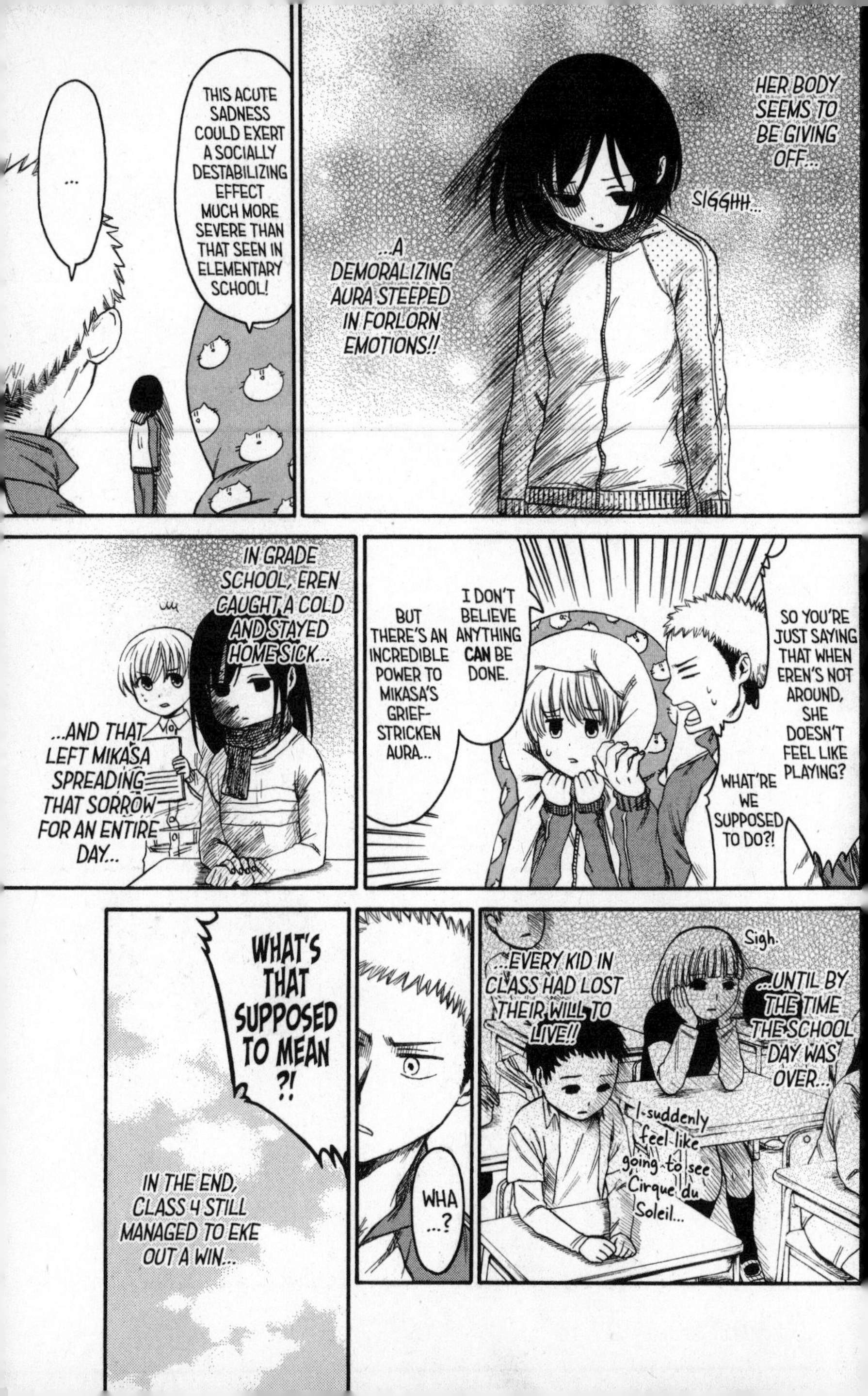

HER BODY SEEMS TO BE GIVING OFF...
SIGGHH...
...A DEMORALIZING AURA STEEPED IN FORLORN EMOTIONS!!
THIS ACUTE SADNESS COULD EXERT A SOCIALLY DESTABILIZING EFFECT MUCH MORE SEVERE THAN THAT SEEN IN ELEMENTARY SCHOOL!
...
SO YOU'RE JUST SAYING THAT WHEN EREN'S NOT AROUND, SHE DOESN'T FEEL LIKE PLAYING?
WHAT'RE WE SUPPOSED TO DO?!
I DON'T BELIEVE ANYTHING **CAN** BE DONE.
BUT THERE'S AN INCREDIBLE POWER TO MIKASA'S GRIEF-STRICKEN AURA...
IN GRADE SCHOOL, EREN CAUGHT A COLD AND STAYED HOME SICK...
...AND THAT LEFT MIKASA SPREADING THAT SORROW FOR AN ENTIRE DAY...
Sigh.
...UNTIL BY THE TIME THE SCHOOL DAY WAS OVER...
...EVERY KID IN CLASS HAD LOST THEIR WILL TO LIVE!!
I-suddenly feel like going to see Cirque du Soleil...
WHA...?
WHAT'S THAT SUPPOSED TO MEAN?!
IN THE END, CLASS 4 STILL MANAGED TO EKE OUT A WIN...

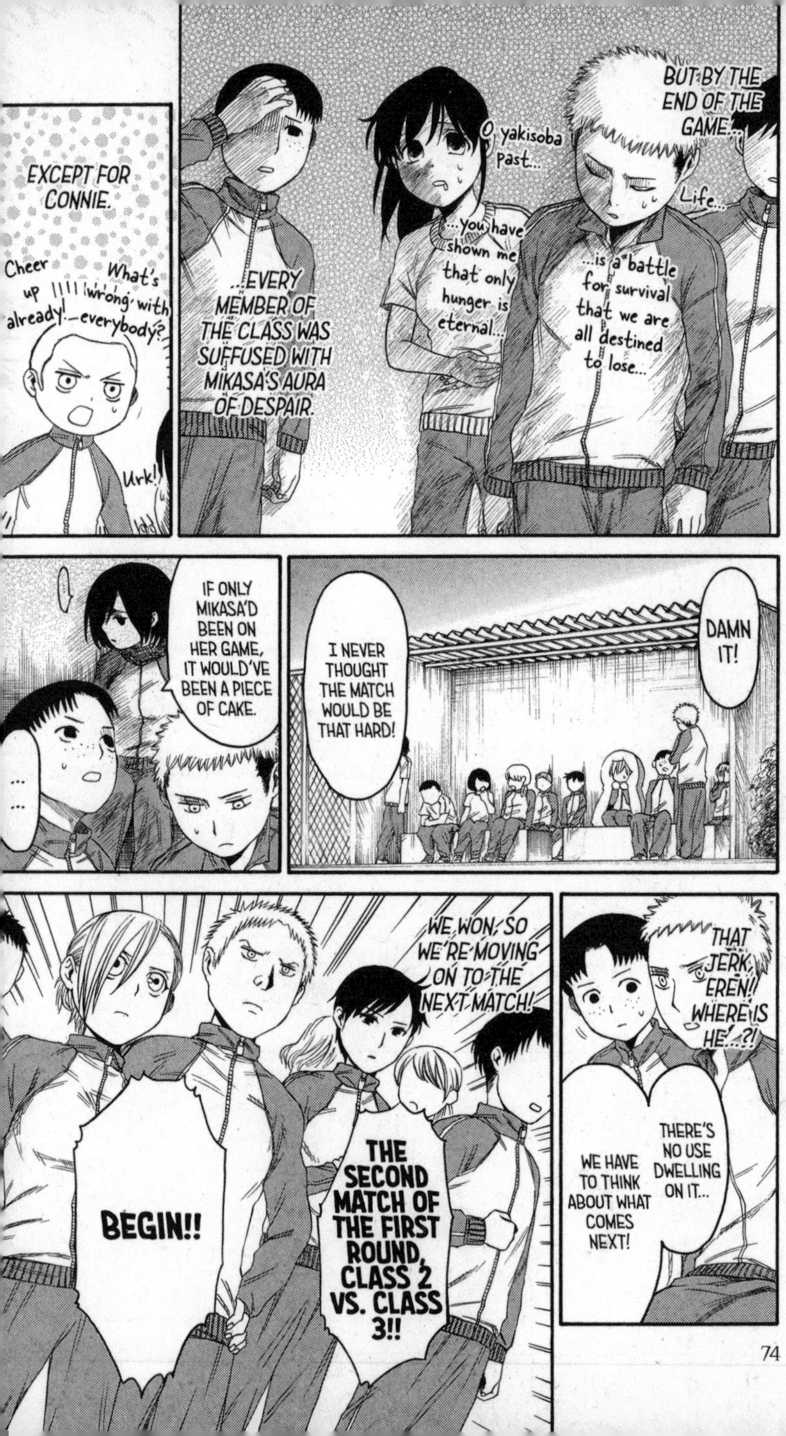

BUT BY THE END OF THE GAME...
Life...
...is a battle for survival that we are all destined to lose...
O yakisoba past...
...you have shown me that only hunger is eternal...
...EVERY MEMBER OF THE CLASS WAS SUFFUSED WITH MIKASA'S AURA OF DESPAIR.
EXCEPT FOR CONNIE.
What's wrong with everybody?
Cheer up already!
Urk!
DAMN IT!
I NEVER THOUGHT THE MATCH WOULD BE THAT HARD!
IF ONLY MIKASA'D BEEN ON HER GAME, IT WOULD'VE BEEN A PIECE OF CAKE.
...
...
THAT JERK EREN! WHERE IS HE...?!
THERE'S NO USE DWELLING ON IT...
WE HAVE TO THINK ABOUT WHAT COMES NEXT!
WE WON, SO WE'RE MOVING ON TO THE NEXT MATCH!
THE SECOND MATCH OF THE FIRST ROUND, CLASS 2 VS. CLASS 3!!
BEGIN!!

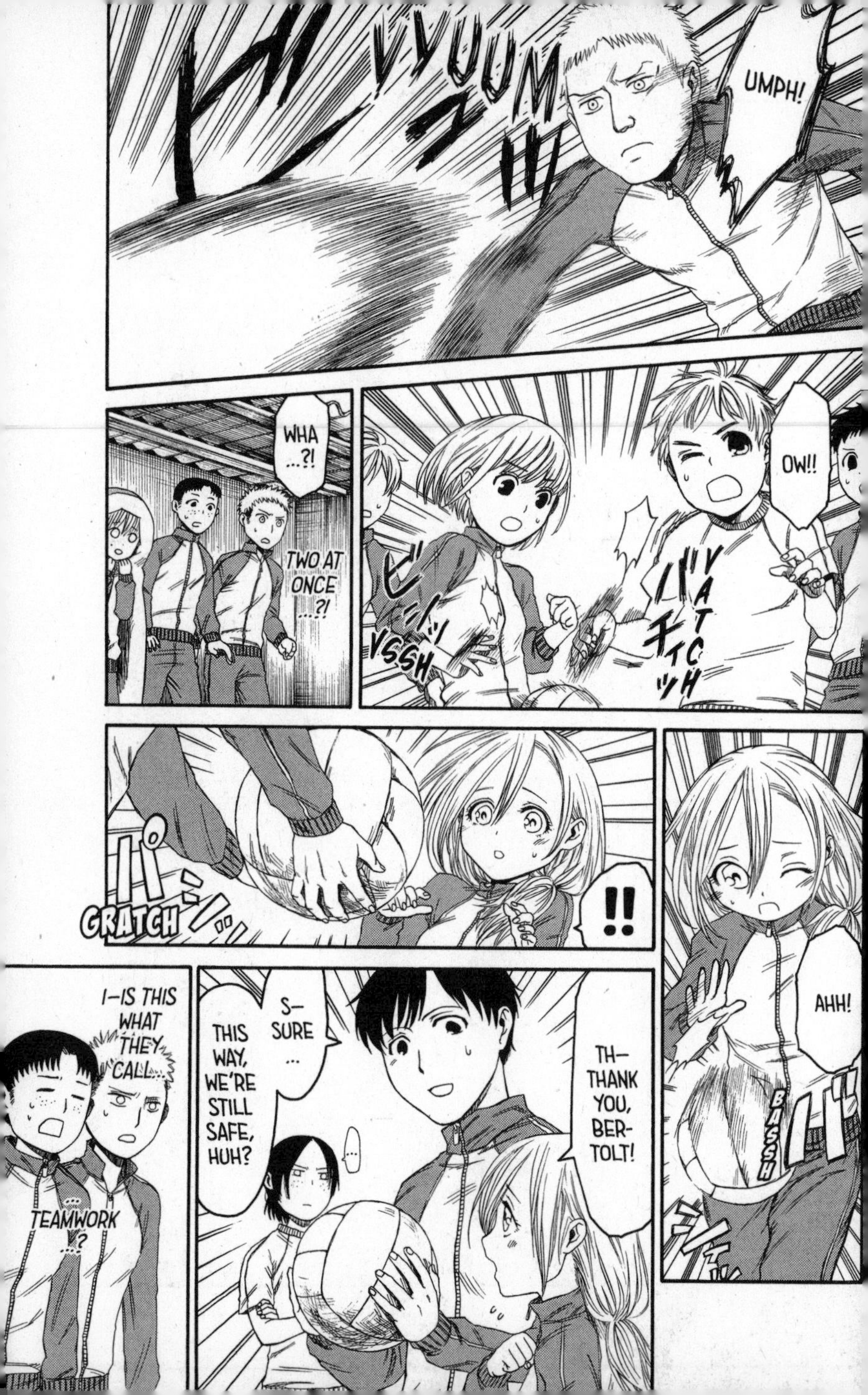
VVUUM
UMPH!
OW!!
VATCH
VSSH
WHA ...?!
TWO AT ONCE ...?!
AHH!
BASSH
!!
GRATCH
TH— THANK YOU, BER-TOLT!
S— SURE ...
THIS WAY, WE'RE STILL SAFE, HUH?
...
I—IS THIS WHAT THEY CALL...
...TEAMWORK ...?

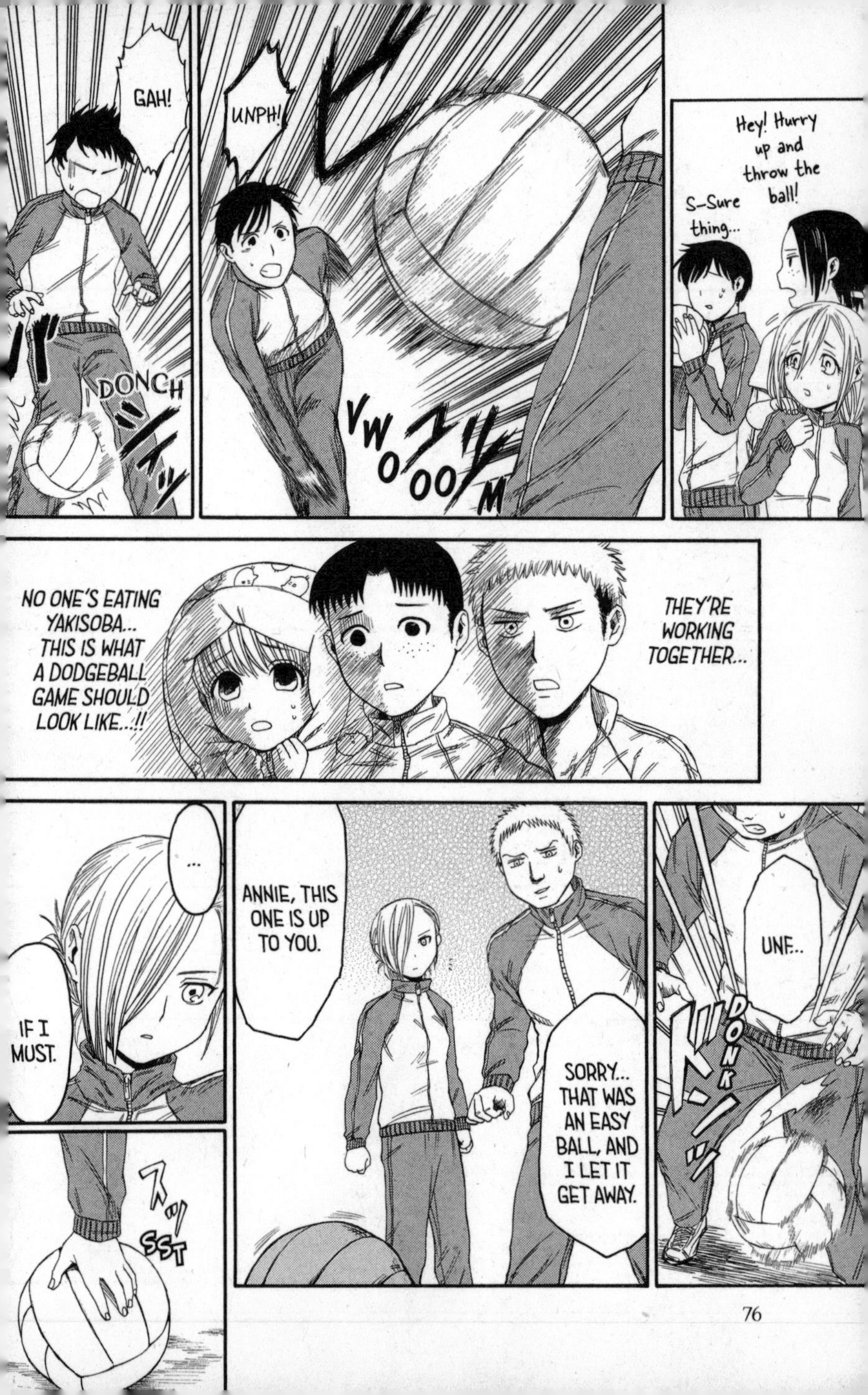
Hey! Hurry up and throw the ball!
S-Sure thing...
UNPH!
VWOOOM
GAH!
DONCH
THEY'RE WORKING TOGETHER...
NO ONE'S EATING YAKISOBA... THIS IS WHAT A DODGEBALL GAME SHOULD LOOK LIKE...!!
UNF...
DONK
ANNIE, THIS ONE IS UP TO YOU.
SORRY... THAT WAS AN EASY BALL, AND I LET IT GET AWAY.
...
IF I MUST.
SST

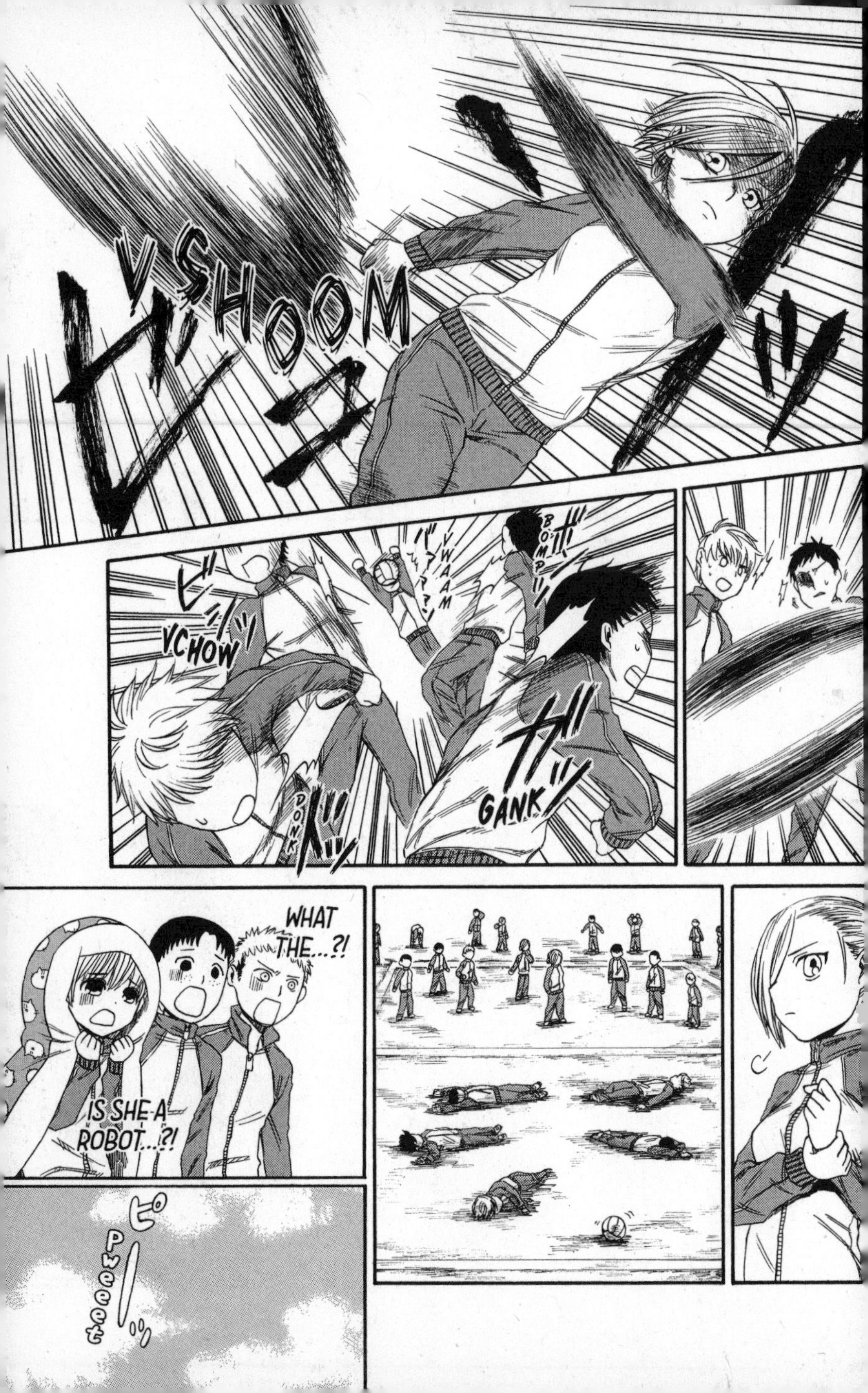
VSHOOM
BOMP!!
VWAAM
VCHOW
GANK!
DONK
WHAT THE...?!
IS SHE A ROBOT...?!
Pweeet

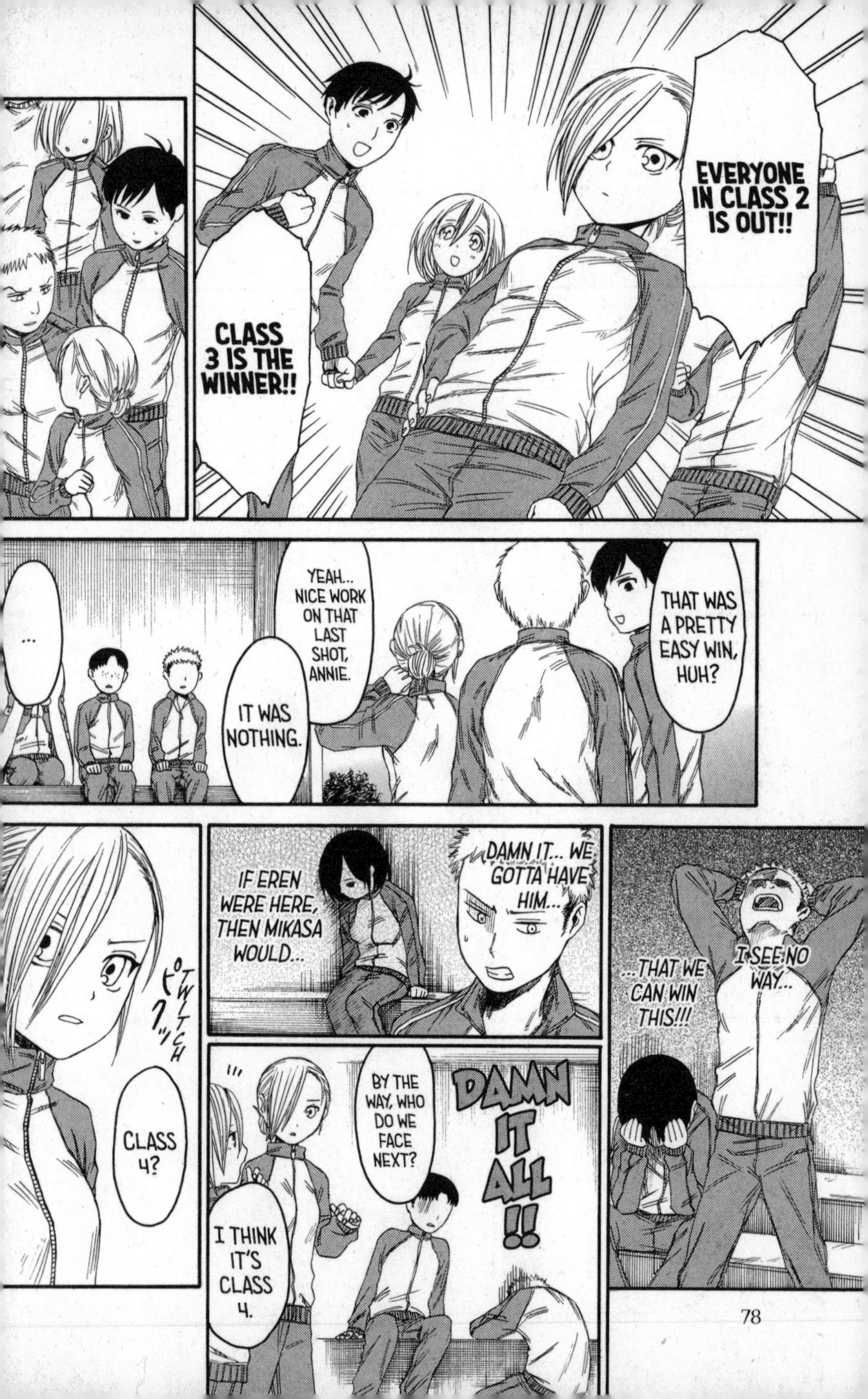
EVERYONE IN CLASS 2 IS OUT!!
CLASS 3 IS THE WINNER!!
THAT WAS A PRETTY EASY WIN, HUH?
YEAH... NICE WORK ON THAT LAST SHOT, ANNIE.
IT WAS NOTHING.
...
I SEE NO WAY...
...THAT WE CAN WIN THIS!!!
DAMN IT... WE GOTTA HAVE HIM...
IF EREN WERE HERE, THEN MIKASA WOULD...
DAMN IT ALL!!
BY THE WAY, WHO DO WE FACE NEXT?
I THINK IT'S CLASS 4.
TWITCH
CLASS 4?

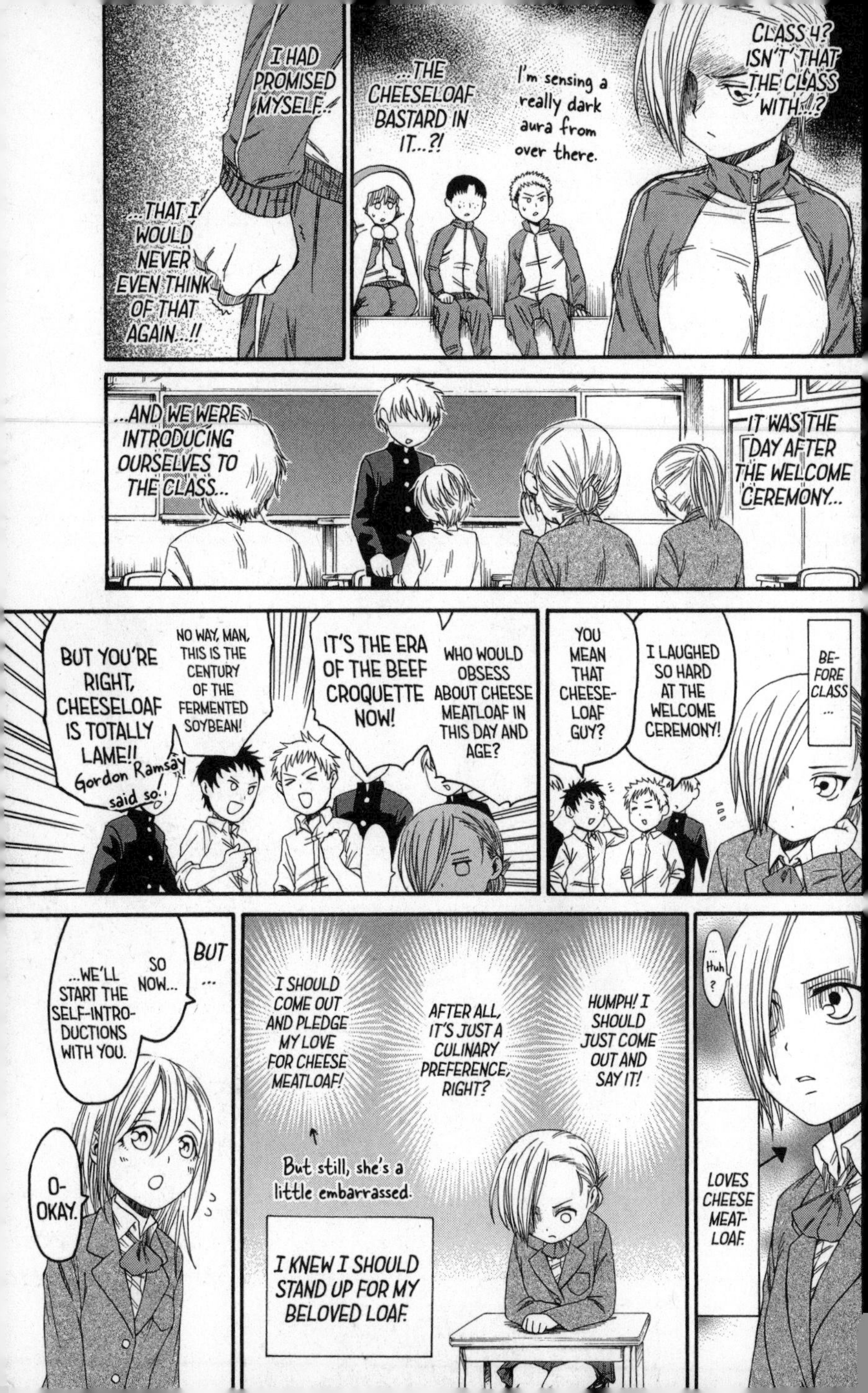
CLASS 4? ISN'T THAT THE CLASS WITH...?
I'm sensing a really dark aura from over there.
...THE CHEESELOAF BASTARD IN IT...?!
I HAD PROMISED MYSELF...
...THAT I WOULD NEVER EVEN THINK OF THAT AGAIN...!!
IT WAS THE DAY AFTER THE WELCOME CEREMONY...
...AND WE WERE INTRODUCING OURSELVES TO THE CLASS...
BEFORE CLASS...
I LAUGHED SO HARD AT THE WELCOME CEREMONY!
YOU MEAN THAT CHEESE-LOAF GUY?
WHO WOULD OBSESS ABOUT CHEESE MEATLOAF IN THIS DAY AND AGE?
IT'S THE ERA OF THE BEEF CROQUETTE NOW!
NO WAY, MAN, THIS IS THE CENTURY OF THE FERMENTED SOYBEAN!
BUT YOU'RE RIGHT, CHEESELOAF IS TOTALLY LAME!!
Gordon Ramsay said so!
...Huh?
LOVES CHEESE MEAT-LOAF.
HUMPH! I SHOULD JUST COME OUT AND SAY IT!
AFTER ALL, IT'S JUST A CULINARY PREFERENCE, RIGHT?
I SHOULD COME OUT AND PLEDGE MY LOVE FOR CHEESE MEATLOAF!
But still, she's a little embarrassed.
I KNEW I SHOULD STAND UP FOR MY BELOVED LOAF.
BUT...
SO NOW...
...WE'LL START THE SELF-INTRO-DUCTIONS WITH YOU.
O-OKAY.

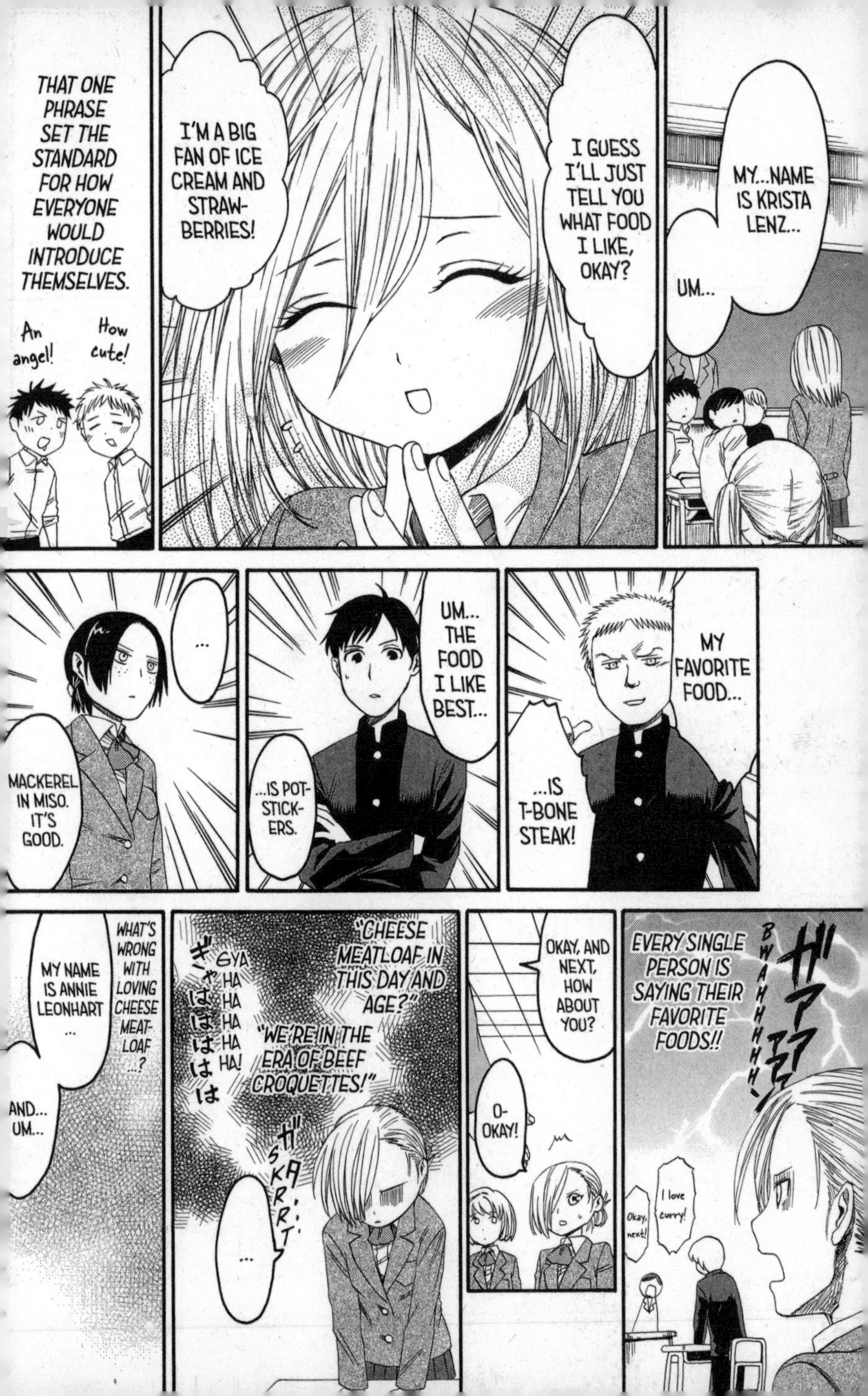
MY...NAME IS KRISTA LENZ...
UM...
I GUESS I'LL JUST TELL YOU WHAT FOOD I LIKE, OKAY?
I'M A BIG FAN OF ICE CREAM AND STRAW-BERRIES!
THAT ONE PHRASE SET THE STANDARD FOR HOW EVERYONE WOULD INTRODUCE THEMSELVES.
How cute!
An angel!
MY FAVORITE FOOD...
...IS T-BONE STEAK!
UM... THE FOOD I LIKE BEST...
...IS POT-STICK-ERS.
...
MACKEREL IN MISO. IT'S GOOD.
ガァァァ
BWAHHHHH
EVERY SINGLE PERSON IS SAYING THEIR FAVORITE FOODS!!
I love curry!
Okay, next!
OKAY, AND NEXT, HOW ABOUT YOU?
O-OKAY!
"CHEESE MEATLOAF IN THIS DAY AND AGE?"
ぎゃははははは
GYA HA HA HA HA HA!
"WE'RE IN THE ERA OF BEEF CROQUETTES!"
ガタ
SKRRT
...
WHAT'S WRONG WITH LOVING CHEESE MEAT-LOAF...?
MY NAME IS ANNIE LEONHART...
AND... UM...

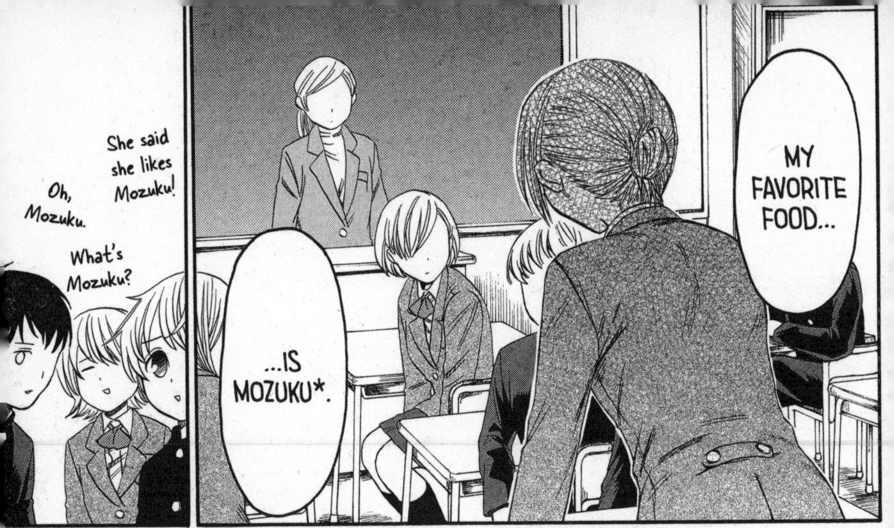
MY FAVORITE FOOD...
...IS MOZUKU*.
She said she likes Mozuku!
Oh, Mozuku.
What's Mozuku?

*A type of edible seaweed. (See note on page 325.)

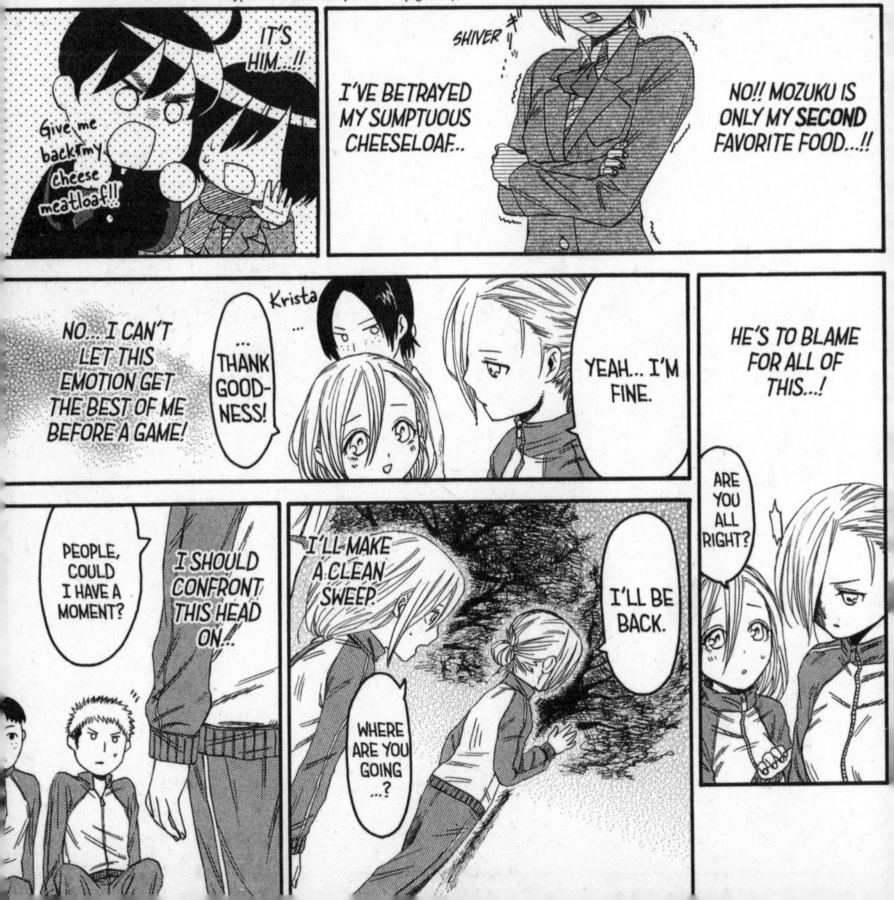
NO!! MOZUKU IS ONLY MY **SECOND** FAVORITE FOOD...!!
SHIVER
I'VE BETRAYED MY SUMPTUOUS CHEESELOAF...
IT'S HIM...!!
Give me back my cheese meatloaf!!
HE'S TO BLAME FOR ALL OF THIS...!
ARE YOU ALL RIGHT?
YEAH... I'M FINE.
Krista...
...THANK GOODNESS!
NO... I CAN'T LET THIS EMOTION GET THE BEST OF ME BEFORE A GAME!
I'LL BE BACK.
WHERE ARE YOU GOING...?
I'LL MAKE A CLEAN SWEEP.
PEOPLE, COULD I HAVE A MOMENT?
I SHOULD CONFRONT THIS HEAD ON...

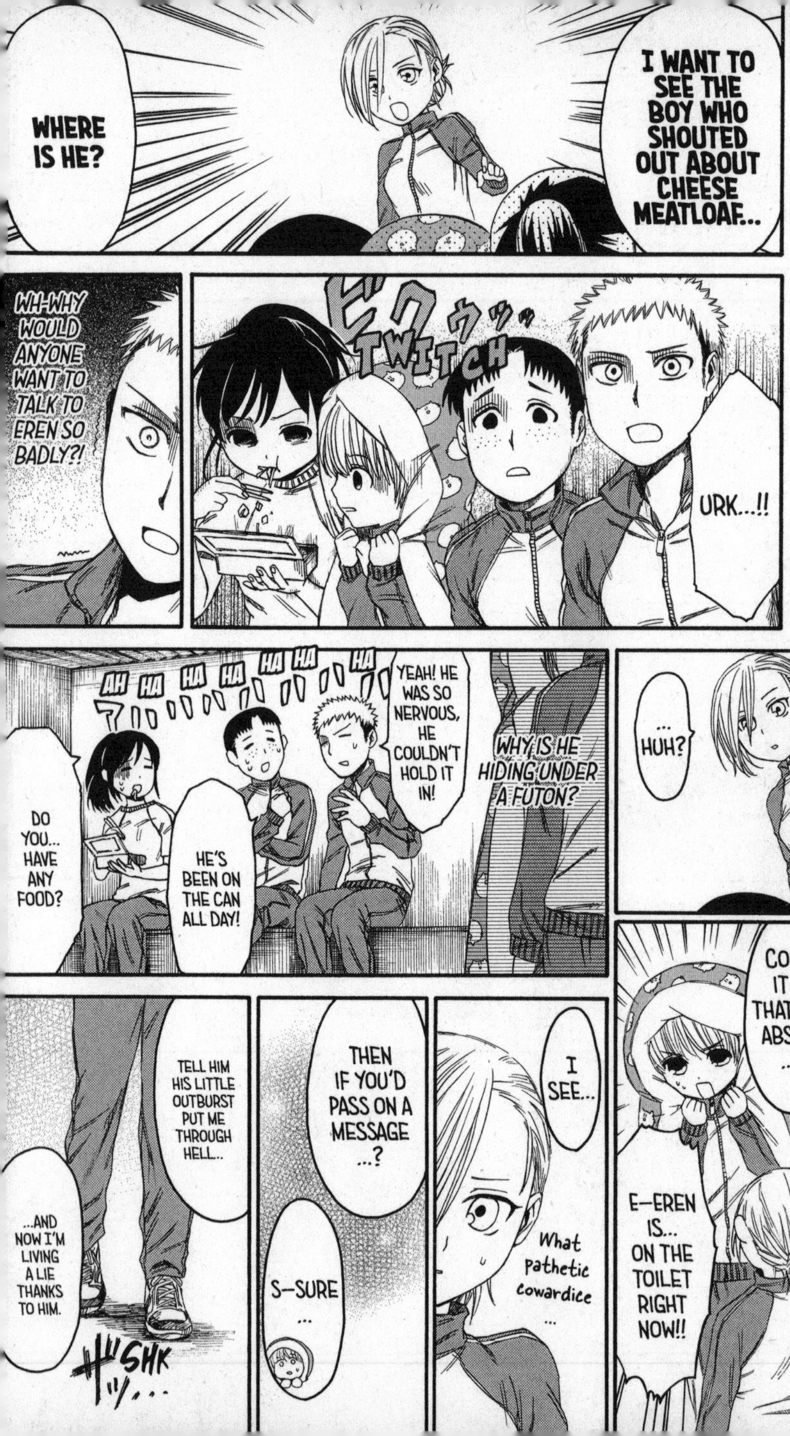
I WANT TO SEE THE BOY WHO SHOUTED OUT ABOUT CHEESE MEATLOAF...
WHERE IS HE?
ビクッ TWITCH
URK...!!
WH-WHY WOULD ANYONE WANT TO TALK TO EREN SO BADLY?!
... HUH?
COULD IT BE THAT HE'S ABSENT ...?
E-EREN IS... ON THE TOILET RIGHT NOW!!
WHY IS HE HIDING UNDER A FUTON?
YEAH! HE WAS SO NERVOUS, HE COULDN'T HOLD IT IN!
AH HA HA HA HA HA HA
HE'S BEEN ON THE CAN ALL DAY!
DO YOU... HAVE ANY FOOD?
I SEE...
What pathetic cowardice ...
THEN IF YOU'D PASS ON A MESSAGE ...?
S-SURE ...
TELL HIM HIS LITTLE OUTBURST PUT ME THROUGH HELL..
...AND NOW I'M LIVING A LIE THANKS TO HIM.
ザッ SHK

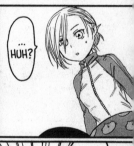

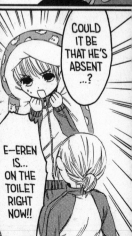

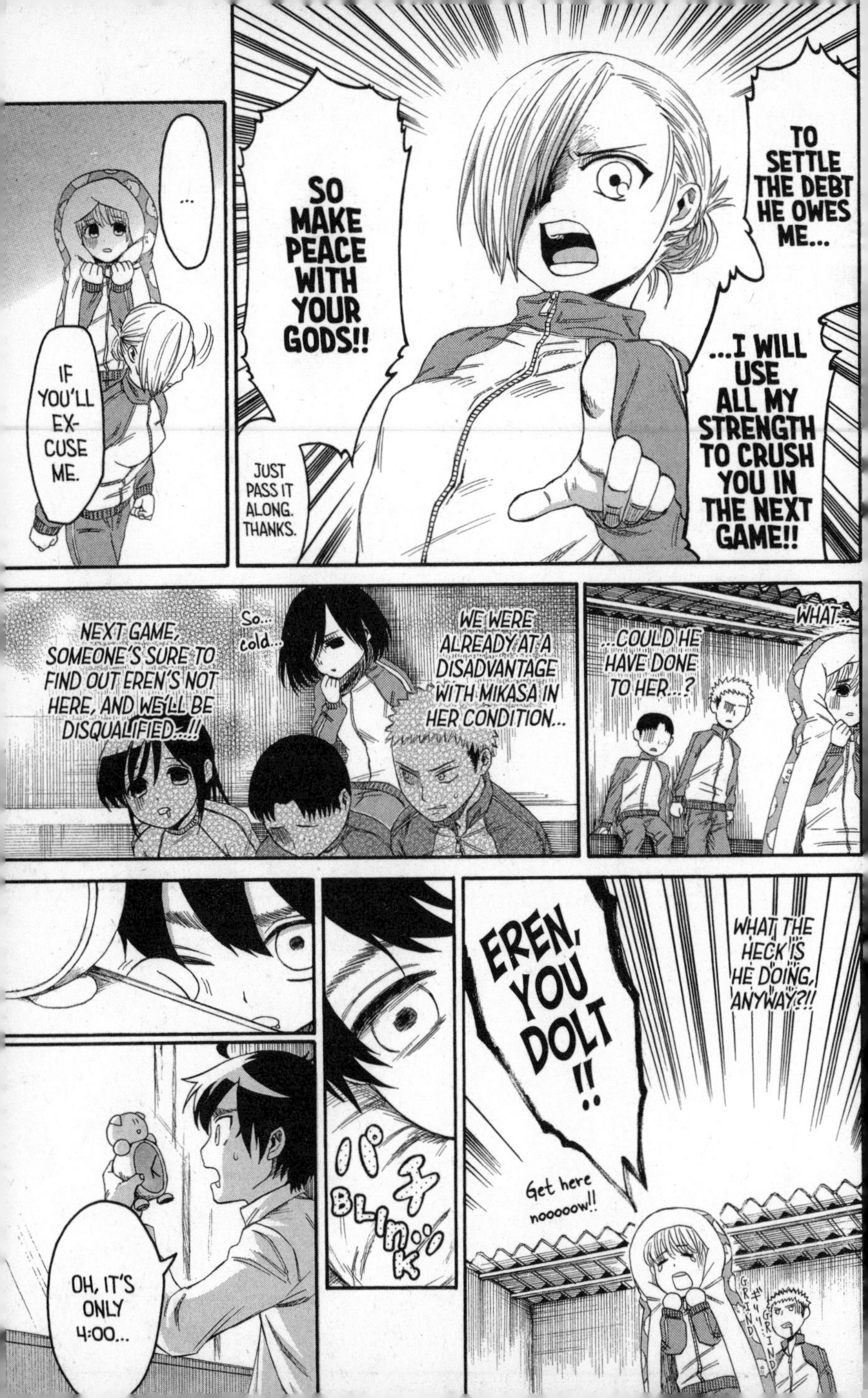
TO SETTLE THE DEBT HE OWES ME...
...I WILL USE ALL MY STRENGTH TO CRUSH YOU IN THE NEXT GAME!!
SO MAKE PEACE WITH YOUR GODS!!
JUST PASS IT ALONG. THANKS.
...
IF YOU'LL EX-CUSE ME.
WHAT...
...COULD HE HAVE DONE TO HER...?
WE WERE ALREADY AT A DISADVANTAGE WITH MIKASA IN HER CONDITION...
So... cold...
NEXT GAME, SOMEONE'S SURE TO FIND OUT EREN'S NOT HERE, AND WE'LL BE DISQUALIFIED...!!
WHAT THE HECK IS HE DOING, ANYWAY?!!
EREN, YOU DOLT!!
Get here nooooow!!
GRIND GRIND
BLINK
OH, IT'S ONLY 4:00...

HAJIME ISAYAMA × SAKI NAKAGAWA

TALK ABOUT TITAN! 2

TELL US ABOUT THE FIRST "JR. HIGH" CHAPTER.

I: IF I REMEMBER, AT OUR FIRST MEETING, NAKAGAWA-SAN HAD A CHART OF THE CHARACTERS AND WHAT KIND OF PATTERNS THEY WOULD FOLLOW, RIGHT?

N: I CHARTED OUT THREE PATTERNS, EACH WITH DIFFERENT HEAD-TO-BODY RATIOS. I WAS REALLY INTO DRAWING THEM BECAUSE I KNEW ISAYAMA-SENSEI WAS GOING TO SEE THEM! THEN WHAT HAPPENED NEXT...

I: HUH? WHAT HAPPENED?

N: YOU GOT UP AND LEFT HALFWAY THROUGH THE MEETING!

I: ...OH, THAT'S RIGHT! MY TOOTH WAS ACHING LIKE CRAZY, AND I HAD TO GET TO A DENTIST QUICK!

N: HERE I WAS SO NERVOUS ABOUT IT, AND SUDDENLY, "HUH? HE'S LEAVING IN THE MIDDLE?" (LAUGHS)

I: WHEN I GOT TO THE DENTIST, HE SAID THAT ALL BUT TWO TEETH HAD CAVITIES...

N: "IT'S HARD DOING A REGULAR COMIC, HUH?" I REMEMBER THINKING THAT AT THE TIME.

GIVE US YOUR THOUGHTS ON THE SPIN-OFF.

I: IT'S A WEIRD FEELING TO HAVE A DIFFERENT EREN IN THE SAME MAGAZINE, BUT NOT IN "ATTACK ON TITAN." HOW DO YOU FEEL, NAKAGAWA-SAN?

N: UP TO THIS POINT, I WAS JUST A READER LOVING HOW COOL "ATTACK ON TITAN" IS! BUT NOW, READING "ATTACK ON TITAN" WAS A LITTLE BIT OF A SCARY EXPERIENCE.

I: HUH?

N: I'M ASSUMING A LOT ABOUT THE CHARACTERS WHEN I READ "ATTACK ON TITAN," AND IF I'M WRONG ABOUT THEM, I FEEL THAT'S A FAILURE ON MY PART.

I: YOU DON'T HAVE TO WORRY ABOUT THAT! I WAS THERE WHILE THEY WERE MAKING SOME OF THE ANIME VERSION OF "ATTACK ON TITAN," AND I FINALLY REALIZED THAT THESE CHARACTERS CAN BE DIFFERENT FROM THE CHARACTERS I HAVE IN MY HEAD.

N: WHAT DO YOU MEAN?

I: THESE CHARACTERS AREN'T JUST MINE. EVERYBODY BRINGS THEIR OWN EXPERIENCES TO THEM, AND THAT'S WHAT GIVES THEM THEIR CHARM! AT LEAST, THAT'S WHAT I THINK!

N: I AM SO HAPPY YOU SAID THAT!

I: IN ATTACK ON TITAN: JR. HIGH, WHEN EREN AND THE GROUP ALL SNUCK INTO THE TITANS' CLASSROOM, I REALIZED IT WAS SOMETHING I WOULD NEVER HAVE COME UP WITH.

N: THAT'S A DEEPLY EMOTIONAL CHAPTER FOR ME. I TOOK THE STORY TO MY MEETING WITH THE EDITOR, AND HE GAVE ME AN, "OKAY," WITHOUT HARDLY ANY ALTERATIONS!

I: ALSO THE SCENE WHERE EREN WAS SUCKED ON BY A TITAN THEN SPIT OUT LEFT A BIG IMPRESSION ON ME.

N: THAT WAS TAKEN FROM YOUR SUGGESTION WHEN YOU SAID, "EREN IS TAKEN INTO A TITAN'S MOUTH AND BY THE TIME HE COMES OUT, HIS CELL PHONE IS WATERLOGGED AND BROKEN."

I: BUT SINCE THAT JOKE TURNED INTO A CHINESE FOOD JOKE, I HAVE TO SAY THAT I HAVEN'T BEEN MUCH HELP TO YOU, HUH? (LAUGHS)

←-------- CONTINUED ON P. 124.

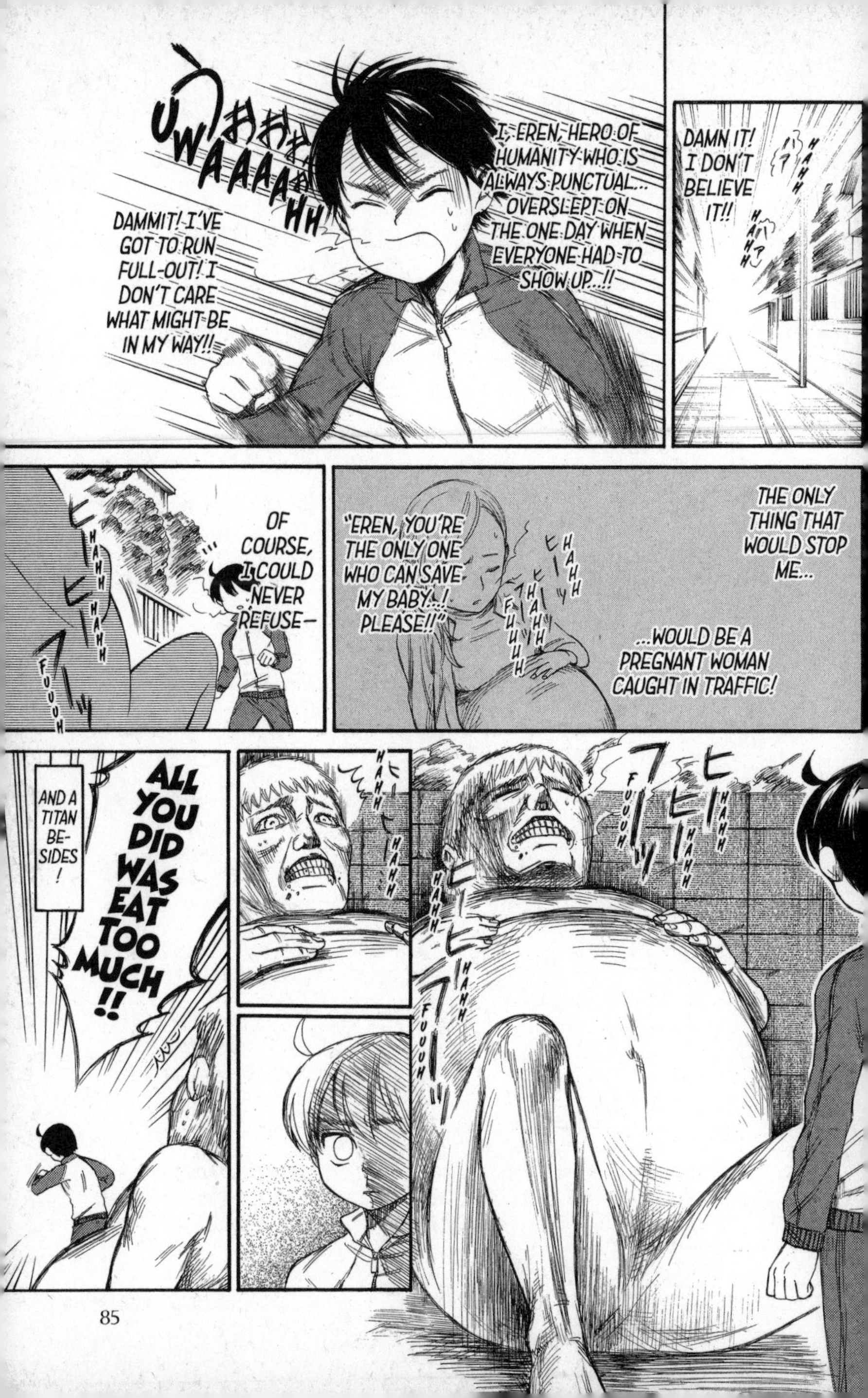

DAMN IT! I DON'T BELIEVE IT!!
HAHH
HAHH
UWAAAAAHH
I, EREN, HERO OF HUMANITY WHO IS ALWAYS PUNCTUAL... OVERSLEPT ON THE ONE DAY WHEN EVERYONE HAD TO SHOW UP...!!
DAMMIT! I'VE GOT TO RUN FULL-OUT! I DON'T CARE WHAT MIGHT BE IN MY WAY!!
THE ONLY THING THAT WOULD STOP ME...
"EREN, YOU'RE THE ONLY ONE WHO CAN SAVE MY BABY...! PLEASE!!"
HAHH
HAHH
FUUUH
...WOULD BE A PREGNANT WOMAN CAUGHT IN TRAFFIC!
OF COURSE, I COULD NEVER REFUSE—
HAHH
HAHH
FUUUH
FUUUH
HAHH
HAHH
HAHH
HAHH
FUUUH
HAHH
HAHH
AND A TITAN BESIDES!
ALL YOU DID WAS EAT TOO MUCH!!

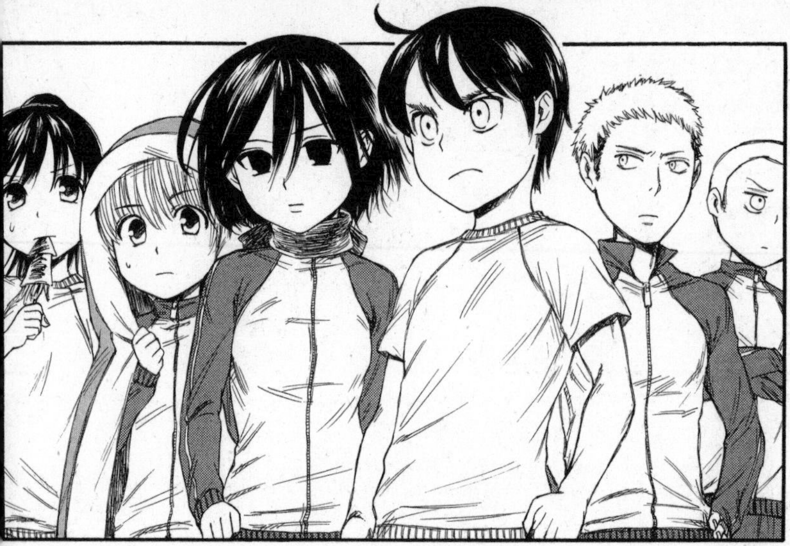

FIFTH PERIOD: THE TITAN ALWAYS RINGS TWICE

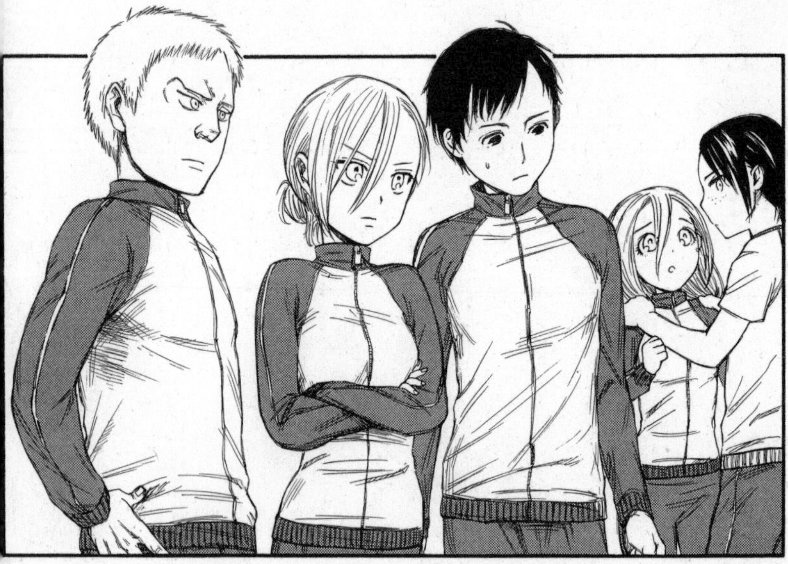

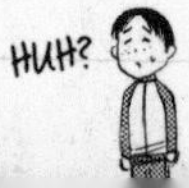
HUH?

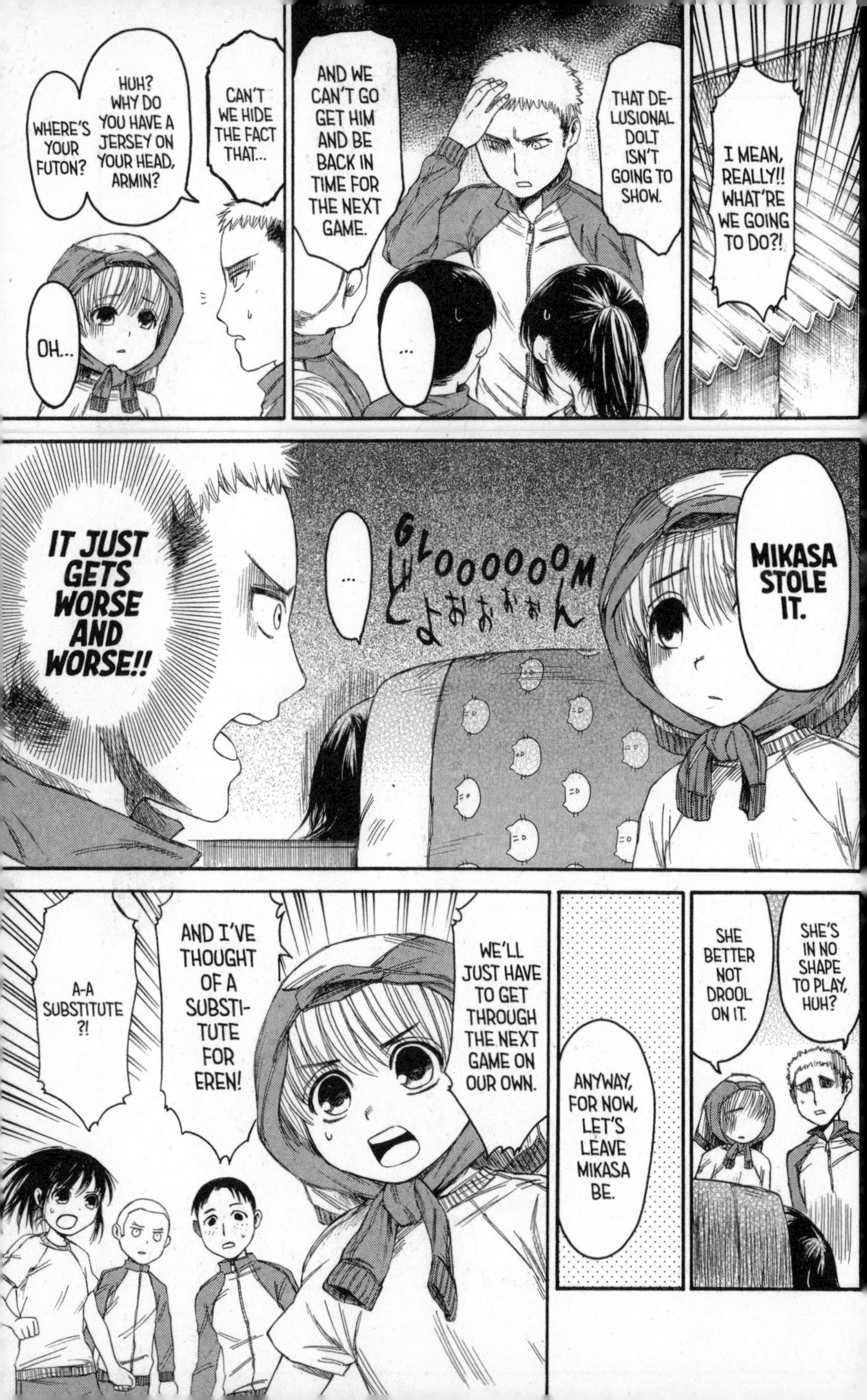
I MEAN, REALLY!! WHAT'RE WE GOING TO DO?!
THAT DE-LUSIONAL DOLT ISN'T GOING TO SHOW.
AND WE CAN'T GO GET HIM AND BE BACK IN TIME FOR THE NEXT GAME.
...
CAN'T WE HIDE THE FACT THAT...
HUH? WHY DO YOU HAVE A JERSEY ON YOUR HEAD, ARMIN?
WHERE'S YOUR FUTON?
OH...
MIKASA STOLE IT.
GLOOOOOOOM
どよおおぉぉん
...
IT JUST GETS WORSE AND WORSE!!
SHE'S IN NO SHAPE TO PLAY, HUH?
SHE BETTER NOT DROOL ON IT.
ANYWAY, FOR NOW, LET'S LEAVE MIKASA BE.
WE'LL JUST HAVE TO GET THROUGH THE NEXT GAME ON OUR OWN.
AND I'VE THOUGHT OF A SUBSTI-TUTE FOR EREN!
A-A SUBSTITUTE?!

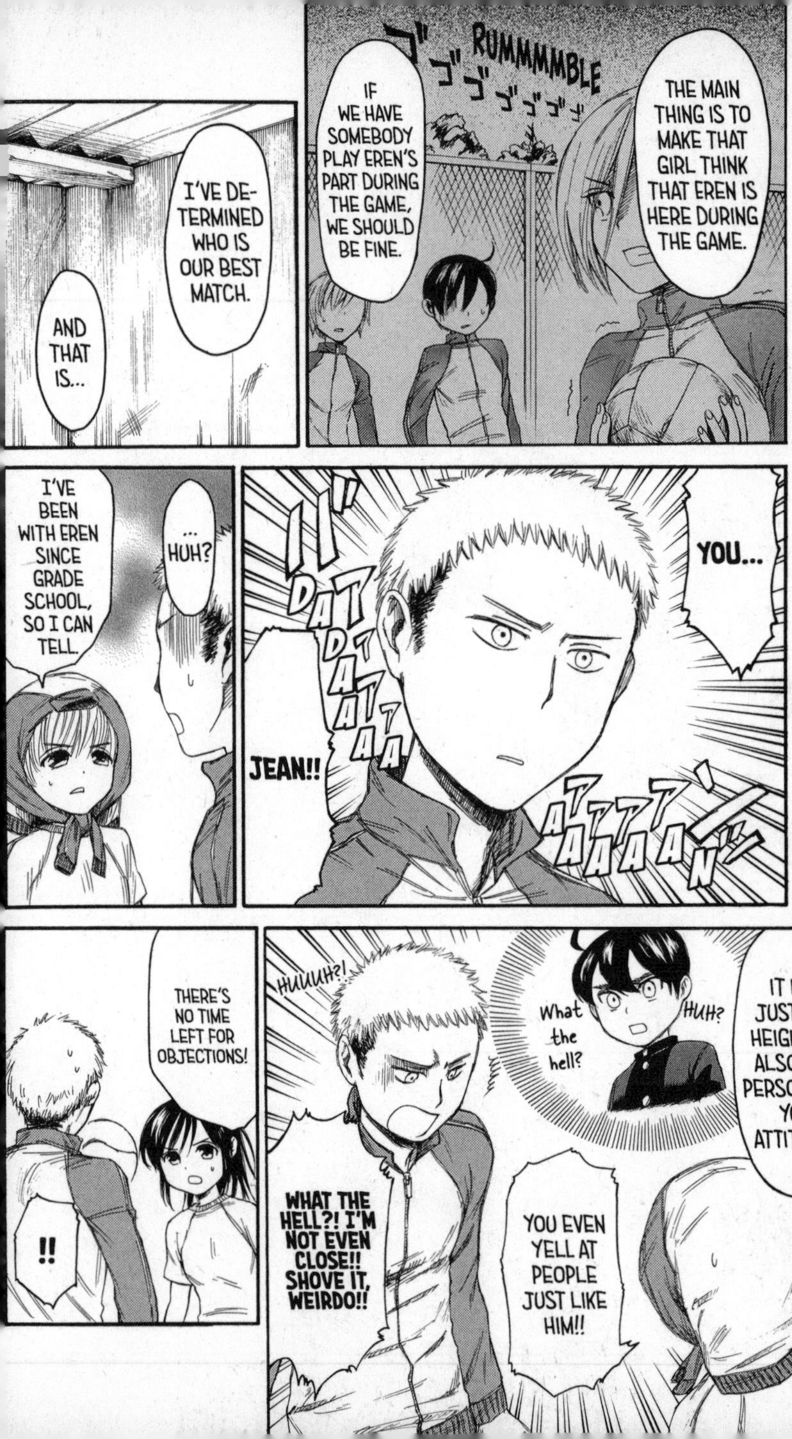
ゴゴゴゴゴ
RUMMMMBLE
THE MAIN THING IS TO MAKE THAT GIRL THINK THAT EREN IS HERE DURING THE GAME.
IF WE HAVE SOMEBODY PLAY EREN'S PART DURING THE GAME, WE SHOULD BE FINE.
I'VE DETERMINED WHO IS OUR BEST MATCH.
AND THAT IS...
YOU...
JEAN!!
I'VE BEEN WITH EREN SINCE GRADE SCHOOL, SO I CAN TELL.
...HUH?
IT ISN'T JUST YOUR HEIGHT, BUT ALSO YOUR PERSONALITY, YOUR ATTITUDE...
HUH?
What the hell?
HUUUH?!
YOU EVEN YELL AT PEOPLE JUST LIKE HIM!!
WHAT THE HELL?! I'M NOT EVEN CLOSE!! SHOVE IT, WEIRDO!!
THERE'S NO TIME LEFT FOR OBJECTIONS!
!!

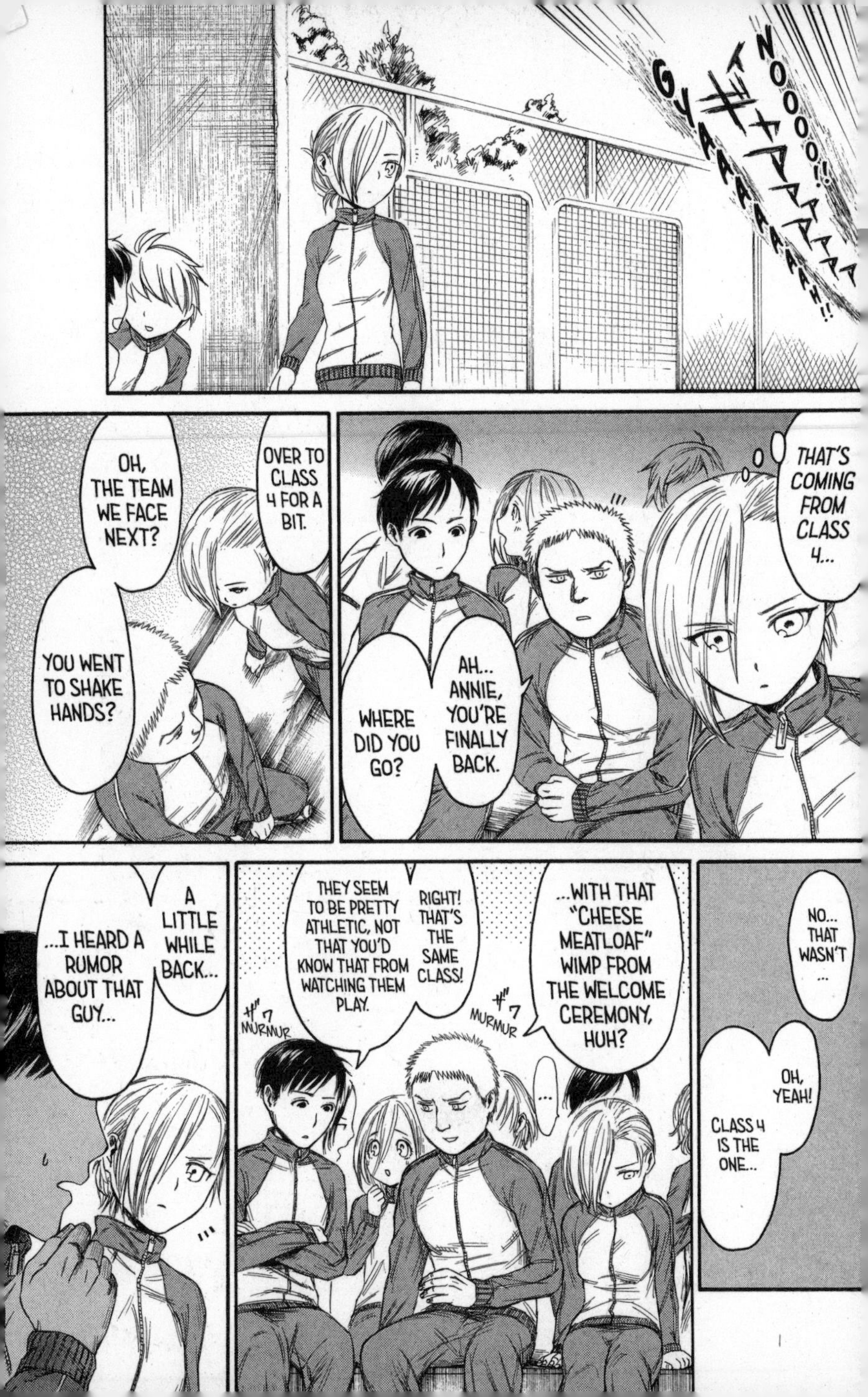
NOOOOO!!
GYAAAAAAAAAH!!
THAT'S COMING FROM CLASS 4...
AH... ANNIE, YOU'RE FINALLY BACK.
WHERE DID YOU GO?
OVER TO CLASS 4 FOR A BIT.
OH, THE TEAM WE FACE NEXT?
YOU WENT TO SHAKE HANDS?
NO... THAT WASN'T ...
OH, YEAH! CLASS 4 IS THE ONE...
...WITH THAT "CHEESE MEATLOAF" WIMP FROM THE WELCOME CEREMONY, HUH?
RIGHT! THAT'S THE SAME CLASS!
THEY SEEM TO BE PRETTY ATHLETIC, NOT THAT YOU'D KNOW THAT FROM WATCHING THEM PLAY.
MURMUR
MURMUR
...
A LITTLE WHILE BACK...
...I HEARD A RUMOR ABOUT THAT GUY...

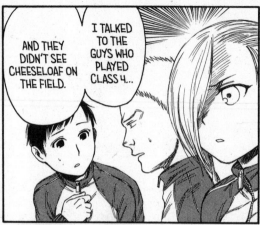

I TALKED TO THE GUYS WHO PLAYED CLASS 4...
AND THEY DIDN'T SEE CHEESELOAF ON THE FIELD.
THAT CAN'T BE RIGHT... THEY MUST HAVE MISSED...
YOU'RE RIGHT. I MEAN OTHERWISE, THEY'D BE DISQUALI-FIED.
...
E-EREN IS...ON THE TOILET RIGHT NOW!!
HE'S BEEN ON THE CAN ALL DAY!
AH HA HA HA HA HA
DO YOU HAVE ANY FOOD?!
WHOOSH
DASH
H-HEY, ANNIE!!
COULD IT BE THAT HE'S...
The game's about to begin!!

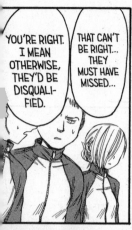

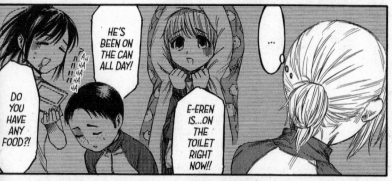

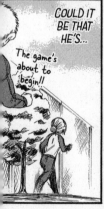

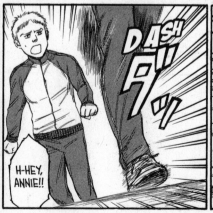

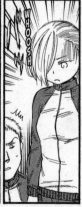

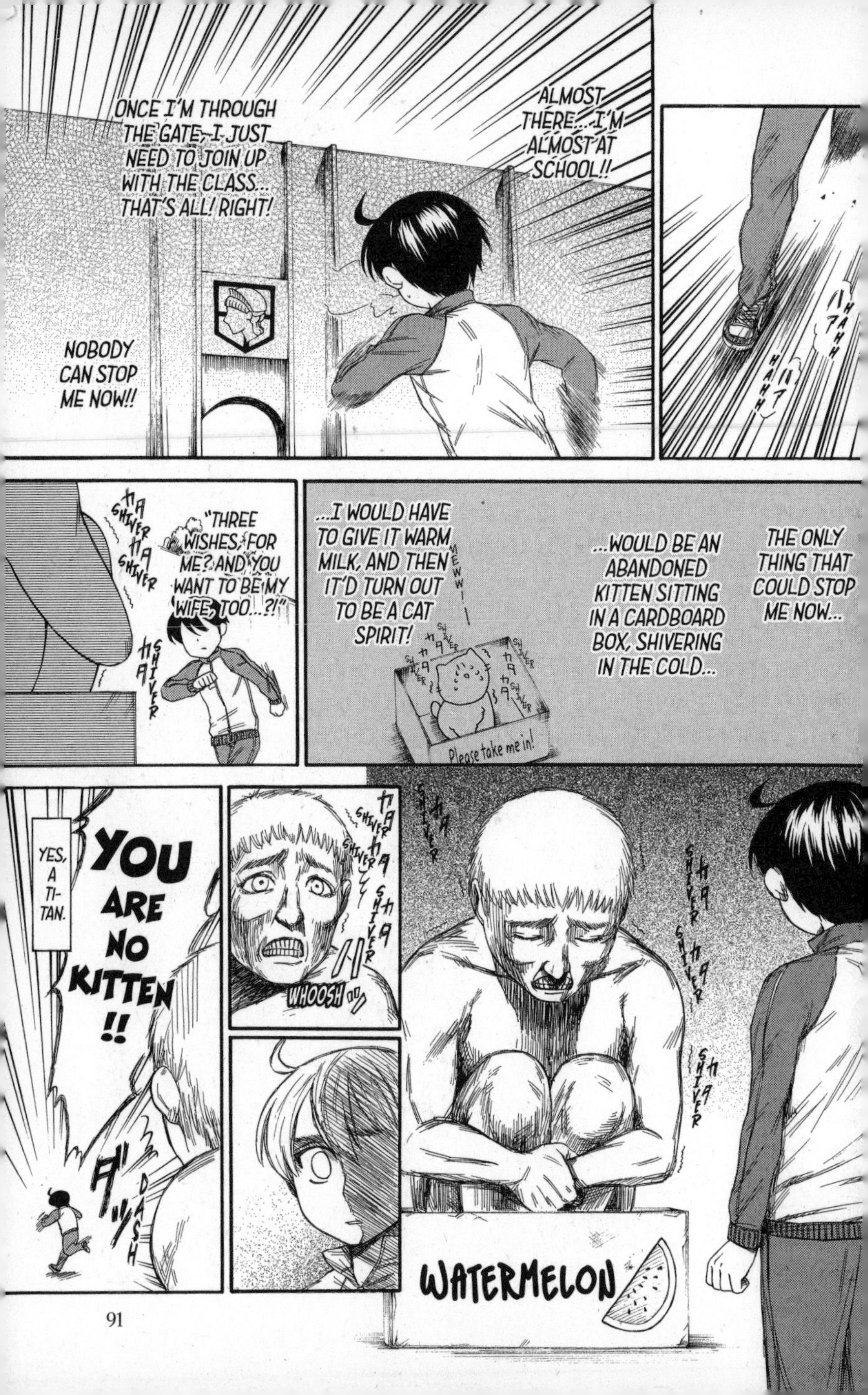
HAHH HAHH
ALMOST THERE... I'M ALMOST AT SCHOOL!!
ONCE I'M THROUGH THE GATE, I JUST NEED TO JOIN UP WITH THE CLASS... THAT'S ALL! RIGHT!
NOBODY CAN STOP ME NOW!!
THE ONLY THING THAT COULD STOP ME NOW...
...WOULD BE AN ABANDONED KITTEN SITTING IN A CARDBOARD BOX, SHIVERING IN THE COLD...
MEW!
...I WOULD HAVE TO GIVE IT WARM MILK, AND THEN IT'D TURN OUT TO BE A CAT SPIRIT!
SHIVER SHIVER SHIVER
Please take me in!
"THREE WISHES, FOR ME? AND YOU WANT TO BE MY WIFE, TOO...?!"
SHIVER SHIVER SHIVER
SHIVER SHIVER SHIVER SHIVER
WATERMELON
SHIVER SHIVER SHIVER
WHOOSH
YOU ARE NO KITTEN!!
YES, A TITAN.
DASH

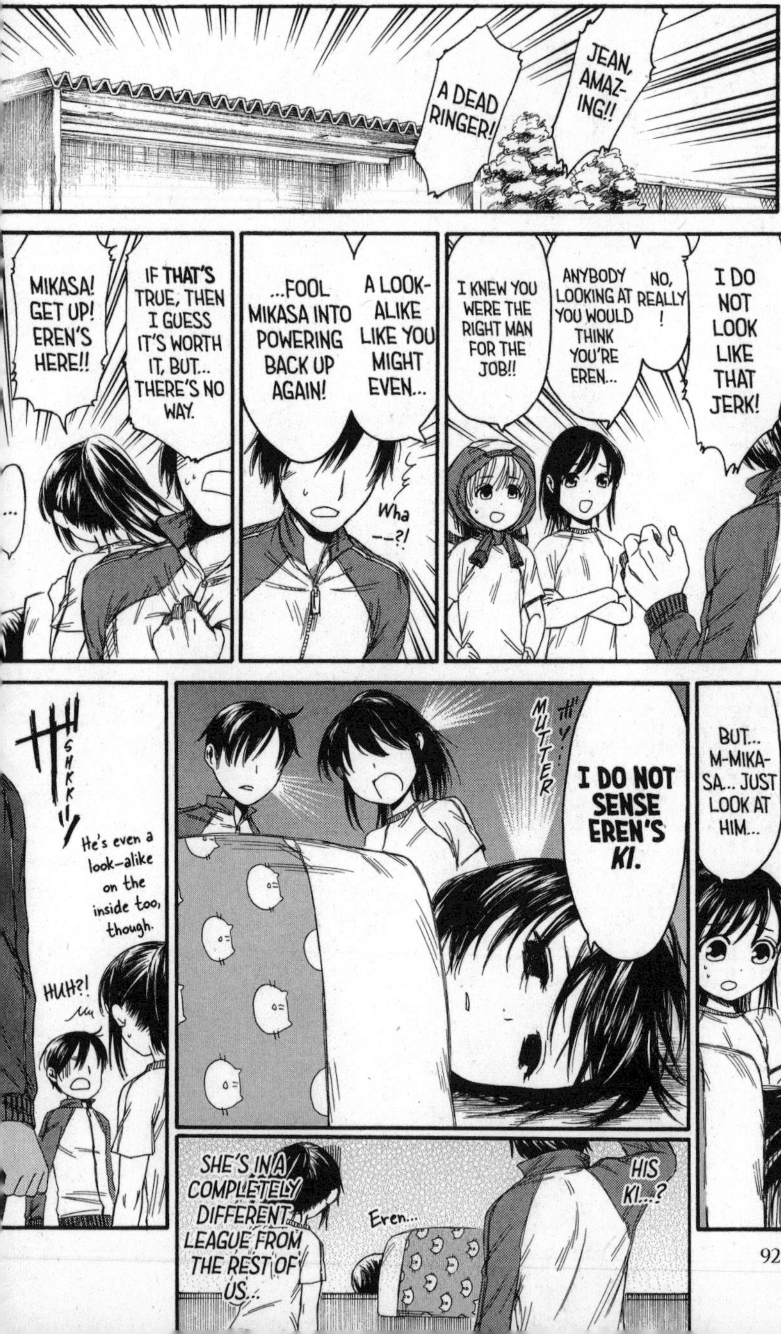
JEAN, AMAZ-ING!!
A DEAD RINGER!
DON'T LIE TO ME!
I DO NOT LOOK LIKE THAT JERK!
NO, REALLY!
ANYBODY LOOKING AT YOU WOULD THINK YOU'RE EREN...
I KNEW YOU WERE THE RIGHT MAN FOR THE JOB!!
A LOOK-ALIKE LIKE YOU MIGHT EVEN...
...FOOL MIKASA INTO POWERING BACK UP AGAIN!
Wha--?!
IF THAT'S TRUE, THEN I GUESS IT'S WORTH IT, BUT... THERE'S NO WAY.
MIKASA! GET UP! EREN'S HERE!!
...
YOU'RE WRONG...
BUT... M-MIKASA... JUST LOOK AT HIM...
I DO NOT SENSE EREN'S KI.
MUTTER
HIS KI...?
Eren...
SHE'S IN A COMPLETELY DIFFERENT LEAGUE FROM THE REST OF US...
SHKK
He's even a look-alike on the inside too, though.
HUH?!

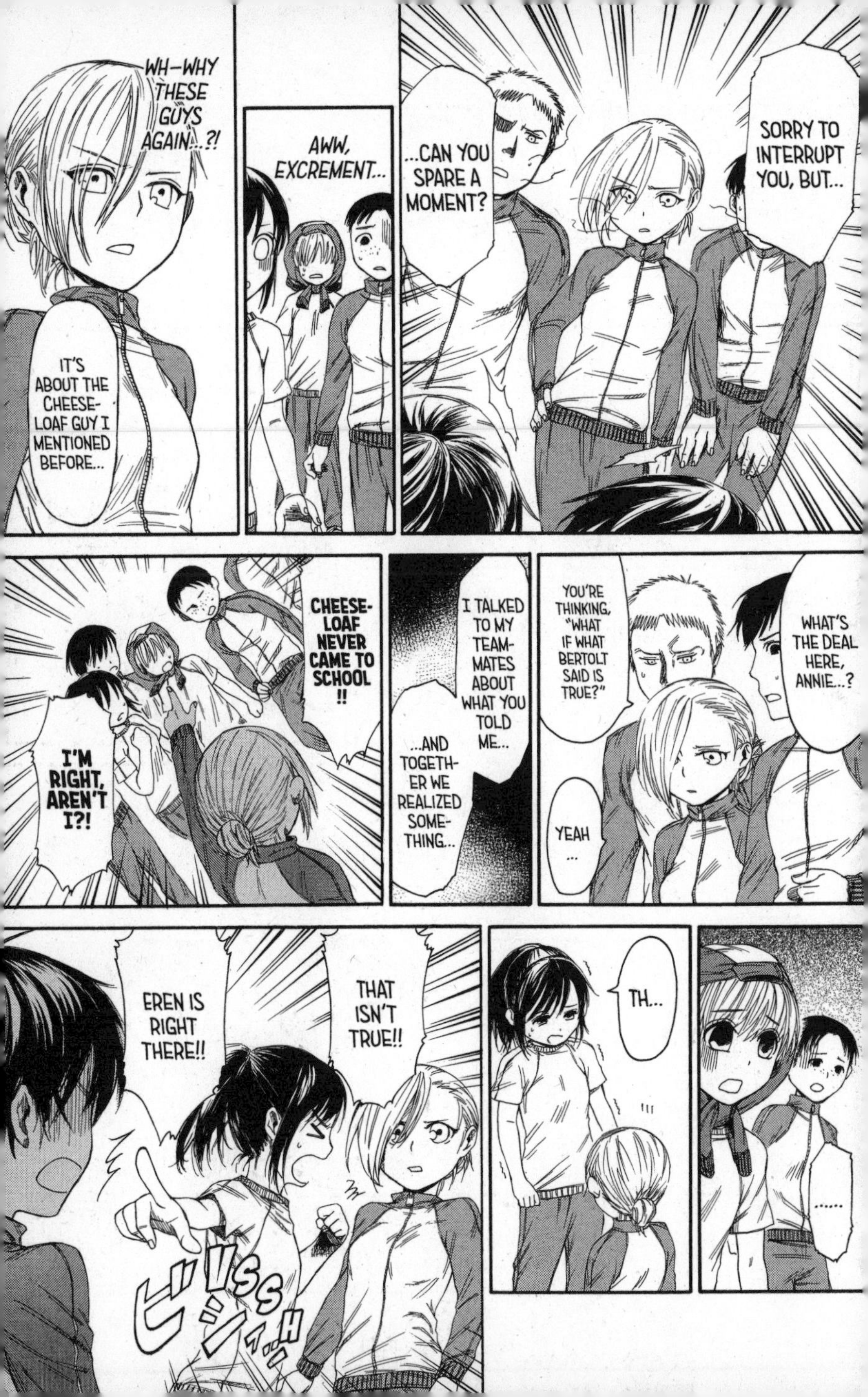
SORRY TO INTERRUPT YOU, BUT...
...CAN YOU SPARE A MOMENT?
AWW, EXCREMENT...
WH-WHY THESE GUYS AGAIN...?!
IT'S ABOUT THE CHEESE-LOAF GUY I MENTIONED BEFORE...
WHAT'S THE DEAL HERE, ANNIE...?
YOU'RE THINKING, "WHAT IF WHAT BERTOLT SAID IS TRUE?"
YEAH ...
I TALKED TO MY TEAM-MATES ABOUT WHAT YOU TOLD ME...
...AND TOGETH-ER WE REALIZED SOME-THING...
CHEESE-LOAF NEVER CAME TO SCHOOL !!
I'M RIGHT, AREN'T I?!
......
TH...
!!!
THAT ISN'T TRUE!!
EREN IS RIGHT THERE!!
VSSSH

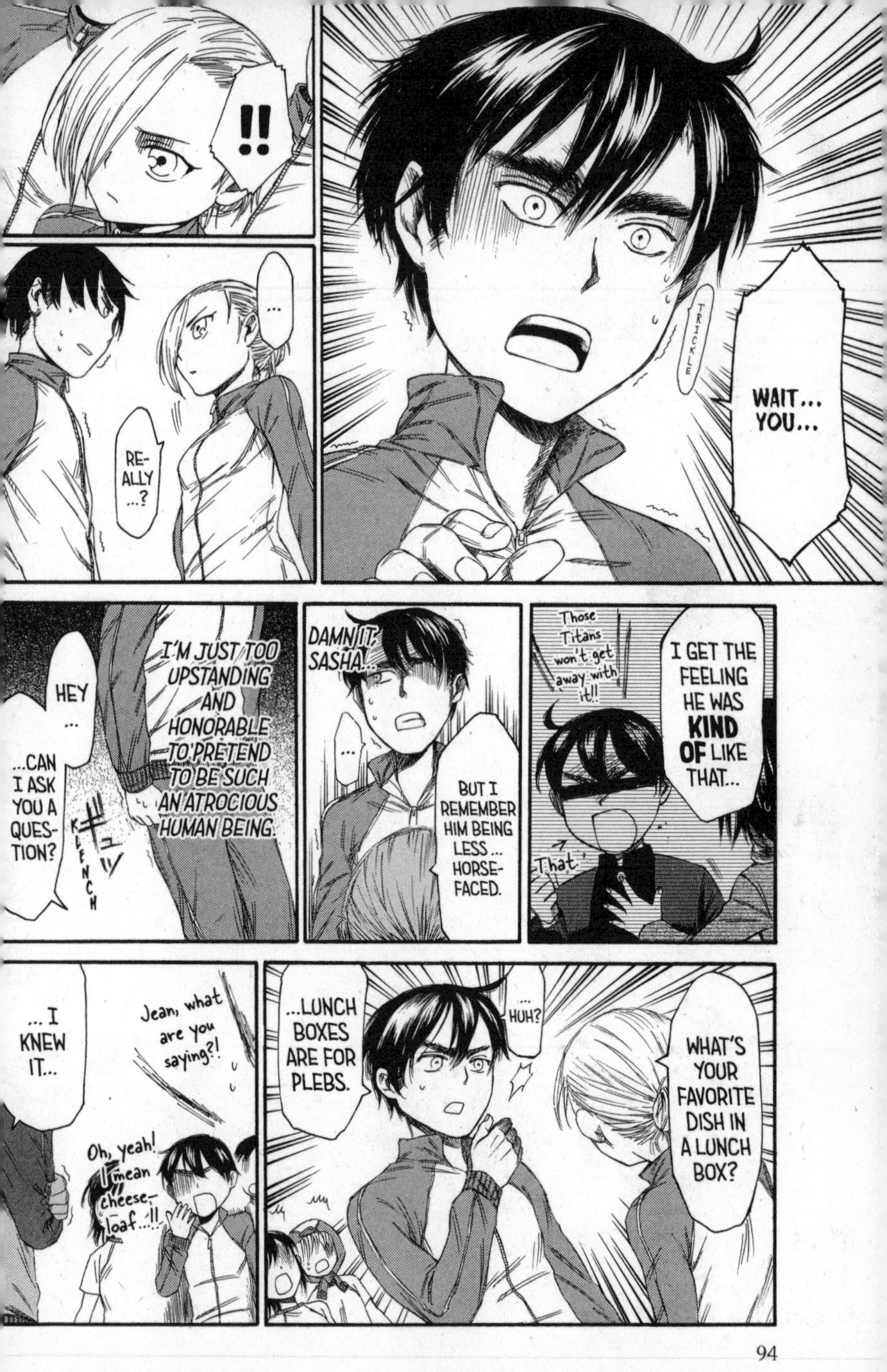
TRICKLE
WAIT... YOU...
!!
...
RE-ALLY ...?
Those Titans won't get away with it!!
I GET THE FEELING HE WAS **KIND OF** LIKE THAT...
That
DAMN IT, SASHA...
...
BUT I REMEMBER HIM BEING LESS ... HORSE-FACED.
I'M JUST TOO UPSTANDING AND HONORABLE TO PRETEND TO BE SUCH AN ATROCIOUS HUMAN BEING.
HEY ...
...CAN I ASK YOU A QUESTION?
KLENCH
WHAT'S YOUR FAVORITE DISH IN A LUNCH BOX?
... HUH?
...LUNCH BOXES ARE FOR PLEBS.
Jean, what are you saying?!
... I KNEW IT...
Oh, yeah! I mean cheese-loaf...!!

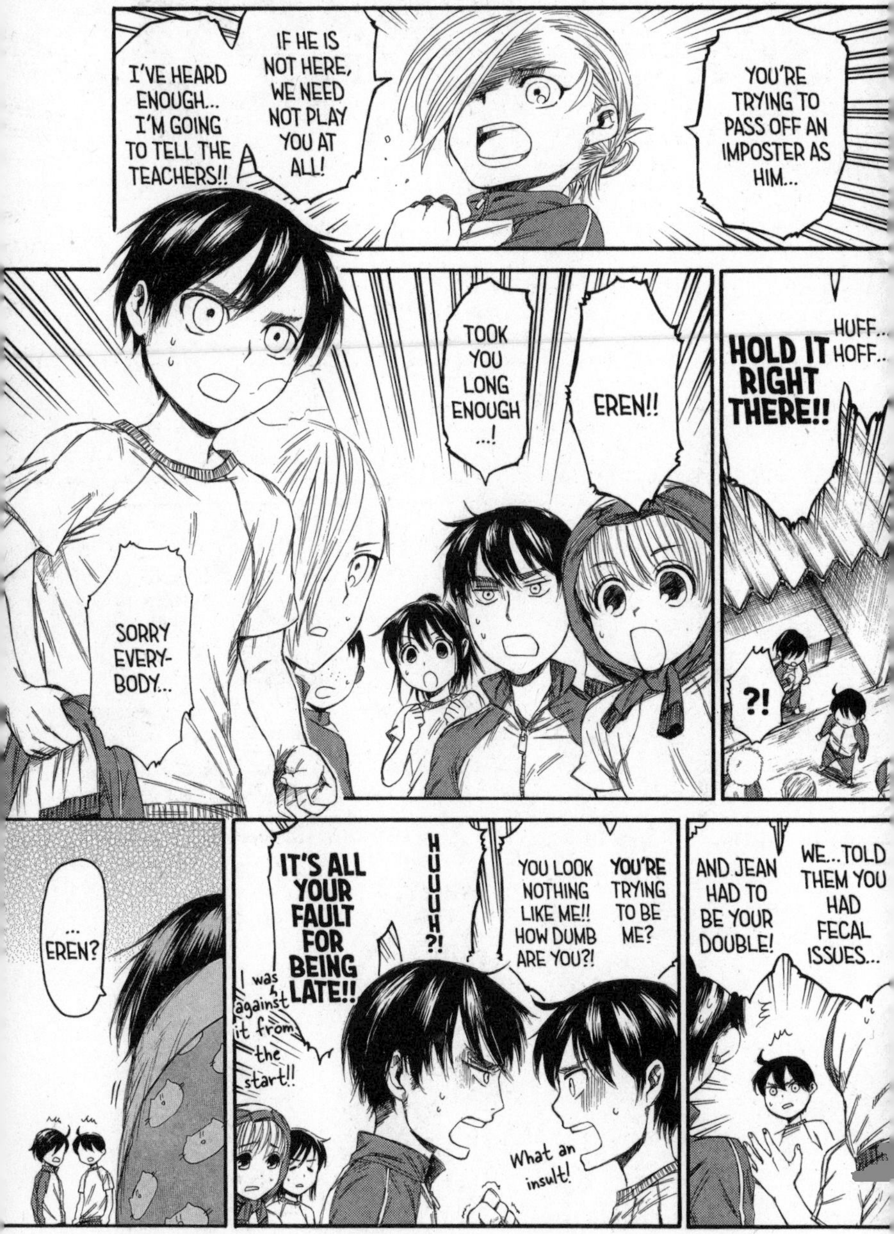
YOU'RE TRYING TO PASS OFF AN IMPOSTER AS HIM...
IF HE IS NOT HERE, WE NEED NOT PLAY YOU AT ALL!
I'VE HEARD ENOUGH... I'M GOING TO TELL THE TEACHERS!!
HUFF... HOFF...
HOLD IT RIGHT THERE!!
?!
EREN!!
TOOK YOU LONG ENOUGH ...!
SORRY EVERY-BODY...
WE...TOLD THEM YOU HAD FECAL ISSUES...
AND JEAN HAD TO BE YOUR DOUBLE!
YOU'RE TRYING TO BE ME?
YOU LOOK NOTHING LIKE ME!! HOW DUMB ARE YOU?!
HUUUH?!
IT'S ALL YOUR FAULT FOR BEING LATE!!
I was against it from the start!!
What an insult!
... EREN?

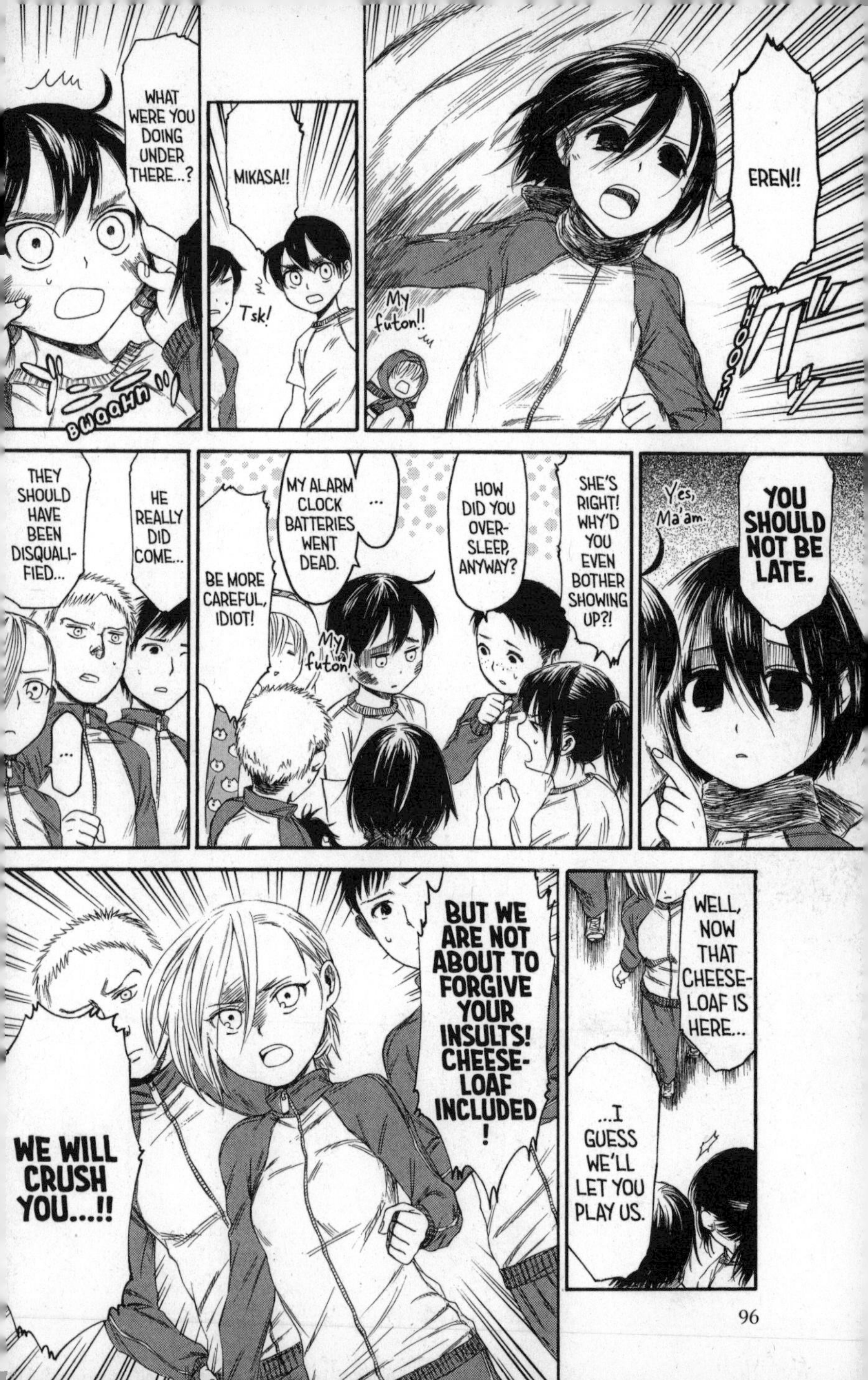
EREN!!
WHOOSH
My futon!!
MIKASA!!
Tsk!
WHAT WERE YOU DOING UNDER THERE...?
BWAAHH
YOU SHOULD NOT BE LATE.
Yes, Ma'am.
SHE'S RIGHT! WHY'D YOU EVEN BOTHER SHOWING UP?!
HOW DID YOU OVER-SLEEP, ANYWAY?
...
MY ALARM CLOCK BATTERIES WENT DEAD.
BE MORE CAREFUL, IDIOT!
My futon!
HE REALLY DID COME...
THEY SHOULD HAVE BEEN DISQUALI-FIED...
...
WELL, NOW THAT CHEESE-LOAF IS HERE...
...I GUESS WE'LL LET YOU PLAY US.
BUT WE ARE NOT ABOUT TO FORGIVE YOUR INSULTS! CHEESE-LOAF INCLUDED!
WE WILL CRUSH YOU...!!

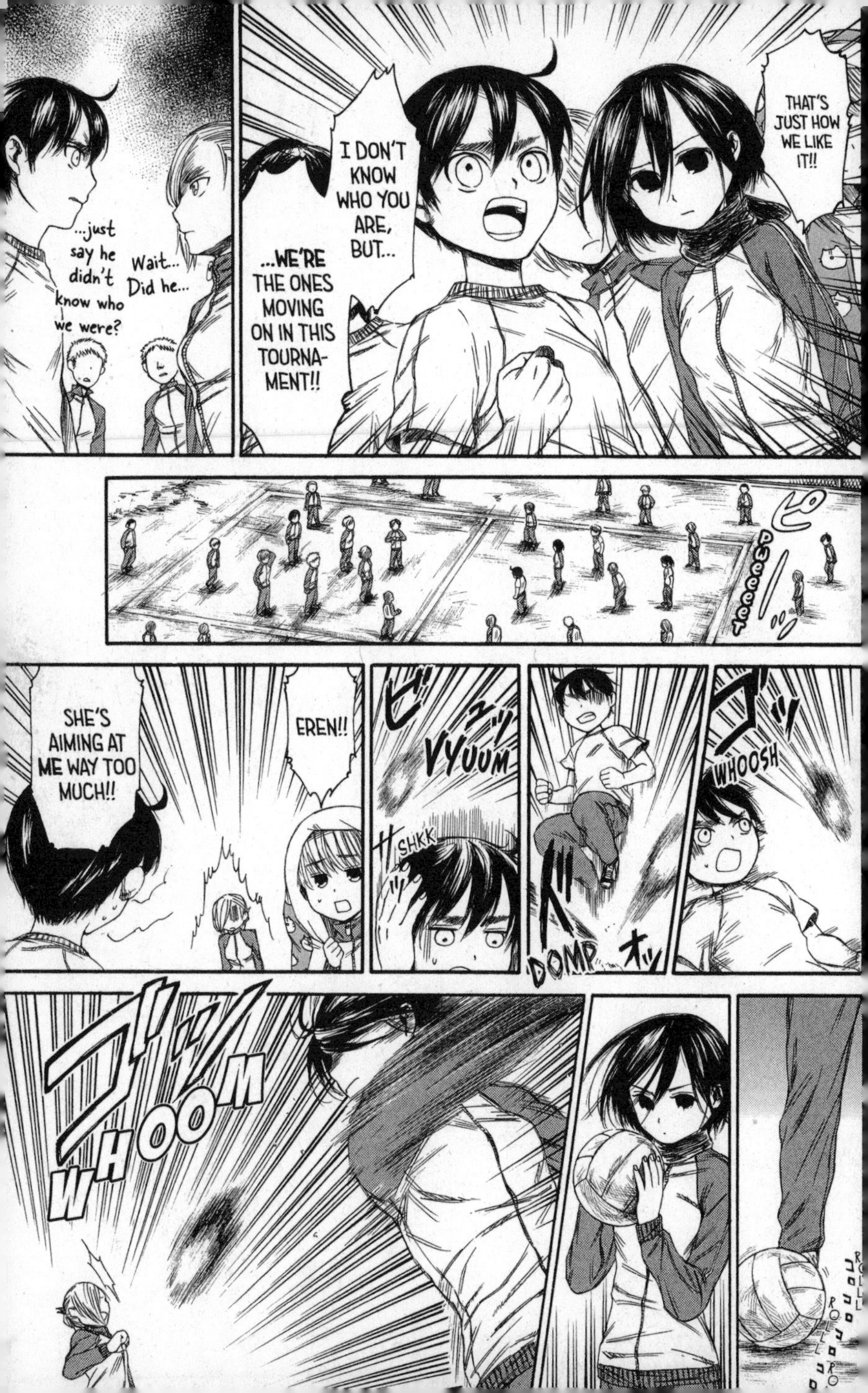
THAT'S JUST HOW WE LIKE IT!!
I DON'T KNOW WHO YOU ARE, BUT...
...WE'RE THE ONES MOVING ON IN THIS TOURNAMENT!!
Wait... Did he...
...just say he didn't know who we were?
PWEEEEET
WHOOSH
DOMP
VYUUM
SHKK
EREN!!
SHE'S AIMING AT ME WAY TOO MUCH!!
ROLL ROLL
WHOOOM

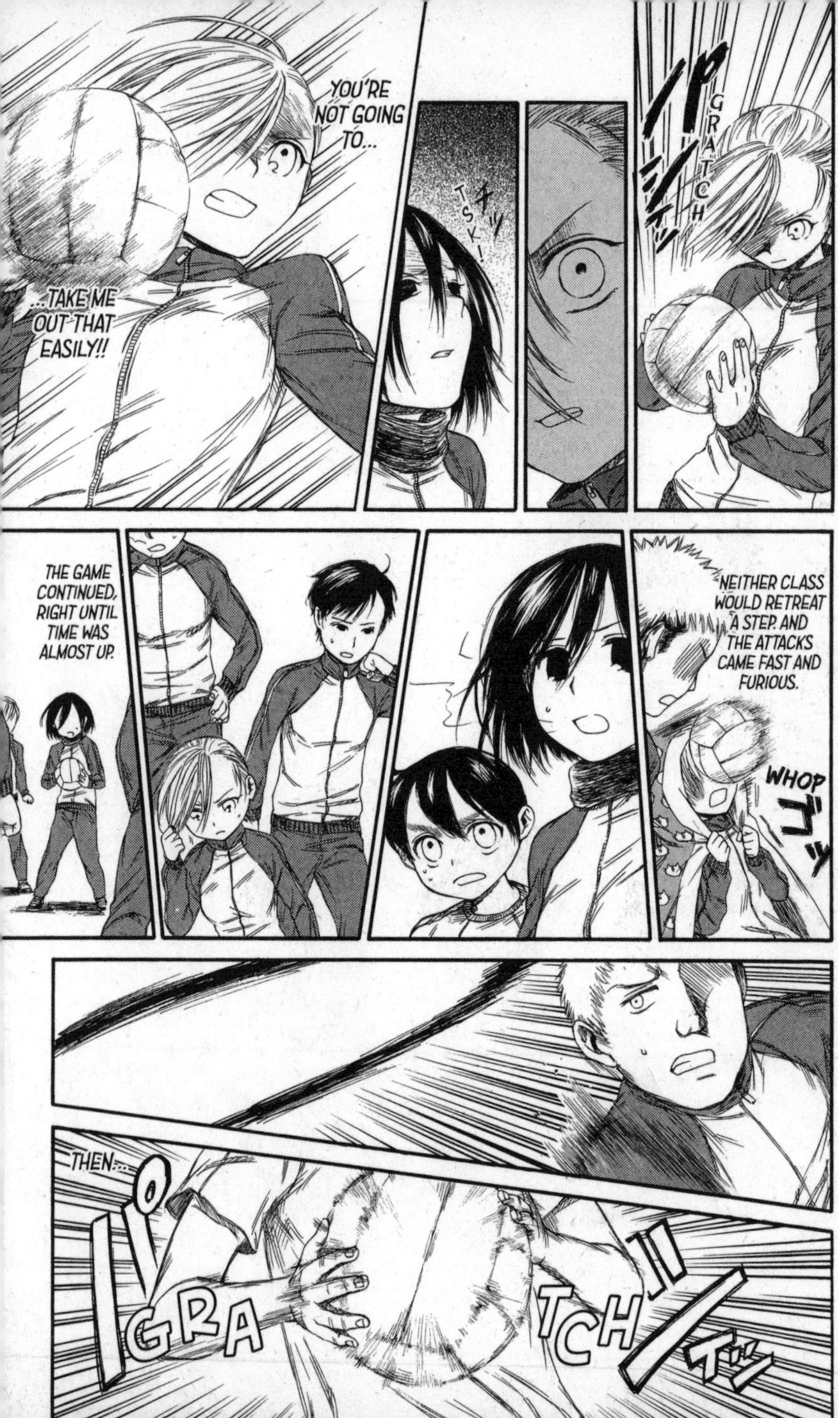
GRATCH
TSK!
YOU'RE NOT GOING TO...
...TAKE ME OUT THAT EASILY!!
NEITHER CLASS WOULD RETREAT A STEP. AND THE ATTACKS CAME FAST AND FURIOUS.
WHOP
THE GAME CONTINUED, RIGHT UNTIL TIME WAS ALMOST UP.
THEN...
GRATCH

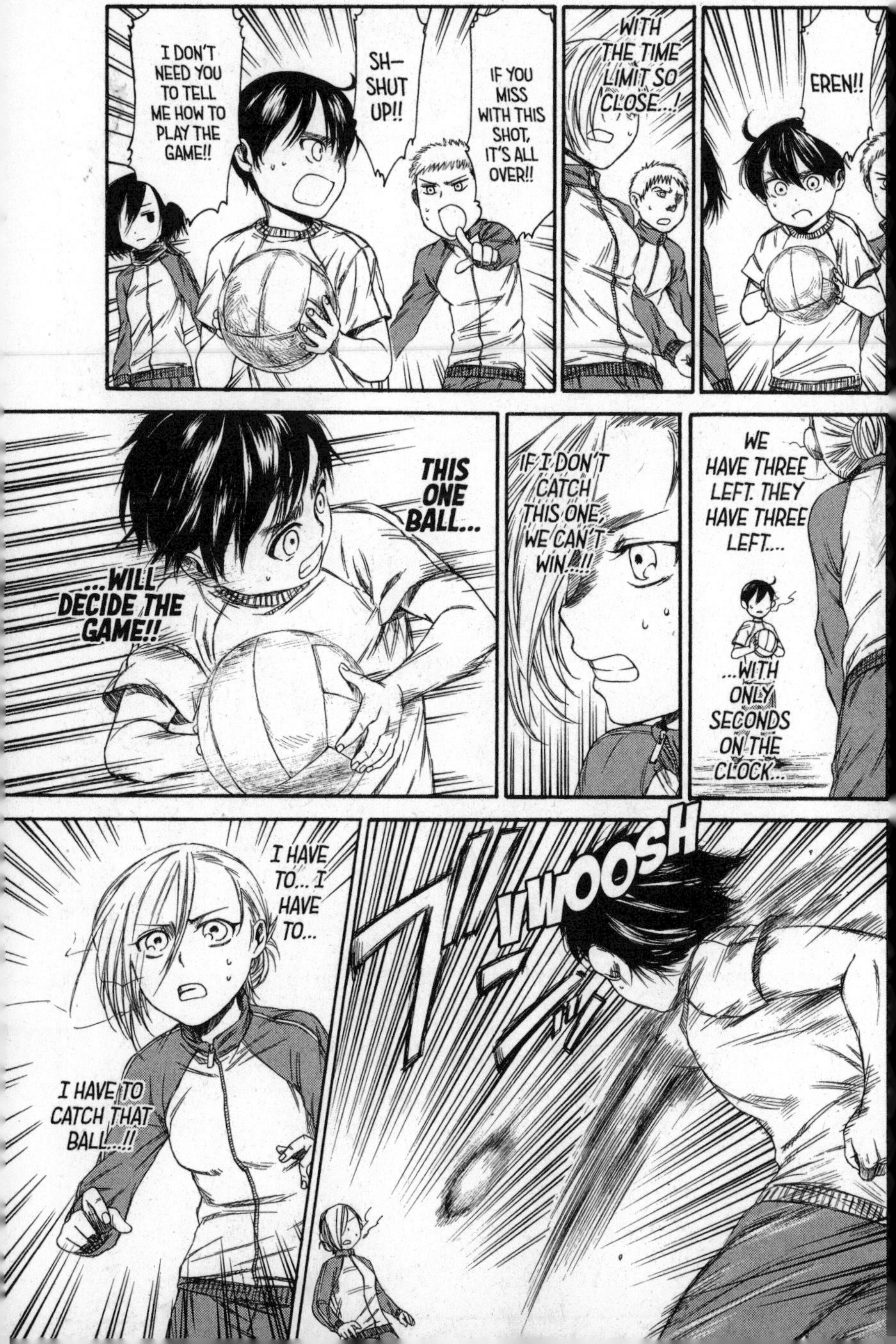
EREN!!
WITH THE TIME LIMIT SO CLOSE...!
IF YOU MISS WITH THIS SHOT, IT'S ALL OVER!!
SH— SHUT UP!!
I DON'T NEED YOU TO TELL ME HOW TO PLAY THE GAME!!
WE HAVE THREE LEFT. THEY HAVE THREE LEFT....
...WITH ONLY SECONDS ON THE CLOCK...
IF I DON'T CATCH THIS ONE, WE CAN'T WIN...!!
THIS ONE BALL...
...WILL DECIDE THE GAME!!
VWOOSH
I HAVE TO... I HAVE TO...
I HAVE TO CATCH THAT BALL...!!

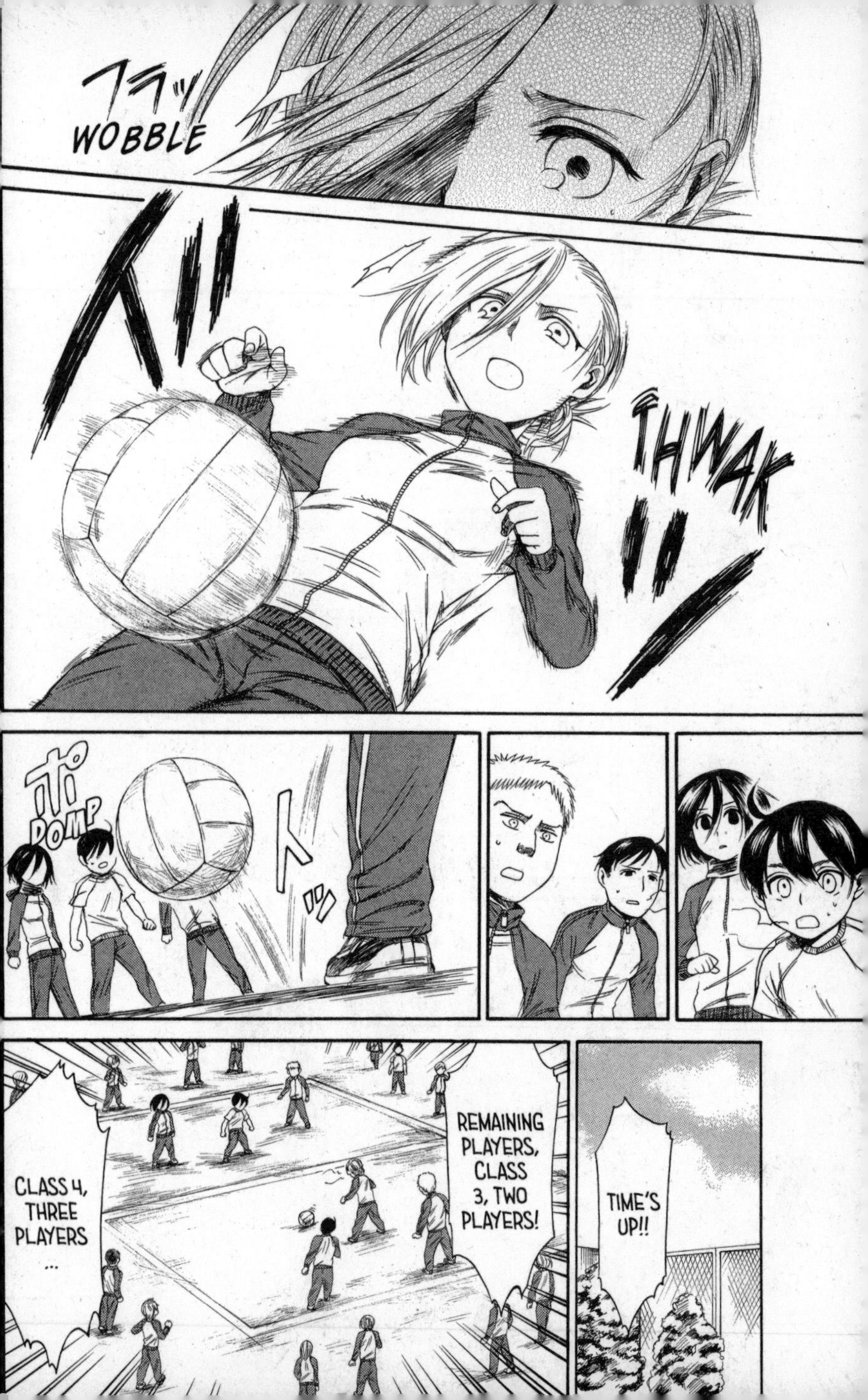
フラッ
WOBBLE
THWAK
DOMP
TIME'S UP!!
REMAINING PLAYERS, CLASS 3, TWO PLAYERS!
CLASS 4, THREE PLAYERS
...

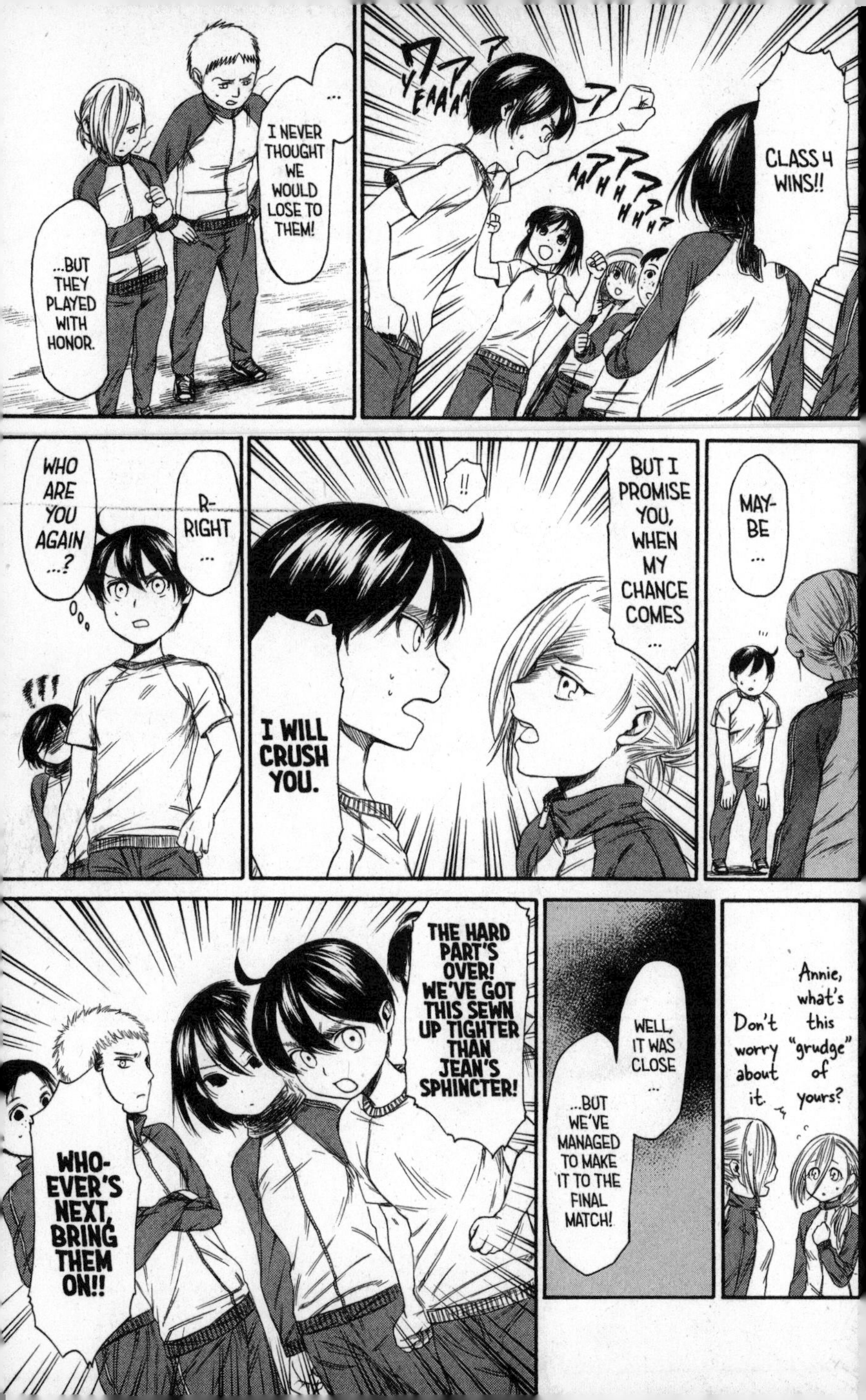
CLASS 4 WINS!!
YEAAAAA
AAHHHHHH
...
I NEVER THOUGHT WE WOULD LOSE TO THEM!
...BUT THEY PLAYED WITH HONOR.
MAY-BE ...
BUT I PROMISE YOU, WHEN MY CHANCE COMES ...
!!
I WILL CRUSH YOU.
R-RIGHT ...
WHO ARE YOU AGAIN ...?
Annie, what's this "grudge" of yours?
Don't worry about it.
WELL, IT WAS CLOSE ...
...BUT WE'VE MANAGED TO MAKE IT TO THE FINAL MATCH!
THE HARD PART'S OVER! WE'VE GOT THIS SEWN UP TIGHTER THAN JEAN'S SPHINCTER!
WHO-EVER'S NEXT, BRING THEM ON!!

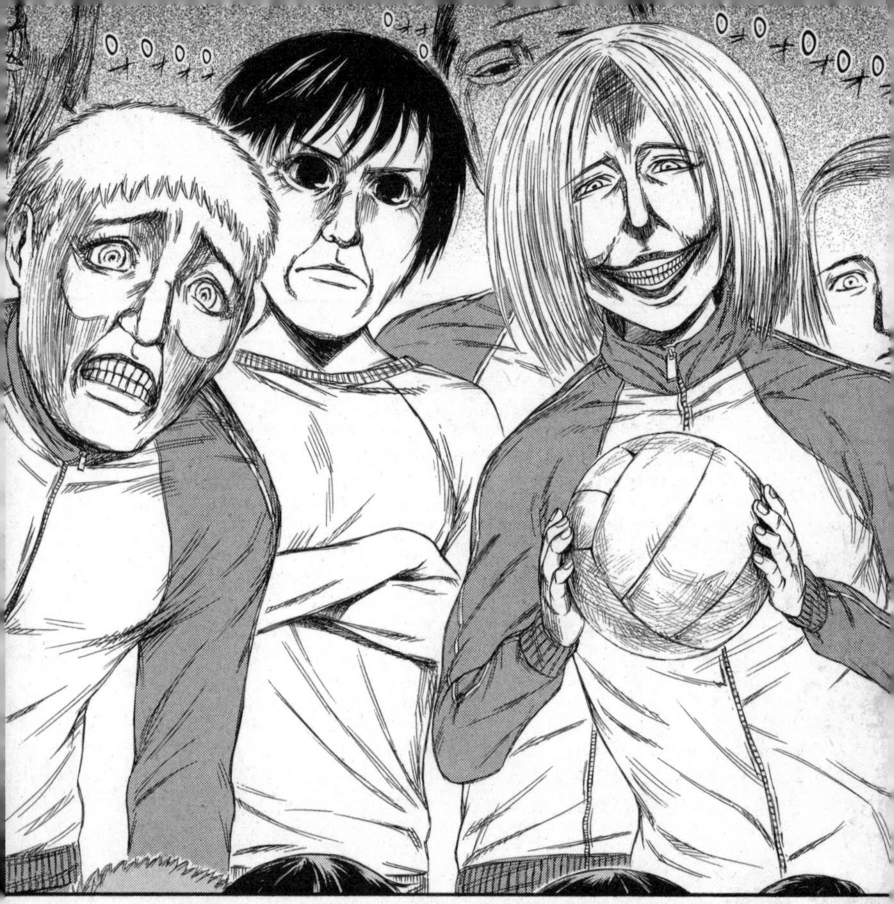

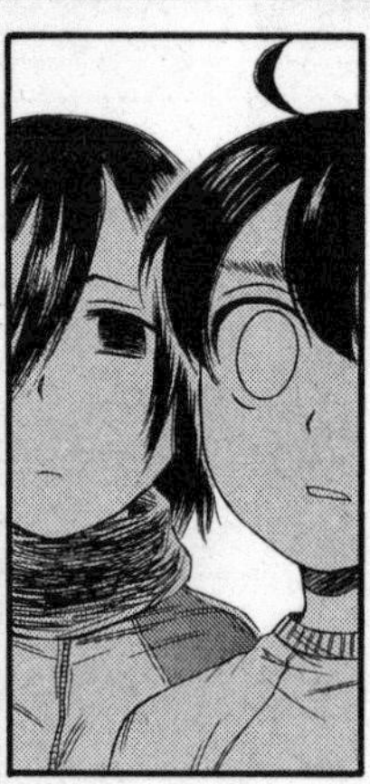

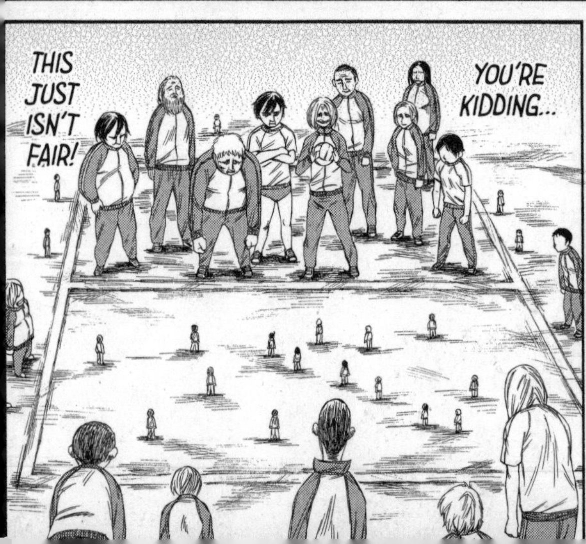
YOU'RE KIDDING...
THIS JUST ISN'T FAIR!

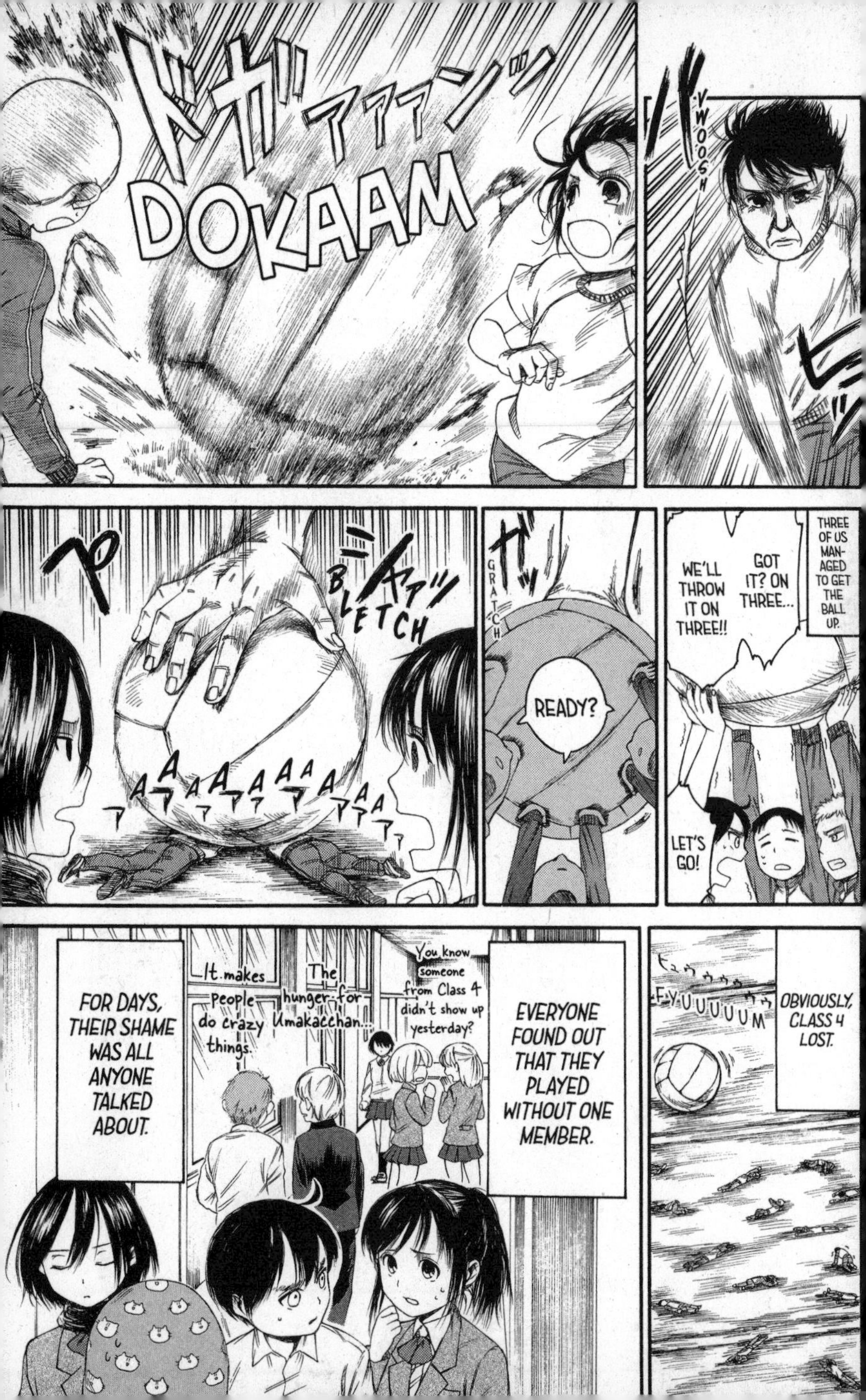
VWOOSH
DOKAAM
THREE OF US MANAGED TO GET THE BALL UP.
GOT IT? ON THREE...
WE'LL THROW IT ON THREE!!
LET'S GO!
GRATCH
READY?
BLETCH
AAAAAAAAAAAA
OBVIOUSLY, CLASS 4 LOST.
FYUUUUUUM
EVERYONE FOUND OUT THAT THEY PLAYED WITHOUT ONE MEMBER.
You know someone from Class 4 didn't show up yesterday?
The hunger for Umakacchan...
It makes people do crazy things.
FOR DAYS, THEIR SHAME WAS ALL ANYONE TALKED ABOUT.

POOR MOZUKU

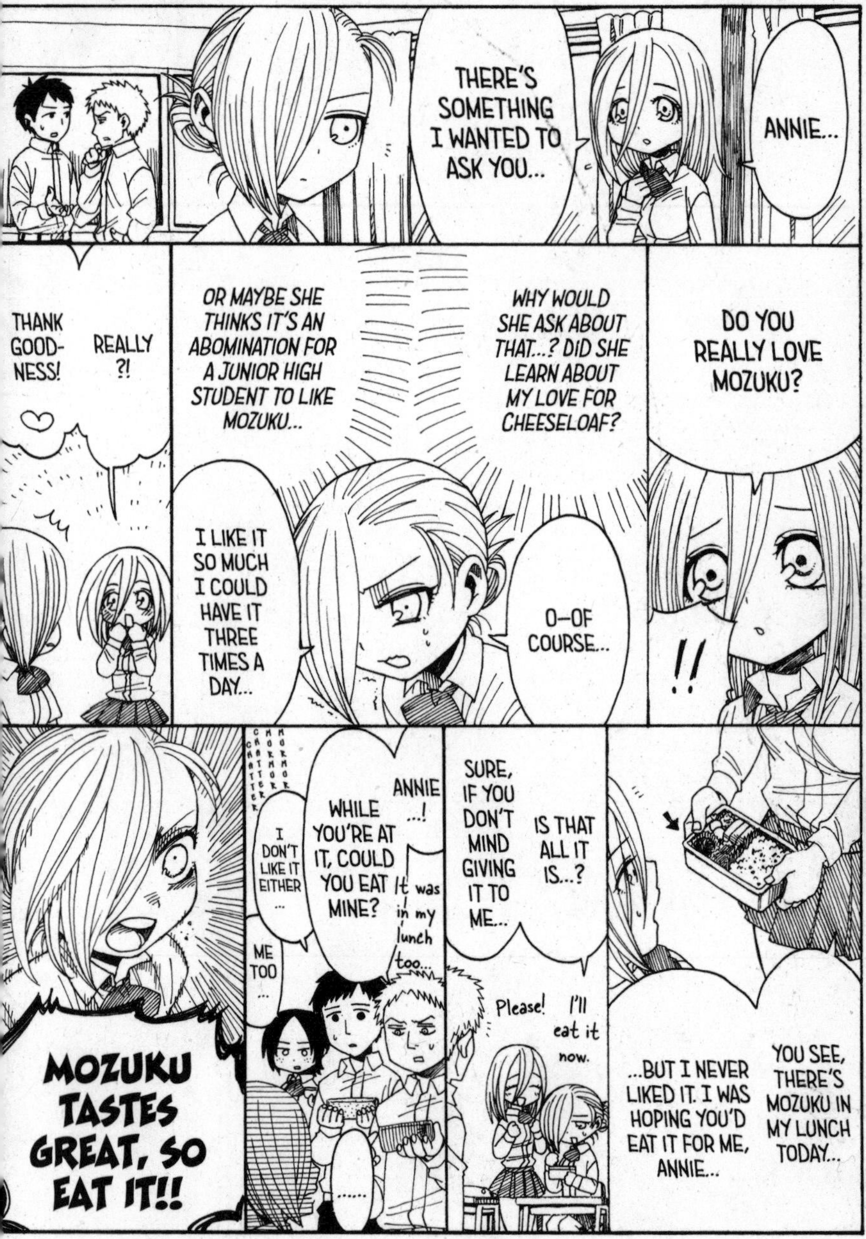
ANNIE...
THERE'S SOMETHING I WANTED TO ASK YOU...
DO YOU REALLY LOVE MOZUKU?
!!
WHY WOULD SHE ASK ABOUT THAT...? DID SHE LEARN ABOUT MY LOVE FOR CHEESELOAF?
OR MAYBE SHE THINKS IT'S AN ABOMINATION FOR A JUNIOR HIGH STUDENT TO LIKE MOZUKU...
O-OF COURSE...
I LIKE IT SO MUCH I COULD HAVE IT THREE TIMES A DAY...
REALLY ?!
THANK GOODNESS!
YOU SEE, THERE'S MOZUKU IN MY LUNCH TODAY...
...BUT I NEVER LIKED IT. I WAS HOPING YOU'D EAT IT FOR ME, ANNIE...
IS THAT ALL IT IS...?
SURE, IF YOU DON'T MIND GIVING IT TO ME...
I'll eat it now.
Please!
ANNIE ...!
WHILE YOU'RE AT IT, COULD YOU EAT MINE?
It was in my lunch too...
CHATTER
MURMUR
MURMUR
I DON'T LIKE IT EITHER...
ME TOO...
......
MOZUKU TASTES GREAT, SO EAT IT!!

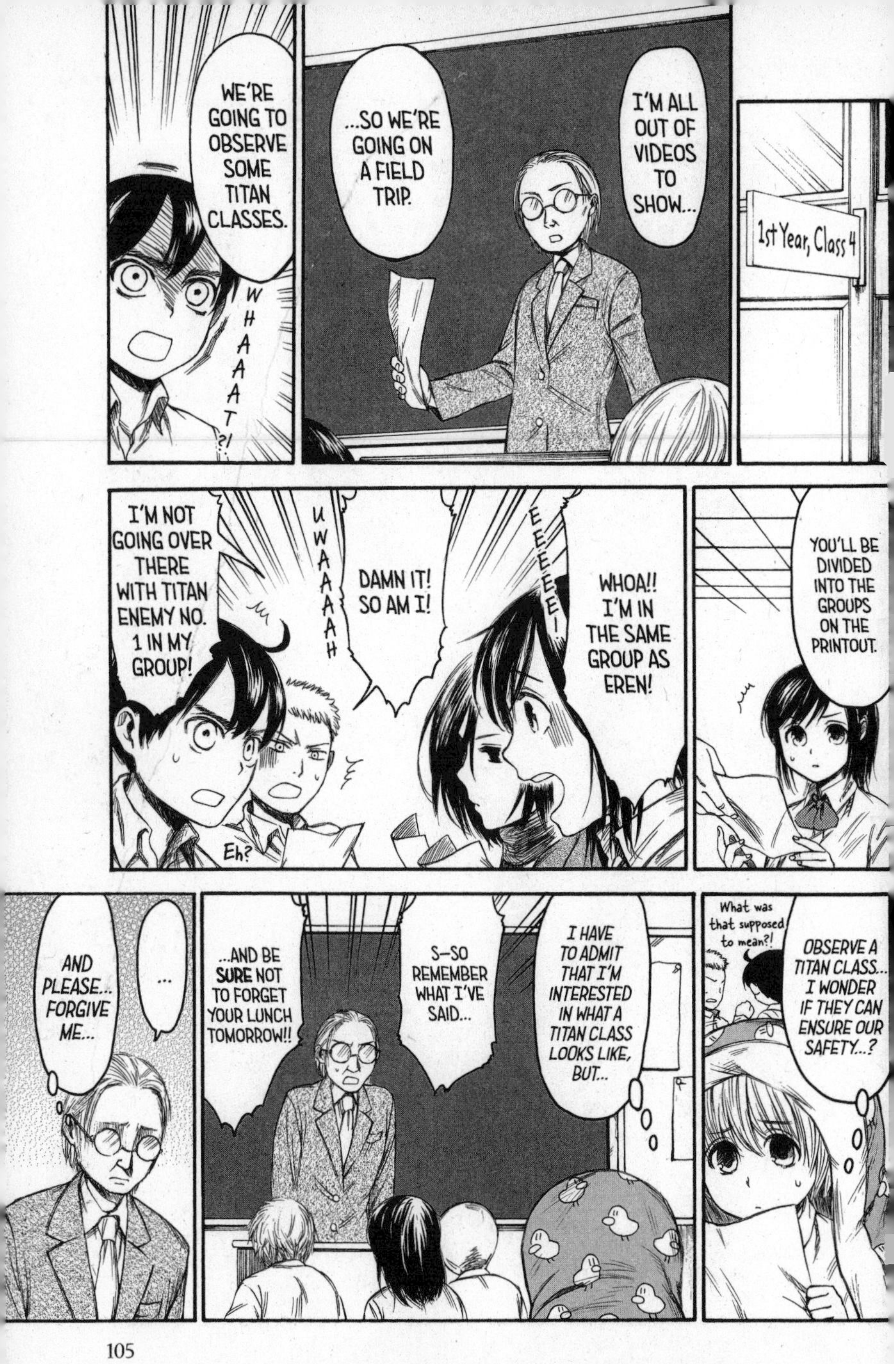
1st Year, Class 4
I'M ALL OUT OF VIDEOS TO SHOW...
...SO WE'RE GOING ON A FIELD TRIP.
WE'RE GOING TO OBSERVE SOME TITAN CLASSES.
WHAAAAT?!
YOU'LL BE DIVIDED INTO THE GROUPS ON THE PRINTOUT.
EEEEE!
WHOA!! I'M IN THE SAME GROUP AS EREN!
DAMN IT! SO AM I!
UWAAAAAH
I'M NOT GOING OVER THERE WITH TITAN ENEMY NO. 1 IN MY GROUP!
Eh?
What was that supposed to mean?!
OBSERVE A TITAN CLASS... I WONDER IF THEY CAN ENSURE OUR SAFETY...?
I HAVE TO ADMIT THAT I'M INTERESTED IN WHAT A TITAN CLASS LOOKS LIKE, BUT...
S-SO REMEMBER WHAT I'VE SAID...
...AND BE SURE NOT TO FORGET YOUR LUNCH TOMORROW!!
...
AND PLEASE... FORGIVE ME...

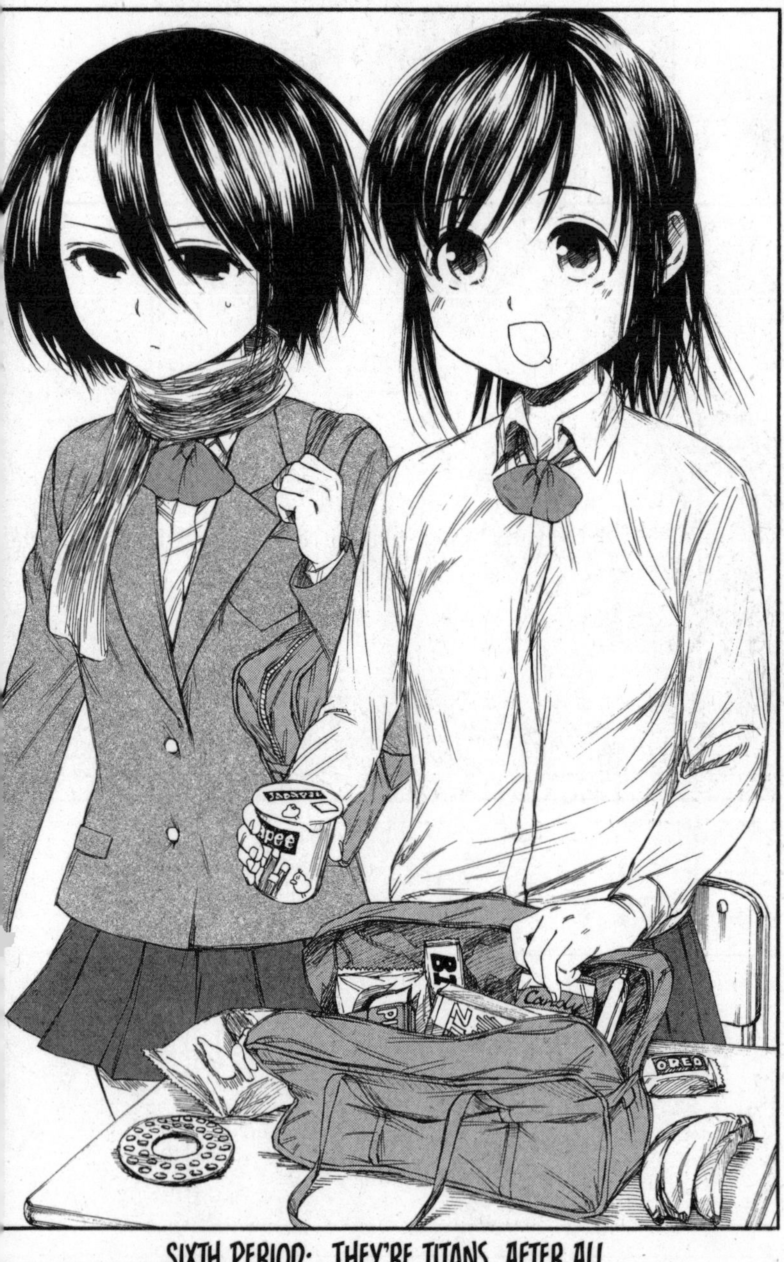
apeé
Candy
OREO

SIXTH PERIOD: THEY'RE TITANS, AFTER ALL

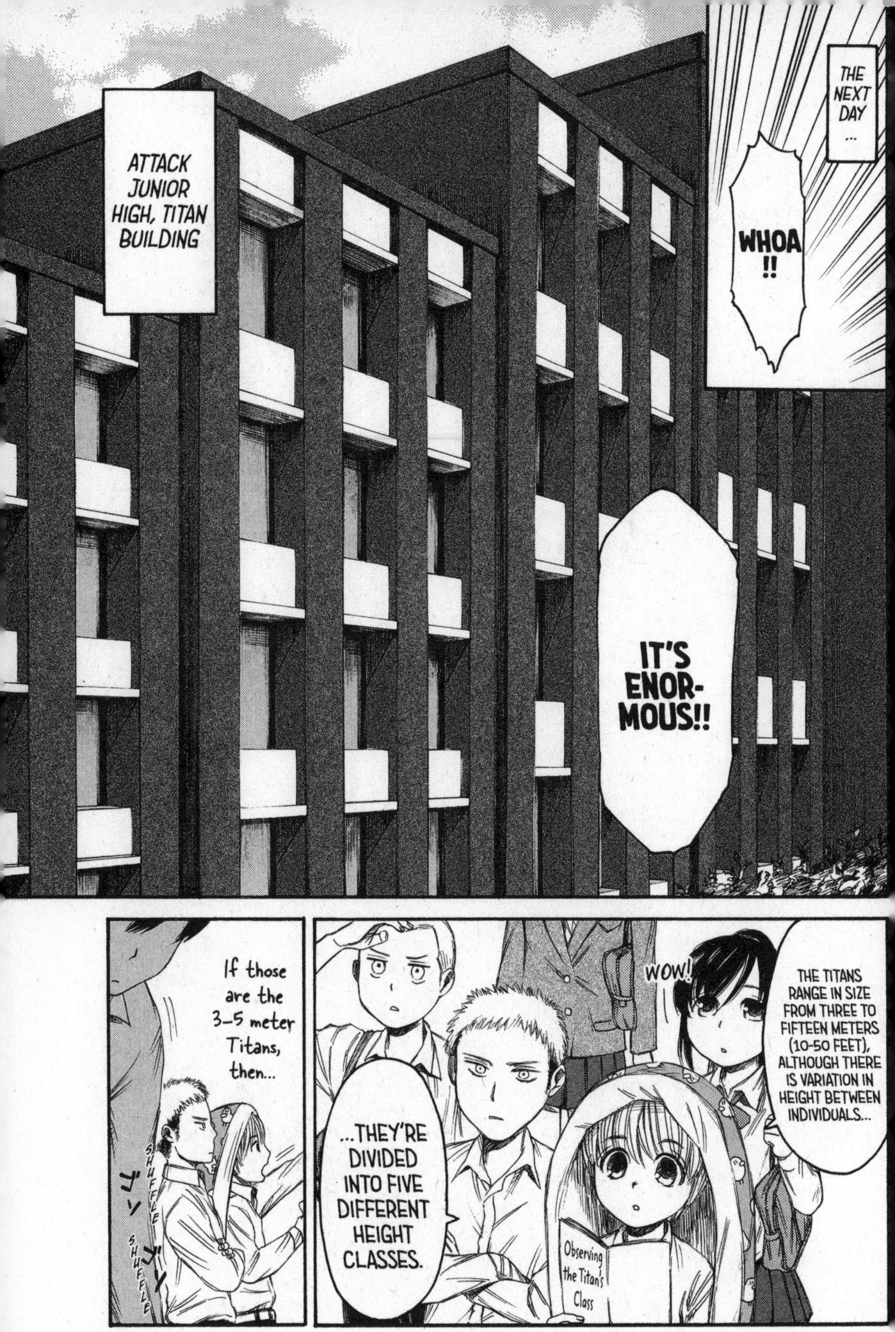
THE NEXT DAY ...
WHOA !!
ATTACK JUNIOR HIGH, TITAN BUILDING
IT'S ENOR-MOUS!!
WOW!
THE TITANS RANGE IN SIZE FROM THREE TO FIFTEEN METERS (10-50 FEET), ALTHOUGH THERE IS VARIATION IN HEIGHT BETWEEN INDIVIDUALS...
...THEY'RE DIVIDED INTO FIVE DIFFERENT HEIGHT CLASSES.
Observing the Titan's Class
If those are the 3–5 meter Titans, then...
SHUFFLE
SHUFFLE

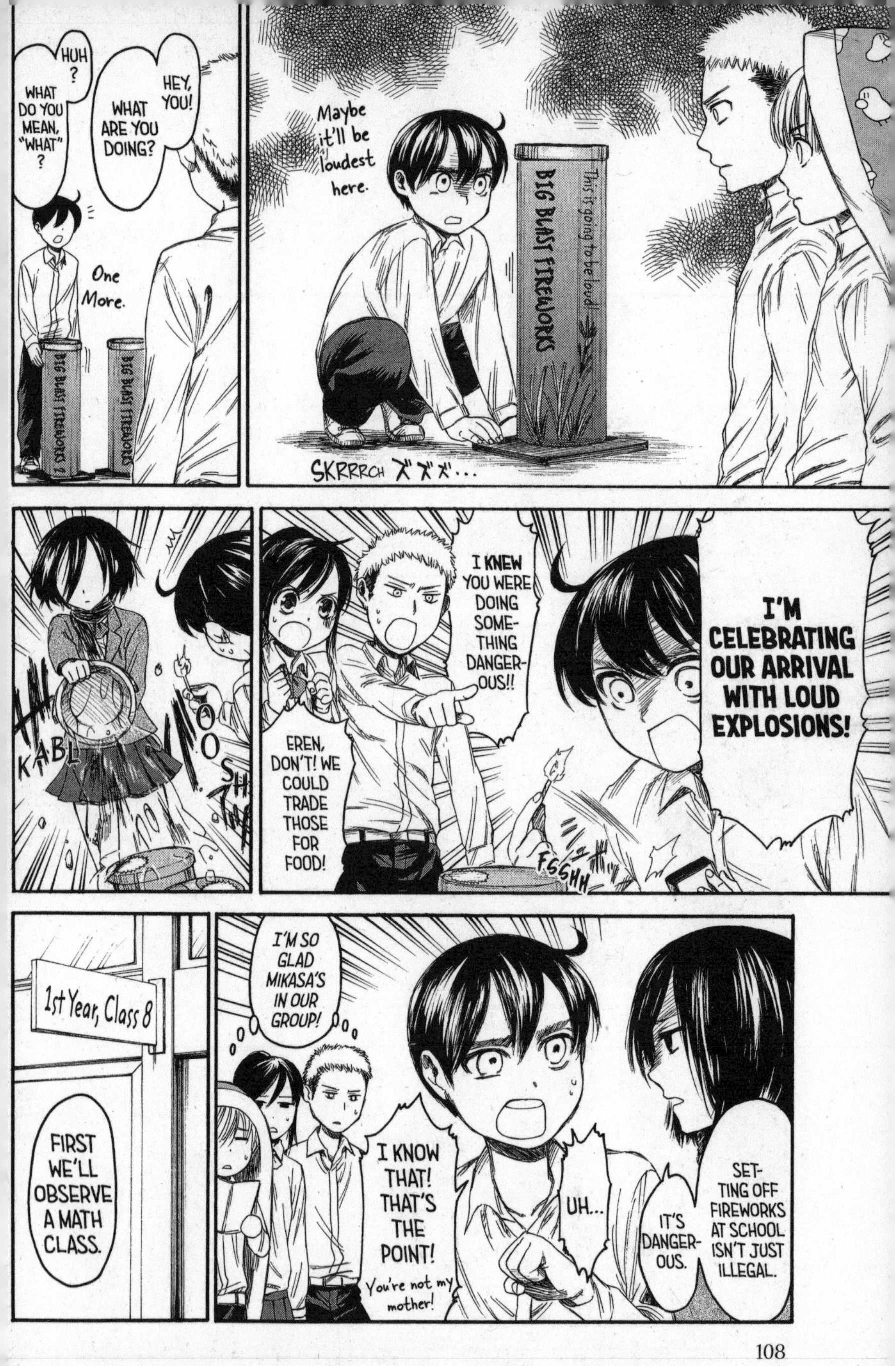
Maybe it'll be loudest here.
BIG BLAST FIREWORKS
This is going to be loud
SKRRRCH ズズズ...
HEY, YOU! WHAT ARE YOU DOING?
HUH? WHAT DO YOU MEAN, "WHAT"?
One More.
BIG BLAST FIREWORKS
BIG BLAST FIREWORKS
I'M CELEBRATING OUR ARRIVAL WITH LOUD EXPLOSIONS!
I KNEW YOU WERE DOING SOME-THING DANGER-OUS!!
EREN, DON'T! WE COULD TRADE THOSE FOR FOOD!
FSSHH
KABL
SET-TING OFF FIREWORKS AT SCHOOL ISN'T JUST ILLEGAL.
IT'S DANGER-OUS.
UH...
I KNOW THAT! THAT'S THE POINT!
You're not my mother!
I'M SO GLAD MIKASA'S IN OUR GROUP!
1st Year, Class 8
FIRST WE'LL OBSERVE A MATH CLASS.

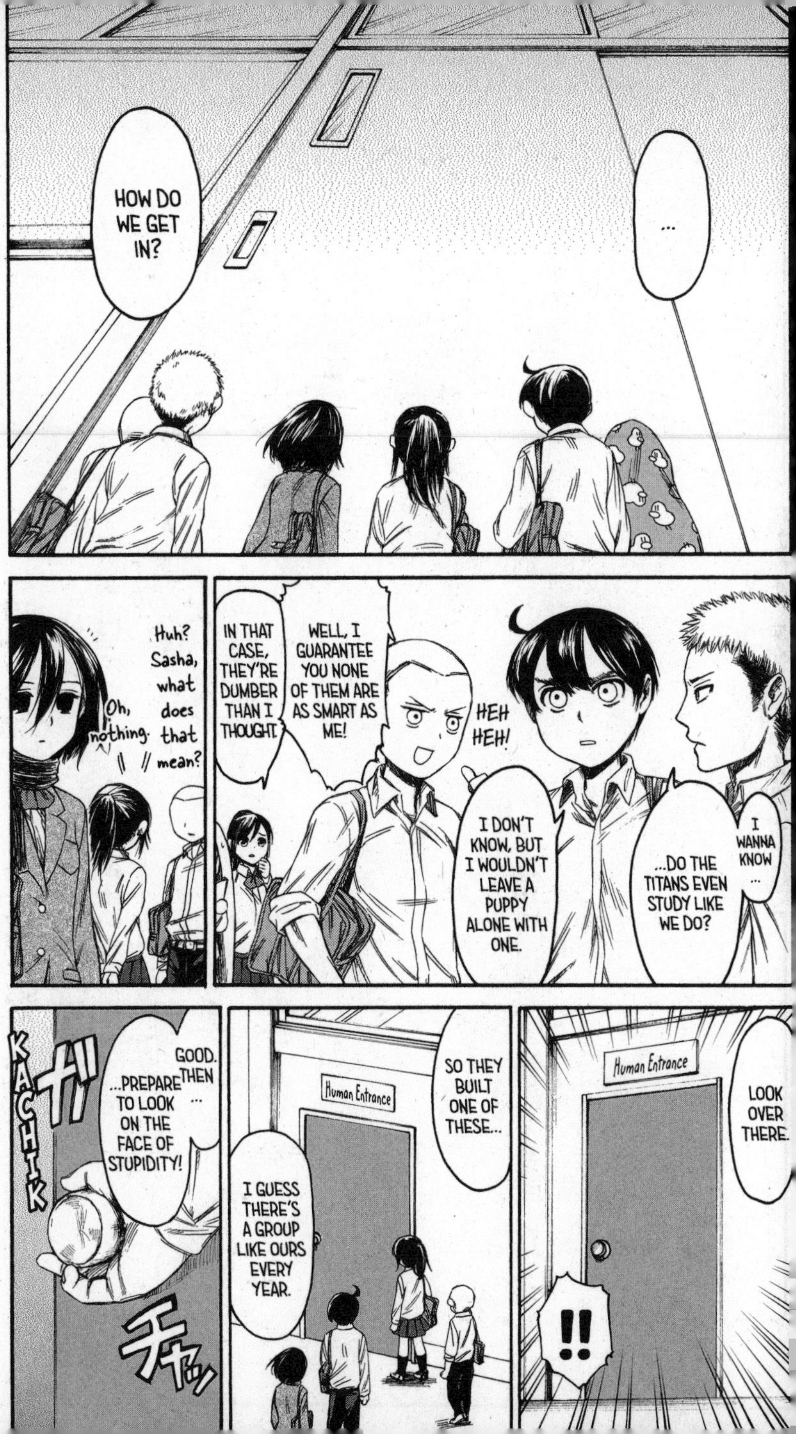
...
HOW DO WE GET IN?
I WANNA KNOW ...
...DO THE TITANS EVEN STUDY LIKE WE DO?
I DON'T KNOW, BUT I WOULDN'T LEAVE A PUPPY ALONE WITH ONE.
HEH HEH!
WELL, I GUARANTEE YOU NONE OF THEM ARE AS SMART AS ME!
IN THAT CASE, THEY'RE DUMBER THAN I THOUGHT.
Huh? Sasha, what does that mean?
Oh, nothing.
LOOK OVER THERE.
Human Entrance
!!
SO THEY BUILT ONE OF THESE...
Human Entrance
I GUESS THERE'S A GROUP LIKE OURS EVERY YEAR.
GOOD. THEN ...
...PREPARE TO LOOK ON THE FACE OF STUPIDITY!
KACHIK
チャッ

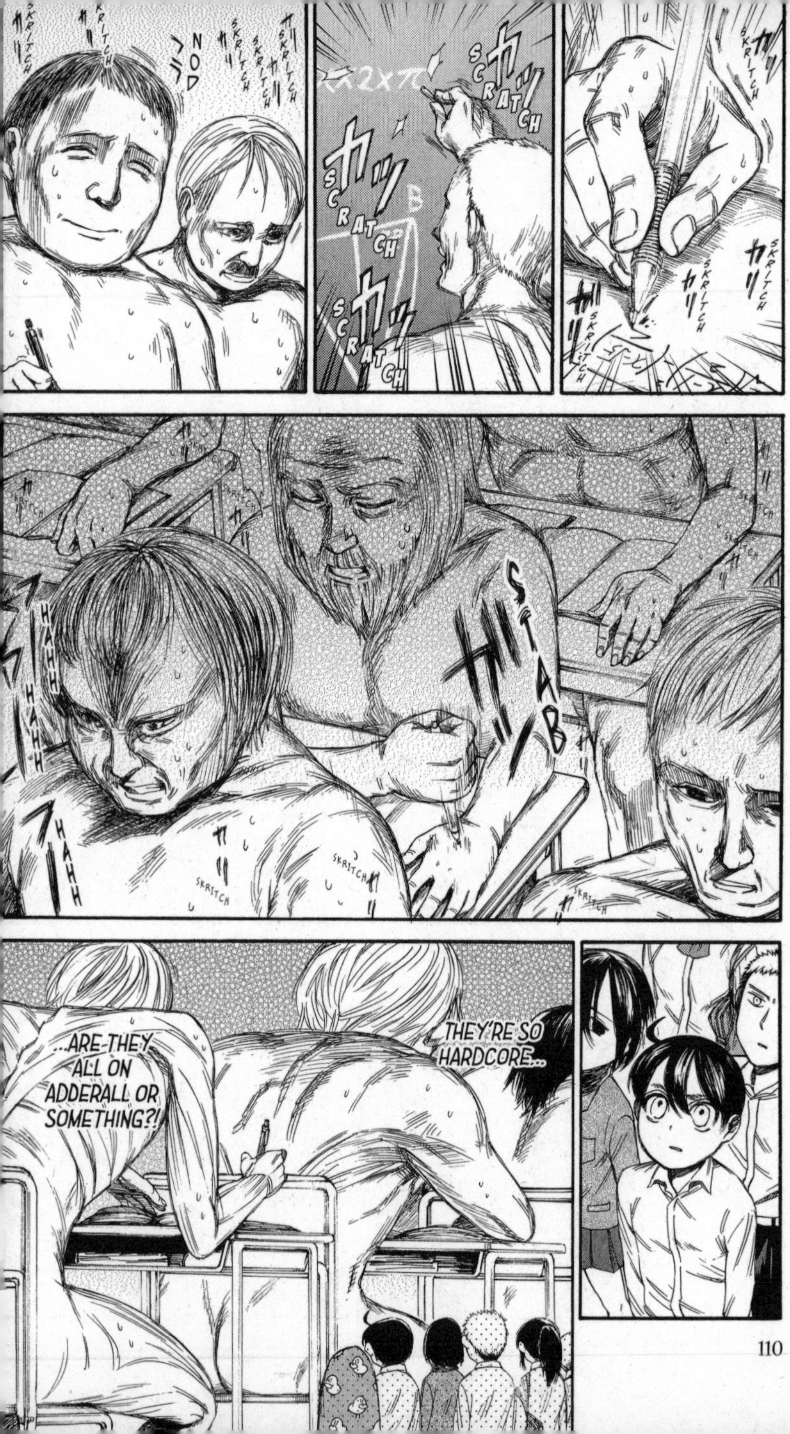
SKRITCH
SKRITCH
SCRATCH
SCRATCH
SCRATCH
NOD
SKRITCH
SKRITCH
SKRITCH
SKRITCH
STAB
HAHH
HAHH
HAHH
HAHH
SKRITCH
SKRITCH
SKRITCH
SKRITCH
THEY'RE SO HARDCORE...
...ARE THEY ALL ON ADDERALL OR SOMETHING?!

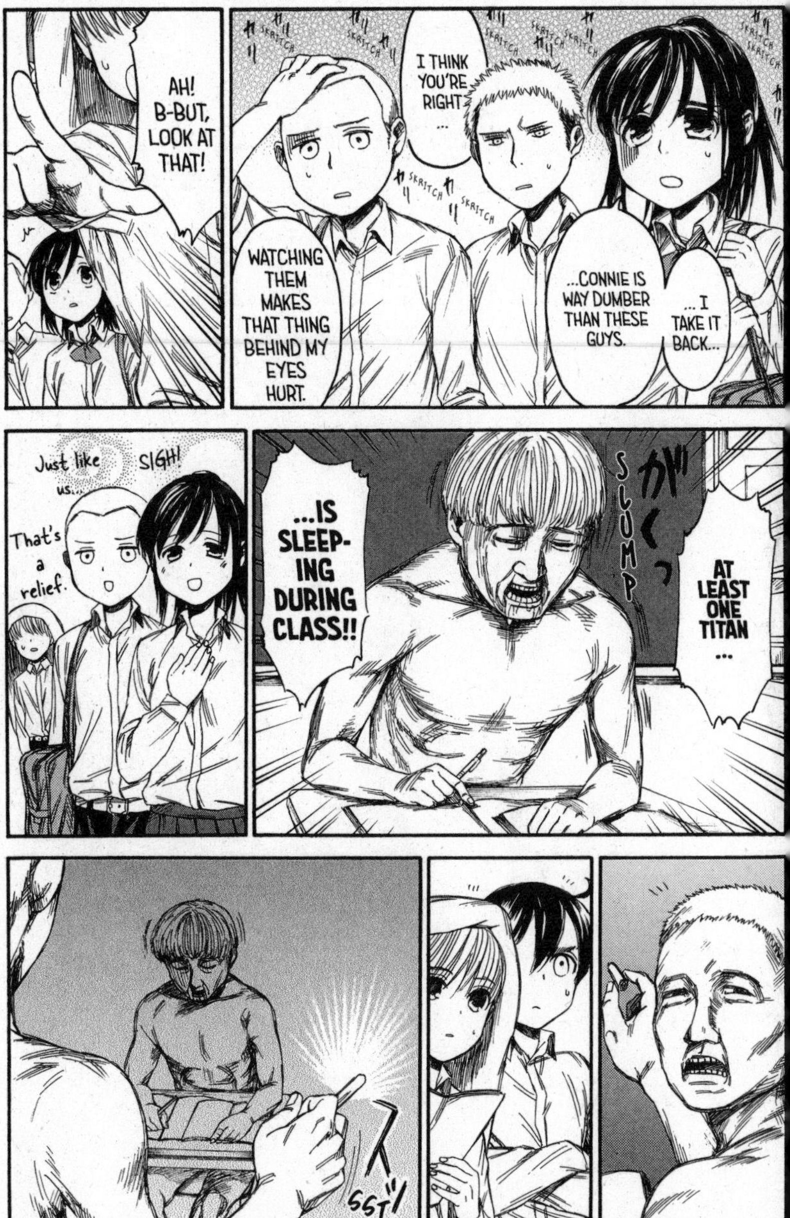
SKRITCH
SKRITCH
SKRITCH
SKRITCH
SKRITCH
I THINK YOU'RE RIGHT ...
... I TAKE IT BACK...
...CONNIE IS WAY DUMBER THAN THESE GUYS.
SKRITCH
SKRITCH
WATCHING THEM MAKES THAT THING BEHIND MY EYES HURT.
AH! B-BUT, LOOK AT THAT!
AT LEAST ONE TITAN ...
SLUMP
...IS SLEEPING DURING CLASS!!
SIGH!
Just like us...
That's a relief.
SST

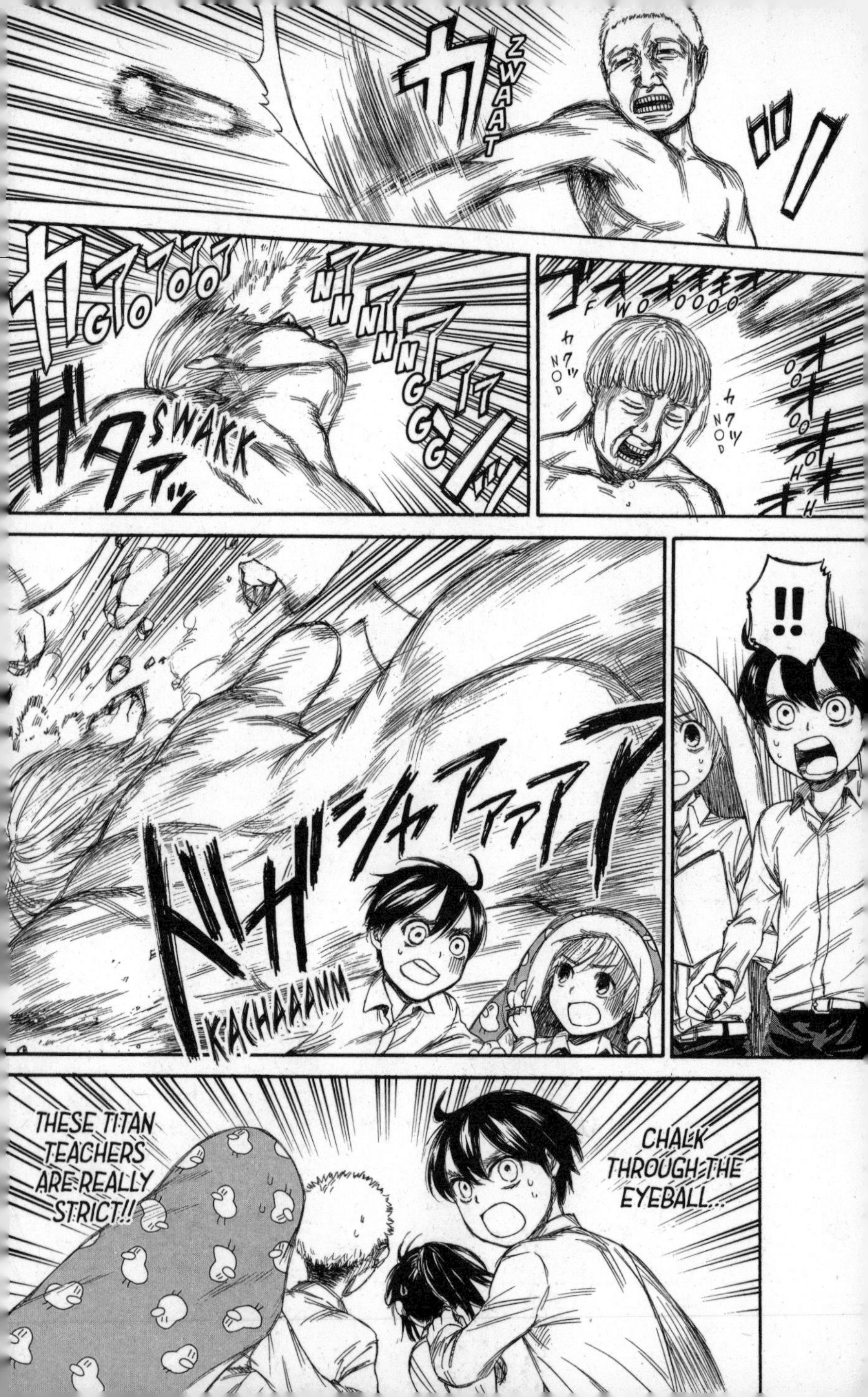
ZWAAT
FWOOOOOO
NOD
NOD
OOOOOHH
GOOOOO
NNNNGGG
SWAKK
!!
KACHAAANM
CHALK THROUGH THE EYEBALL...
THESE TITAN TEACHERS ARE REALLY STRICT!!

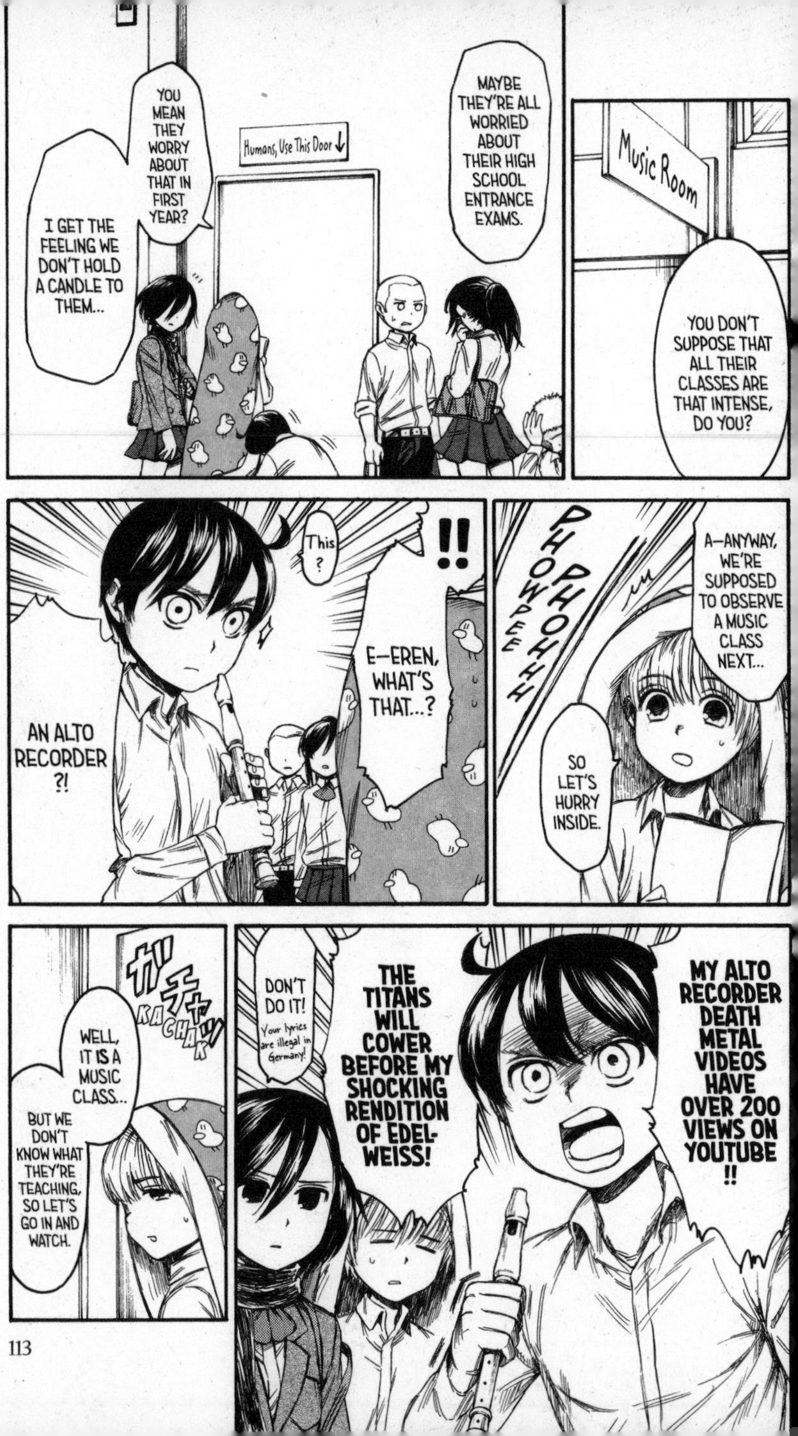
Music Room
YOU DON'T SUPPOSE THAT ALL THEIR CLASSES ARE THAT INTENSE, DO YOU?
MAYBE THEY'RE ALL WORRIED ABOUT THEIR HIGH SCHOOL ENTRANCE EXAMS.
Humans, Use This Door ↓
YOU MEAN THEY WORRY ABOUT THAT IN FIRST YEAR?
I GET THE FEELING WE DON'T HOLD A CANDLE TO THEM...
PHOPHOHHHH
PHOWPEE
A—ANYWAY, WE'RE SUPPOSED TO OBSERVE A MUSIC CLASS NEXT...
SO LET'S HURRY INSIDE.
!!
This?
E—EREN, WHAT'S THAT...?
AN ALTO RECORDER ?!
MY ALTO RECORDER DEATH METAL VIDEOS HAVE OVER 200 VIEWS ON YOUTUBE !!
THE TITANS WILL COWER BEFORE MY SHOCKING RENDITION OF EDEL-WEISS!
DON'T DO IT!
Your lyrics are illegal in Germany!
KACHAK
WELL, IT IS A MUSIC CLASS...
BUT WE DON'T KNOW WHAT THEY'RE TEACHING, SO LET'S GO IN AND WATCH.

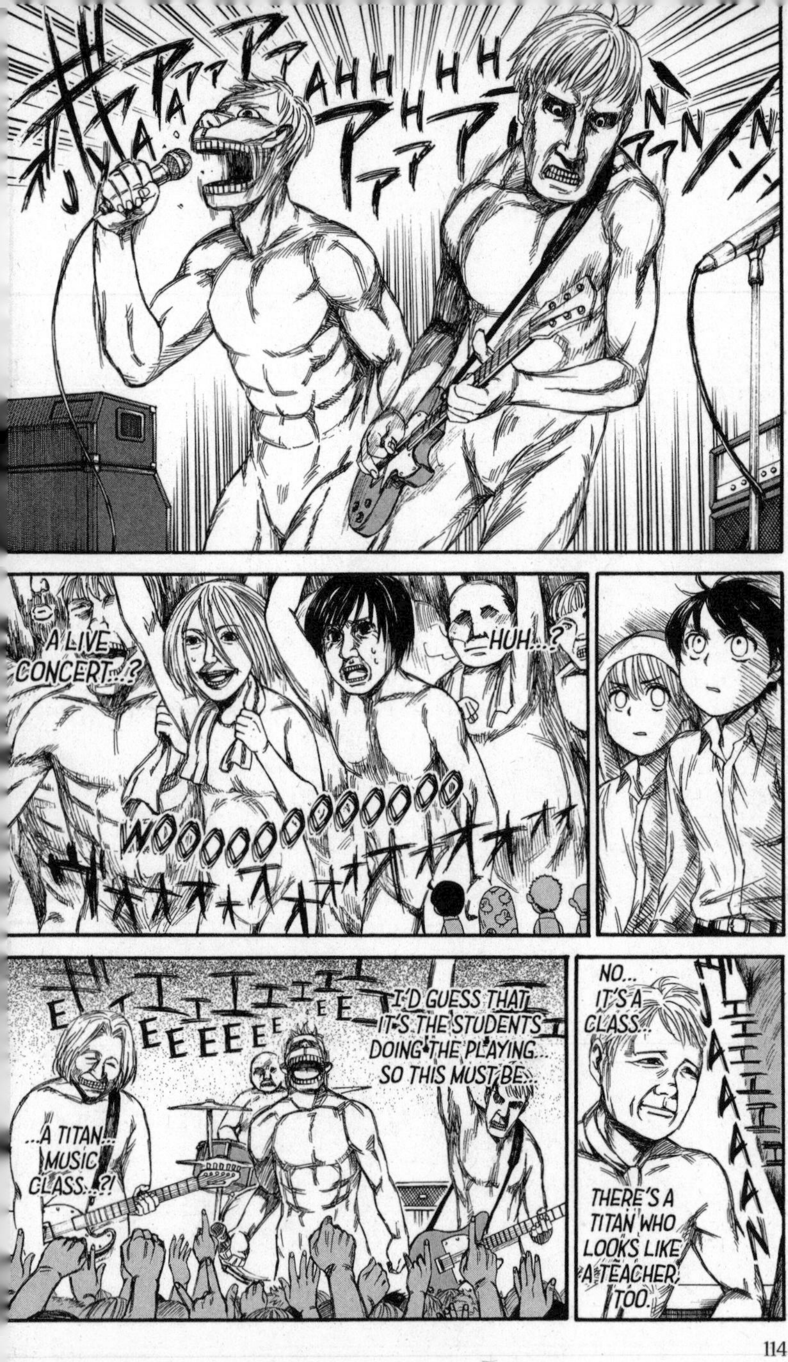

JYAAAAAAHHHHHH
NNN
HUH...?
A LIVE CONCERT...?
WOOOOOOOOOOOOOO
NO... IT'S A CLASS...
JAAAAAAN
THERE'S A TITAN WHO LOOKS LIKE A TEACHER, TOO.
EEEEEEEEE
I'D GUESS THAT IT'S THE STUDENTS DOING THE PLAYING... SO THIS MUST BE...
...A TITAN MUSIC CLASS...?!

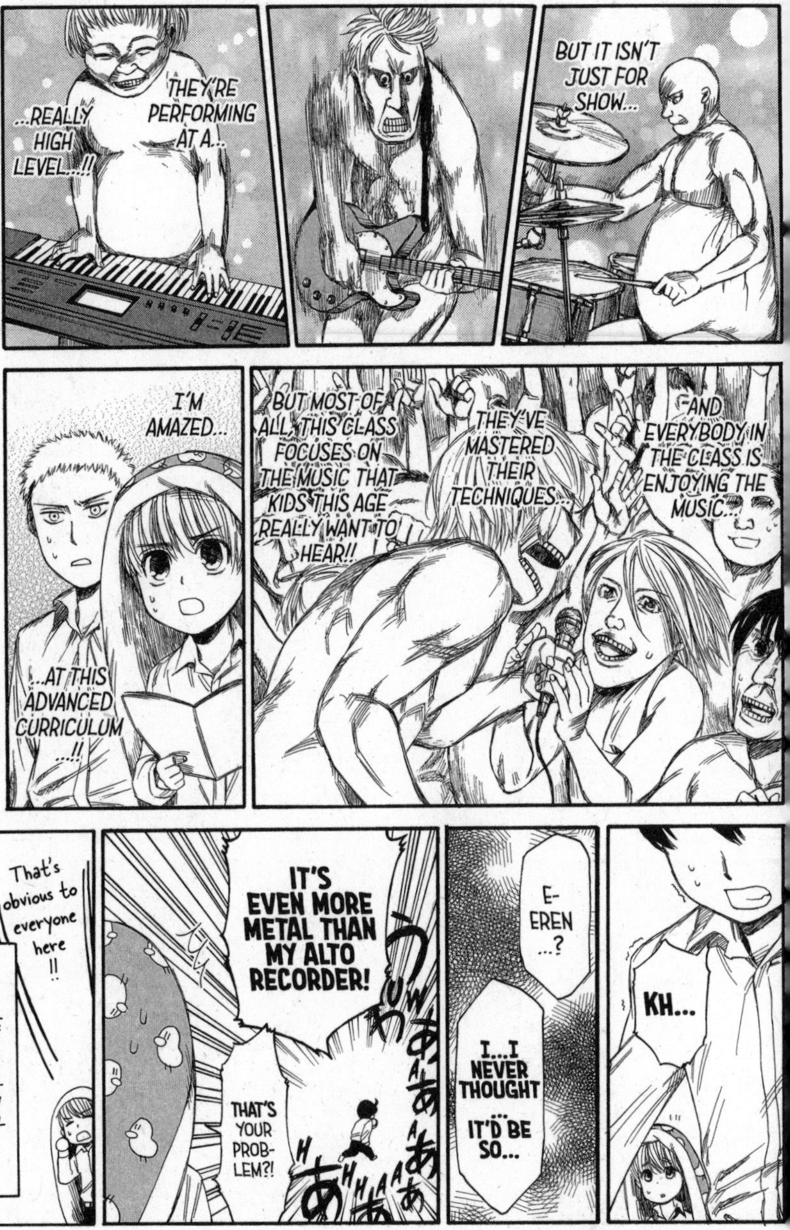
BUT IT ISN'T JUST FOR SHOW...
THEY'RE PERFORMING AT A...
...REALLY HIGH LEVEL...!!
THEY'VE MASTERED THEIR TECHNIQUES...
-AND EVERYBODY IN THE CLASS IS ENJOYING THE MUSIC...
BUT MOST OF ALL, THIS CLASS FOCUSES ON THE MUSIC THAT KIDS THIS AGE REALLY WANT TO HEAR!!
I'M AMAZED...
...AT THIS ADVANCED CURRICULUM...!!
KH...
E-EREN...?
I...I NEVER THOUGHT... IT'D BE SO...
IT'S EVEN MORE METAL THAN MY ALTO RECORDER!
THAT'S YOUR PROBLEM?!
That's obvious to everyone here!!
AND SO THE TITAN CLASS OBSERVATION CONTINUED...

Self-portrait sculpture.

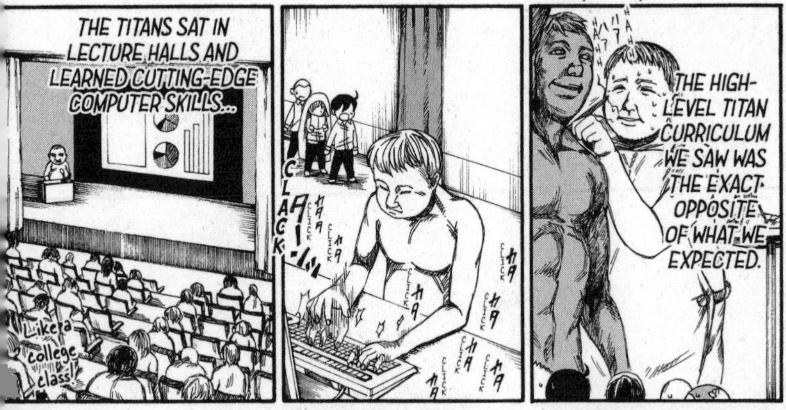
THE HIGH-LEVEL TITAN CURRICULUM WE SAW WAS THE EXACT OPPOSITE OF WHAT WE EXPECTED.
CLACK
CLICK
CLICK
CLICK
CLICK
CLICK
CLICK
THE TITANS SAT IN LECTURE HALLS AND LEARNED CUTTING-EDGE COMPUTER SKILLS...
Like a college class!

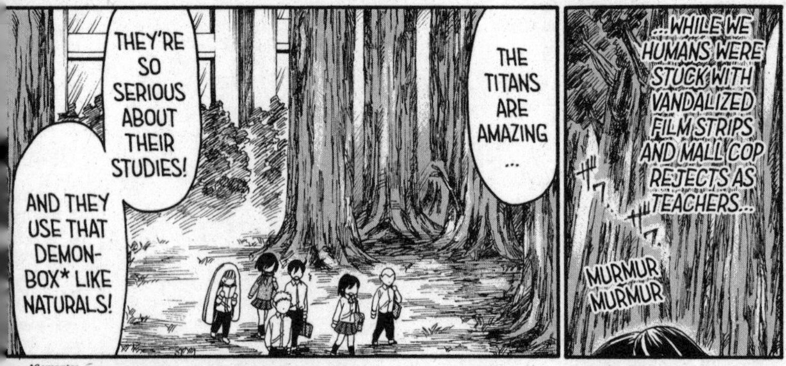
...WHILE WE HUMANS WERE STUCK WITH VANDALIZED FILM STRIPS AND MALL COP REJECTS AS TEACHERS...
MURMUR MURMUR
THE TITANS ARE AMAZING ...
THEY'RE SO SERIOUS ABOUT THEIR STUDIES!
AND THEY USE THAT DEMON-BOX* LIKE NATURALS!

*Computer

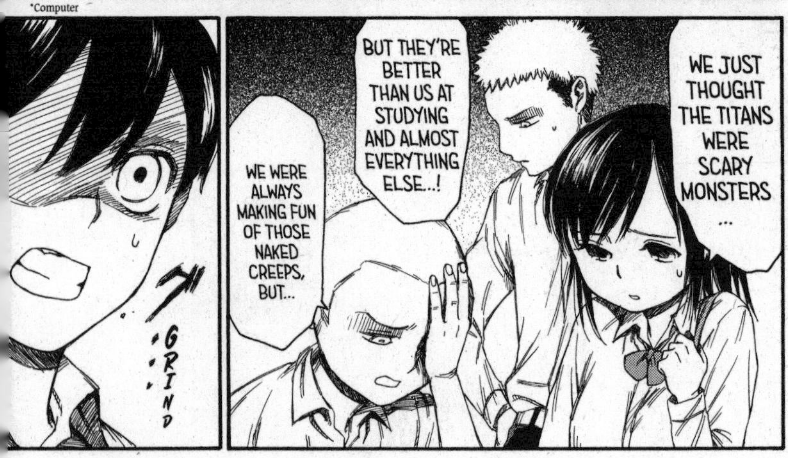
WE JUST THOUGHT THE TITANS WERE SCARY MONSTERS ...
BUT THEY'RE BETTER THAN US AT STUDYING AND ALMOST EVERYTHING ELSE...!
WE WERE ALWAYS MAKING FUN OF THOSE NAKED CREEPS, BUT...
GRIND

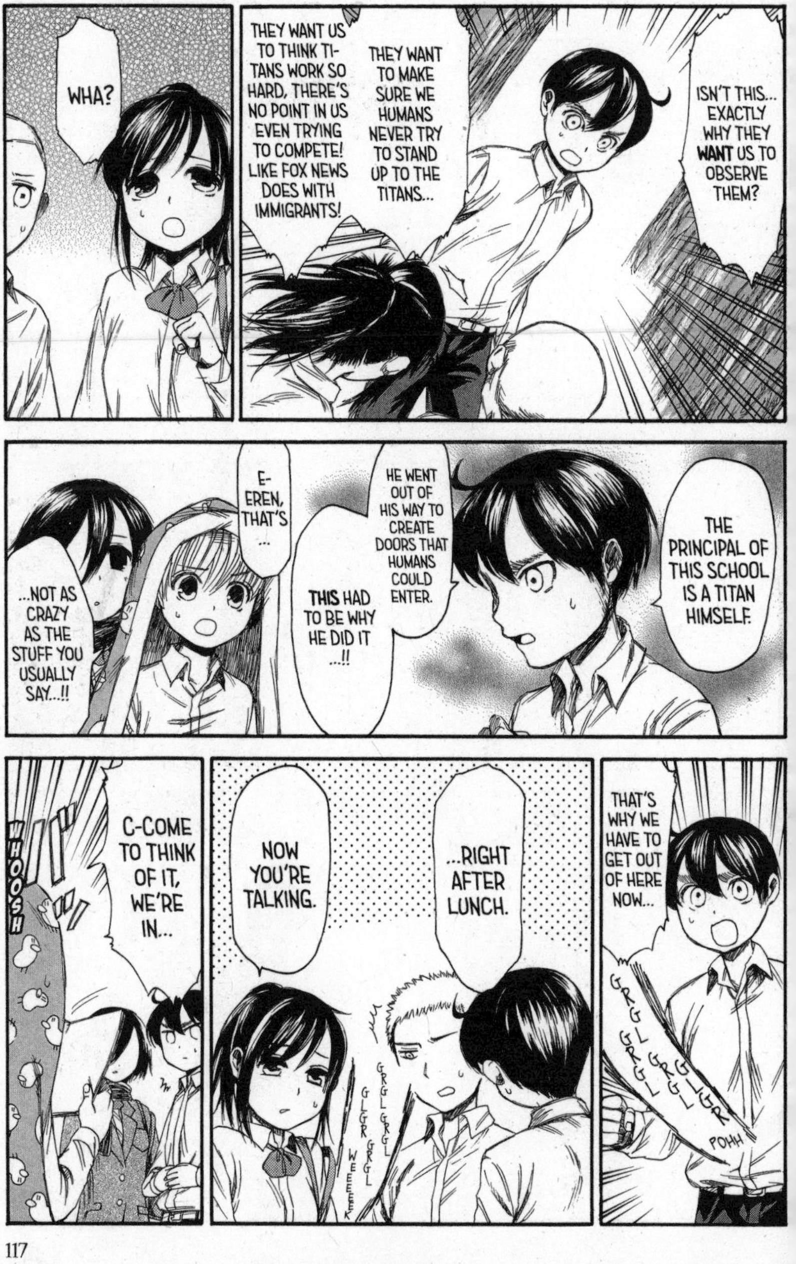
ISN'T THIS... EXACTLY WHY THEY **WANT** US TO OBSERVE THEM?
THEY WANT TO MAKE SURE WE HUMANS NEVER TRY TO STAND UP TO THE TITANS...
THEY WANT US TO THINK TI-TANS WORK SO HARD, THERE'S NO POINT IN US EVEN TRYING TO COMPETE! LIKE FOX NEWS DOES WITH IMMIGRANTS!
WHA?
THE PRINCIPAL OF THIS SCHOOL IS A TITAN HIMSELF.
HE WENT OUT OF HIS WAY TO CREATE DOORS THAT HUMANS COULD ENTER.
THIS HAD TO BE WHY HE DID IT ...!!
E-EREN, THAT'S ...
...NOT AS CRAZY AS THE STUFF YOU USUALLY SAY...!!
THAT'S WHY WE HAVE TO GET OUT OF HERE NOW...
GRGL GRGL GRGL GLGR
POHH
...RIGHT AFTER LUNCH.
NOW YOU'RE TALKING.
GRGL GRGL GLGR GRGL
WEEEEK
WHOOSH
C-COME TO THINK OF IT, WE'RE IN...

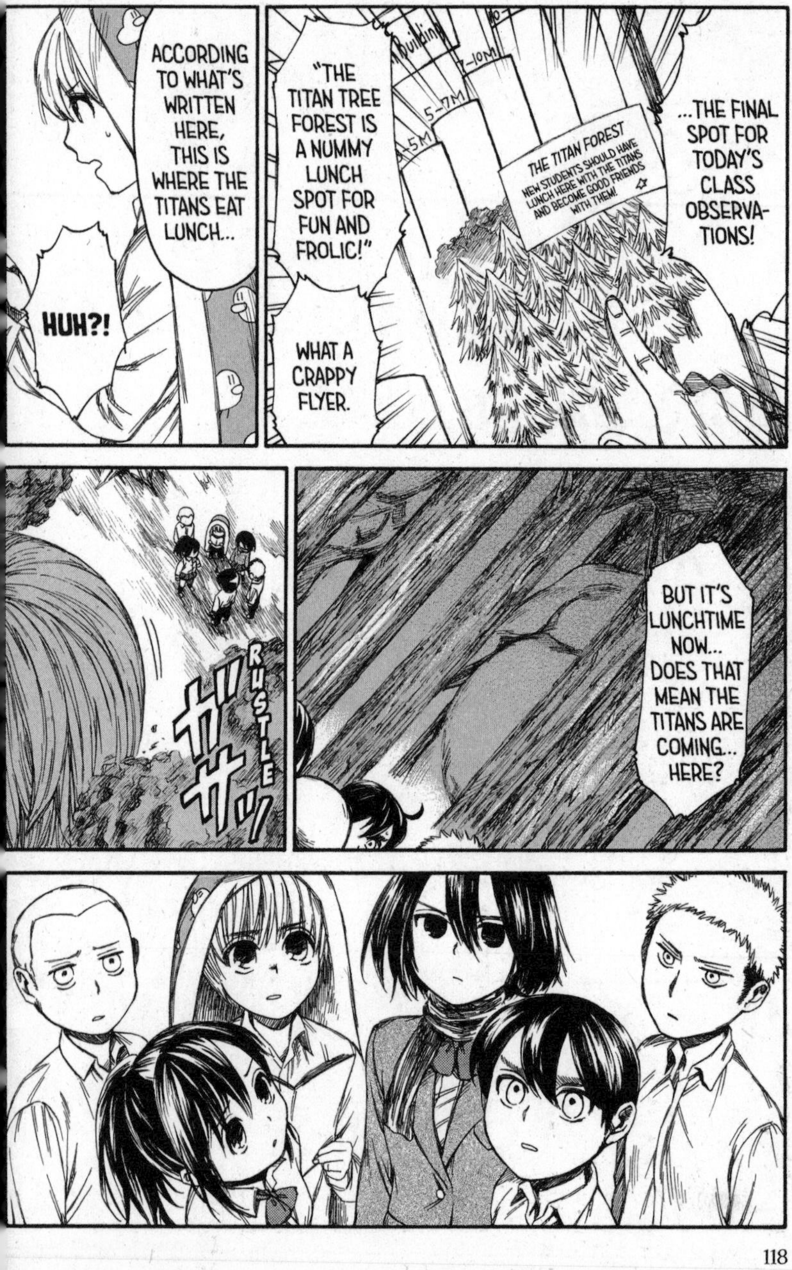
...THE FINAL SPOT FOR TODAY'S CLASS OBSERVATIONS!
Building
7~10M
5~7M
THE TITAN FOREST
NEW STUDENTS SHOULD HAVE LUNCH HERE WITH THE TITANS AND BECOME GOOD FRIENDS WITH THEM!
"THE TITAN TREE FOREST IS A NUMMY LUNCH SPOT FOR FUN AND FROLIC!"
WHAT A CRAPPY FLYER.
ACCORDING TO WHAT'S WRITTEN HERE, THIS IS WHERE THE TITANS EAT LUNCH...
HUH?!
BUT IT'S LUNCHTIME NOW... DOES THAT MEAN THE TITANS ARE COMING... HERE?
RUSTLE

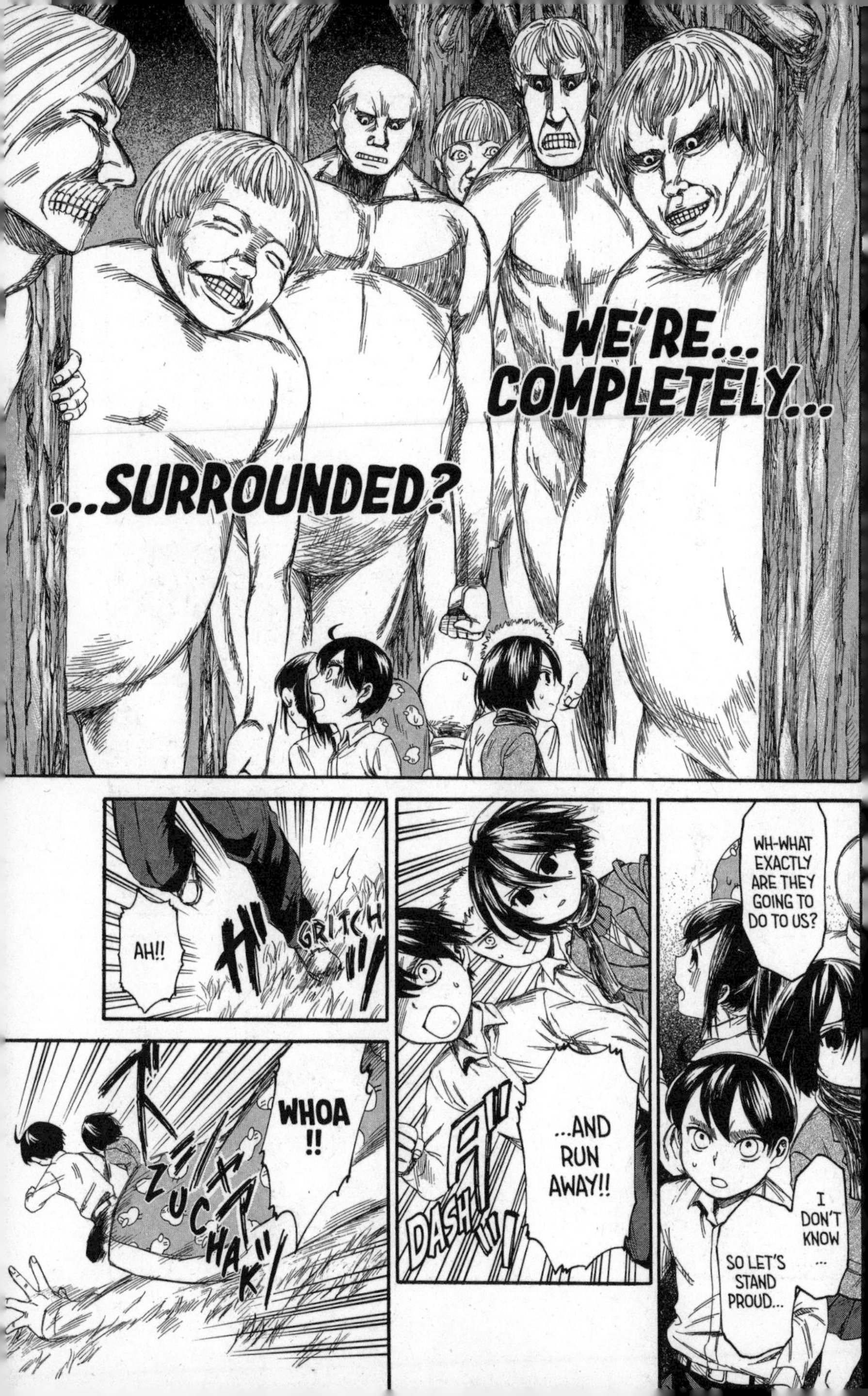
WE'RE... COMPLETELY...
...SURROUNDED?
WH-WHAT EXACTLY ARE THEY GOING TO DO TO US?
I DON'T KNOW ...
SO LET'S STAND PROUD...
...AND RUN AWAY!!
DASH
AH!!
GRITCH
WHOA !!
ZUCHAK

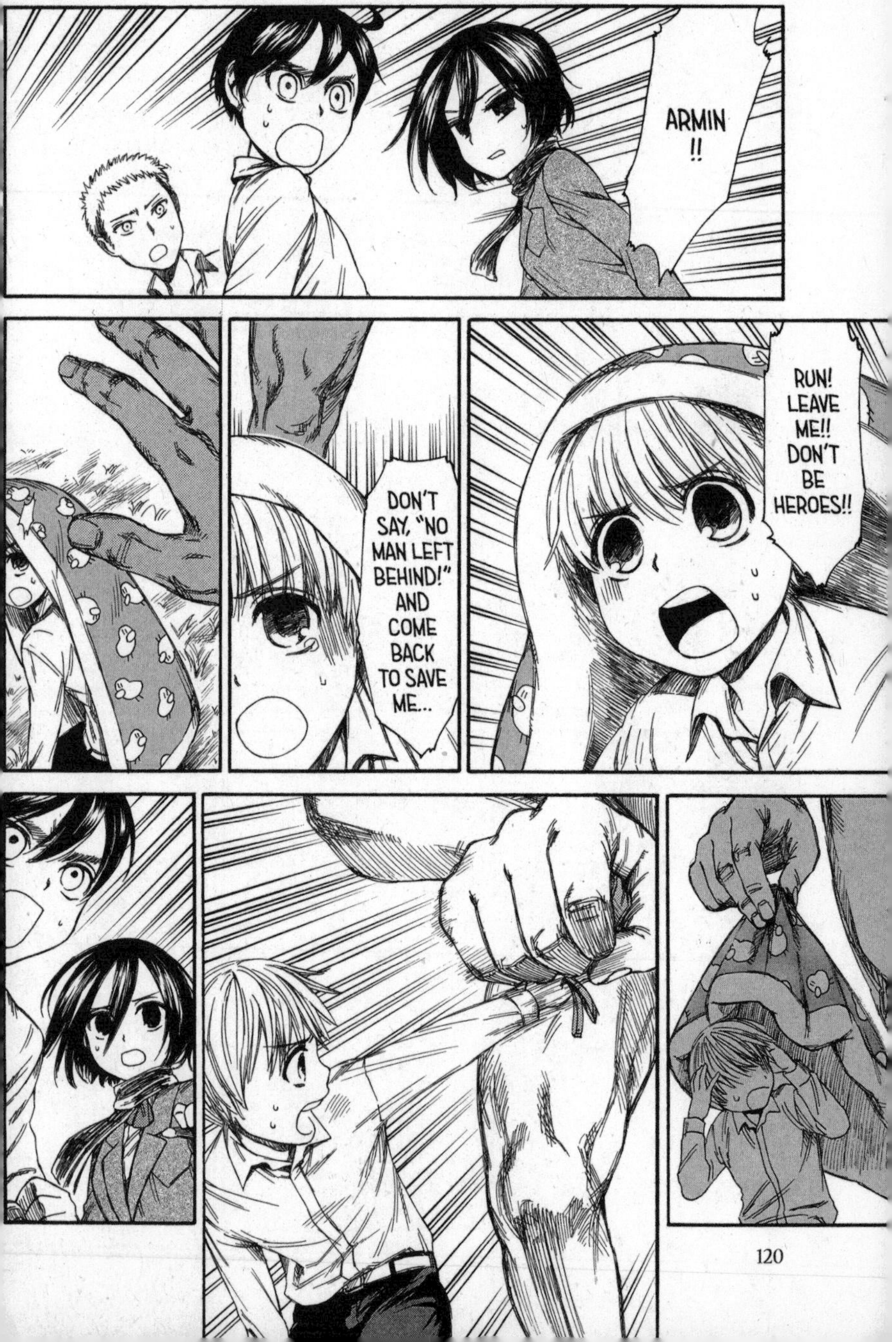
ARMIN !!
RUN! LEAVE ME!! DON'T BE HEROES!!
DON'T SAY, "NO MAN LEFT BEHIND!" AND COME BACK TO SAVE ME...

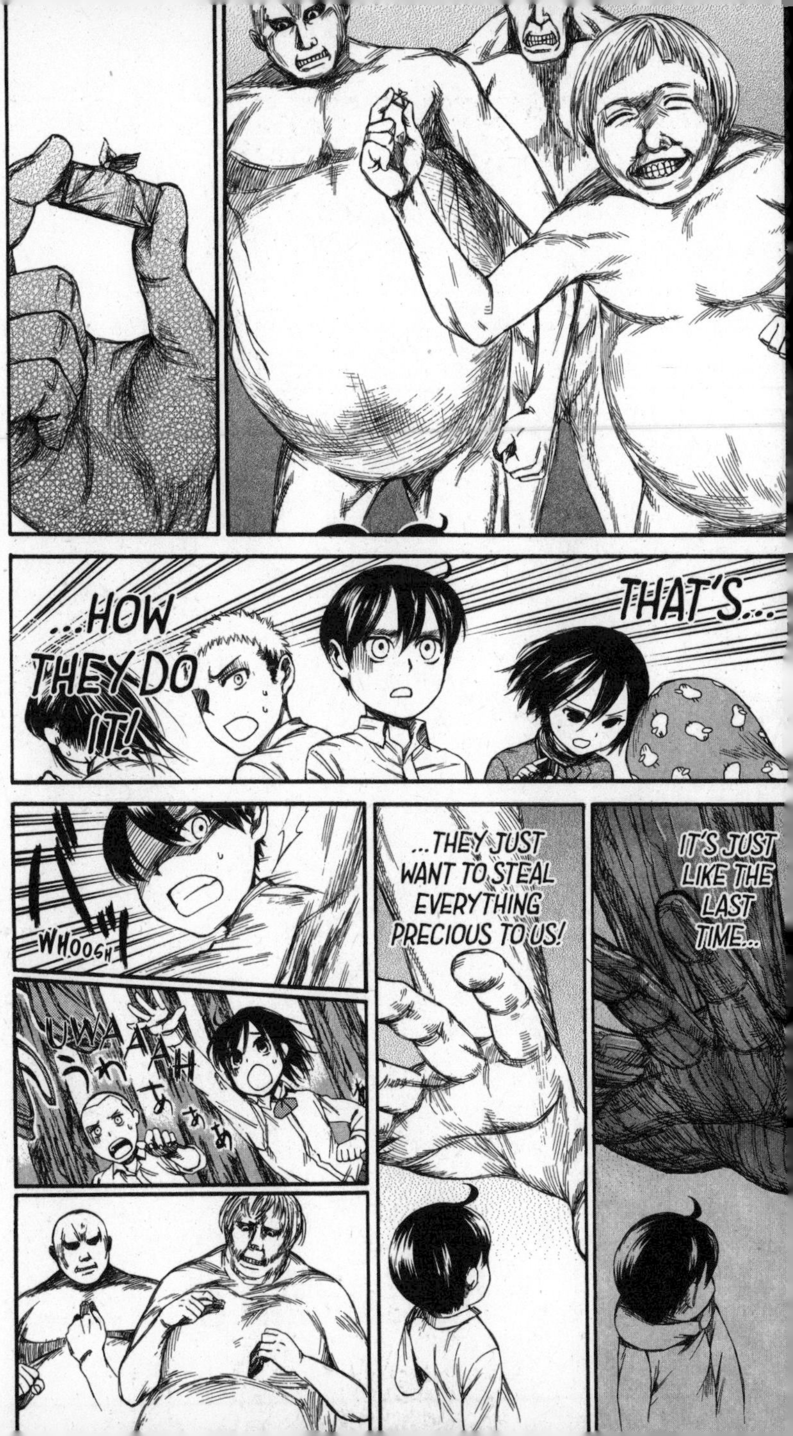

THAT'S...
...HOW THEY DO IT!
IT'S JUST LIKE THE LAST TIME...
...THEY JUST WANT TO STEAL EVERYTHING PRECIOUS TO US!
WHOOSH
UWAAAAH
うわぁぁぁ

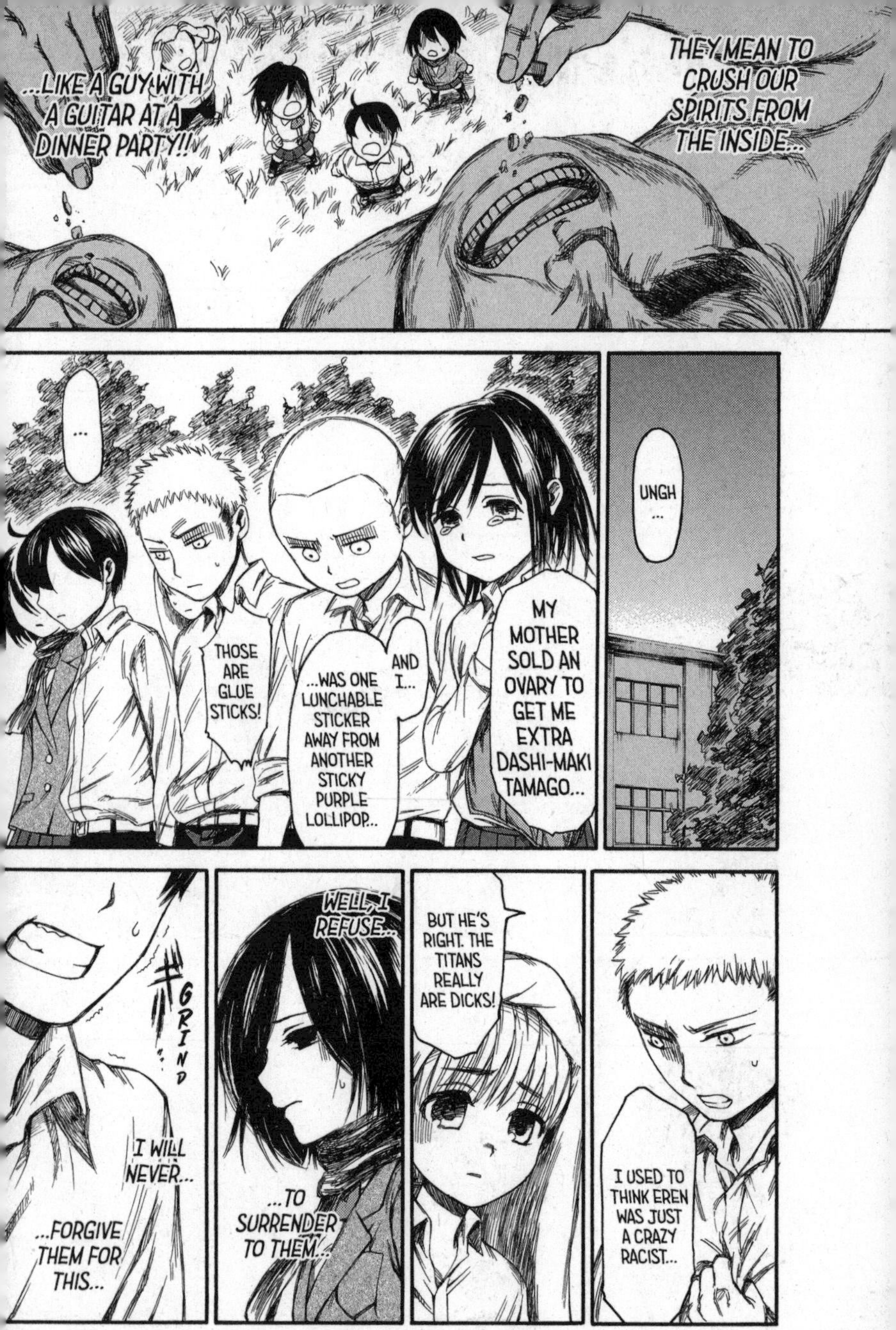
THEY MEAN TO CRUSH OUR SPIRITS FROM THE INSIDE...
...LIKE A GUY WITH A GUITAR AT A DINNER PARTY!!
UNGH ...
MY MOTHER SOLD AN OVARY TO GET ME EXTRA DASHI-MAKI TAMAGO...
AND I...
...WAS ONE LUNCHABLE STICKER AWAY FROM ANOTHER STICKY PURPLE LOLLIPOP...
THOSE ARE GLUE STICKS!
...
I USED TO THINK EREN WAS JUST A CRAZY RACIST...
BUT HE'S RIGHT. THE TITANS REALLY ARE DICKS!
WELL, I REFUSE...
...TO SURRENDER TO THEM...
GRIND
I WILL NEVER...
...FORGIVE THEM FOR THIS...

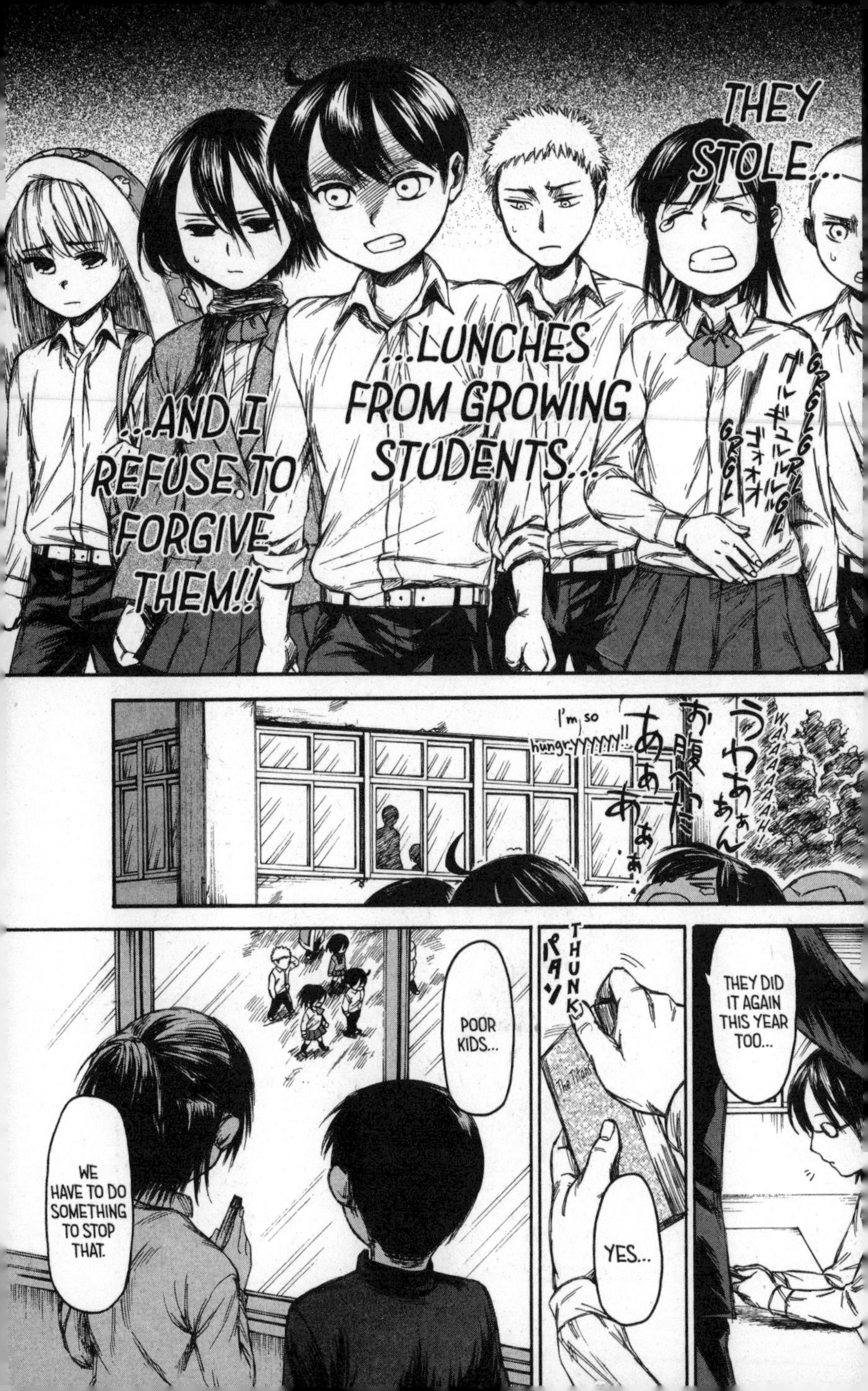
THEY STOLE...
...LUNCHES FROM GROWING STUDENTS...
...AND I REFUSE TO FORGIVE THEM!!
グルギュルルゴォオオ
GRGLGRGL GRGL
うやあぁあん
WAAAAAAAH!!
お腹へったあぁぁあぁぁ
I'm so hungryyyyyy!!
THEY DID IT AGAIN THIS YEAR TOO...
パタン
THUNK
YES...
POOR KIDS...
WE HAVE TO DO SOMETHING TO STOP THAT.

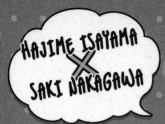

HAJIME ISAYAMA × SAKI NAKAGAWA

TALK ABOUT TITAN! 3

WHAT COMES AFTER THIS?

I: THIS MAY SOUND A LITTLE WEIRD, BUT I WANT NAKAGAWA-SAN TO USE "TITAN JUNIOR HIGH" AS A STEPPING STONE. I KNOW IT CAME OUT REALLY WEIRD, SO I WANT SOME ORIGINAL NAKAGAWA-SAN WORK TO COME OUT.

N: BUT MORE THAN THAT, I WANT TO KEEP DOING "TITAN JUNIOR HIGH" AS LONG AS POSSIBLE. ACTUALLY, I'VE LEARNED A SECRET ABOUT ISAYAMA-SAN, SO AFTER A LONG TIME WORKING ON THIS, I WANT TO HAVE A MEETING WHERE I REVEAL IT ALL!

I: WH—WHAT DOES THAT MEAN? NOW I'M ALL NERVOUS... BUT HOWEVER IT GOES, I'M LOOKING FORWARD TO THE NEXT VOLUME AND THE VOLUMES FOLLOWING THAT!

N: PLEASE SUPPORT ME, EVERYONE!

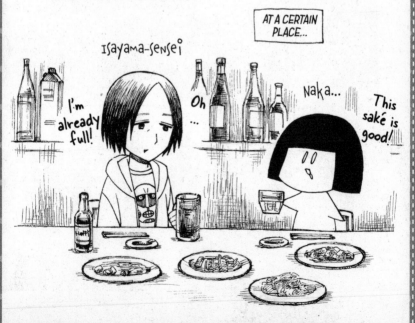

AT A CERTAIN PLACE...
This saké is good!
Naka...
Oh ...
I'm already full!
Isayama-sensei

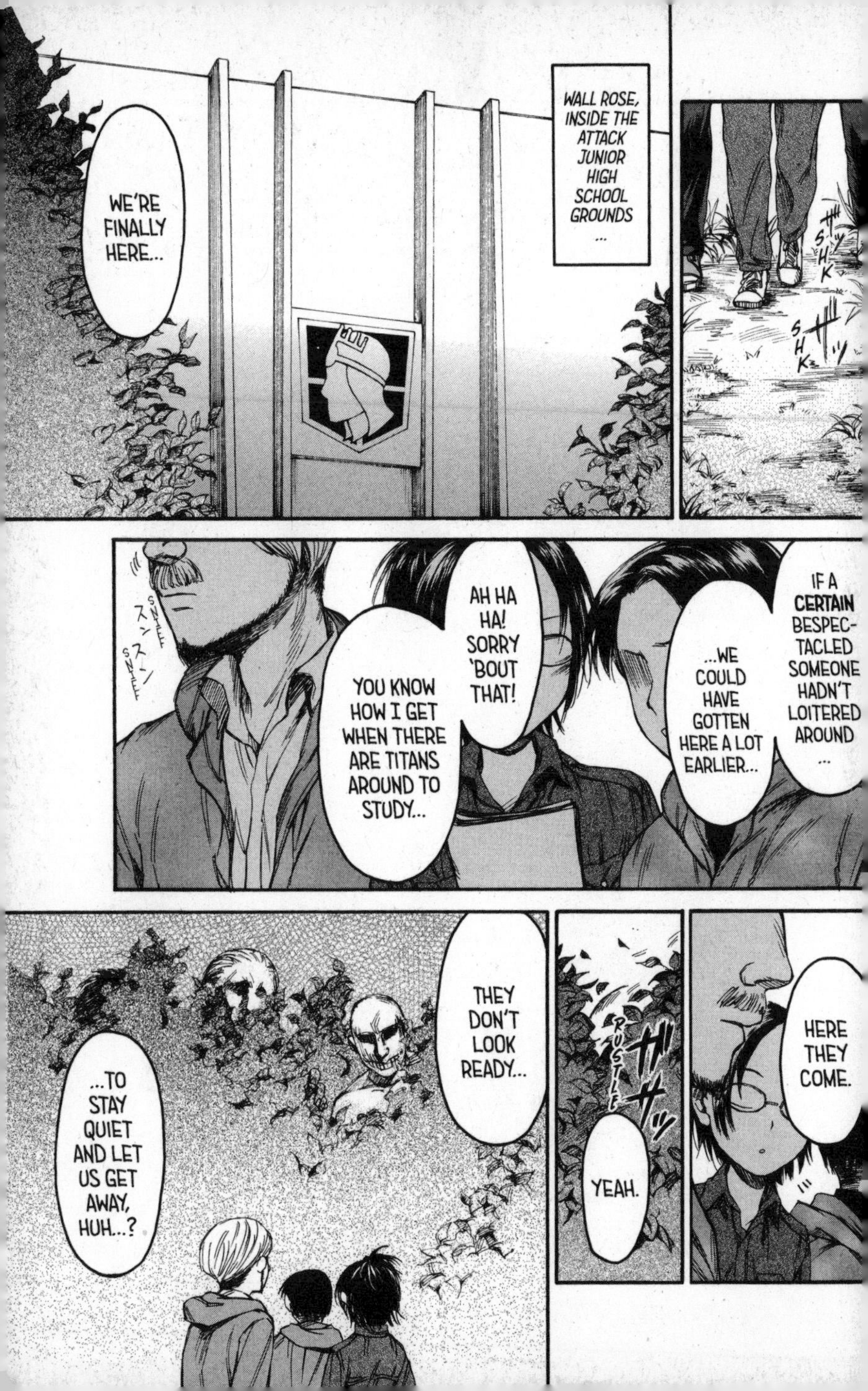

SHK
SHK
WALL ROSE, INSIDE THE ATTACK JUNIOR HIGH SCHOOL GROUNDS ...
WE'RE FINALLY HERE...
IF A CERTAIN BESPECTACLED SOMEONE HADN'T LOITERED AROUND ...
...WE COULD HAVE GOTTEN HERE A LOT EARLIER...
AH HA HA! SORRY 'BOUT THAT!
YOU KNOW HOW I GET WHEN THERE ARE TITANS AROUND TO STUDY...
SNIFF
SNIFF
HERE THEY COME.
RUSTLE
YEAH.
THEY DON'T LOOK READY...
...TO STAY QUIET AND LET US GET AWAY, HUH...?

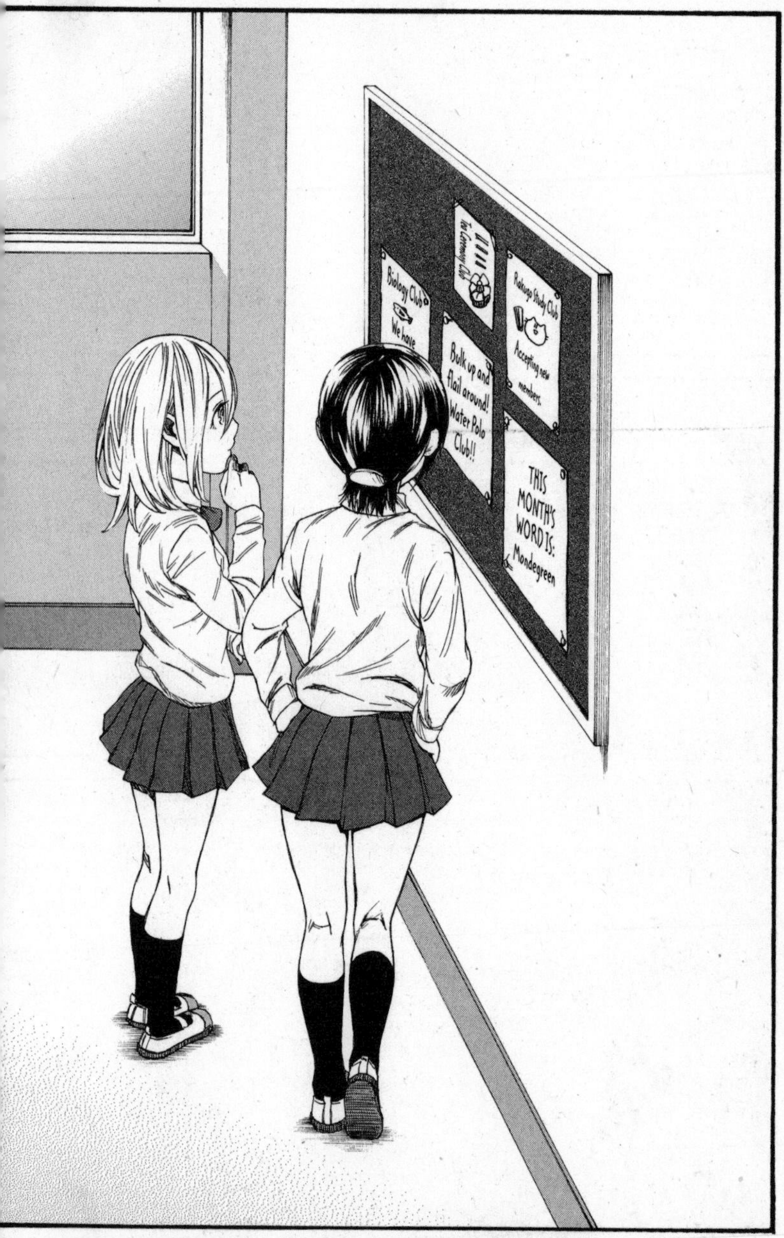
Tea Ceremony Club
Biology Club
We have
Rakugo Study Club
Accepting new members.
Bulk up and flail around! Water Polo Club!!
THIS MONTH'S WORD IS: Mondegreen

SEVENTH PERIOD: A WHIFF OF SOMETHING INTERESTING

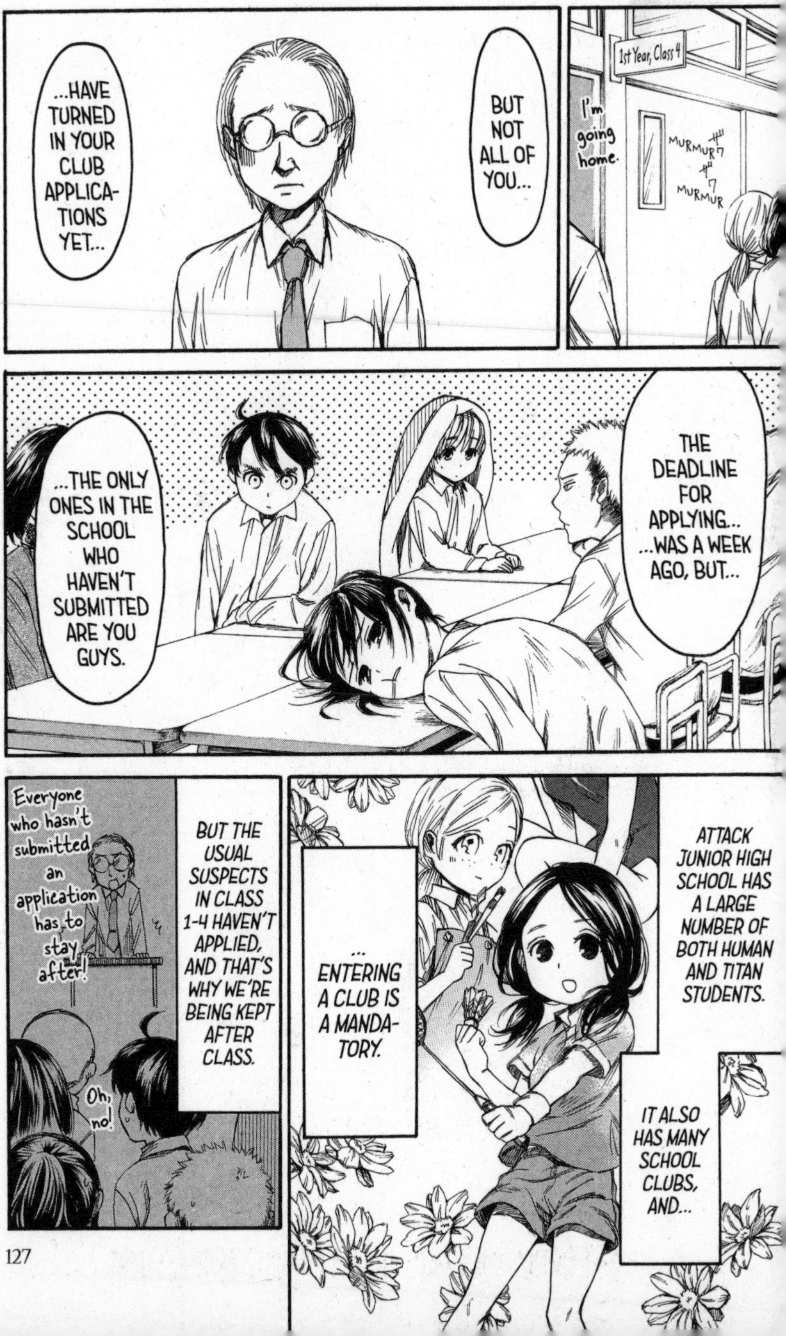
1st Year, Class 4
I'm going home.
MURMUR MURMUR
BUT NOT ALL OF YOU...
...HAVE TURNED IN YOUR CLUB APPLICATIONS YET...
THE DEADLINE FOR APPLYING... ...WAS A WEEK AGO, BUT...
...THE ONLY ONES IN THE SCHOOL WHO HAVEN'T SUBMITTED ARE YOU GUYS.
ATTACK JUNIOR HIGH SCHOOL HAS A LARGE NUMBER OF BOTH HUMAN AND TITAN STUDENTS.
IT ALSO HAS MANY SCHOOL CLUBS, AND...
...ENTERING A CLUB IS A MANDATORY.
BUT THE USUAL SUSPECTS IN CLASS 1-4 HAVEN'T APPLIED, AND THAT'S WHY WE'RE BEING KEPT AFTER CLASS.
Everyone who hasn't submitted an application has to stay after!
Oh, no!

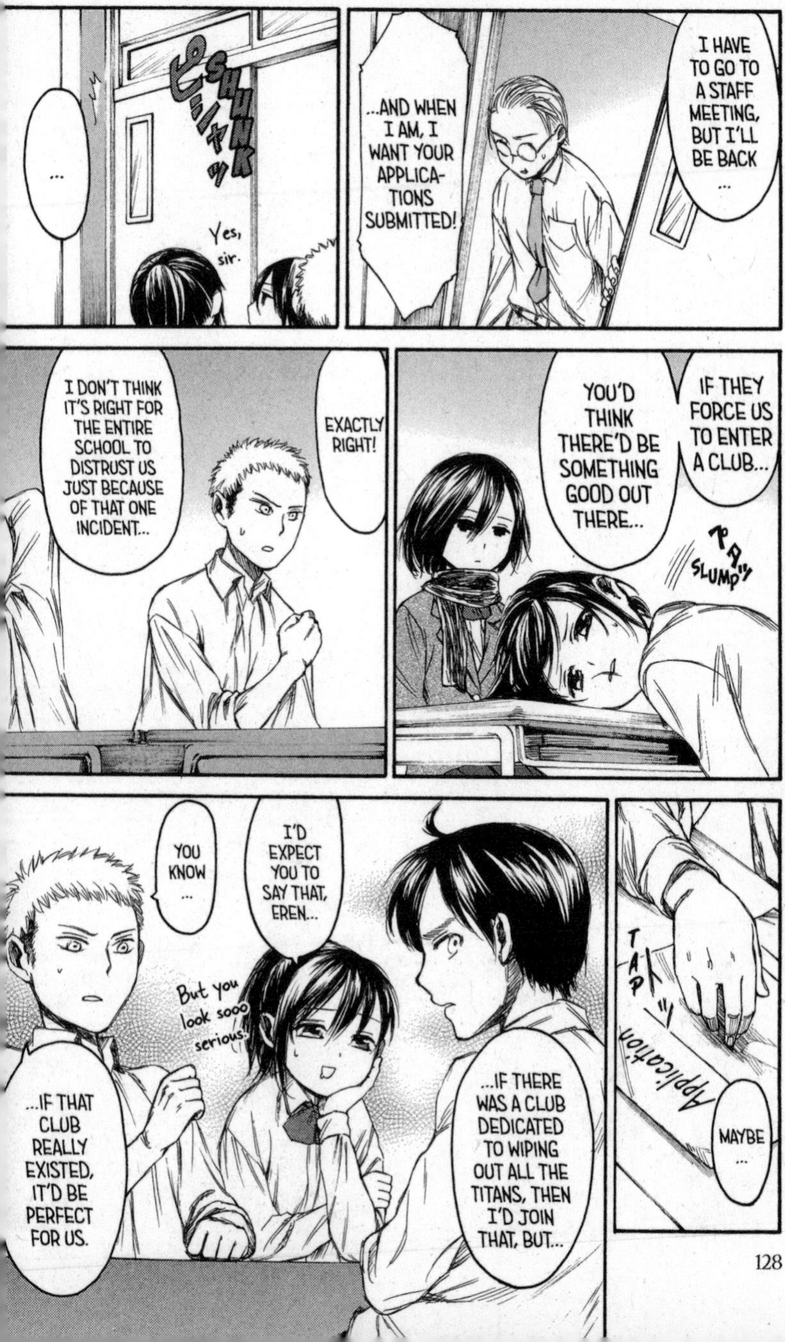

I HAVE TO GO TO A STAFF MEETING, BUT I'LL BE BACK...
...AND WHEN I AM, I WANT YOUR APPLICATIONS SUBMITTED!
ピシャッ
SHUNK
Yes, sir.
...
IF THEY FORCE US TO ENTER A CLUB...
YOU'D THINK THERE'D BE SOMETHING GOOD OUT THERE...
ペタッ
SLUMP
EXACTLY RIGHT!
I DON'T THINK IT'S RIGHT FOR THE ENTIRE SCHOOL TO DISTRUST US JUST BECAUSE OF THAT ONE INCIDENT...
TAP
Application
MAYBE...
...IF THERE WAS A CLUB DEDICATED TO WIPING OUT ALL THE TITANS, THEN I'D JOIN THAT, BUT...
I'D EXPECT YOU TO SAY THAT, EREN...
YOU KNOW...
...IF THAT CLUB REALLY EXISTED, IT'D BE PERFECT FOR US.
But you look sooo serious.

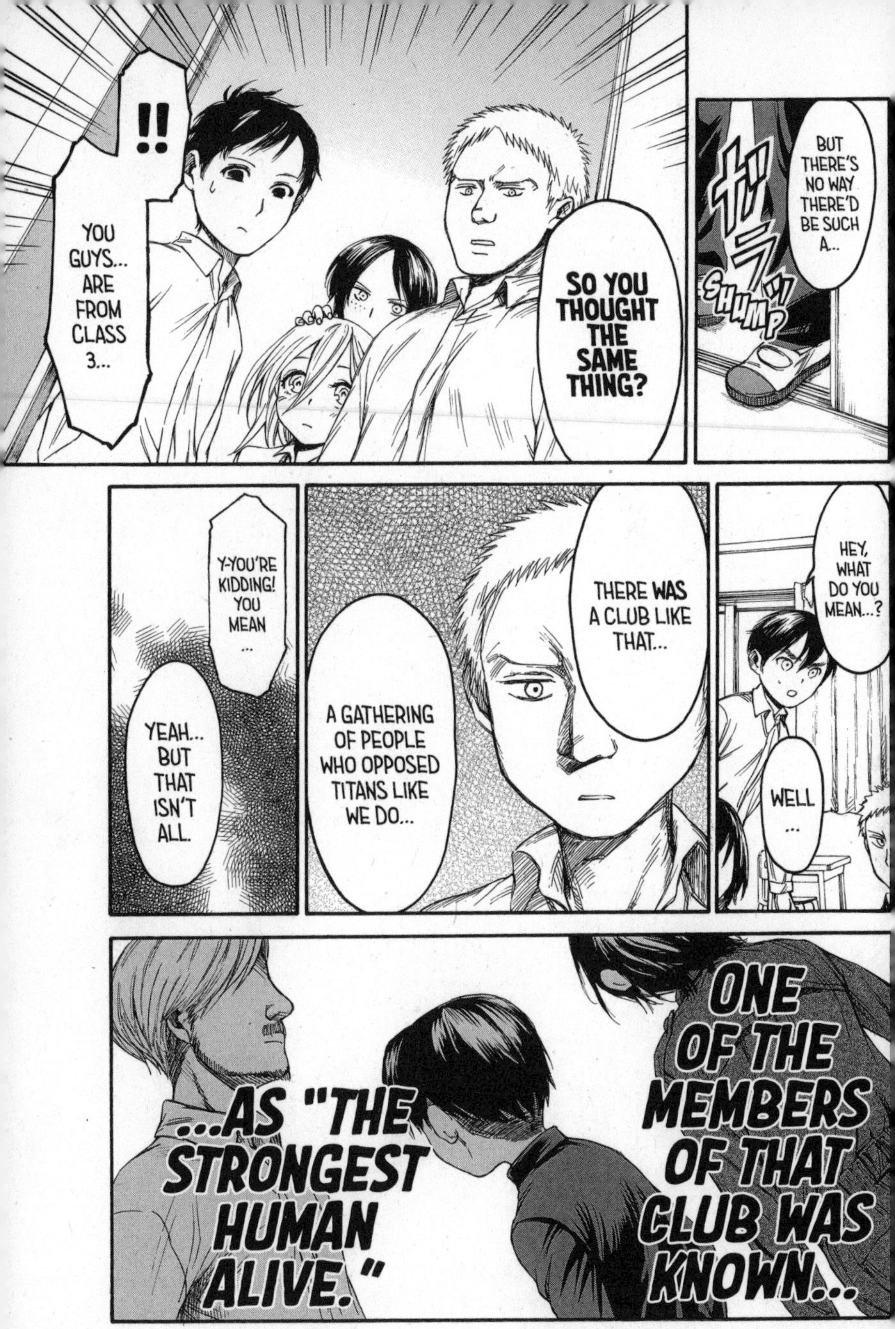
BUT THERE'S NO WAY THERE'D BE SUCH A...
SHUMP
SO YOU THOUGHT THE SAME THING?
!!
YOU GUYS... ARE FROM CLASS 3...
HEY, WHAT DO YOU MEAN...?
WELL ...
THERE WAS A CLUB LIKE THAT...
A GATHERING OF PEOPLE WHO OPPOSED TITANS LIKE WE DO...
Y-YOU'RE KIDDING! YOU MEAN ...
YEAH... BUT THAT ISN'T ALL.
ONE OF THE MEMBERS OF THAT CLUB WAS KNOWN...
...AS "THE STRONGEST HUMAN ALIVE."

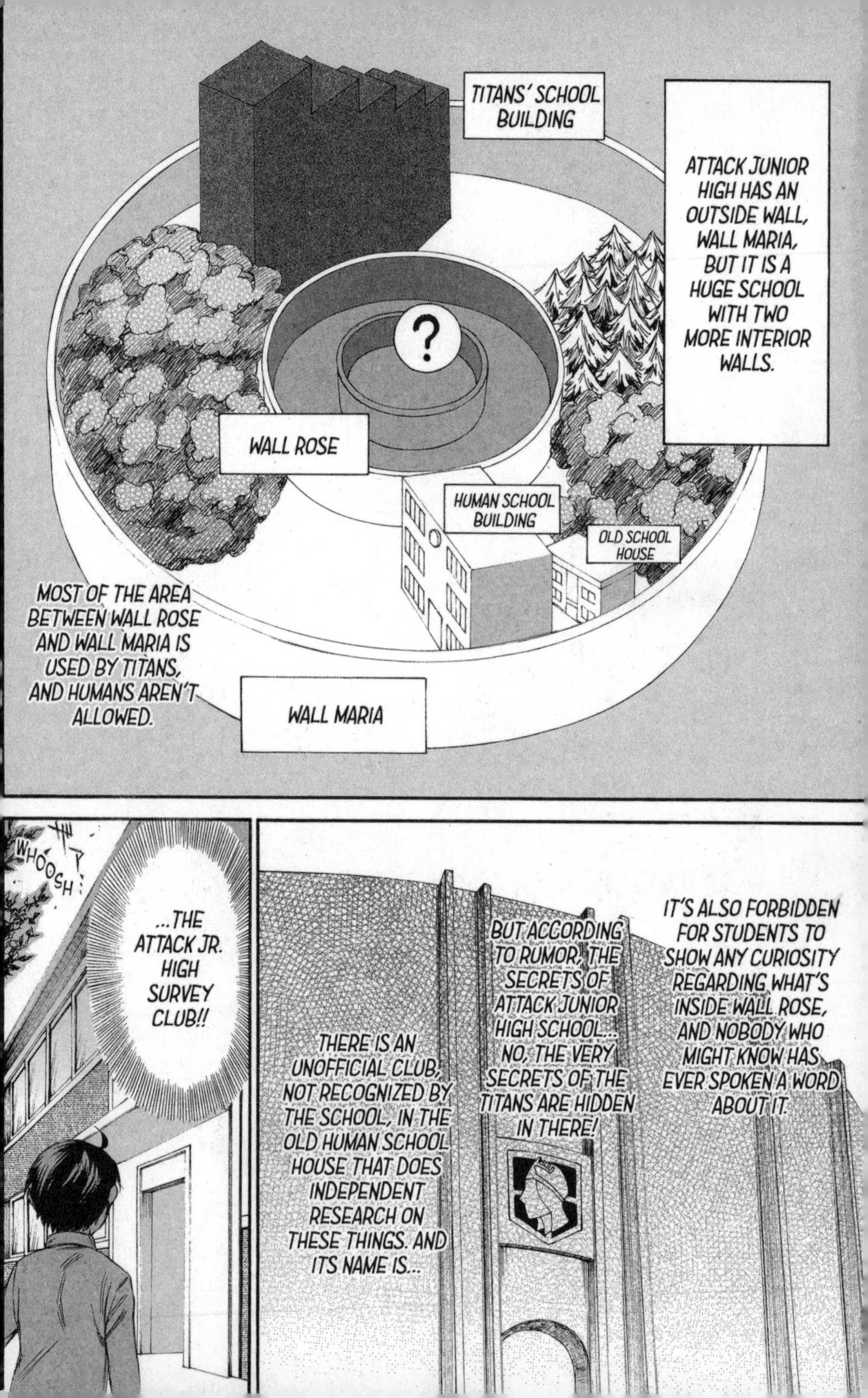
ATTACK JUNIOR HIGH HAS AN OUTSIDE WALL, WALL MARIA, BUT IT IS A HUGE SCHOOL WITH TWO MORE INTERIOR WALLS.
TITANS' SCHOOL BUILDING
?
WALL ROSE
HUMAN SCHOOL BUILDING
OLD SCHOOL HOUSE
MOST OF THE AREA BETWEEN WALL ROSE AND WALL MARIA IS USED BY TITANS, AND HUMANS AREN'T ALLOWED.
WALL MARIA
IT'S ALSO FORBIDDEN FOR STUDENTS TO SHOW ANY CURIOSITY REGARDING WHAT'S INSIDE WALL ROSE, AND NOBODY WHO MIGHT KNOW HAS EVER SPOKEN A WORD ABOUT IT.
BUT ACCORDING TO RUMOR, THE SECRETS OF ATTACK JUNIOR HIGH SCHOOL... NO, THE VERY SECRETS OF THE TITANS ARE HIDDEN IN THERE!
THERE IS AN UNOFFICIAL CLUB, NOT RECOGNIZED BY THE SCHOOL, IN THE OLD HUMAN SCHOOL HOUSE THAT DOES INDEPENDENT RESEARCH ON THESE THINGS. AND ITS NAME IS...
WHOOSH
...THE ATTACK JR. HIGH SURVEY CLUB!!

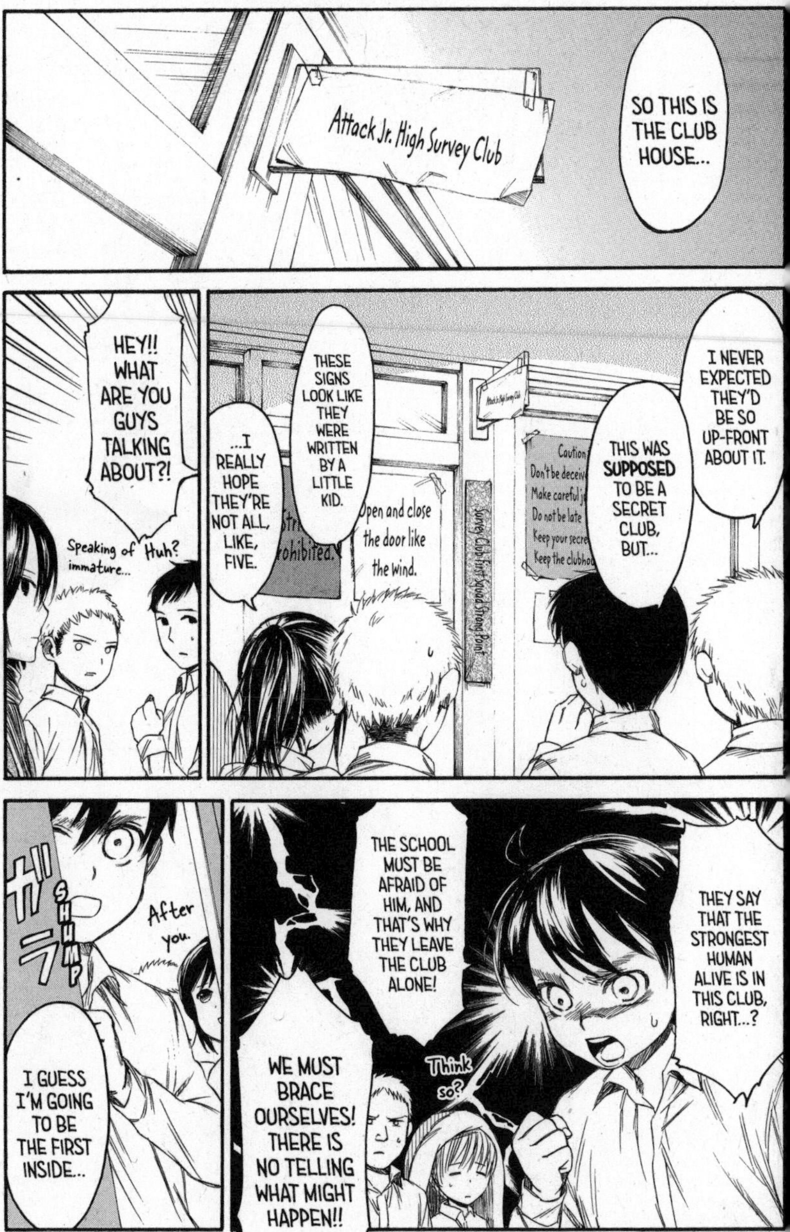
Attack Jr. High Survey Club
SO THIS IS THE CLUB HOUSE...
I NEVER EXPECTED THEY'D BE SO UP-FRONT ABOUT IT.
THIS WAS **SUPPOSED** TO BE A SECRET CLUB, BUT...
Caution
Survey Club First Squad Strong Point
THESE SIGNS LOOK LIKE THEY WERE WRITTEN BY A LITTLE KID.
...I REALLY HOPE THEY'RE NOT ALL, LIKE, FIVE.
Open and close the door like the wind.
HEY!! WHAT ARE YOU GUYS TALKING ABOUT?!
Huh?
Speaking of immature...
THEY SAY THAT THE STRONGEST HUMAN ALIVE IS IN THIS CLUB, RIGHT...?
THE SCHOOL MUST BE AFRAID OF HIM, AND THAT'S WHY THEY LEAVE THE CLUB ALONE!
Think so?
WE MUST BRACE OURSELVES! THERE IS NO TELLING WHAT MIGHT HAPPEN!!
SHUMP
After you.
I GUESS I'M GOING TO BE THE FIRST INSIDE...

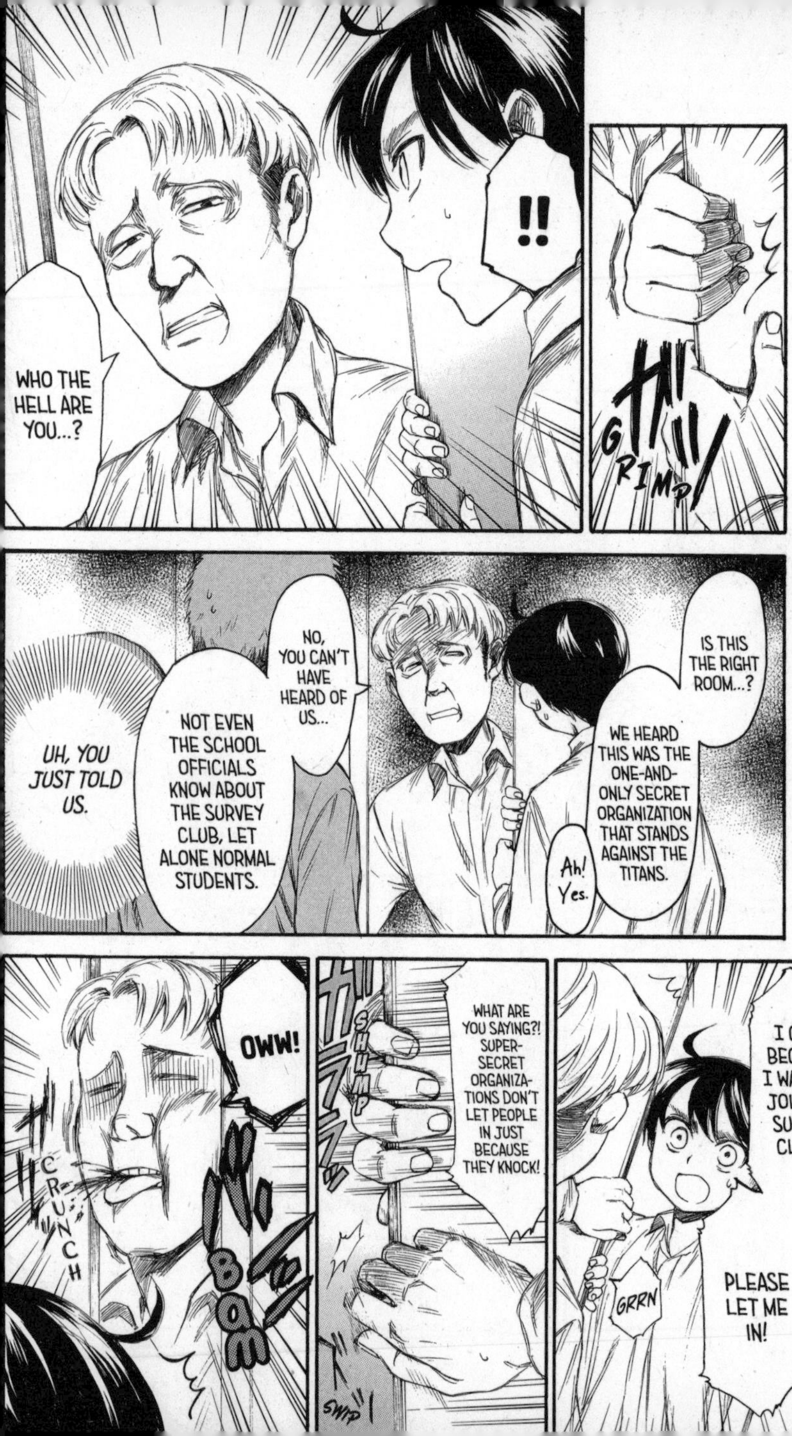
GRIMP
!!
WHO THE HELL ARE YOU...?
IS THIS THE RIGHT ROOM...?
WE HEARD THIS WAS THE ONE-AND-ONLY SECRET ORGANIZATION THAT STANDS AGAINST THE TITANS.
Ah! Yes.
NO, YOU CAN'T HAVE HEARD OF US...
NOT EVEN THE SCHOOL OFFICIALS KNOW ABOUT THE SURVEY CLUB, LET ALONE NORMAL STUDENTS.
UH, YOU JUST TOLD US.
I CAME BECAUSE I WANT TO JOIN THE SURVEY CLUB!!
GRRN
PLEASE LET ME IN!
SHUMP
WHAT ARE YOU SAYING?! SUPER-SECRET ORGANIZA-TIONS DON'T LET PEOPLE IN JUST BECAUSE THEY KNOCK!
SHIP
OWW!
BAM
CRUNCH

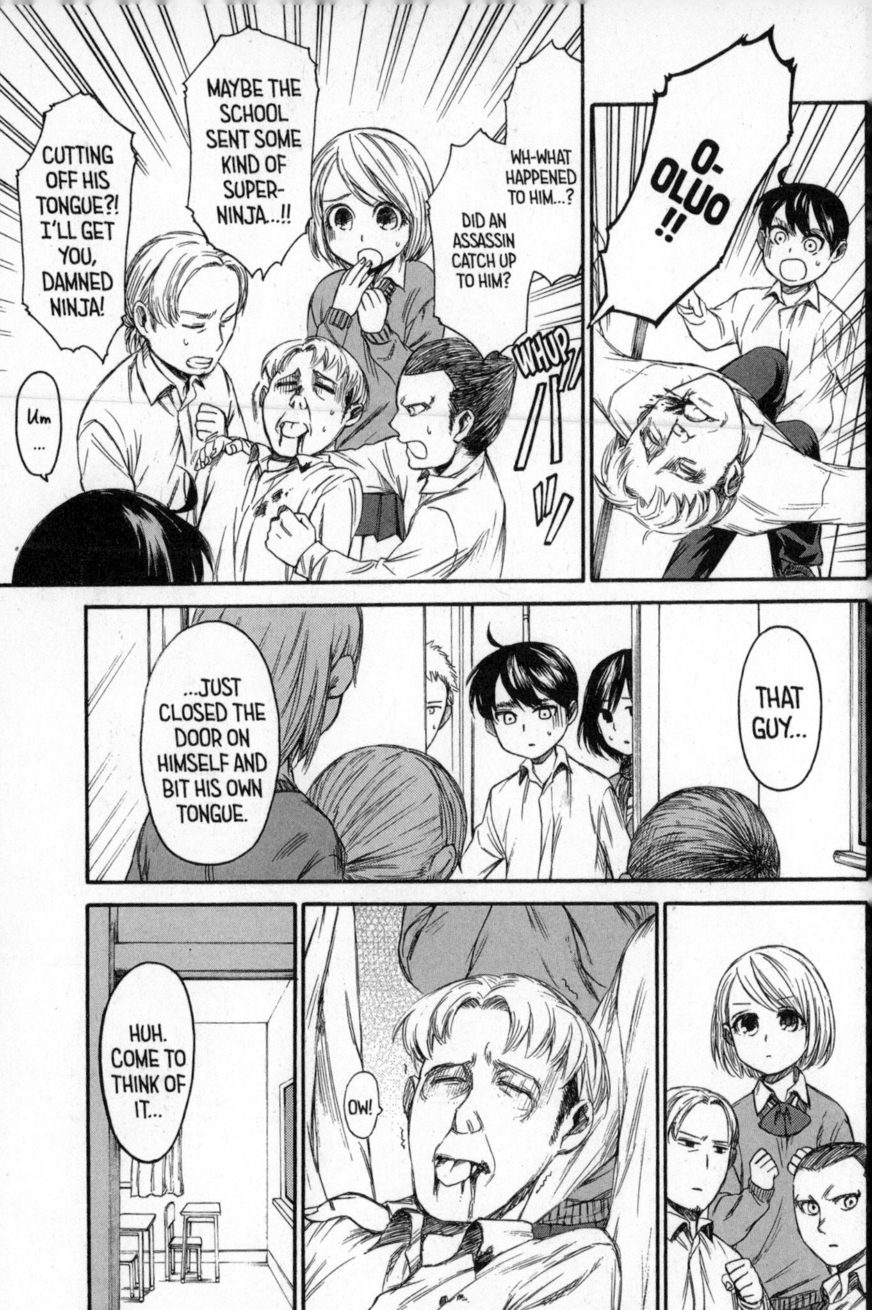
O-OLUO!!
WH-WHAT HAPPENED TO HIM...?
DID AN ASSASSIN CATCH UP TO HIM?
WHUP
MAYBE THE SCHOOL SENT SOME KIND OF SUPER-NINJA...!!
CUTTING OFF HIS TONGUE?! I'LL GET YOU, DAMNED NINJA!
Um ...
THAT GUY...
...JUST CLOSED THE DOOR ON HIMSELF AND BIT HIS OWN TONGUE.
OW!
HUH. COME TO THINK OF IT...

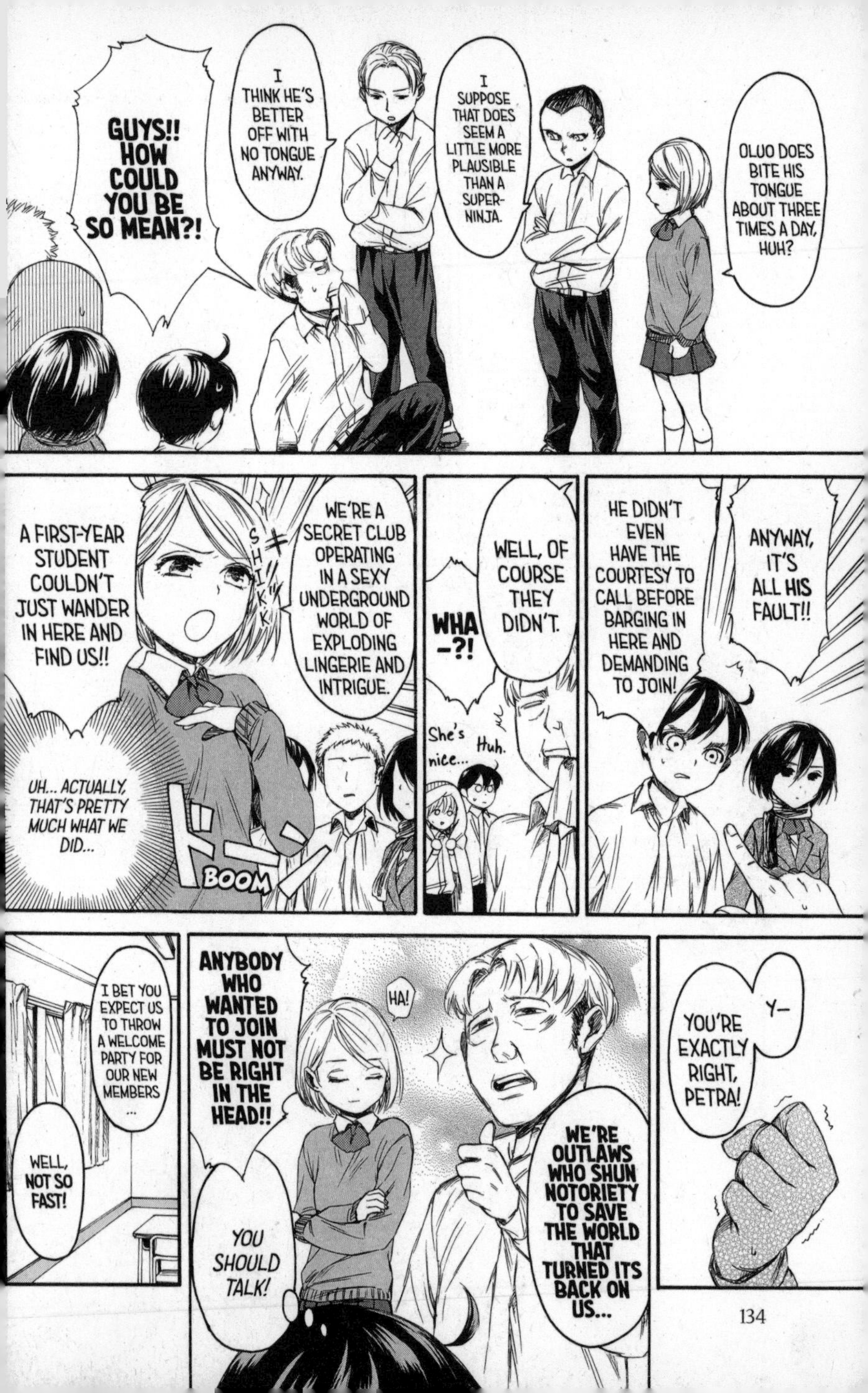
OLUO DOES BITE HIS TONGUE ABOUT THREE TIMES A DAY, HUH?
I SUPPOSE THAT DOES SEEM A LITTLE MORE PLAUSIBLE THAN A SUPER-NINJA.
I THINK HE'S BETTER OFF WITH NO TONGUE ANYWAY.
GUYS!! HOW COULD YOU BE SO MEAN?!
ANYWAY, IT'S ALL HIS FAULT!!
HE DIDN'T EVEN HAVE THE COURTESY TO CALL BEFORE BARGING IN HERE AND DEMANDING TO JOIN!
WELL, OF COURSE THEY DIDN'T.
WHA—?!
Huh.
She's nice...
WE'RE A SECRET CLUB OPERATING IN A SEXY UNDERGROUND WORLD OF EXPLODING LINGERIE AND INTRIGUE.
SHIKK
A FIRST-YEAR STUDENT COULDN'T JUST WANDER IN HERE AND FIND US!!
UH... ACTUALLY, THAT'S PRETTY MUCH WHAT WE DID...
BOOM
Y—
YOU'RE EXACTLY RIGHT, PETRA!
WE'RE OUTLAWS WHO SHUN NOTORIETY TO SAVE THE WORLD THAT TURNED ITS BACK ON US...
HA!
ANYBODY WHO WANTED TO JOIN MUST NOT BE RIGHT IN THE HEAD!!
YOU SHOULD TALK!
I BET YOU EXPECT US TO THROW A WELCOME PARTY FOR OUR NEW MEMBERS ...
WELL, NOT SO FAST!

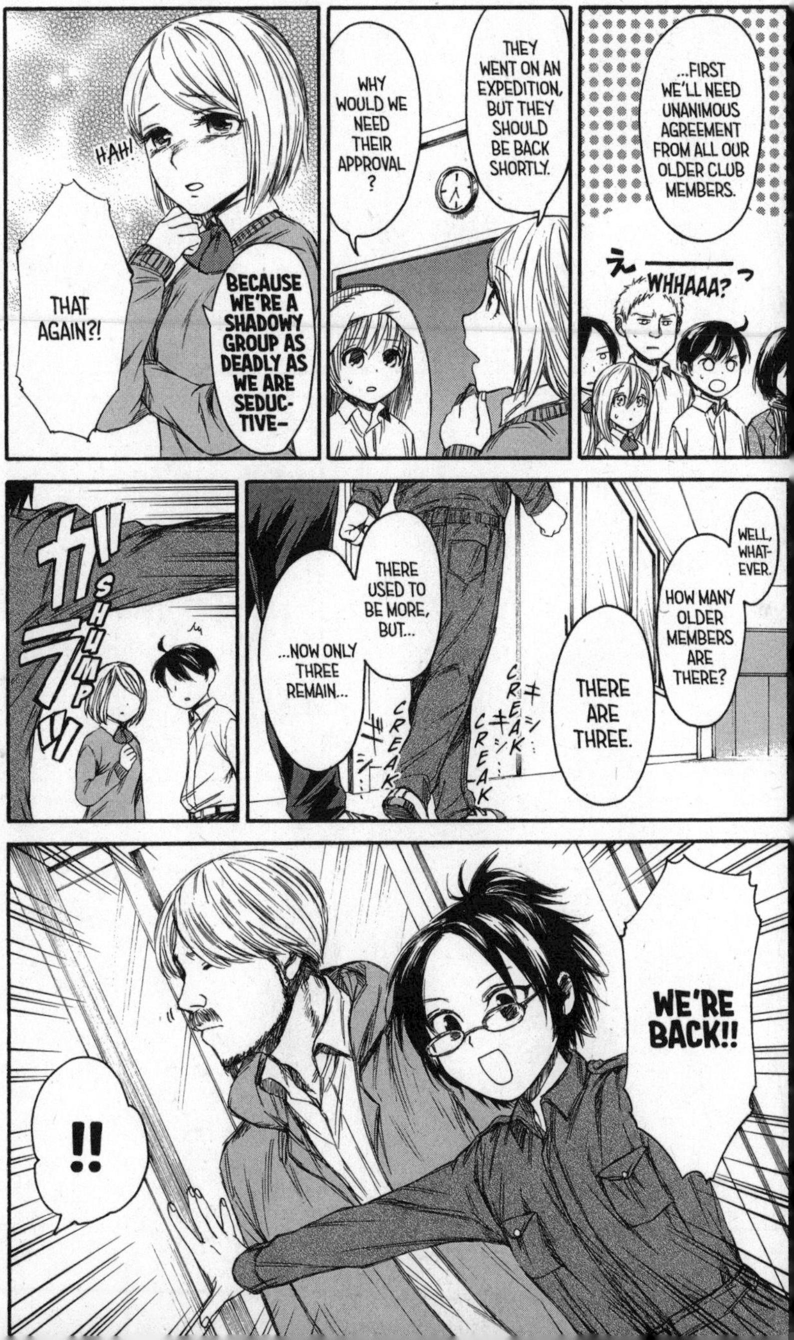
...FIRST WE'LL NEED UNANIMOUS AGREEMENT FROM ALL OUR OLDER CLUB MEMBERS.
え——WHHAAA?
THEY WENT ON AN EXPEDITION, BUT THEY SHOULD BE BACK SHORTLY.
WHY WOULD WE NEED THEIR APPROVAL?
BECAUSE WE'RE A SHADOWY GROUP AS DEADLY AS WE ARE SEDUC-TIVE–
HAH!
THAT AGAIN?!
WELL, WHAT-EVER.
HOW MANY OLDER MEMBERS ARE THERE?
THERE ARE THREE.
CREAK
CREAK
THERE USED TO BE MORE, BUT...
...NOW ONLY THREE REMAIN...
CREAK
SHUMP
WE'RE BACK!!
!!

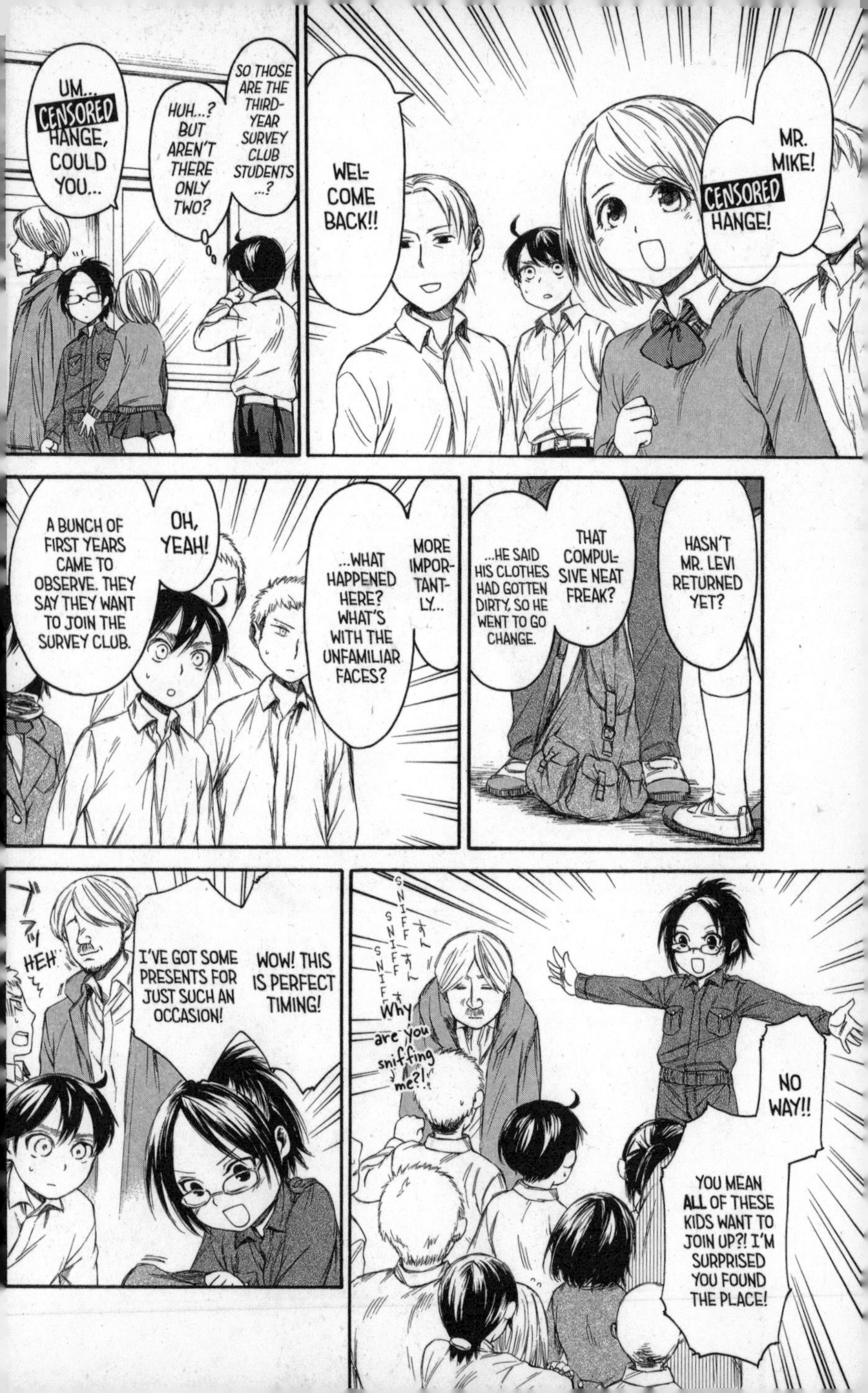
MR. MIKE! CENSORED HANGE!
WEL-COME BACK!!
SO THOSE ARE THE THIRD-YEAR SURVEY CLUB STUDENTS ...?
HUH...? BUT AREN'T THERE ONLY TWO?
UM... CENSORED HANGE, COULD YOU...
HASN'T MR. LEVI RETURNED YET?
THAT COMPUL-SIVE NEAT FREAK?
...HE SAID HIS CLOTHES HAD GOTTEN DIRTY, SO HE WENT TO GO CHANGE.
MORE IMPOR-TANT-LY...
...WHAT HAPPENED HERE? WHAT'S WITH THE UNFAMILIAR FACES?
OH, YEAH!
A BUNCH OF FIRST YEARS CAME TO OBSERVE. THEY SAY THEY WANT TO JOIN THE SURVEY CLUB.
NO WAY!!
YOU MEAN ALL OF THESE KIDS WANT TO JOIN UP?! I'M SURPRISED YOU FOUND THE PLACE!
SNIFF すん SNIFF すん SNIFF す
Why are you sniffing me?!
WOW! THIS IS PERFECT TIMING!
I'VE GOT SOME PRESENTS FOR JUST SUCH AN OCCASION!
HEH

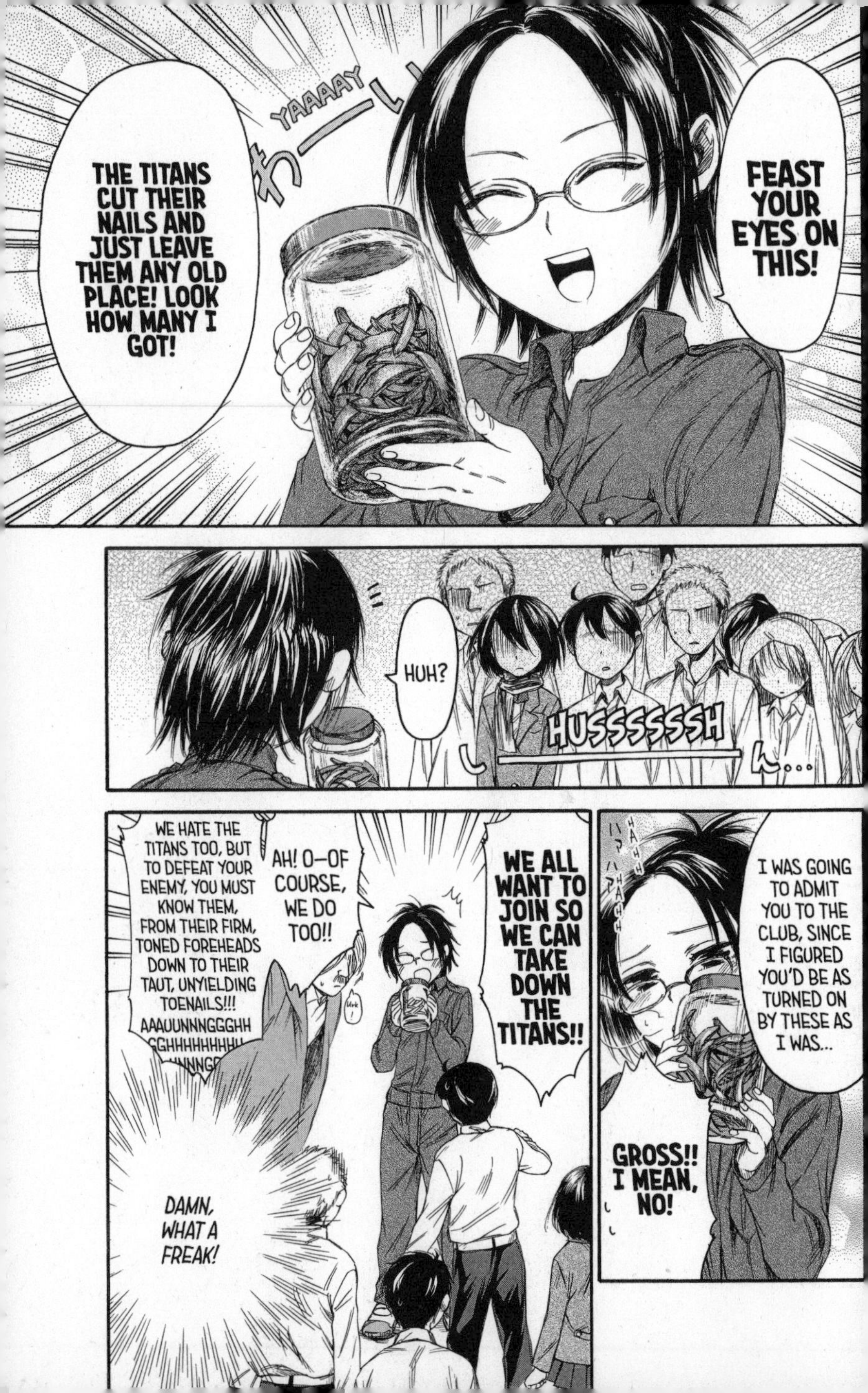
FEAST YOUR EYES ON THIS!
YAAAAY
THE TITANS CUT THEIR NAILS AND JUST LEAVE THEM ANY OLD PLACE! LOOK HOW MANY I GOT!
HUH?
HUSSSSSSH
I WAS GOING TO ADMIT YOU TO THE CLUB, SINCE I FIGURED YOU'D BE AS TURNED ON BY THESE AS I WAS...
GROSS!! I MEAN, NO!
WE ALL WANT TO JOIN SO WE CAN TAKE DOWN THE TITANS!!
AH! O-OF COURSE, WE DO TOO!!
WE HATE THE TITANS TOO, BUT TO DEFEAT YOUR ENEMY, YOU MUST KNOW THEM, FROM THEIR FIRM, TONED FOREHEADS DOWN TO THEIR TAUT, UNYIELDING TOENAILS!!! AAAUUNNNGGGHH
DAMN, WHAT A FREAK!

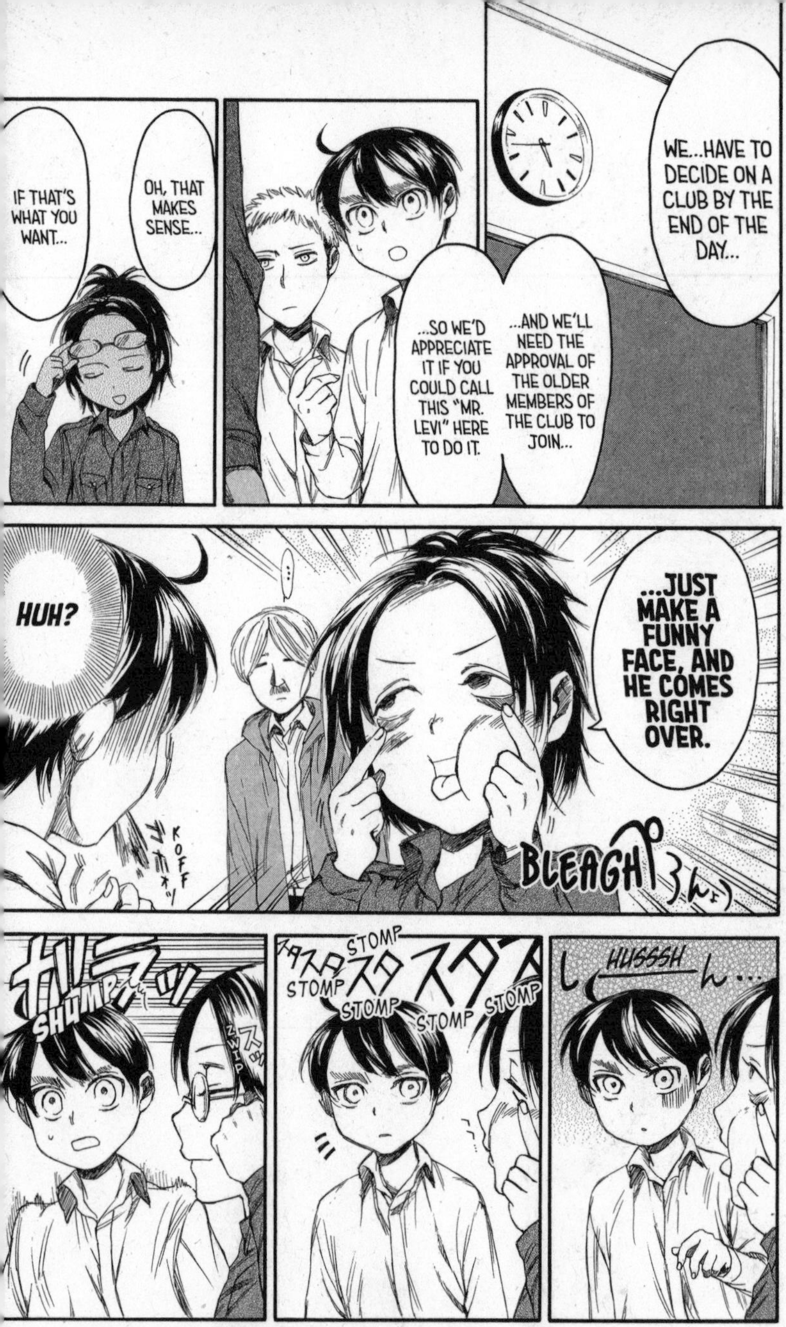
WE...HAVE TO DECIDE ON A CLUB BY THE END OF THE DAY...
...AND WE'LL NEED THE APPROVAL OF THE OLDER MEMBERS OF THE CLUB TO JOIN...
...SO WE'D APPRECIATE IT IF YOU COULD CALL THIS "MR. LEVI" HERE TO DO IT.
OH, THAT MAKES SENSE...
IF THAT'S WHAT YOU WANT...
...JUST MAKE A FUNNY FACE, AND HE COMES RIGHT OVER.
BLEAGH
HUH?
KOFF
HUSSSH
STOMP STOMP STOMP STOMP STOMP STOMP
SHUMP
ZWIP

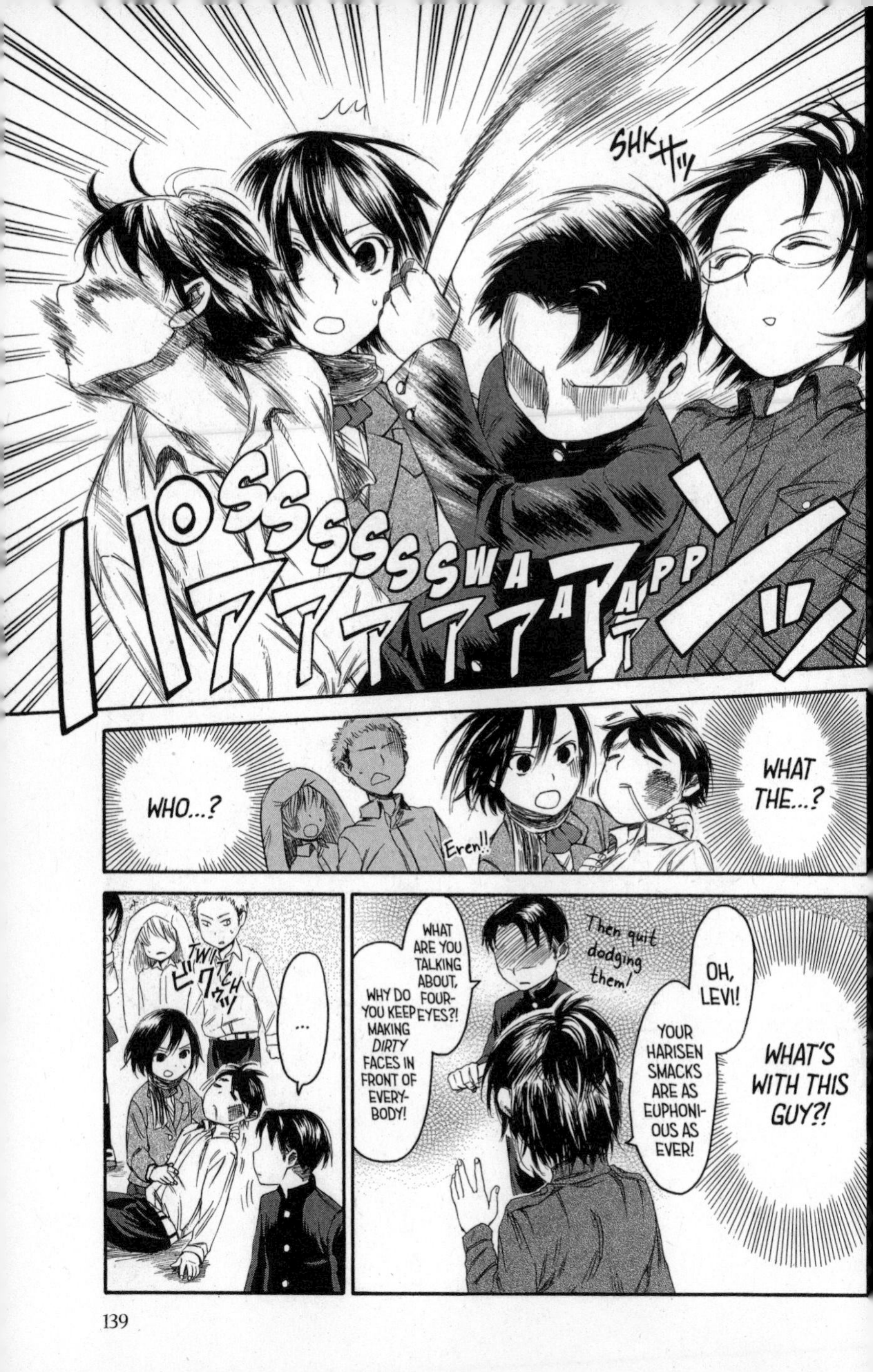
SHK
SSSSSSWAAAPP
WHAT THE...?
Eren!!
WHO...?
WHAT'S WITH THIS GUY?!
OH, LEVI!
YOUR HARISEN SMACKS ARE AS EUPHONIOUS AS EVER!
Then quit dodging them!
WHAT ARE YOU TALKING ABOUT, FOUR-EYES?!
WHY DO YOU KEEP MAKING DIRTY FACES IN FRONT OF EVERYBODY!
TWITCH
...

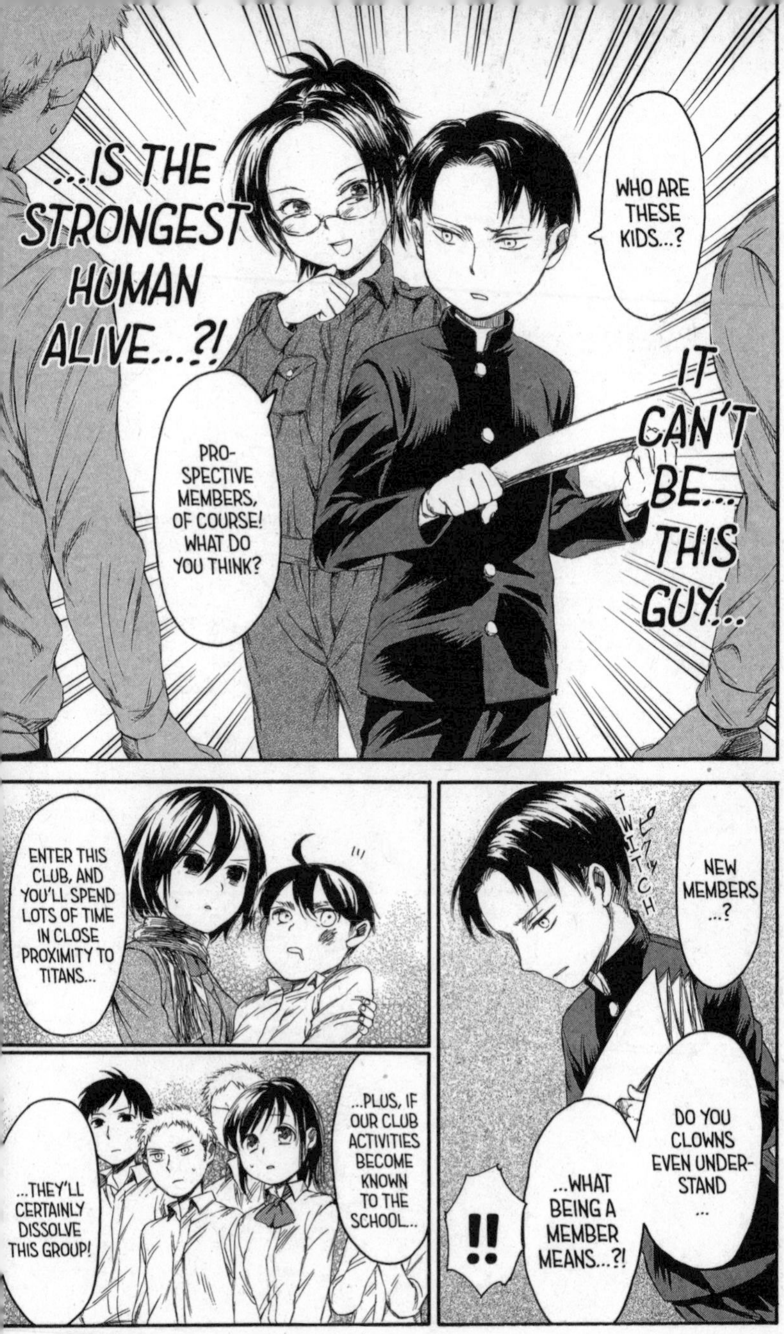
WHO ARE THESE KIDS...?
IT CAN'T BE... THIS GUY...
...IS THE STRONGEST HUMAN ALIVE...?!
PRO-SPECTIVE MEMBERS, OF COURSE! WHAT DO YOU THINK?
TWITCH
NEW MEMBERS ...?
DO YOU CLOWNS EVEN UNDER-STAND ...
...WHAT BEING A MEMBER MEANS...?!
!!
ENTER THIS CLUB, AND YOU'LL SPEND LOTS OF TIME IN CLOSE PROXIMITY TO TITANS...
...PLUS, IF OUR CLUB ACTIVITIES BECOME KNOWN TO THE SCHOOL...
...THEY'LL CERTAINLY DISSOLVE THIS GROUP!

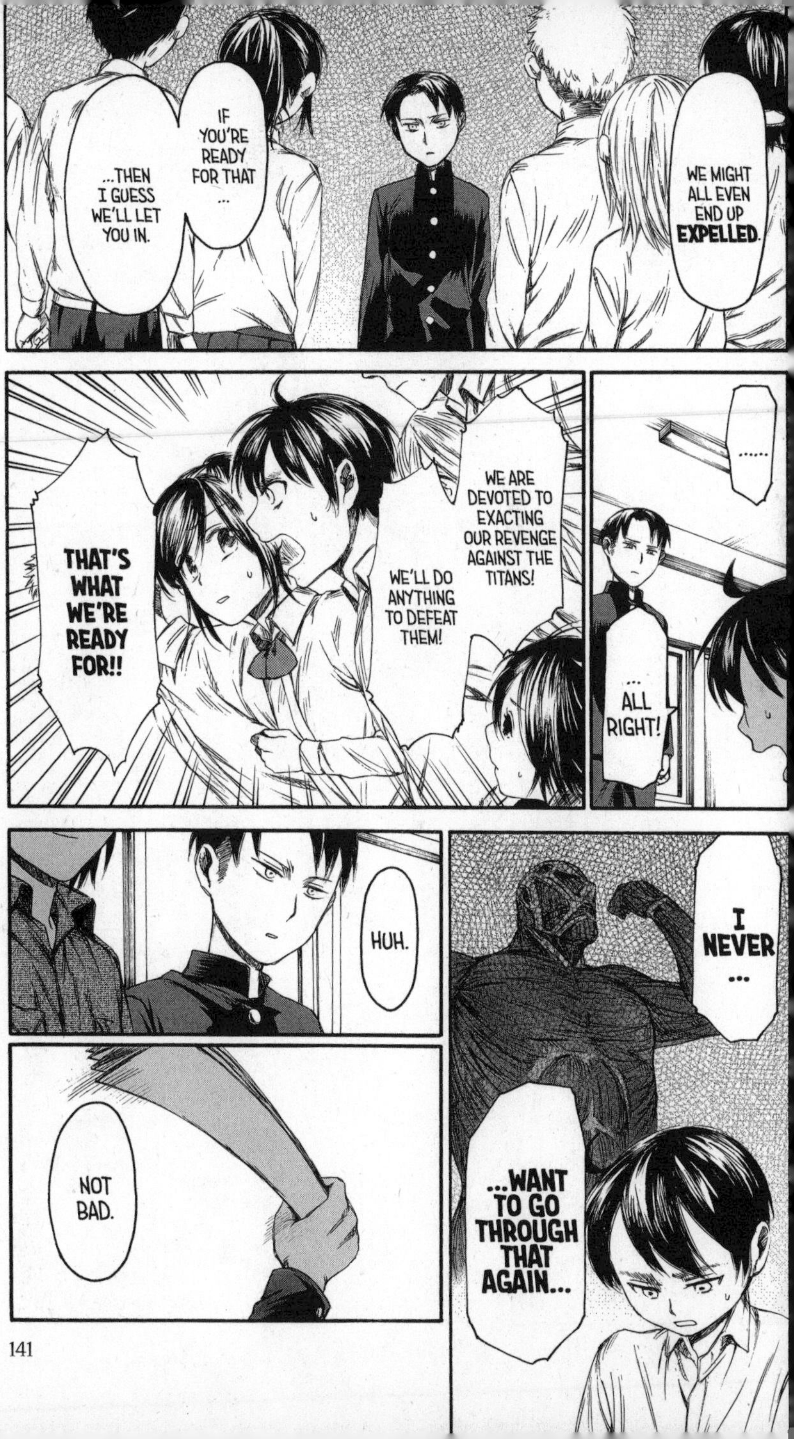
WE MIGHT ALL EVEN END UP **EXPELLED**.
IF YOU'RE READY FOR THAT ...
...THEN I GUESS WE'LL LET YOU IN.
......
... ALL RIGHT!
WE ARE DEVOTED TO EXACTING OUR REVENGE AGAINST THE TITANS!
WE'LL DO ANYTHING TO DEFEAT THEM!
THAT'S WHAT WE'RE READY FOR!!
I NEVER ...
...WANT TO GO THROUGH THAT AGAIN...
HUH.
NOT BAD.

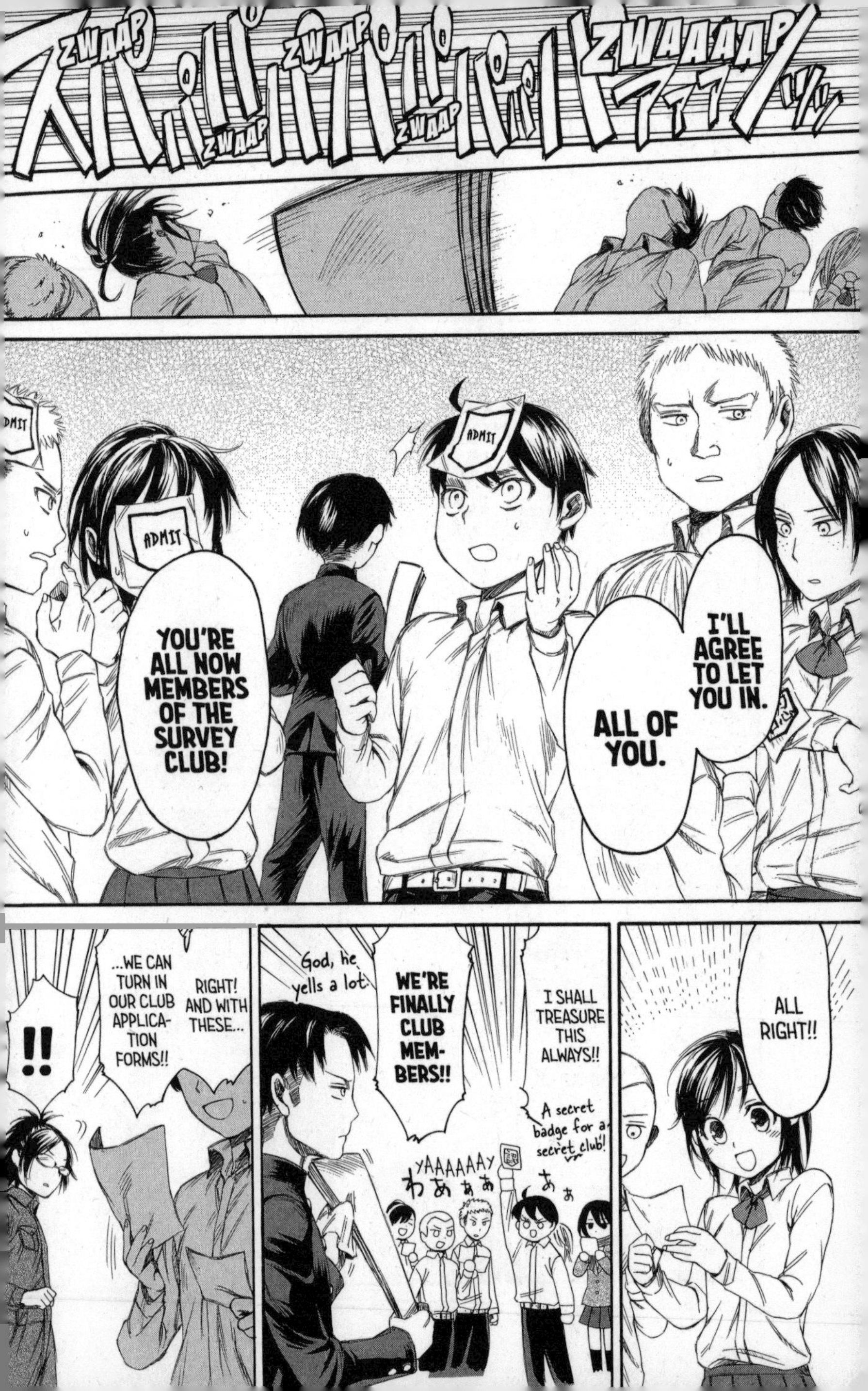
ZWAAAAP
ZWAAP
ZWAAP
ZWAAP
ZWAAP
I'LL AGREE TO LET YOU IN.
ALL OF YOU.
YOU'RE ALL NOW MEMBERS OF THE SURVEY CLUB!
ADMIT
ALL RIGHT!!
I SHALL TREASURE THIS ALWAYS!!
A secret badge for a secret club!
WE'RE FINALLY CLUB MEMBERS!!
God, he yells a lot.
YAAAAAAY
RIGHT! AND WITH THESE...
...WE CAN TURN IN OUR CLUB APPLICA-TION FORMS!!
!!

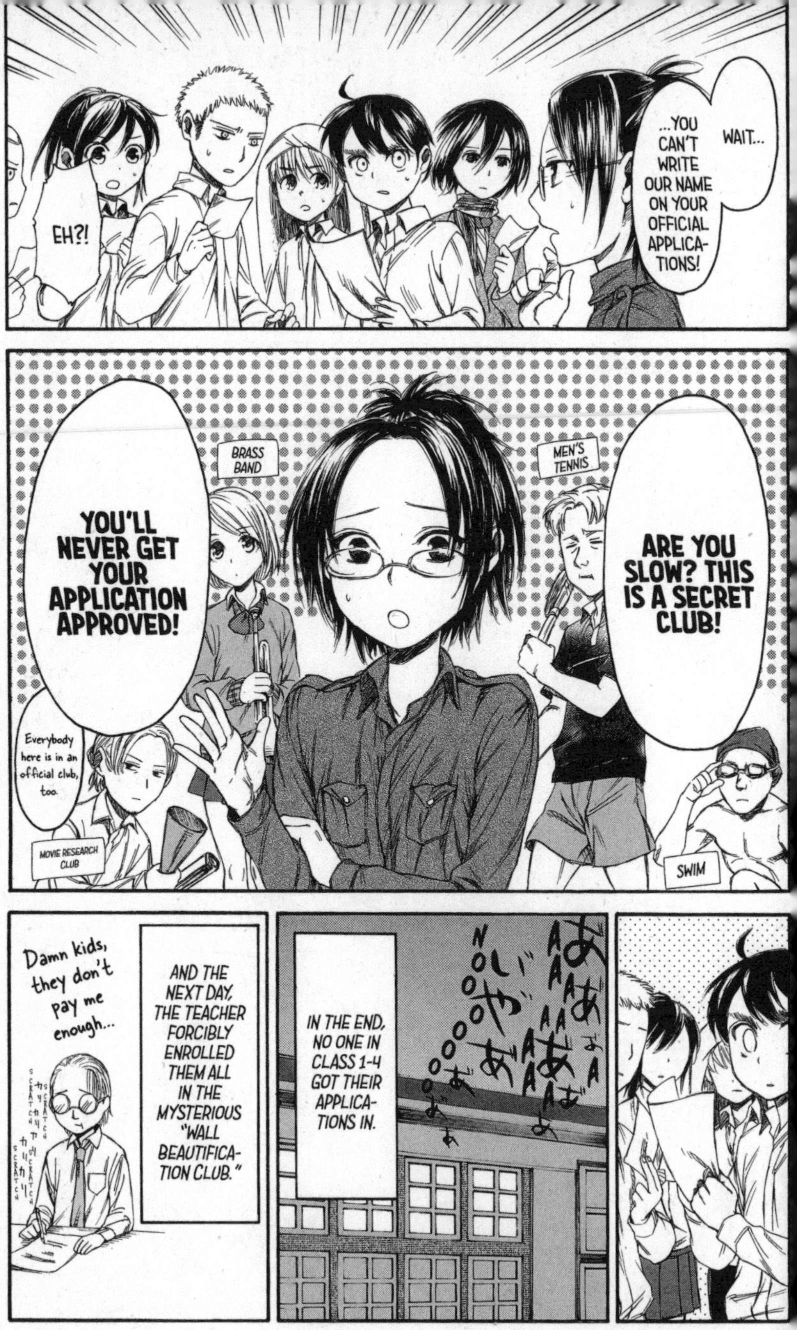
WAIT...
...YOU CAN'T WRITE OUR NAME ON YOUR OFFICIAL APPLICATIONS!
EH?!
ARE YOU SLOW? THIS IS A SECRET CLUB!
MEN'S TENNIS
SWIM
YOU'LL NEVER GET YOUR APPLICATION APPROVED!
BRASS BAND
Everybody here is in an official club, too.
MOVIE RESEARCH CLUB
IN THE END, NO ONE IN CLASS 1-4 GOT THEIR APPLICATIONS IN.
AND THE NEXT DAY, THE TEACHER FORCIBLY ENROLLED THEM ALL IN THE MYSTERIOUS "WALL BEAUTIFICATION CLUB."
Damn kids, they don't pay me enough...
SCRATCH SCRATCH SCRATCH SCRATCH

FUN AND GAMES IN CLUB LIFE

OR, MIKASA'S FACE POWERS

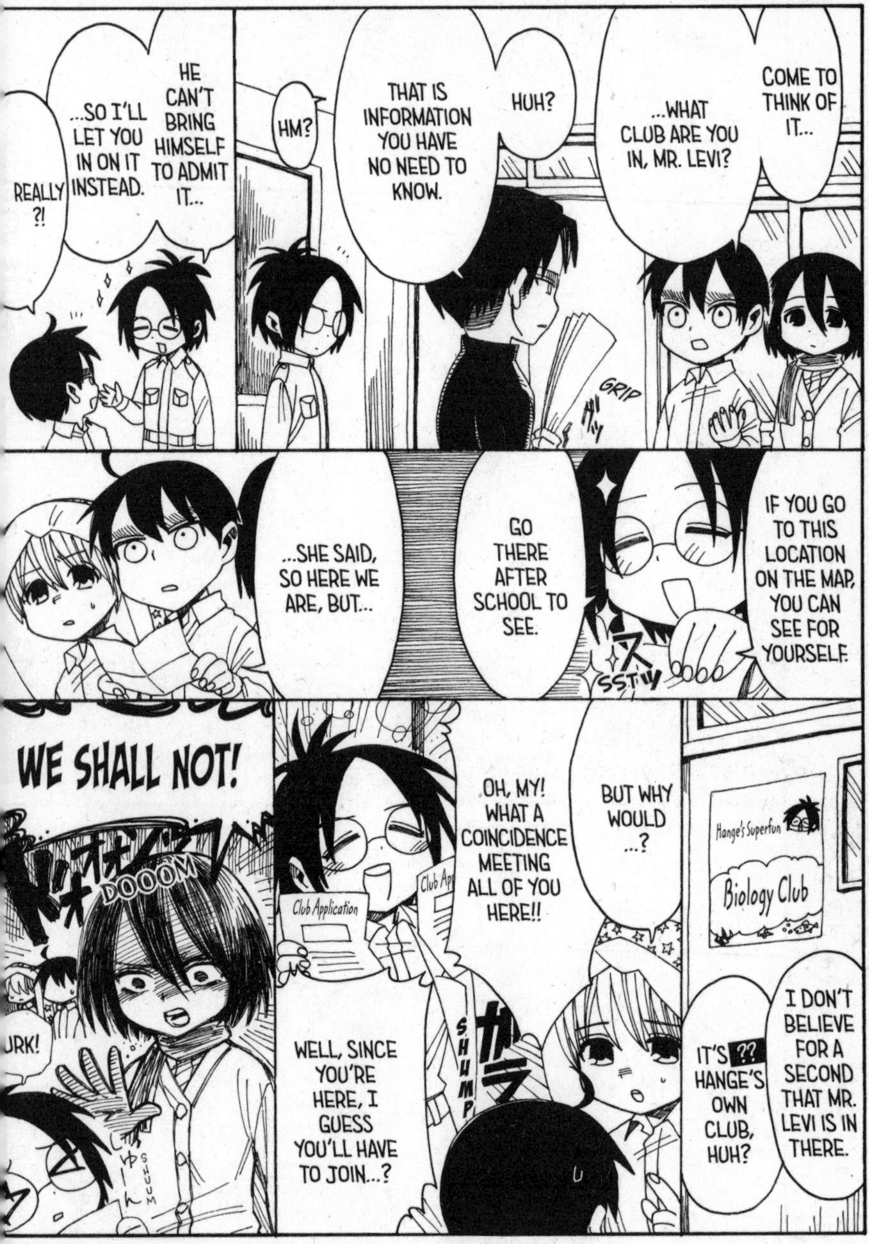
COME TO THINK OF IT...
...WHAT CLUB ARE YOU IN, MR. LEVI?
GRIP
HUH?
THAT IS INFORMATION YOU HAVE NO NEED TO KNOW.
HM?
HE CAN'T BRING HIMSELF TO ADMIT IT...
...SO I'LL LET YOU IN ON IT INSTEAD.
REALLY?!
IF YOU GO TO THIS LOCATION ON THE MAP, YOU CAN SEE FOR YOURSELF.
SST
GO THERE AFTER SCHOOL TO SEE.
...SHE SAID, SO HERE WE ARE, BUT...
I DON'T BELIEVE FOR A SECOND THAT MR. LEVI IS IN THERE.
IT'S ?? HANGE'S OWN CLUB, HUH?
Hange's Superfun
Biology Club
BUT WHY WOULD...?
OH, MY! WHAT A COINCIDENCE MEETING ALL OF YOU HERE!!
SHUMP
WELL, SINCE YOU'RE HERE, I GUESS YOU'LL HAVE TO JOIN...?
Club Application
WE SHALL NOT!
DOOOM
URK!
SHUUM

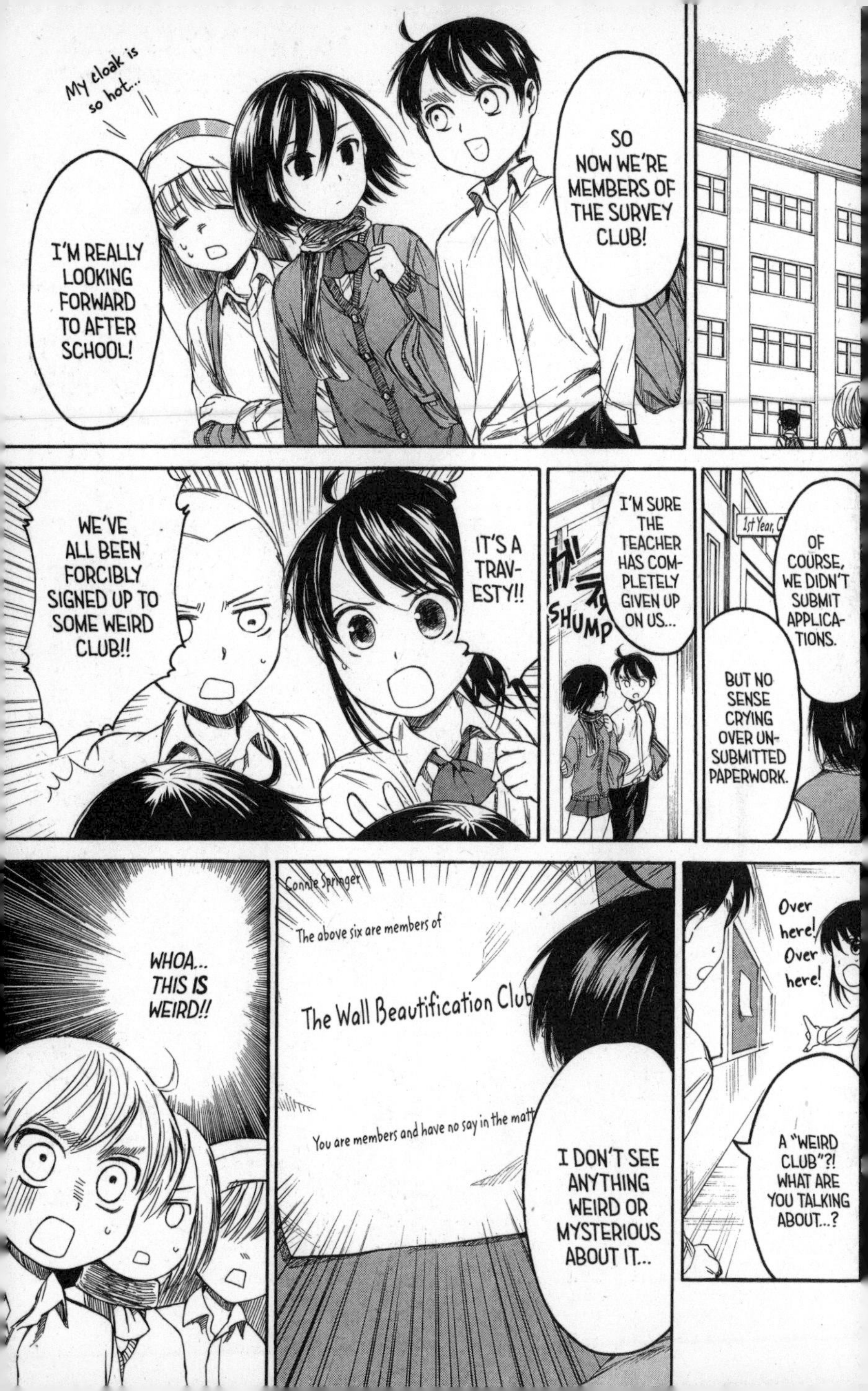
SO NOW WE'RE MEMBERS OF THE SURVEY CLUB!
My cloak is so hot...
I'M REALLY LOOKING FORWARD TO AFTER SCHOOL!
1st Year, C
OF COURSE, WE DIDN'T SUBMIT APPLICATIONS.
BUT NO SENSE CRYING OVER UNSUBMITTED PAPERWORK.
I'M SURE THE TEACHER HAS COMPLETELY GIVEN UP ON US...
SHUMP
IT'S A TRAVESTY!!
WE'VE ALL BEEN FORCIBLY SIGNED UP TO SOME WEIRD CLUB!!
Over here! Over here!
A "WEIRD CLUB"?! WHAT ARE YOU TALKING ABOUT...?
Connie Springer
The above six are members of
The Wall Beautification Club
You are members and have no say in the matt
I DON'T SEE ANYTHING WEIRD OR MYSTERIOUS ABOUT IT...
WHOA... THIS IS WEIRD!!

EIGHTH PERIOD: THE BEAUTIFIERS

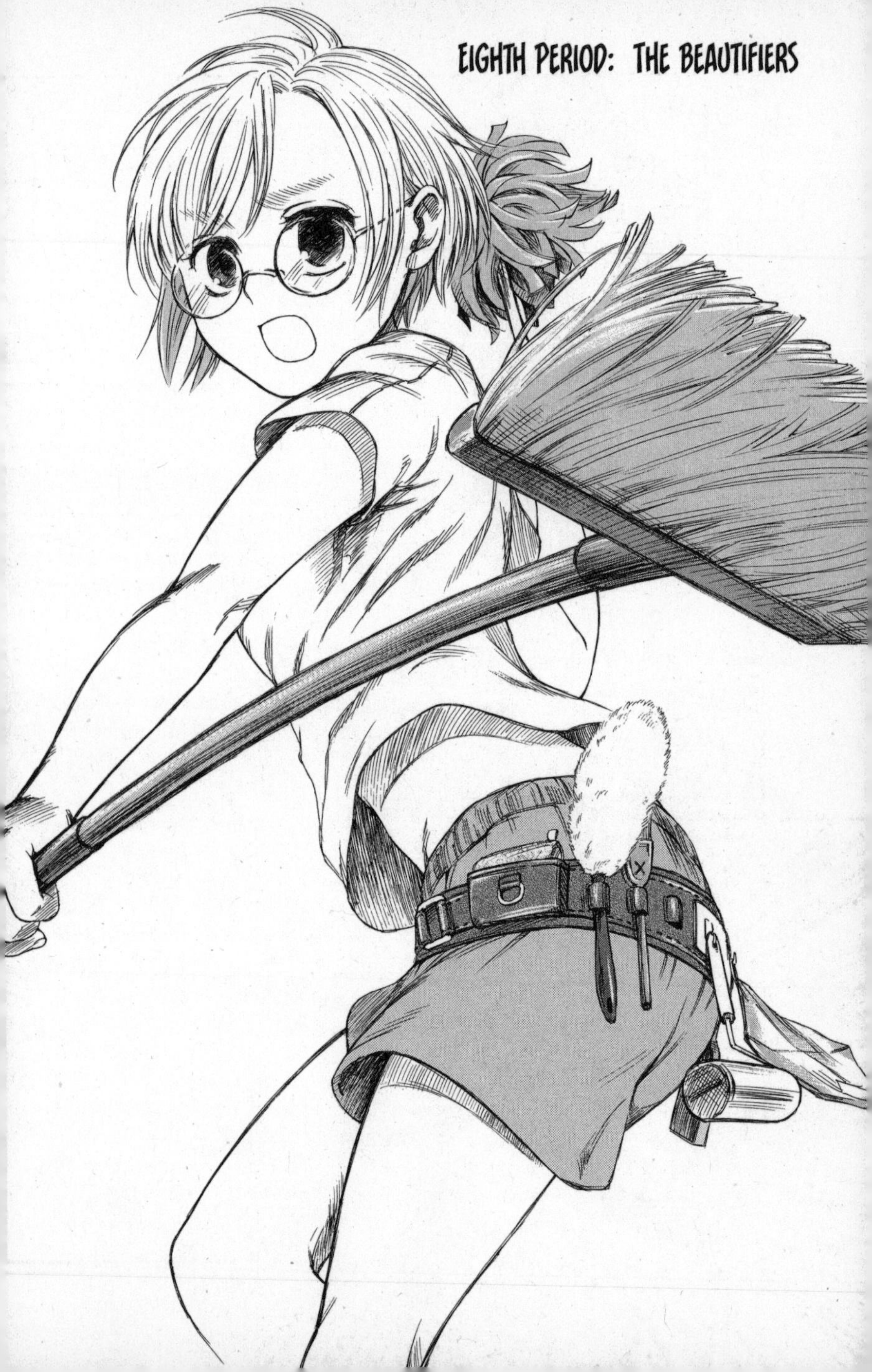

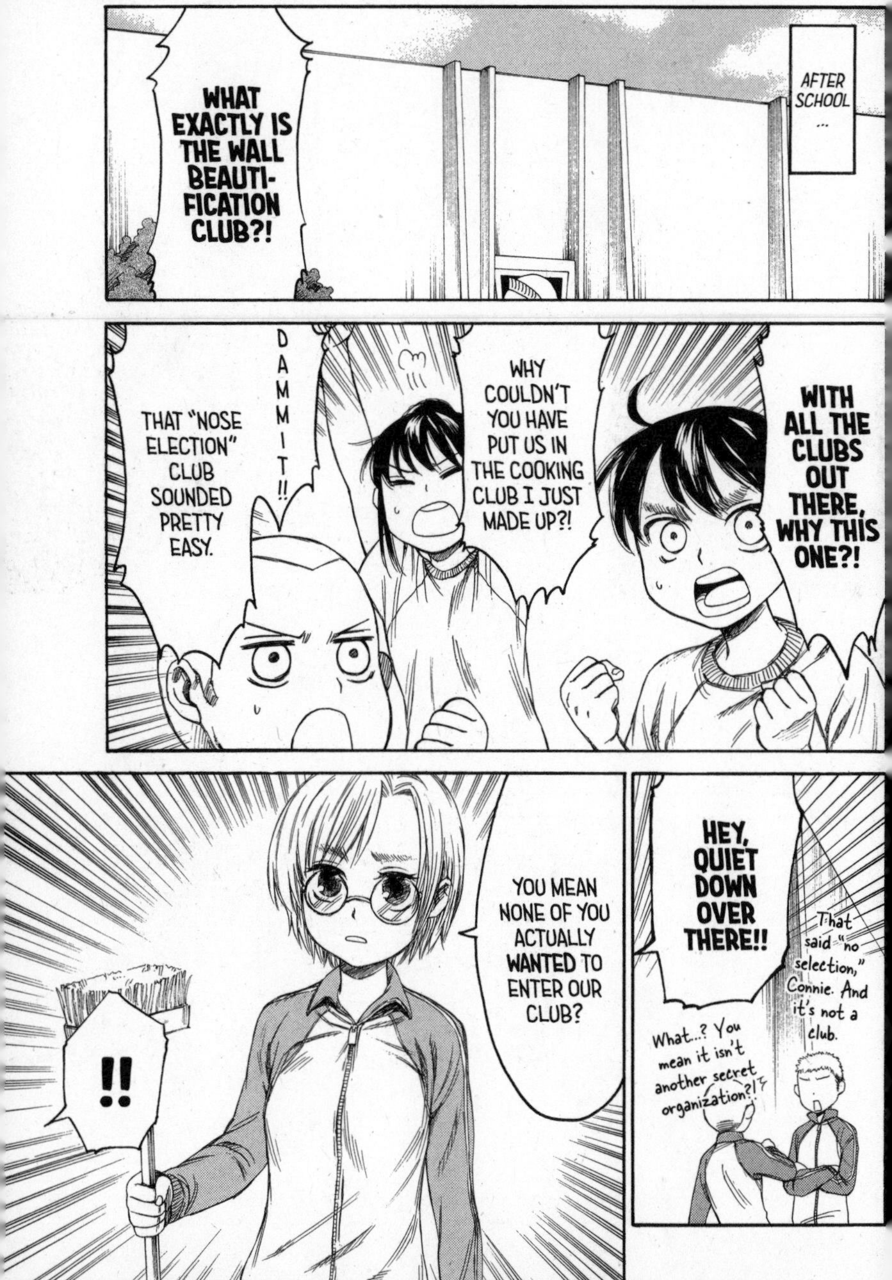
AFTER SCHOOL ...
WHAT EXACTLY IS THE WALL BEAUTI-FICATION CLUB?!
WITH ALL THE CLUBS OUT THERE, WHY THIS ONE?!
WHY COULDN'T YOU HAVE PUT US IN THE COOKING CLUB I JUST MADE UP?!
DAMMIT!!
THAT "NOSE ELECTION" CLUB SOUNDED PRETTY EASY.
HEY, QUIET DOWN OVER THERE!!
That said "no selection," Connie. And it's not a club.
What...? You mean it isn't another secret organization?!
YOU MEAN NONE OF YOU ACTUALLY WANTED TO ENTER OUR CLUB?
!!

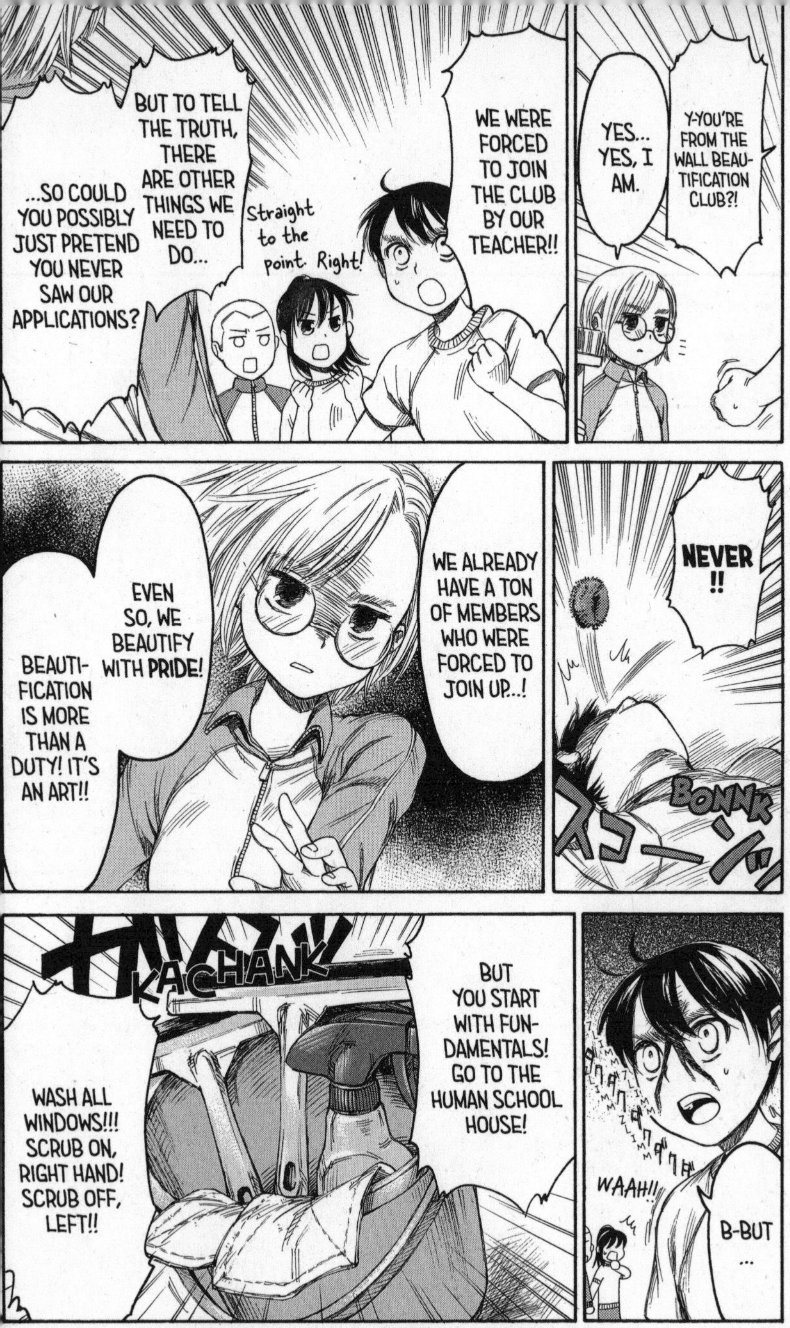
Y-YOU'RE FROM THE WALL BEAU-TIFICATION CLUB?!
YES... YES, I AM.
WE WERE FORCED TO JOIN THE CLUB BY OUR TEACHER!!
Straight to the point. Right!
BUT TO TELL THE TRUTH, THERE ARE OTHER THINGS WE NEED TO DO...
...SO COULD YOU POSSIBLY JUST PRETEND YOU NEVER SAW OUR APPLICATIONS?
NEVER!!
BONNK
WE ALREADY HAVE A TON OF MEMBERS WHO WERE FORCED TO JOIN UP...!
EVEN SO, WE BEAUTIFY WITH PRIDE!
BEAUTI-FICATION IS MORE THAN A DUTY! IT'S AN ART!!
WAAH!!
B-BUT...
KACHANK
BUT YOU START WITH FUN-DAMENTALS! GO TO THE HUMAN SCHOOL HOUSE!
WASH ALL WINDOWS!!! SCRUB ON, RIGHT HAND! SCRUB OFF, LEFT!!

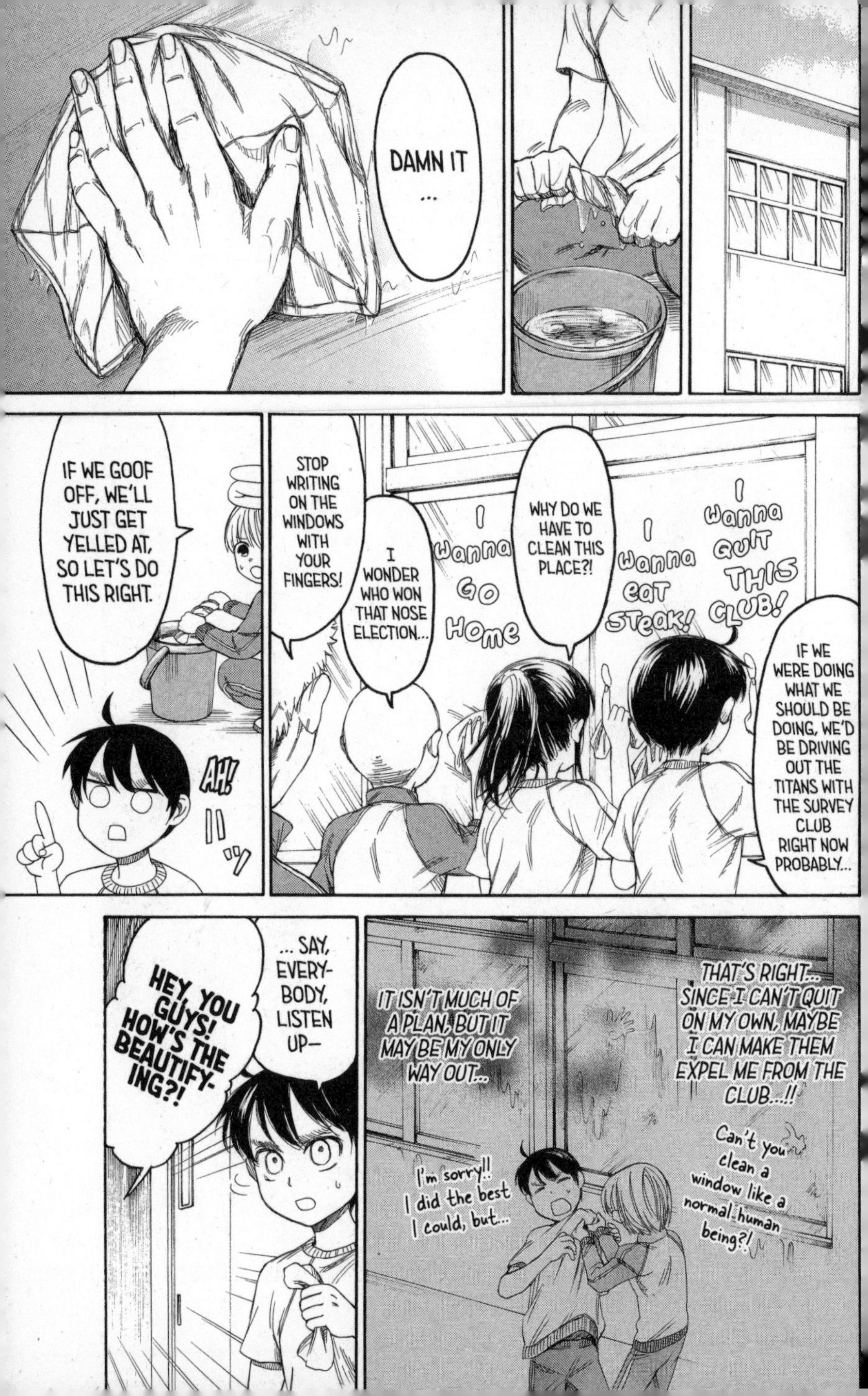
DAMN IT ...
I wanna QUIT THIS CLUB!
IF WE WERE DOING WHAT WE SHOULD BE DOING, WE'D BE DRIVING OUT THE TITANS WITH THE SURVEY CLUB RIGHT NOW PROBABLY...
I wanna eat STEAK!
WHY DO WE HAVE TO CLEAN THIS PLACE?!
I wanna GO Home
I WONDER WHO WON THAT NOSE ELECTION...
STOP WRITING ON THE WINDOWS WITH YOUR FINGERS!
IF WE GOOF OFF, WE'LL JUST GET YELLED AT, SO LET'S DO THIS RIGHT.
AH!
THAT'S RIGHT... SINCE I CAN'T QUIT ON MY OWN, MAYBE I CAN MAKE THEM EXPEL ME FROM THE CLUB...!!
IT ISN'T MUCH OF A PLAN, BUT IT MAY BE MY ONLY WAY OUT...
Can't you clean a window like a normal human being?!
I'm sorry!! I did the best I could, but...
... SAY, EVERY-BODY, LISTEN UP—
HEY, YOU GUYS! HOW'S THE BEAUTIFY-ING?!

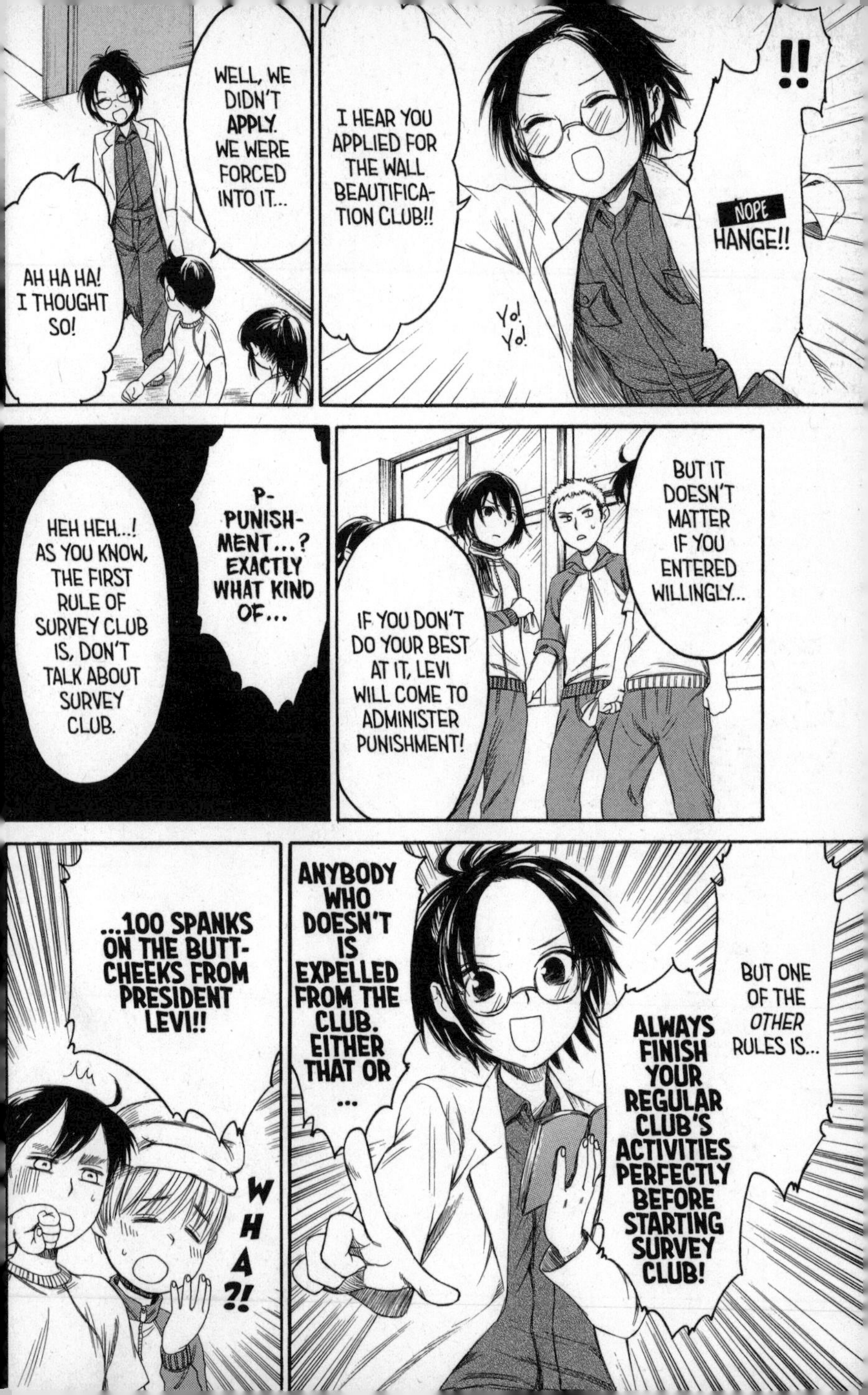
!!
NOPE
HANGE!!
Yo! Yo!
I HEAR YOU APPLIED FOR THE WALL BEAUTIFICATION CLUB!!
WELL, WE DIDN'T APPLY. WE WERE FORCED INTO IT...
AH HA HA! I THOUGHT SO!
BUT IT DOESN'T MATTER IF YOU ENTERED WILLINGLY...
IF YOU DON'T DO YOUR BEST AT IT, LEVI WILL COME TO ADMINISTER PUNISHMENT!
P-PUNISHMENT...? EXACTLY WHAT KIND OF...
HEH HEH...! AS YOU KNOW, THE FIRST RULE OF SURVEY CLUB IS, DON'T TALK ABOUT SURVEY CLUB.
BUT ONE OF THE OTHER RULES IS...
ALWAYS FINISH YOUR REGULAR CLUB'S ACTIVITIES PERFECTLY BEFORE STARTING SURVEY CLUB!
ANYBODY WHO DOESN'T IS EXPELLED FROM THE CLUB. EITHER THAT OR ...
...100 SPANKS ON THE BUTT-CHEEKS FROM PRESIDENT LEVI!!
WHA?!

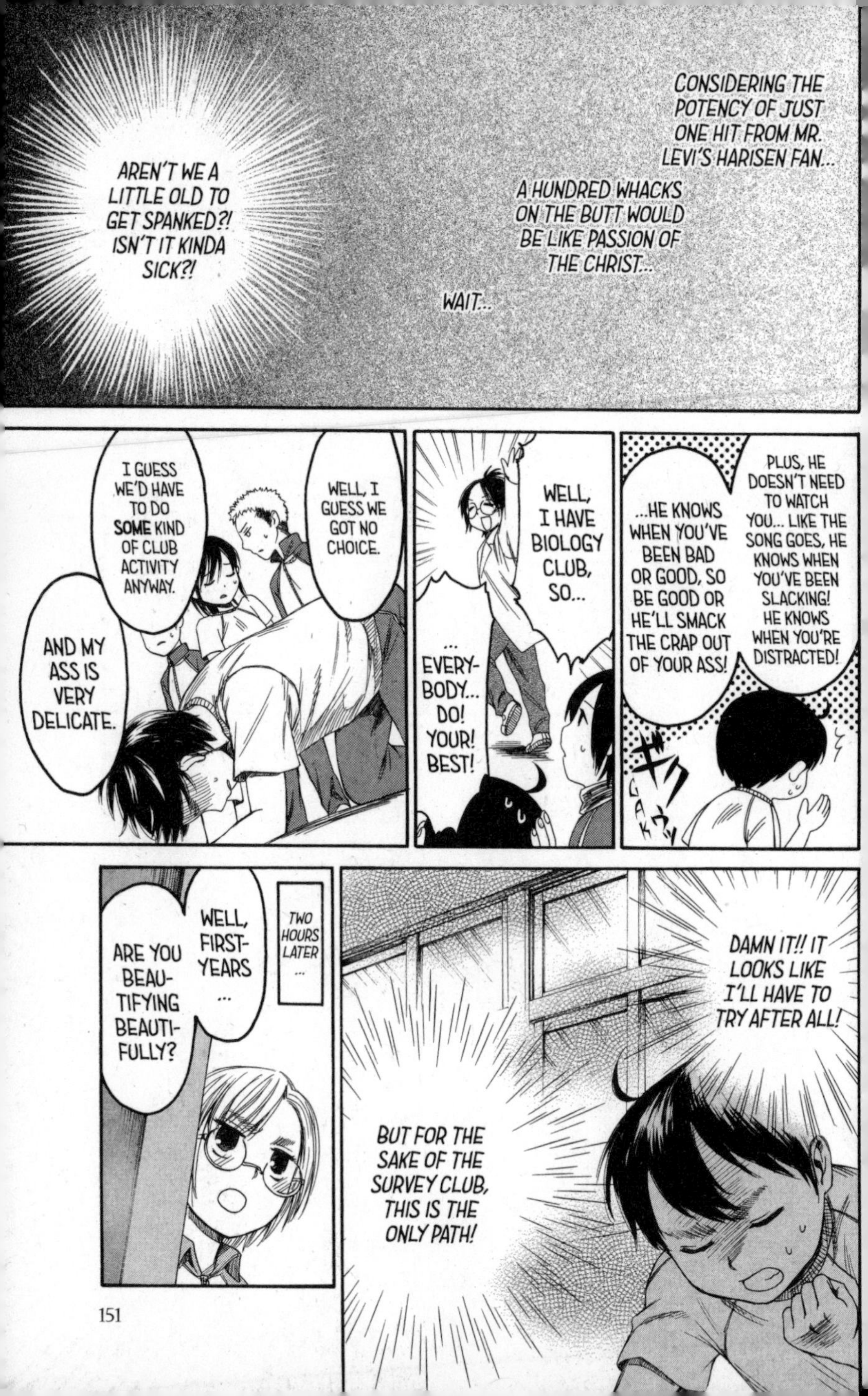
CONSIDERING THE POTENCY OF JUST ONE HIT FROM MR. LEVI'S HARISEN FAN...
A HUNDRED WHACKS ON THE BUTT WOULD BE LIKE PASSION OF THE CHRIST...
WAIT...
AREN'T WE A LITTLE OLD TO GET SPANKED?! ISN'T IT KINDA SICK?!
PLUS, HE DOESN'T NEED TO WATCH YOU... LIKE THE SONG GOES, HE KNOWS WHEN YOU'VE BEEN SLACKING! HE KNOWS WHEN YOU'RE DISTRACTED!
...HE KNOWS WHEN YOU'VE BEEN BAD OR GOOD, SO BE GOOD OR HE'LL SMACK THE CRAP OUT OF YOUR ASS!
WELL, I HAVE BIOLOGY CLUB, SO...
... EVERYBODY... DO! YOUR! BEST!
WELL, I GUESS WE GOT NO CHOICE.
I GUESS WE'D HAVE TO DO SOME KIND OF CLUB ACTIVITY ANYWAY.
AND MY ASS IS VERY DELICATE.
DAMN IT!! IT LOOKS LIKE I'LL HAVE TO TRY AFTER ALL!
BUT FOR THE SAKE OF THE SURVEY CLUB, THIS IS THE ONLY PATH!
TWO HOURS LATER ...
WELL, FIRST-YEARS ...
ARE YOU BEAUTIFYING BEAUTIFULLY?

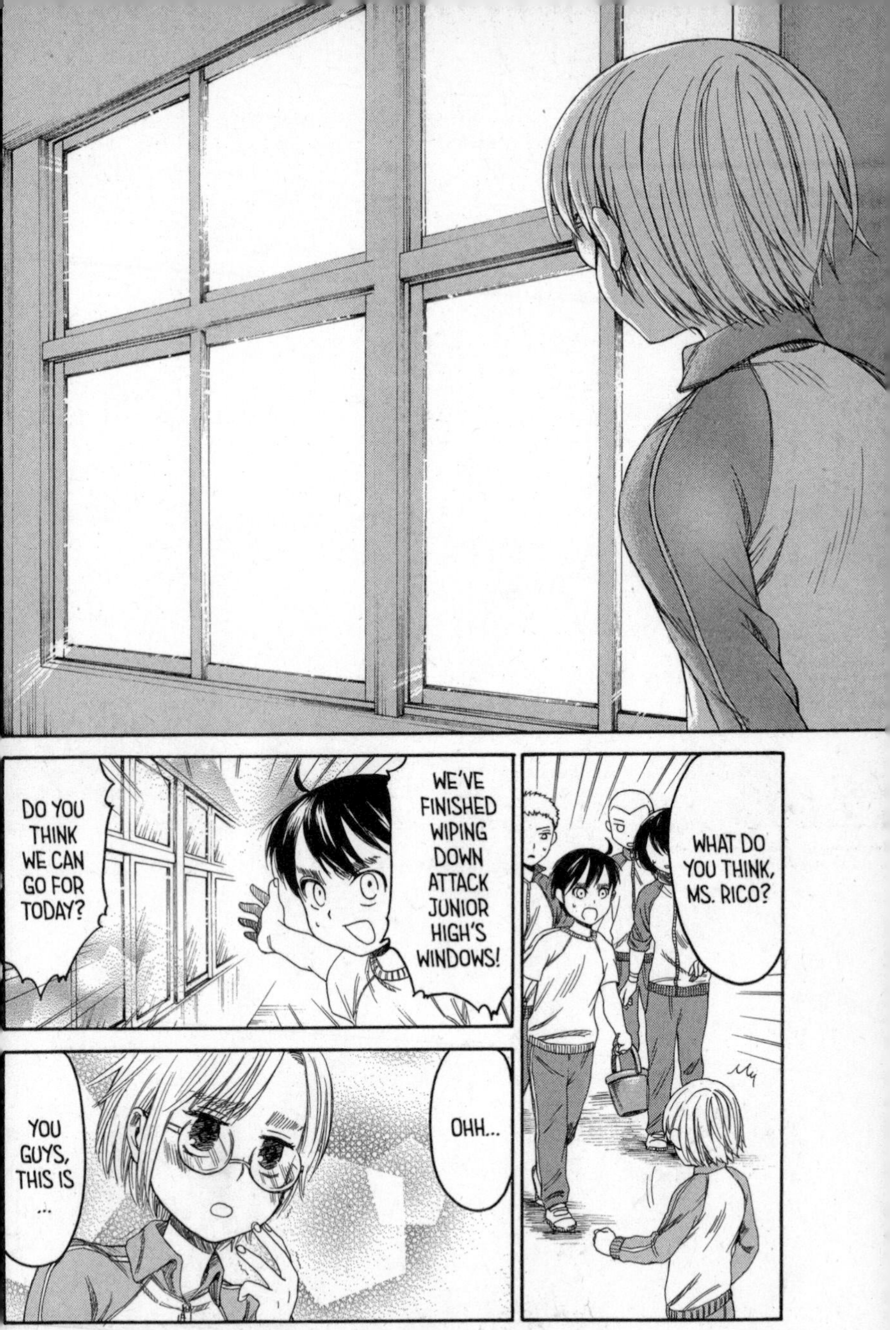
WHAT DO YOU THINK, MS. RICO?
WE'VE FINISHED WIPING DOWN ATTACK JUNIOR HIGH'S WINDOWS!
DO YOU THINK WE CAN GO FOR TODAY?
OHH...
YOU GUYS, THIS IS ...

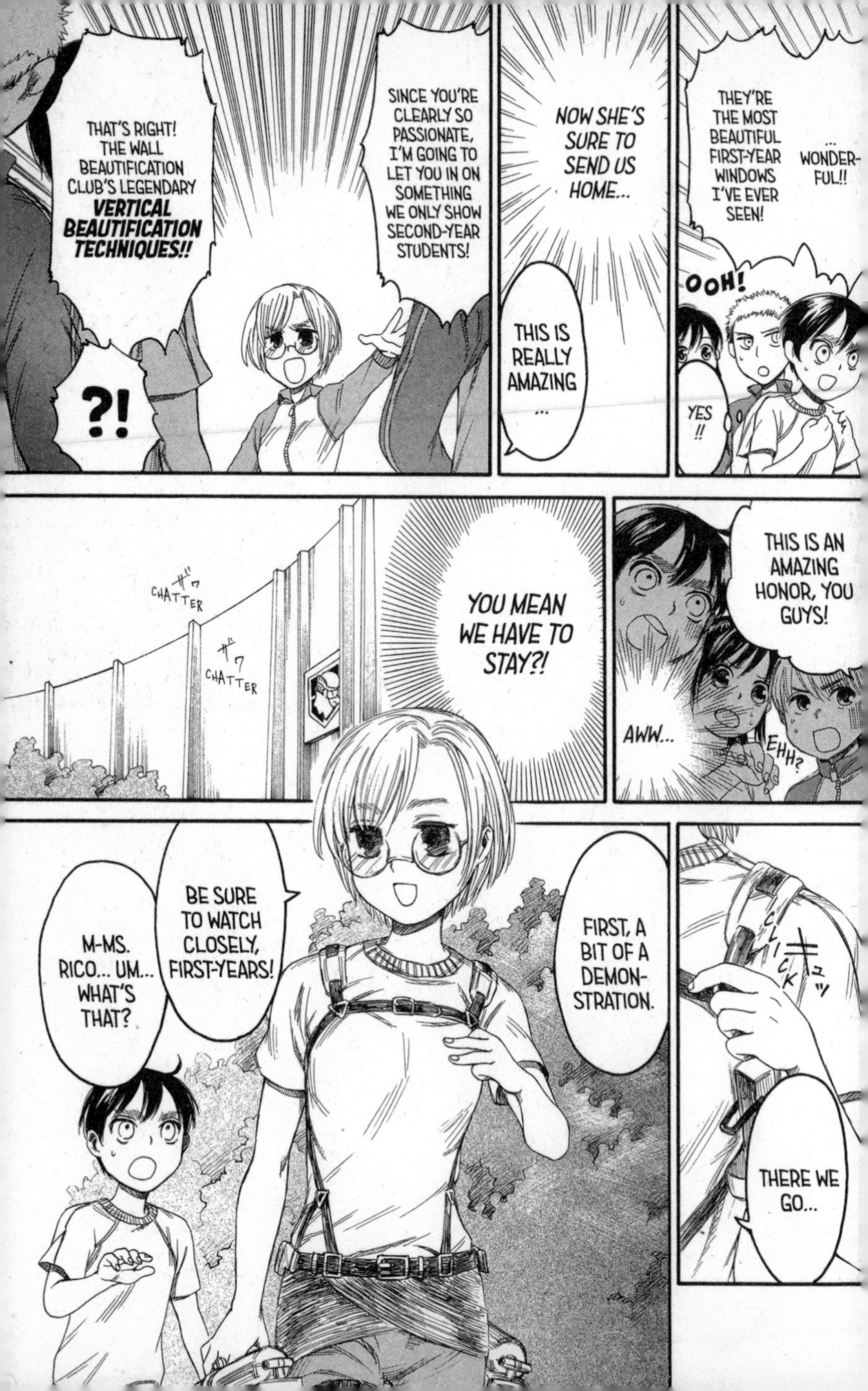
... WONDER-FUL!!
THEY'RE THE MOST BEAUTIFUL FIRST-YEAR WINDOWS I'VE EVER SEEN!
OOH!
YES!!
NOW SHE'S SURE TO SEND US HOME...
THIS IS REALLY AMAZING...
SINCE YOU'RE CLEARLY SO PASSIONATE, I'M GOING TO LET YOU IN ON SOMETHING WE ONLY SHOW SECOND-YEAR STUDENTS!
THAT'S RIGHT! THE WALL BEAUTIFICATION CLUB'S LEGENDARY **VERTICAL BEAUTIFICATION TECHNIQUES!!**
?!
THIS IS AN AMAZING HONOR, YOU GUYS!
AWW...
EHH?
YOU MEAN WE HAVE TO STAY?!
ザワ CHATTER
ザワ CHATTER
キュッ CLICK
THERE WE GO...
FIRST, A BIT OF A DEMON-STRATION.
BE SURE TO WATCH CLOSELY, FIRST-YEARS!
M-MS. RICO... UM... WHAT'S THAT?

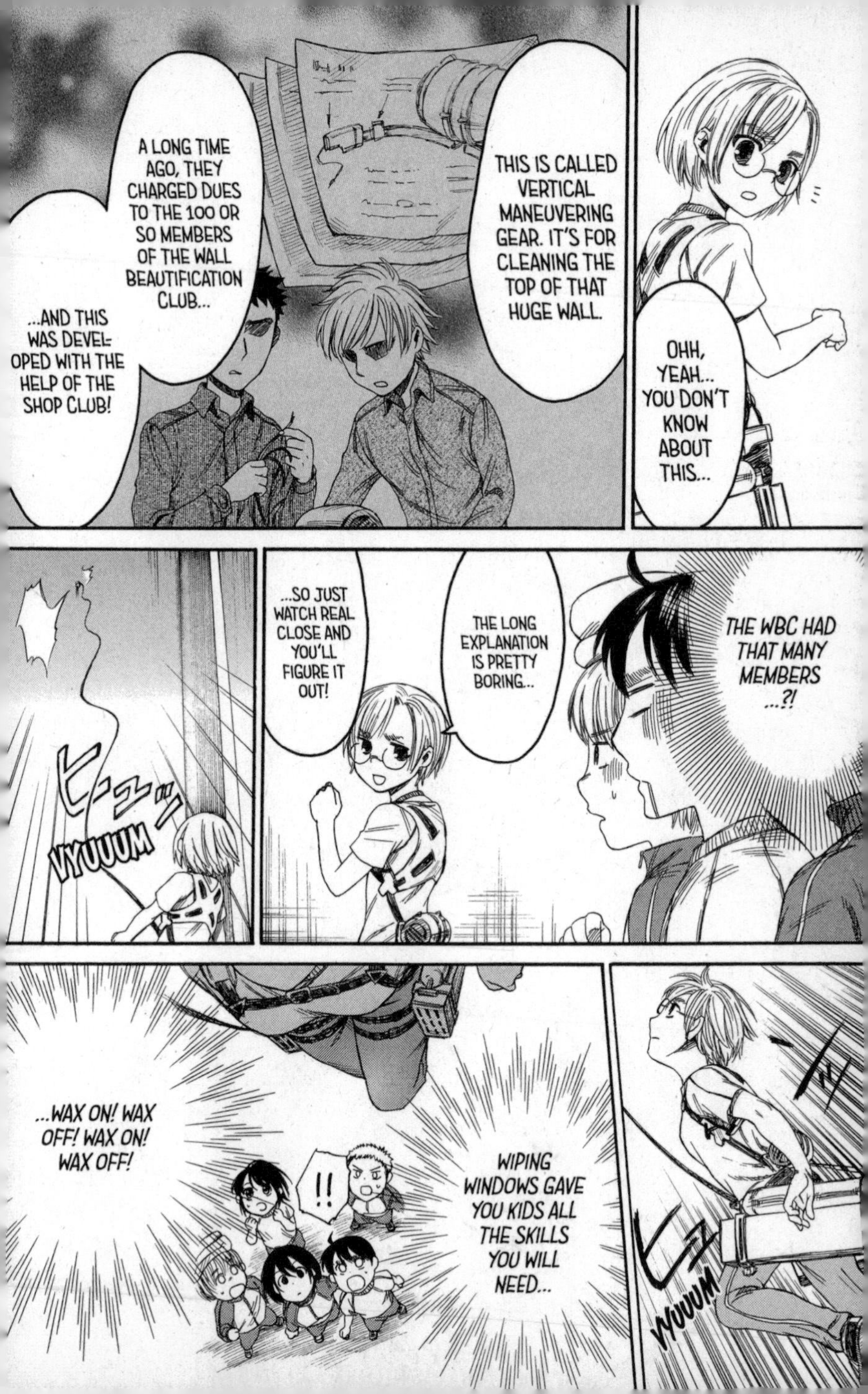
OHH, YEAH... YOU DON'T KNOW ABOUT THIS...
THIS IS CALLED VERTICAL MANEUVERING GEAR. IT'S FOR CLEANING THE TOP OF THAT HUGE WALL.
A LONG TIME AGO, THEY CHARGED DUES TO THE 100 OR SO MEMBERS OF THE WALL BEAUTIFICATION CLUB...
...AND THIS WAS DEVEL-OPED WITH THE HELP OF THE SHOP CLUB!
THE WBC HAD THAT MANY MEMBERS ...?!
THE LONG EXPLANATION IS PRETTY BORING...
...SO JUST WATCH REAL CLOSE AND YOU'LL FIGURE IT OUT!
VYUUUM
VYUUUM
WIPING WINDOWS GAVE YOU KIDS ALL THE SKILLS YOU WILL NEED...
!!
...WAX ON! WAX OFF! WAX ON! WAX OFF!

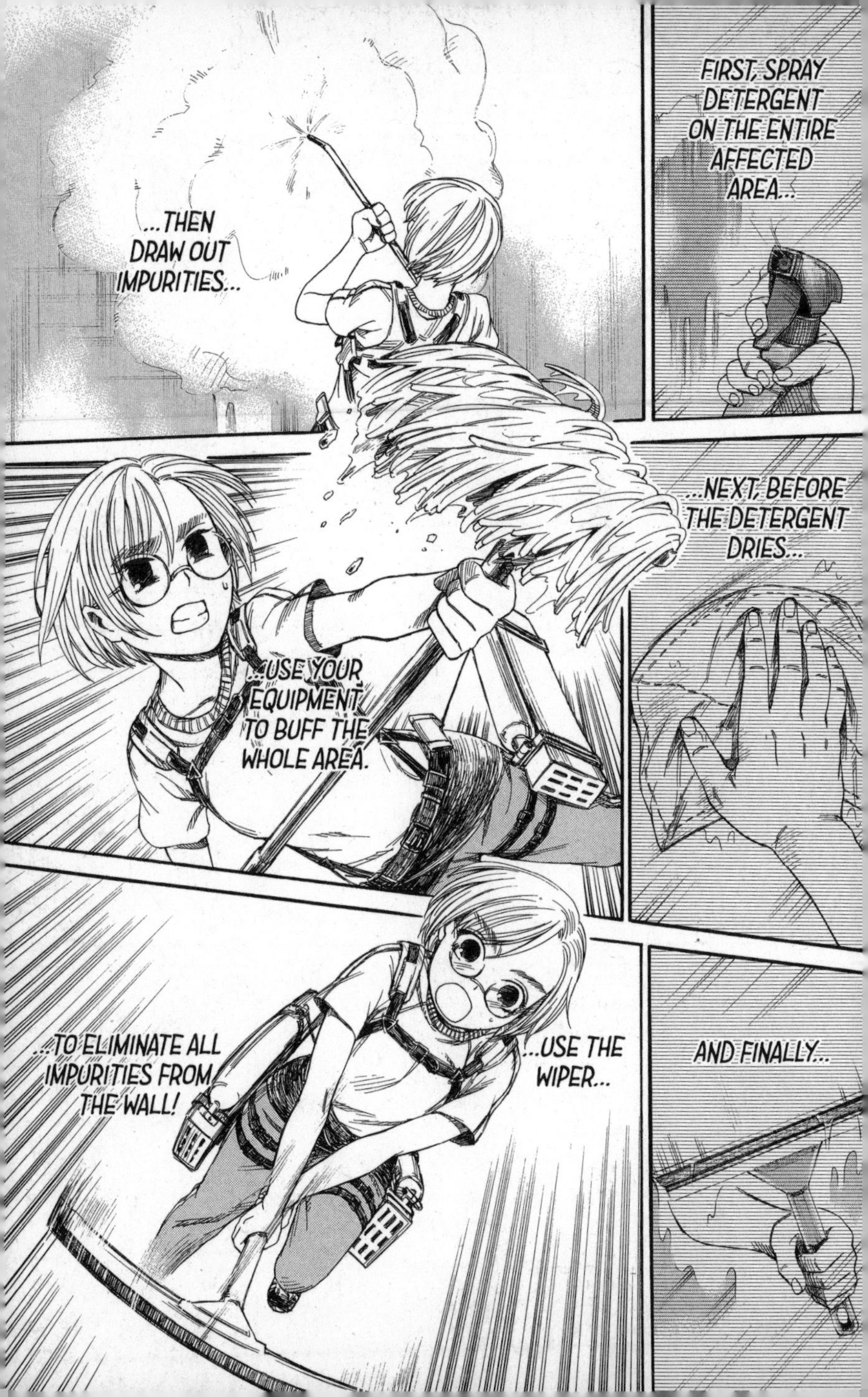
FIRST, SPRAY DETERGENT ON THE ENTIRE AFFECTED AREA...
...THEN DRAW OUT IMPURITIES...
...NEXT, BEFORE THE DETERGENT DRIES...
...USE YOUR EQUIPMENT TO BUFF THE WHOLE AREA.
AND FINALLY...
...USE THE WIPER...
...TO ELIMINATE ALL IMPURITIES FROM THE WALL!

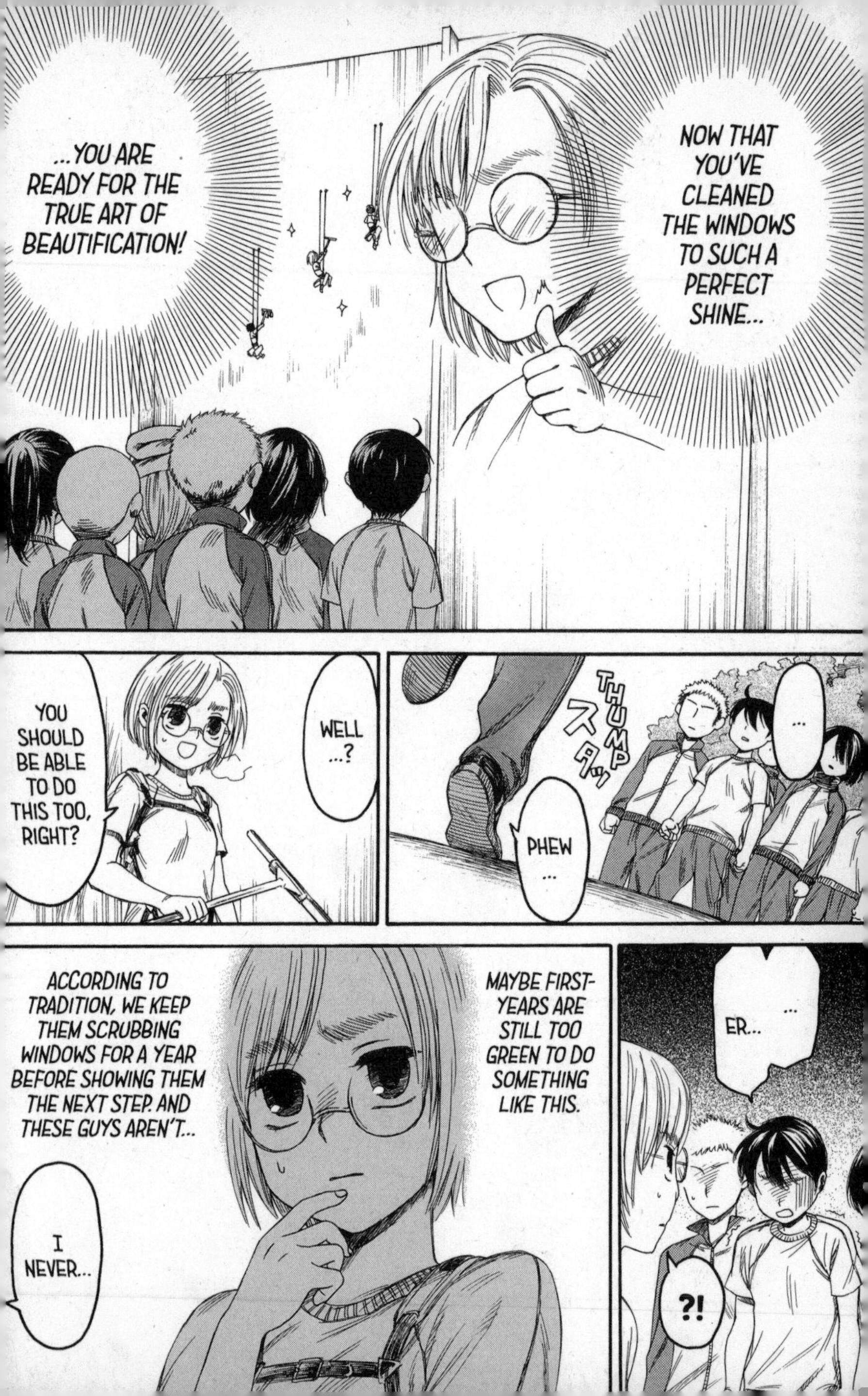
NOW THAT YOU'VE CLEANED THE WINDOWS TO SUCH A PERFECT SHINE...
...YOU ARE READY FOR THE TRUE ART OF BEAUTIFICATION!
...
THUMP
スタッ
PHEW ...
WELL ...?
YOU SHOULD BE ABLE TO DO THIS TOO, RIGHT?
... ER...
?!
MAYBE FIRST-YEARS ARE STILL TOO GREEN TO DO SOMETHING LIKE THIS.
ACCORDING TO TRADITION, WE KEEP THEM SCRUBBING WINDOWS FOR A YEAR BEFORE SHOWING THEM THE NEXT STEP. AND THESE GUYS AREN'T...
I NEVER...

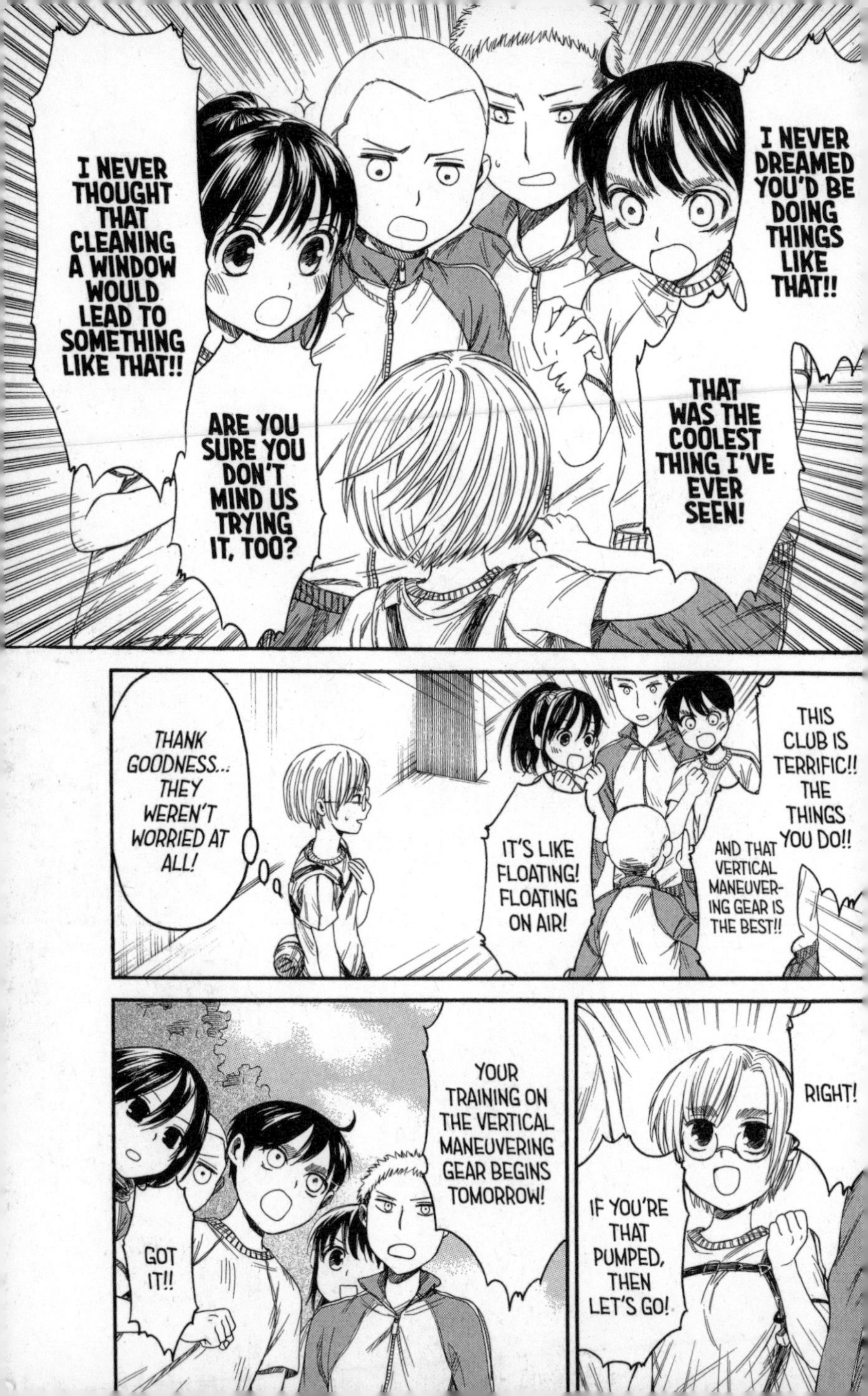
I NEVER DREAMED YOU'D BE DOING THINGS LIKE THAT!!
I NEVER THOUGHT THAT CLEANING A WINDOW WOULD LEAD TO SOMETHING LIKE THAT!!
THAT WAS THE COOLEST THING I'VE EVER SEEN!
ARE YOU SURE YOU DON'T MIND US TRYING IT, TOO?
THIS CLUB IS TERRIFIC!! THE THINGS YOU DO!!
AND THAT VERTICAL MANEUVER-ING GEAR IS THE BEST!!
IT'S LIKE FLOATING! FLOATING ON AIR!
THANK GOODNESS... THEY WEREN'T WORRIED AT ALL!
RIGHT!
IF YOU'RE THAT PUMPED, THEN LET'S GO!
YOUR TRAINING ON THE VERTICAL MANEUVERING GEAR BEGINS TOMORROW!
GOT IT!!

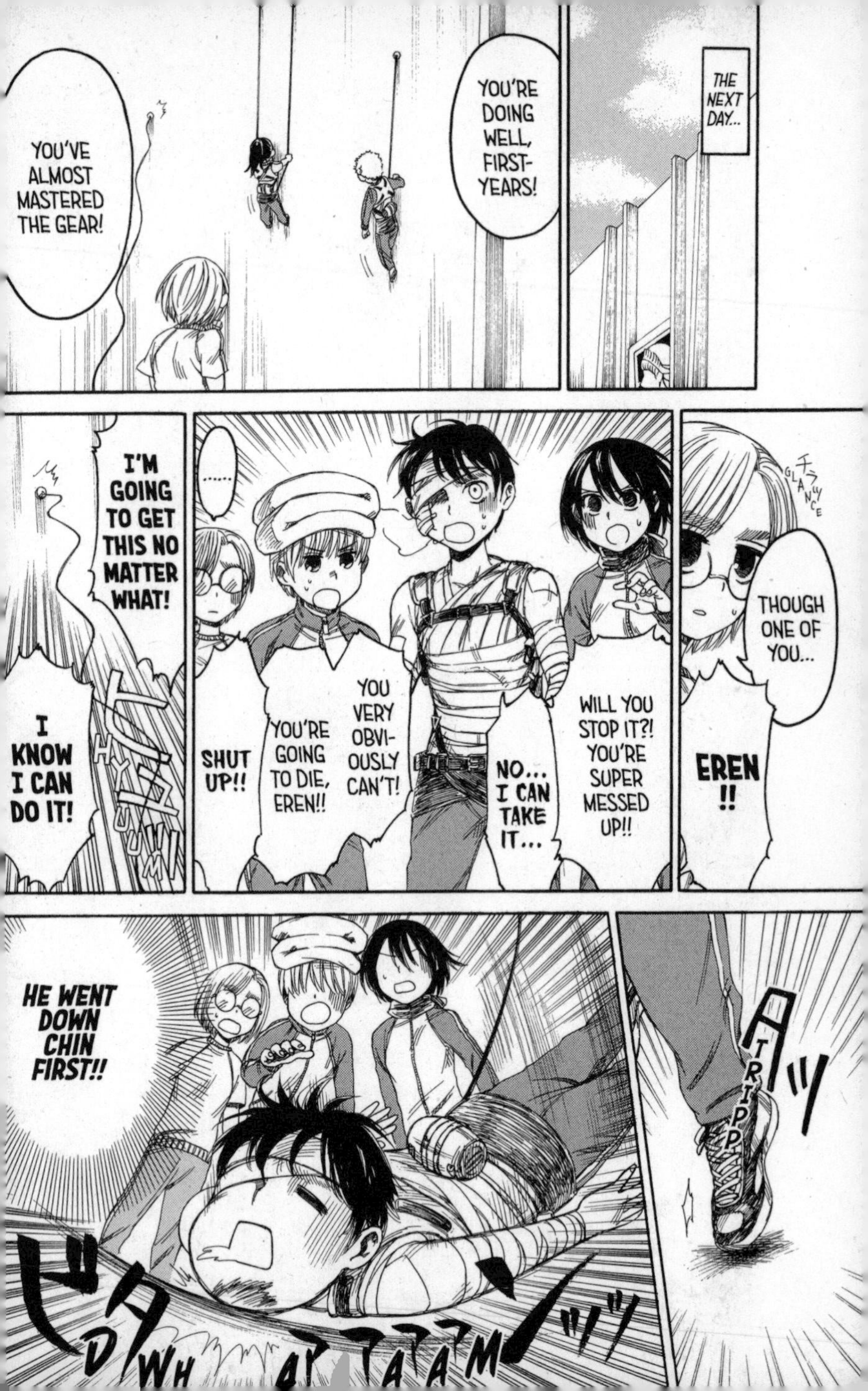
THE NEXT DAY...
YOU'RE DOING WELL, FIRST-YEARS!
YOU'VE ALMOST MASTERED THE GEAR!
GLANCE
THOUGH ONE OF YOU...
EREN!!
......
WILL YOU STOP IT?! YOU'RE SUPER MESSED UP!!
NO... I CAN TAKE IT...
YOU VERY OBVIOUSLY CAN'T!
YOU'RE GOING TO DIE, EREN!!
SHUT UP!!
I'M GOING TO GET THIS NO MATTER WHAT!
I KNOW I CAN DO IT!
TRIPP
HE WENT DOWN CHIN FIRST!!

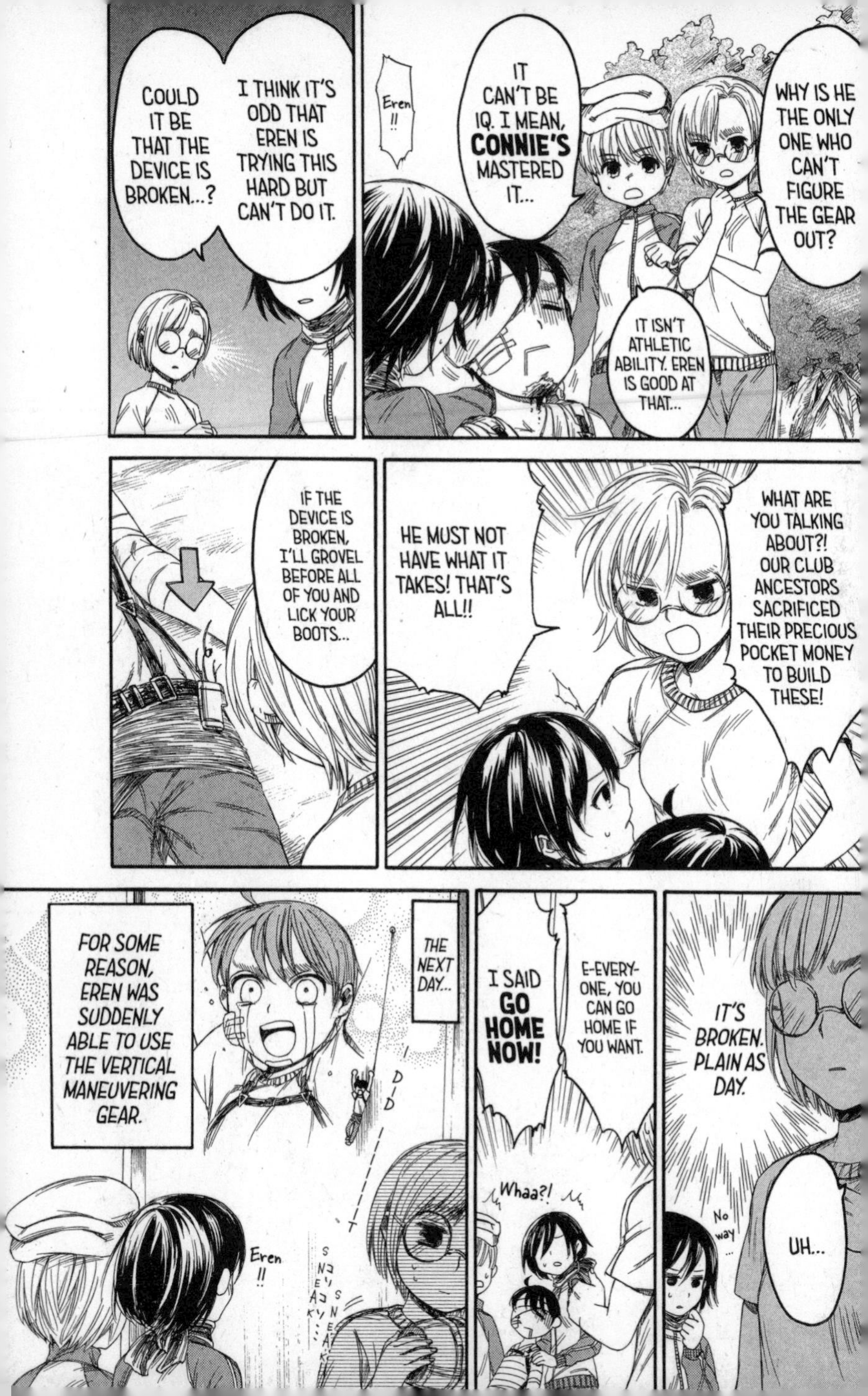
WHY IS HE THE ONLY ONE WHO CAN'T FIGURE THE GEAR OUT?
IT CAN'T BE IQ. I MEAN, **CONNIE'S** MASTERED IT...
IT ISN'T ATHLETIC ABILITY. EREN IS GOOD AT THAT...
Eren !!
I THINK IT'S ODD THAT EREN IS TRYING THIS HARD BUT CAN'T DO IT.
COULD IT BE THAT THE DEVICE IS BROKEN...?
WHAT ARE YOU TALKING ABOUT?! OUR CLUB ANCESTORS SACRIFICED THEIR PRECIOUS POCKET MONEY TO BUILD THESE!
HE MUST NOT HAVE WHAT IT TAKES! THAT'S ALL!!
IF THE DEVICE IS BROKEN, I'LL GROVEL BEFORE ALL OF YOU AND LICK YOUR BOOTS...
IT'S BROKEN. PLAIN AS DAY.
UH...
No way...
E-EVERY-ONE, YOU CAN GO HOME IF YOU WANT.
I SAID **GO HOME NOW!**
Whaa?!
THE NEXT DAY...
FOR SOME REASON, EREN WAS SUDDENLY ABLE TO USE THE VERTICAL MANEUVERING GEAR.
I DID IT
Eren !!
SNEAK SNEAK

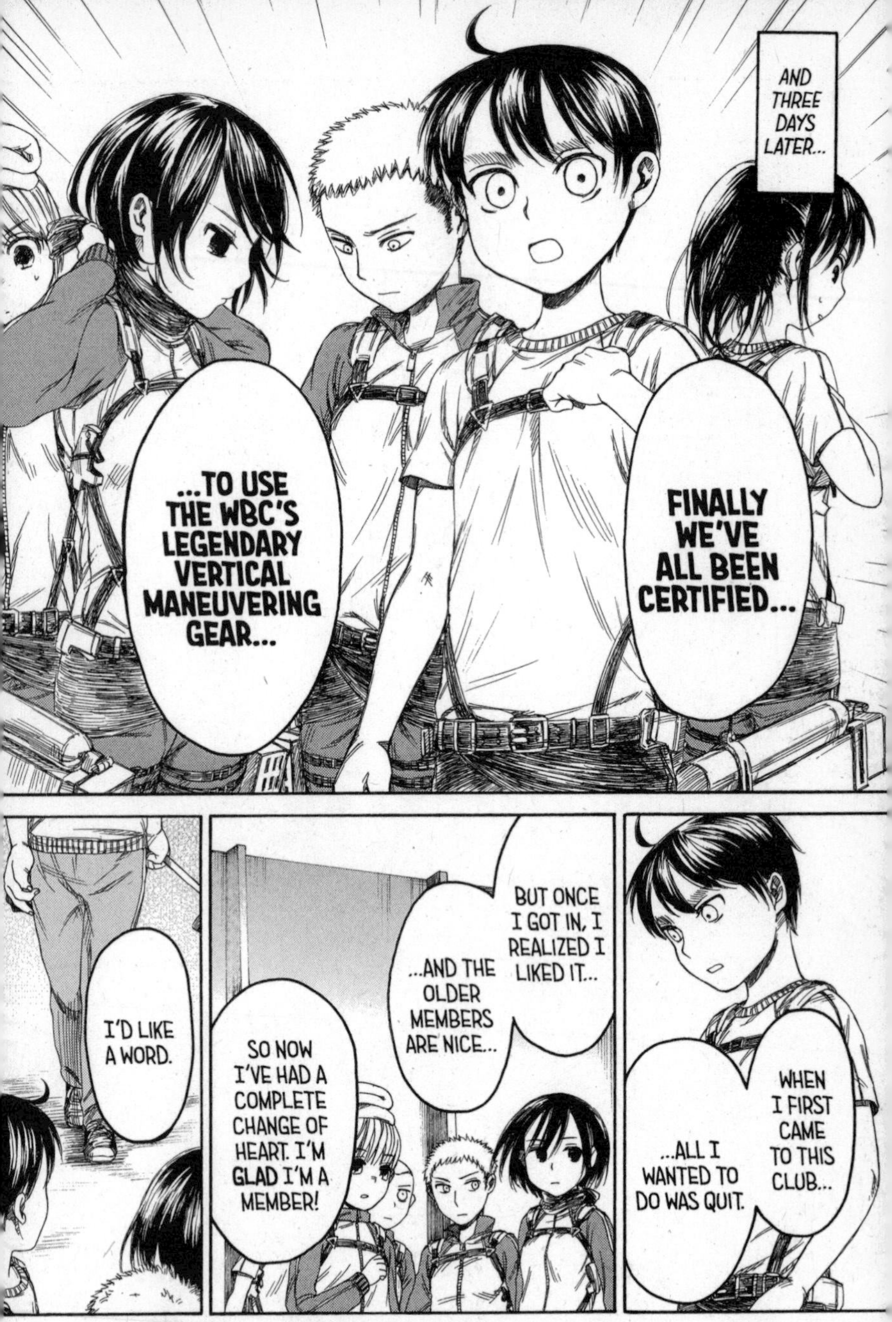
AND THREE DAYS LATER...
FINALLY WE'VE ALL BEEN CERTIFIED...
...TO USE THE WBC'S LEGENDARY VERTICAL MANEUVERING GEAR...
WHEN I FIRST CAME TO THIS CLUB...
...ALL I WANTED TO DO WAS QUIT.
BUT ONCE I GOT IN, I REALIZED I LIKED IT...
...AND THE OLDER MEMBERS ARE NICE...
SO NOW I'VE HAD A COMPLETE CHANGE OF HEART. I'M GLAD I'M A MEMBER!
I'D LIKE A WORD.

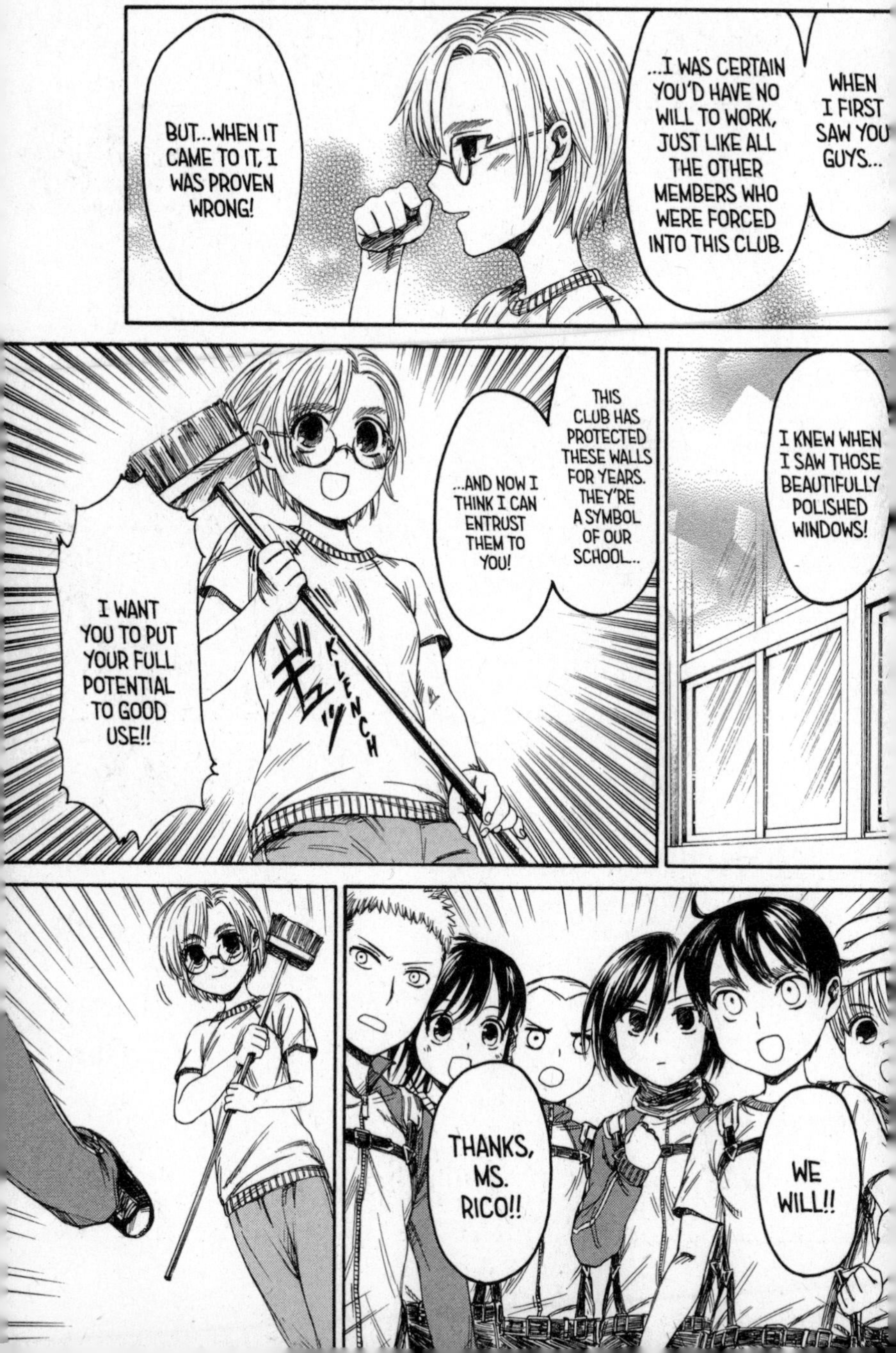
WHEN I FIRST SAW YOU GUYS...
...I WAS CERTAIN YOU'D HAVE NO WILL TO WORK, JUST LIKE ALL THE OTHER MEMBERS WHO WERE FORCED INTO THIS CLUB.
BUT...WHEN IT CAME TO IT, I WAS PROVEN WRONG!
I KNEW WHEN I SAW THOSE BEAUTIFULLY POLISHED WINDOWS!
THIS CLUB HAS PROTECTED THESE WALLS FOR YEARS. THEY'RE A SYMBOL OF OUR SCHOOL...
...AND NOW I THINK I CAN ENTRUST THEM TO YOU!
KLENCH
I WANT YOU TO PUT YOUR FULL POTENTIAL TO GOOD USE!!
WE WILL!!
THANKS, MS. RICO!!

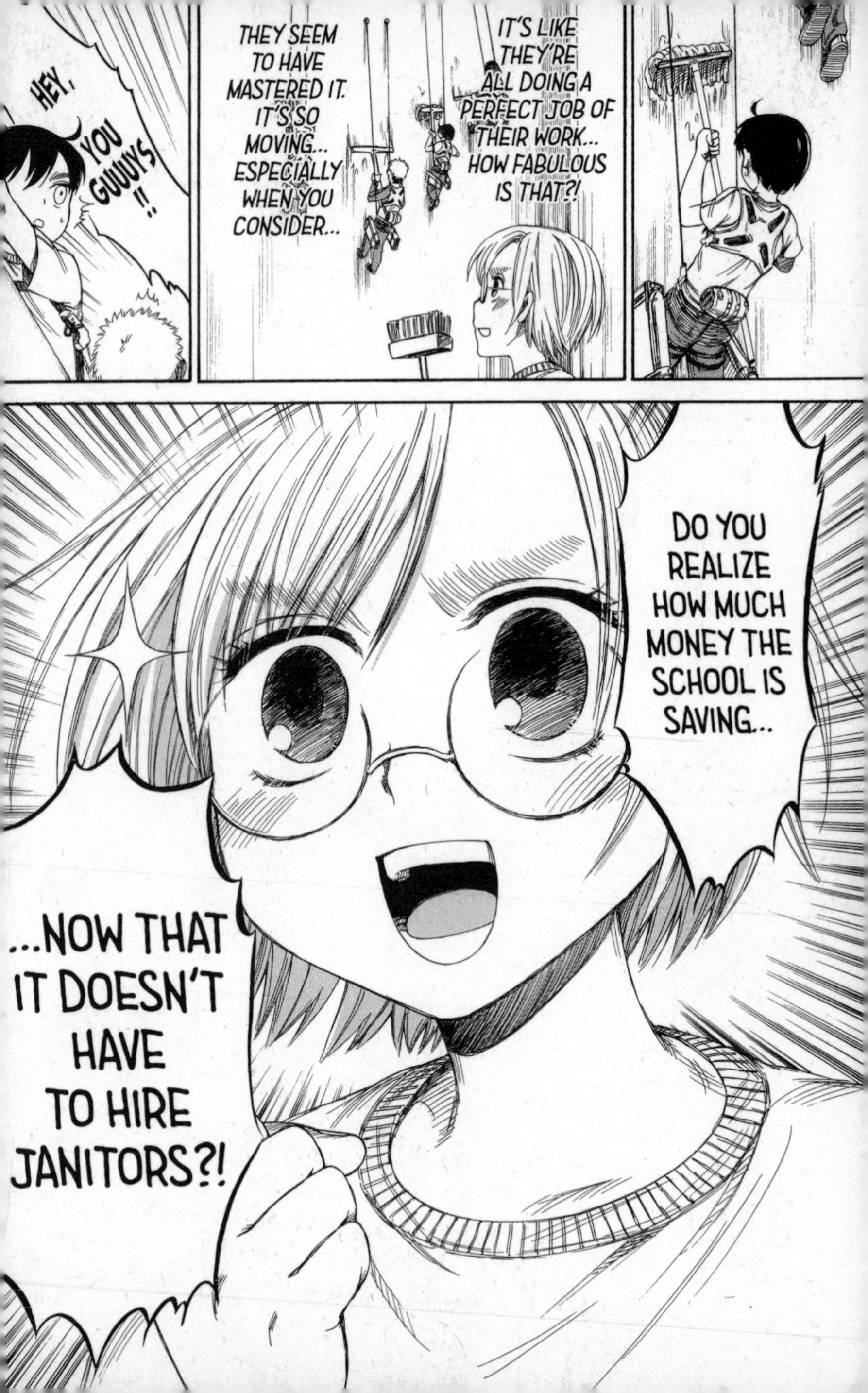
IT'S LIKE THEY'RE ALL DOING A PERFECT JOB OF THEIR WORK... HOW FABULOUS IS THAT?!
THEY SEEM TO HAVE MASTERED IT. IT'S SO MOVING... ESPECIALLY WHEN YOU CONSIDER...
HEY, YOU GUUUYS!!
DO YOU REALIZE HOW MUCH MONEY THE SCHOOL IS SAVING...
...NOW THAT IT DOESN'T HAVE TO HIRE JANITORS?!

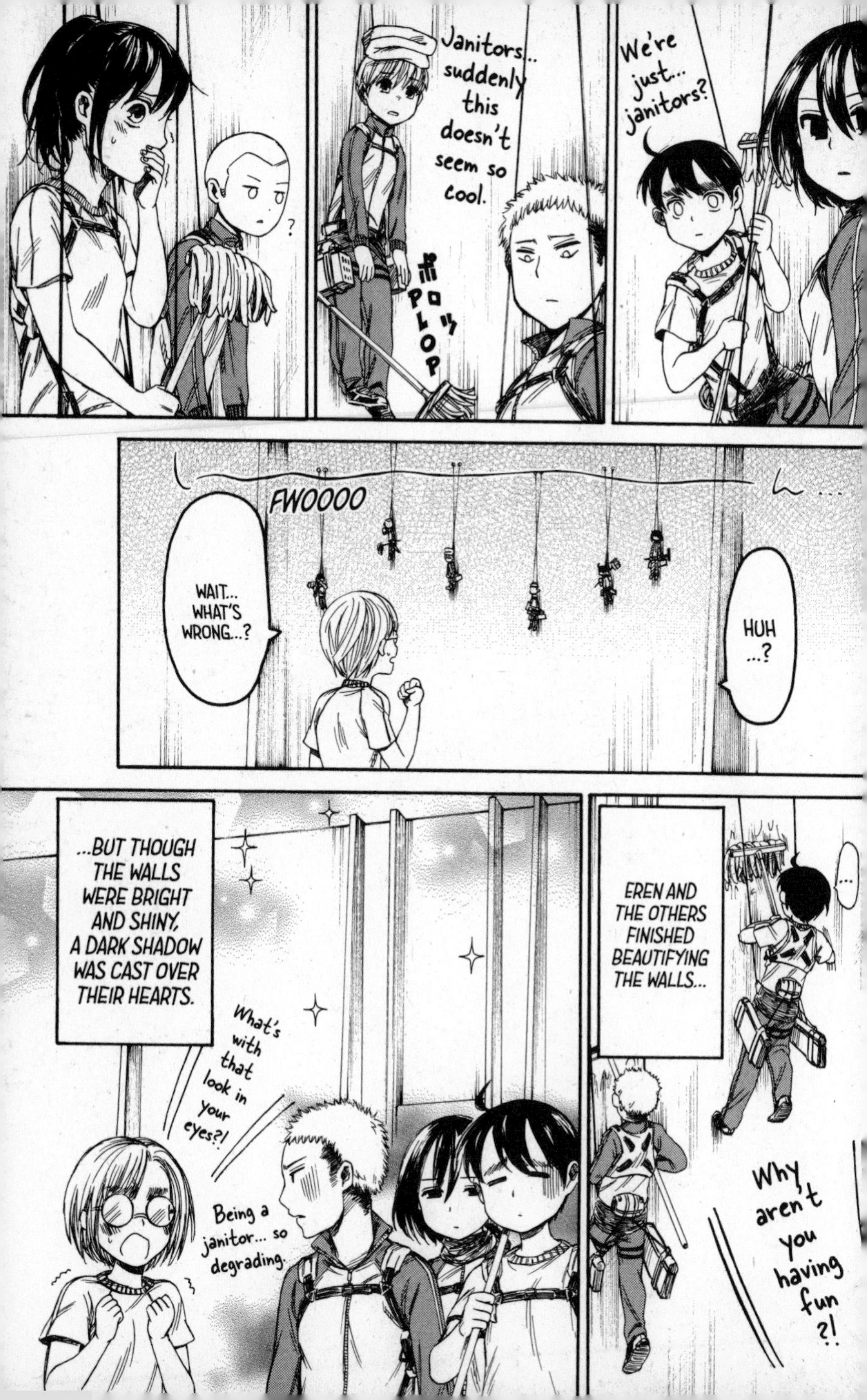
We're just... janitors?
Janitors... suddenly this doesn't seem so cool.
ポロッ
PLOP
?
HUH ...?
FWOOOO
WAIT... WHAT'S WRONG...?
EREN AND THE OTHERS FINISHED BEAUTIFYING THE WALLS...
...
Why aren't you having fun?!
...BUT THOUGH THE WALLS WERE BRIGHT AND SHINY, A DARK SHADOW WAS CAST OVER THEIR HEARTS.
What's with that look in your eyes?!
Being a janitor... so degrading.

This is
a weird
book...

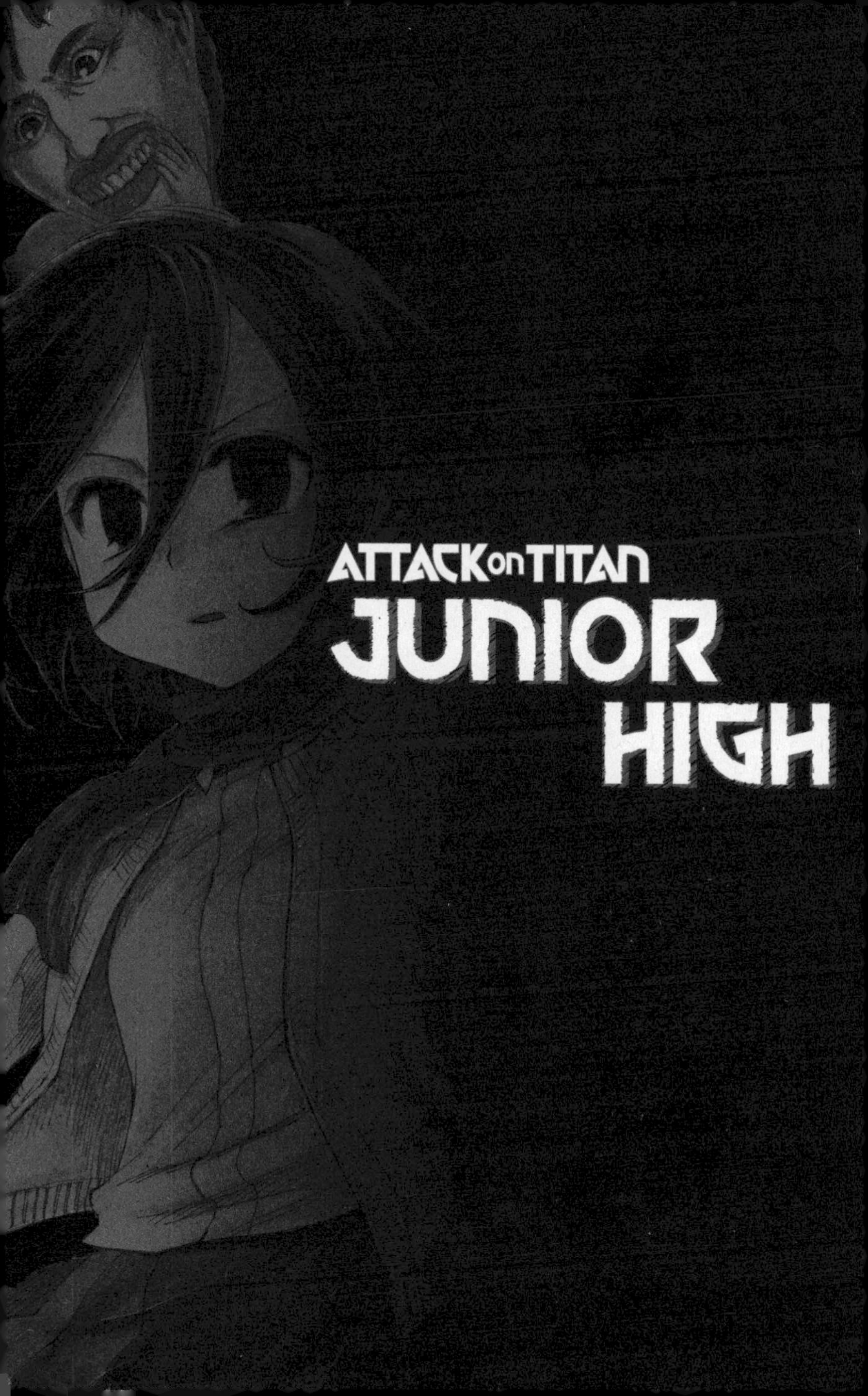
ATTACK on TITAN
JUNIOR HIGH

Contents

SCHEDULE FOR FRIDAY, AUGUST 9

MIKASA

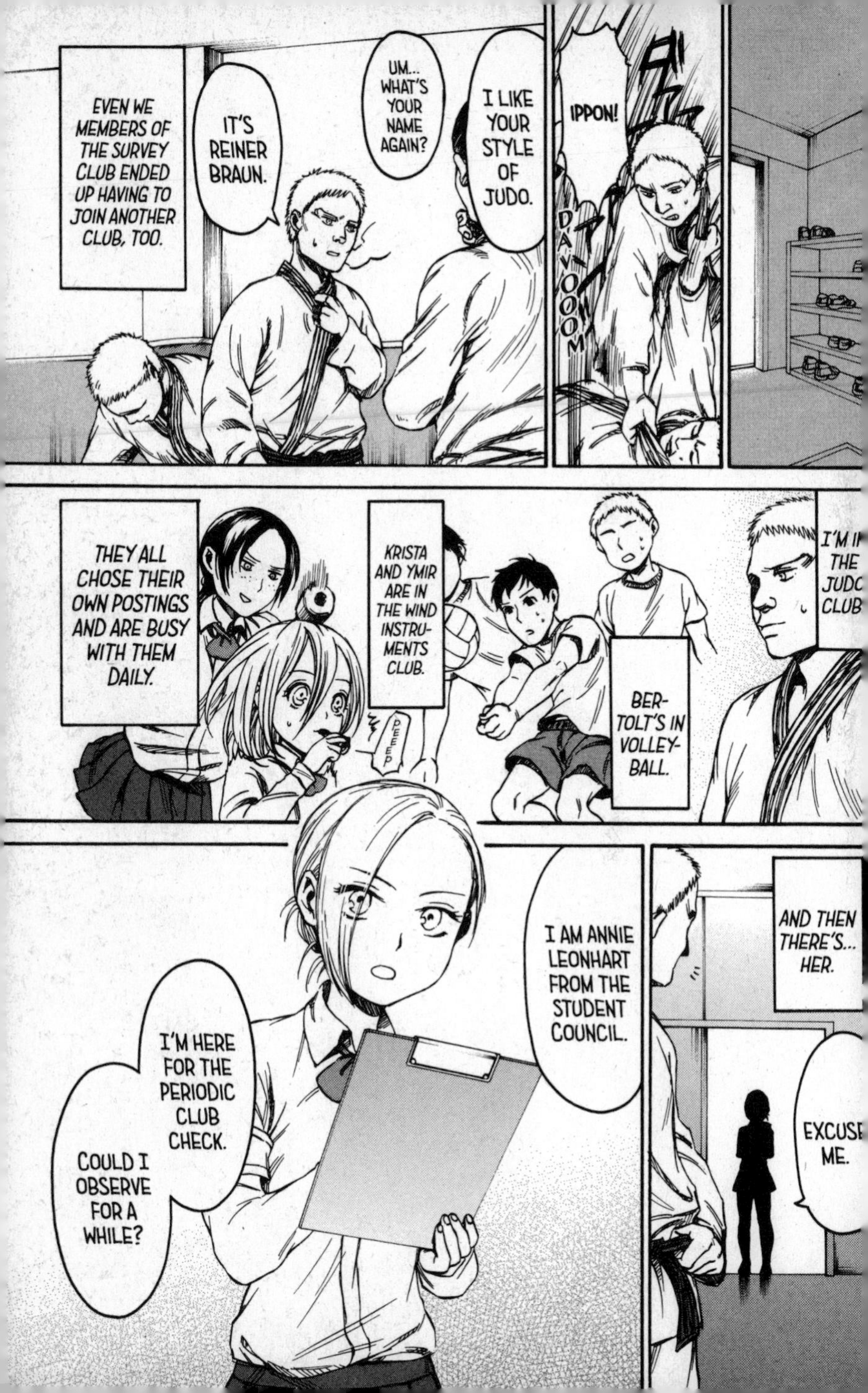
IPPON!
DAVOOOOM
I LIKE YOUR STYLE OF JUDO.
UM... WHAT'S YOUR NAME AGAIN?
IT'S REINER BRAUN.
EVEN WE MEMBERS OF THE SURVEY CLUB ENDED UP HAVING TO JOIN ANOTHER CLUB, TOO.
I'M I THE JUDC CLUB
BER-TOLT'S IN VOLLEY-BALL.
KRISTA AND YMIR ARE IN THE WIND INSTRU-MENTS CLUB.
PEEEP
THEY ALL CHOSE THEIR OWN POSTINGS AND ARE BUSY WITH THEM DAILY.
AND THEN THERE'S... HER.
EXCUSI ME.
I AM ANNIE LEONHART FROM THE STUDENT COUNCIL.
I'M HERE FOR THE PERIODIC CLUB CHECK.
COULD I OBSERVE FOR A WHILE?

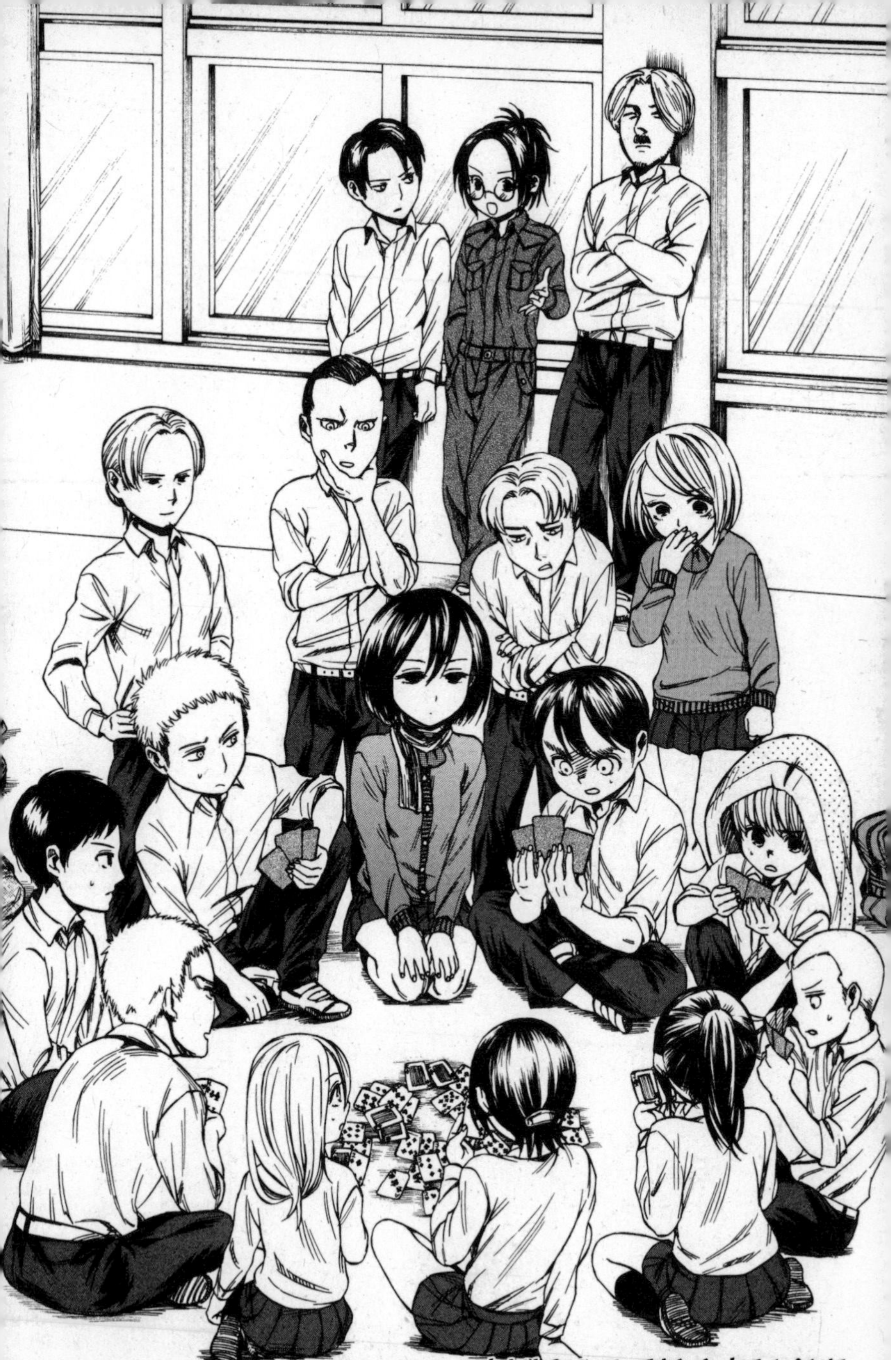

NINTH PERIOD: THIS IS NOT A GAME

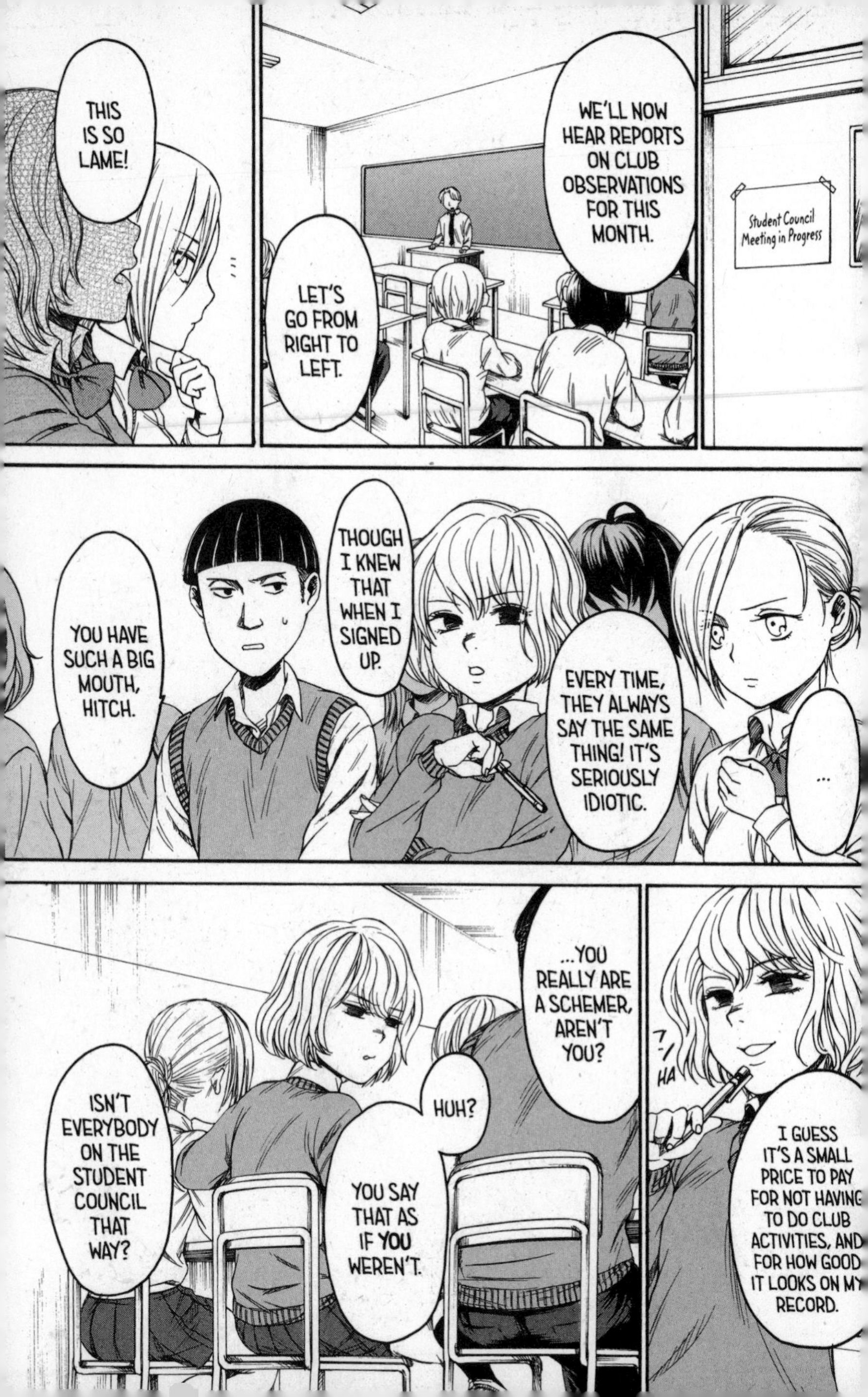
Student Council Meeting in Progress
WE'LL NOW HEAR REPORTS ON CLUB OBSERVATIONS FOR THIS MONTH.
LET'S GO FROM RIGHT TO LEFT.
THIS IS SO LAME!
...
EVERY TIME, THEY ALWAYS SAY THE SAME THING! IT'S SERIOUSLY IDIOTIC.
THOUGH I KNEW THAT WHEN I SIGNED UP.
YOU HAVE SUCH A BIG MOUTH, HITCH.
I GUESS IT'S A SMALL PRICE TO PAY FOR NOT HAVING TO DO CLUB ACTIVITIES, AND FOR HOW GOOD IT LOOKS ON MY RECORD.
HA
...YOU REALLY ARE A SCHEMER, AREN'T YOU?
HUH?
YOU SAY THAT AS IF YOU WEREN'T.
ISN'T EVERYBODY ON THE STUDENT COUNCIL THAT WAY?

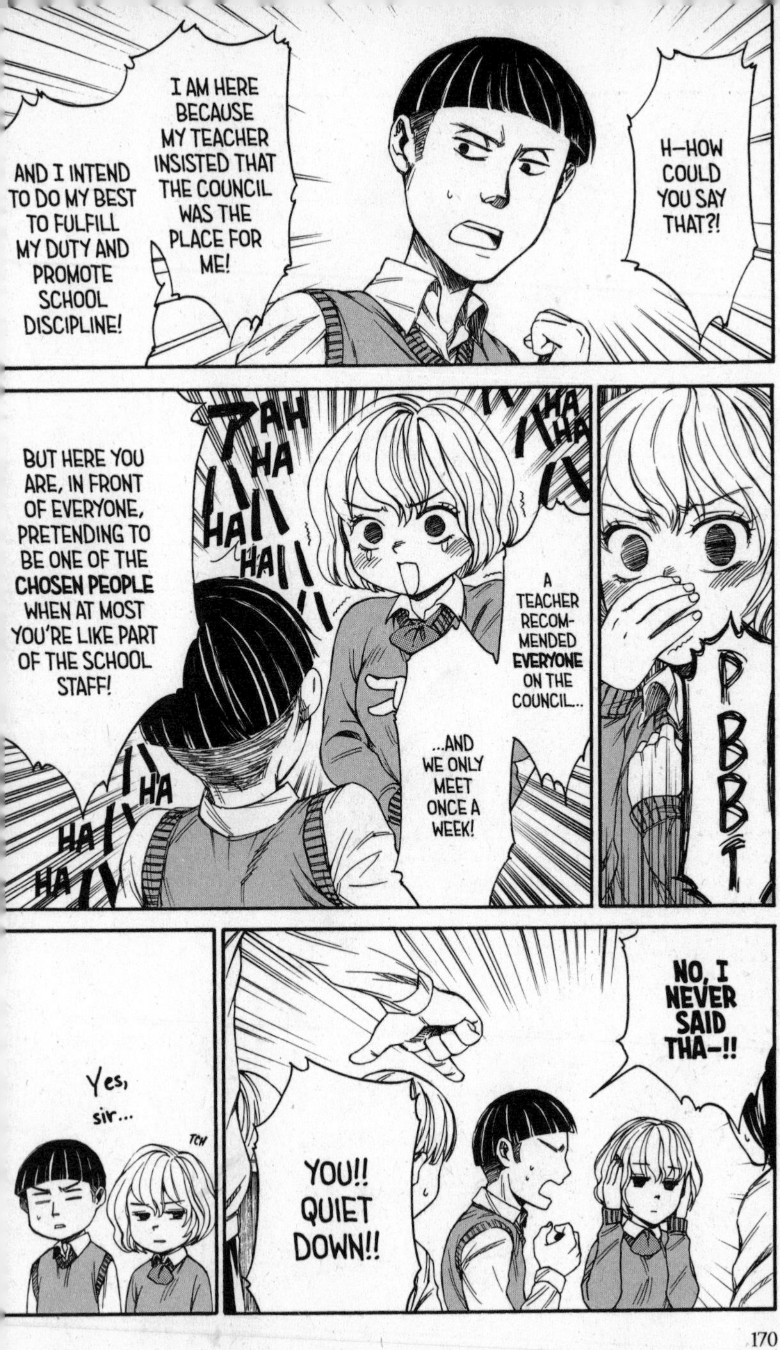
H-HOW COULD YOU SAY THAT?!
I AM HERE BECAUSE MY TEACHER INSISTED THAT THE COUNCIL WAS THE PLACE FOR ME!
AND I INTEND TO DO MY BEST TO FULFILL MY DUTY AND PROMOTE SCHOOL DISCIPLINE!
PBBT
HAHA
A TEACHER RECOMENDED EVERYONE ON THE COUNCIL...
...AND WE ONLY MEET ONCE A WEEK!
PAH HA HA HA
BUT HERE YOU ARE, IN FRONT OF EVERYONE, PRETENDING TO BE ONE OF THE CHOSEN PEOPLE WHEN AT MOST YOU'RE LIKE PART OF THE SCHOOL STAFF!
HA HA HA
NO, I NEVER SAID THA-!!
YOU!! QUIET DOWN!!
Yes, sir...
TCH

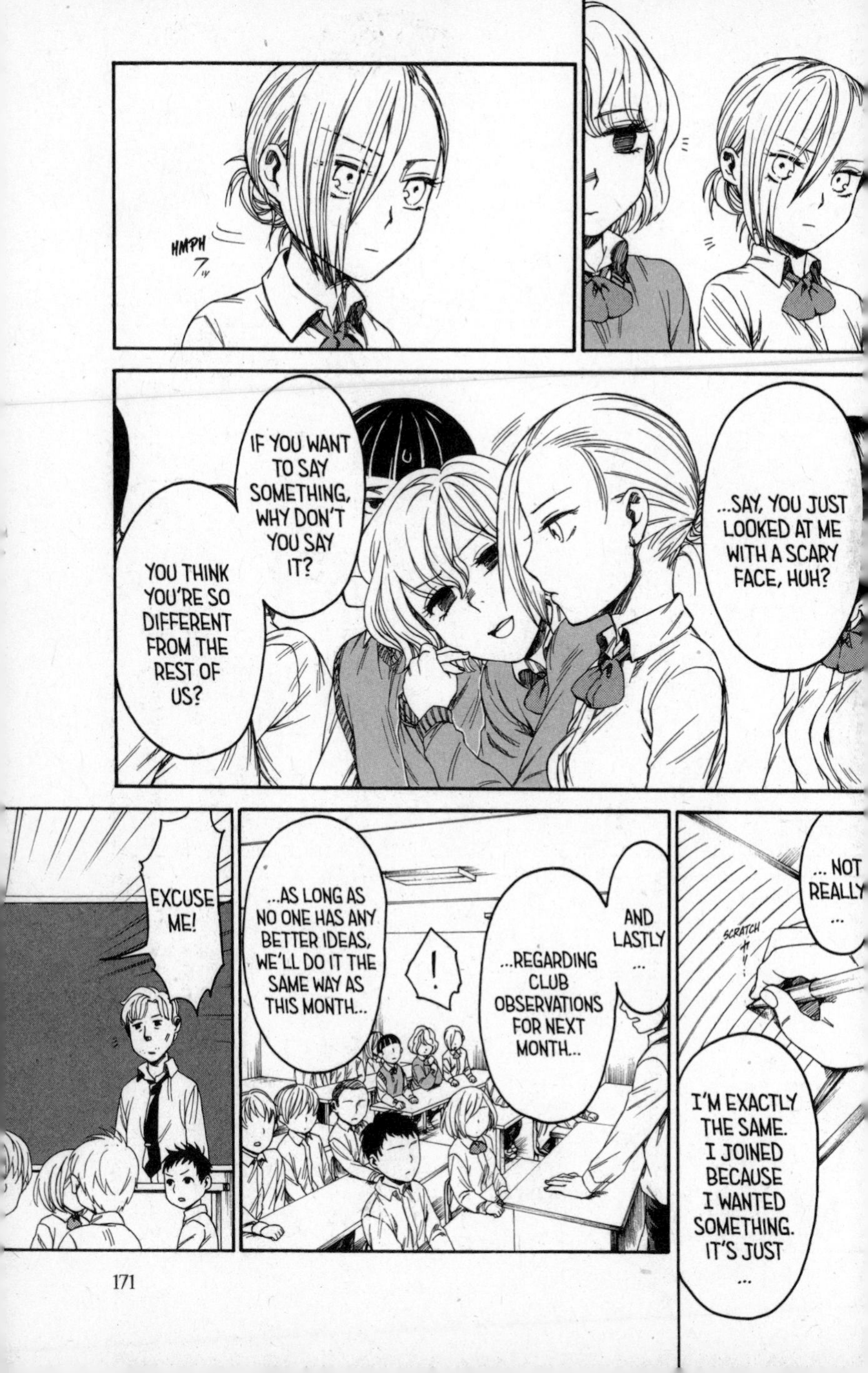
HMPH
...SAY, YOU JUST LOOKED AT ME WITH A SCARY FACE, HUH?
IF YOU WANT TO SAY SOMETHING, WHY DON'T YOU SAY IT?
YOU THINK YOU'RE SO DIFFERENT FROM THE REST OF US?
... NOT REALLY ...
SCRATCH
I'M EXACTLY THE SAME. I JOINED BECAUSE I WANTED SOMETHING. IT'S JUST ...
AND LASTLY ...
...REGARDING CLUB OBSERVATIONS FOR NEXT MONTH...
!
...AS LONG AS NO ONE HAS ANY BETTER IDEAS, WE'LL DO IT THE SAME WAY AS THIS MONTH...
EXCUSE ME!

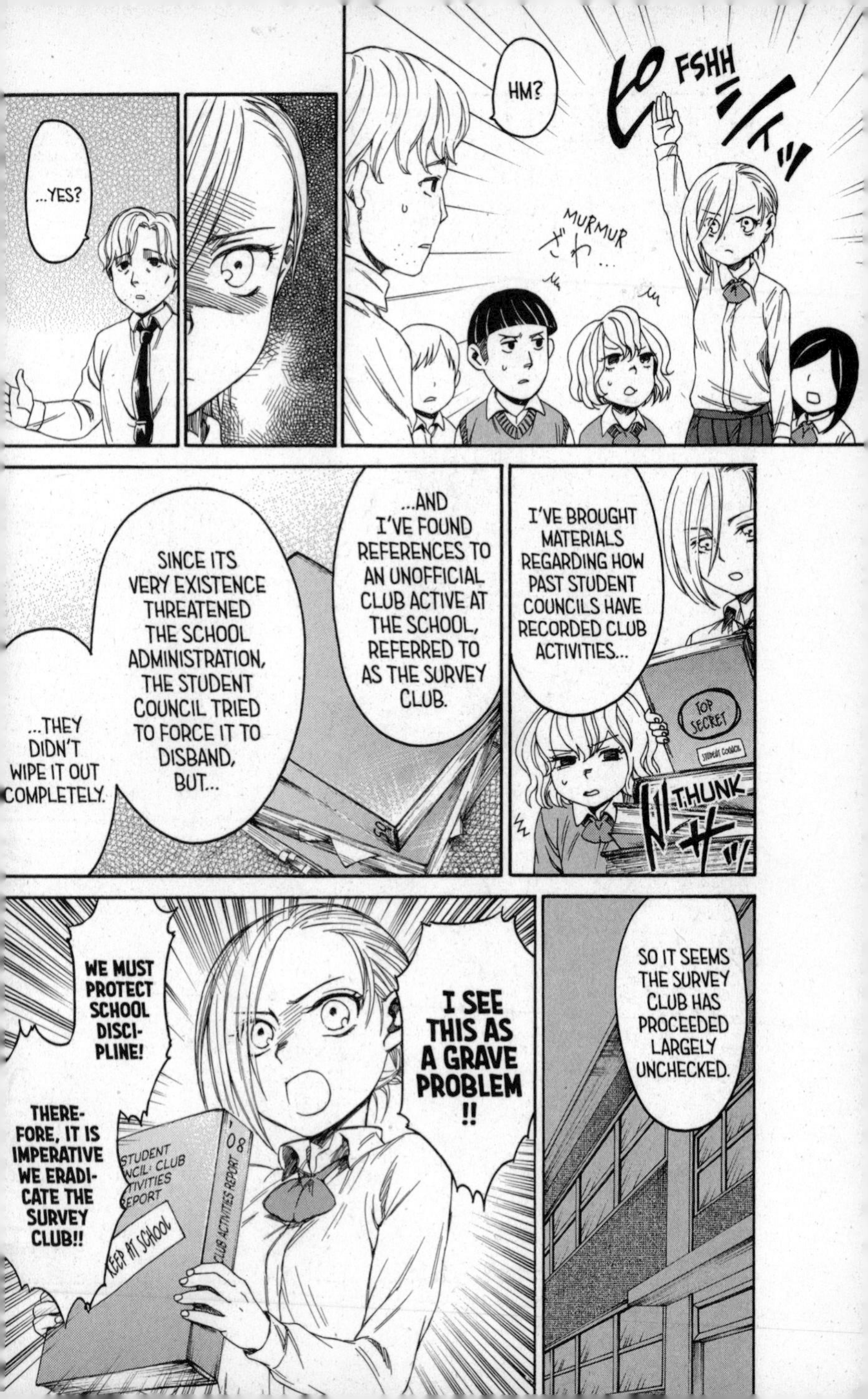
ピシッ FSHH
ざわ… MURMUR
HM?
...YES?
I'VE BROUGHT MATERIALS REGARDING HOW PAST STUDENT COUNCILS HAVE RECORDED CLUB ACTIVITIES...
TOP SECRET
STUDENT COUNCIL
ドサッ THUNK
...AND I'VE FOUND REFERENCES TO AN UNOFFICIAL CLUB ACTIVE AT THE SCHOOL, REFERRED TO AS THE SURVEY CLUB.
SINCE ITS VERY EXISTENCE THREATENED THE SCHOOL ADMINISTRATION, THE STUDENT COUNCIL TRIED TO FORCE IT TO DISBAND, BUT...
...THEY DIDN'T WIPE IT OUT COMPLETELY.
SO IT SEEMS THE SURVEY CLUB HAS PROCEEDED LARGELY UNCHECKED.
I SEE THIS AS A GRAVE PROBLEM!!
WE MUST PROTECT SCHOOL DISCI-PLINE!
THERE-FORE, IT IS IMPERATIVE WE ERADI-CATE THE SURVEY CLUB!!
'08
CLUB ACTIVITIES REPORT
KEEP AT SCHOOL

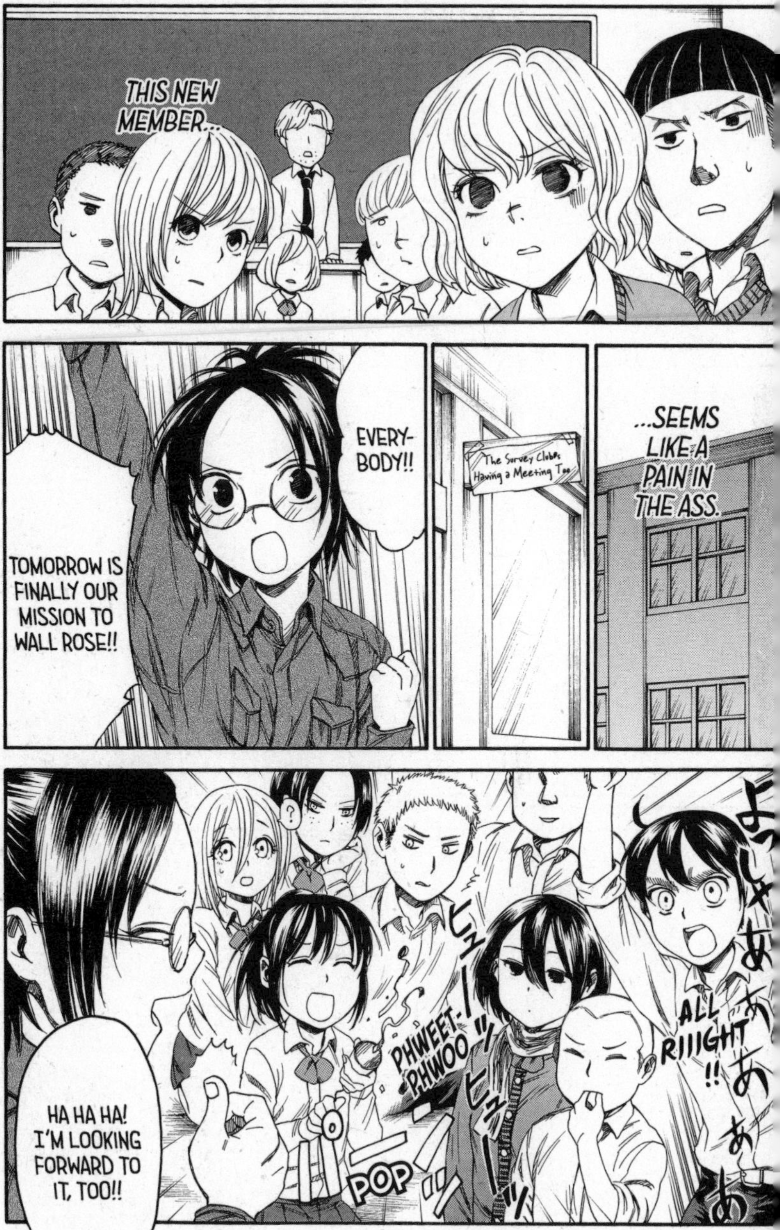
THIS NEW MEMBER...
...SEEMS LIKE A PAIN IN THE ASS.
The Survey Club's Having a Meeting Too
EVERY-BODY!!
TOMORROW IS FINALLY OUR MISSION TO WALL ROSE!!
よっしゃあああああ
ALL RIIIGHT!!
PHWEET-PHWOO
POP
HA HA HA! I'M LOOKING FORWARD TO IT, TOO!!

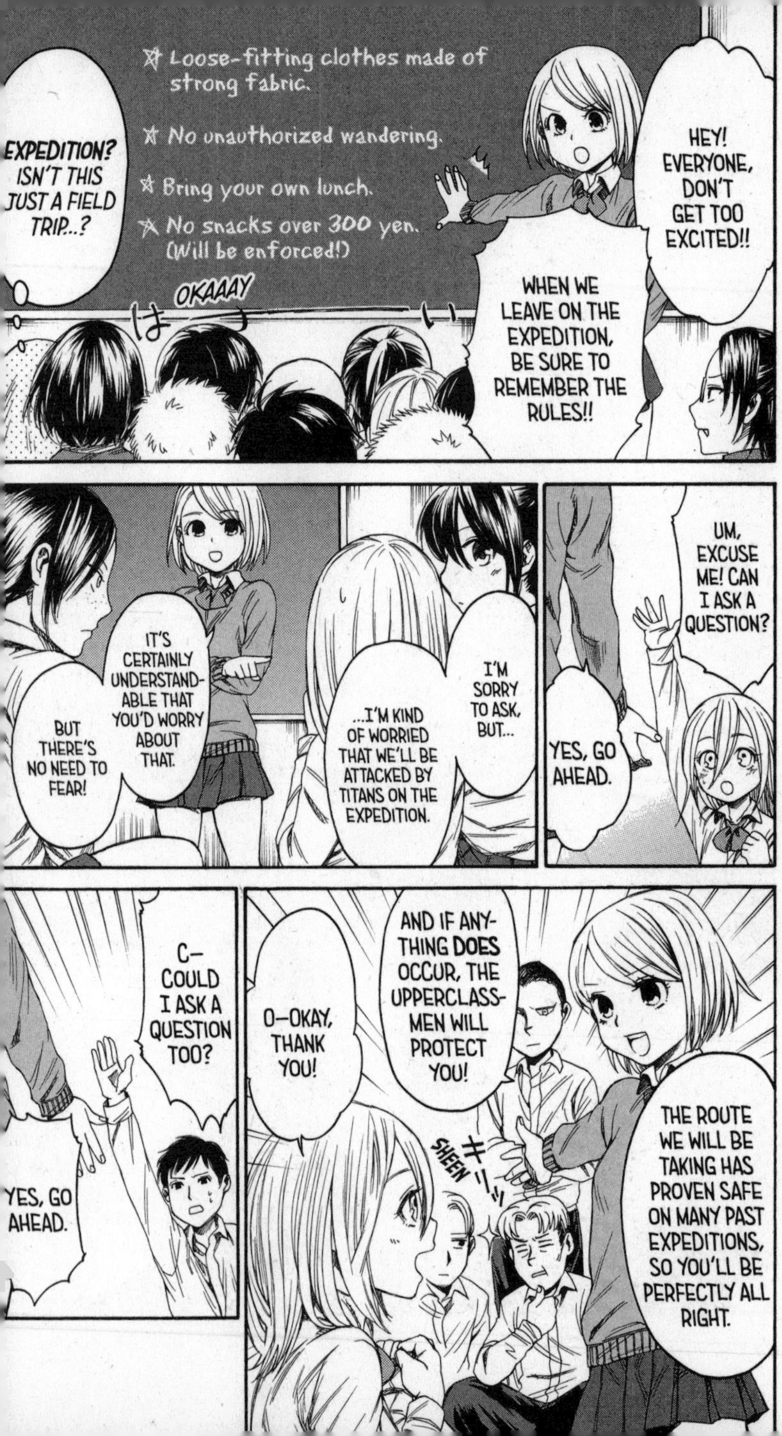
HEY! EVERYONE, DON'T GET TOO EXCITED!!
WHEN WE LEAVE ON THE EXPEDITION, BE SURE TO REMEMBER THE RULES!!
☆ Loose-fitting clothes made of strong fabric.
☆ No unauthorized wandering.
☆ Bring your own lunch.
☆ No snacks over 300 yen. (Will be enforced!)
OKAAAY
EXPEDITION? ISN'T THIS JUST A FIELD TRIP...?
UM, EXCUSE ME! CAN I ASK A QUESTION?
YES, GO AHEAD.
I'M SORRY TO ASK, BUT...
...I'M KIND OF WORRIED THAT WE'LL BE ATTACKED BY TITANS ON THE EXPEDITION.
IT'S CERTAINLY UNDERSTAND-ABLE THAT YOU'D WORRY ABOUT THAT.
BUT THERE'S NO NEED TO FEAR!
THE ROUTE WE WILL BE TAKING HAS PROVEN SAFE ON MANY PAST EXPEDITIONS, SO YOU'LL BE PERFECTLY ALL RIGHT.
AND IF ANY-THING DOES OCCUR, THE UPPERCLASS-MEN WILL PROTECT YOU!
SHEEN
O-OKAY, THANK YOU!
C-COULD I ASK A QUESTION TOO?
YES, GO AHEAD.

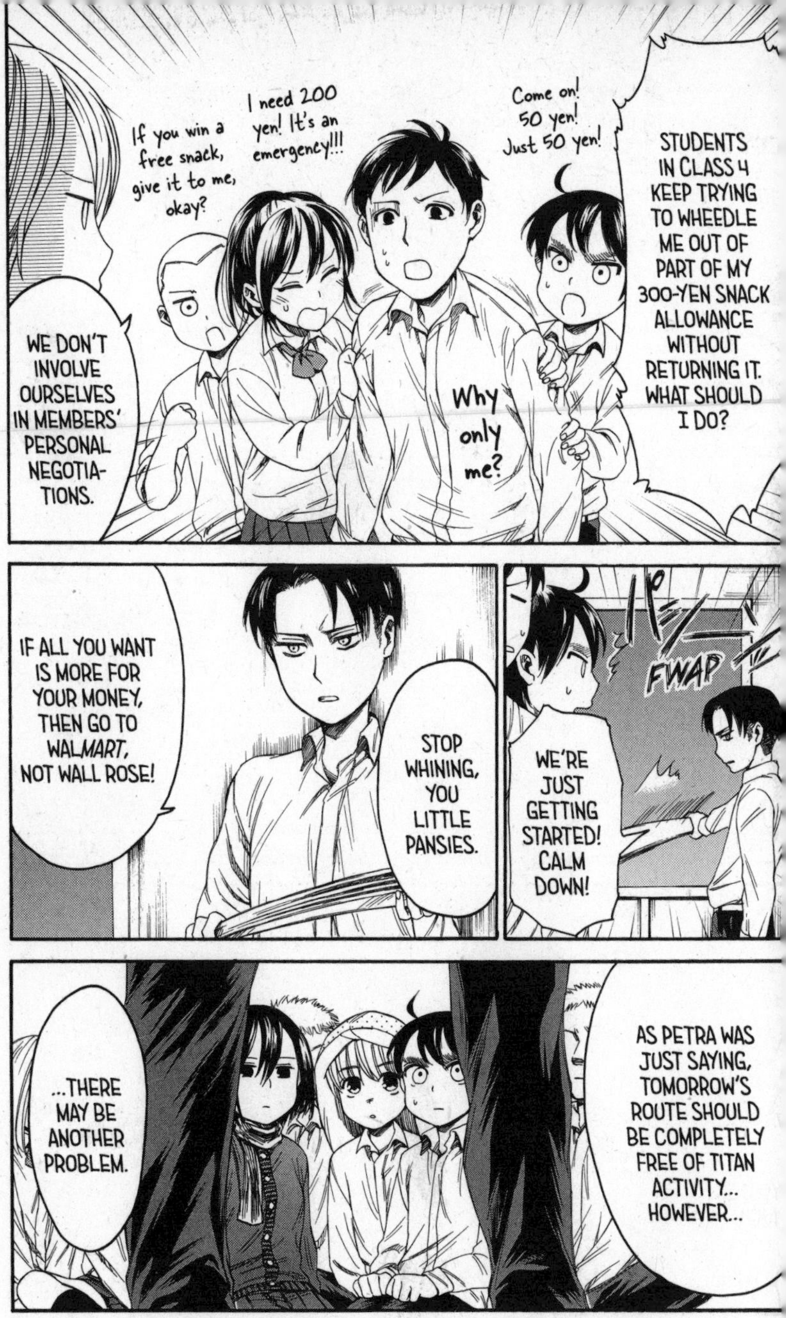
STUDENTS IN CLASS 4 KEEP TRYING TO WHEEDLE ME OUT OF PART OF MY 300-YEN SNACK ALLOWANCE WITHOUT RETURNING IT. WHAT SHOULD I DO?
Come on! 50 yen! Just 50 yen!
I need 200 yen! It's an emergency!!!
If you win a free snack, give it to me, okay?
Why only me?
WE DON'T INVOLVE OURSELVES IN MEMBERS' PERSONAL NEGOTIA-TIONS.
FWAP
WE'RE JUST GETTING STARTED! CALM DOWN!
STOP WHINING, YOU LITTLE PANSIES.
IF ALL YOU WANT IS MORE FOR YOUR MONEY, THEN GO TO WALMART, NOT WALL ROSE!
AS PETRA WAS JUST SAYING, TOMORROW'S ROUTE SHOULD BE COMPLETELY FREE OF TITAN ACTIVITY... HOWEVER...
...THERE MAY BE ANOTHER PROBLEM.

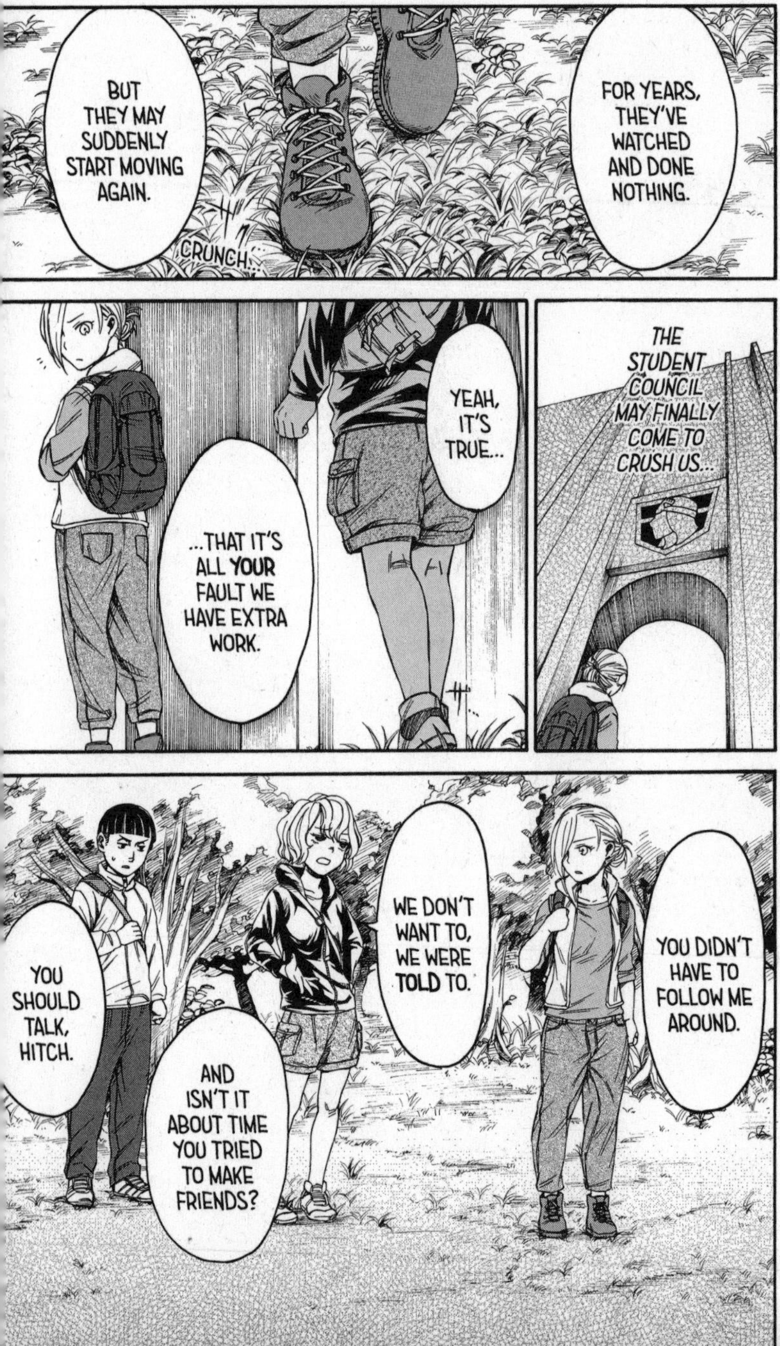
FOR YEARS, THEY'VE WATCHED AND DONE NOTHING.
BUT THEY MAY SUDDENLY START MOVING AGAIN.
CRUNCH...
THE STUDENT COUNCIL MAY FINALLY COME TO CRUSH US...
YEAH, IT'S TRUE...
...THAT IT'S ALL YOUR FAULT WE HAVE EXTRA WORK.
YOU DIDN'T HAVE TO FOLLOW ME AROUND.
WE DON'T WANT TO, WE WERE TOLD TO.
AND ISN'T IT ABOUT TIME YOU TRIED TO MAKE FRIENDS?
YOU SHOULD TALK, HITCH.

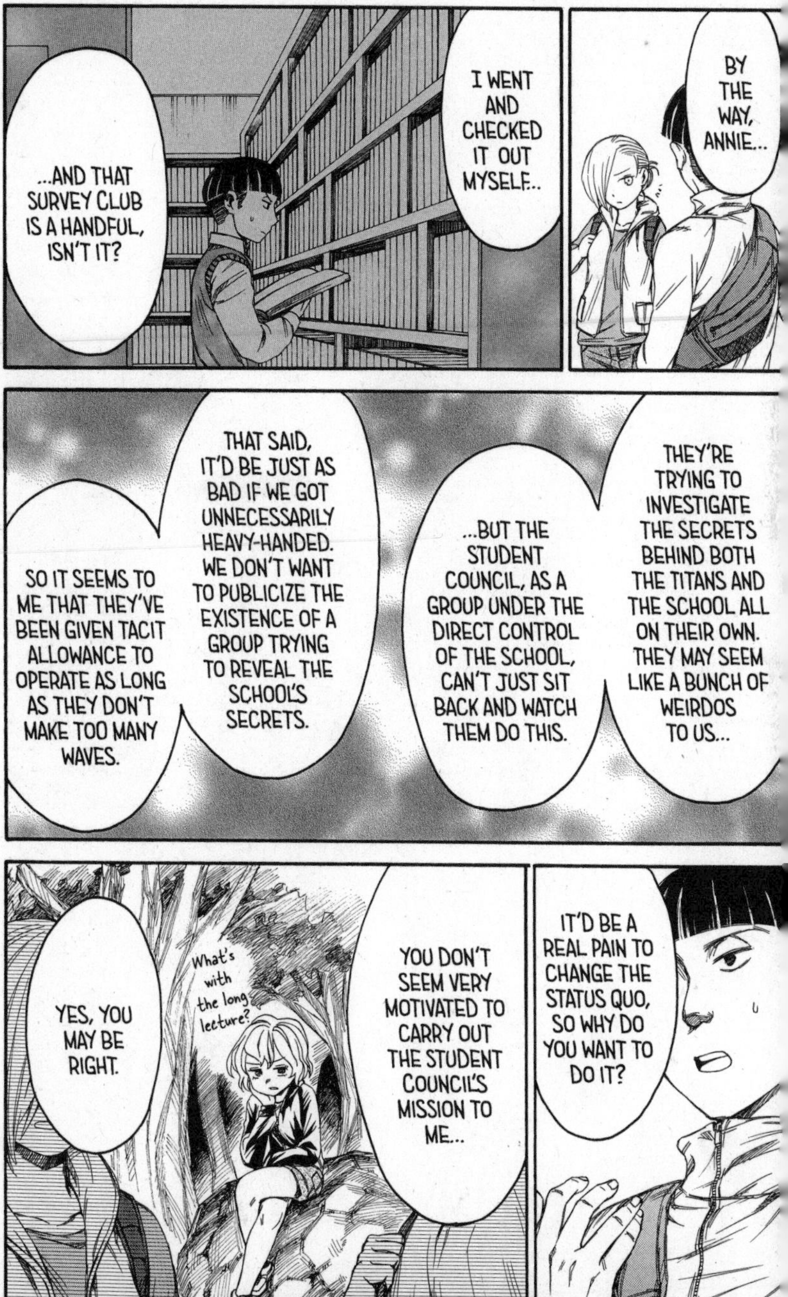
BY THE WAY, ANNIE...
I WENT AND CHECKED IT OUT MYSELF...
...AND THAT SURVEY CLUB IS A HANDFUL, ISN'T IT?
THEY'RE TRYING TO INVESTIGATE THE SECRETS BEHIND BOTH THE TITANS AND THE SCHOOL ALL ON THEIR OWN. THEY MAY SEEM LIKE A BUNCH OF WEIRDOS TO US...
...BUT THE STUDENT COUNCIL, AS A GROUP UNDER THE DIRECT CONTROL OF THE SCHOOL, CAN'T JUST SIT BACK AND WATCH THEM DO THIS.
THAT SAID, IT'D BE JUST AS BAD IF WE GOT UNNECESSARILY HEAVY-HANDED. WE DON'T WANT TO PUBLICIZE THE EXISTENCE OF A GROUP TRYING TO REVEAL THE SCHOOL'S SECRETS.
SO IT SEEMS TO ME THAT THEY'VE BEEN GIVEN TACIT ALLOWANCE TO OPERATE AS LONG AS THEY DON'T MAKE TOO MANY WAVES.
IT'D BE A REAL PAIN TO CHANGE THE STATUS QUO, SO WHY DO YOU WANT TO DO IT?
YOU DON'T SEEM VERY MOTIVATED TO CARRY OUT THE STUDENT COUNCIL'S MISSION TO ME...
What's with the long lecture?
YES, YOU MAY BE RIGHT.

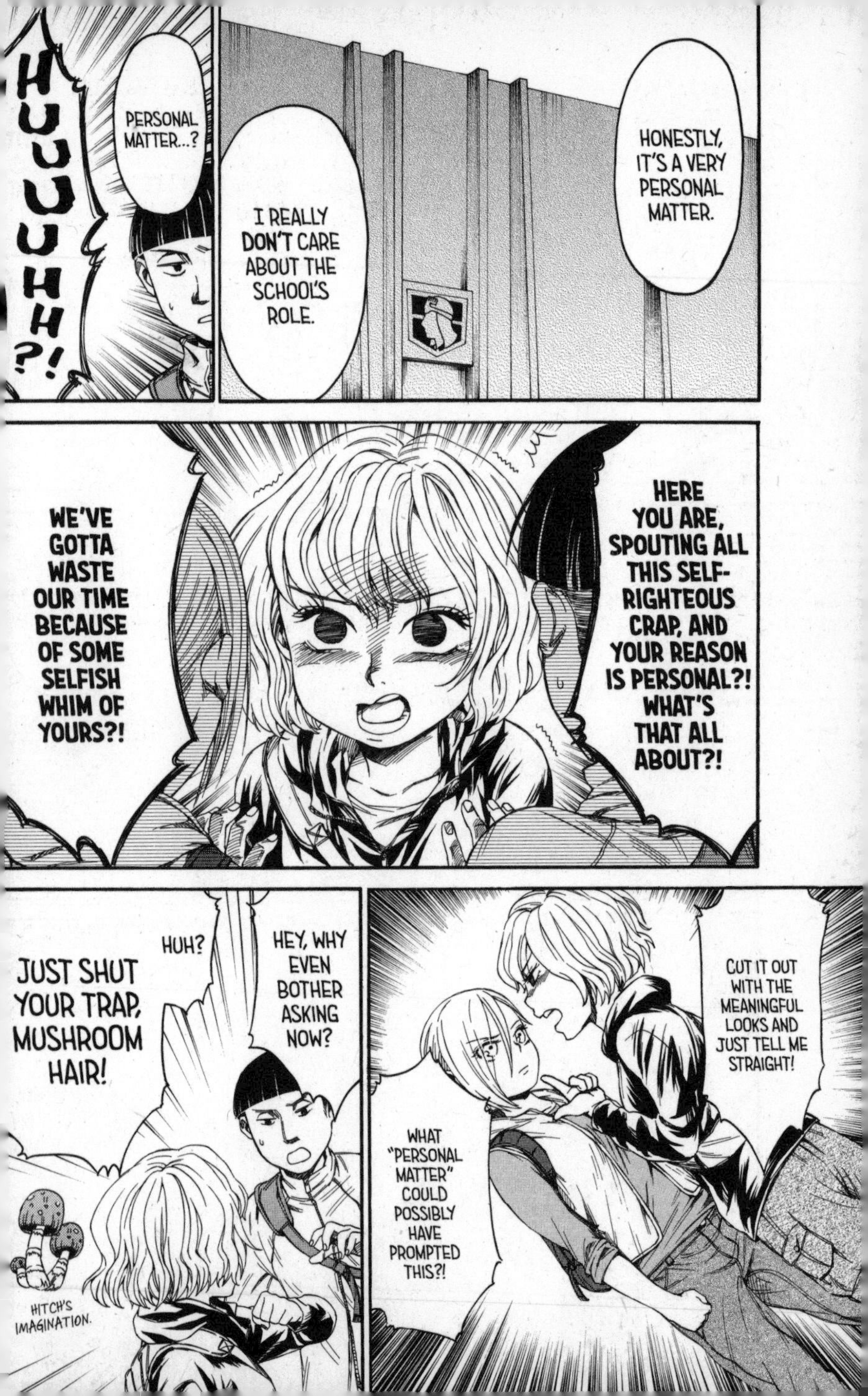
HONESTLY, IT'S A VERY PERSONAL MATTER.
I REALLY DON'T CARE ABOUT THE SCHOOL'S ROLE.
PERSONAL MATTER...?
HUUUUHH?!
HERE YOU ARE, SPOUTING ALL THIS SELF-RIGHTEOUS CRAP, AND YOUR REASON IS PERSONAL?! WHAT'S THAT ALL ABOUT?!
WE'VE GOTTA WASTE OUR TIME BECAUSE OF SOME SELFISH WHIM OF YOURS?!
CUT IT OUT WITH THE MEANINGFUL LOOKS AND JUST TELL ME STRAIGHT!
WHAT "PERSONAL MATTER" COULD POSSIBLY HAVE PROMPTED THIS?!
HEY, WHY EVEN BOTHER ASKING NOW?
HUH?
JUST SHUT YOUR TRAP, MUSHROOM HAIR!
HITCH'S IMAGINATION.

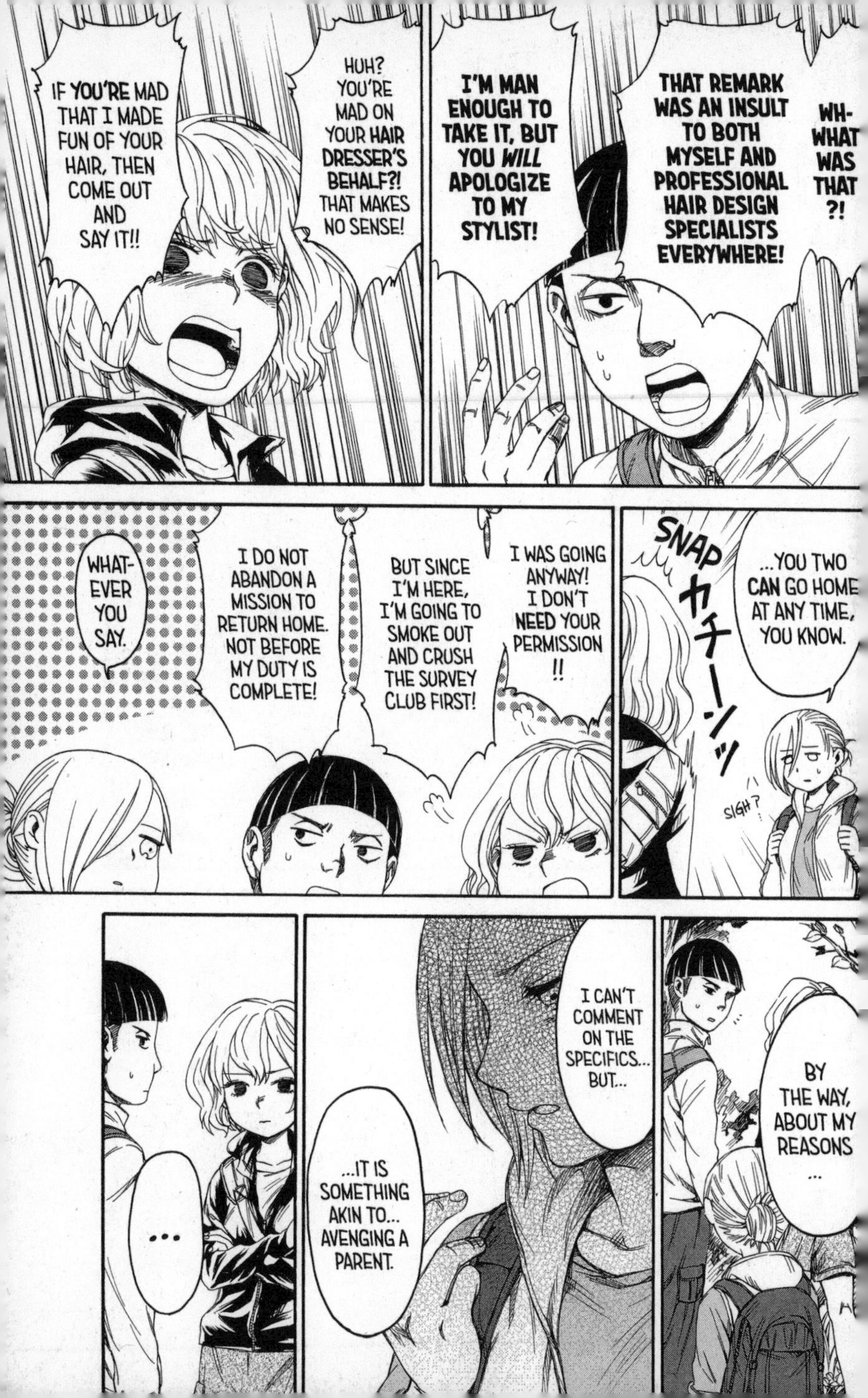
WH-WHAT WAS THAT?!
THAT REMARK WAS AN INSULT TO BOTH MYSELF AND PROFESSIONAL HAIR DESIGN SPECIALISTS EVERYWHERE!
I'M MAN ENOUGH TO TAKE IT, BUT YOU *WILL* APOLOGIZE TO MY STYLIST!
HUH? YOU'RE MAD ON YOUR HAIR DRESSER'S BEHALF?! THAT MAKES NO SENSE!
IF YOU'RE MAD THAT I MADE FUN OF YOUR HAIR, THEN COME OUT AND SAY IT!!
...YOU TWO CAN GO HOME AT ANY TIME, YOU KNOW.
SNAP
カチーンッ
SIGH?
I WAS GOING ANYWAY! I DON'T NEED YOUR PERMISSION!!
BUT SINCE I'M HERE, I'M GOING TO SMOKE OUT AND CRUSH THE SURVEY CLUB FIRST!
I DO NOT ABANDON A MISSION TO RETURN HOME. NOT BEFORE MY DUTY IS COMPLETE!
WHAT-EVER YOU SAY.
BY THE WAY, ABOUT MY REASONS...
I CAN'T COMMENT ON THE SPECIFICS... BUT...
...IT IS SOMETHING AKIN TO... AVENGING A PARENT.
...

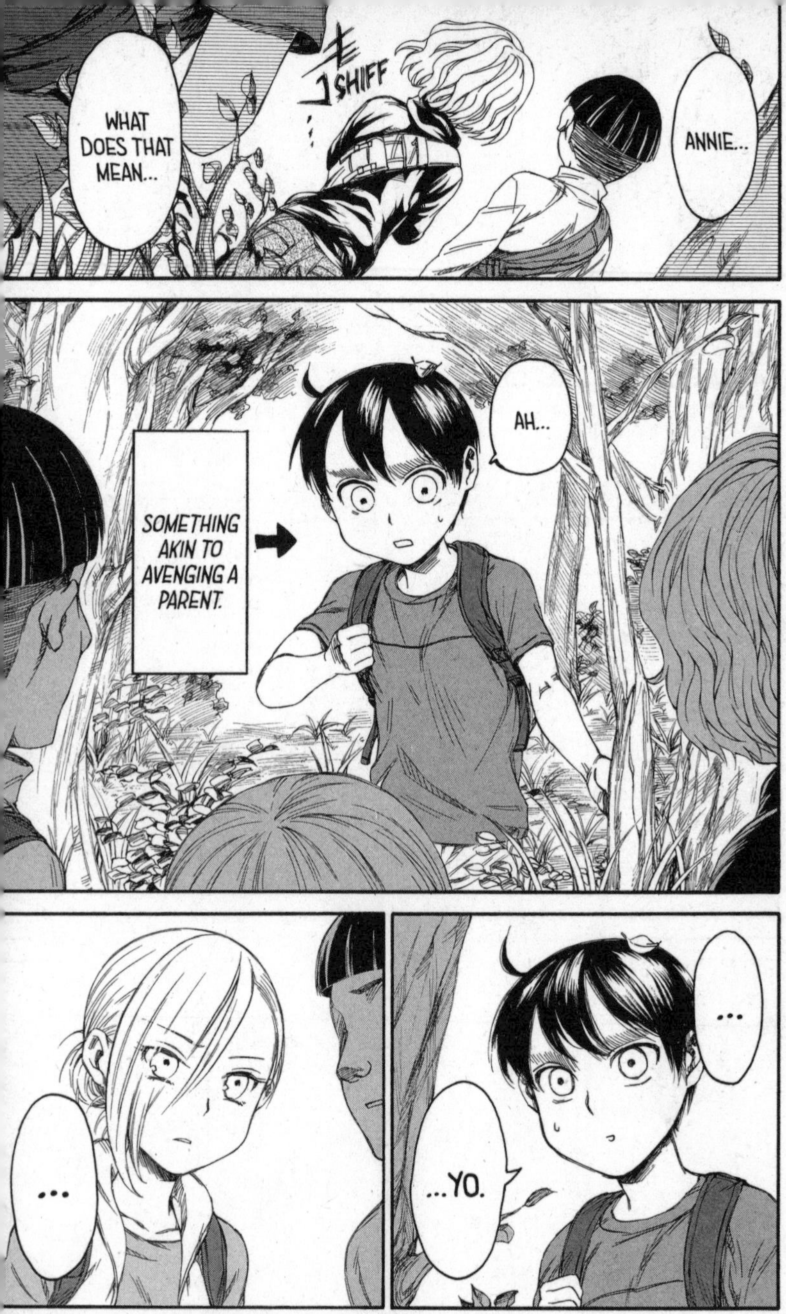
ANNIE...
SHIFF
WHAT DOES THAT MEAN...
AH...
SOMETHING AKIN TO AVENGING A PARENT.
...
...YO.
...

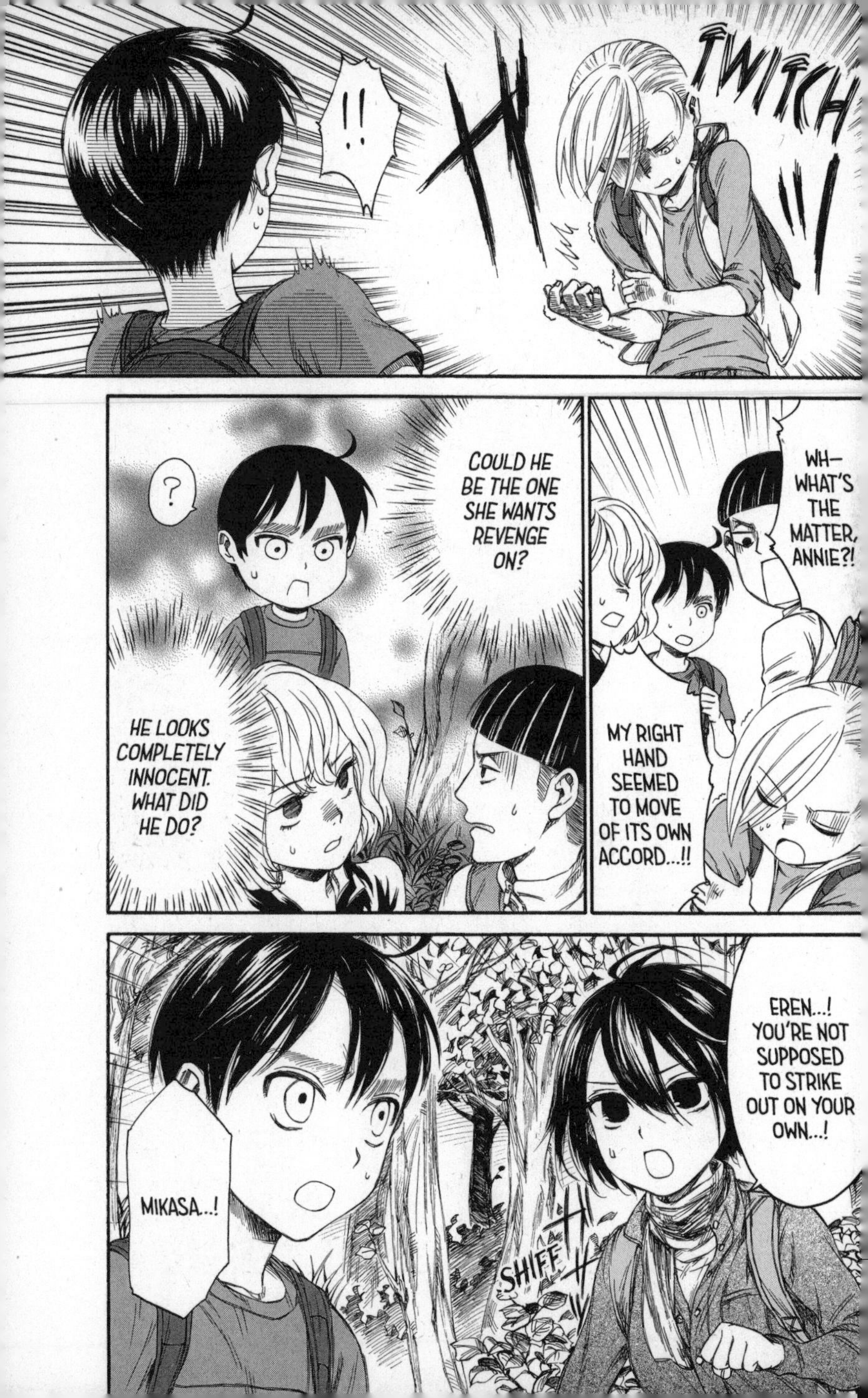
TWITCH
!!
WH— WHAT'S THE MATTER, ANNIE?!
MY RIGHT HAND SEEMED TO MOVE OF ITS OWN ACCORD...!!
COULD HE BE THE ONE SHE WANTS REVENGE ON?
?
HE LOOKS COMPLETELY INNOCENT. WHAT DID HE DO?
EREN...! YOU'RE NOT SUPPOSED TO STRIKE OUT ON YOUR OWN...!
SHIFF
MIKASA...!

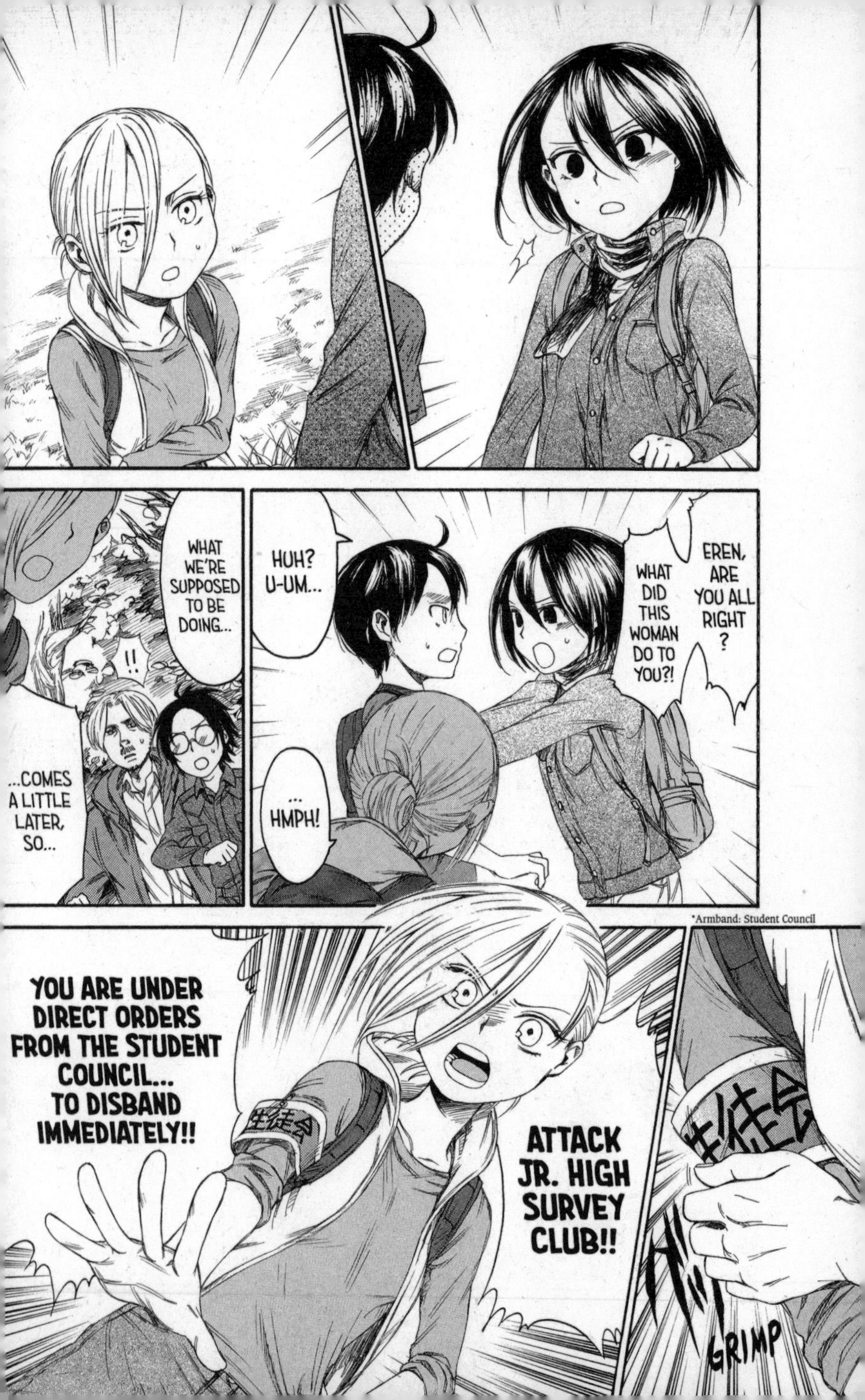
EREN, ARE YOU ALL RIGHT?
WHAT DID THIS WOMAN DO TO YOU?!
HUH? U-UM...
... HMPH!
WHAT WE'RE SUPPOSED TO BE DOING...
!!
...COMES A LITTLE LATER, SO...
生徒会
GRIMP
生徒会
YOU ARE UNDER DIRECT ORDERS FROM THE STUDENT COUNCIL... TO DISBAND IMMEDIATELY!!
ATTACK JR. HIGH SURVEY CLUB!!

*Armband: Student Council

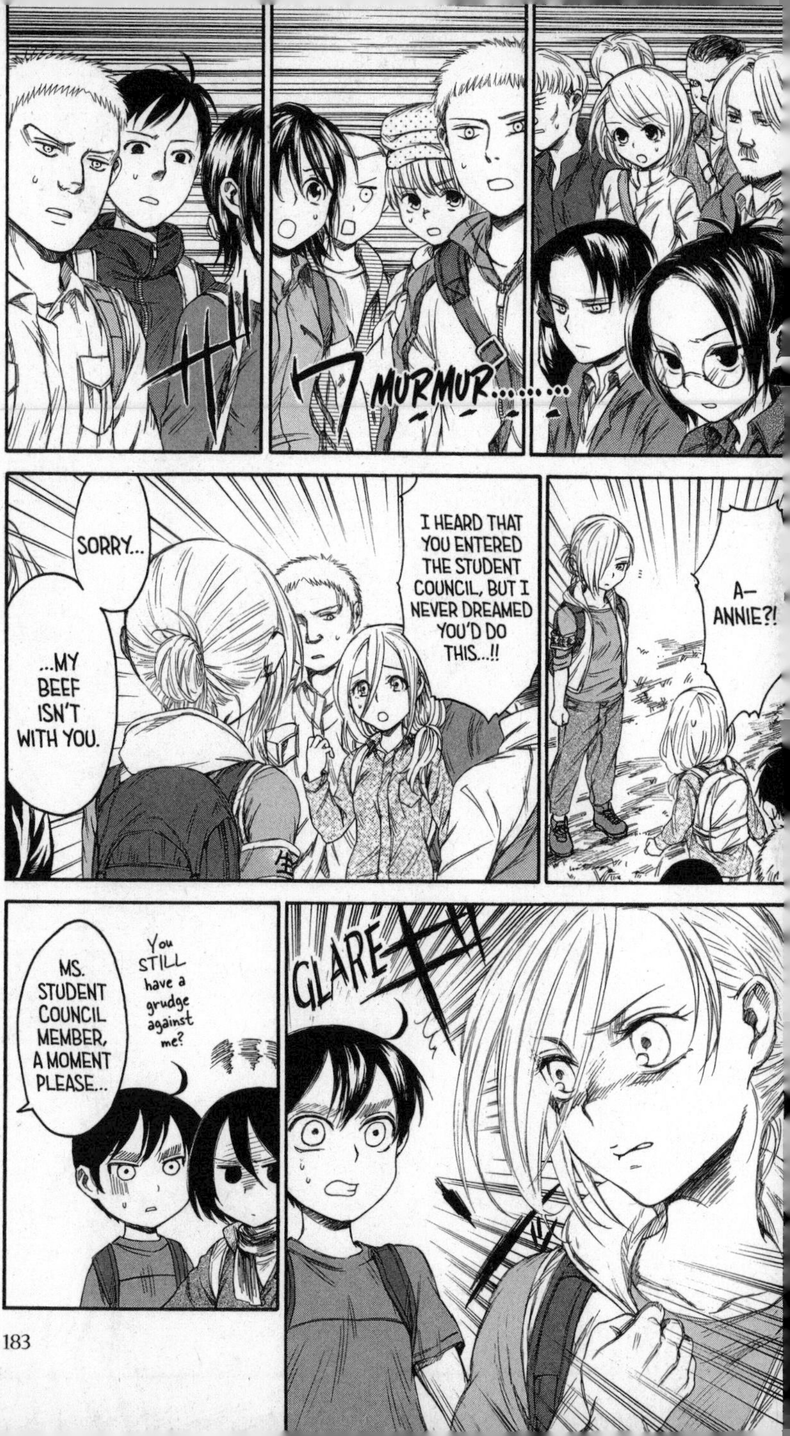
MURMUR.......
A— ANNIE?!
I HEARD THAT YOU ENTERED THE STUDENT COUNCIL, BUT I NEVER DREAMED YOU'D DO THIS...!!
SORRY...
...MY BEEF ISN'T WITH YOU.
GLARE
You STILL have a grudge against me?
MS. STUDENT COUNCIL MEMBER, A MOMENT PLEASE...

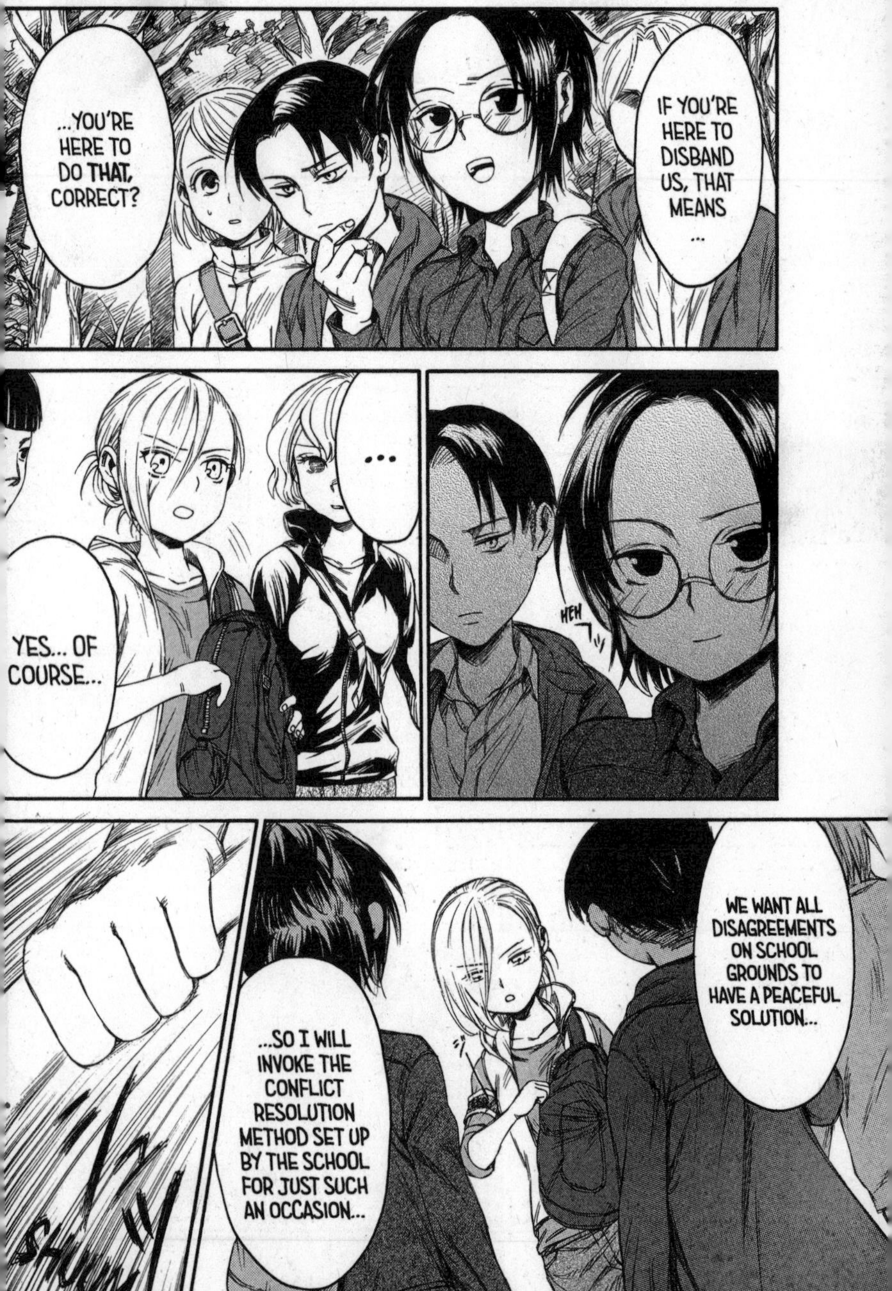
IF YOU'RE HERE TO DISBAND US, THAT MEANS ...
...YOU'RE HERE TO DO THAT, CORRECT?
HEH
...
YES... OF COURSE...
WE WANT ALL DISAGREEMENTS ON SCHOOL GROUNDS TO HAVE A PEACEFUL SOLUTION...
...SO I WILL INVOKE THE CONFLICT RESOLUTION METHOD SET UP BY THE SCHOOL FOR JUST SUCH AN OCCASION...
SHUUM

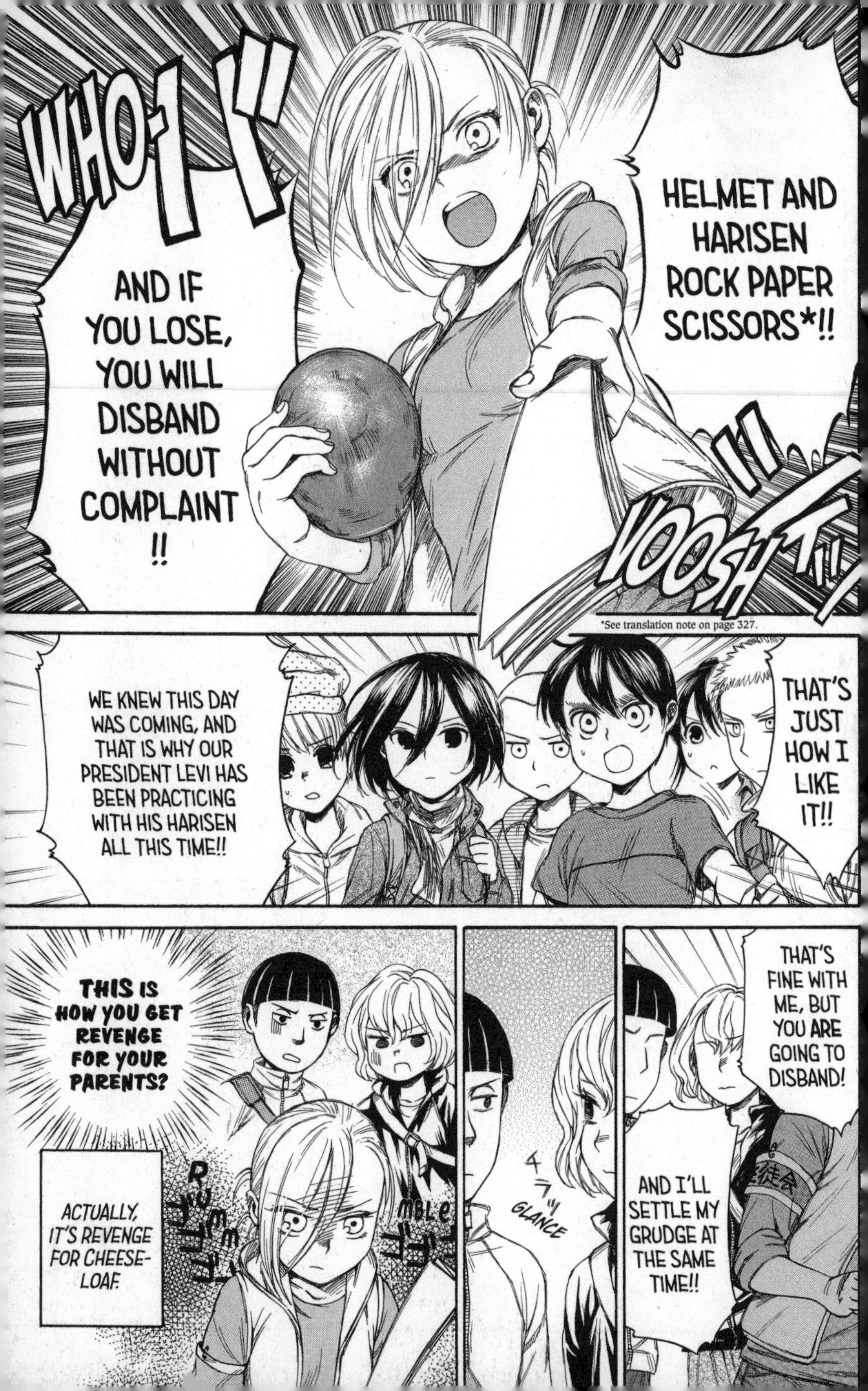
HELMET AND HARISEN ROCK PAPER SCISSORS*!!
WHO-I-I
AND IF YOU LOSE, YOU WILL DISBAND WITHOUT COMPLAINT !!
VOOSH
THAT'S JUST HOW I LIKE IT!!
WE KNEW THIS DAY WAS COMING, AND THAT IS WHY OUR PRESIDENT LEVI HAS BEEN PRACTICING WITH HIS HARISEN ALL THIS TIME!!
THAT'S FINE WITH ME, BUT YOU ARE GOING TO DISBAND!
AND I'LL SETTLE MY GRUDGE AT THE SAME TIME!!
GLANCE
THIS IS HOW YOU GET REVENGE FOR YOUR PARENTS?
RUMBLE
ACTUALLY, IT'S REVENGE FOR CHEESE-LOAF.
*See translation note on page 327.

YET AGAIN WITH THE BONUS MANGA

D-DÉJÁ VU...

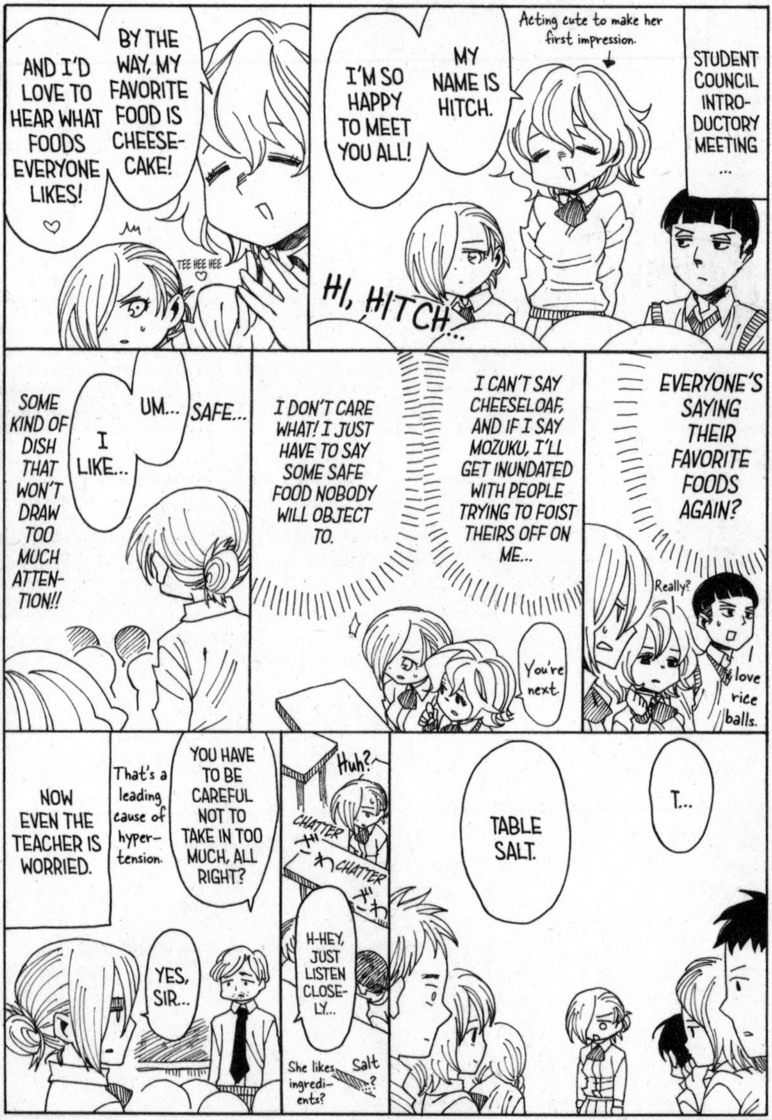
STUDENT COUNCIL INTRODUCTORY MEETING...
Acting cute to make her first impression.
MY NAME IS HITCH.
I'M SO HAPPY TO MEET YOU ALL!
HI, HITCH...
BY THE WAY, MY FAVORITE FOOD IS CHEESECAKE!
AND I'D LOVE TO HEAR WHAT FOODS EVERYONE LIKES! ♡
TEE HEE HEE ♡
EVERYONE'S SAYING THEIR FAVORITE FOODS AGAIN?
Really?
I love rice balls.
I CAN'T SAY CHEESELOAF, AND IF I SAY MOZUKU, I'LL GET INUNDATED WITH PEOPLE TRYING TO FOIST THEIRS OFF ON ME...
I DON'T CARE WHAT! I JUST HAVE TO SAY SOME SAFE FOOD NOBODY WILL OBJECT TO.
You're next.
SAFE...
UM... I LIKE...
SOME KIND OF DISH THAT WON'T DRAW TOO MUCH ATTENTION!!
T...
TABLE SALT.
Huh?
CHATTER
CHATTER
H-HEY, JUST LISTEN CLOSELY...
She likes ingredients?
Salt?
YOU HAVE TO BE CAREFUL NOT TO TAKE IN TOO MUCH, ALL RIGHT?
That's a leading cause of hypertension.
NOW EVEN THE TEACHER IS WORRIED.
YES, SIR...

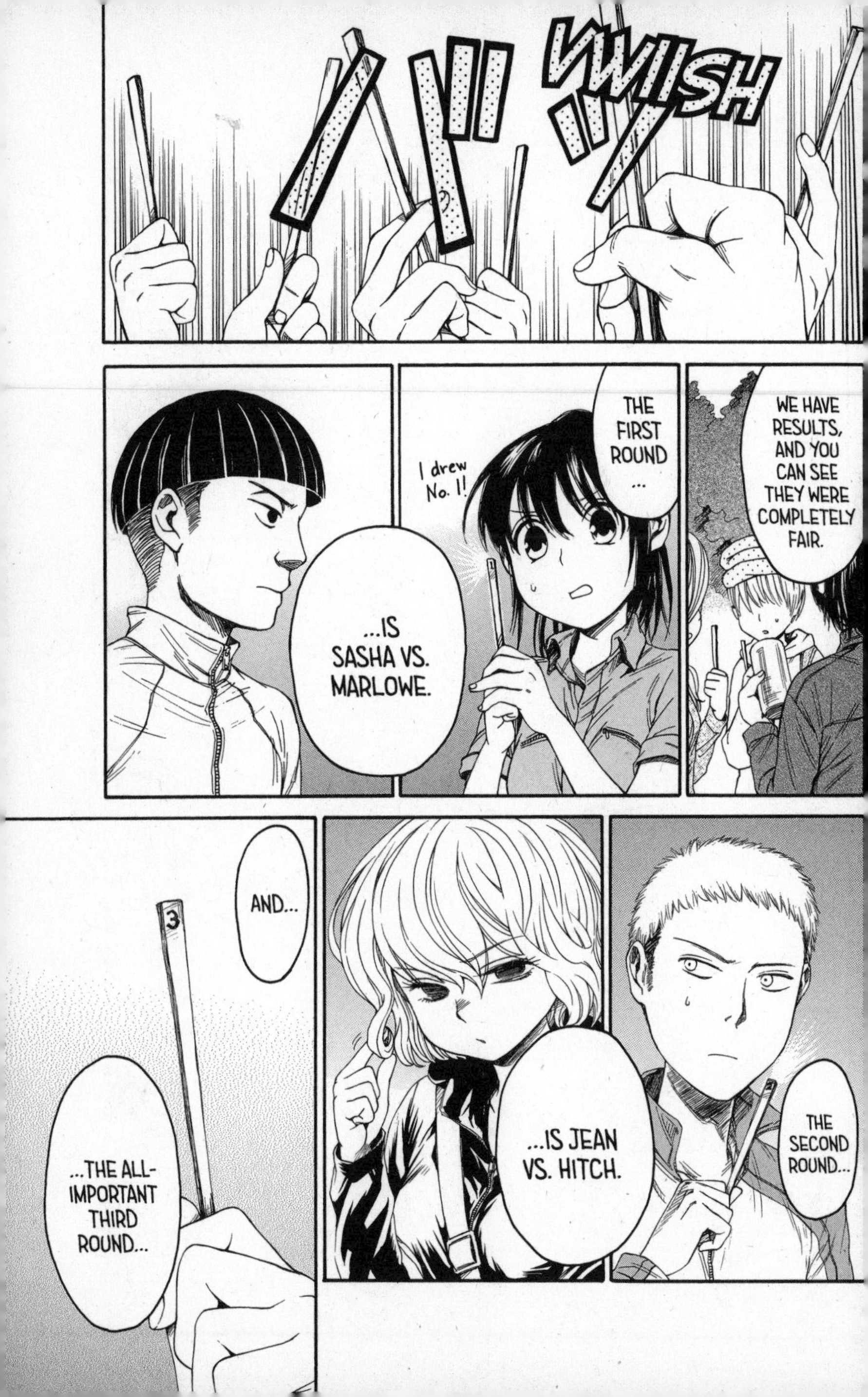
VVISH
WE HAVE RESULTS, AND YOU CAN SEE THEY WERE COMPLETELY FAIR.
THE FIRST ROUND ...
I drew No. 1!
...IS SASHA VS. MARLOWE.
THE SECOND ROUND...
...IS JEAN VS. HITCH.
AND...
...THE ALL-IMPORTANT THIRD ROUND...

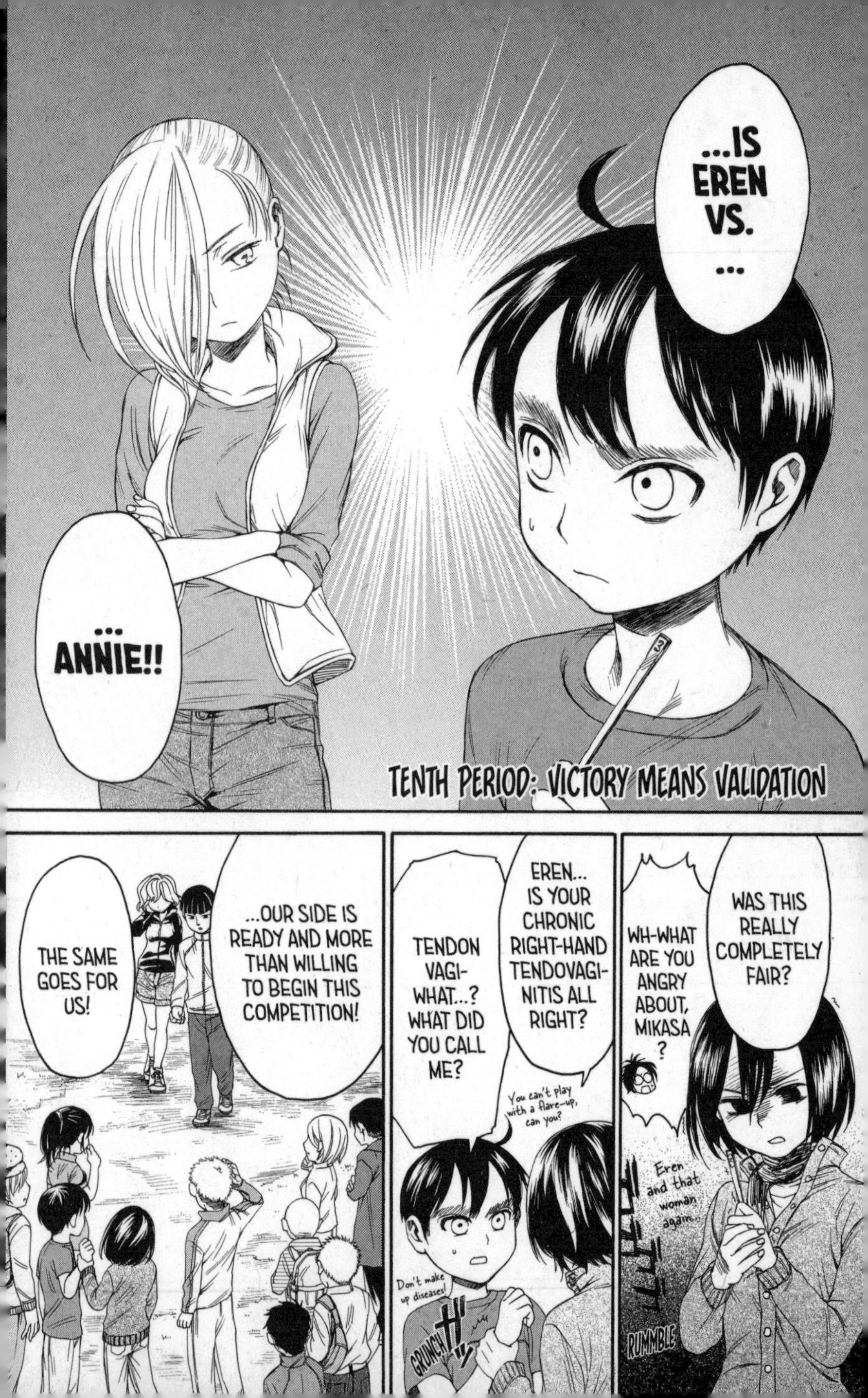
...IS EREN VS. ...
... ANNIE!!
TENTH PERIOD: VICTORY MEANS VALIDATION
WAS THIS REALLY COMPLETELY FAIR?
WH-WHAT ARE YOU ANGRY ABOUT, MIKASA?
Eren and that woman again...
RUMMBLE
EREN... IS YOUR CHRONIC RIGHT-HAND TENDOVAGINITIS ALL RIGHT?
You can't play with a flare-up, can you?
TENDON VAGI-WHAT...? WHAT DID YOU CALL ME?
Don't make up diseases!
GRUNCH
...OUR SIDE IS READY AND MORE THAN WILLING TO BEGIN THIS COMPETITION!
THE SAME GOES FOR US!

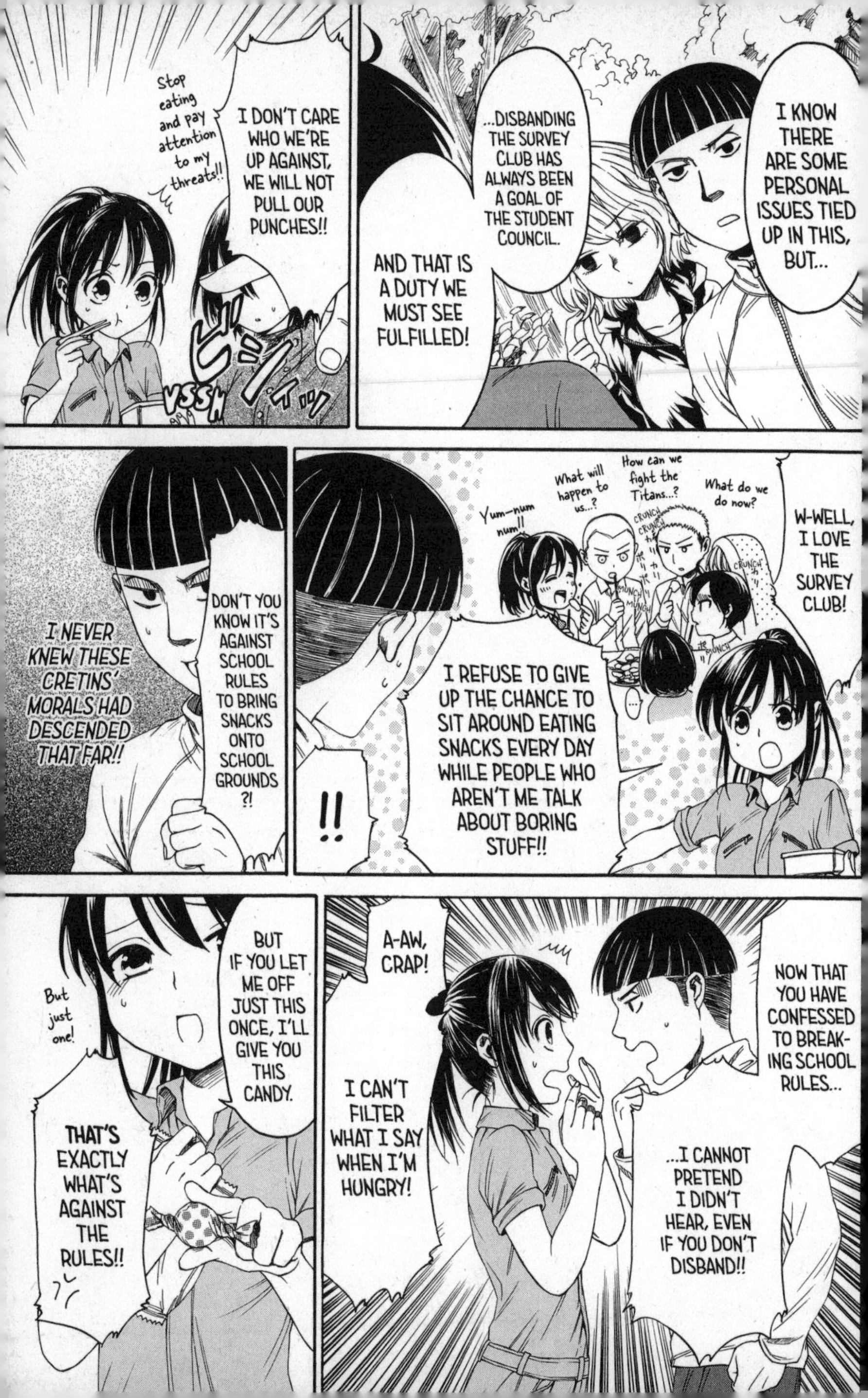
I KNOW THERE ARE SOME PERSONAL ISSUES TIED UP IN THIS, BUT...
...DISBANDING THE SURVEY CLUB HAS ALWAYS BEEN A GOAL OF THE STUDENT COUNCIL.
AND THAT IS A DUTY WE MUST SEE FULFILLED!
I DON'T CARE WHO WE'RE UP AGAINST, WE WILL NOT PULL OUR PUNCHES!!
Stop eating and pay attention to my threats!!
VSSH
W-WELL, I LOVE THE SURVEY CLUB!
What do we do now?
How can we fight the Titans...?
What will happen to us...?
Yum-num num!!
CRUNCH CRUNCH
CRUNCH
MUNCH MUNCH
MUNCH
I REFUSE TO GIVE UP THE CHANCE TO SIT AROUND EATING SNACKS EVERY DAY WHILE PEOPLE WHO AREN'T ME TALK ABOUT BORING STUFF!!
...
!!
DON'T YOU KNOW IT'S AGAINST SCHOOL RULES TO BRING SNACKS ONTO SCHOOL GROUNDS?!
I NEVER KNEW THESE CRETINS' MORALS HAD DESCENDED THAT FAR!!
NOW THAT YOU HAVE CONFESSED TO BREAK-ING SCHOOL RULES...
...I CANNOT PRETEND I DIDN'T HEAR, EVEN IF YOU DON'T DISBAND!!
A-AW, CRAP!
I CAN'T FILTER WHAT I SAY WHEN I'M HUNGRY!
BUT IF YOU LET ME OFF JUST THIS ONCE, I'LL GIVE YOU THIS CANDY.
But just one!
THAT'S EXACTLY WHAT'S AGAINST THE RULES!!

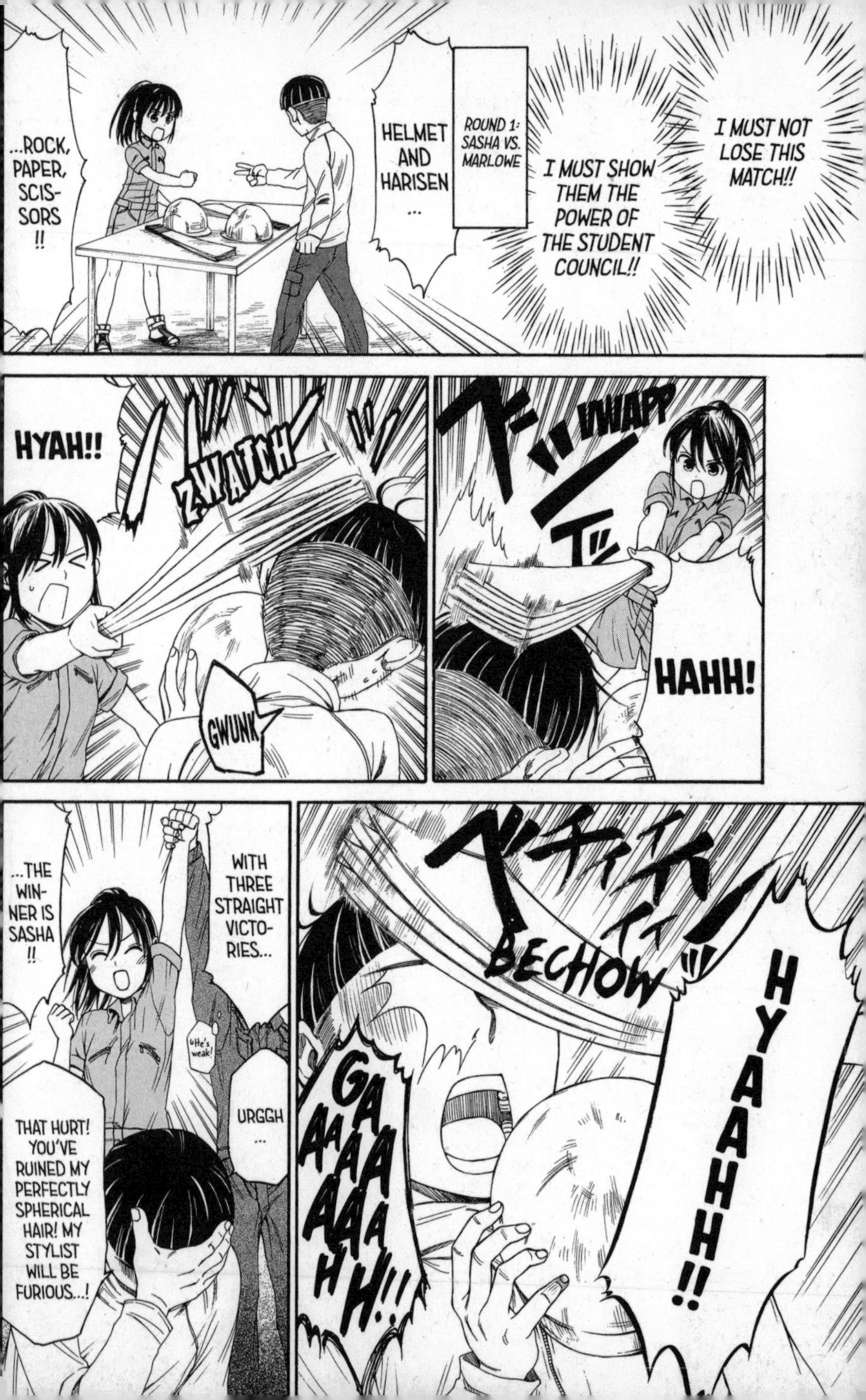
I MUST NOT LOSE THIS MATCH!!
I MUST SHOW THEM THE POWER OF THE STUDENT COUNCIL!!
ROUND 1: SASHA VS. MARLOWE
HELMET AND HARISEN ...
...ROCK, PAPER, SCIS-SORS !!
VWAPP
HAHH!
HYAH!!
ZWATCH
GWUNK
BECHOW
HYAAAHH!!
GAAAAAAAAAAH!!
WITH THREE STRAIGHT VICTO-RIES...
...THE WIN-NER IS SASHA !!
He's weak!
URGGH ...
THAT HURT! YOU'VE RUINED MY PERFECTLY SPHERICAL HAIR! MY STYLIST WILL BE FURIOUS...!

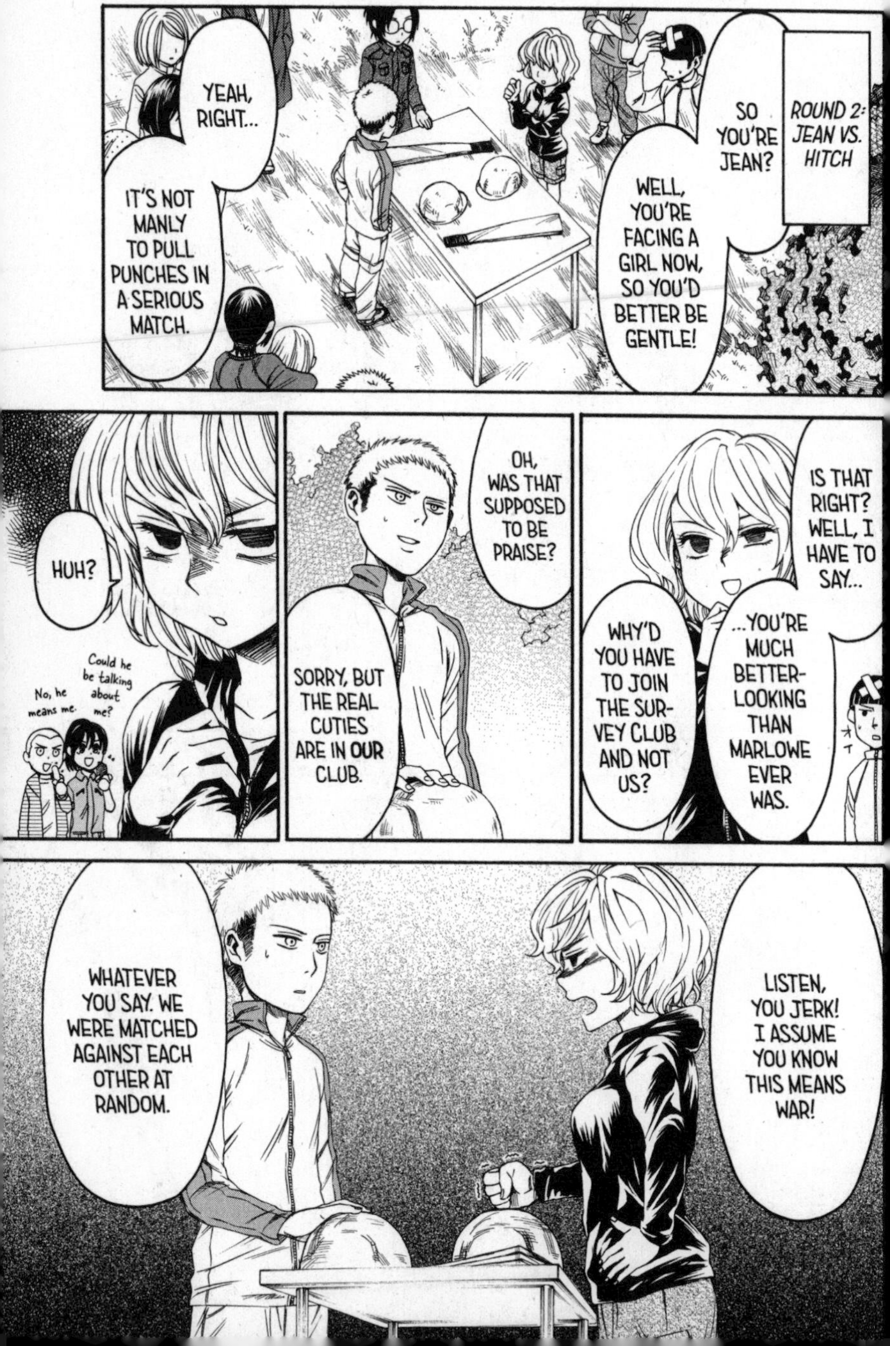
ROUND 2: JEAN VS. HITCH
SO YOU'RE JEAN?
WELL, YOU'RE FACING A GIRL NOW, SO YOU'D BETTER BE GENTLE!
YEAH, RIGHT...
IT'S NOT MANLY TO PULL PUNCHES IN A SERIOUS MATCH.
IS THAT RIGHT? WELL, I HAVE TO SAY...
...YOU'RE MUCH BETTER-LOOKING THAN MARLOWE EVER WAS.
WHY'D YOU HAVE TO JOIN THE SURVEY CLUB AND NOT US?
OH, WAS THAT SUPPOSED TO BE PRAISE?
SORRY, BUT THE REAL CUTIES ARE IN **OUR** CLUB.
HUH?
Could he be talking about me?
No, he means me.
LISTEN, YOU JERK! I ASSUME YOU KNOW THIS MEANS WAR!
WHATEVER YOU SAY. WE WERE MATCHED AGAINST EACH OTHER AT RANDOM.

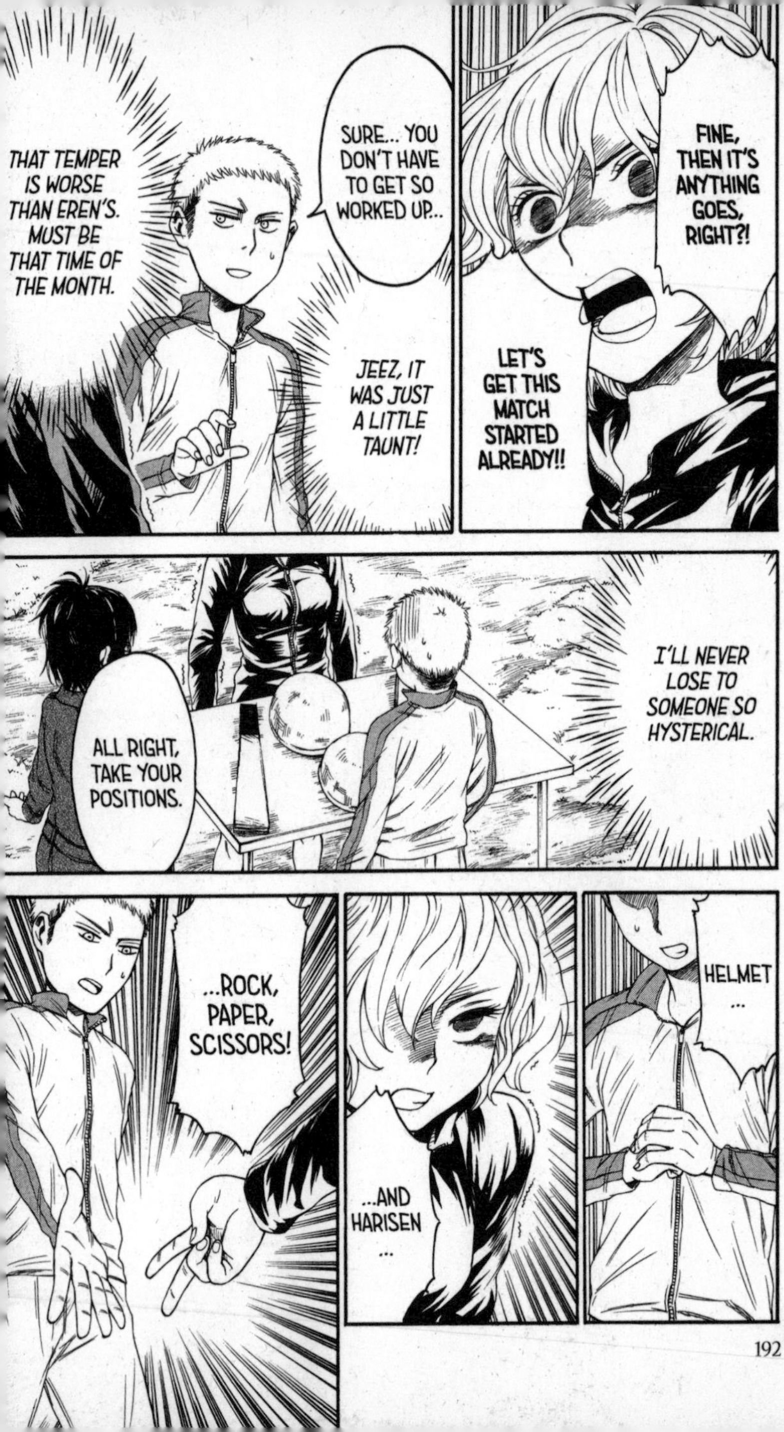
FINE, THEN IT'S ANYTHING GOES, RIGHT?!
LET'S GET THIS MATCH STARTED ALREADY!!
SURE... YOU DON'T HAVE TO GET SO WORKED UP...
JEEZ, IT WAS JUST A LITTLE TAUNT!
THAT TEMPER IS WORSE THAN EREN'S. MUST BE THAT TIME OF THE MONTH.
I'LL NEVER LOSE TO SOMEONE SO HYSTERICAL.
ALL RIGHT, TAKE YOUR POSITIONS.
HELMET ...
...AND HARISEN ...
...ROCK, PAPER, SCISSORS!

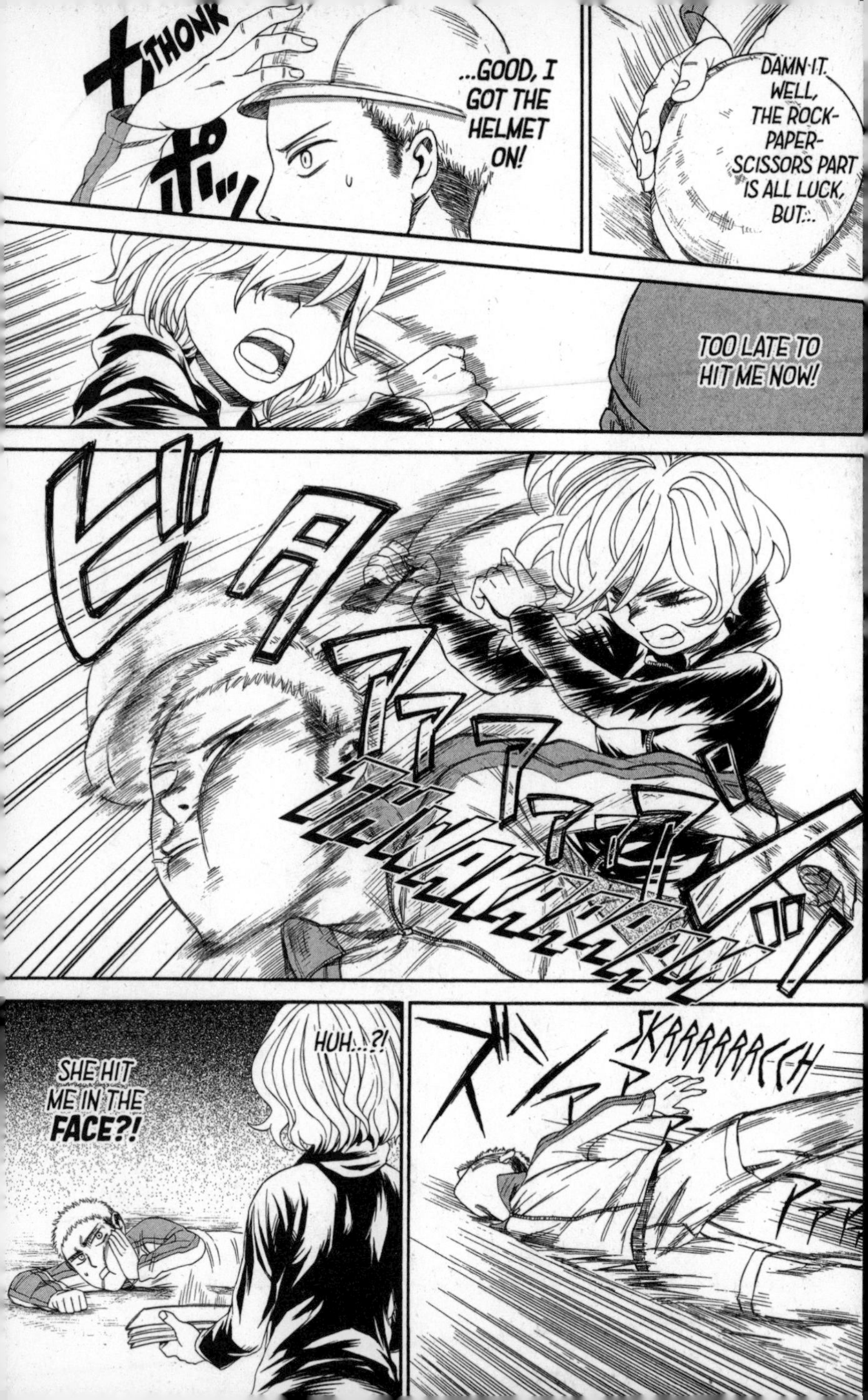
DAMN IT. WELL, THE ROCK-PAPER-SCISSORS PART IS ALL LUCK, BUT...
THONK
...GOOD, I GOT THE HELMET ON!
TOO LATE TO HIT ME NOW!
THWAAAAACK
SKRRRRRRCCH
HUH...?!
SHE HIT ME IN THE FACE?!

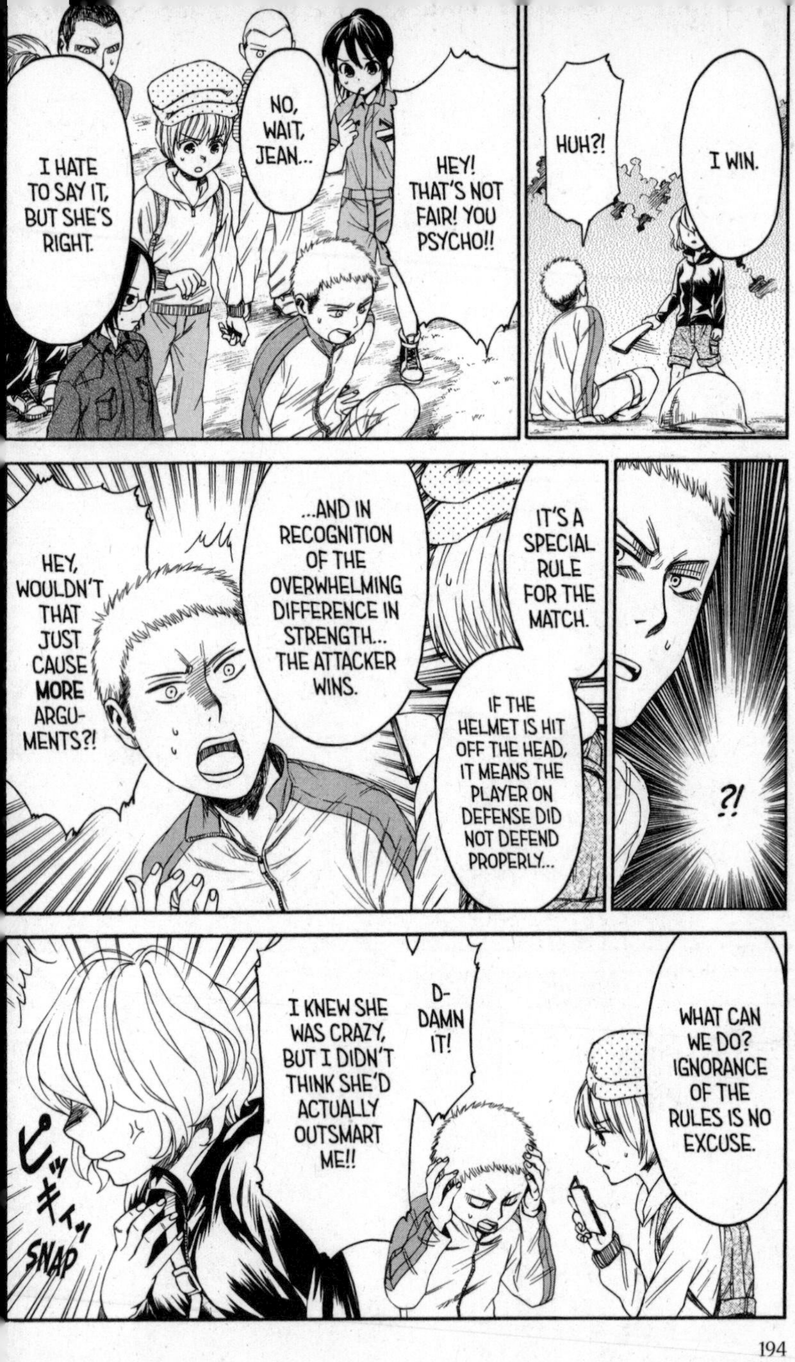
I WIN.
HUH?!
HEY! THAT'S NOT FAIR! YOU PSYCHO!!
NO, WAIT, JEAN...
I HATE TO SAY IT, BUT SHE'S RIGHT.
?!
IT'S A SPECIAL RULE FOR THE MATCH.
IF THE HELMET IS HIT OFF THE HEAD, IT MEANS THE PLAYER ON DEFENSE DID NOT DEFEND PROPERLY...
...AND IN RECOGNITION OF THE OVERWHELMING DIFFERENCE IN STRENGTH... THE ATTACKER WINS.
HEY, WOULDN'T THAT JUST CAUSE **MORE** ARGU- MENTS?!
WHAT CAN WE DO? IGNORANCE OF THE RULES IS NO EXCUSE.
D- DAMN IT!
I KNEW SHE WAS CRAZY, BUT I DIDN'T THINK SHE'D ACTUALLY OUTSMART ME!!
ピッキィッ
SNAP

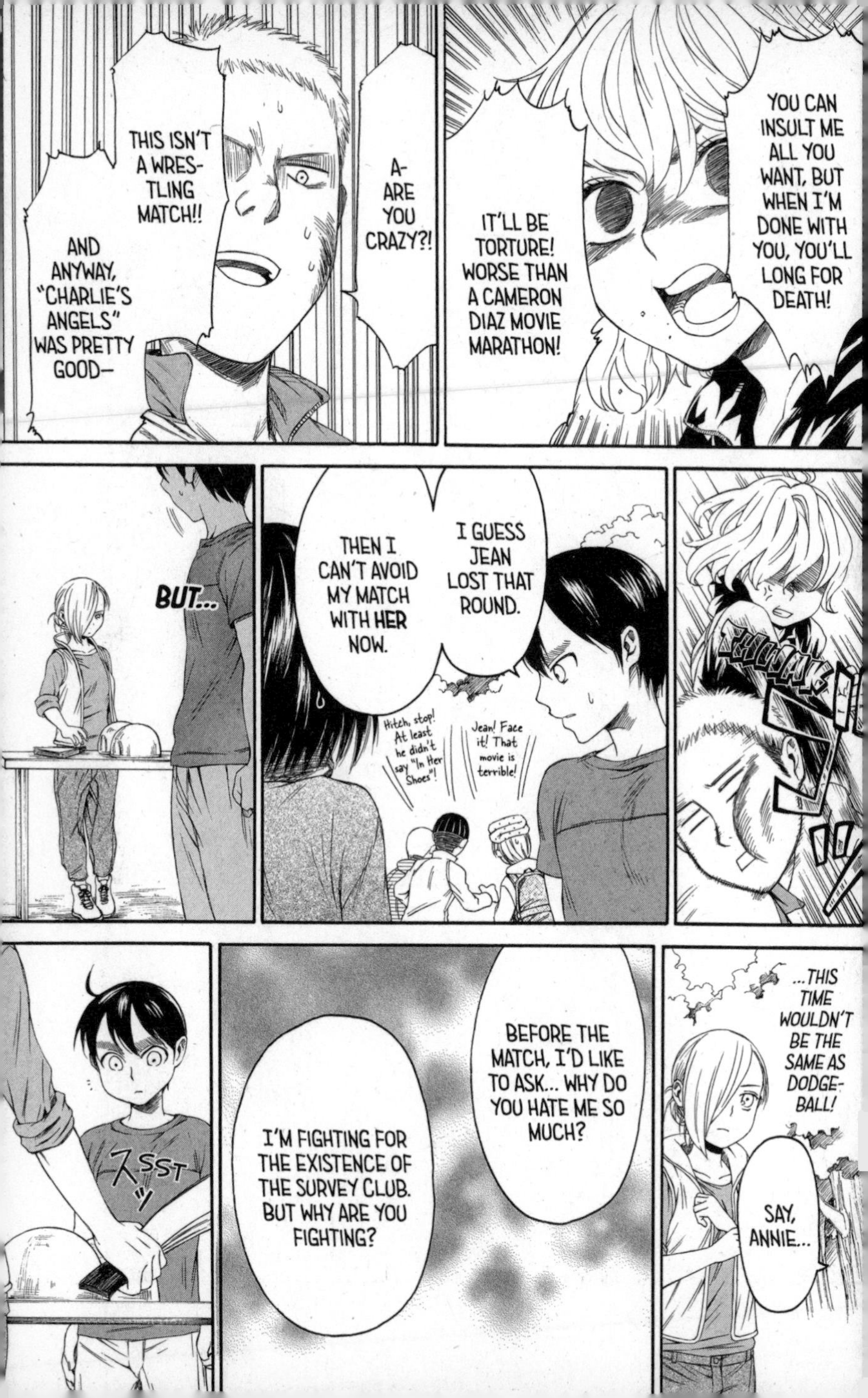
YOU CAN INSULT ME ALL YOU WANT, BUT WHEN I'M DONE WITH YOU, YOU'LL LONG FOR DEATH!
IT'LL BE TORTURE! WORSE THAN A CAMERON DIAZ MOVIE MARATHON!
A- ARE YOU CRAZY?!
THIS ISN'T A WRES- TLING MATCH!!
AND ANYWAY, "CHARLIE'S ANGELS" WAS PRETTY GOOD—
I GUESS JEAN LOST THAT ROUND.
THEN I CAN'T AVOID MY MATCH WITH HER NOW.
Jean! Face it! That movie is terrible!
Hitch, stop! At least he didn't say "In Her Shoes"!
BUT...
...THIS TIME WOULDN'T BE THE SAME AS DODGE- BALL!
SAY, ANNIE...
BEFORE THE MATCH, I'D LIKE TO ASK... WHY DO YOU HATE ME SO MUCH?
I'M FIGHTING FOR THE EXISTENCE OF THE SURVEY CLUB. BUT WHY ARE YOU FIGHTING?
スッ
SST

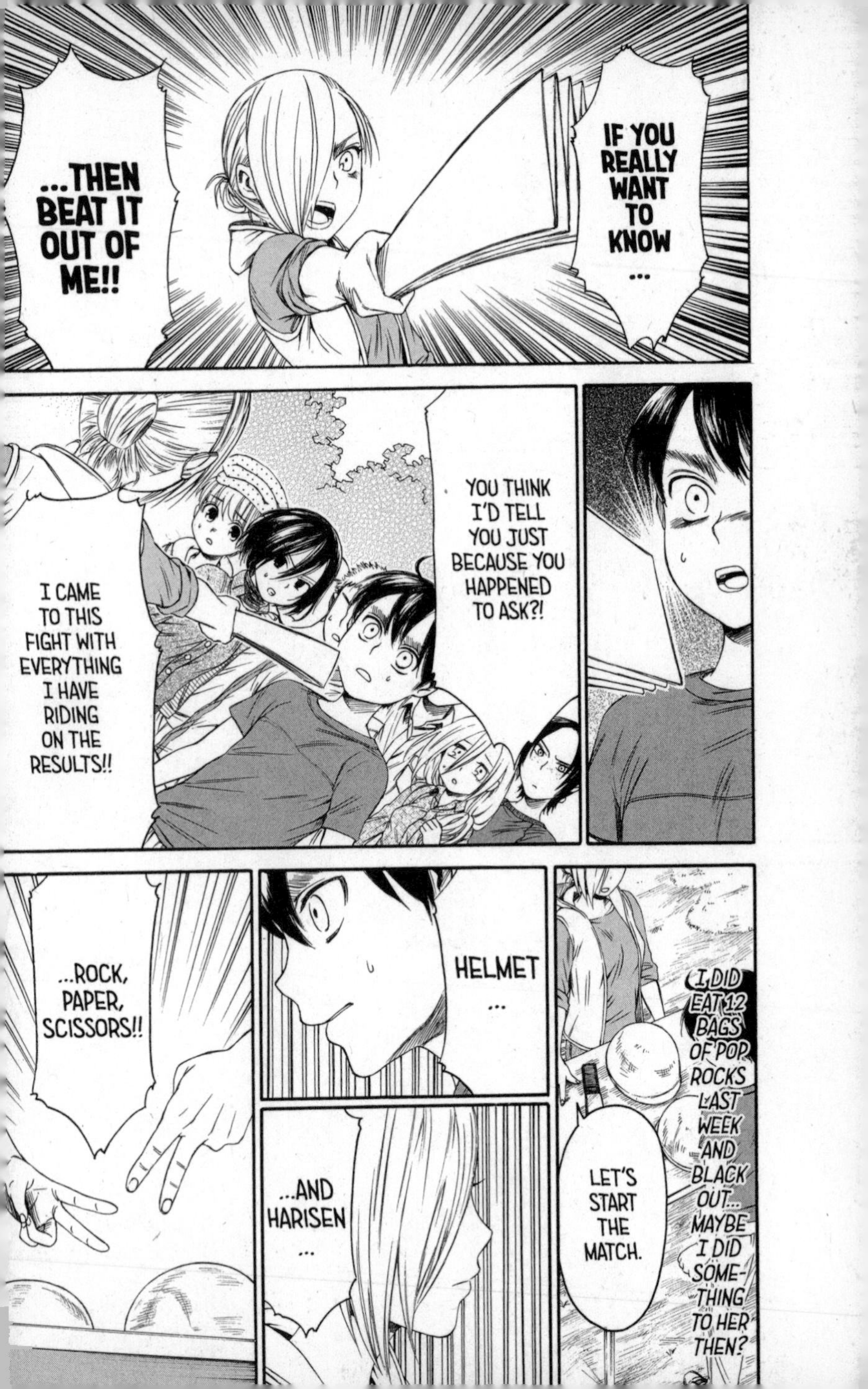
IF YOU REALLY WANT TO KNOW...
...THEN BEAT IT OUT OF ME!!
YOU THINK I'D TELL YOU JUST BECAUSE YOU HAPPENED TO ASK?!
I CAME TO THIS FIGHT WITH EVERYTHING I HAVE RIDING ON THE RESULTS!!
I DID EAT 12 BAGS OF POP ROCKS LAST WEEK AND BLACK OUT... MAYBE I DID SOMETHING TO HER THEN?
LET'S START THE MATCH.
HELMET...
...AND HARISEN...
...ROCK, PAPER, SCISSORS!!

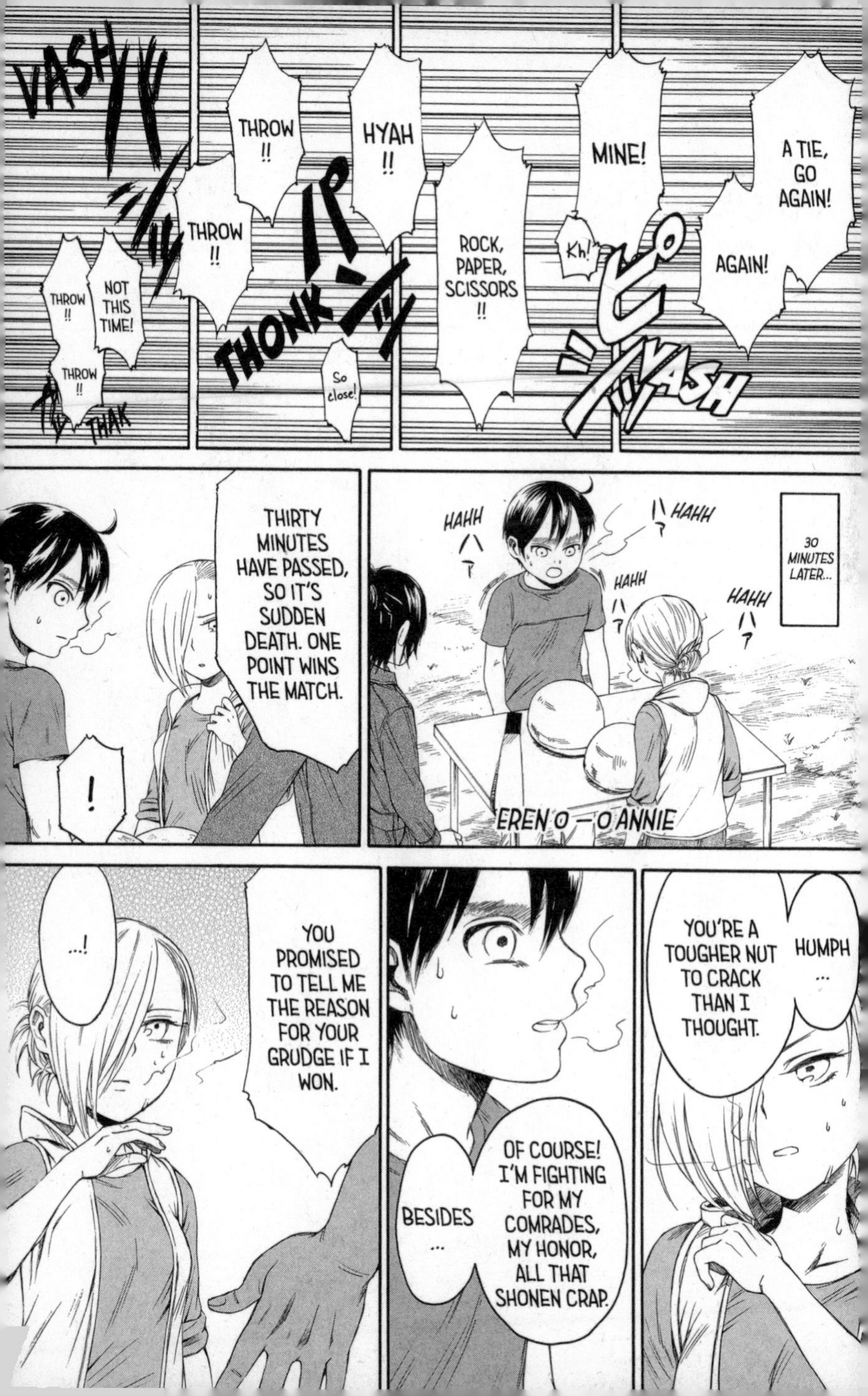
A TIE, GO AGAIN!
AGAIN!
VASH
MINE!
Kh!
ROCK, PAPER, SCISSORS!!
HYAH!!
THROW!!
THROW!!
THONK
So close!
VASH
NOT THIS TIME!
THROW!!
THROW!!
THAK
30 MINUTES LATER...
HAHH
HAHH
HAHH
HAHH
EREN 0 — 0 ANNIE
THIRTY MINUTES HAVE PASSED, SO IT'S SUDDEN DEATH. ONE POINT WINS THE MATCH.
!
HUMPH...
YOU'RE A TOUGHER NUT TO CRACK THAN I THOUGHT.
OF COURSE! I'M FIGHTING FOR MY COMRADES, MY HONOR, ALL THAT SHONEN CRAP.
BESIDES...
YOU PROMISED TO TELL ME THE REASON FOR YOUR GRUDGE IF I WON.
...!

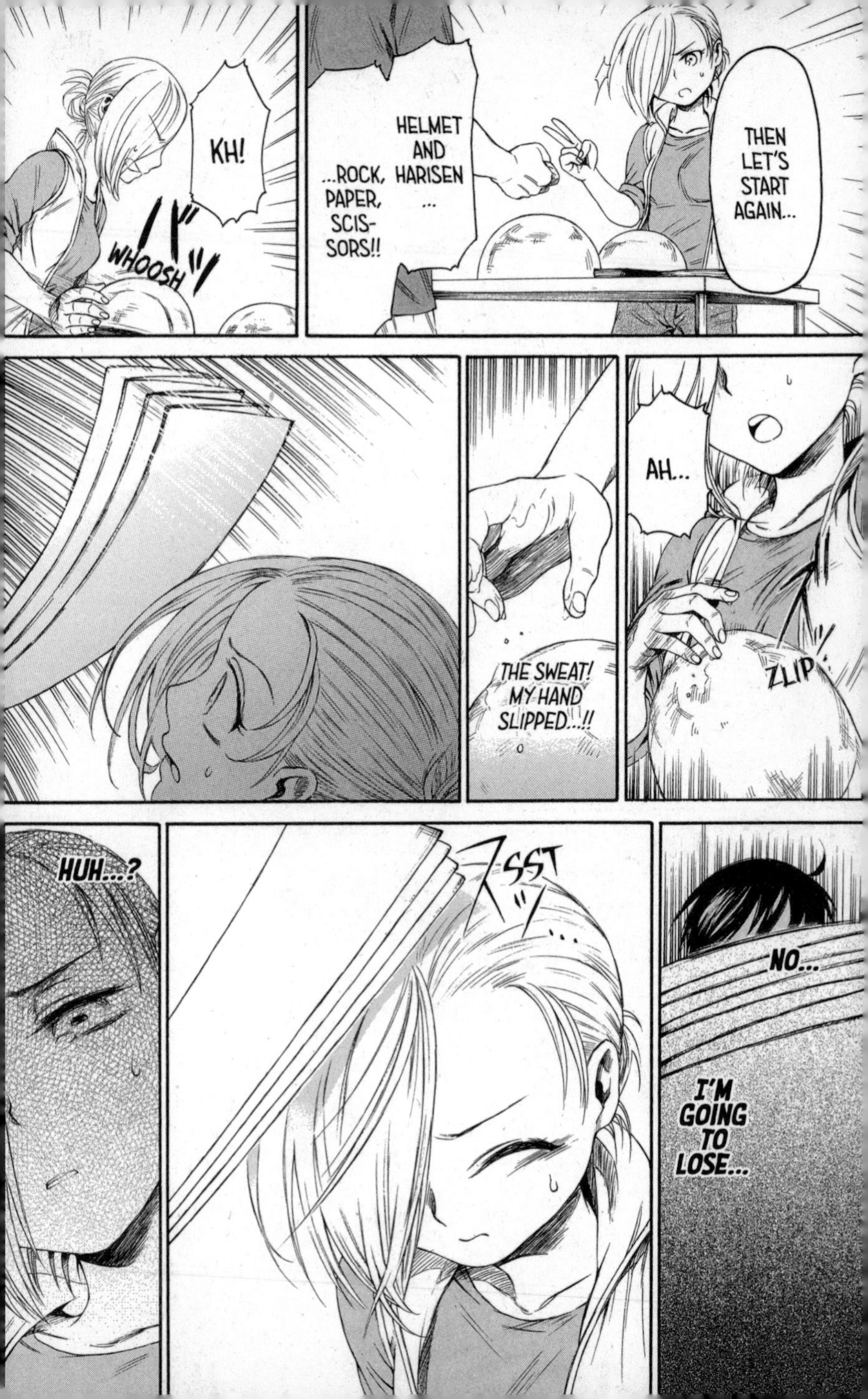
THEN LET'S START AGAIN...
HELMET AND HARISEN...
...ROCK, PAPER, SCISSORS!!
KH!
WHOOSH
AH...
ZLIP
THE SWEAT! MY HAND SLIPPED...!!
NO...
I'M GOING TO LOSE...
RSST
...
HUH...?

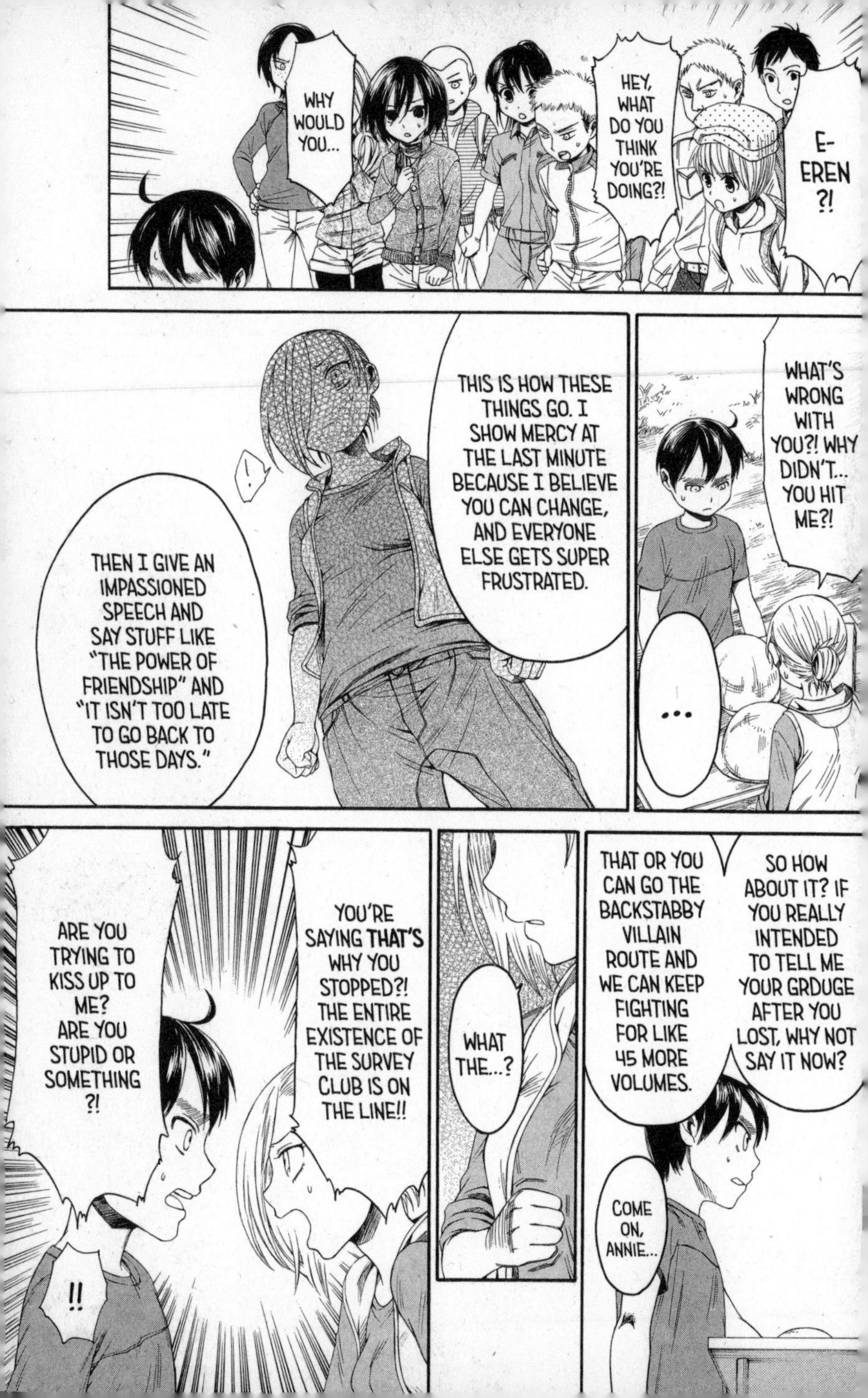
E-EREN?!
HEY, WHAT DO YOU THINK YOU'RE DOING?!
WHY WOULD YOU...
WHAT'S WRONG WITH YOU?! WHY DIDN'T... YOU HIT ME?!
...
THIS IS HOW THESE THINGS GO. I SHOW MERCY AT THE LAST MINUTE BECAUSE I BELIEVE YOU CAN CHANGE, AND EVERYONE ELSE GETS SUPER FRUSTRATED.
!
THEN I GIVE AN IMPASSIONED SPEECH AND SAY STUFF LIKE "THE POWER OF FRIENDSHIP" AND "IT ISN'T TOO LATE TO GO BACK TO THOSE DAYS."
SO HOW ABOUT IT? IF YOU REALLY INTENDED TO TELL ME YOUR GRDUGE AFTER YOU LOST, WHY NOT SAY IT NOW?
THAT OR YOU CAN GO THE BACKSTABBY VILLAIN ROUTE AND WE CAN KEEP FIGHTING FOR LIKE 45 MORE VOLUMES.
COME ON, ANNIE...
WHAT THE...?
YOU'RE SAYING **THAT'S** WHY YOU STOPPED?! THE ENTIRE EXISTENCE OF THE SURVEY CLUB IS ON THE LINE!!
ARE YOU TRYING TO KISS UP TO ME? ARE YOU STUPID OR SOMETHING?!
!!

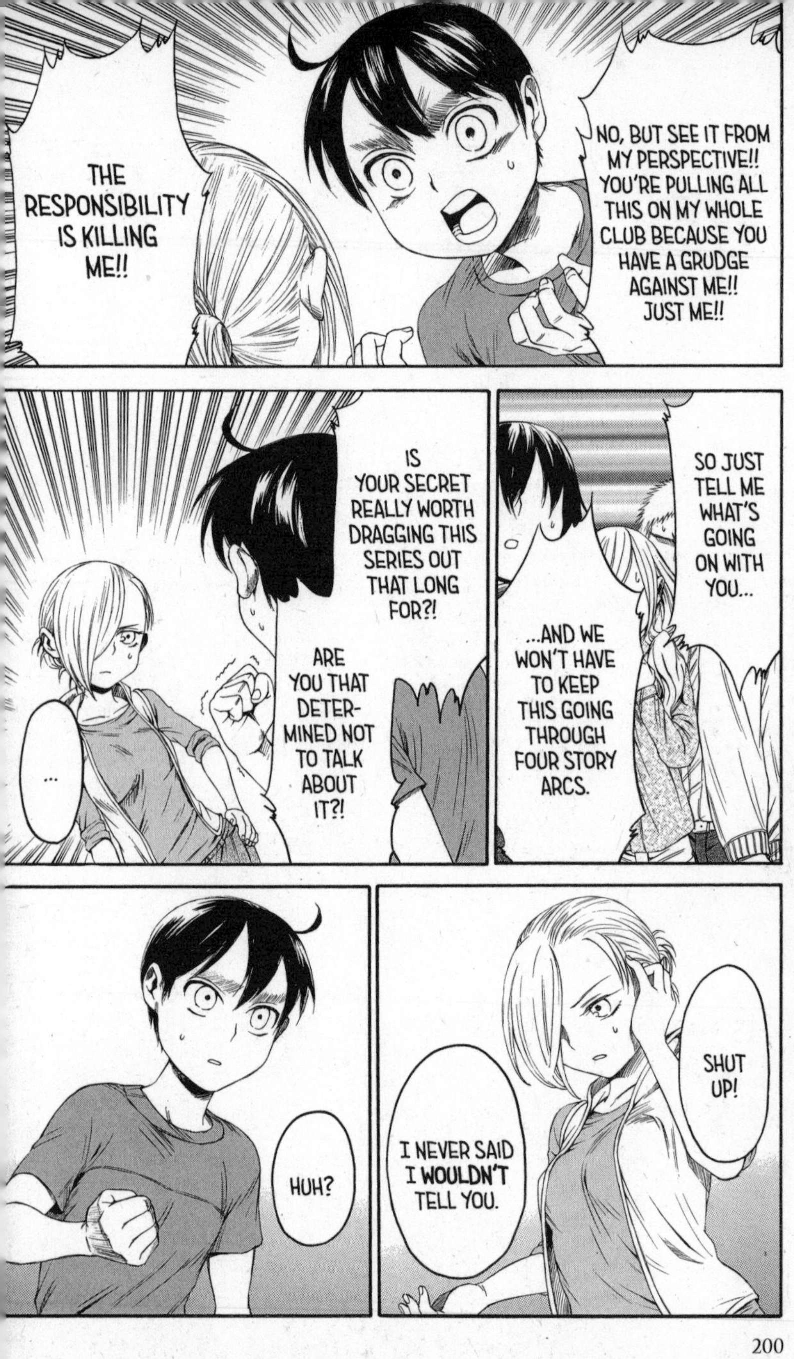
NO, BUT SEE IT FROM MY PERSPECTIVE!! YOU'RE PULLING ALL THIS ON MY WHOLE CLUB BECAUSE YOU HAVE A GRUDGE AGAINST ME!! JUST ME!!
THE RESPONSIBILITY IS KILLING ME!!
SO JUST TELL ME WHAT'S GOING ON WITH YOU...
...AND WE WON'T HAVE TO KEEP THIS GOING THROUGH FOUR STORY ARCS.
IS YOUR SECRET REALLY WORTH DRAGGING THIS SERIES OUT THAT LONG FOR?!
ARE YOU THAT DETERMINED NOT TO TALK ABOUT IT?!
...
SHUT UP!
I NEVER SAID I **WOULDN'T** TELL YOU.
HUH?

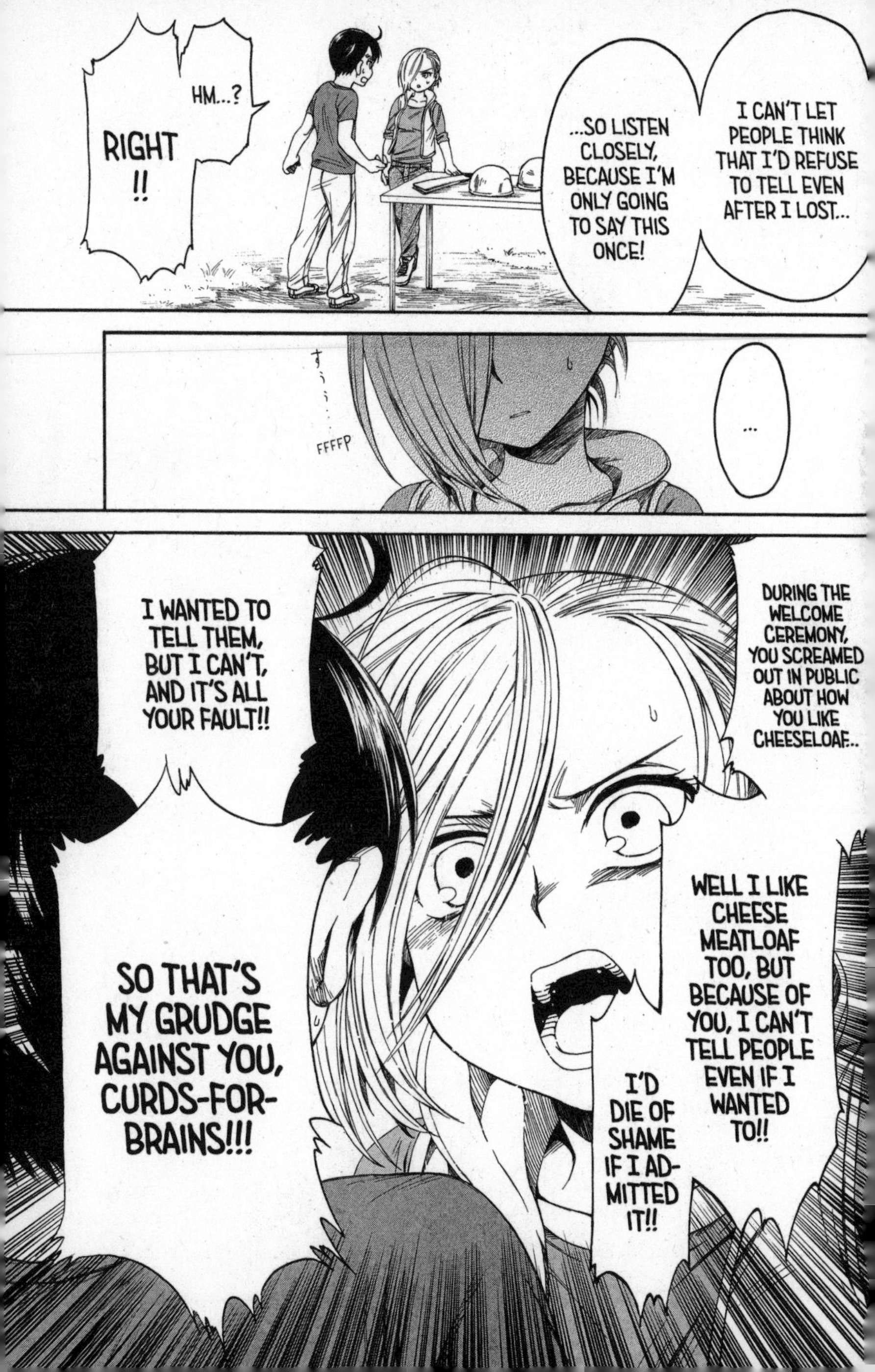

I CAN'T LET PEOPLE THINK THAT I'D REFUSE TO TELL EVEN AFTER I LOST...
...SO LISTEN CLOSELY, BECAUSE I'M ONLY GOING TO SAY THIS ONCE!
HM...?
RIGHT !!
...
FFFFP
DURING THE WELCOME CEREMONY, YOU SCREAMED OUT IN PUBLIC ABOUT HOW YOU LIKE CHEESELOAF...
WELL I LIKE CHEESE MEATLOAF TOO, BUT BECAUSE OF YOU, I CAN'T TELL PEOPLE EVEN IF I WANTED TO!!
I'D DIE OF SHAME IF I ADMITTED IT!!
I WANTED TO TELL THEM, BUT I CAN'T, AND IT'S ALL YOUR FAULT!!
SO THAT'S MY GRUDGE AGAINST YOU, CURDS-FOR-BRAINS!!!

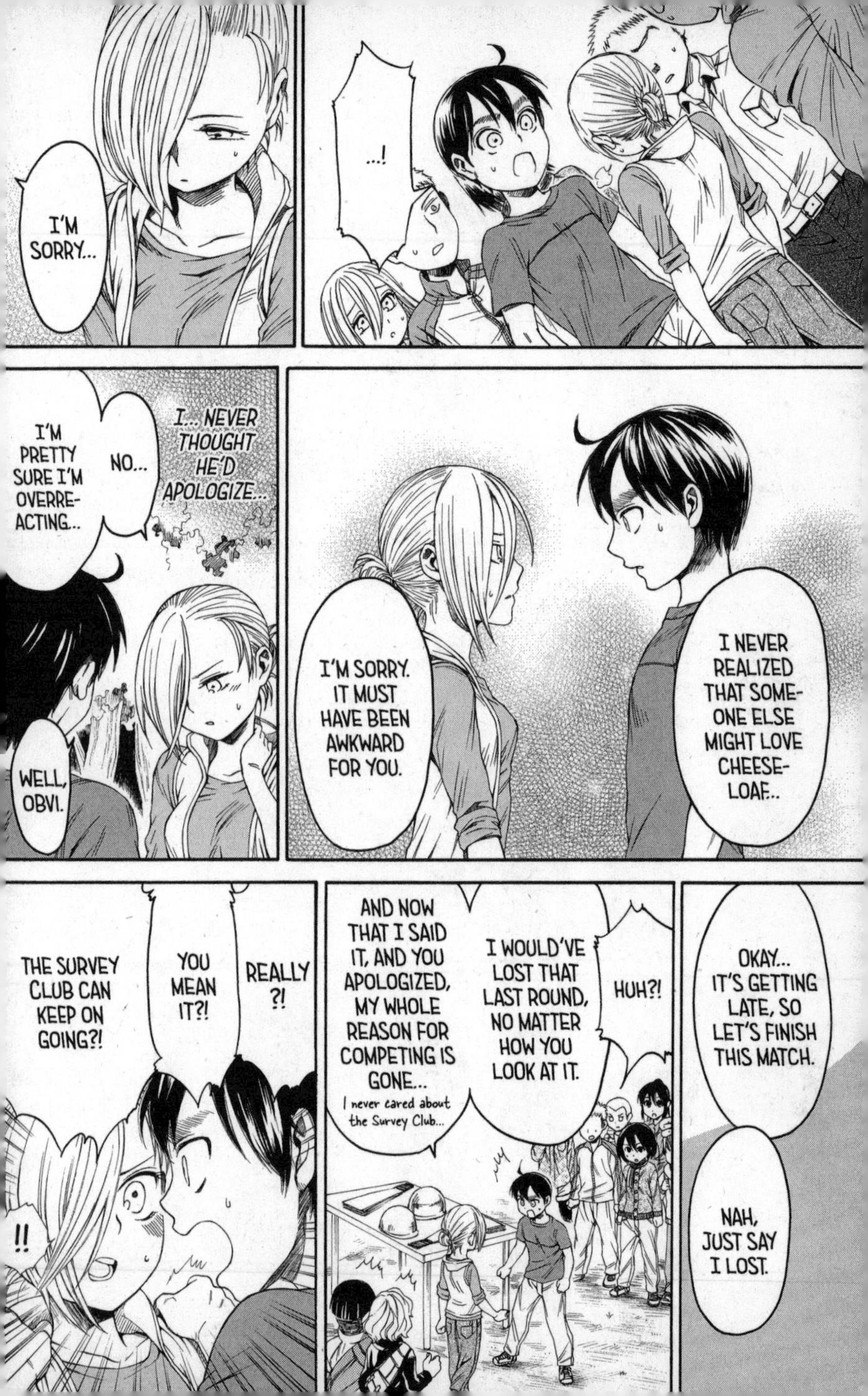
...!
I'M SORRY...
I NEVER REALIZED THAT SOMEONE ELSE MIGHT LOVE CHEESELOAF...
I'M SORRY. IT MUST HAVE BEEN AWKWARD FOR YOU.
I... NEVER THOUGHT HE'D APOLOGIZE...
NO...
I'M PRETTY SURE I'M OVERREACTING...
WELL, OBVI.
OKAY... IT'S GETTING LATE, SO LET'S FINISH THIS MATCH.
NAH, JUST SAY I LOST.
HUH?!
I WOULD'VE LOST THAT LAST ROUND, NO MATTER HOW YOU LOOK AT IT.
AND NOW THAT I SAID IT, AND YOU APOLOGIZED, MY WHOLE REASON FOR COMPETING IS GONE...
I never cared about the Survey Club...
REALLY?!
YOU MEAN IT?!
THE SURVEY CLUB CAN KEEP ON GOING?!
!!

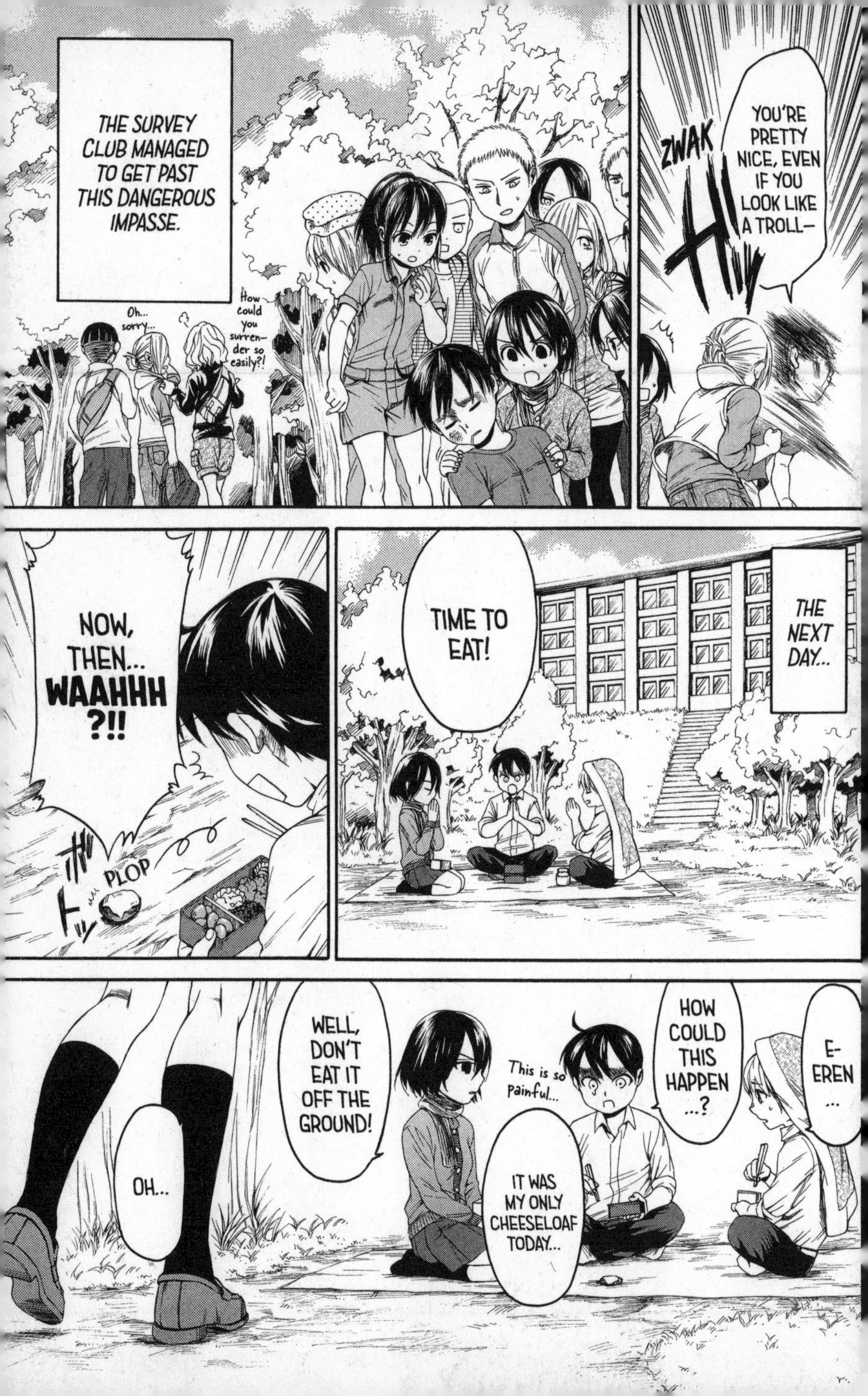
ZWAK
YOU'RE PRETTY NICE, EVEN IF YOU LOOK LIKE A TROLL—
THE SURVEY CLUB MANAGED TO GET PAST THIS DANGEROUS IMPASSE.
How could you surren-der so easily?!
Oh... sorry...
THE NEXT DAY...
TIME TO EAT!
NOW, THEN... WAAHHH ?!!
PLOP
E-EREN...
HOW COULD THIS HAPPEN ...?
This is so painful...
IT WAS MY ONLY CHEESELOAF TODAY...
WELL, DON'T EAT IT OFF THE GROUND!
OH...

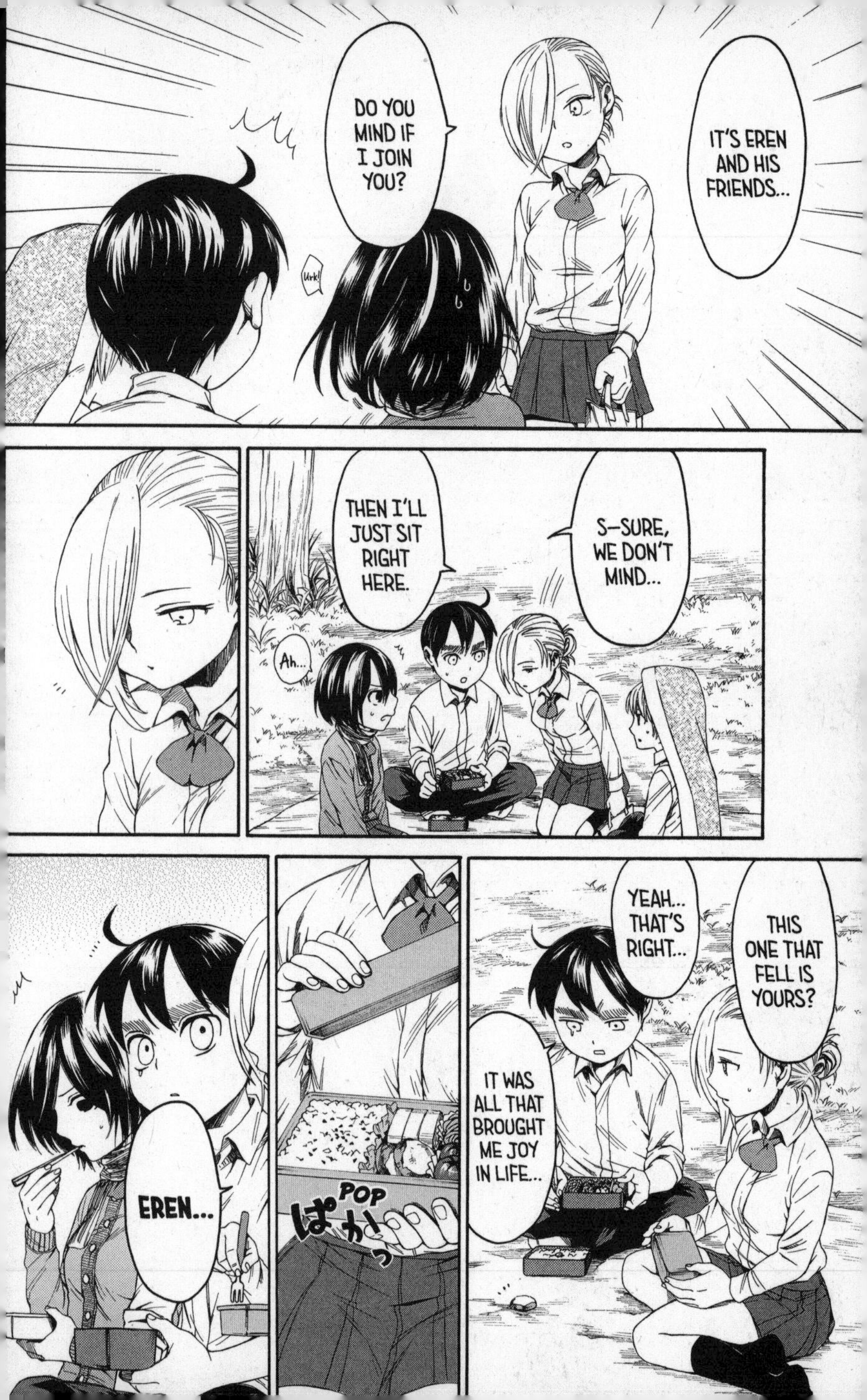
IT'S EREN AND HIS FRIENDS...
DO YOU MIND IF I JOIN YOU?
Urk!
S-SURE, WE DON'T MIND...
THEN I'LL JUST SIT RIGHT HERE.
Ah...
THIS ONE THAT FELL IS YOURS?
YEAH... THAT'S RIGHT...
IT WAS ALL THAT BROUGHT ME JOY IN LIFE...
POP
ぱかっ
EREN...

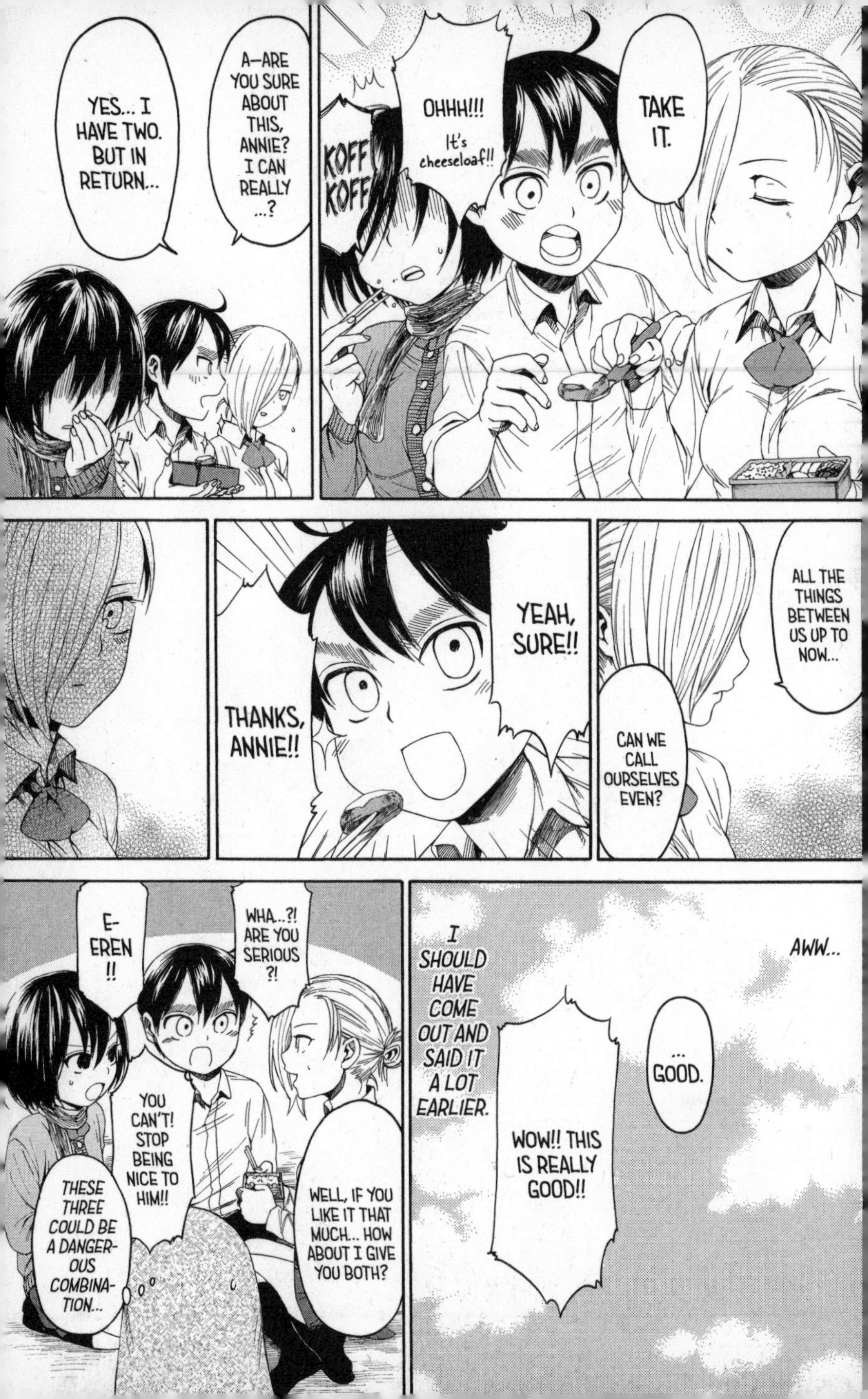
TAKE IT.
OHHH!!!
It's cheeseloaf!!
KOFF KOFF
A—ARE YOU SURE ABOUT THIS, ANNIE? I CAN REALLY ...?
YES... I HAVE TWO. BUT IN RETURN...
ALL THE THINGS BETWEEN US UP TO NOW...
CAN WE CALL OURSELVES EVEN?
YEAH, SURE!!
THANKS, ANNIE!!
AWW...
... GOOD.
WOW!! THIS IS REALLY GOOD!!
I SHOULD HAVE COME OUT AND SAID IT A LOT EARLIER.
WHA...?! ARE YOU SERIOUS ?!
E- EREN !!
WELL, IF YOU LIKE IT THAT MUCH... HOW ABOUT I GIVE YOU BOTH?
YOU CAN'T! STOP BEING NICE TO HIM!!
THESE THREE COULD BE A DANGER-OUS COMBINA-TION...

SIZZLE SIZZLE BONUS MANGA

LET'S HAVE THE BEST SUMMER EVER!!

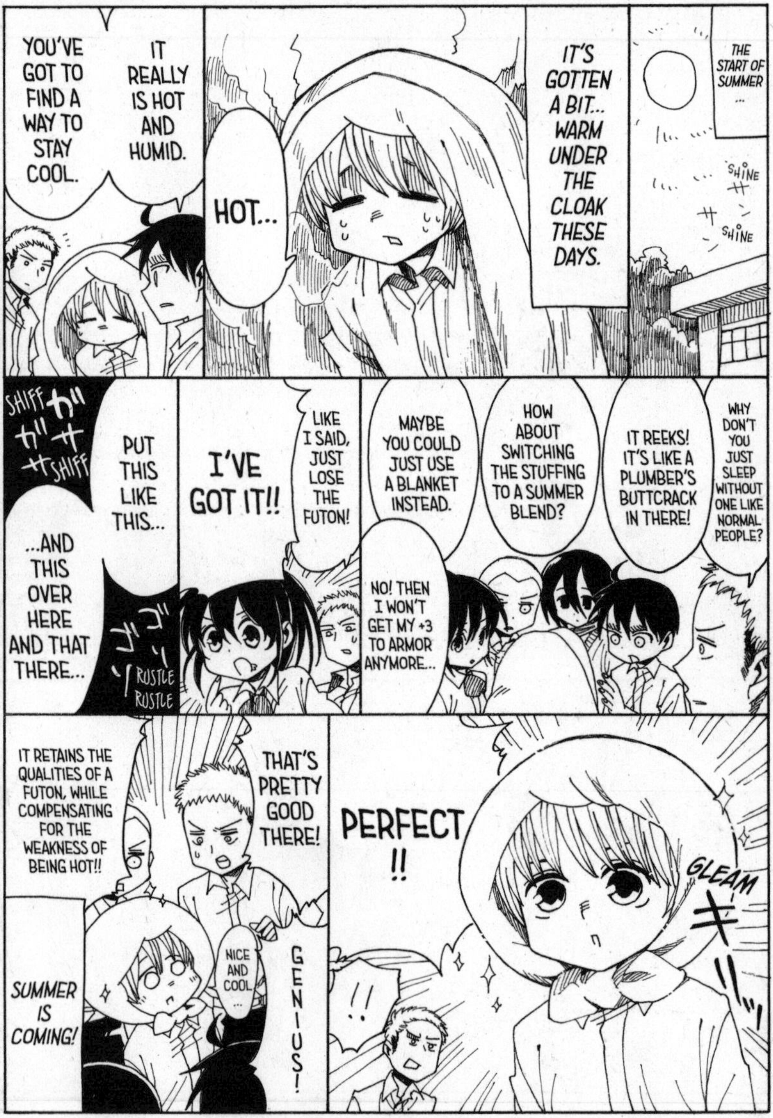
THE START OF SUMMER...
SHINE
SHINE
IT'S GOTTEN A BIT... WARM UNDER THE CLOAK THESE DAYS.
HOT...
IT REALLY IS HOT AND HUMID.
YOU'VE GOT TO FIND A WAY TO STAY COOL.
WHY DON'T YOU JUST SLEEP WITHOUT ONE LIKE NORMAL PEOPLE?
IT REEKS! IT'S LIKE A PLUMBER'S BUTTCRACK IN THERE!
HOW ABOUT SWITCHING THE STUFFING TO A SUMMER BLEND?
MAYBE YOU COULD JUST USE A BLANKET INSTEAD.
LIKE I SAID, JUST LOSE THE FUTON!
NO! THEN I WON'T GET MY +3 TO ARMOR ANYMORE...
I'VE GOT IT!!
RUSTLE RUSTLE
PUT THIS LIKE THIS...
SHIFF SHIFF
...AND THIS OVER HERE AND THAT THERE...
GLEAM
PERFECT!!
THAT'S PRETTY GOOD THERE!
IT RETAINS THE QUALITIES OF A FUTON, WHILE COMPENSATING FOR THE WEAKNESS OF BEING HOT!!
GENIUS!
NICE AND COOL...
SUMMER IS COMING!

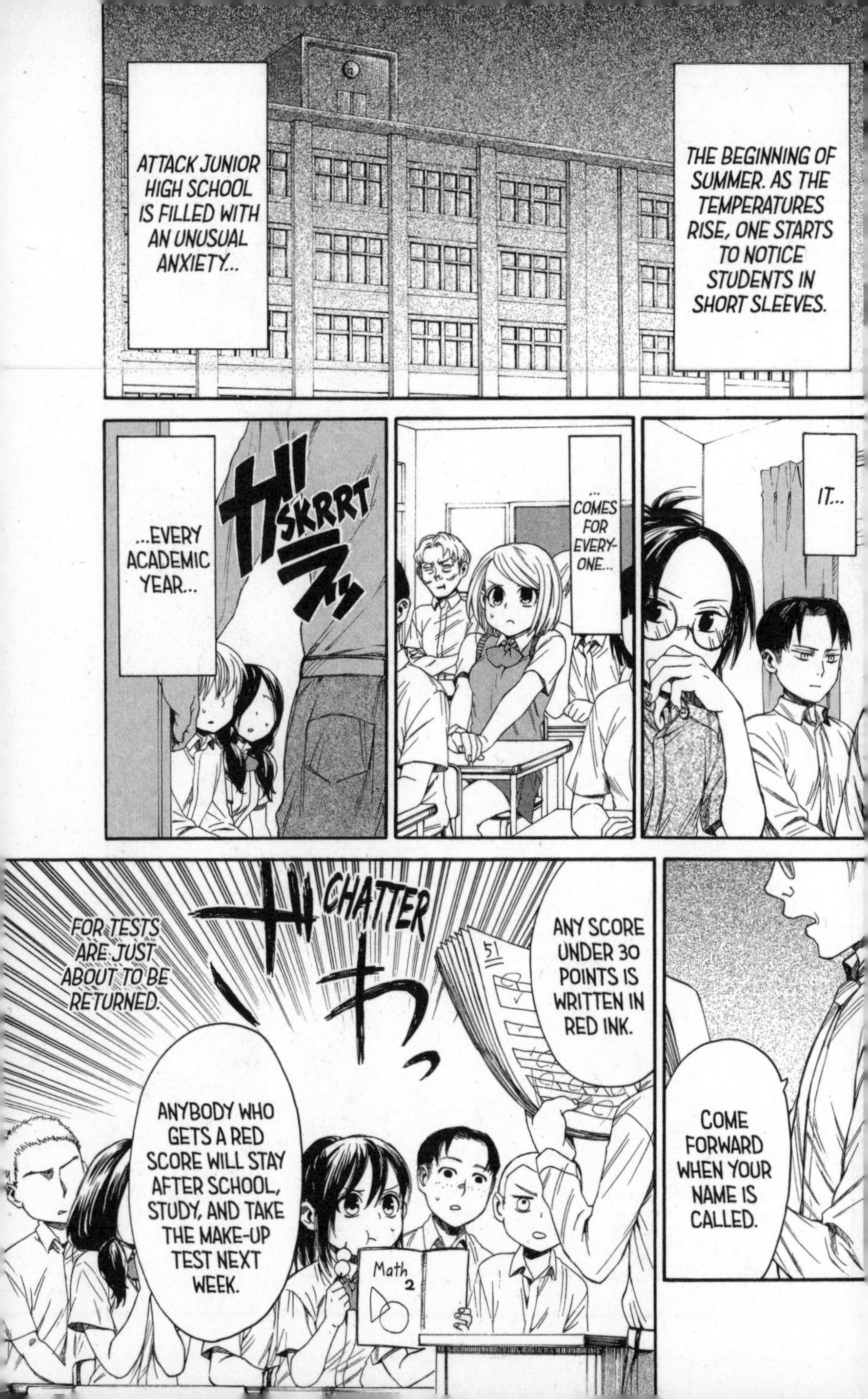
THE BEGINNING OF SUMMER. AS THE TEMPERATURES RISE, ONE STARTS TO NOTICE STUDENTS IN SHORT SLEEVES.
ATTACK JUNIOR HIGH SCHOOL IS FILLED WITH AN UNUSUAL ANXIETY...
IT...
...COMES FOR EVERY-ONE...
SKRRT
...EVERY ACADEMIC YEAR...
COME FORWARD WHEN YOUR NAME IS CALLED.
ANY SCORE UNDER 30 POINTS IS WRITTEN IN RED INK.
CHATTER
FOR TESTS ARE JUST ABOUT TO BE RETURNED.
ANYBODY WHO GETS A RED SCORE WILL STAY AFTER SCHOOL, STUDY, AND TAKE THE MAKE-UP TEST NEXT WEEK.
Math 2

ELEVENTH PERIOD: EVERYONE'S AFTER SCHOOL

Sasha's Remedial After School

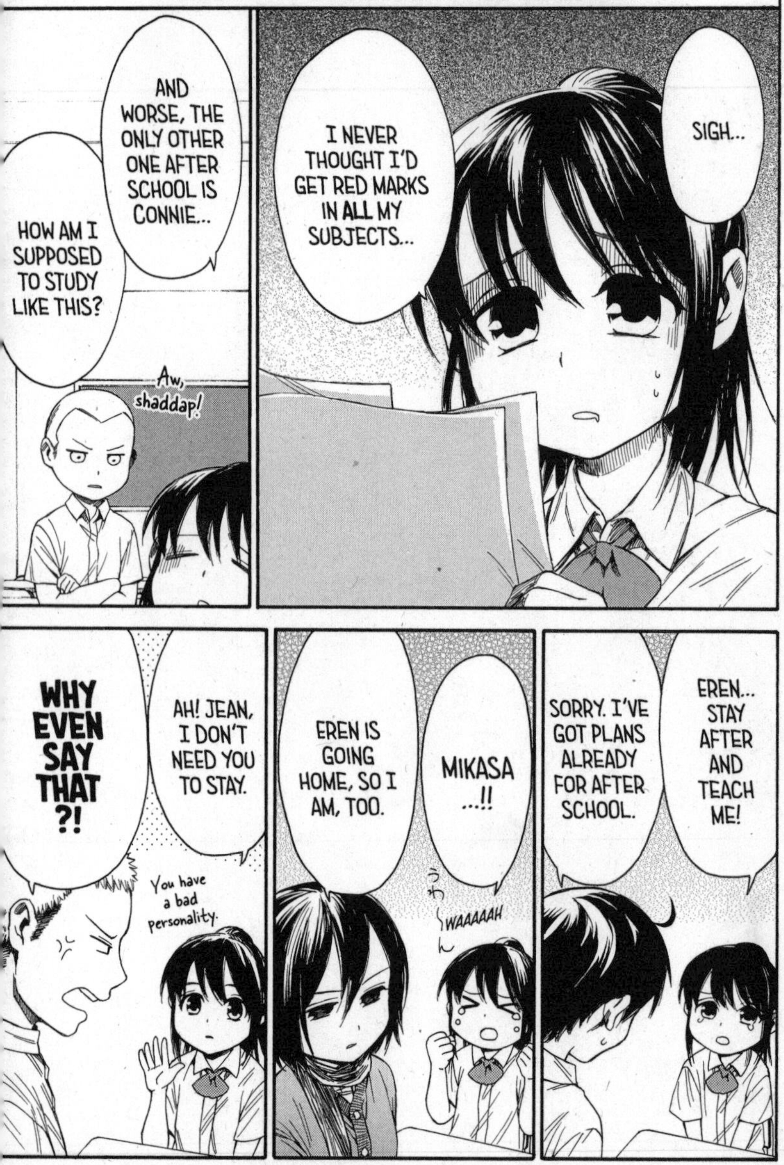
SIGH...
I NEVER THOUGHT I'D GET RED MARKS IN ALL MY SUBJECTS...
AND WORSE, THE ONLY OTHER ONE AFTER SCHOOL IS CONNIE...
HOW AM I SUPPOSED TO STUDY LIKE THIS?
Aw, shaddap!
EREN... STAY AFTER AND TEACH ME!
SORRY. I'VE GOT PLANS ALREADY FOR AFTER SCHOOL.
MIKASA ...!!
EREN IS GOING HOME, SO I AM, TOO.
WAAAAAH
AH! JEAN, I DON'T NEED YOU TO STAY.
WHY EVEN SAY THAT?!
You have a bad personality.

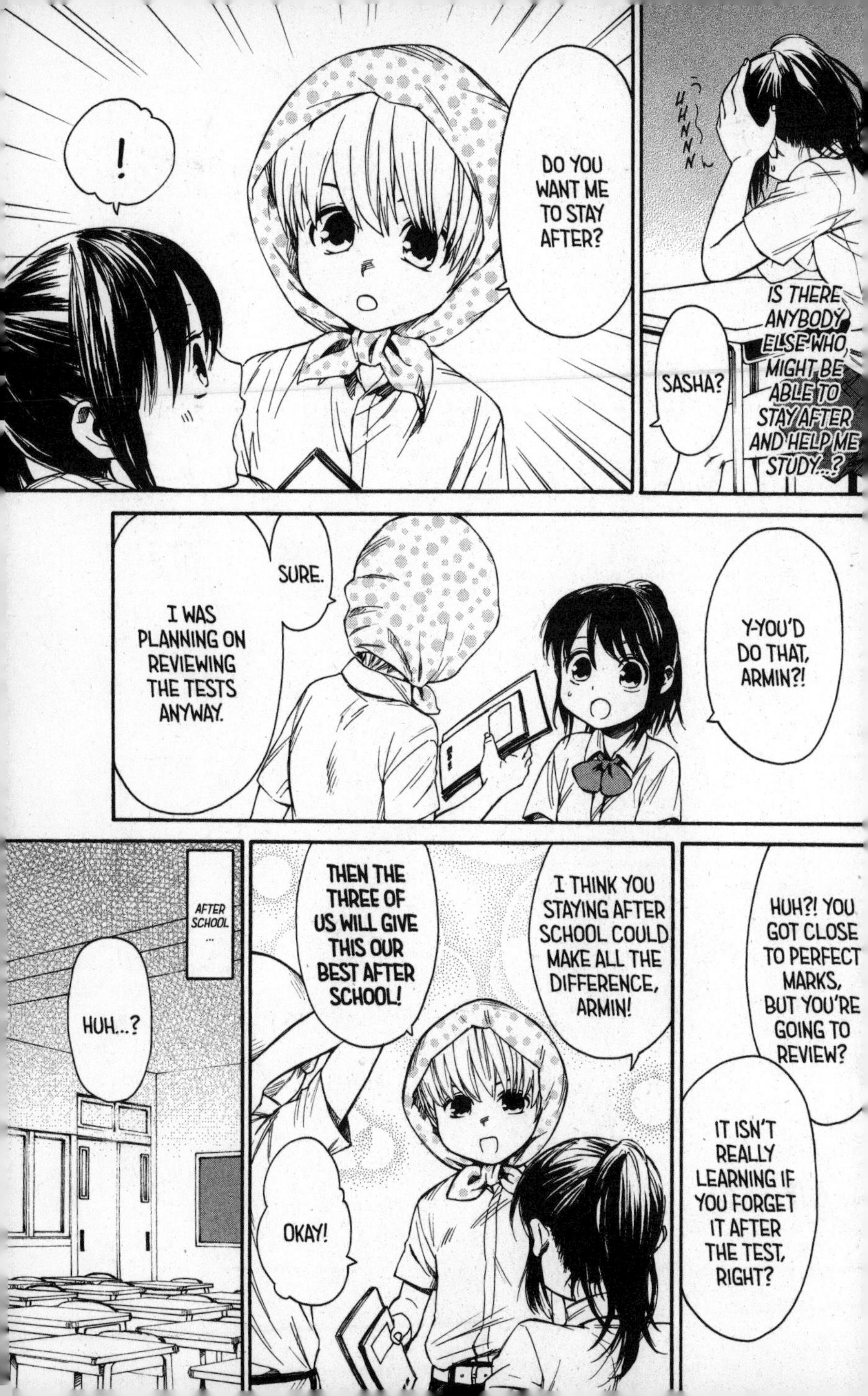
UHHNNN~
IS THERE ANYBODY ELSE WHO MIGHT BE ABLE TO STAY AFTER AND HELP ME STUDY...?
SASHA?
DO YOU WANT ME TO STAY AFTER?
!
Y-YOU'D DO THAT, ARMIN?!
SURE.
I WAS PLANNING ON REVIEWING THE TESTS ANYWAY.
HUH?! YOU GOT CLOSE TO PERFECT MARKS, BUT YOU'RE GOING TO REVIEW?
IT ISN'T REALLY LEARNING IF YOU FORGET IT AFTER THE TEST, RIGHT?
I THINK YOU STAYING AFTER SCHOOL COULD MAKE ALL THE DIFFERENCE, ARMIN!
THEN THE THREE OF US WILL GIVE THIS OUR BEST AFTER SCHOOL!
OKAY!
AFTER SCHOOL...
HUH...?

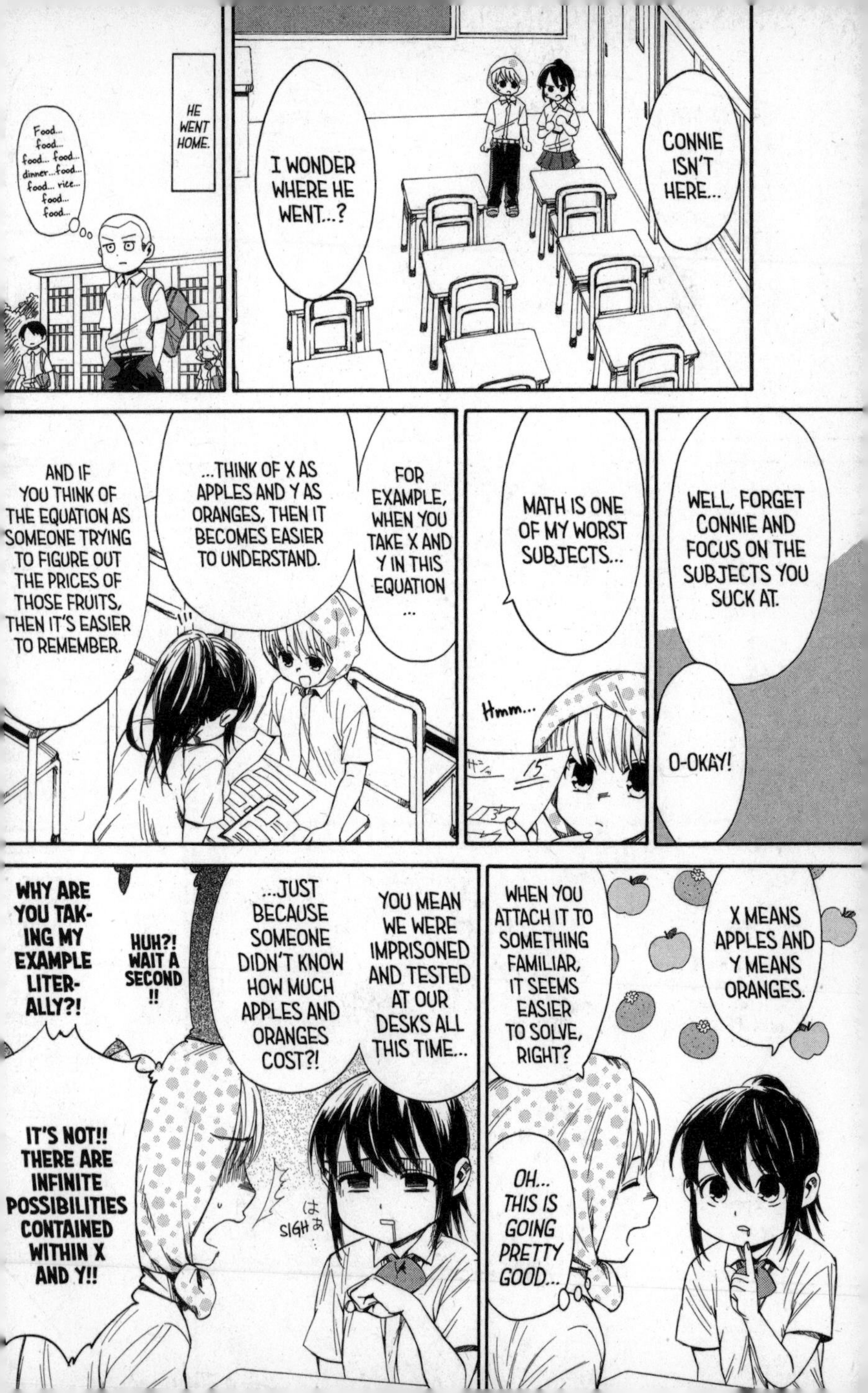
CONNIE ISN'T HERE...
I WONDER WHERE HE WENT...?
HE WENT HOME.
Food... food... food... food... dinner...food... food... rice... food... food...
WELL, FORGET CONNIE AND FOCUS ON THE SUBJECTS YOU SUCK AT.
O-OKAY!
MATH IS ONE OF MY WORST SUBJECTS...
Hmm...
15
FOR EXAMPLE, WHEN YOU TAKE X AND Y IN THIS EQUATION...
...THINK OF X AS APPLES AND Y AS ORANGES, THEN IT BECOMES EASIER TO UNDERSTAND.
AND IF YOU THINK OF THE EQUATION AS SOMEONE TRYING TO FIGURE OUT THE PRICES OF THOSE FRUITS, THEN IT'S EASIER TO REMEMBER.
X MEANS APPLES AND Y MEANS ORANGES.
WHEN YOU ATTACH IT TO SOMETHING FAMILIAR, IT SEEMS EASIER TO SOLVE, RIGHT?
OH... THIS IS GOING PRETTY GOOD...
YOU MEAN WE WERE IMPRISONED AND TESTED AT OUR DESKS ALL THIS TIME...
...JUST BECAUSE SOMEONE DIDN'T KNOW HOW MUCH APPLES AND ORANGES COST?!
SIGH はあ
HUH?! WAIT A SECOND!!
WHY ARE YOU TAKING MY EXAMPLE LITERALLY?!
IT'S NOT!! THERE ARE INFINITE POSSIBILITIES CONTAINED WITHIN X AND Y!!

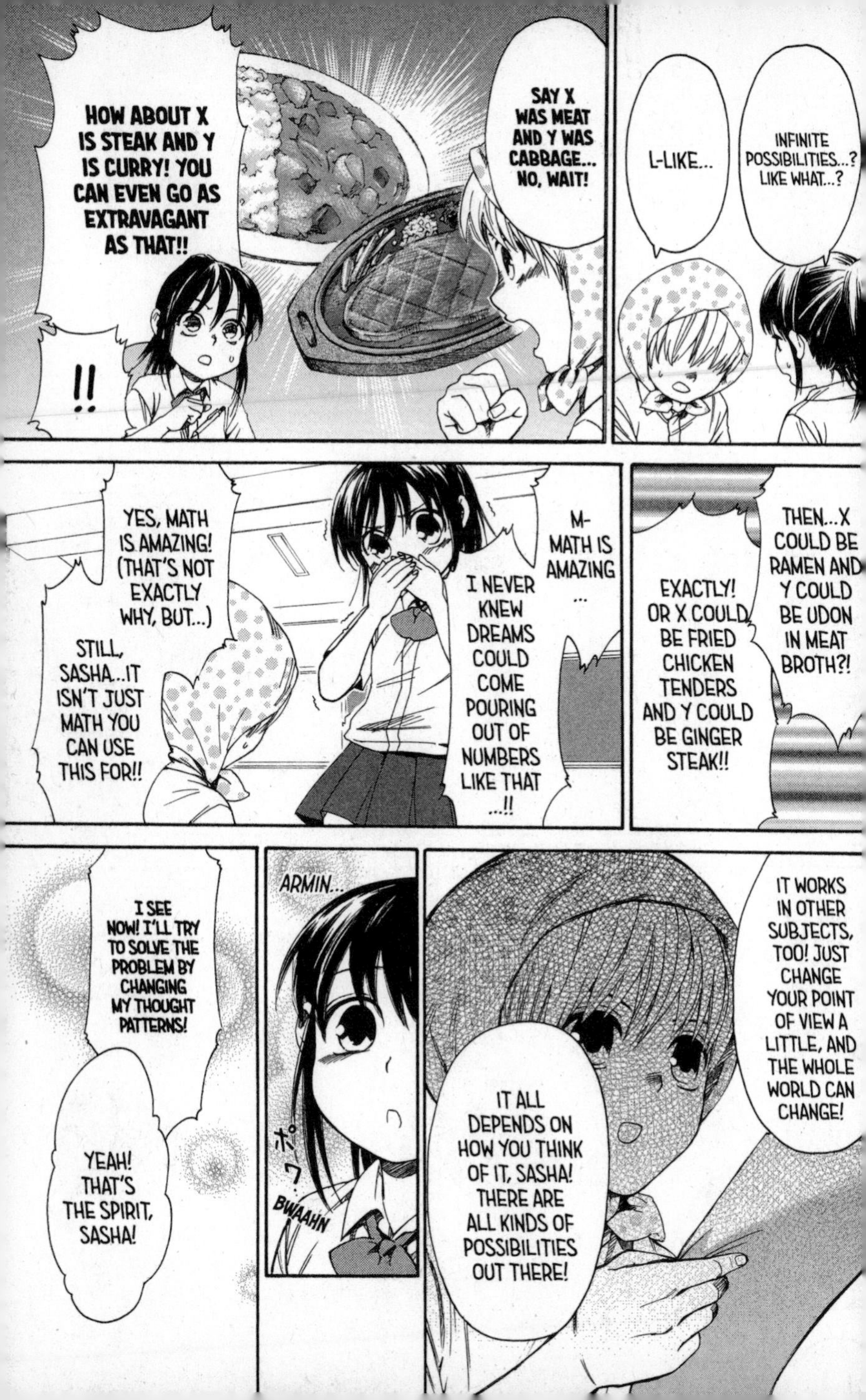
INFINITE POSSIBILITIES...? LIKE WHAT...?
L-LIKE...
SAY X WAS MEAT AND Y WAS CABBAGE... NO, WAIT!
HOW ABOUT X IS STEAK AND Y IS CURRY! YOU CAN EVEN GO AS EXTRAVAGANT AS THAT!!
!!
THEN...X COULD BE RAMEN AND Y COULD BE UDON IN MEAT BROTH?!
EXACTLY! OR X COULD BE FRIED CHICKEN TENDERS AND Y COULD BE GINGER STEAK!!
M-MATH IS AMAZING...
I NEVER KNEW DREAMS COULD COME POURING OUT OF NUMBERS LIKE THAT...!!
YES, MATH IS AMAZING! (THAT'S NOT EXACTLY WHY, BUT...)
STILL, SASHA...IT ISN'T JUST MATH YOU CAN USE THIS FOR!!
IT WORKS IN OTHER SUBJECTS, TOO! JUST CHANGE YOUR POINT OF VIEW A LITTLE, AND THE WHOLE WORLD CAN CHANGE!
IT ALL DEPENDS ON HOW YOU THINK OF IT, SASHA! THERE ARE ALL KINDS OF POSSIBILITIES OUT THERE!
ARMIN...
ポワ
BWAAHN
I SEE NOW! I'LL TRY TO SOLVE THE PROBLEM BY CHANGING MY THOUGHT PATTERNS!
YEAH! THAT'S THE SPIRIT, SASHA!

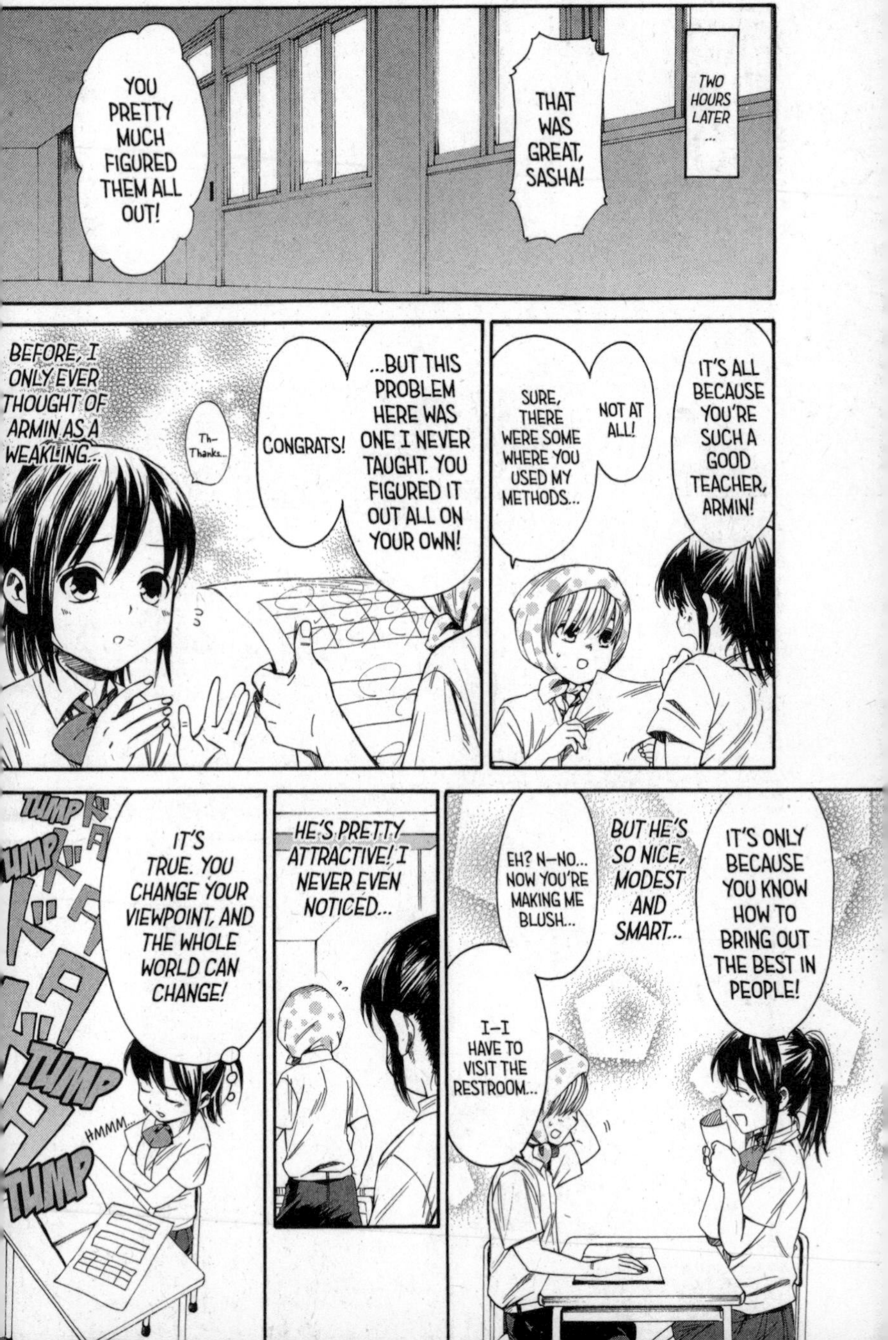
TWO HOURS LATER ...
THAT WAS GREAT, SASHA!
YOU PRETTY MUCH FIGURED THEM ALL OUT!
IT'S ALL BECAUSE YOU'RE SUCH A GOOD TEACHER, ARMIN!
NOT AT ALL!
SURE, THERE WERE SOME WHERE YOU USED MY METHODS...
...BUT THIS PROBLEM HERE WAS ONE I NEVER TAUGHT. YOU FIGURED IT OUT ALL ON YOUR OWN!
CONGRATS!
Th- Thanks...
BEFORE, I ONLY EVER THOUGHT OF ARMIN AS A WEAKLING...
IT'S ONLY BECAUSE YOU KNOW HOW TO BRING OUT THE BEST IN PEOPLE!
BUT HE'S SO NICE, MODEST AND SMART...
EH? N-NO... NOW YOU'RE MAKING ME BLUSH...
I-I HAVE TO VISIT THE RESTROOM...
HE'S PRETTY ATTRACTIVE! I NEVER EVEN NOTICED...
IT'S TRUE. YOU CHANGE YOUR VIEWPOINT, AND THE WHOLE WORLD CAN CHANGE!
TUMP
TUMP
TUMP
HMMM...
TUMP

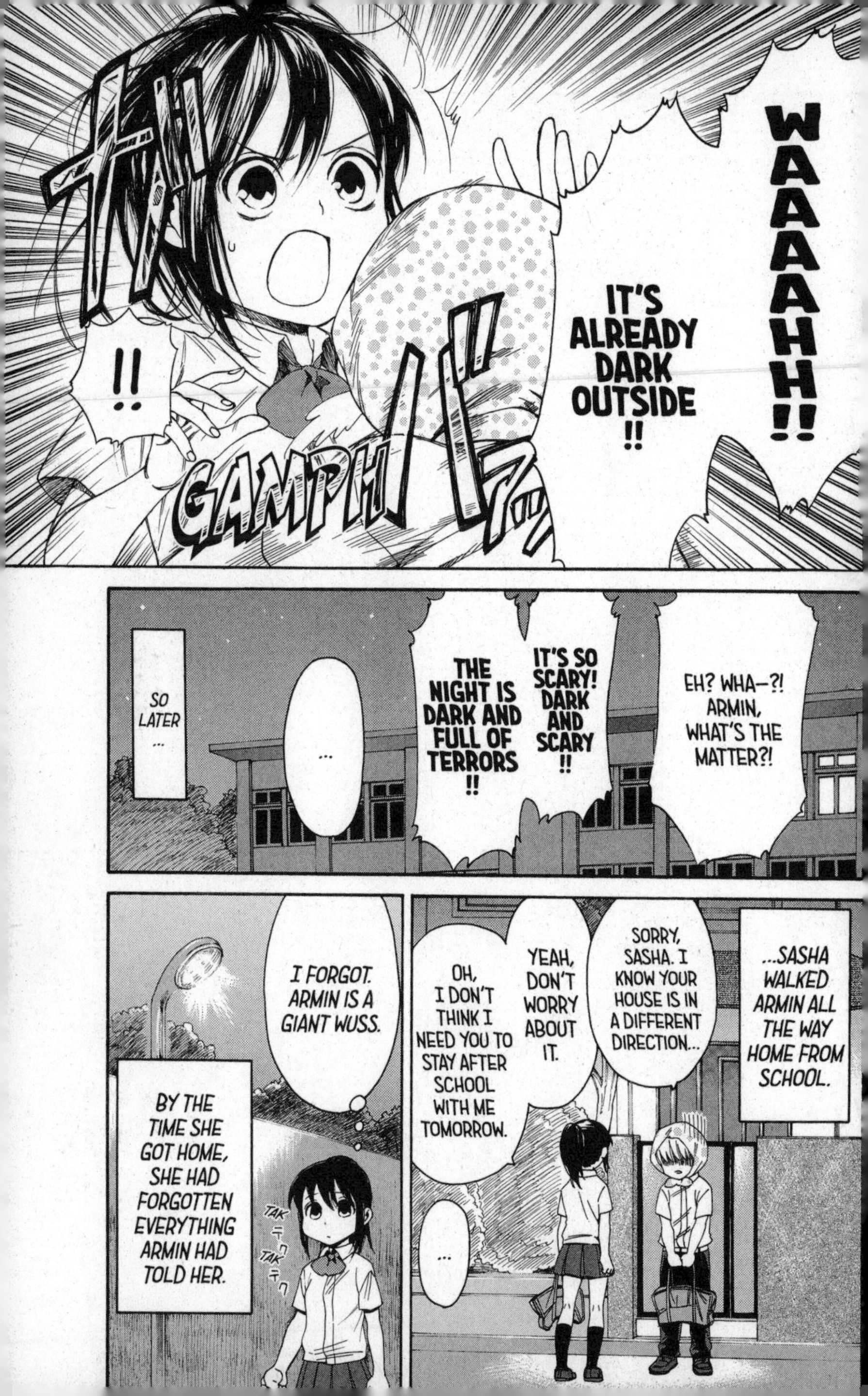
WAAAAAHH!!
IT'S ALREADY DARK OUTSIDE!!
!!
GAMPH
EH? WHA—?! ARMIN, WHAT'S THE MATTER?!
IT'S SO SCARY! DARK AND SCARY!!
THE NIGHT IS DARK AND FULL OF TERRORS!!
...
SO LATER...
...SASHA WALKED ARMIN ALL THE WAY HOME FROM SCHOOL.
SORRY, SASHA. I KNOW YOUR HOUSE IS IN A DIFFERENT DIRECTION...
YEAH, DON'T WORRY ABOUT IT.
OH, I DON'T THINK I NEED YOU TO STAY AFTER SCHOOL WITH ME TOMORROW.
...
I FORGOT. ARMIN IS A GIANT WUSS.
BY THE TIME SHE GOT HOME, SHE HAD FORGOTTEN EVERYTHING ARMIN HAD TOLD HER.
TAK
TAK

Oluo's Worries

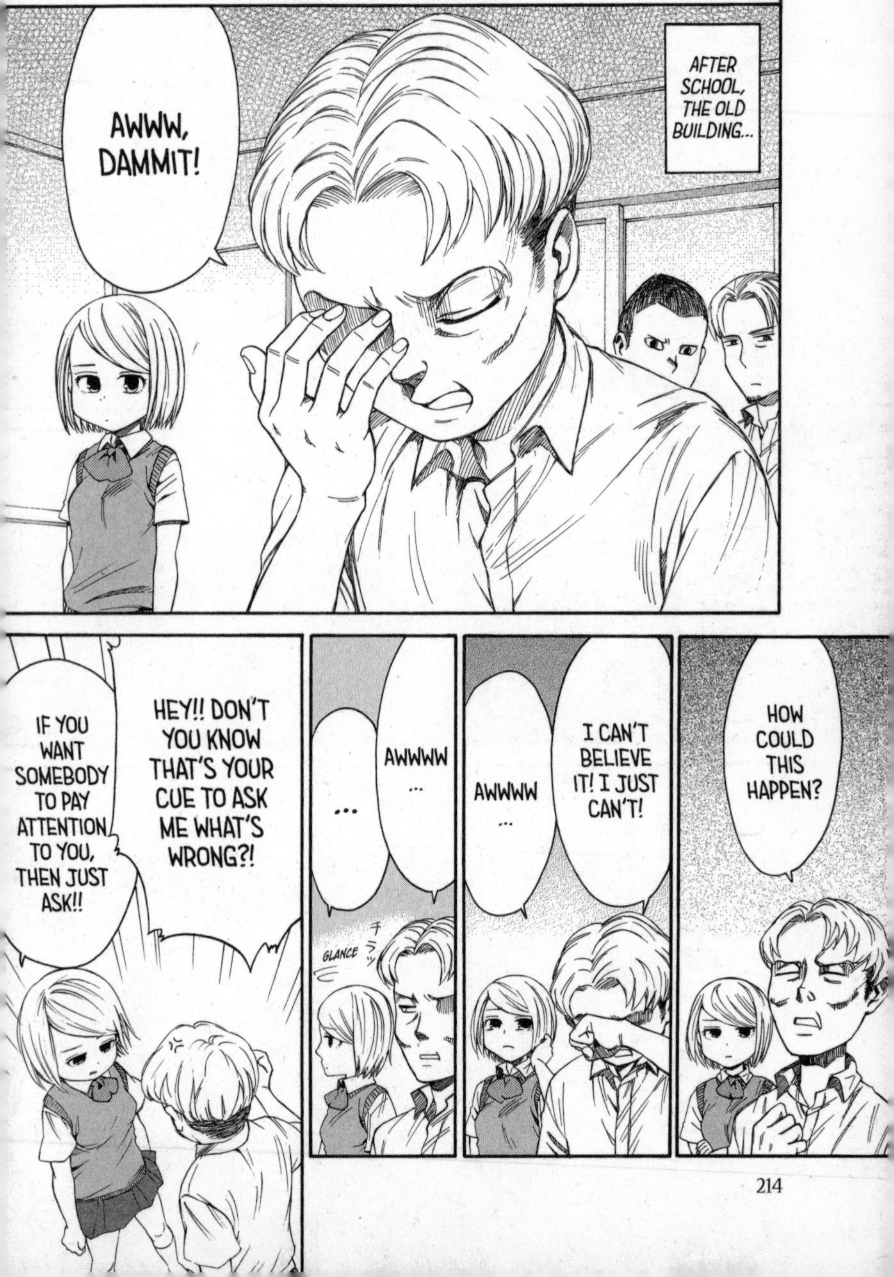
AFTER SCHOOL, THE OLD BUILDING...
AWWW, DAMMIT!
HOW COULD THIS HAPPEN?
I CAN'T BELIEVE IT! I JUST CAN'T!
AWWWW ...
AWWWW ...
...
GLANCE
チラッ
HEY!! DON'T YOU KNOW THAT'S YOUR CUE TO ASK ME WHAT'S WRONG?!
IF YOU WANT SOMEBODY TO PAY ATTENTION TO YOU, THEN JUST ASK!!

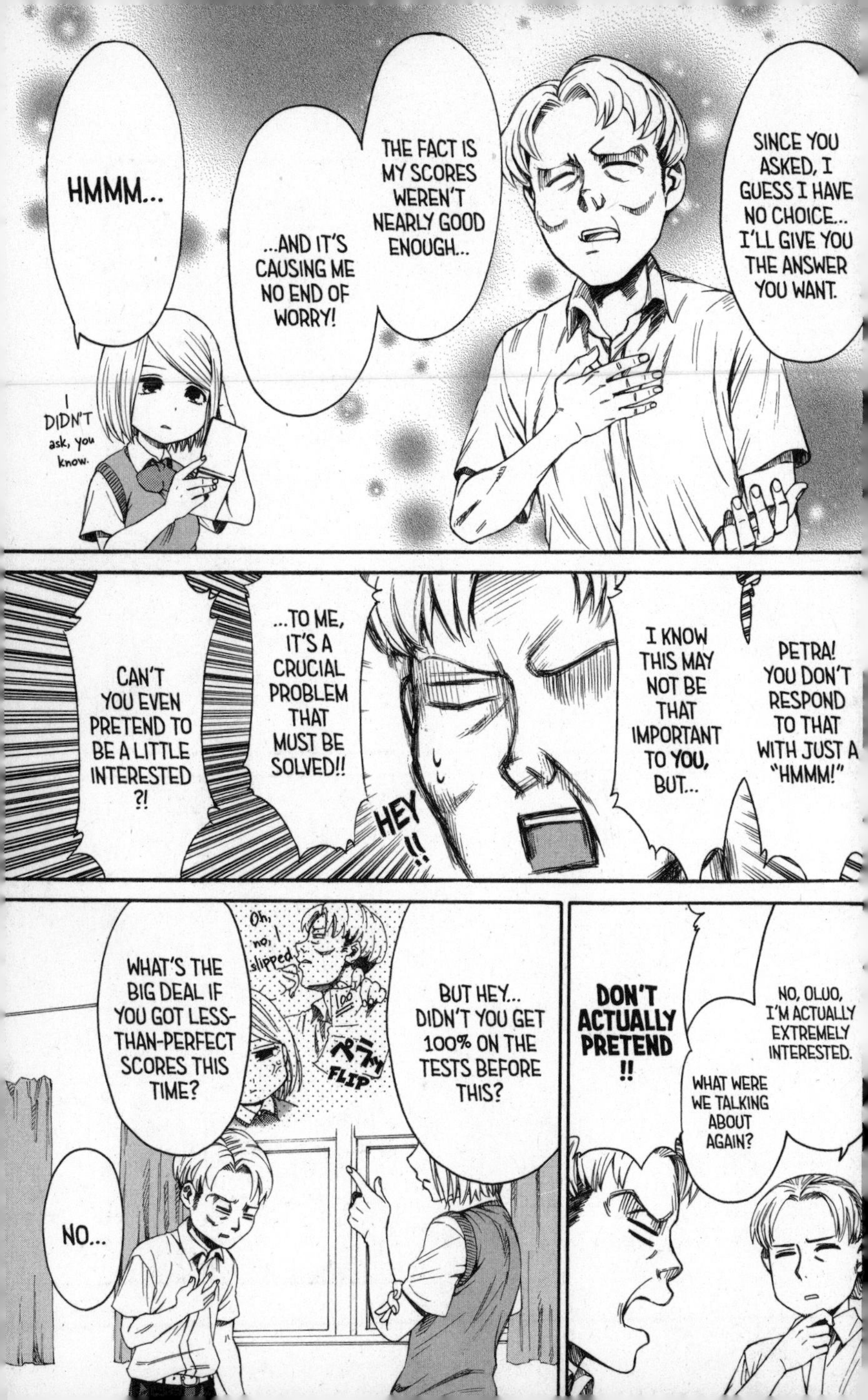
SINCE YOU ASKED, I GUESS I HAVE NO CHOICE... I'LL GIVE YOU THE ANSWER YOU WANT.
THE FACT IS MY SCORES WEREN'T NEARLY GOOD ENOUGH...
...AND IT'S CAUSING ME NO END OF WORRY!
HMMM...
I DIDN'T ask, you know.
PETRA! YOU DON'T RESPOND TO THAT WITH JUST A "HMMM!"
I KNOW THIS MAY NOT BE THAT IMPORTANT TO YOU, BUT...
HEY!!
...TO ME, IT'S A CRUCIAL PROBLEM THAT MUST BE SOLVED!!
CAN'T YOU EVEN PRETEND TO BE A LITTLE INTERESTED?!
NO, OLUO, I'M ACTUALLY EXTREMELY INTERESTED.
WHAT WERE WE TALKING ABOUT AGAIN?
DON'T ACTUALLY PRETEND!!
BUT HEY... DIDN'T YOU GET 100% ON THE TESTS BEFORE THIS?
Oh, no, I slipped.
ペラッ FLIP
WHAT'S THE BIG DEAL IF YOU GOT LESS-THAN-PERFECT SCORES THIS TIME?
NO...

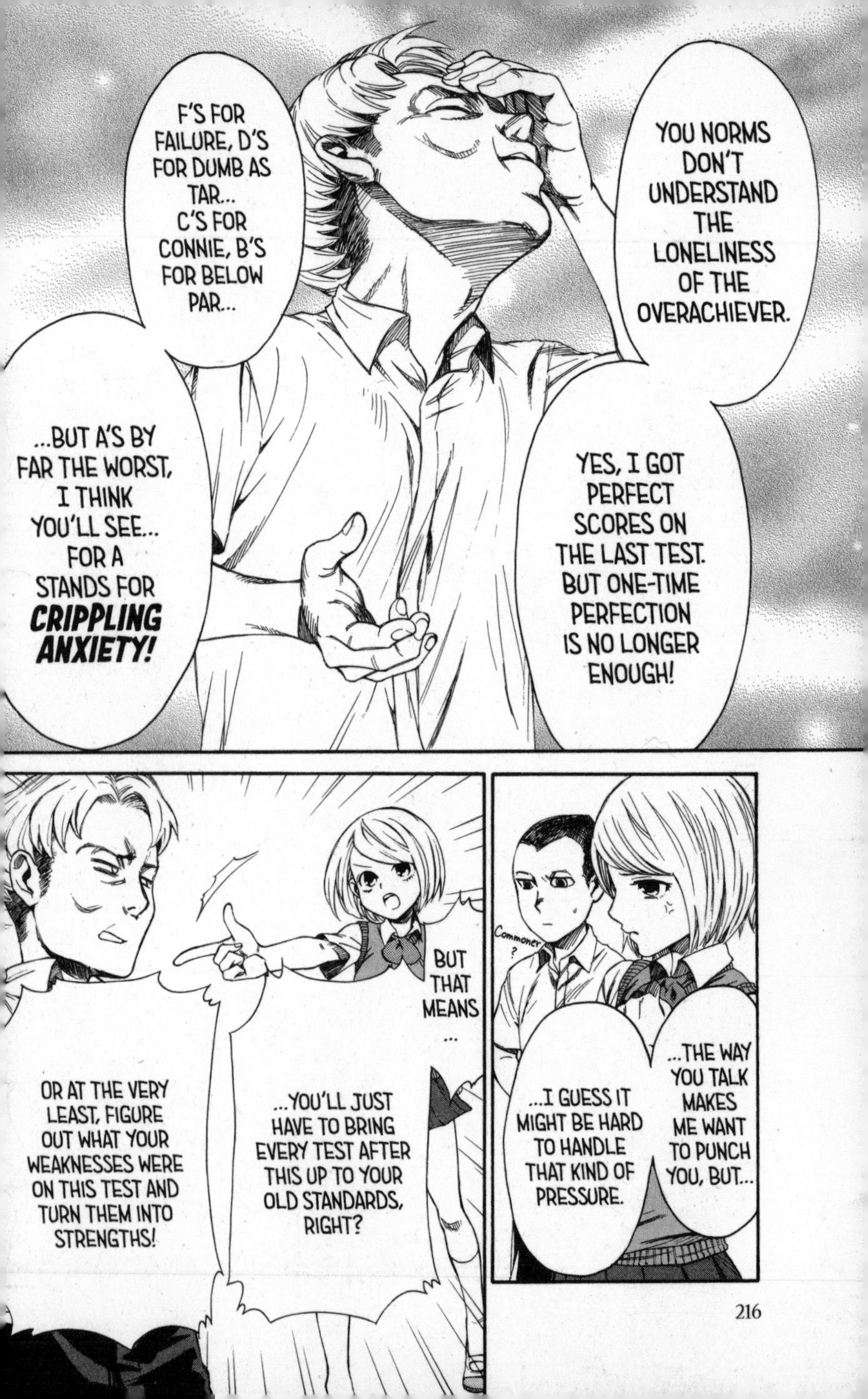
YOU NORMS DON'T UNDERSTAND THE LONELINESS OF THE OVERACHIEVER.
F'S FOR FAILURE, D'S FOR DUMB AS TAR... C'S FOR CONNIE, B'S FOR BELOW PAR...
YES, I GOT PERFECT SCORES ON THE LAST TEST. BUT ONE-TIME PERFECTION IS NO LONGER ENOUGH!
...BUT A'S BY FAR THE WORST, I THINK YOU'LL SEE... FOR A STANDS FOR **CRIPPLING ANXIETY!**
Commoner?
...THE WAY YOU TALK MAKES ME WANT TO PUNCH YOU, BUT...
...I GUESS IT MIGHT BE HARD TO HANDLE THAT KIND OF PRESSURE.
BUT THAT MEANS...
...YOU'LL JUST HAVE TO BRING EVERY TEST AFTER THIS UP TO YOUR OLD STANDARDS, RIGHT?
OR AT THE VERY LEAST, FIGURE OUT WHAT YOUR WEAKNESSES WERE ON THIS TEST AND TURN THEM INTO STRENGTHS!

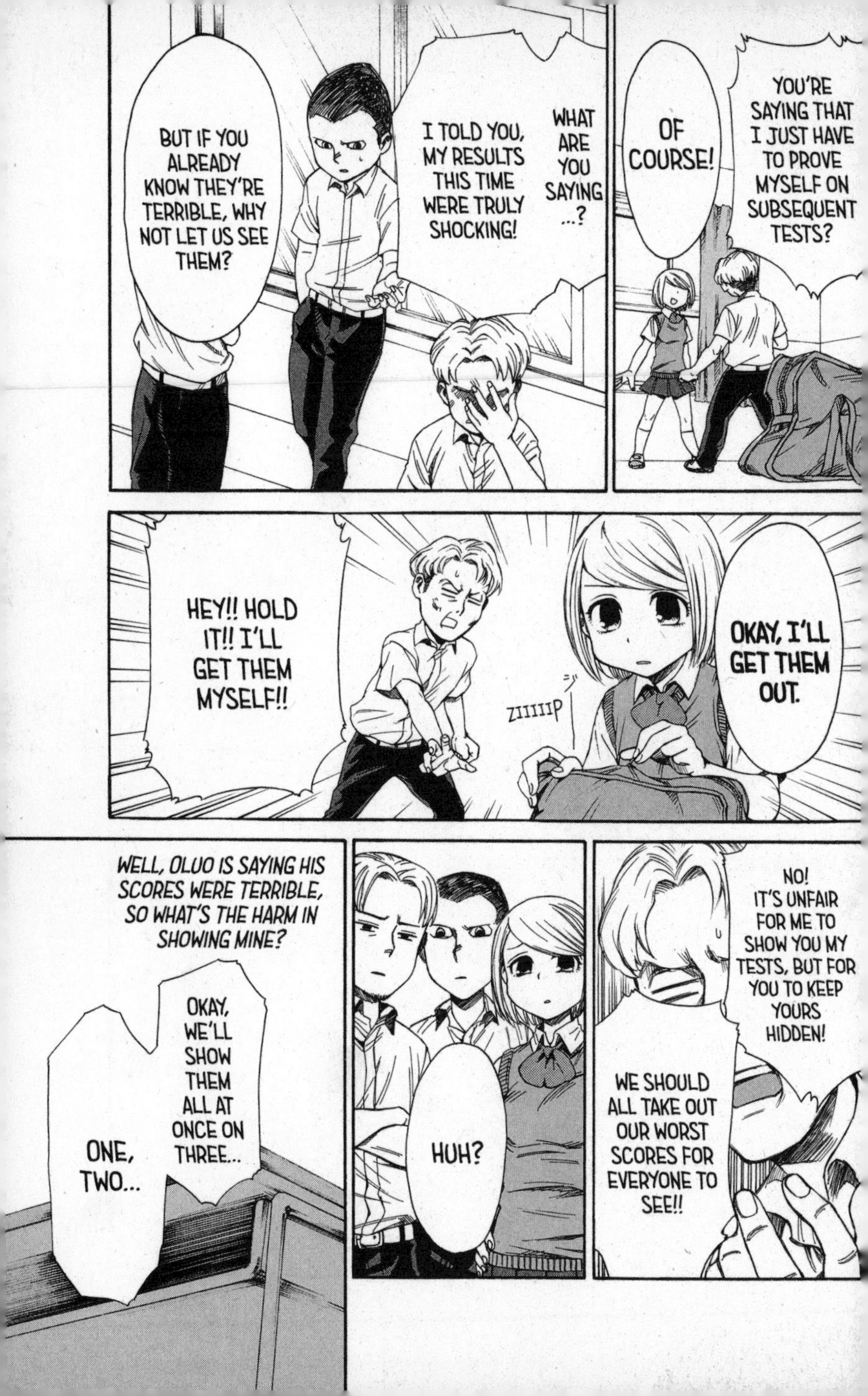

YOU'RE SAYING THAT I JUST HAVE TO PROVE MYSELF ON SUBSEQUENT TESTS?
OF COURSE!
WHAT ARE YOU SAYING ...?
I TOLD YOU, MY RESULTS THIS TIME WERE TRULY SHOCKING!
BUT IF YOU ALREADY KNOW THEY'RE TERRIBLE, WHY NOT LET US SEE THEM?
OKAY, I'LL GET THEM OUT.
ZIIIIIP
HEY!! HOLD IT!! I'LL GET THEM MYSELF!!
NO! IT'S UNFAIR FOR ME TO SHOW YOU MY TESTS, BUT FOR YOU TO KEEP YOURS HIDDEN!
WE SHOULD ALL TAKE OUT OUR WORST SCORES FOR EVERYONE TO SEE!!
HUH?
WELL, OLUO IS SAYING HIS SCORES WERE TERRIBLE, SO WHAT'S THE HARM IN SHOWING MINE?
OKAY, WE'LL SHOW THEM ALL AT ONCE ON THREE...
ONE, TWO...

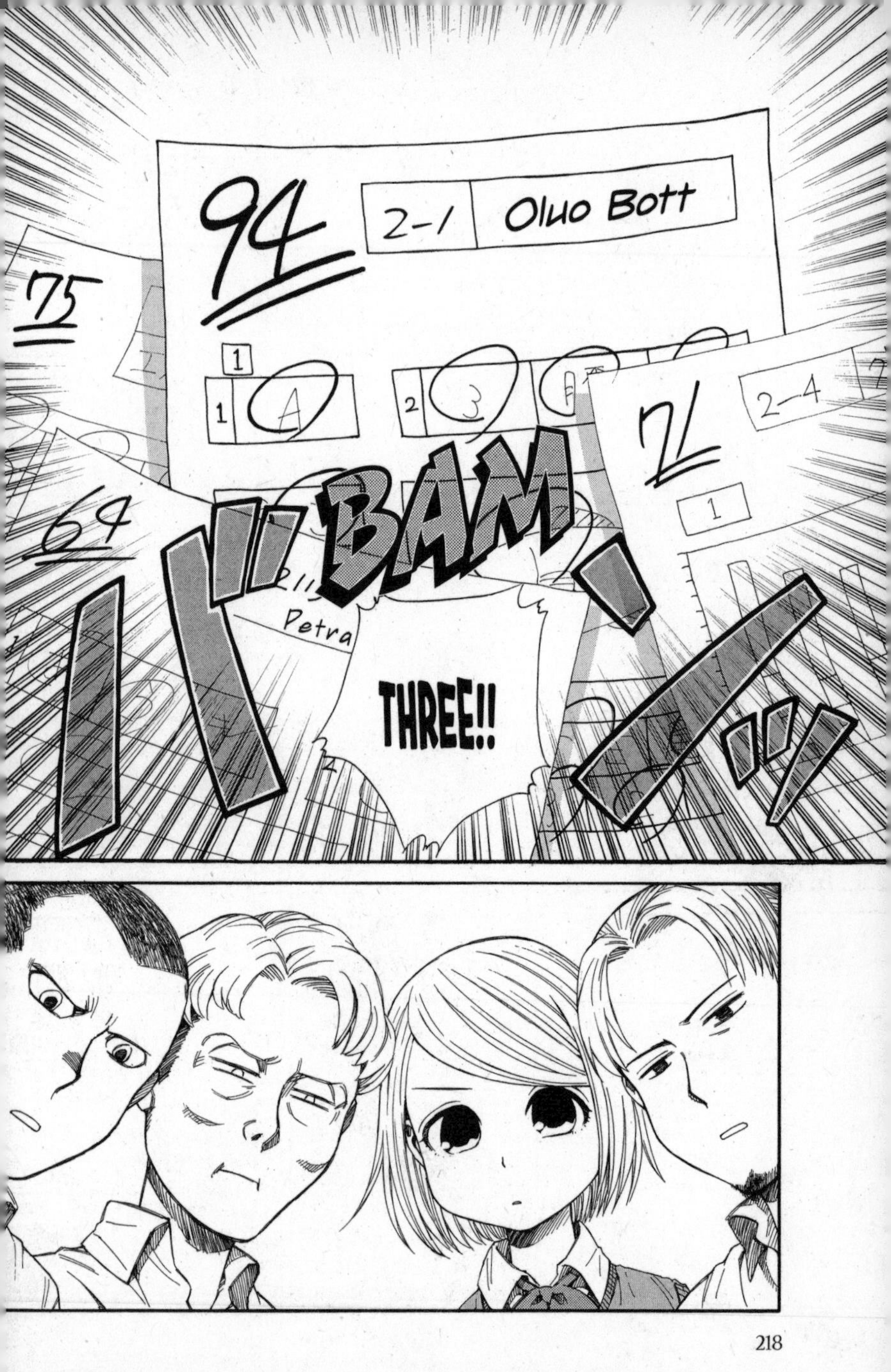
94
2-1
Oluo Bott
75
64
Petra
BAM
THREE!!
2-4

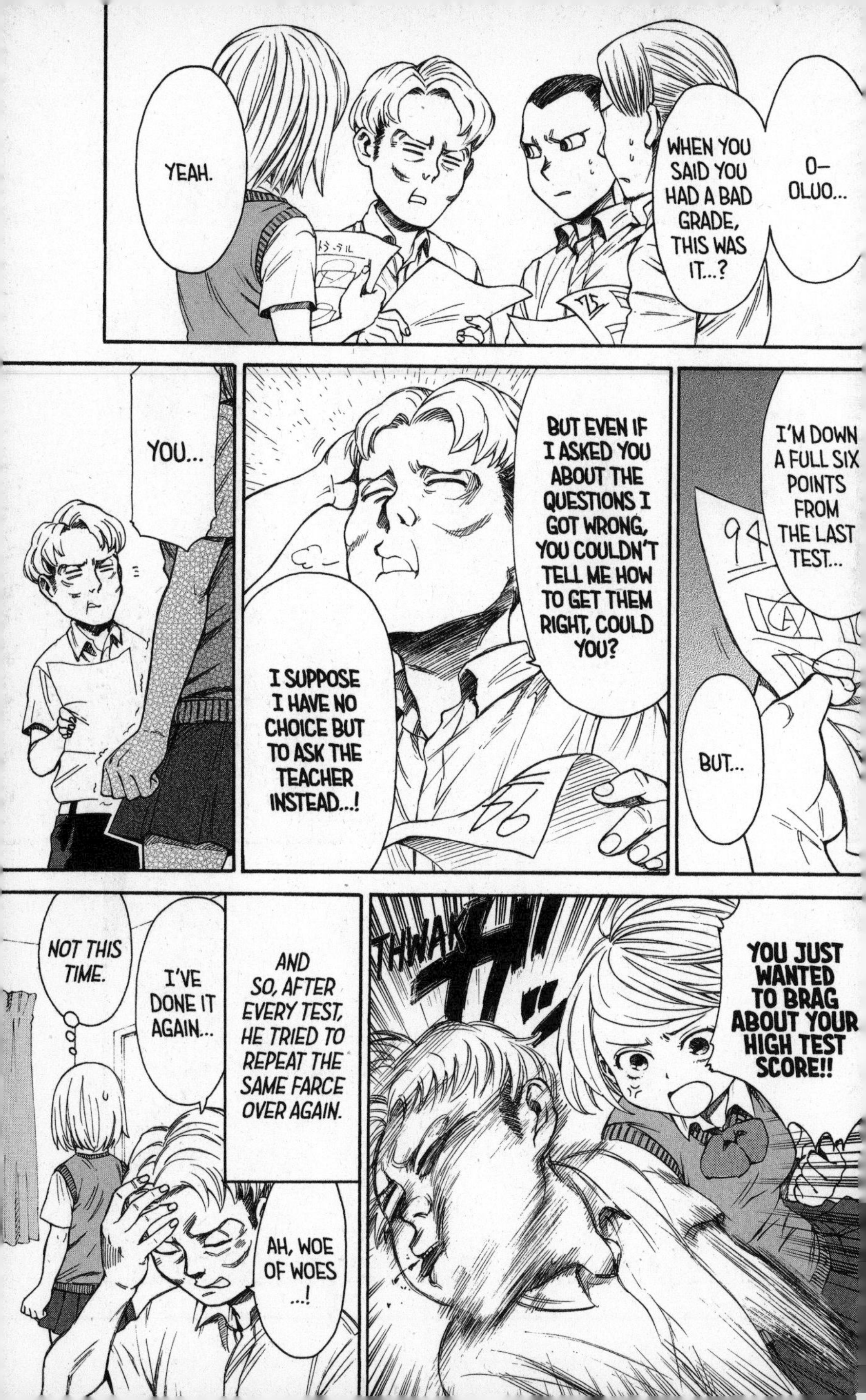
O— OLUO...
WHEN YOU SAID YOU HAD A BAD GRADE, THIS WAS IT...?
YEAH.
I'M DOWN A FULL SIX POINTS FROM THE LAST TEST...
BUT...
BUT EVEN IF I ASKED YOU ABOUT THE QUESTIONS I GOT WRONG, YOU COULDN'T TELL ME HOW TO GET THEM RIGHT, COULD YOU?
I SUPPOSE I HAVE NO CHOICE BUT TO ASK THE TEACHER INSTEAD...!
YOU...
THWAK
YOU JUST WANTED TO BRAG ABOUT YOUR HIGH TEST SCORE!!
AND SO, AFTER EVERY TEST, HE TRIED TO REPEAT THE SAME FARCE OVER AGAIN.
I'VE DONE IT AGAIN...
NOT THIS TIME.
AH, WOE OF WOES ...!

Poor Hange

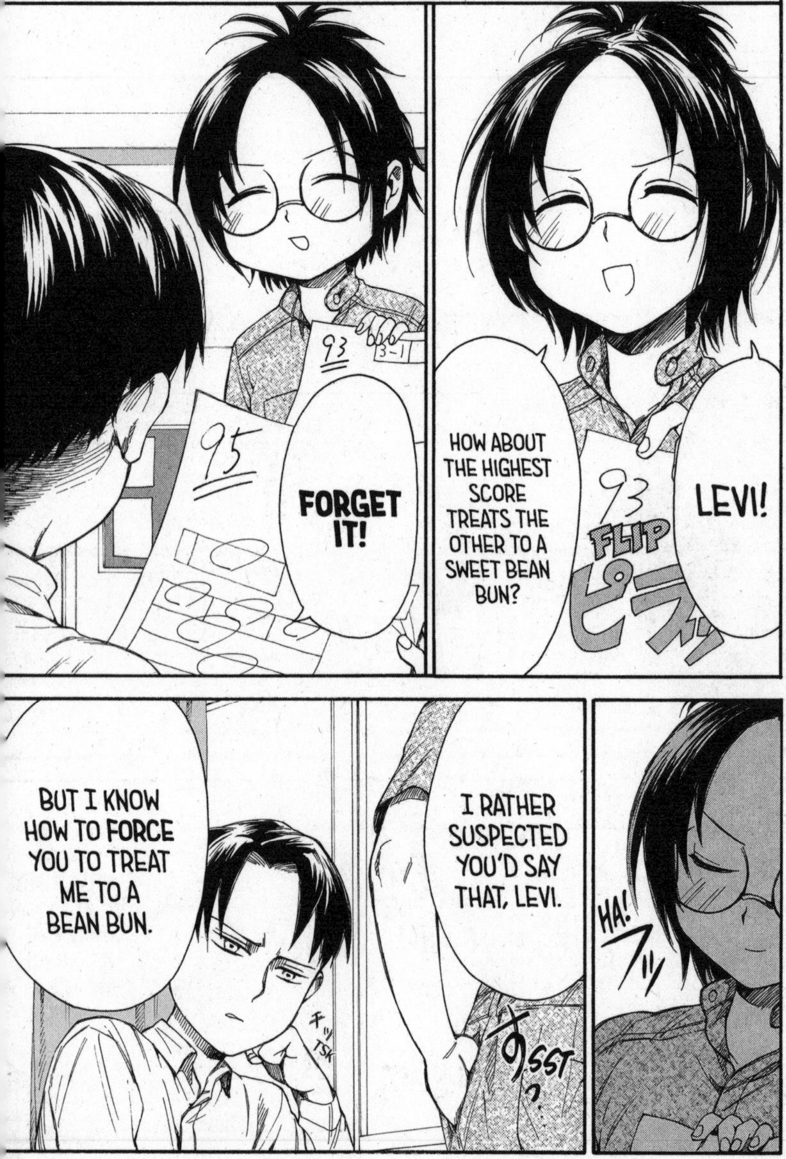

LEVI!
HOW ABOUT THE HIGHEST SCORE TREATS THE OTHER TO A SWEET BEAN BUN?
FLIP
FORGET IT!
HA!
I RATHER SUSPECTED YOU'D SAY THAT, LEVI.
SST
BUT I KNOW HOW TO FORCE YOU TO TREAT ME TO A BEAN BUN.
TSK

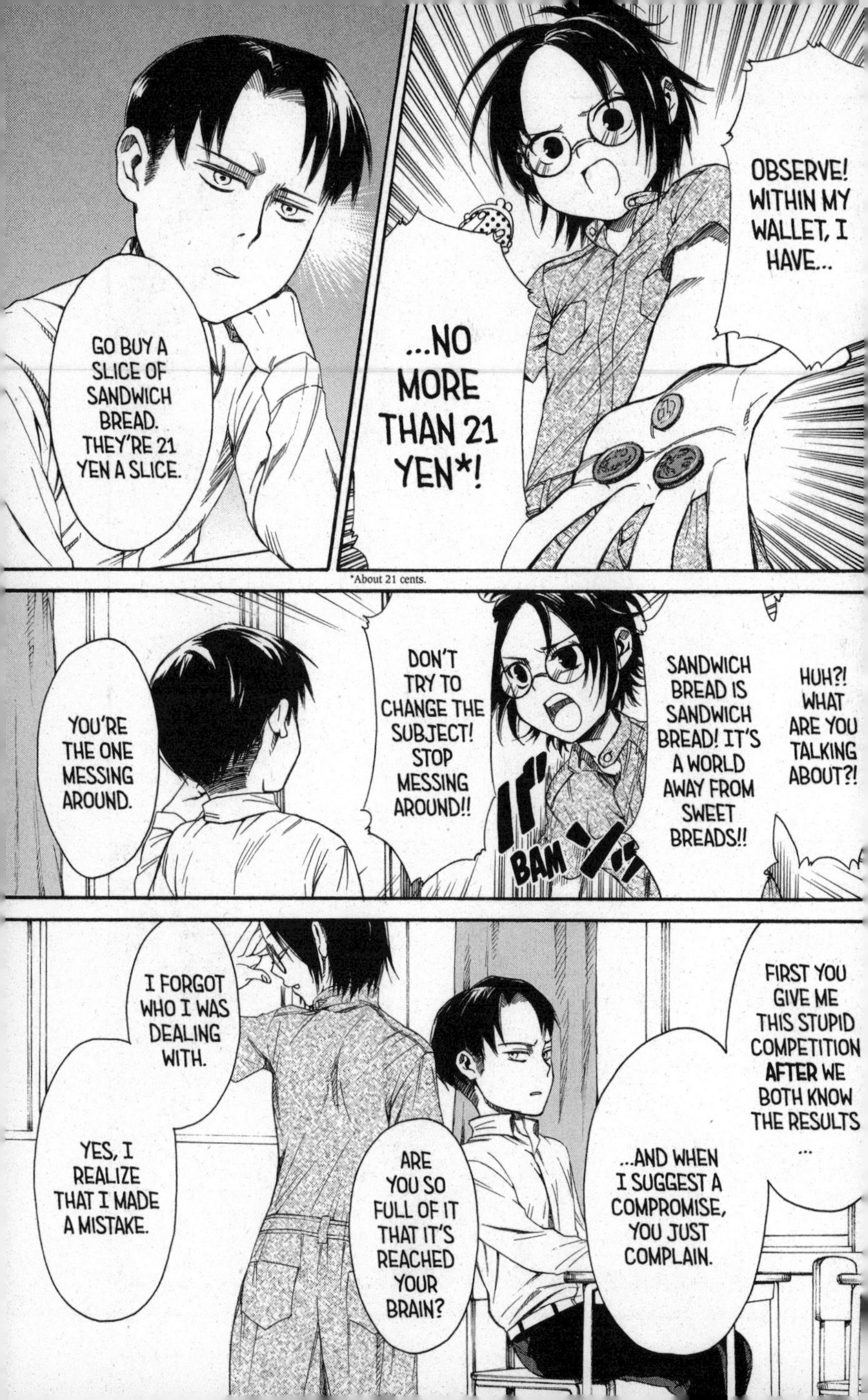
OBSERVE! WITHIN MY WALLET, I HAVE...
...NO MORE THAN 21 YEN*!
GO BUY A SLICE OF SANDWICH BREAD. THEY'RE 21 YEN A SLICE.
HUH?! WHAT ARE YOU TALKING ABOUT?!
SANDWICH BREAD IS SANDWICH BREAD! IT'S A WORLD AWAY FROM SWEET BREADS!!
DON'T TRY TO CHANGE THE SUBJECT! STOP MESSING AROUND!!
BAM
YOU'RE THE ONE MESSING AROUND.
FIRST YOU GIVE ME THIS STUPID COMPETITION **AFTER** WE BOTH KNOW THE RESULTS ...
...AND WHEN I SUGGEST A COMPROMISE, YOU JUST COMPLAIN.
ARE YOU SO FULL OF IT THAT IT'S REACHED YOUR BRAIN?
I FORGOT WHO I WAS DEALING WITH.
YES, I REALIZE THAT I MADE A MISTAKE.

*About 21 cents.

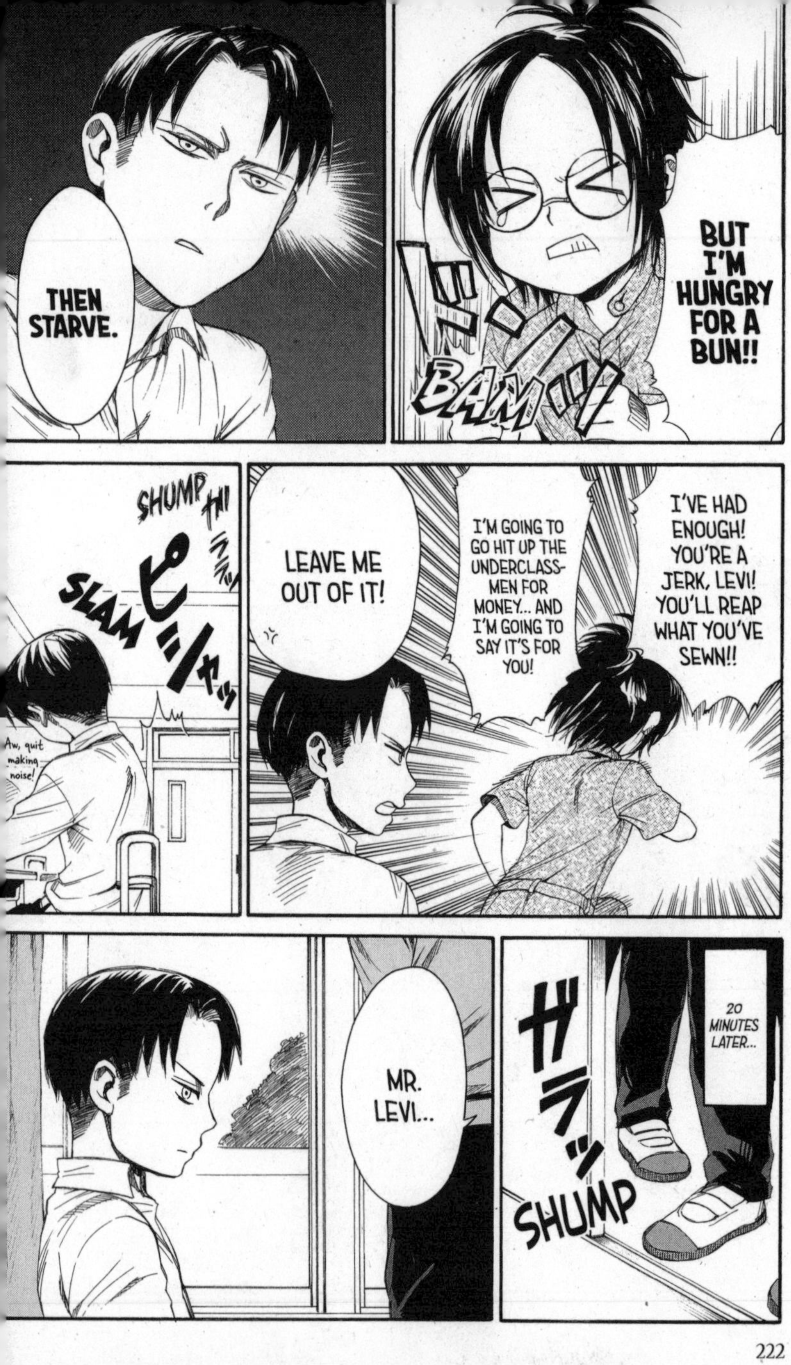
BUT I'M HUNGRY FOR A BUN!!
BAM
THEN STARVE.
I'VE HAD ENOUGH! YOU'RE A JERK, LEVI! YOU'LL REAP WHAT YOU'VE SEWN!!
I'M GOING TO GO HIT UP THE UNDERCLASSMEN FOR MONEY... AND I'M GOING TO SAY IT'S FOR YOU!
LEAVE ME OUT OF IT!
SHUMP
SLAM
Aw, quit making noise!
20 MINUTES LATER...
SHUMP
MR. LEVI...

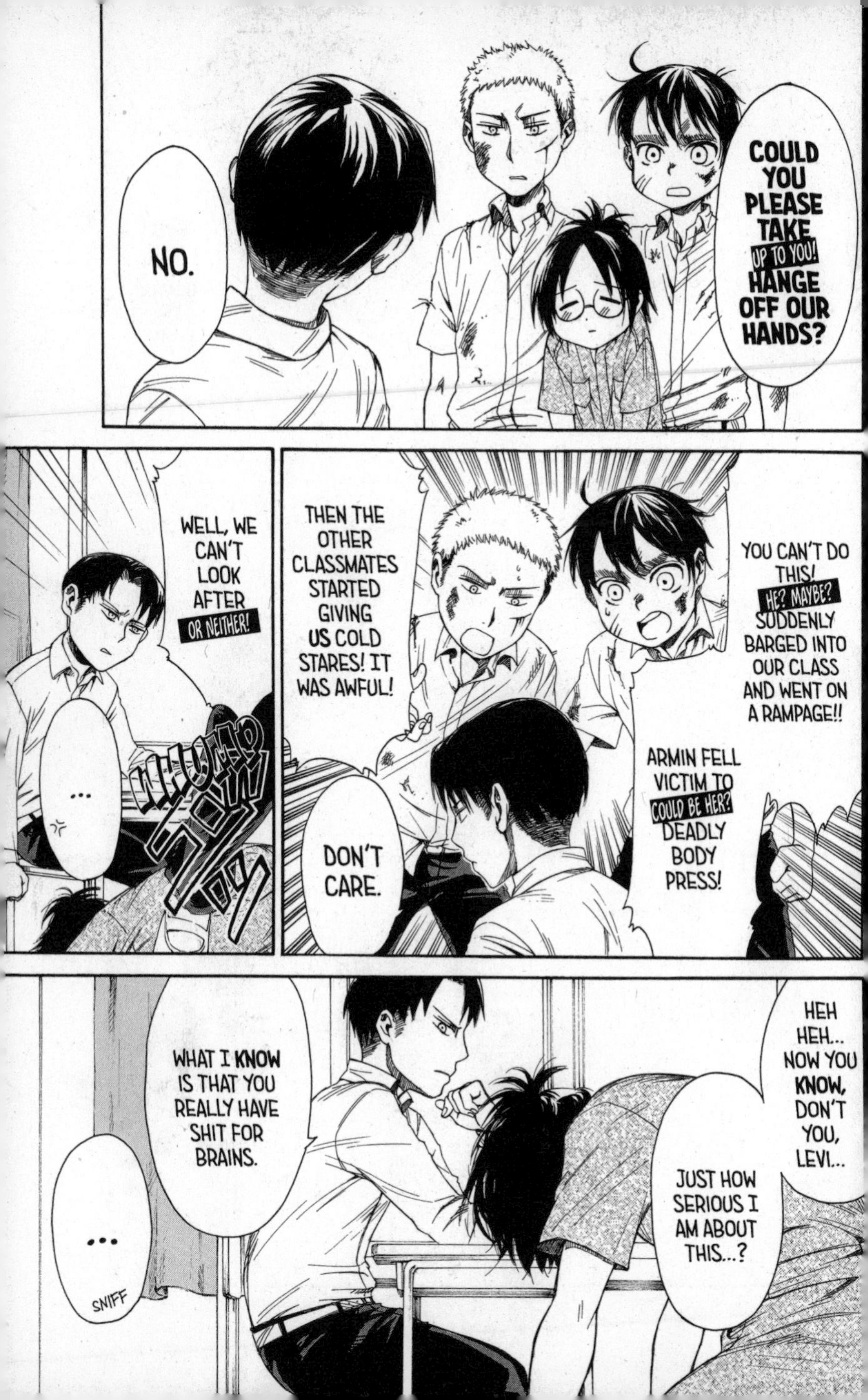
COULD YOU PLEASE TAKE UP TO YOU! HANGE OFF OUR HANDS?
NO.
YOU CAN'T DO THIS! HE? MAYBE? SUDDENLY BARGED INTO OUR CLASS AND WENT ON A RAMPAGE!!
ARMIN FELL VICTIM TO COULD BE HER? DEADLY BODY PRESS!
THEN THE OTHER CLASSMATES STARTED GIVING US COLD STARES! IT WAS AWFUL!
DON'T CARE.
WELL, WE CAN'T LOOK AFTER OR NEITHER!
...
HEH HEH... NOW YOU KNOW, DON'T YOU, LEVI...
JUST HOW SERIOUS I AM ABOUT THIS...?
WHAT I KNOW IS THAT YOU REALLY HAVE SHIT FOR BRAINS.
...
SNIFF

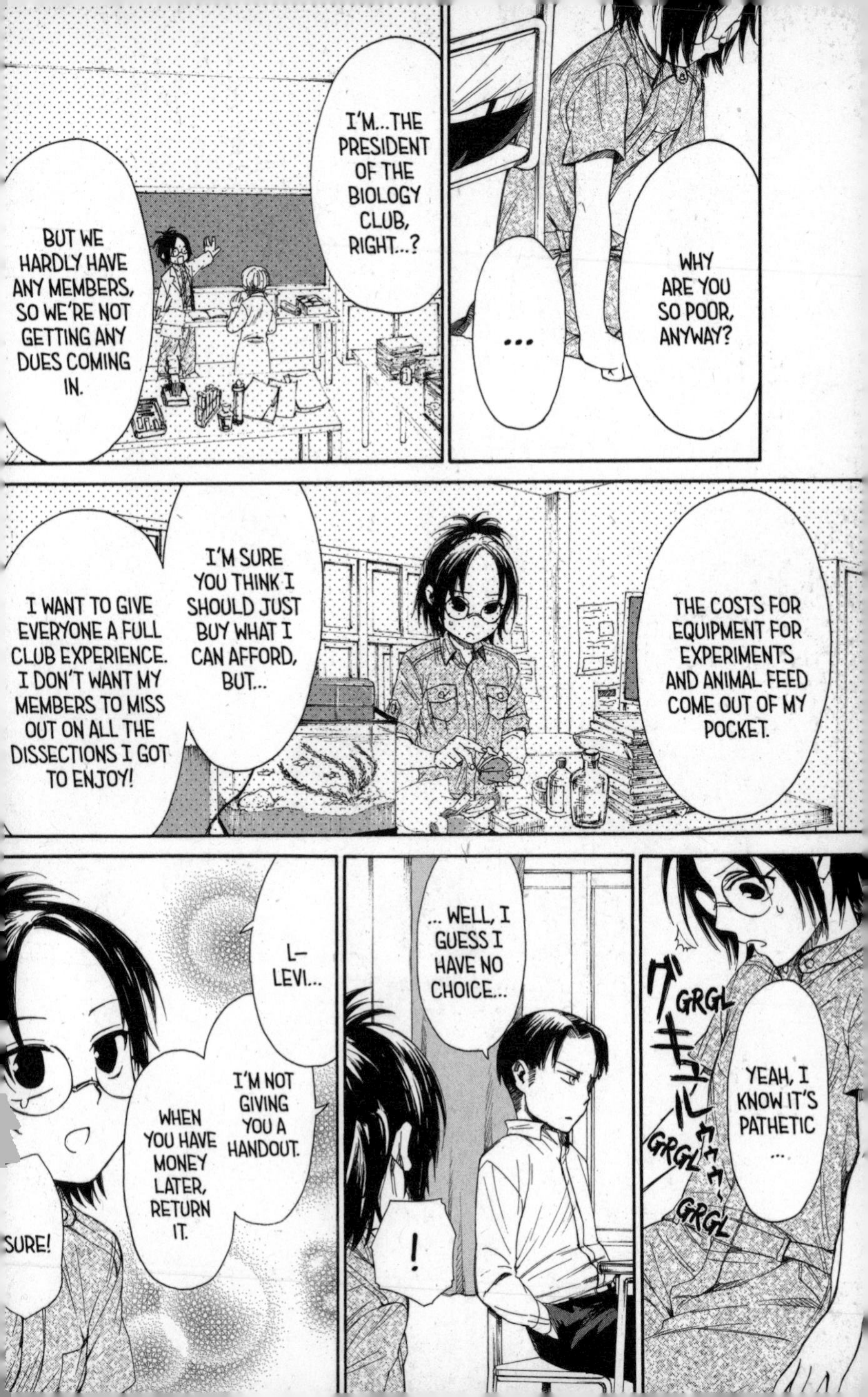
WHY ARE YOU SO POOR, ANYWAY?
...
I'M...THE PRESIDENT OF THE BIOLOGY CLUB, RIGHT...?
BUT WE HARDLY HAVE ANY MEMBERS, SO WE'RE NOT GETTING ANY DUES COMING IN.
THE COSTS FOR EQUIPMENT FOR EXPERIMENTS AND ANIMAL FEED COME OUT OF MY POCKET.
I'M SURE YOU THINK I SHOULD JUST BUY WHAT I CAN AFFORD, BUT...
I WANT TO GIVE EVERYONE A FULL CLUB EXPERIENCE. I DON'T WANT MY MEMBERS TO MISS OUT ON ALL THE DISSECTIONS I GOT TO ENJOY!
GRGL
YEAH, I KNOW IT'S PATHETIC...
GRGL
GRGL
... WELL, I GUESS I HAVE NO CHOICE...
!
L- LEVI...
I'M NOT GIVING YOU A HANDOUT.
WHEN YOU HAVE MONEY LATER, RETURN IT.
SURE!

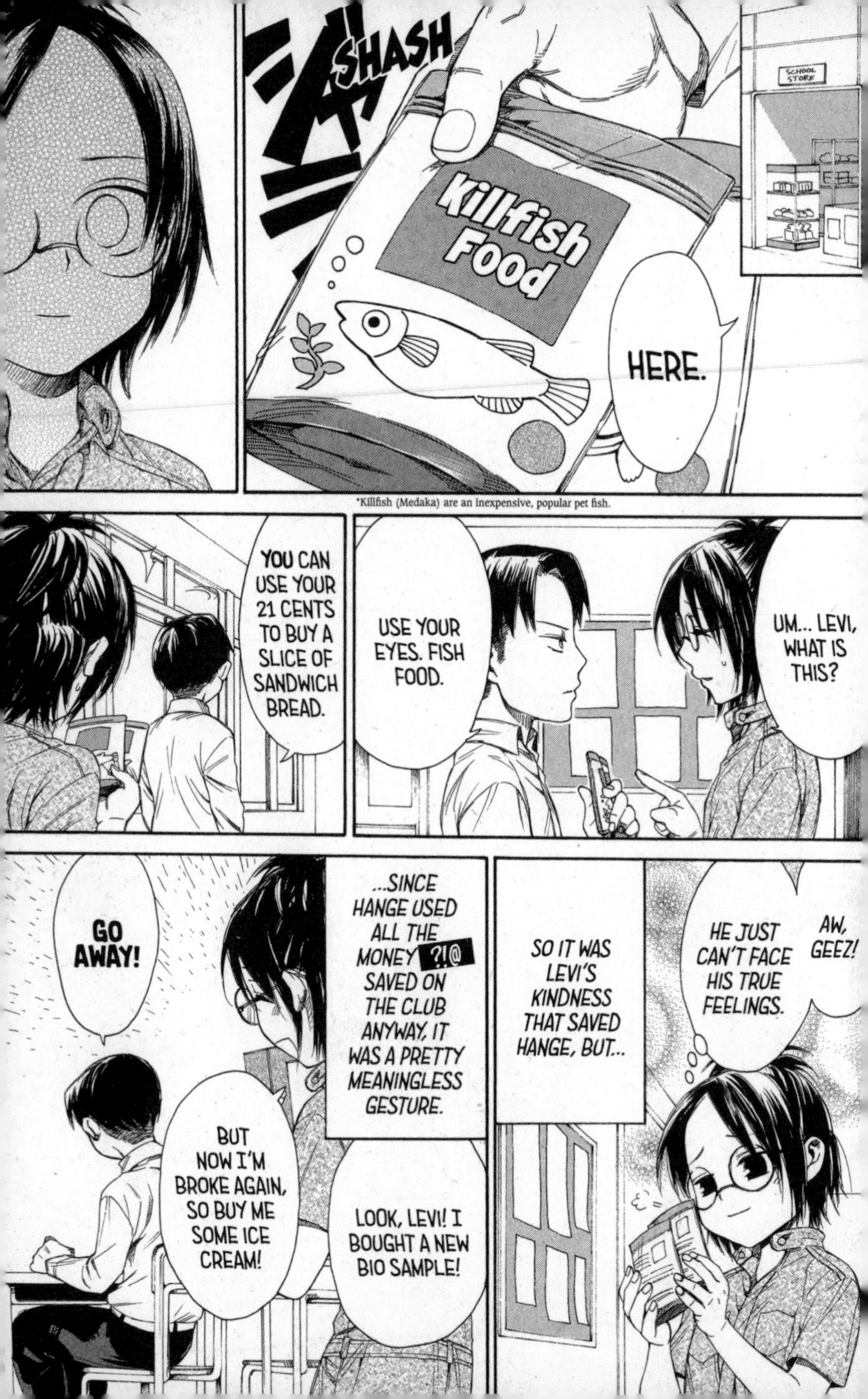
SCHOOL STORE
SHASH
Killfish Food
HERE.
UM... LEVI, WHAT IS THIS?
USE YOUR EYES. FISH FOOD.
YOU CAN USE YOUR 21 CENTS TO BUY A SLICE OF SANDWICH BREAD.
AW, GEEZ!
HE JUST CAN'T FACE HIS TRUE FEELINGS.
SO IT WAS LEVI'S KINDNESS THAT SAVED HANGE, BUT...
...SINCE HANGE USED ALL THE MONEY ?!@ SAVED ON THE CLUB ANYWAY, IT WAS A PRETTY MEANINGLESS GESTURE.
LOOK, LEVI! I BOUGHT A NEW BIO SAMPLE!
BUT NOW I'M BROKE AGAIN, SO BUY ME SOME ICE CREAM!
GO AWAY!

*Killfish (Medaka) are an inexpensive, popular pet fish.

FULL POINTS
BONUS MANGA

HANGE PAYS BACK A DEBT!!

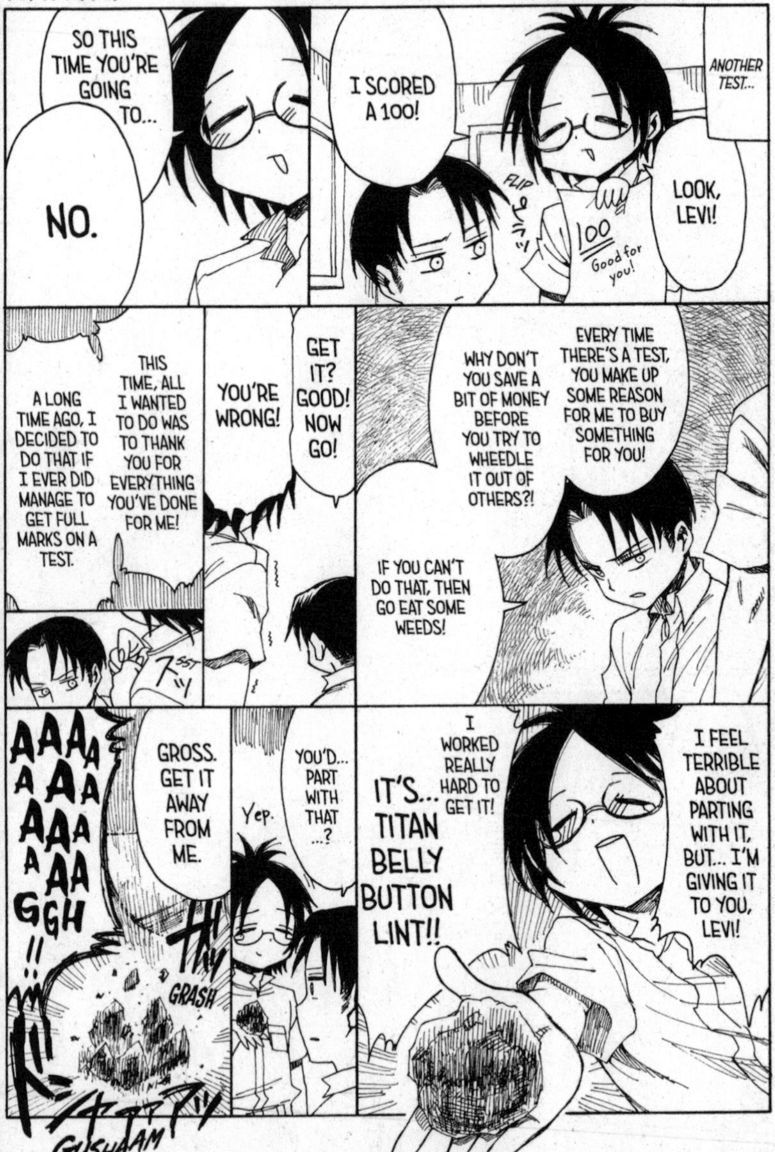
ANOTHER TEST...
I SCORED A 100!
LOOK, LEVI!
FLIP
100
Good for you!
SO THIS TIME YOU'RE GOING TO...
NO.
EVERY TIME THERE'S A TEST, YOU MAKE UP SOME REASON FOR ME TO BUY SOMETHING FOR YOU!
WHY DON'T YOU SAVE A BIT OF MONEY BEFORE YOU TRY TO WHEEDLE IT OUT OF OTHERS?!
IF YOU CAN'T DO THAT, THEN GO EAT SOME WEEDS!
GET IT? GOOD! NOW GO!
YOU'RE WRONG!
THIS TIME, ALL I WANTED TO DO WAS TO THANK YOU FOR EVERYTHING YOU'VE DONE FOR ME!
A LONG TIME AGO, I DECIDED TO DO THAT IF I EVER DID MANAGE TO GET FULL MARKS ON A TEST.
SST
I FEEL TERRIBLE ABOUT PARTING WITH IT, BUT... I'M GIVING IT TO YOU, LEVI!
I WORKED REALLY HARD TO GET IT!
IT'S... TITAN BELLY BUTTON LINT!!
YOU'D... PART WITH THAT ...?
Yep.
GROSS. GET IT AWAY FROM ME.
AAAAAAAAAAAAAAAGGH!!
GRASH
GUSHAAM

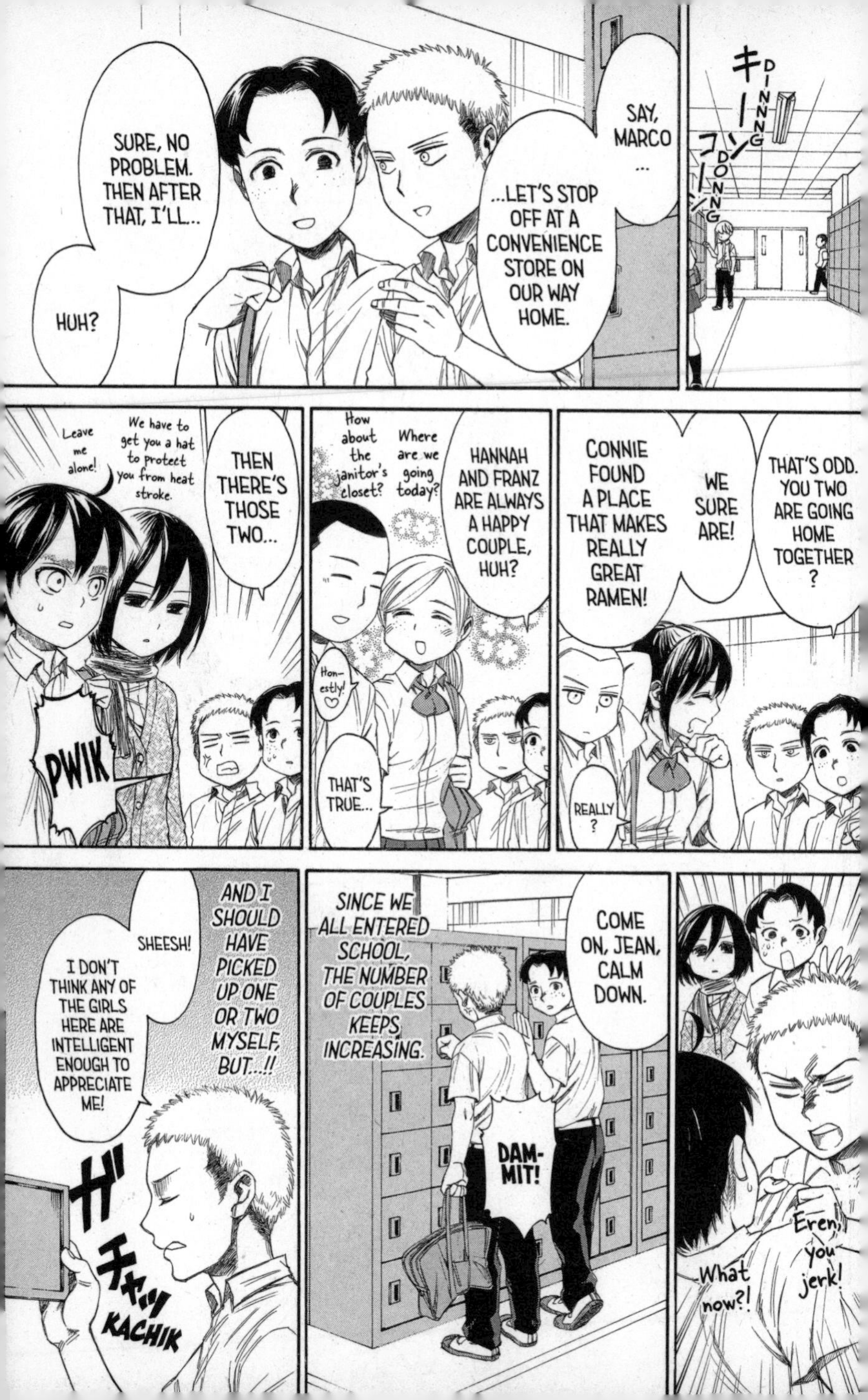
キーンコーン
DINNNG DONNNG
SAY, MARCO...
...LET'S STOP OFF AT A CONVENIENCE STORE ON OUR WAY HOME.
SURE, NO PROBLEM. THEN AFTER THAT, I'LL...
HUH?
THAT'S ODD. YOU TWO ARE GOING HOME TOGETHER?
WE SURE ARE!
CONNIE FOUND A PLACE THAT MAKES REALLY GREAT RAMEN!
REALLY?
HANNAH AND FRANZ ARE ALWAYS A HAPPY COUPLE, HUH?
Where are we going today?
How about the janitor's closet?
Hon-estly! ♡
THAT'S TRUE...
THEN THERE'S THOSE TWO...
We have to get you a hat to protect you from heat stroke.
Leave me alone!
PWIK
Eren, you jerk!
What now?!
COME ON, JEAN, CALM DOWN.
SINCE WE ALL ENTERED SCHOOL, THE NUMBER OF COUPLES KEEPS INCREASING.
DAM-MIT!
AND I SHOULD HAVE PICKED UP ONE OR TWO MYSELF, BUT...!!
SHEESH!
I DON'T THINK ANY OF THE GIRLS HERE ARE INTELLIGENT ENOUGH TO APPRECIATE ME!
ガチャッ
KACHIK

TWELFTH PERIOD: TOO BIG A LOVE

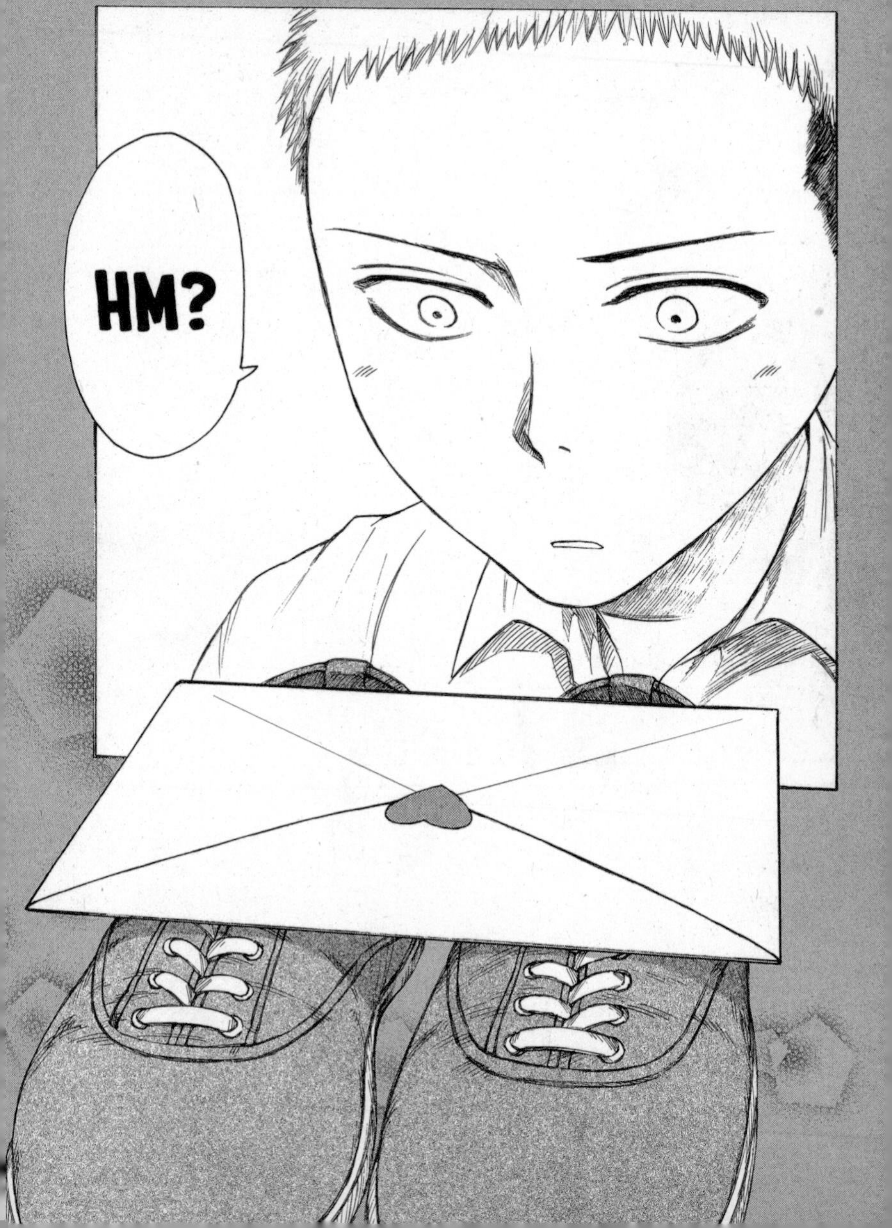
HM?

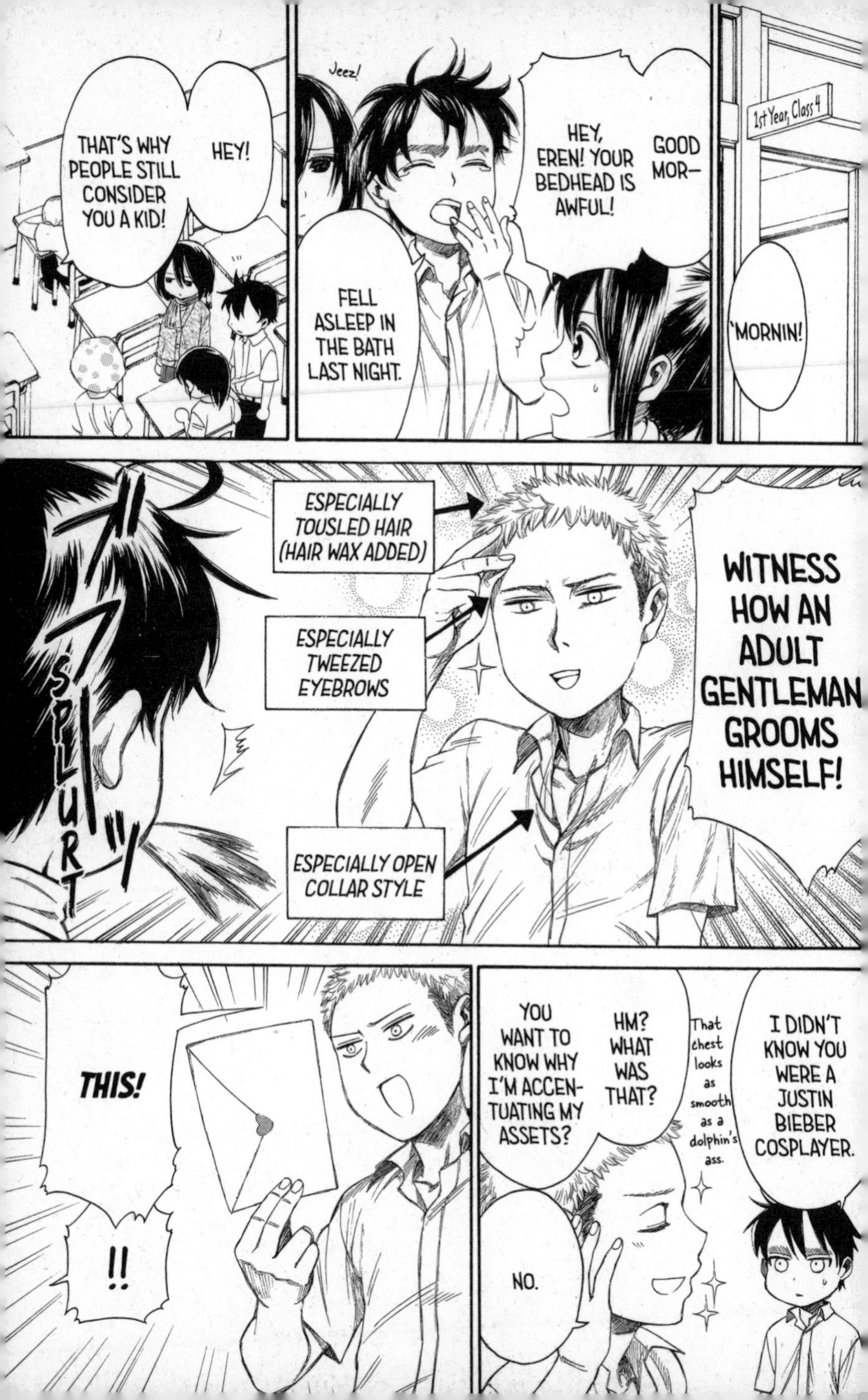
1st Year, Class 4
'MORNIN!
GOOD MOR—
HEY, EREN! YOUR BEDHEAD IS AWFUL!
Jeez!
FELL ASLEEP IN THE BATH LAST NIGHT.
HEY!
THAT'S WHY PEOPLE STILL CONSIDER YOU A KID!
WITNESS HOW AN ADULT GENTLEMAN GROOMS HIMSELF!
ESPECIALLY TOUSLED HAIR (HAIR WAX ADDED)
ESPECIALLY TWEEZED EYEBROWS
ESPECIALLY OPEN COLLAR STYLE
SPLURT
I DIDN'T KNOW YOU WERE A JUSTIN BIEBER COSPLAYER.
That chest looks as smooth as a dolphin's ass.
HM? WHAT WAS THAT?
YOU WANT TO KNOW WHY I'M ACCEN-TUATING MY ASSETS?
NO.
THIS!
!!

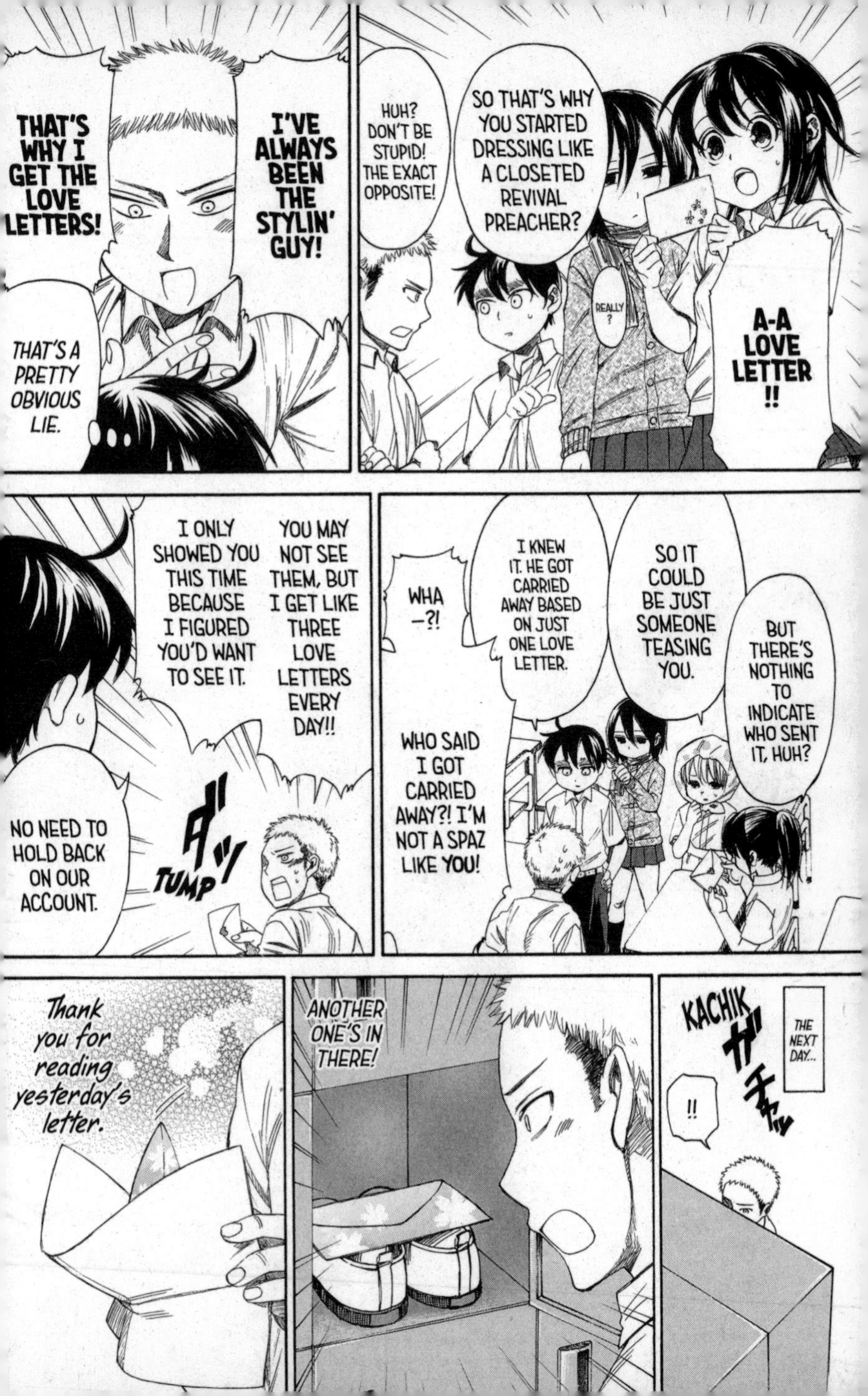
A-A LOVE LETTER!!
REALLY?
SO THAT'S WHY YOU STARTED DRESSING LIKE A CLOSETED REVIVAL PREACHER?
HUH? DON'T BE STUPID! THE EXACT OPPOSITE!
I'VE ALWAYS BEEN THE STYLIN' GUY!
THAT'S WHY I GET THE LOVE LETTERS!
THAT'S A PRETTY OBVIOUS LIE.
...
BUT THERE'S NOTHING TO INDICATE WHO SENT IT, HUH?
SO IT COULD BE JUST SOMEONE TEASING YOU.
I KNEW IT. HE GOT CARRIED AWAY BASED ON JUST ONE LOVE LETTER.
WHA—?!
WHO SAID I GOT CARRIED AWAY?! I'M NOT A SPAZ LIKE YOU!
YOU MAY NOT SEE THEM, BUT I GET LIKE THREE LOVE LETTERS EVERY DAY!!
I ONLY SHOWED YOU THIS TIME BECAUSE I FIGURED YOU'D WANT TO SEE IT.
TUMP
NO NEED TO HOLD BACK ON OUR ACCOUNT.
THE NEXT DAY...
KACHIK
!!
ANOTHER ONE'S IN THERE!
Thank you for reading yesterday's letter.

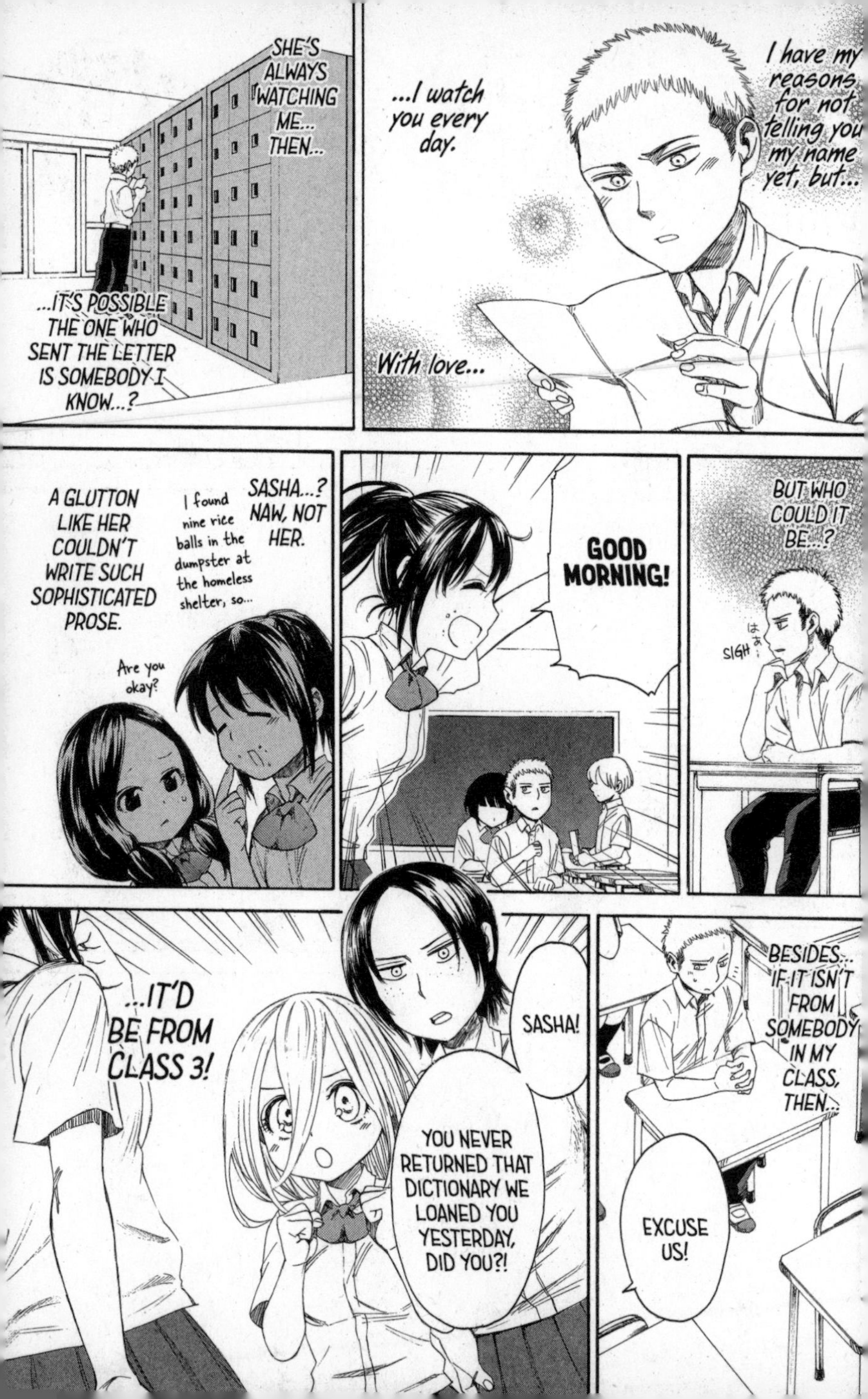
I have my reasons for not telling you my name yet, but...
...I watch you every day.
With love...
SHE'S ALWAYS WATCHING ME... THEN...
...IT'S POSSIBLE THE ONE WHO SENT THE LETTER IS SOMEBODY I KNOW...?
BUT WHO COULD IT BE...?
SIGH
GOOD MORNING!
SASHA...? NAW, NOT HER.
I found nine rice balls in the dumpster at the homeless shelter, so...
A GLUTTON LIKE HER COULDN'T WRITE SUCH SOPHISTICATED PROSE.
Are you okay?
BESIDES... IF IT ISN'T FROM SOMEBODY IN MY CLASS, THEN...
EXCUSE US!
SASHA!
YOU NEVER RETURNED THAT DICTIONARY WE LOANED YOU YESTERDAY, DID YOU?!
...IT'D BE FROM CLASS 3!

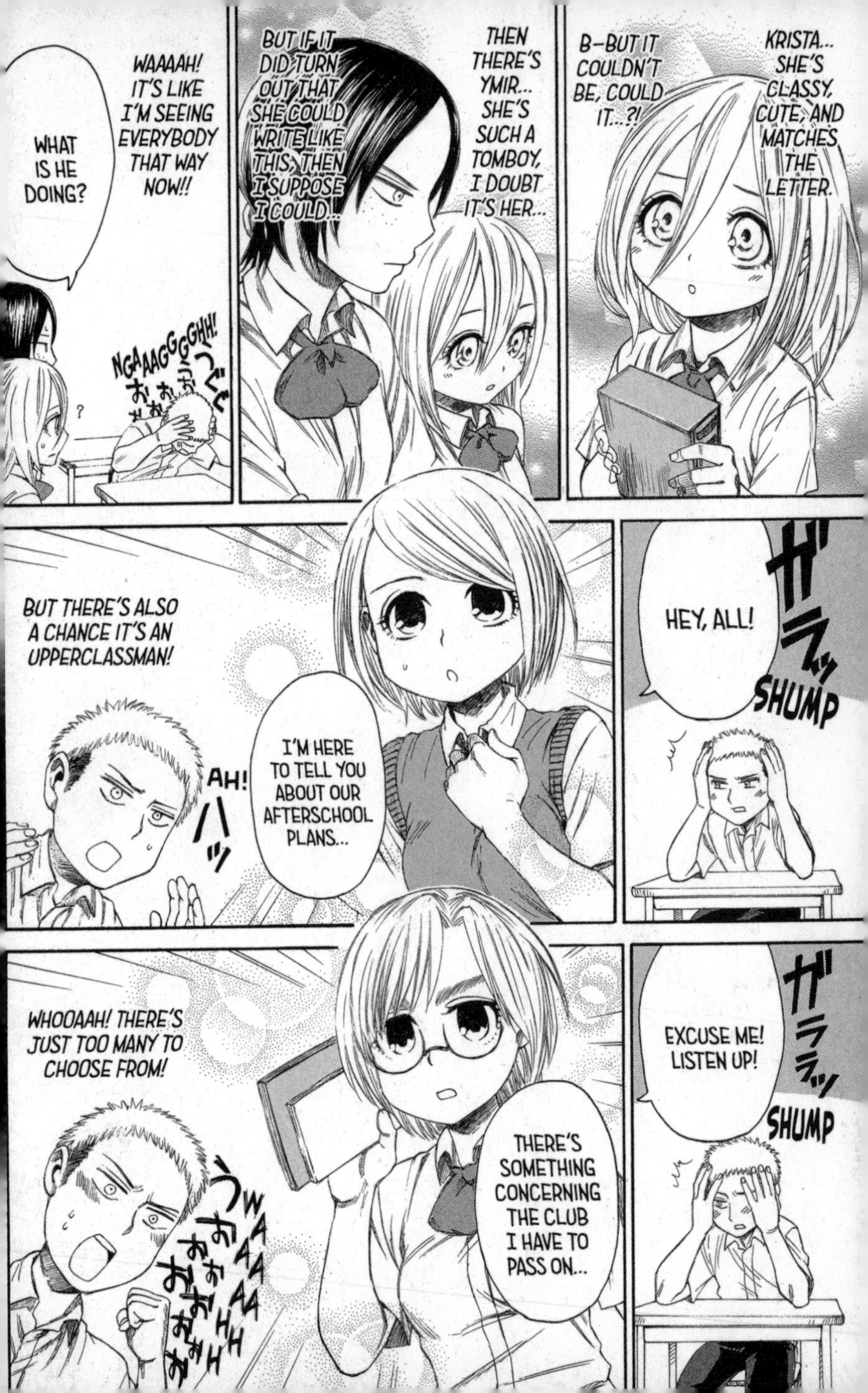
KRISTA... SHE'S CLASSY, CUTE, AND MATCHES THE LETTER.
B-BUT IT COULDN'T BE, COULD IT...?!
THEN THERE'S YMIR... SHE'S SUCH A TOMBOY, I DOUBT IT'S HER...
BUT IF IT DID TURN OUT THAT SHE COULD WRITE LIKE THIS, THEN I SUPPOSE I COULD...
WAAAAH! IT'S LIKE I'M SEEING EVERYBODY THAT WAY NOW!!
WHAT IS HE DOING?
NGAAAGGGHH!
?
ガラッ
SHUMP
HEY, ALL!
I'M HERE TO TELL YOU ABOUT OUR AFTERSCHOOL PLANS...
AH!
ハッ
BUT THERE'S ALSO A CHANCE IT'S AN UPPERCLASSMAN!
ガラララッ
SHUMP
EXCUSE ME! LISTEN UP!
THERE'S SOMETHING CONCERNING THE CLUB I HAVE TO PASS ON...
WHOOAAH! THERE'S JUST TOO MANY TO CHOOSE FROM!
WAAAAHHH

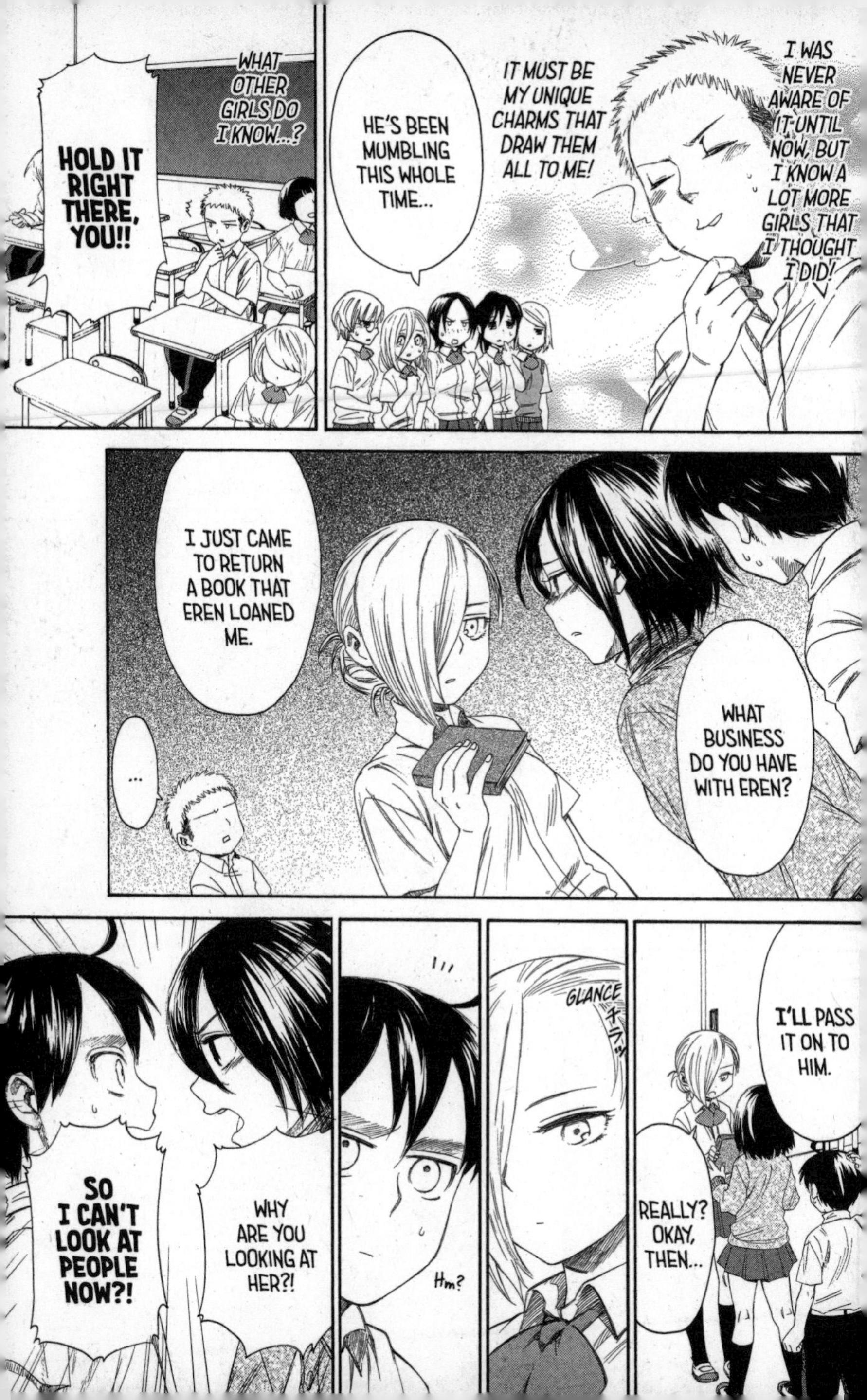
I WAS NEVER AWARE OF IT UNTIL NOW, BUT I KNOW A LOT MORE GIRLS THAT I THOUGHT I DID!
IT MUST BE MY UNIQUE CHARMS THAT DRAW THEM ALL TO ME!
HE'S BEEN MUMBLING THIS WHOLE TIME...
WHAT OTHER GIRLS DO I KNOW...?
HOLD IT RIGHT THERE, YOU!!
WHAT BUSINESS DO YOU HAVE WITH EREN?
I JUST CAME TO RETURN A BOOK THAT EREN LOANED ME.
...
I'LL PASS IT ON TO HIM.
REALLY? OKAY, THEN...
GLANCE
チラッ
!!!
Hm?
WHY ARE YOU LOOKING AT HER?!
SO I CAN'T LOOK AT PEOPLE NOW?!

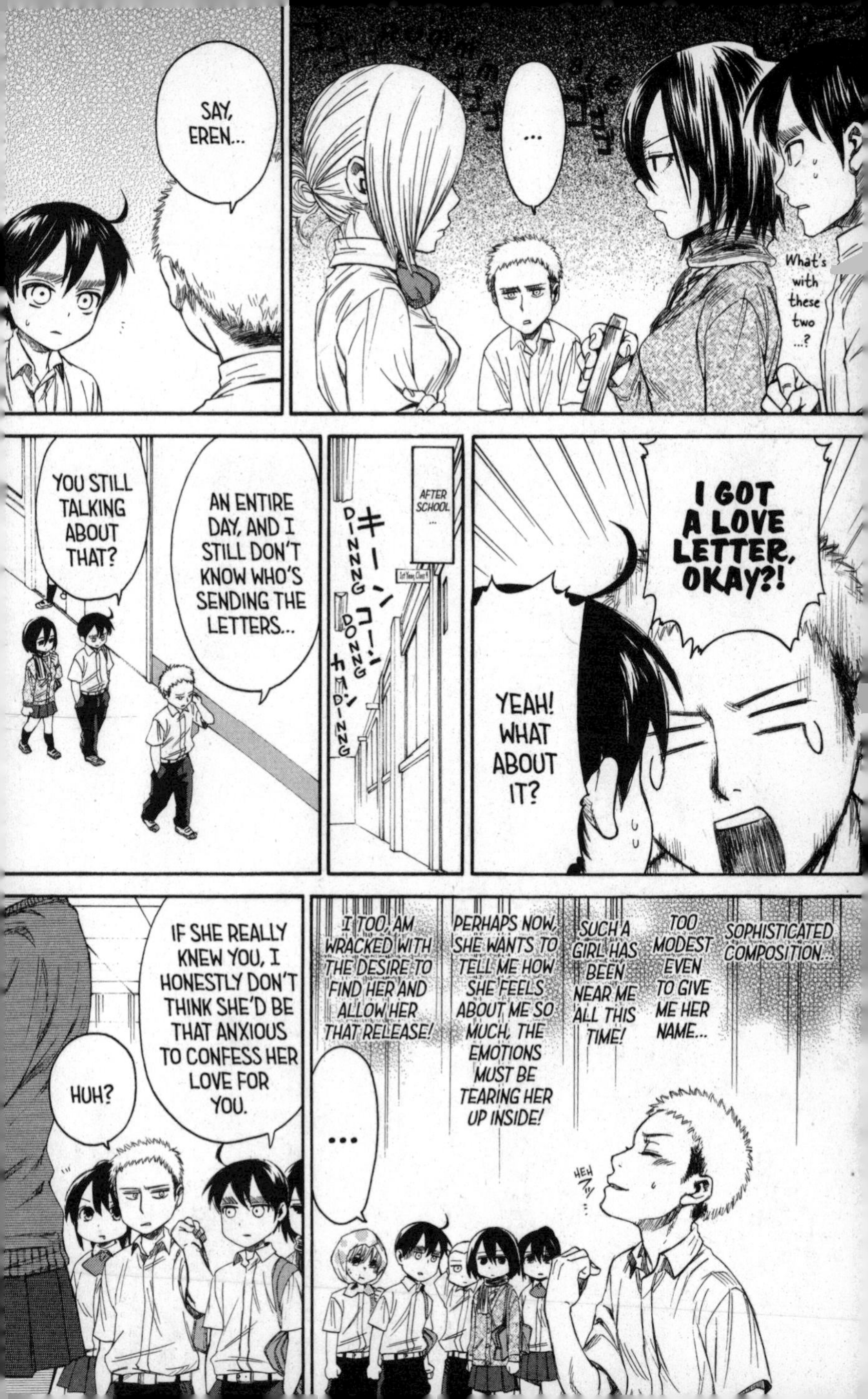
...
What's with these two ...?
SAY, EREN...
I GOT A LOVE LETTER, OKAY?!
YEAH! WHAT ABOUT IT?
AFTER SCHOOL...
DINNNG DONNG DINNNG
AN ENTIRE DAY, AND I STILL DON'T KNOW WHO'S SENDING THE LETTERS...
YOU STILL TALKING ABOUT THAT?
SOPHISTICATED COMPOSITION...
TOO MODEST EVEN TO GIVE ME HER NAME...
SUCH A GIRL HAS BEEN NEAR ME ALL THIS TIME!
PERHAPS NOW, SHE WANTS TO TELL ME HOW SHE FEELS ABOUT ME SO MUCH, THE EMOTIONS MUST BE TEARING HER UP INSIDE!
I TOO, AM WRACKED WITH THE DESIRE TO FIND HER AND ALLOW HER THAT RELEASE!
HEH
...
IF SHE REALLY KNEW YOU, I HONESTLY DON'T THINK SHE'D BE THAT ANXIOUS TO CONFESS HER LOVE FOR YOU.
HUH?

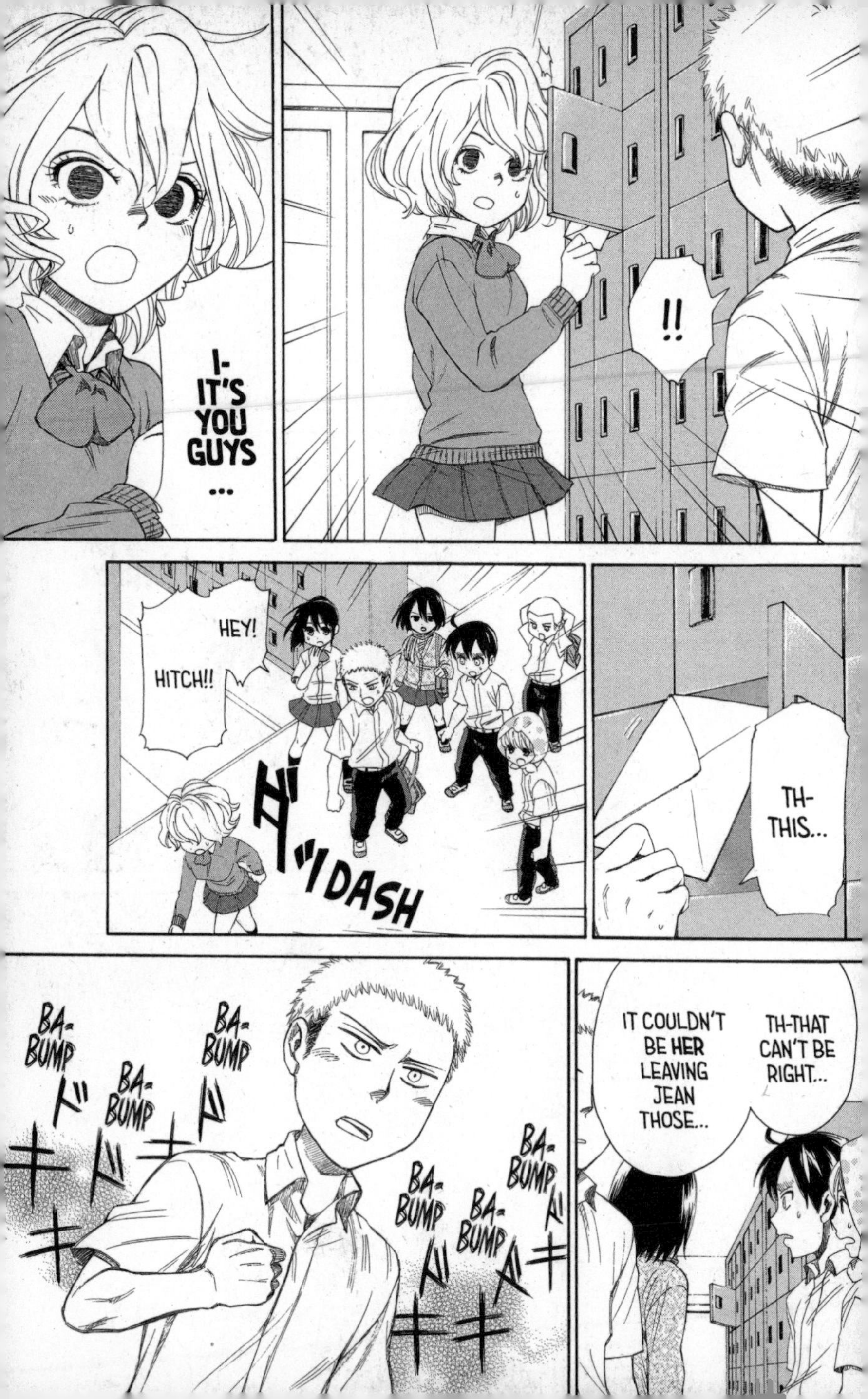
!!
I- IT'S YOU GUYS ...
TH- THIS...
HEY!
HITCH!!
DASH
TH-THAT CAN'T BE RIGHT...
IT COULDN'T BE HER LEAVING JEAN THOSE...
BA-BUMP
BA-BUMP
BA-BUMP
BA-BUMP
BA-BUMP
BA-BUMP

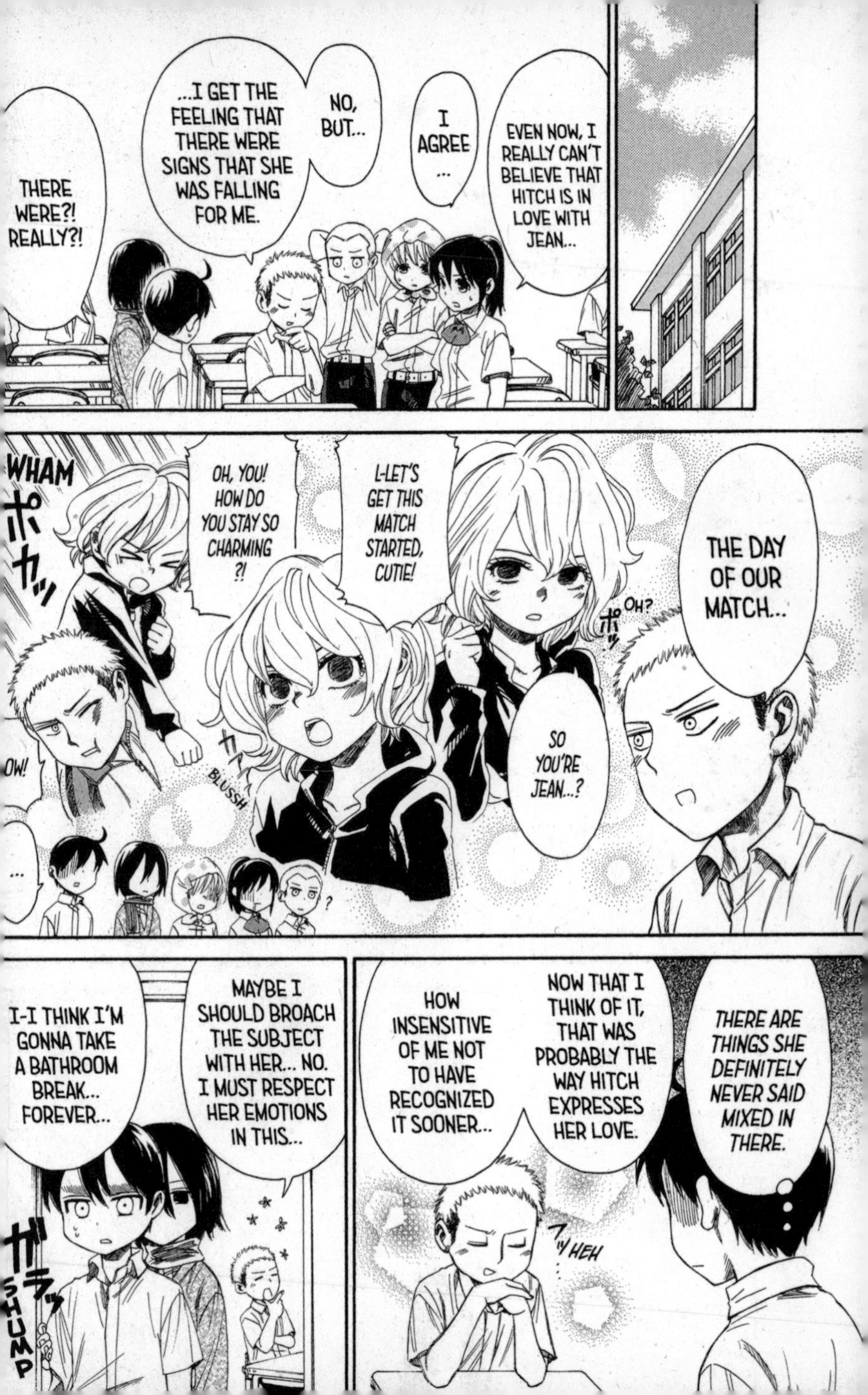
EVEN NOW, I REALLY CAN'T BELIEVE THAT HITCH IS IN LOVE WITH JEAN...
I AGREE ...
NO, BUT...
...I GET THE FEELING THAT THERE WERE SIGNS THAT SHE WAS FALLING FOR ME.
THERE WERE?! REALLY?!
THE DAY OF OUR MATCH...
ポッ OH?
SO YOU'RE JEAN...?
L-LET'S GET THIS MATCH STARTED, CUTIE!
カァ BLUSSH
OH, YOU! HOW DO YOU STAY SO CHARMING?!
WHAM ポカッ
OW!
?
...
THERE ARE THINGS SHE DEFINITELY NEVER SAID MIXED IN THERE.
NOW THAT I THINK OF IT, THAT WAS PROBABLY THE WAY HITCH EXPRESSES HER LOVE.
HOW INSENSITIVE OF ME NOT TO HAVE RECOGNIZED IT SOONER...
フッ HEH
MAYBE I SHOULD BROACH THE SUBJECT WITH HER... NO. I MUST RESPECT HER EMOTIONS IN THIS...
I-I THINK I'M GONNA TAKE A BATHROOM BREAK... FOREVER...
ガラッ SHUMP

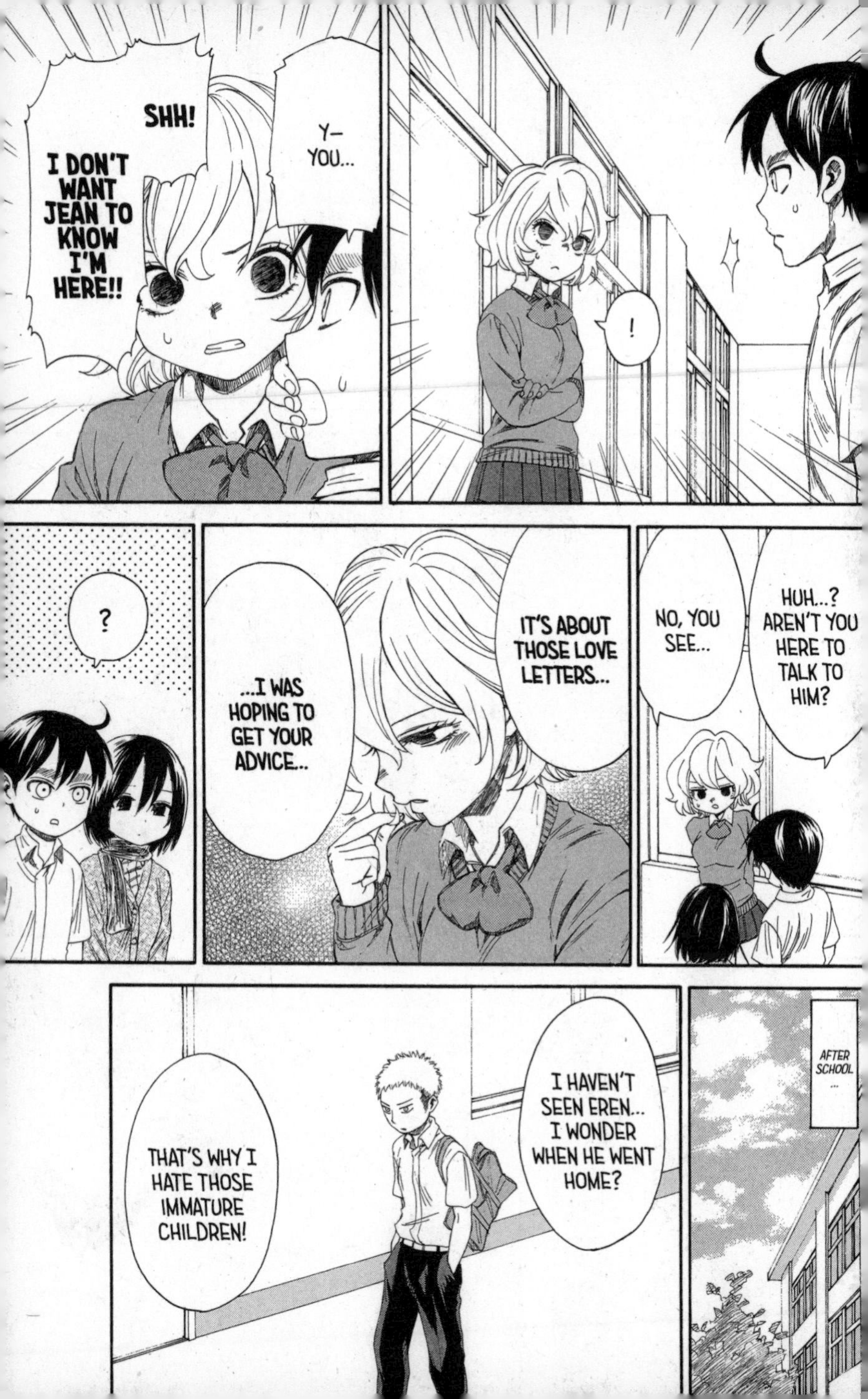
!
Y— YOU...
SHH!
I DON'T WANT JEAN TO KNOW I'M HERE!!
HUH...? AREN'T YOU HERE TO TALK TO HIM?
NO, YOU SEE...
IT'S ABOUT THOSE LOVE LETTERS...
...I WAS HOPING TO GET YOUR ADVICE...
?
AFTER SCHOOL ...
I HAVEN'T SEEN EREN... I WONDER WHEN HE WENT HOME?
THAT'S WHY I HATE THOSE IMMATURE CHILDREN!

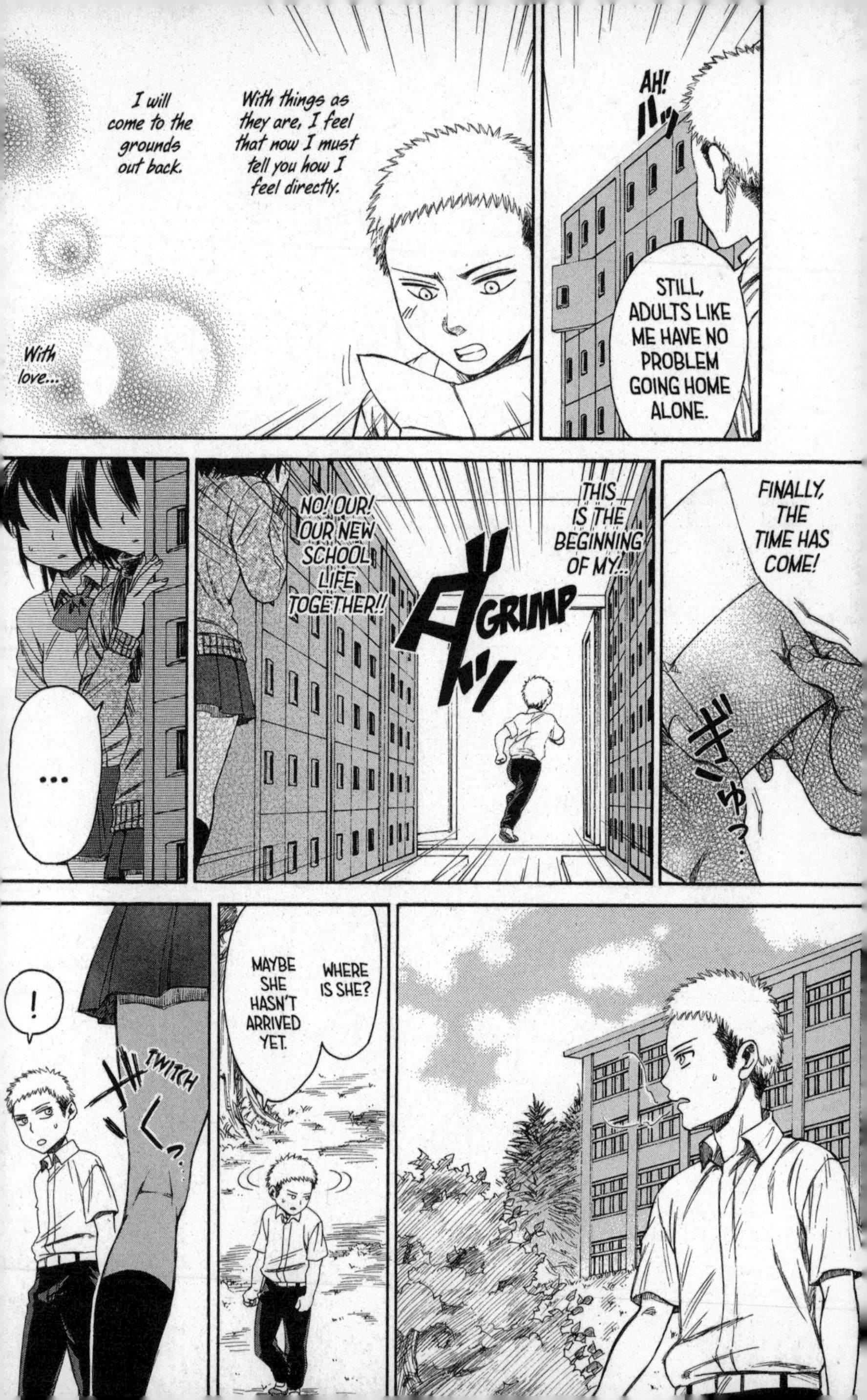
AH!
STILL, ADULTS LIKE ME HAVE NO PROBLEM GOING HOME ALONE.
With things as they are, I feel that now I must tell you how I feel directly.
I will come to the grounds out back.
With love...
FINALLY, THE TIME HAS COME!
THIS IS THE BEGINNING OF MY...
NO! OUR! OUR NEW SCHOOL LIFE TOGETHER!!
GRIMP
...
WHERE IS SHE?
MAYBE SHE HASN'T ARRIVED YET.
!
TWITCH

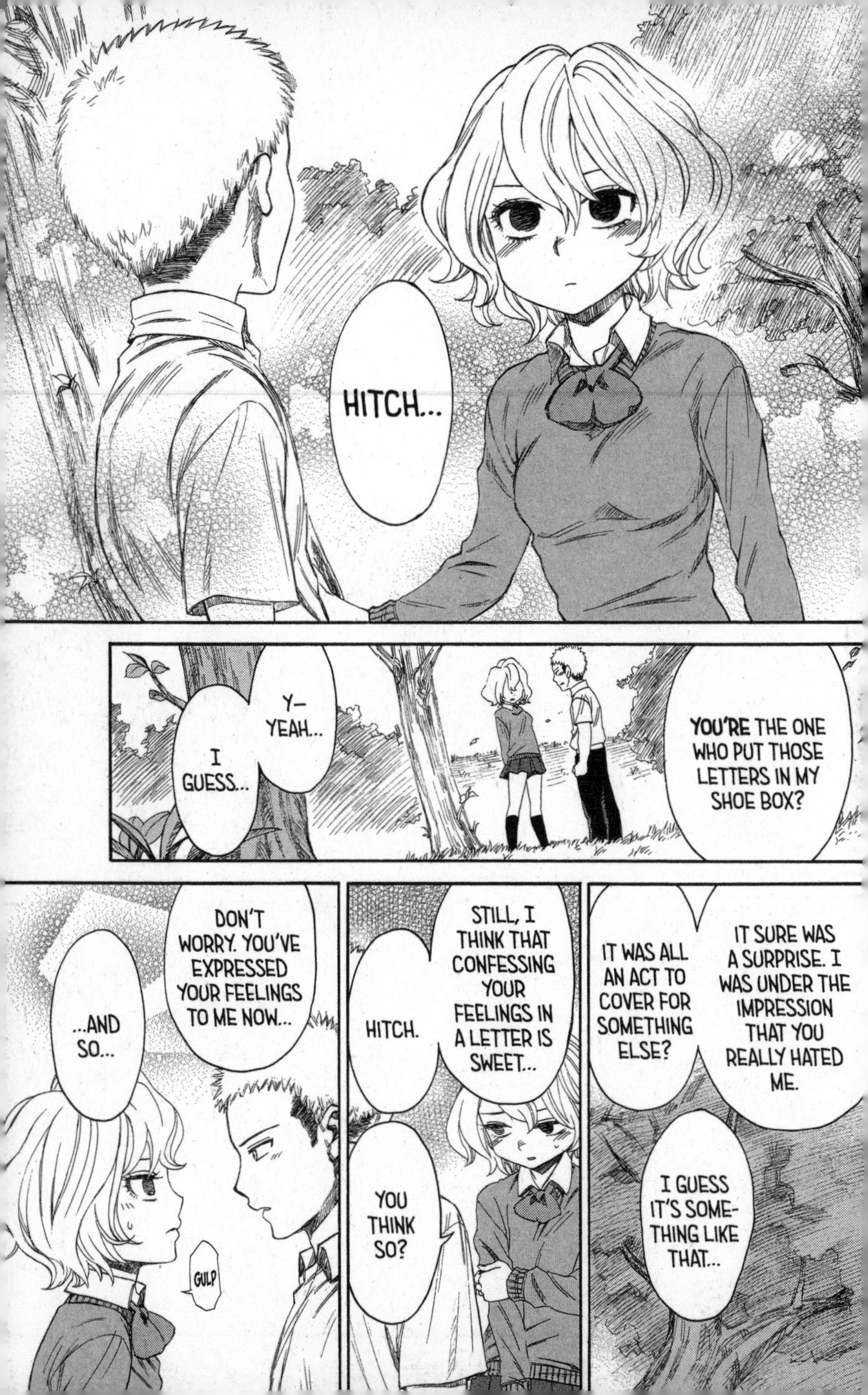
HITCH...
YOU'RE THE ONE WHO PUT THOSE LETTERS IN MY SHOE BOX?
Y— YEAH...
I GUESS...
IT SURE WAS A SURPRISE. I WAS UNDER THE IMPRESSION THAT YOU REALLY HATED ME.
IT WAS ALL AN ACT TO COVER FOR SOMETHING ELSE?
I GUESS IT'S SOME-THING LIKE THAT...
STILL, I THINK THAT CONFESSING YOUR FEELINGS IN A LETTER IS SWEET...
HITCH.
YOU THINK SO?
DON'T WORRY. YOU'VE EXPRESSED YOUR FEELINGS TO ME NOW...
...AND SO...
GULP

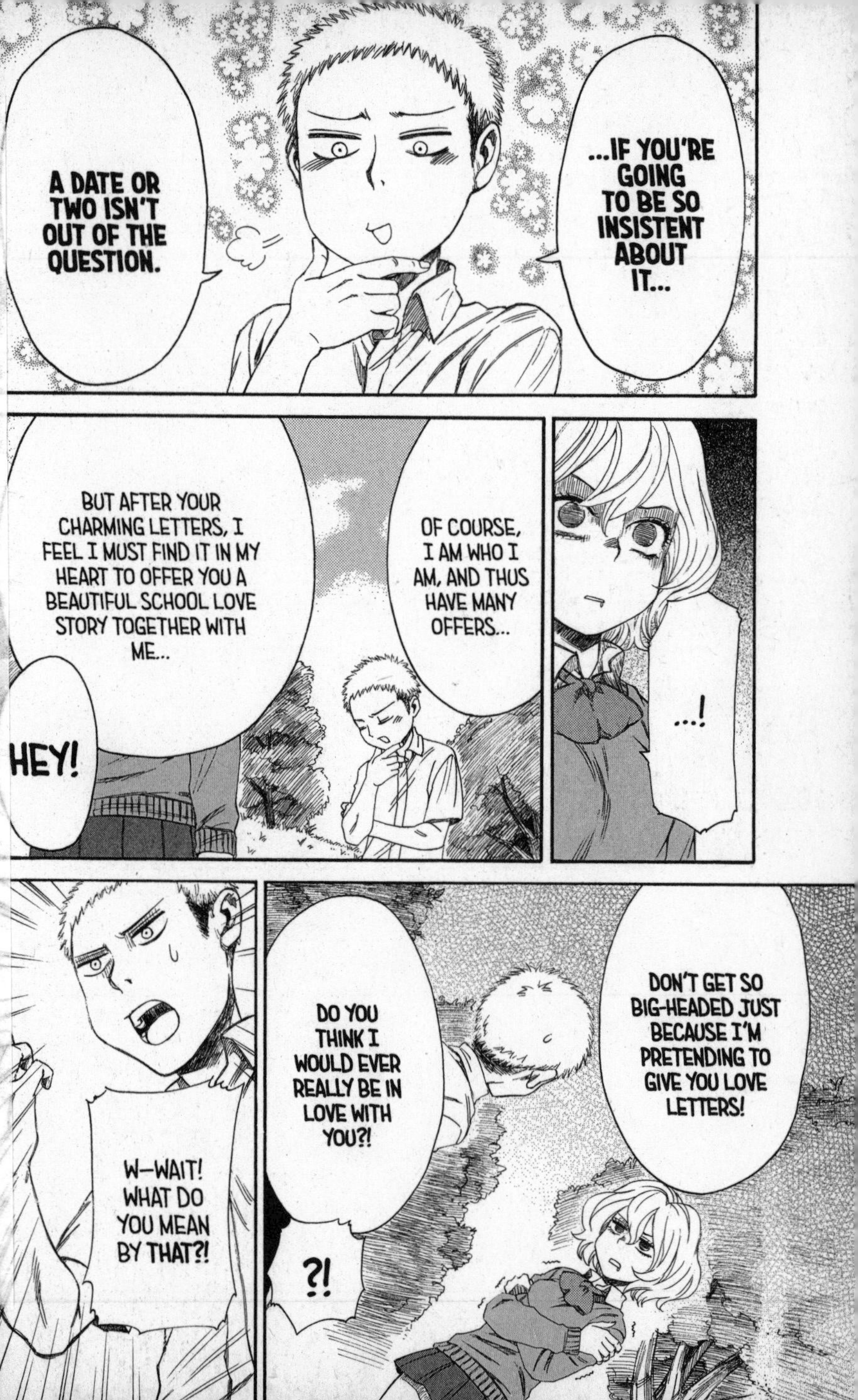
...IF YOU'RE GOING TO BE SO INSISTENT ABOUT IT...
A DATE OR TWO ISN'T OUT OF THE QUESTION.
...!
OF COURSE, I AM WHO I AM, AND THUS HAVE MANY OFFERS...
BUT AFTER YOUR CHARMING LETTERS, I FEEL I MUST FIND IT IN MY HEART TO OFFER YOU A BEAUTIFUL SCHOOL LOVE STORY TOGETHER WITH ME...
HEY!
DON'T GET SO BIG-HEADED JUST BECAUSE I'M PRETENDING TO GIVE YOU LOVE LETTERS!
DO YOU THINK I WOULD EVER REALLY BE IN LOVE WITH YOU?!
?!
W—WAIT! WHAT DO YOU MEAN BY THAT?!

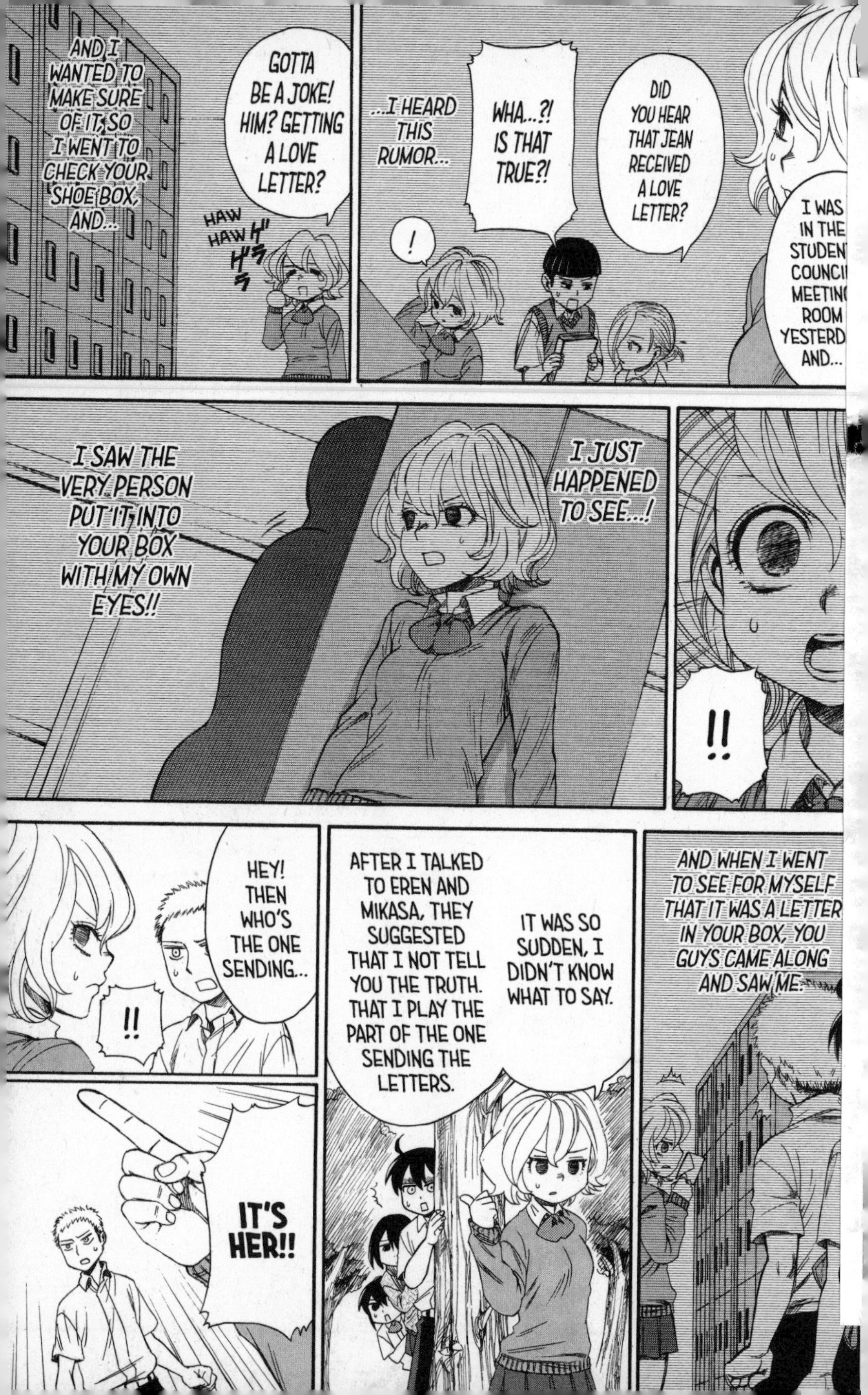
I WAS IN THE STUDENT COUNCIL MEETING ROOM YESTERD AND...
DID YOU HEAR THAT JEAN RECEIVED A LOVE LETTER?
WHA...?! IS THAT TRUE?!
...I HEARD THIS RUMOR...
!
GOTTA BE A JOKE! HIM? GETTING A LOVE LETTER?
HAW HAW ゲラゲラ
AND I WANTED TO MAKE SURE OF IT, SO I WENT TO CHECK YOUR SHOE BOX, AND...
!!
I JUST HAPPENED TO SEE...!
I SAW THE VERY PERSON PUT IT INTO YOUR BOX WITH MY OWN EYES!!
AND WHEN I WENT TO SEE FOR MYSELF THAT IT WAS A LETTER IN YOUR BOX, YOU GUYS CAME ALONG AND SAW ME.
IT WAS SO SUDDEN, I DIDN'T KNOW WHAT TO SAY.
AFTER I TALKED TO EREN AND MIKASA, THEY SUGGESTED THAT I NOT TELL YOU THE TRUTH. THAT I PLAY THE PART OF THE ONE SENDING THE LETTERS.
HEY! THEN WHO'S THE ONE SENDING...
!!
IT'S HER!!

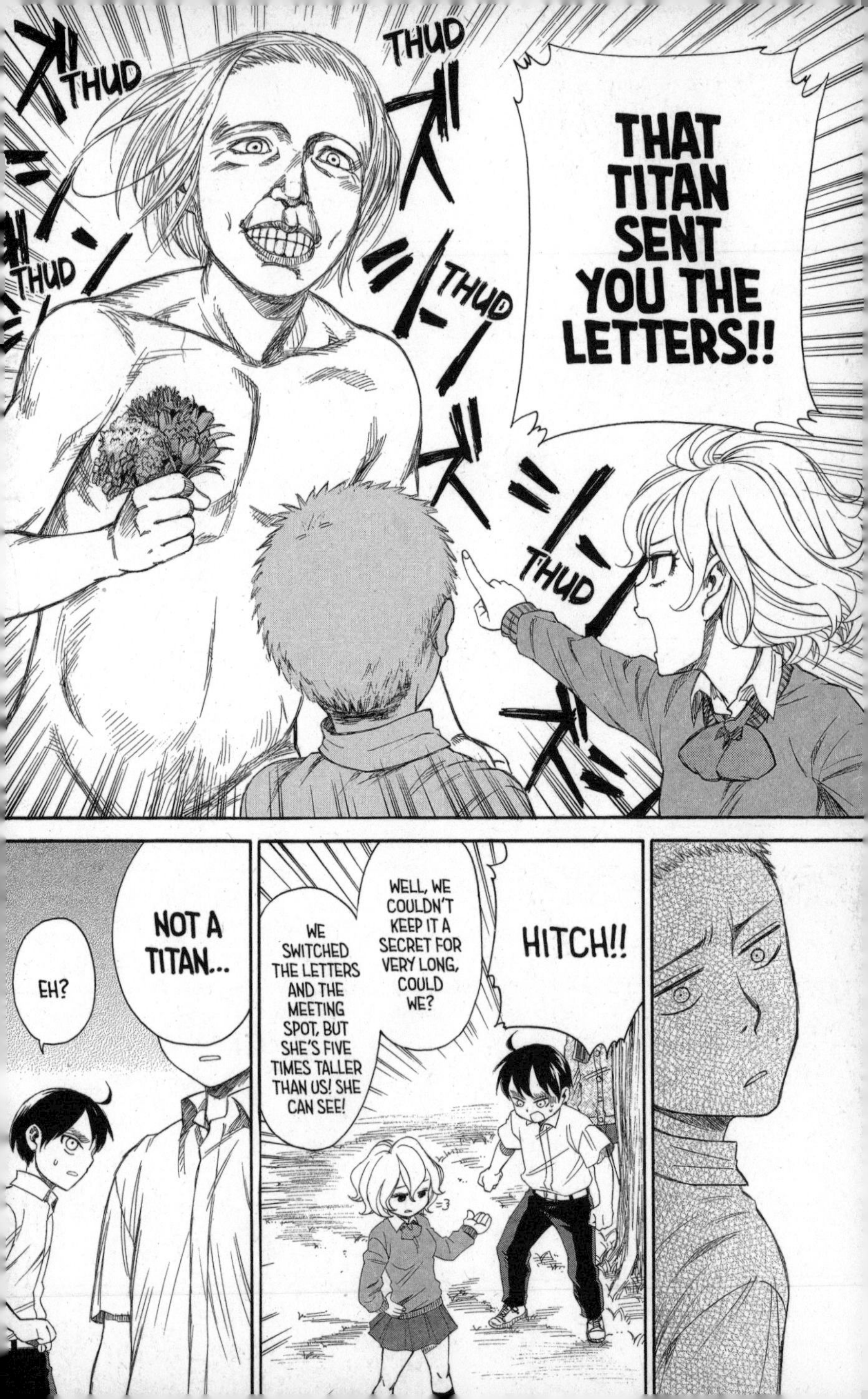
THAT TITAN SENT YOU THE LETTERS!!
THUD
THUD
THUD
THUD
THUD
HITCH!!
WELL, WE COULDN'T KEEP IT A SECRET FOR VERY LONG, COULD WE?
WE SWITCHED THE LETTERS AND THE MEETING SPOT, BUT SHE'S FIVE TIMES TALLER THAN US! SHE CAN SEE!
NOT A TITAN...
EH?

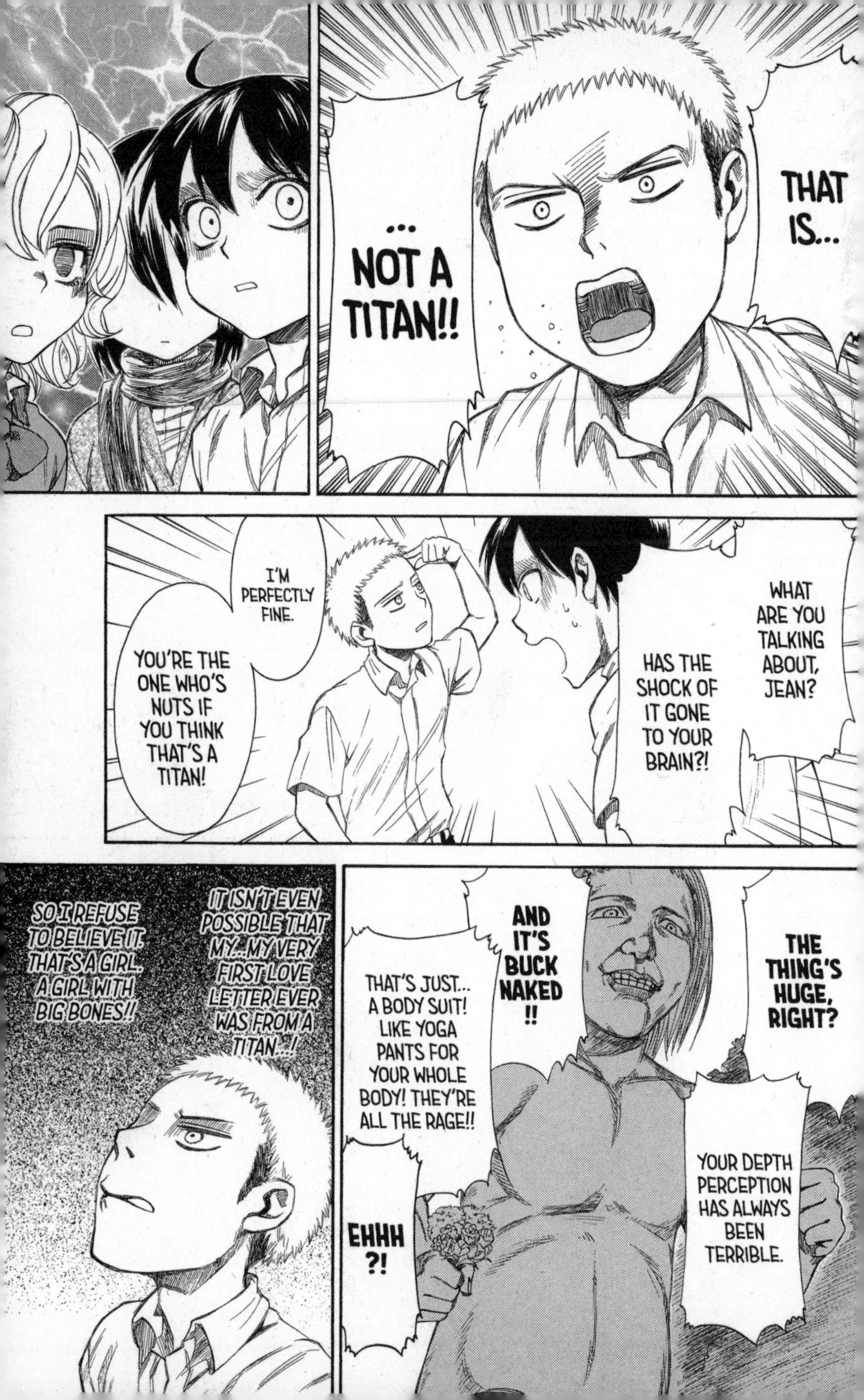
THAT IS...
...NOT A TITAN!!
WHAT ARE YOU TALKING ABOUT, JEAN?
HAS THE SHOCK OF IT GONE TO YOUR BRAIN?!
I'M PERFECTLY FINE.
YOU'RE THE ONE WHO'S NUTS IF YOU THINK THAT'S A TITAN!
THE THING'S HUGE, RIGHT?
AND IT'S BUCK NAKED!!
YOUR DEPTH PERCEPTION HAS ALWAYS BEEN TERRIBLE.
THAT'S JUST... A BODY SUIT! LIKE YOGA PANTS FOR YOUR WHOLE BODY! THEY'RE ALL THE RAGE!!
EHHH?!
IT ISN'T EVEN POSSIBLE THAT MY...MY VERY FIRST LOVE LETTER EVER WAS FROM A TITAN...!
SO I REFUSE TO BELIEVE IT. THAT'S A GIRL. A GIRL WITH BIG BONES!!

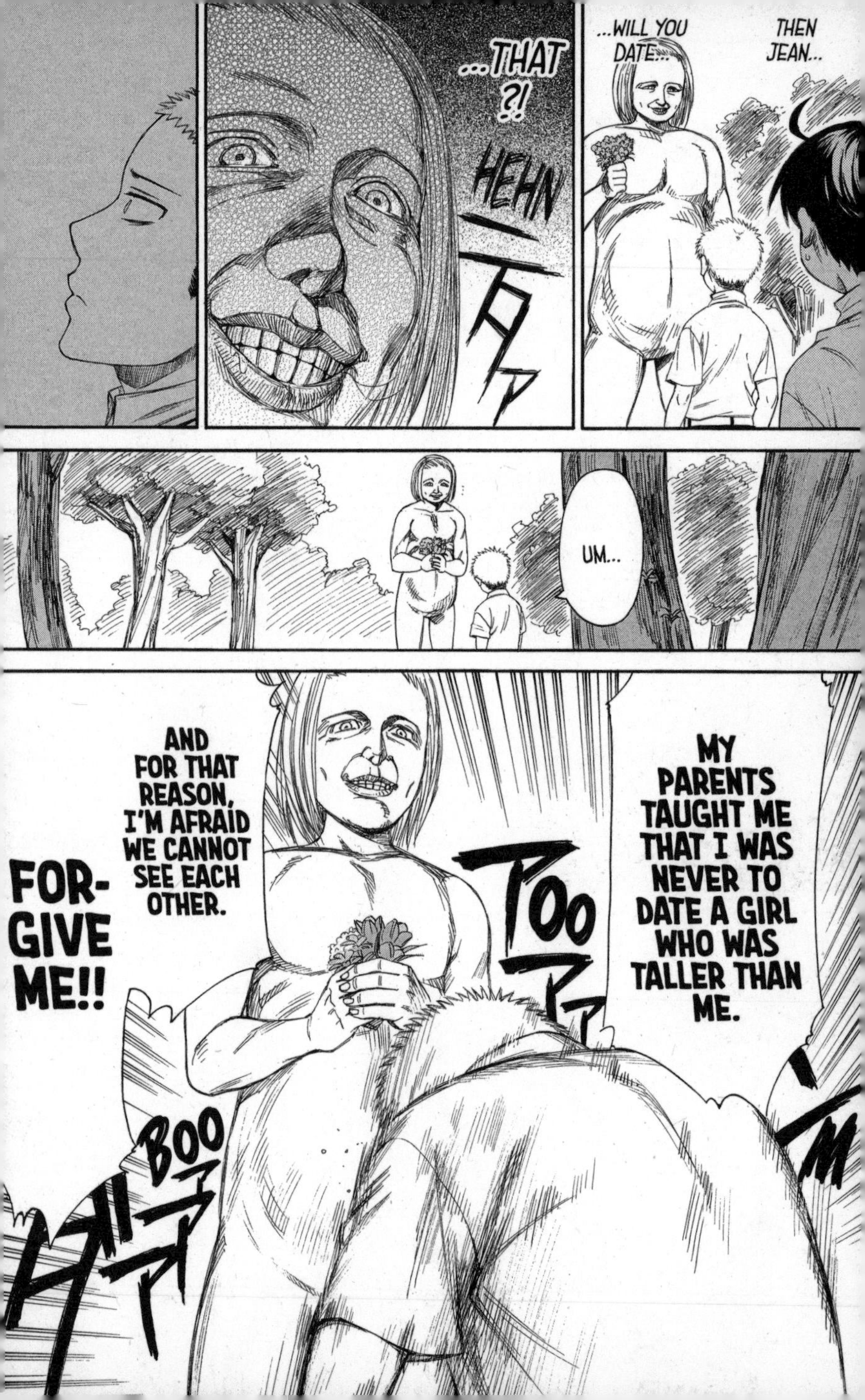
THEN JEAN...
...WILL YOU DATE...
...THAT ?!
HEHN
UM...
MY PARENTS TAUGHT ME THAT I WAS NEVER TO DATE A GIRL WHO WAS TALLER THAN ME.
POO
AND FOR THAT REASON, I'M AFRAID WE CANNOT SEE EACH OTHER.
FOR-GIVE ME!!
BOO

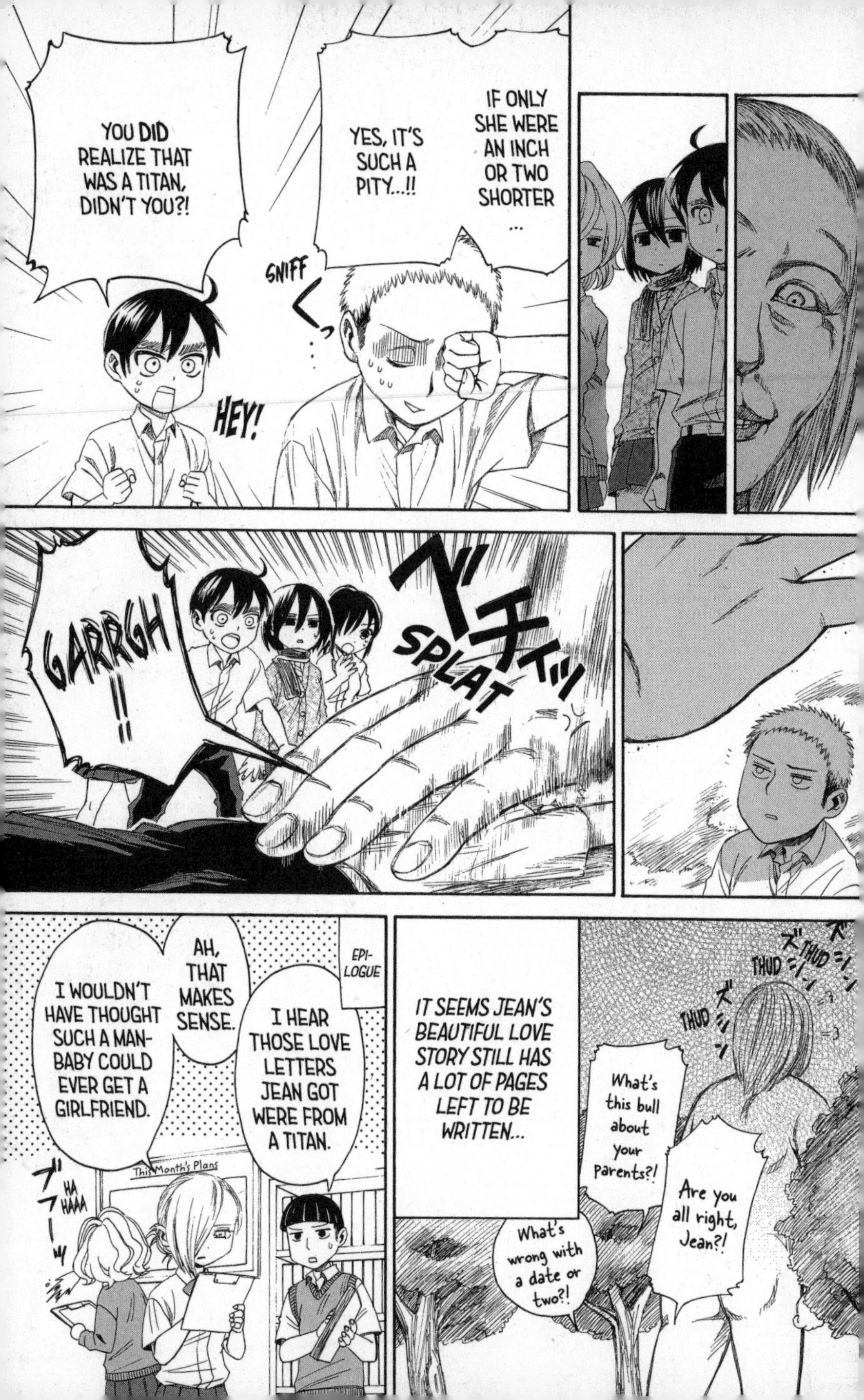
IF ONLY SHE WERE AN INCH OR TWO SHORTER...
YES, IT'S SUCH A PITY...!!
SNIFF
YOU DID REALIZE THAT WAS A TITAN, DIDN'T YOU?!
HEY!
SPLAT
GARRGH !!
THUD
THUD
Are you all right, Jean?!
What's this bull about your parents?!
What's wrong with a date or two?!
IT SEEMS JEAN'S BEAUTIFUL LOVE STORY STILL HAS A LOT OF PAGES LEFT TO BE WRITTEN...
EPILOGUE
I HEAR THOSE LOVE LETTERS JEAN GOT WERE FROM A TITAN.
AH, THAT MAKES SENSE.
I WOULDN'T HAVE THOUGHT SUCH A MAN-BABY COULD EVER GET A GIRLFRIEND.
HA HAAA
This Month's Plans

MR. POPULAR
BONUS MANGA

OVERFLOWING YOUTH!

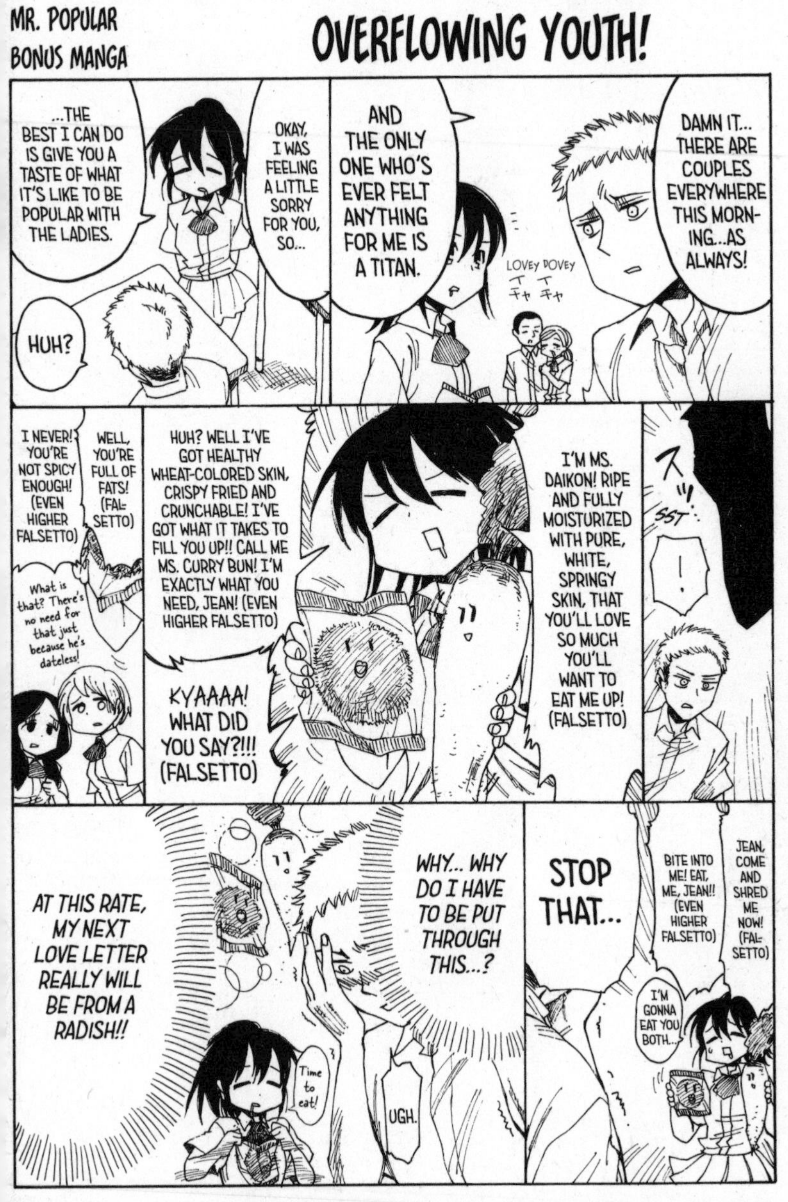
DAMN IT... THERE ARE COUPLES EVERYWHERE THIS MORNING...AS ALWAYS!
LOVEY DOVEY
イチャ イチャ
AND THE ONLY ONE WHO'S EVER FELT ANYTHING FOR ME IS A TITAN.
OKAY, I WAS FEELING A LITTLE SORRY FOR YOU, SO...
...THE BEST I CAN DO IS GIVE YOU A TASTE OF WHAT IT'S LIKE TO BE POPULAR WITH THE LADIES.
HUH?
スッ
SST
!
I'M MS. DAIKON! RIPE AND FULLY MOISTURIZED WITH PURE, WHITE, SPRINGY SKIN, THAT YOU'LL LOVE SO MUCH YOU'LL WANT TO EAT ME UP! (FALSETTO)
HUH? WELL I'VE GOT HEALTHY WHEAT-COLORED SKIN, CRISPY FRIED AND CRUNCHABLE! I'VE GOT WHAT IT TAKES TO FILL YOU UP!! CALL ME MS. CURRY BUN! I'M EXACTLY WHAT YOU NEED, JEAN! (EVEN HIGHER FALSETTO)
KYAAAA! WHAT DID YOU SAY?!!! (FALSETTO)
WELL, YOU'RE FULL OF FATS! (FAL-SETTO)
I NEVER! YOU'RE NOT SPICY ENOUGH! (EVEN HIGHER FALSETTO)
What is that? There's no need for that just because he's dateless!
JEAN, COME AND SHRED ME NOW! (FAL-SETTO)
BITE INTO ME! EAT, ME, JEAN!! (EVEN HIGHER FALSETTO)
STOP THAT...
I'M GONNA EAT YOU BOTH...
WHY... WHY DO I HAVE TO BE PUT THROUGH THIS...?
UGH.
AT THIS RATE, MY NEXT LOVE LETTER REALLY WILL BE FROM A RADISH!!
Time to eat!

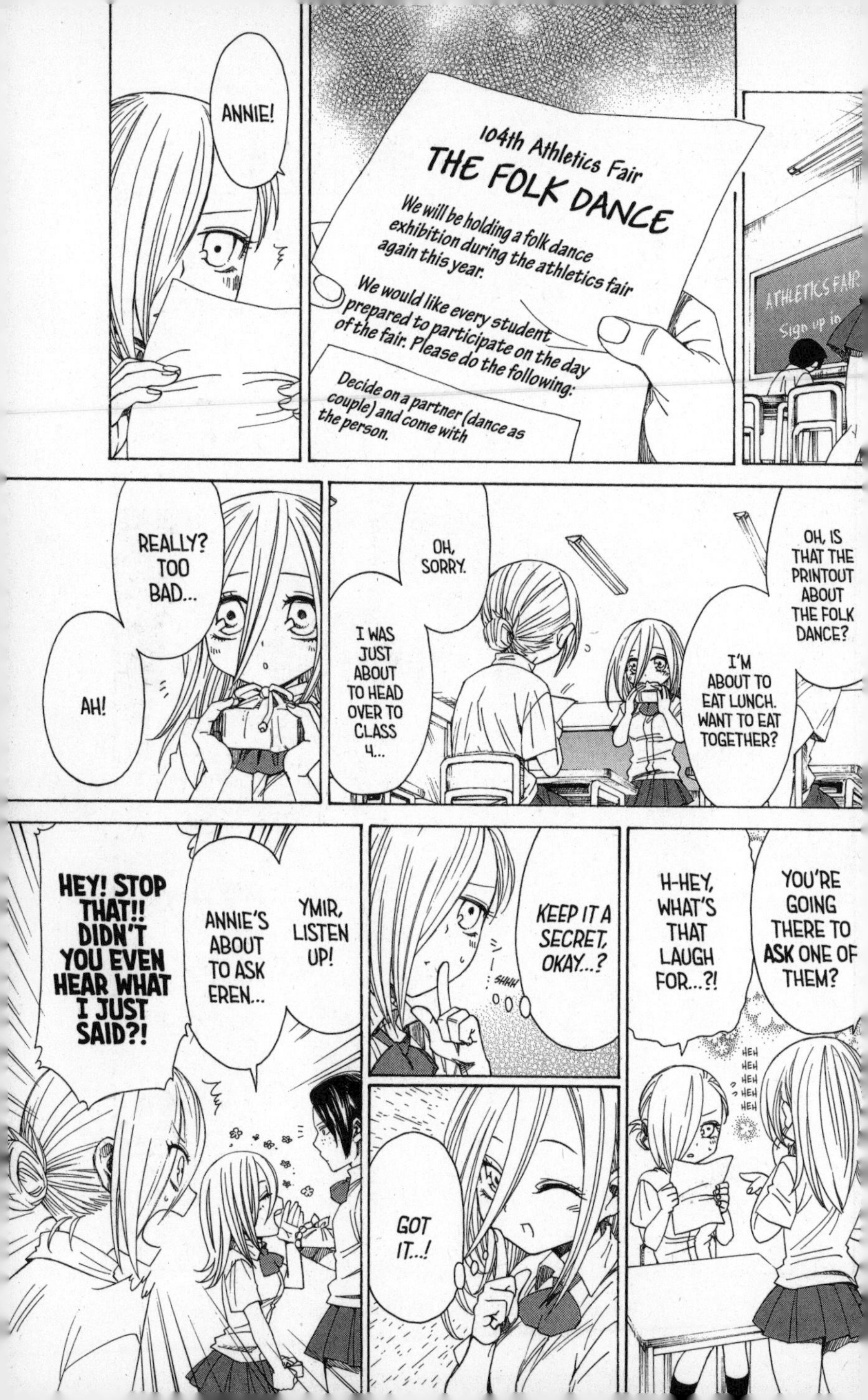
ATHLETICS FAIR
Sign up in
104th Athletics Fair
THE FOLK DANCE
We will be holding a folk dance exhibition during the athletics fair again this year.
We would like every student prepared to participate on the day of the fair. Please do the following:
Decide on a partner (dance as couple) and come with the person.
ANNIE!
OH, IS THAT THE PRINTOUT ABOUT THE FOLK DANCE?
I'M ABOUT TO EAT LUNCH. WANT TO EAT TOGETHER?
OH, SORRY.
I WAS JUST ABOUT TO HEAD OVER TO CLASS 4...
REALLY? TOO BAD...
AH!
YOU'RE GOING THERE TO ASK ONE OF THEM?
H-HEY, WHAT'S THAT LAUGH FOR...?!
HEH HEH HEH HEH HEH
KEEP IT A SECRET, OKAY...?
SHHH
GOT IT...!
YMIR, LISTEN UP!
ANNIE'S ABOUT TO ASK EREN...
HEY! STOP THAT!! DIDN'T YOU EVEN HEAR WHAT I JUST SAID?!

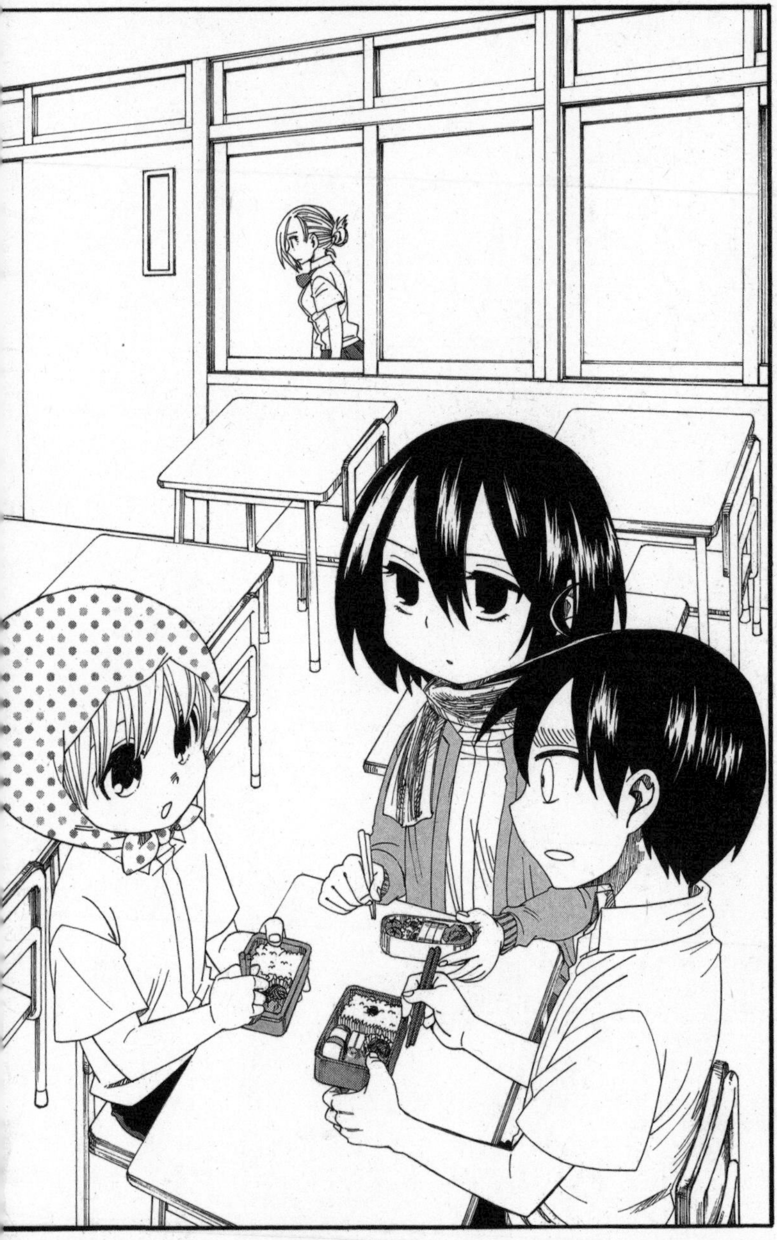

THIRTEENTH PERIOD: COUPLING

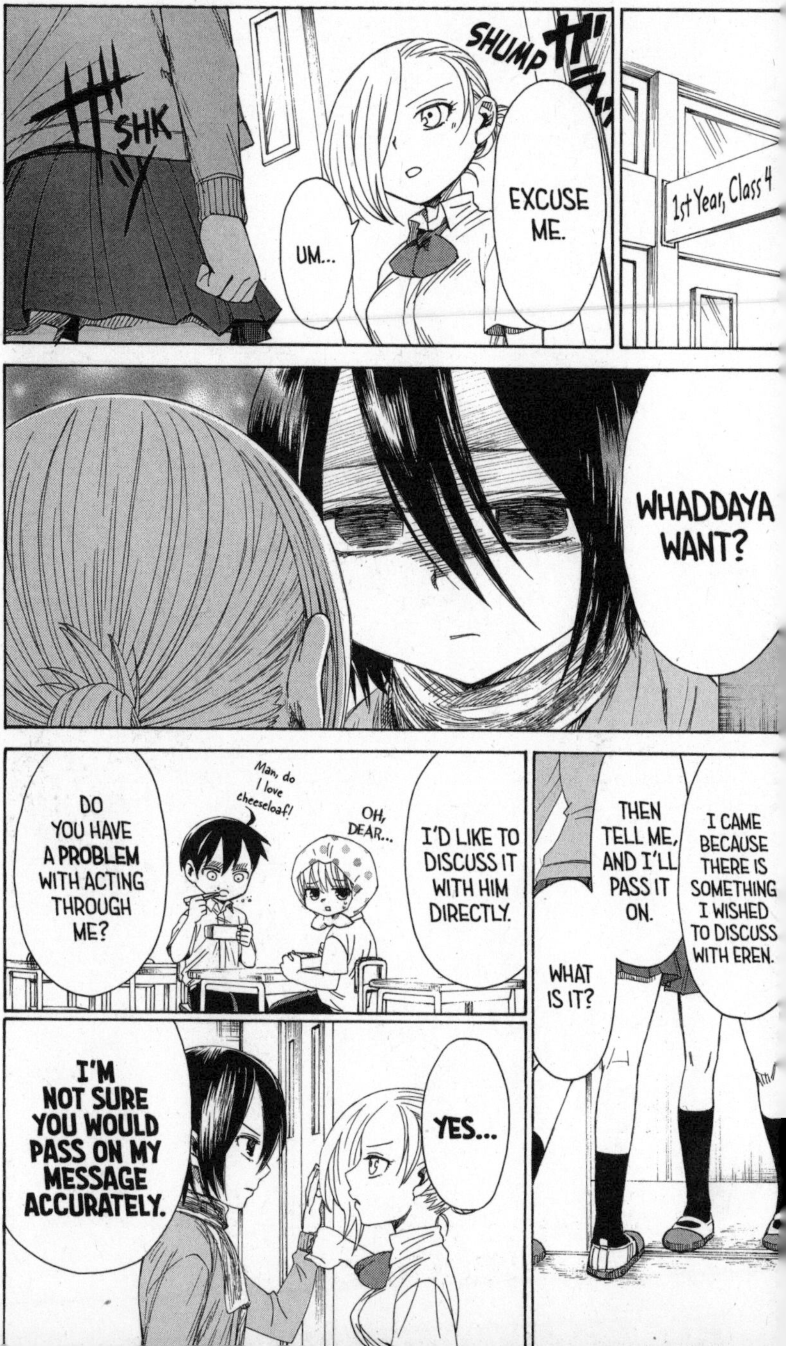
1st Year, Class 4
SHUMP
EXCUSE ME.
UM...
SHK
WHADDAYA WANT?
I CAME BECAUSE THERE IS SOMETHING I WISHED TO DISCUSS WITH EREN.
WHAT IS IT?
I'D LIKE TO DISCUSS IT WITH HIM DIRECTLY.
THEN TELL ME, AND I'LL PASS IT ON.
OH, DEAR...
Man, do I love cheeseloaf!
DO YOU HAVE A PROBLEM WITH ACTING THROUGH ME?
YES...
I'M NOT SURE YOU WOULD PASS ON MY MESSAGE ACCURATELY.

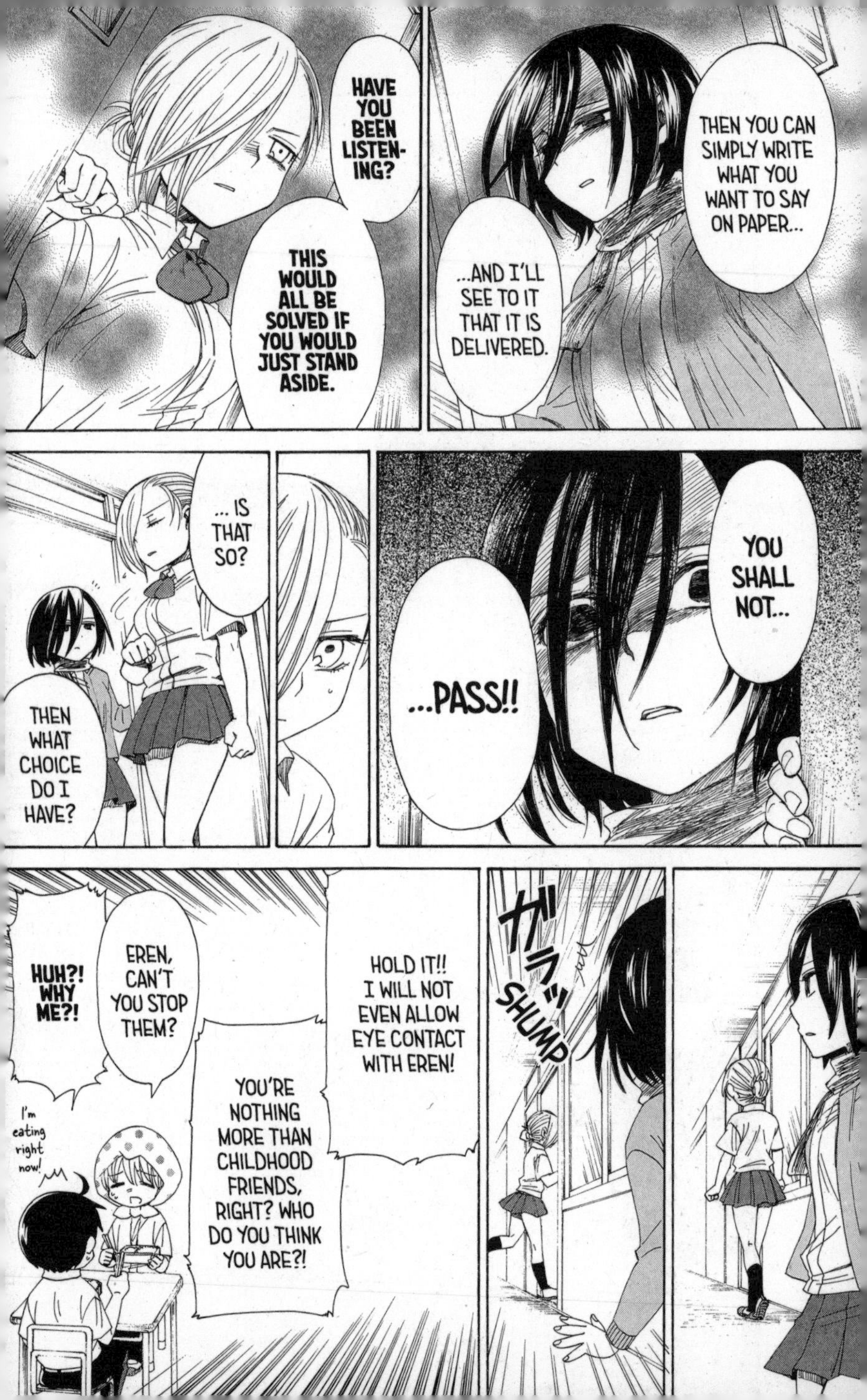
THEN YOU CAN SIMPLY WRITE WHAT YOU WANT TO SAY ON PAPER...
...AND I'LL SEE TO IT THAT IT IS DELIVERED.
HAVE YOU BEEN LISTEN-ING?
THIS WOULD ALL BE SOLVED IF YOU WOULD JUST STAND ASIDE.
YOU SHALL NOT...
...PASS!!
... IS THAT SO?
THEN WHAT CHOICE DO I HAVE?
ガラッ
SHUMP
HOLD IT!! I WILL NOT EVEN ALLOW EYE CONTACT WITH EREN!
YOU'RE NOTHING MORE THAN CHILDHOOD FRIENDS, RIGHT? WHO DO YOU THINK YOU ARE?!
EREN, CAN'T YOU STOP THEM?
HUH?! WHY ME?!
I'm eating right now!

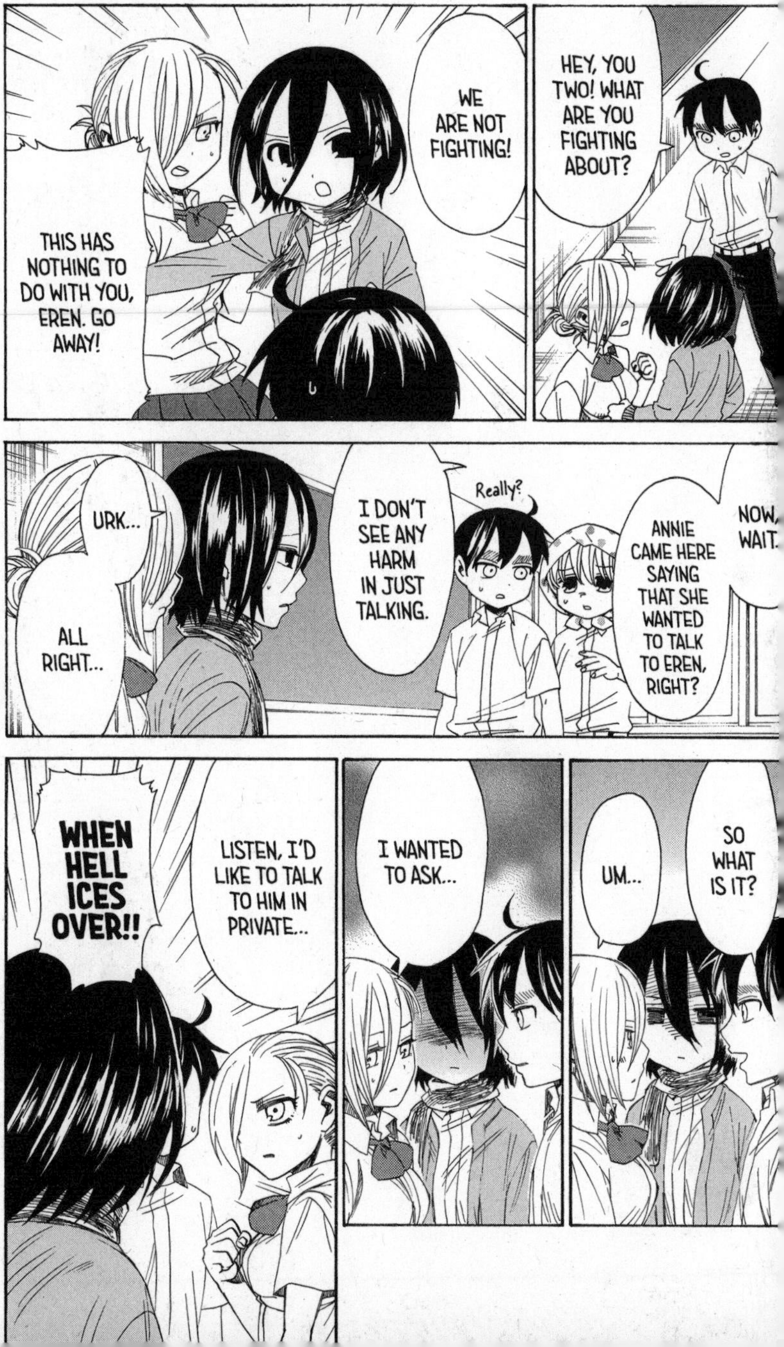
HEY, YOU TWO! WHAT ARE YOU FIGHTING ABOUT?
WE ARE NOT FIGHTING!
THIS HAS NOTHING TO DO WITH YOU, EREN. GO AWAY!
NOW, WAIT.
ANNIE CAME HERE SAYING THAT SHE WANTED TO TALK TO EREN, RIGHT?
Really?
I DON'T SEE ANY HARM IN JUST TALKING.
URK...
ALL RIGHT...
SO WHAT IS IT?
UM...
I WANTED TO ASK...
LISTEN, I'D LIKE TO TALK TO HIM IN PRIVATE...
WHEN HELL ICES OVER!!

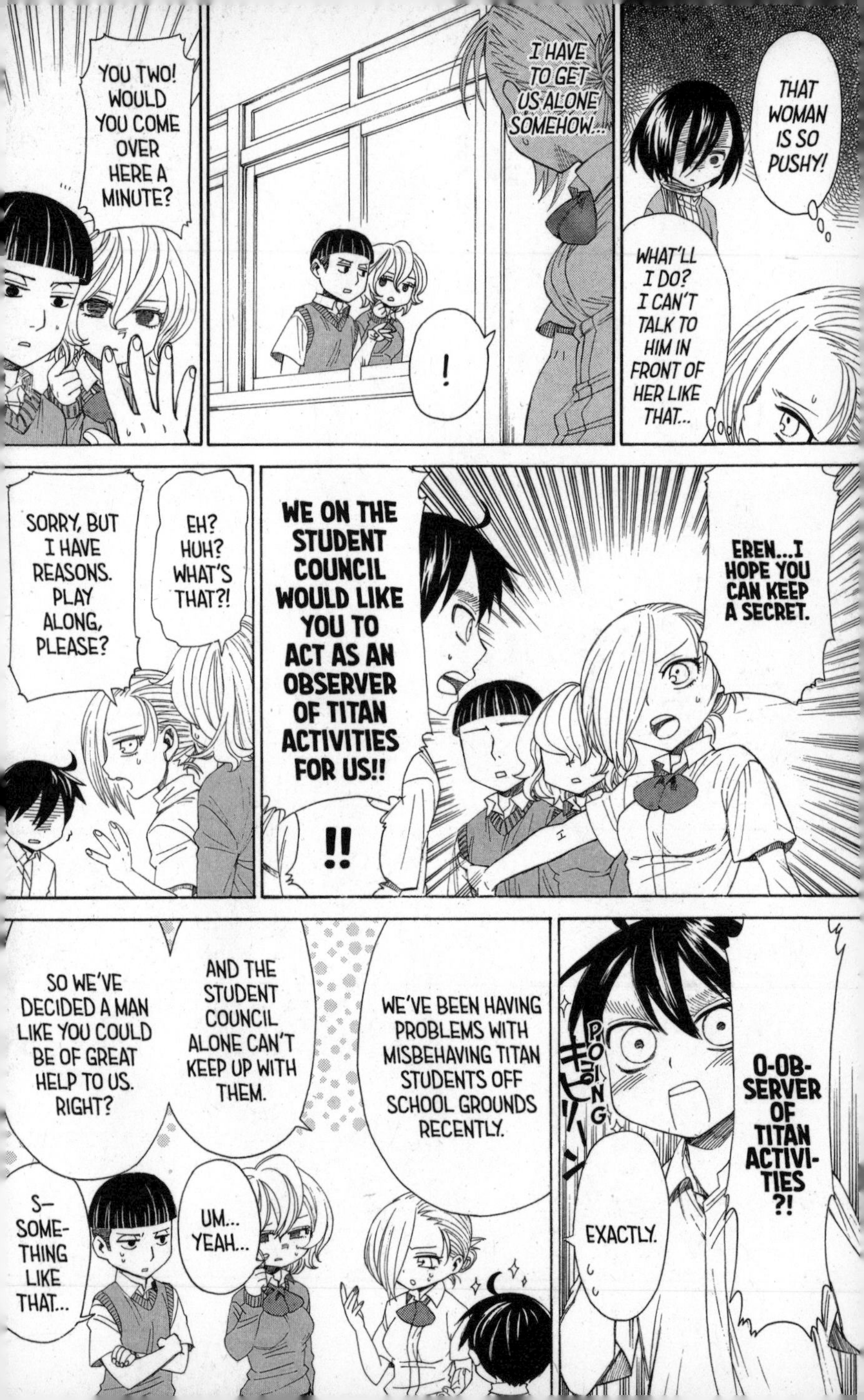
THAT WOMAN IS SO PUSHY!
WHAT'LL I DO? I CAN'T TALK TO HIM IN FRONT OF HER LIKE THAT...
I HAVE TO GET US ALONE SOMEHOW...
!
YOU TWO! WOULD YOU COME OVER HERE A MINUTE?
EREN...I HOPE YOU CAN KEEP A SECRET.
WE ON THE STUDENT COUNCIL WOULD LIKE YOU TO ACT AS AN OBSERVER OF TITAN ACTIVITIES FOR US!!
!!
EH? HUH? WHAT'S THAT?!
SORRY, BUT I HAVE REASONS. PLAY ALONG, PLEASE?
O-OB-SERVER OF TITAN ACTIVI-TIES?!
POING
EXACTLY.
WE'VE BEEN HAVING PROBLEMS WITH MISBEHAVING TITAN STUDENTS OFF SCHOOL GROUNDS RECENTLY.
AND THE STUDENT COUNCIL ALONE CAN'T KEEP UP WITH THEM.
SO WE'VE DECIDED A MAN LIKE YOU COULD BE OF GREAT HELP TO US. RIGHT?
UM... YEAH...
S—SOME-THING LIKE THAT...

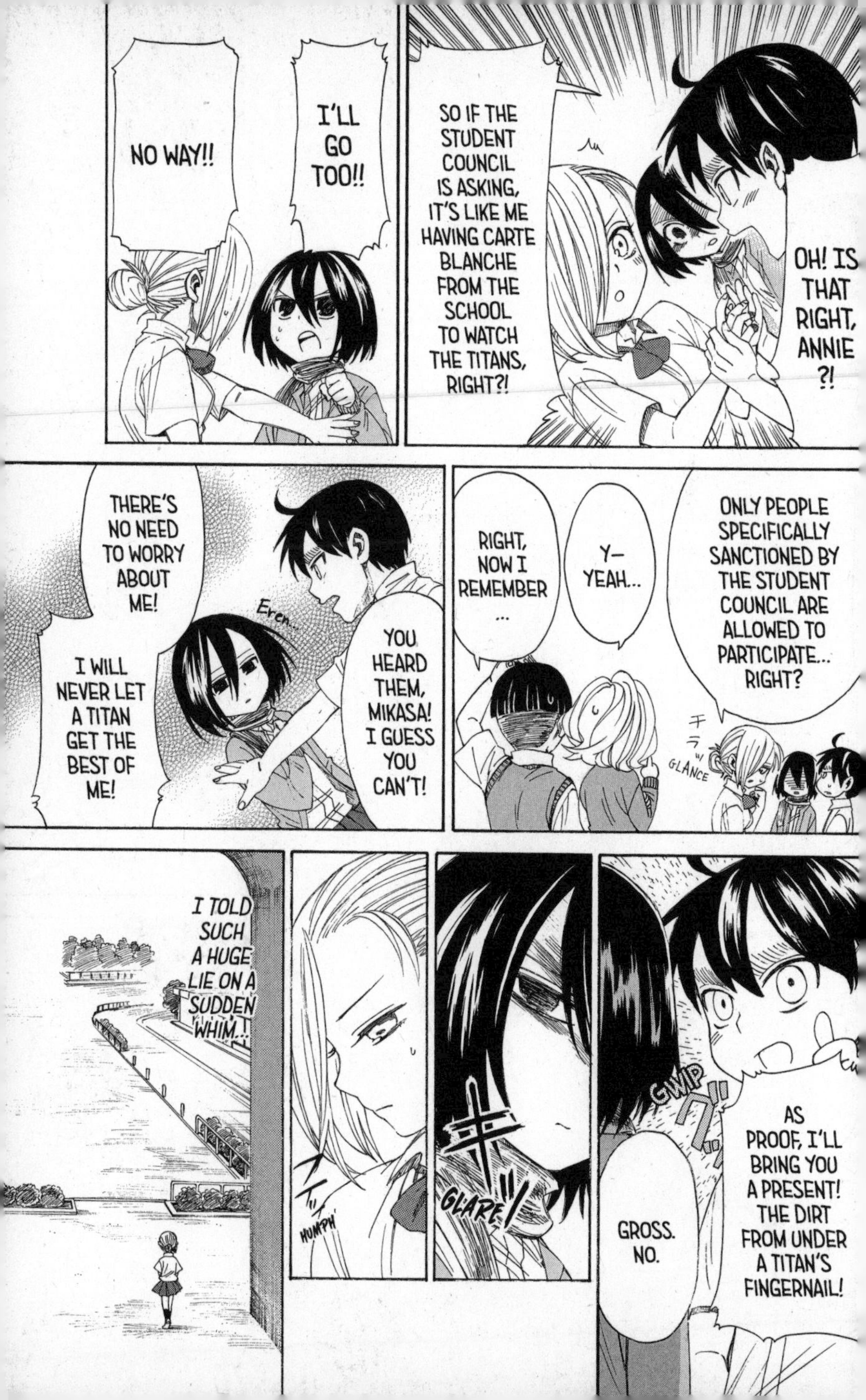
OH! IS THAT RIGHT, ANNIE?!
SO IF THE STUDENT COUNCIL IS ASKING, IT'S LIKE ME HAVING CARTE BLANCHE FROM THE SCHOOL TO WATCH THE TITANS, RIGHT?!
I'LL GO TOO!!
NO WAY!!
ONLY PEOPLE SPECIFICALLY SANCTIONED BY THE STUDENT COUNCIL ARE ALLOWED TO PARTICIPATE... RIGHT?
GLANCE
Y— YEAH...
RIGHT, NOW I REMEMBER ...
YOU HEARD THEM, MIKASA! I GUESS YOU CAN'T!
Eren...
THERE'S NO NEED TO WORRY ABOUT ME!
I WILL NEVER LET A TITAN GET THE BEST OF ME!
AS PROOF, I'LL BRING YOU A PRESENT! THE DIRT FROM UNDER A TITAN'S FINGERNAIL!
GWIP
GROSS. NO.
GLARE
HUMPH
I TOLD SUCH A HUGE LIE ON A SUDDEN WHIM...

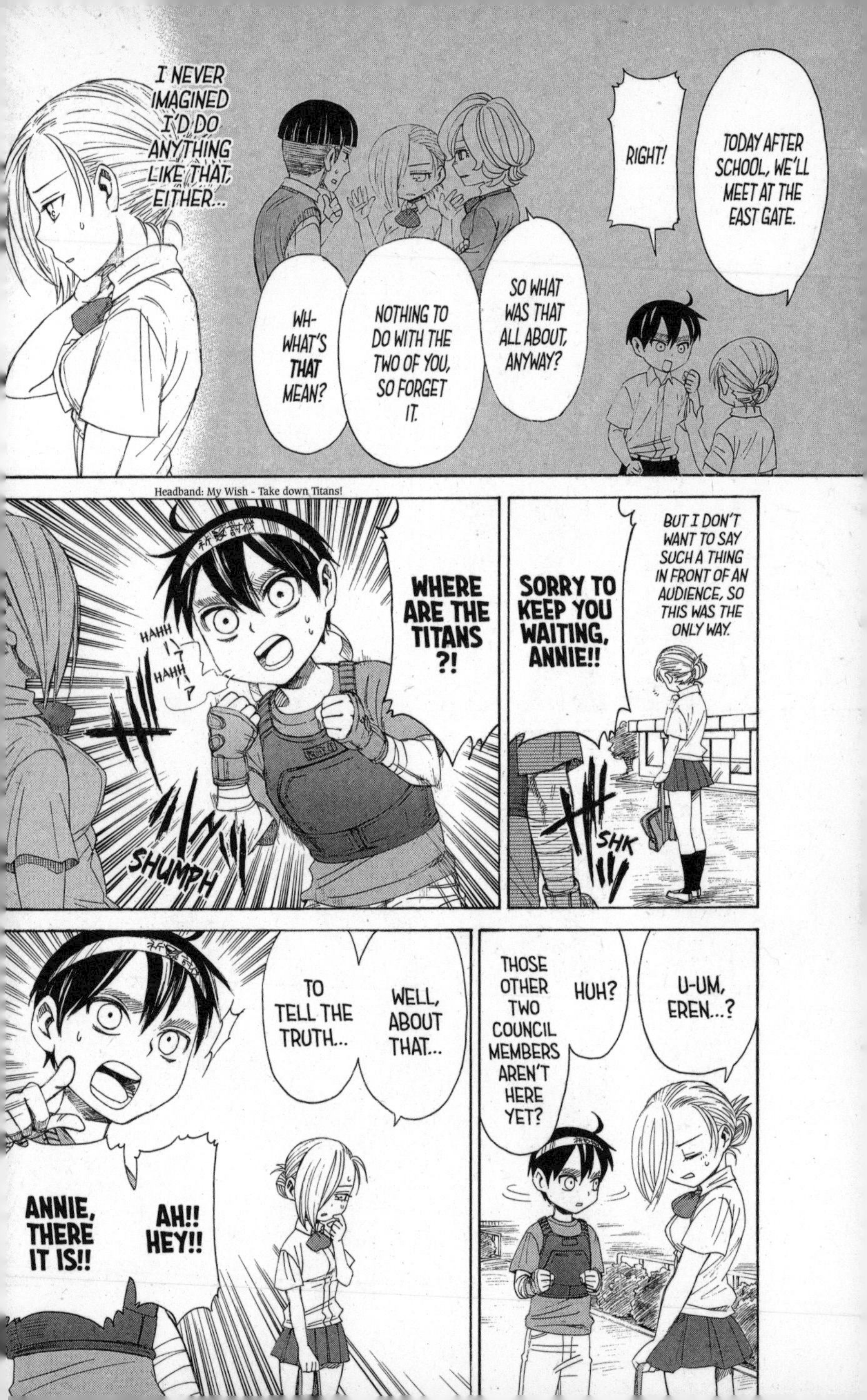
TODAY AFTER SCHOOL, WE'LL MEET AT THE EAST GATE.
RIGHT!
SO WHAT WAS THAT ALL ABOUT, ANYWAY?
NOTHING TO DO WITH THE TWO OF YOU, SO FORGET IT.
WH-WHAT'S THAT MEAN?
I NEVER IMAGINED I'D DO ANYTHING LIKE THAT, EITHER...
Headband: My Wish - Take down Titans!
BUT I DON'T WANT TO SAY SUCH A THING IN FRONT OF AN AUDIENCE, SO THIS WAS THE ONLY WAY.
SORRY TO KEEP YOU WAITING, ANNIE!!
SHK
WHERE ARE THE TITANS ?!
HAHH HAHH
SHUMPH
U-UM, EREN...?
HUH?
THOSE OTHER TWO COUNCIL MEMBERS AREN'T HERE YET?
WELL, ABOUT THAT...
TO TELL THE TRUTH...
AH!! HEY!!
ANNIE, THERE IT IS!!

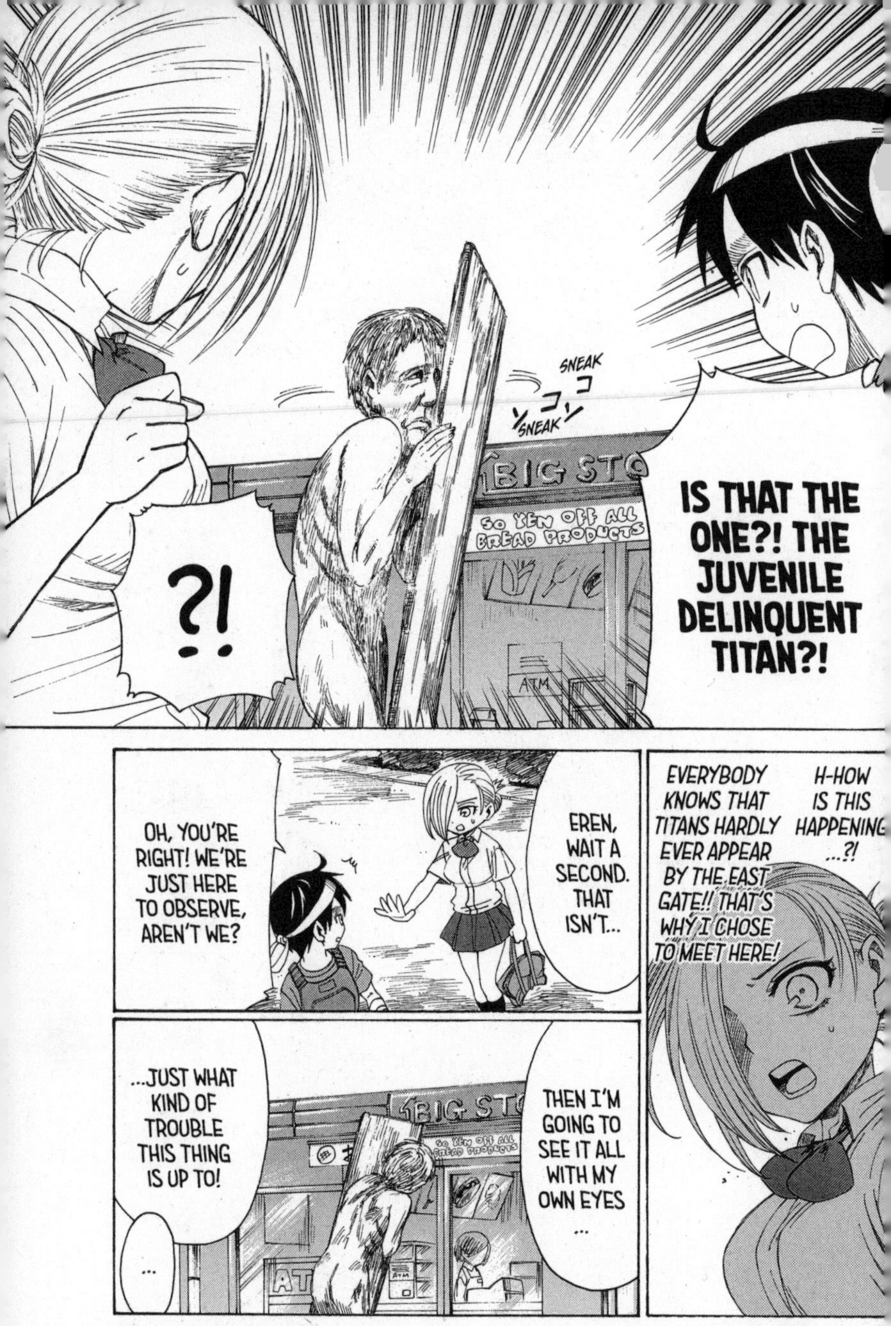
SNEAK
SNEAK
BIG STO
50 YEN OFF ALL BREAD PRODUCTS
ATM
IS THAT THE ONE?! THE JUVENILE DELINQUENT TITAN?!
?!
H-HOW IS THIS HAPPENING...?!
EVERYBODY KNOWS THAT TITANS HARDLY EVER APPEAR BY THE EAST GATE!! THAT'S WHY I CHOSE TO MEET HERE!
EREN, WAIT A SECOND. THAT ISN'T...
OH, YOU'RE RIGHT! WE'RE JUST HERE TO OBSERVE, AREN'T WE?
THEN I'M GOING TO SEE IT ALL WITH MY OWN EYES...
...JUST WHAT KIND OF TROUBLE THIS THING IS UP TO!
...

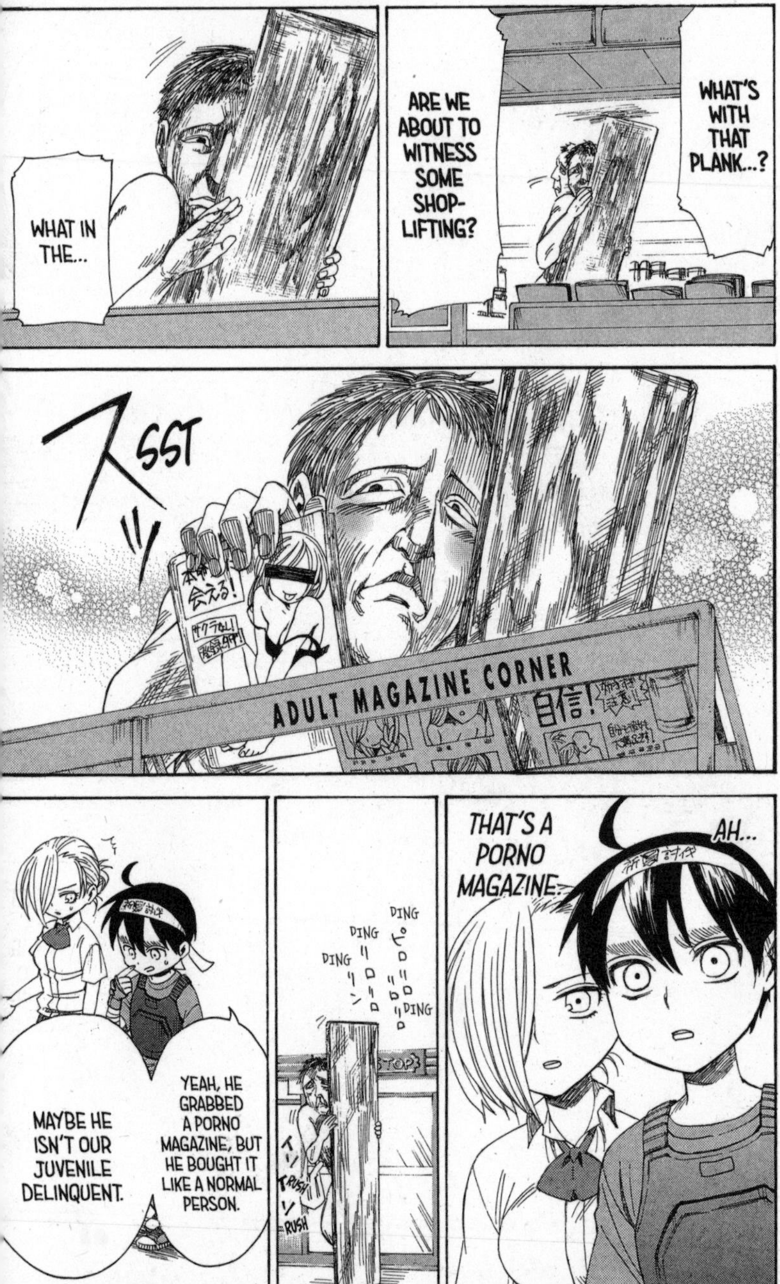
WHAT'S WITH THAT PLANK...?
ARE WE ABOUT TO WITNESS SOME SHOP-LIFTING?
WHAT IN THE...
SST
ADULT MAGAZINE CORNER
AH...
THAT'S A PORNO MAGAZINE.
DING DING DING DING
STOP
RUSH RUSH
YEAH, HE GRABBED A PORNO MAGAZINE, BUT HE BOUGHT IT LIKE A NORMAL PERSON.
MAYBE HE ISN'T OUR JUVENILE DELINQUENT.

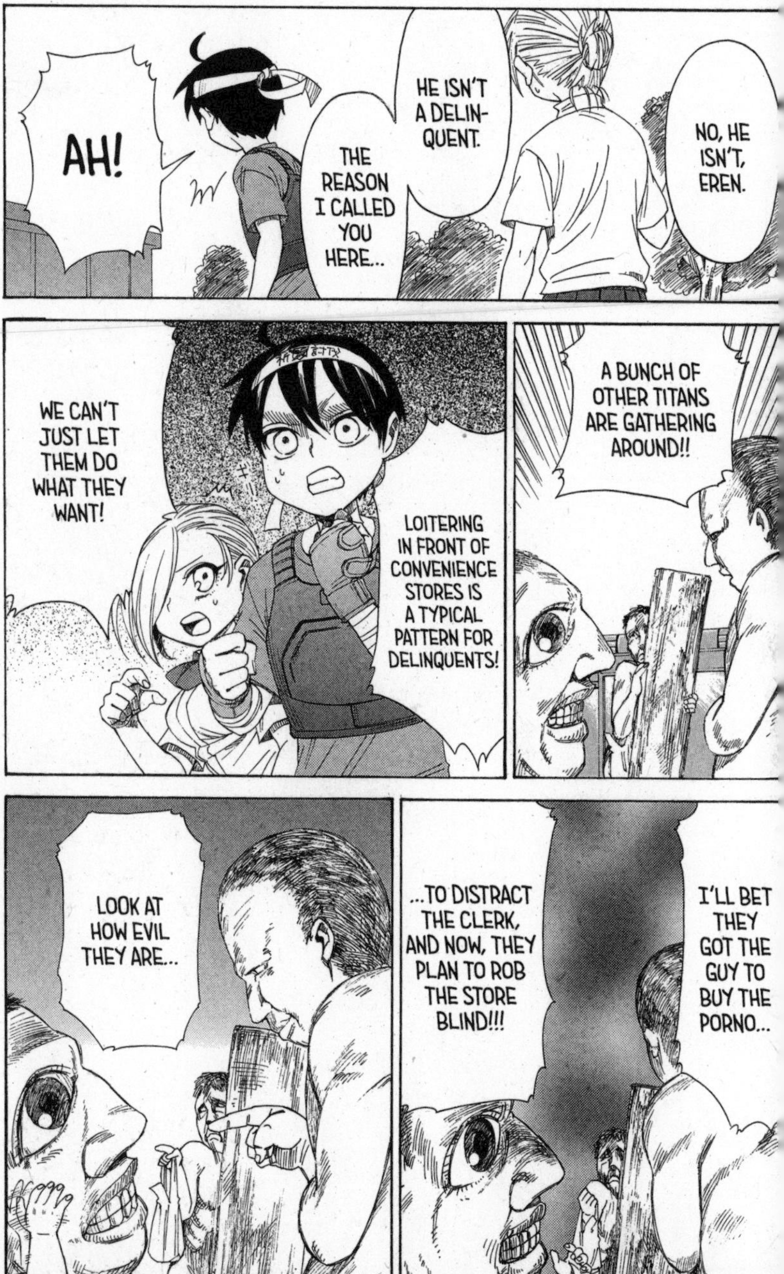
NO, HE ISN'T, EREN.
HE ISN'T A DELINQUENT.
THE REASON I CALLED YOU HERE...
AH!
A BUNCH OF OTHER TITANS ARE GATHERING AROUND!!
LOITERING IN FRONT OF CONVENIENCE STORES IS A TYPICAL PATTERN FOR DELINQUENTS!
WE CAN'T JUST LET THEM DO WHAT THEY WANT!
I'LL BET THEY GOT THE GUY TO BUY THE PORNO...
...TO DISTRACT THE CLERK, AND NOW, THEY PLAN TO ROB THE STORE BLIND!!!
LOOK AT HOW EVIL THEY ARE...

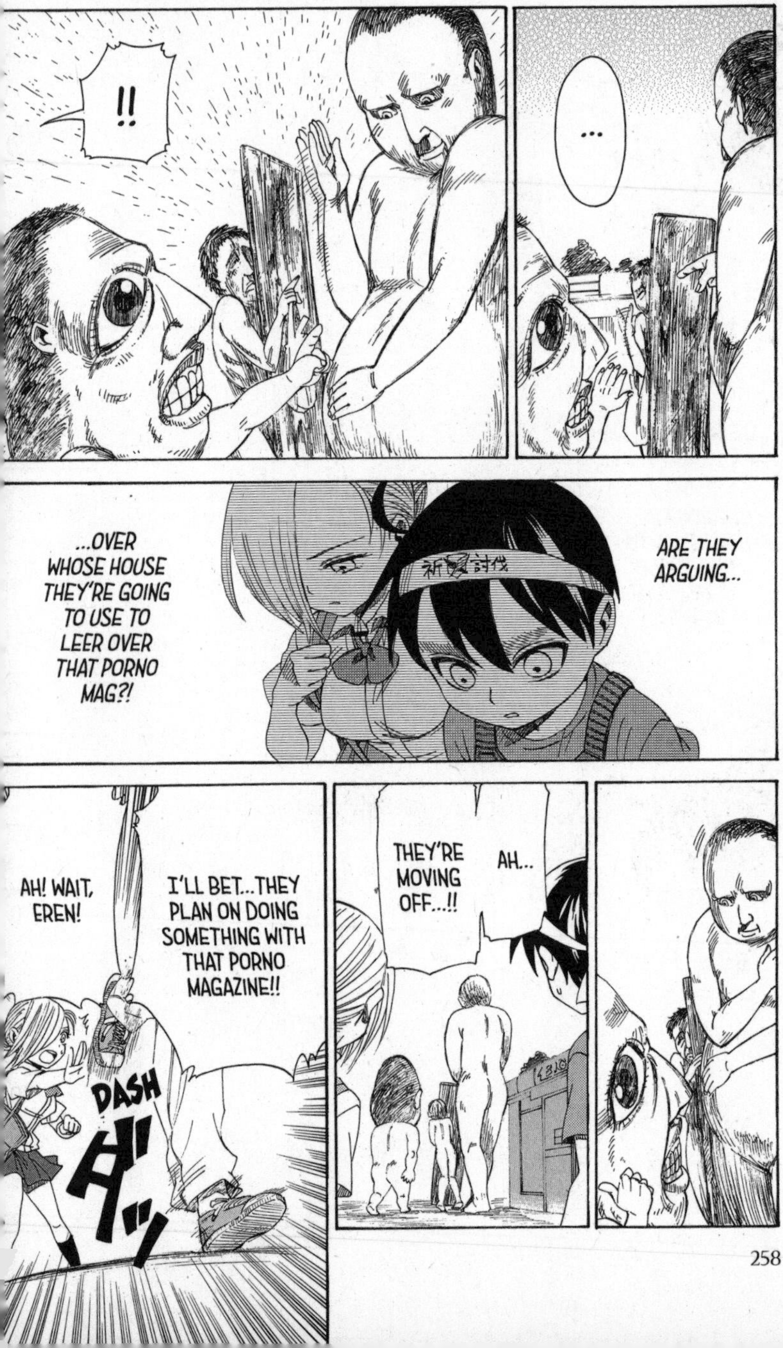
...
!!
ARE THEY ARGUING...
...OVER WHOSE HOUSE THEY'RE GOING TO USE TO LEER OVER THAT PORNO MAG?!
AH...
THEY'RE MOVING OFF...!!
I'LL BET...THEY PLAN ON DOING SOMETHING WITH THAT PORNO MAGAZINE!!
AH! WAIT, EREN!
DASH

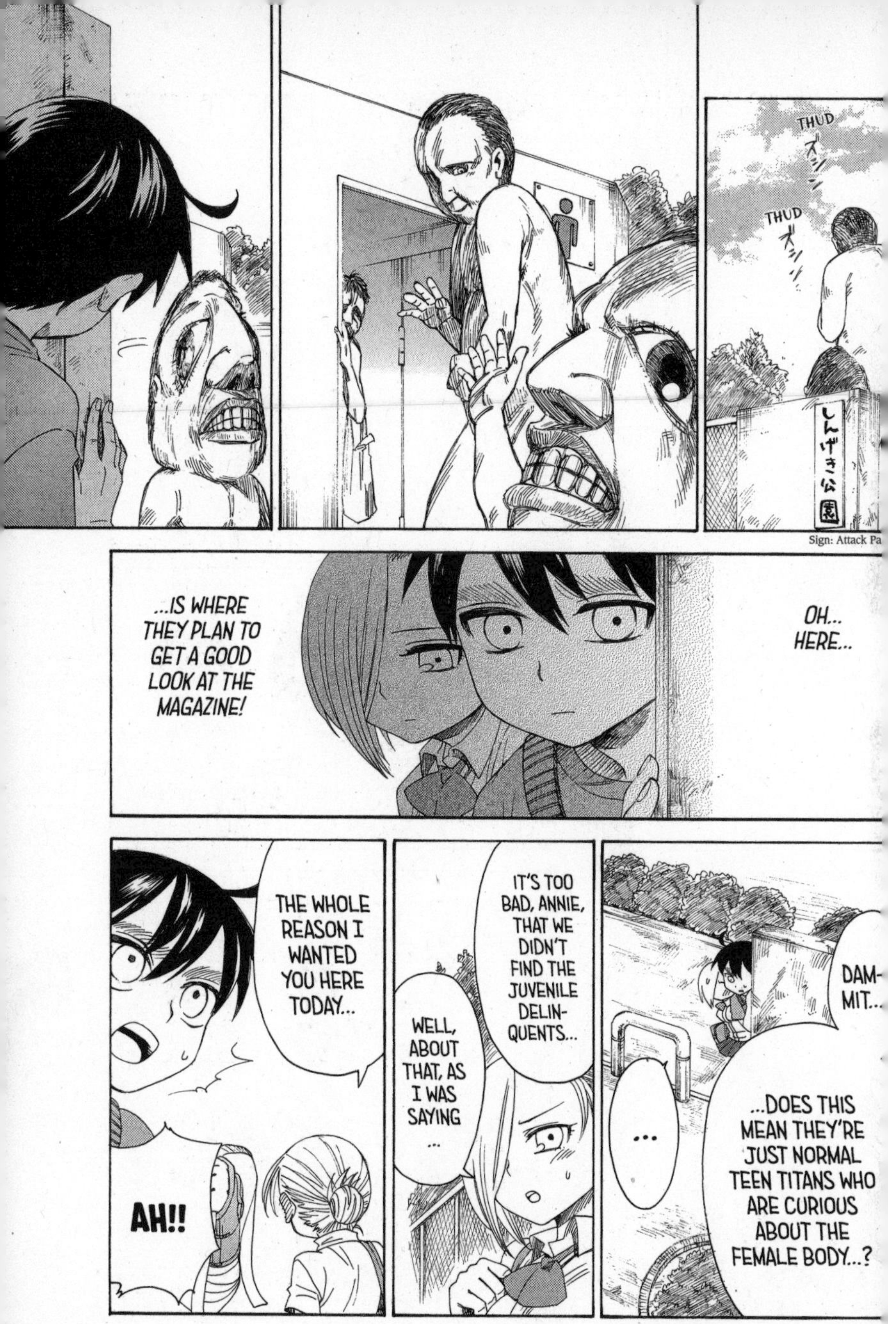
THUD
THUD
しんげき公園
Sign: Attack Pa
OH... HERE...
...IS WHERE THEY PLAN TO GET A GOOD LOOK AT THE MAGAZINE!
DAM-MIT...
...DOES THIS MEAN THEY'RE JUST NORMAL TEEN TITANS WHO ARE CURIOUS ABOUT THE FEMALE BODY...?
...
IT'S TOO BAD, ANNIE, THAT WE DIDN'T FIND THE JUVENILE DELIN-QUENTS...
WELL, ABOUT THAT, AS I WAS SAYING ...
THE WHOLE REASON I WANTED YOU HERE TODAY...
AH!!

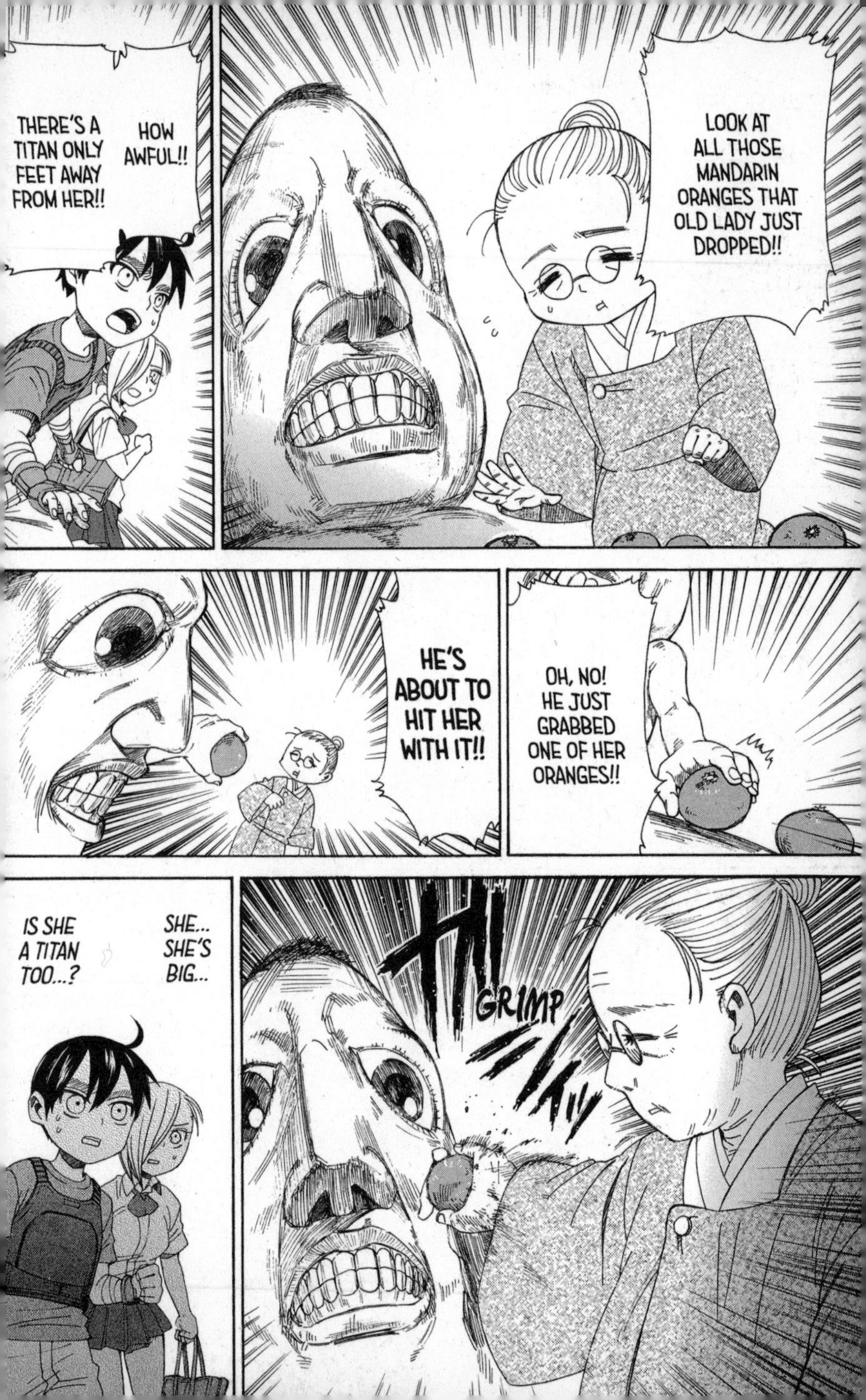
LOOK AT ALL THOSE MANDARIN ORANGES THAT OLD LADY JUST DROPPED!!
HOW AWFUL!!
THERE'S A TITAN ONLY FEET AWAY FROM HER!!
OH, NO! HE JUST GRABBED ONE OF HER ORANGES!!
HE'S ABOUT TO HIT HER WITH IT!!
GRIMP
SHE... SHE'S BIG...
IS SHE A TITAN TOO...?

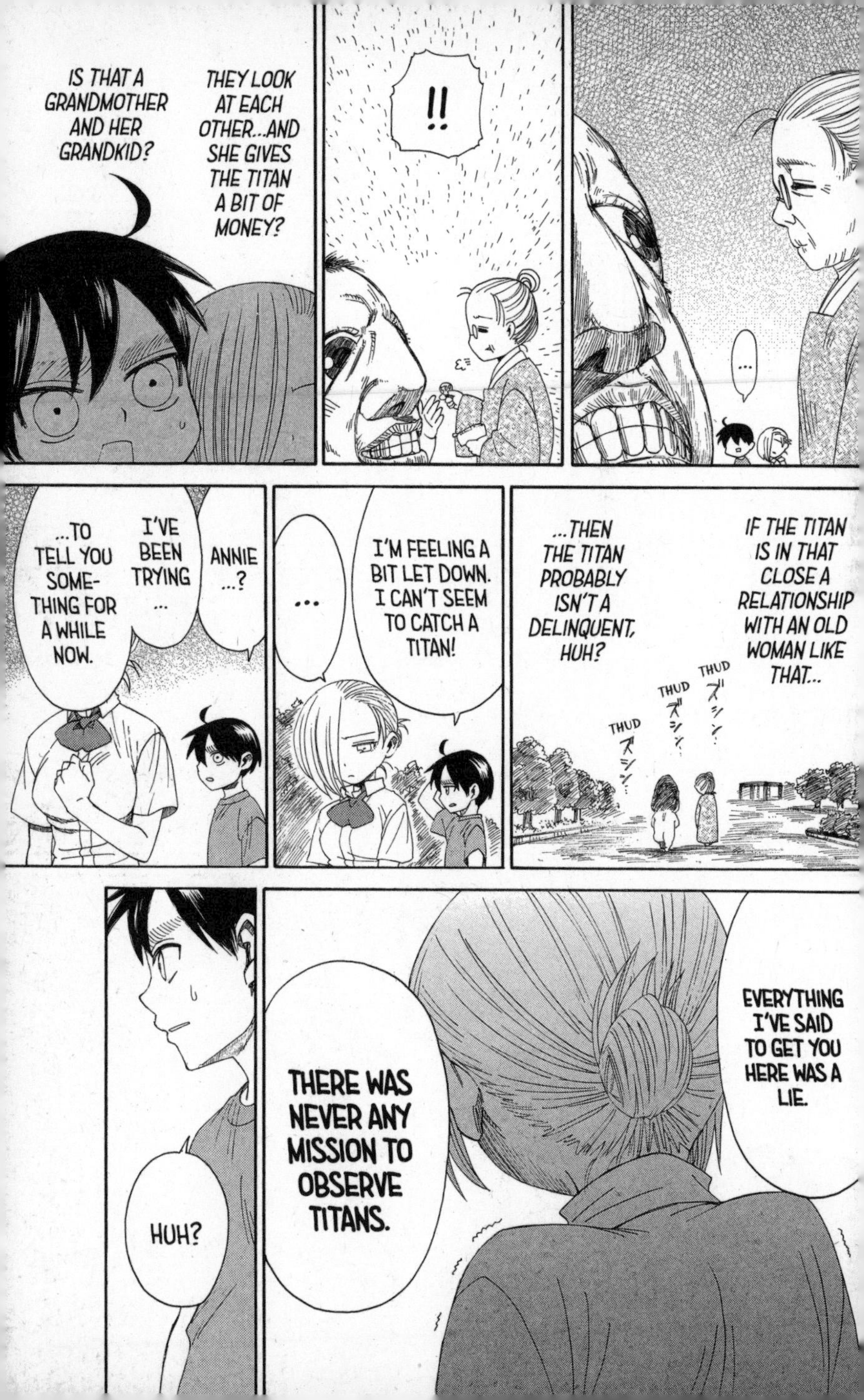
...
!!
THEY LOOK AT EACH OTHER...AND SHE GIVES THE TITAN A BIT OF MONEY?
IS THAT A GRANDMOTHER AND HER GRANDKID?
IF THE TITAN IS IN THAT CLOSE A RELATIONSHIP WITH AN OLD WOMAN LIKE THAT...
...THEN THE TITAN PROBABLY ISN'T A DELINQUENT, HUH?
THUD
THUD
THUD
I'M FEELING A BIT LET DOWN. I CAN'T SEEM TO CATCH A TITAN!
...
ANNIE ...?
I'VE BEEN TRYING ...
...TO TELL YOU SOMETHING FOR A WHILE NOW.
EVERYTHING I'VE SAID TO GET YOU HERE WAS A LIE.
THERE WAS NEVER ANY MISSION TO OBSERVE TITANS.
HUH?

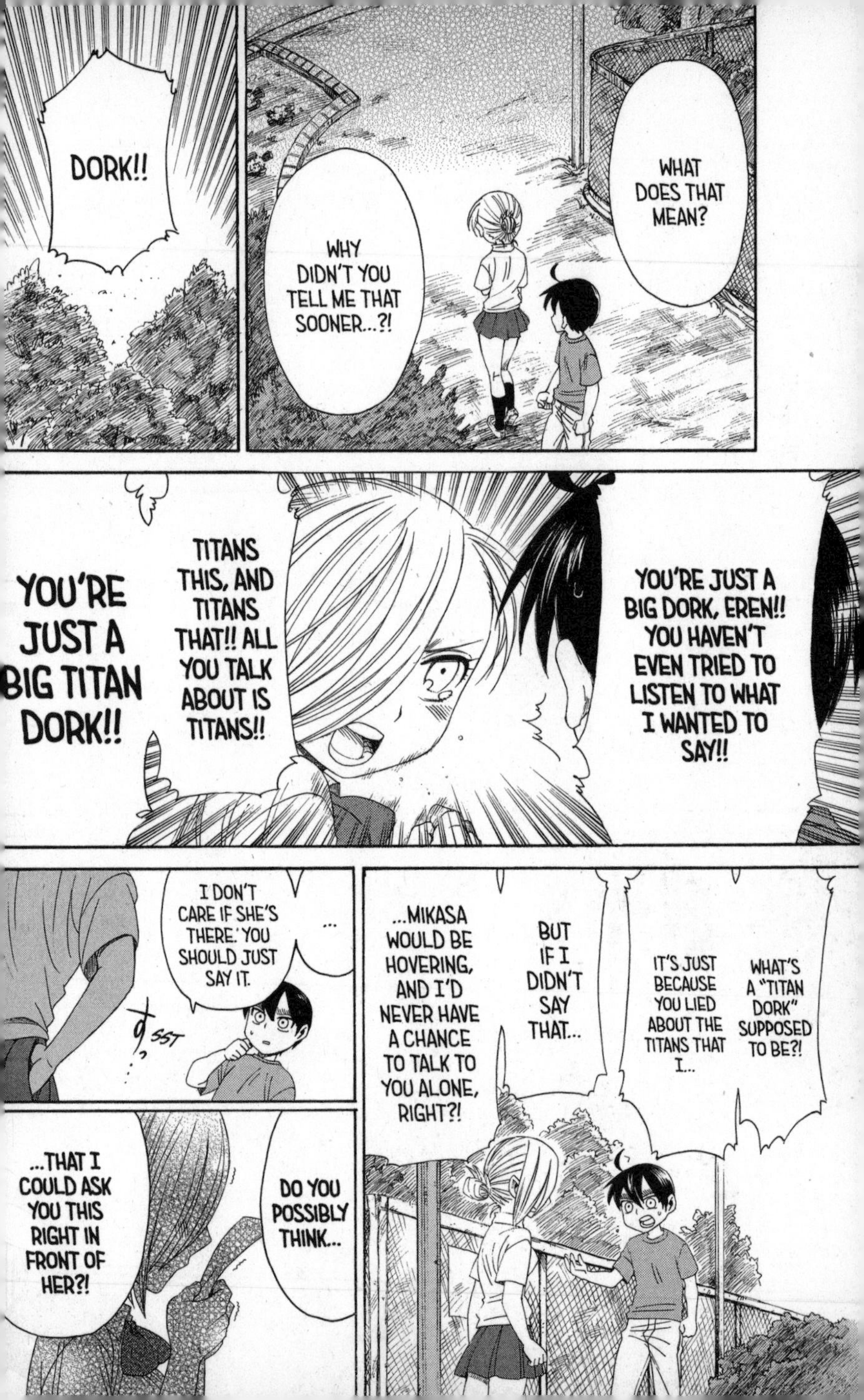
WHAT DOES THAT MEAN?
WHY DIDN'T YOU TELL ME THAT SOONER...?!
DORK!!
YOU'RE JUST A BIG DORK, EREN!! YOU HAVEN'T EVEN TRIED TO LISTEN TO WHAT I WANTED TO SAY!!
TITANS THIS, AND TITANS THAT!! ALL YOU TALK ABOUT IS TITANS!!
YOU'RE JUST A BIG TITAN DORK!!
WHAT'S A "TITAN DORK" SUPPOSED TO BE?!
IT'S JUST BECAUSE YOU LIED ABOUT THE TITANS THAT I...
BUT IF I DIDN'T SAY THAT...
...MIKASA WOULD BE HOVERING, AND I'D NEVER HAVE A CHANCE TO TALK TO YOU ALONE, RIGHT?!
...
I DON'T CARE IF SHE'S THERE. YOU SHOULD JUST SAY IT.
SST
DO YOU POSSIBLY THINK...
...THAT I COULD ASK YOU THIS RIGHT IN FRONT OF HER?!

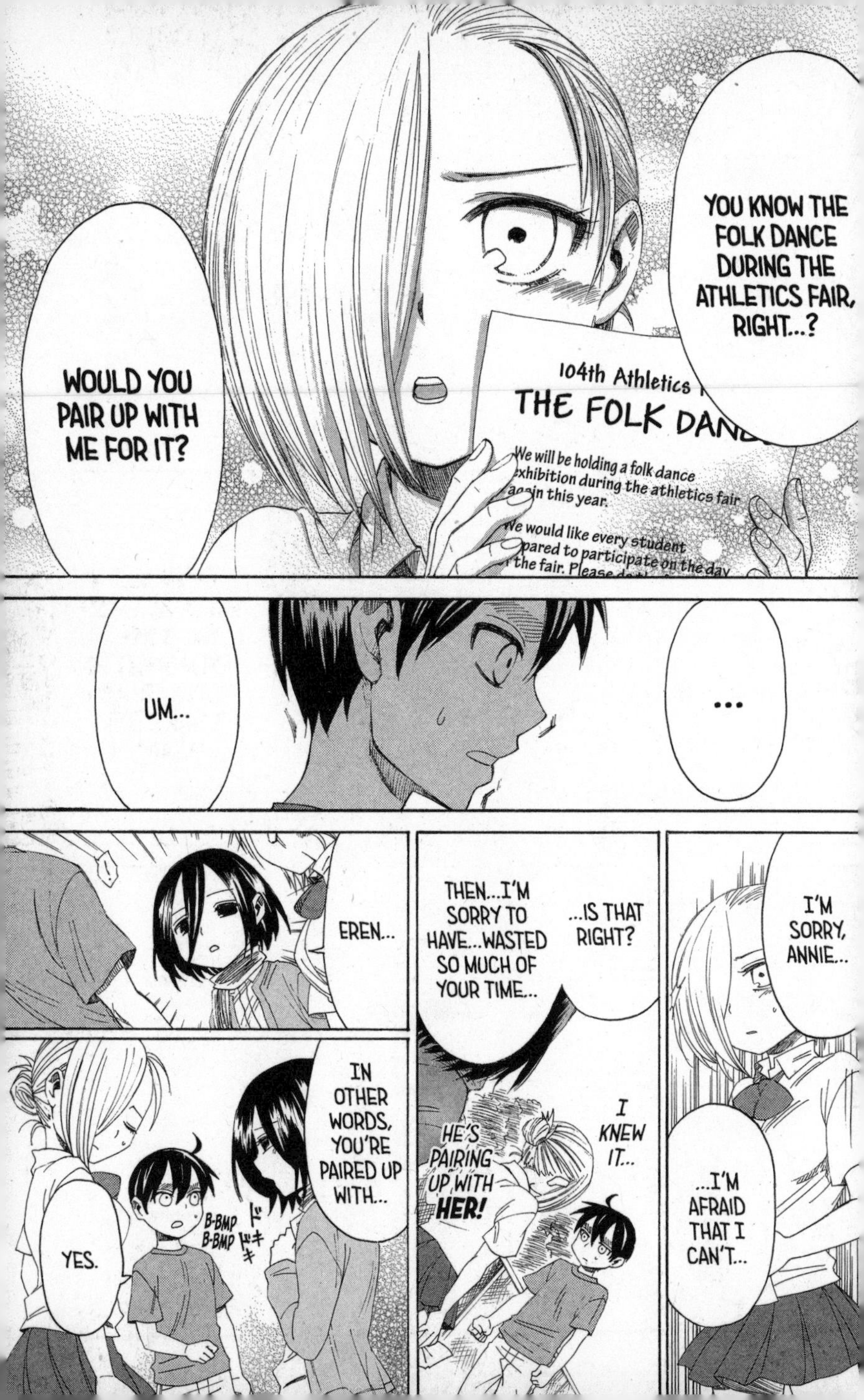

YOU KNOW THE FOLK DANCE DURING THE ATHLETICS FAIR, RIGHT...?
WOULD YOU PAIR UP WITH ME FOR IT?
104th Athletics
THE FOLK DAN
We will be holding a folk dance exhibition during the athletics fair again this year.
We would like every student
...
UM...
I'M SORRY, ANNIE...
...I'M AFRAID THAT I CAN'T...
...IS THAT RIGHT?
THEN...I'M SORRY TO HAVE...WASTED SO MUCH OF YOUR TIME...
!
EREN...
I KNEW IT...
HE'S PAIRING UP WITH **HER!**
IN OTHER WORDS, YOU'RE PAIRED UP WITH...
B-BMP B-BMP
ドキ ドキ
YES.

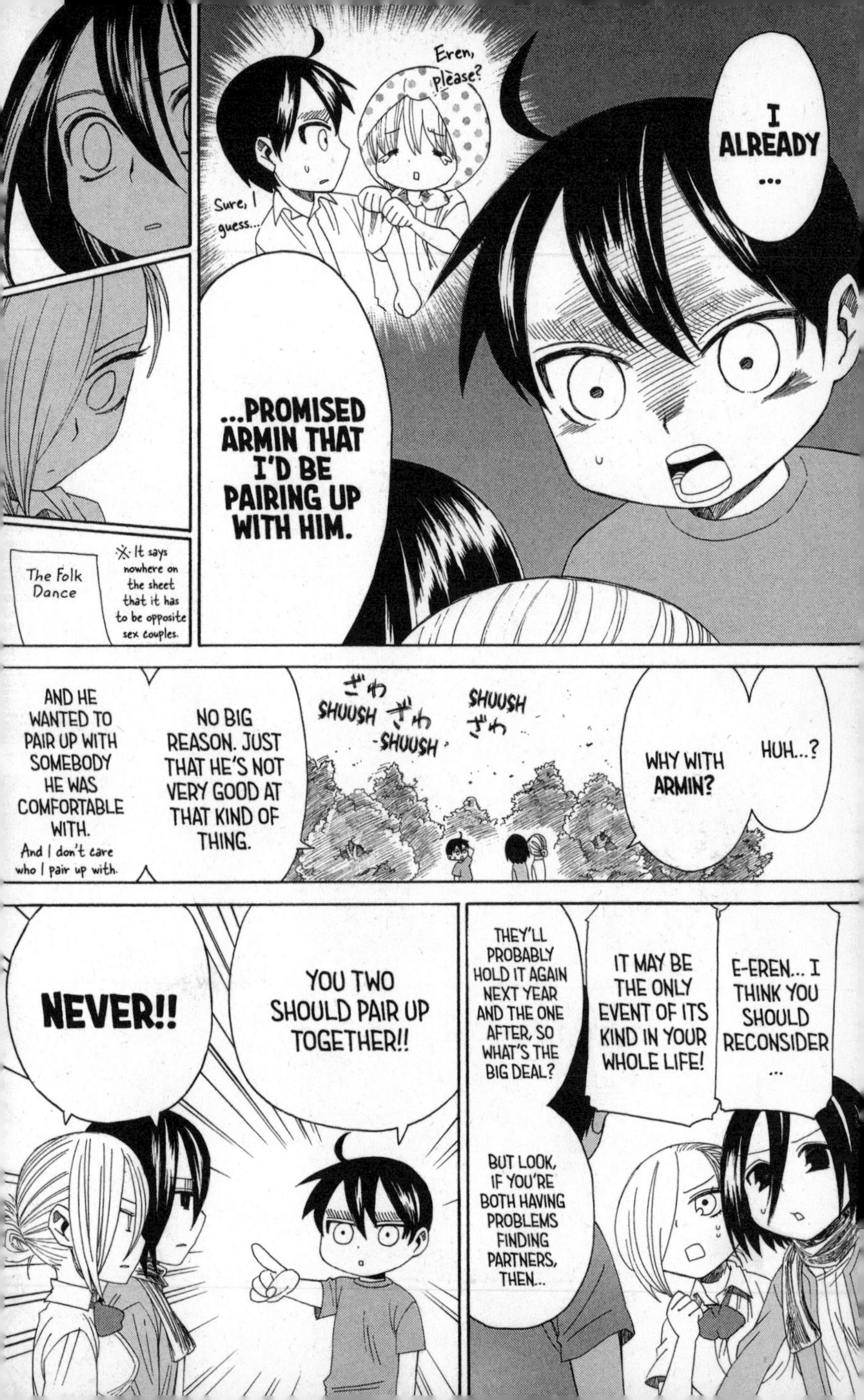
I ALREADY...
...PROMISED ARMIN THAT I'D BE PAIRING UP WITH HIM.
Eren, please?
Sure, I guess...
The Folk Dance
※ It says nowhere on the sheet that it has to be opposite sex couples.
HUH...?
WHY WITH ARMIN?
ざわ SHUUSH ざわ SHUUSH ざわ SHUUSH
NO BIG REASON. JUST THAT HE'S NOT VERY GOOD AT THAT KIND OF THING.
AND HE WANTED TO PAIR UP WITH SOMEBODY HE WAS COMFORTABLE WITH.
And I don't care who I pair up with.
E-EREN... I THINK YOU SHOULD RECONSIDER...
IT MAY BE THE ONLY EVENT OF ITS KIND IN YOUR WHOLE LIFE!
THEY'LL PROBABLY HOLD IT AGAIN NEXT YEAR AND THE ONE AFTER, SO WHAT'S THE BIG DEAL?
BUT LOOK, IF YOU'RE BOTH HAVING PROBLEMS FINDING PARTNERS, THEN...
YOU TWO SHOULD PAIR UP TOGETHER!!
NEVER!!

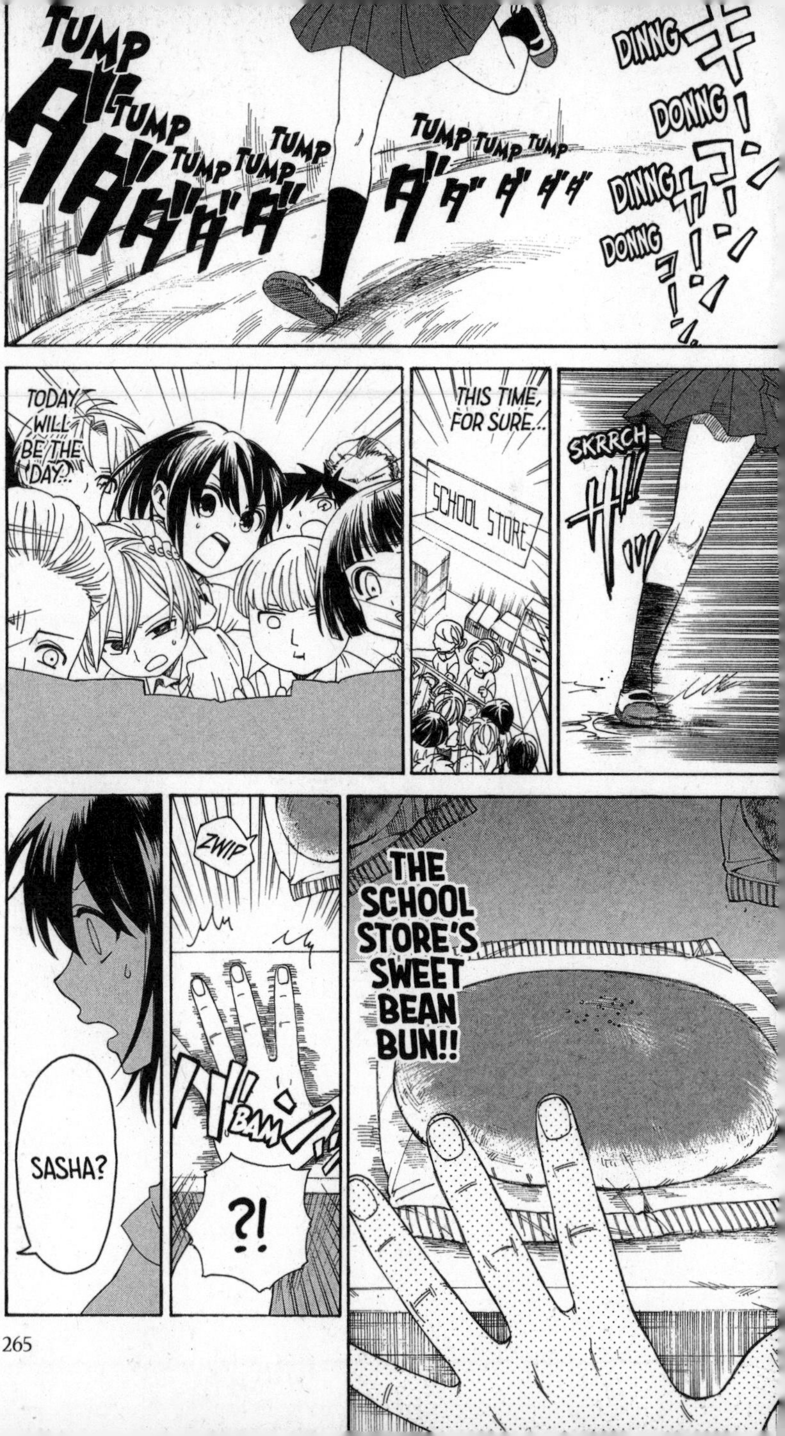
DINNG
DONNG
DINNG
DONNG
TUMP
TUMP
TUMP
TUMP
TUMP
TUMP
TUMP
TUMP
SKRRCH
THIS TIME, FOR SURE...
SCHOOL STORE
TODAY WILL BE THE DAY...
THE SCHOOL STORE'S SWEET BEAN BUN!!
ZWIP
BAM
?!
SASHA?

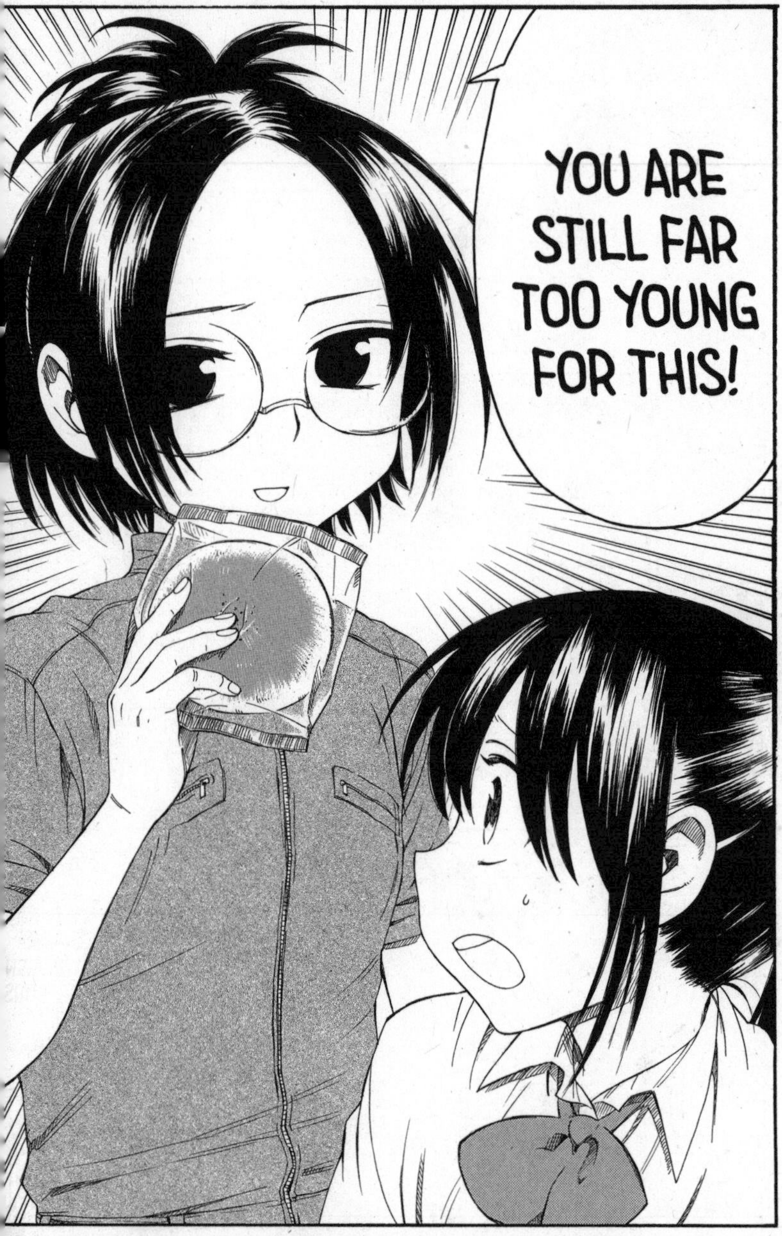
YOU ARE STILL FAR TOO YOUNG FOR THIS!

FOURTEENTH PERIOD: NO, I AM NOT BENEATH YOU

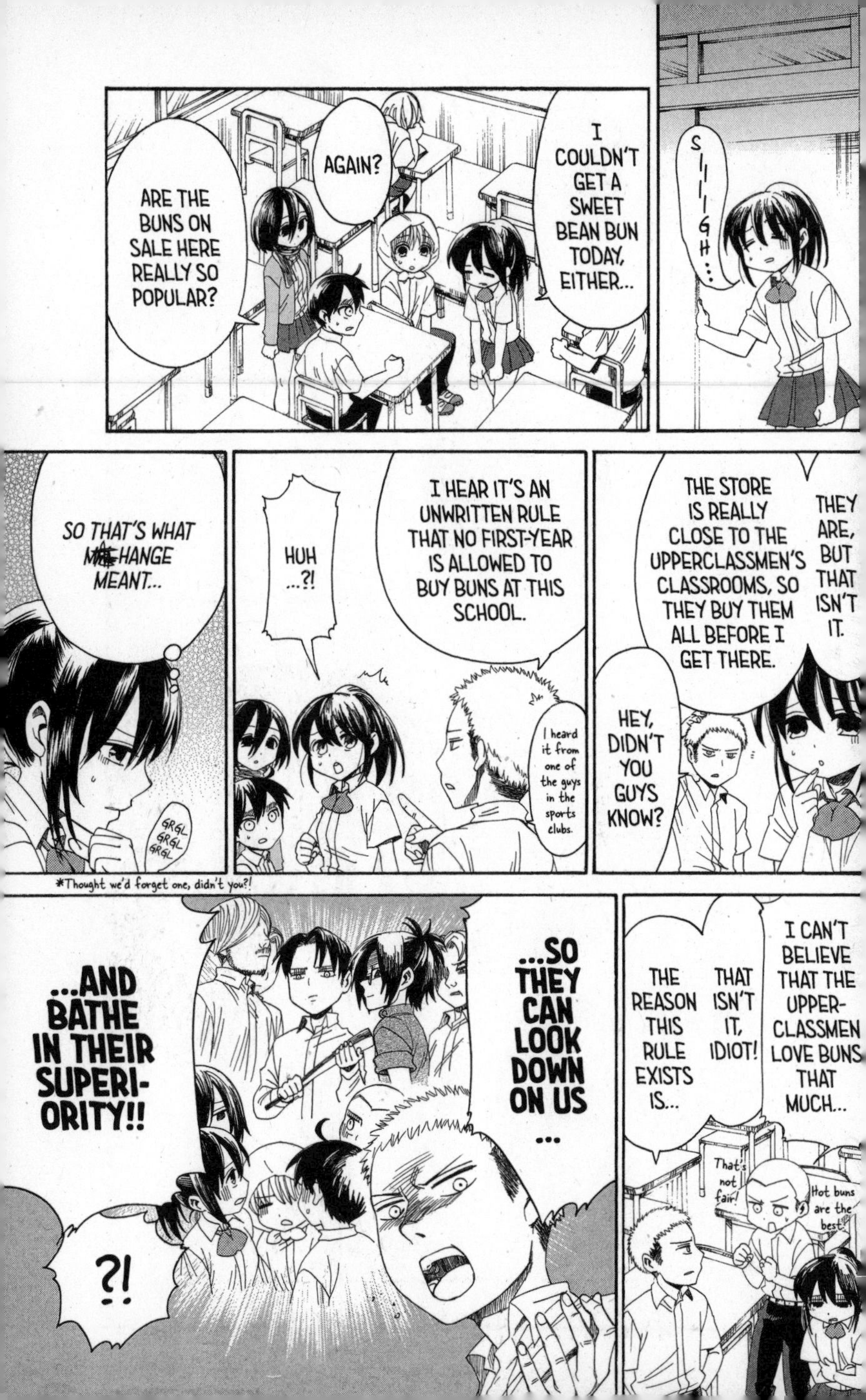
SIIIIGH...
I COULDN'T GET A SWEET BEAN BUN TODAY, EITHER...
AGAIN?
ARE THE BUNS ON SALE HERE REALLY SO POPULAR?
THEY ARE, BUT THAT ISN'T IT.
THE STORE IS REALLY CLOSE TO THE UPPERCLASSMEN'S CLASSROOMS, SO THEY BUY THEM ALL BEFORE I GET THERE.
HEY, DIDN'T YOU GUYS KNOW?
I HEAR IT'S AN UNWRITTEN RULE THAT NO FIRST-YEAR IS ALLOWED TO BUY BUNS AT THIS SCHOOL.
HUH ...?!
I heard it from one of the guys in the sports clubs.
SO THAT'S WHAT ~~M~~HANGE MEANT...
GRGL GRGL GRGL
*Thought we'd forget one, didn't you?!
I CAN'T BELIEVE THAT THE UPPERCLASSMEN LOVE BUNS THAT MUCH...
THAT ISN'T IT, IDIOT!
THE REASON THIS RULE EXISTS IS...
Hot buns are the best.
That's not fair!
...SO THEY CAN LOOK DOWN ON US...
...AND BATHE IN THEIR SUPERIORITY!!
?!

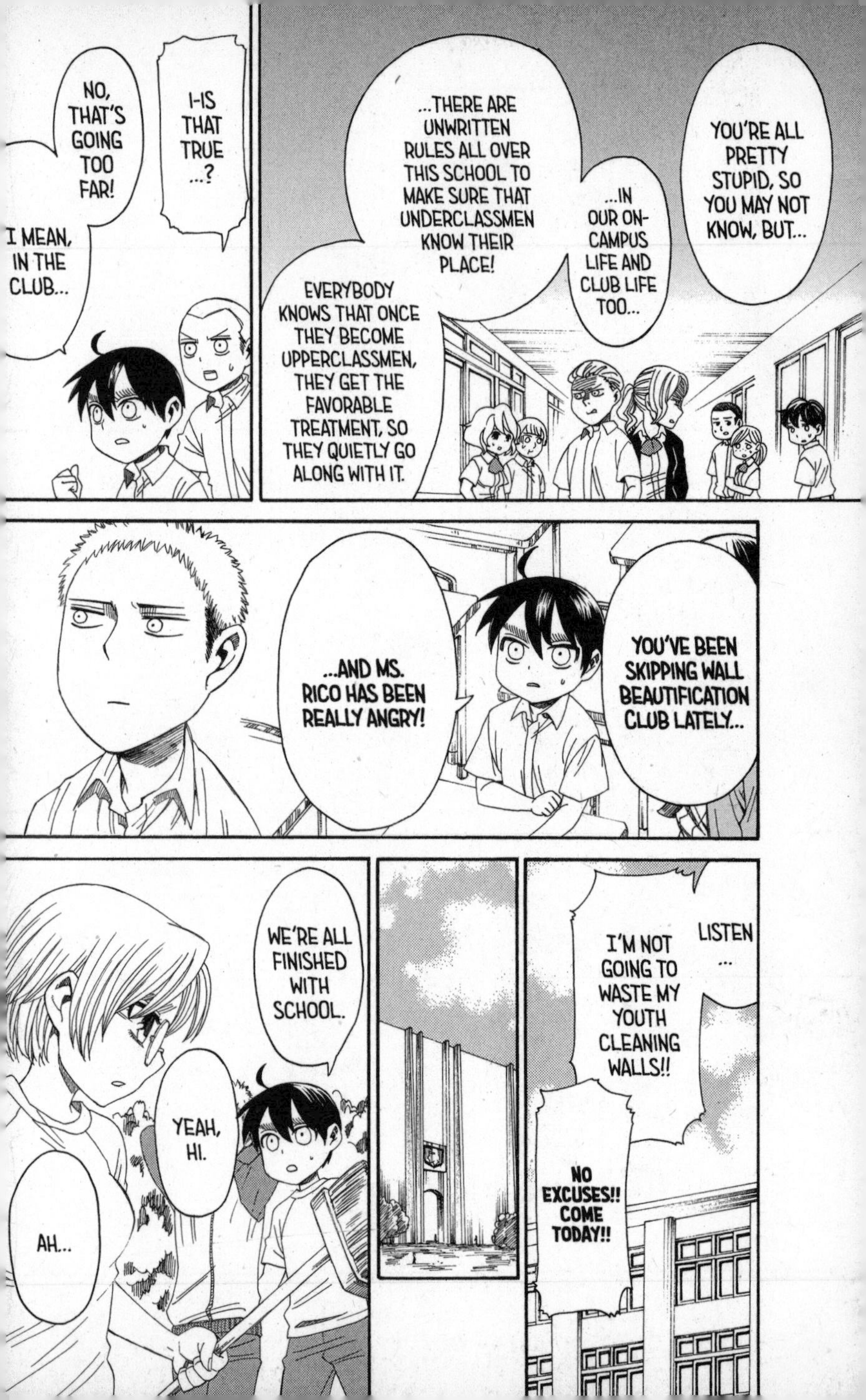
YOU'RE ALL PRETTY STUPID, SO YOU MAY NOT KNOW, BUT...
...IN OUR ON-CAMPUS LIFE AND CLUB LIFE TOO...
...THERE ARE UNWRITTEN RULES ALL OVER THIS SCHOOL TO MAKE SURE THAT UNDERCLASSMEN KNOW THEIR PLACE!
EVERYBODY KNOWS THAT ONCE THEY BECOME UPPERCLASSMEN, THEY GET THE FAVORABLE TREATMENT, SO THEY QUIETLY GO ALONG WITH IT.
I-IS THAT TRUE ...?
NO, THAT'S GOING TOO FAR!
I MEAN, IN THE CLUB...
YOU'VE BEEN SKIPPING WALL BEAUTIFICATION CLUB LATELY...
...AND MS. RICO HAS BEEN REALLY ANGRY!
LISTEN ...
I'M NOT GOING TO WASTE MY YOUTH CLEANING WALLS!!
NO EXCUSES!! COME TODAY!!
WE'RE ALL FINISHED WITH SCHOOL.
YEAH, HI.
AH...

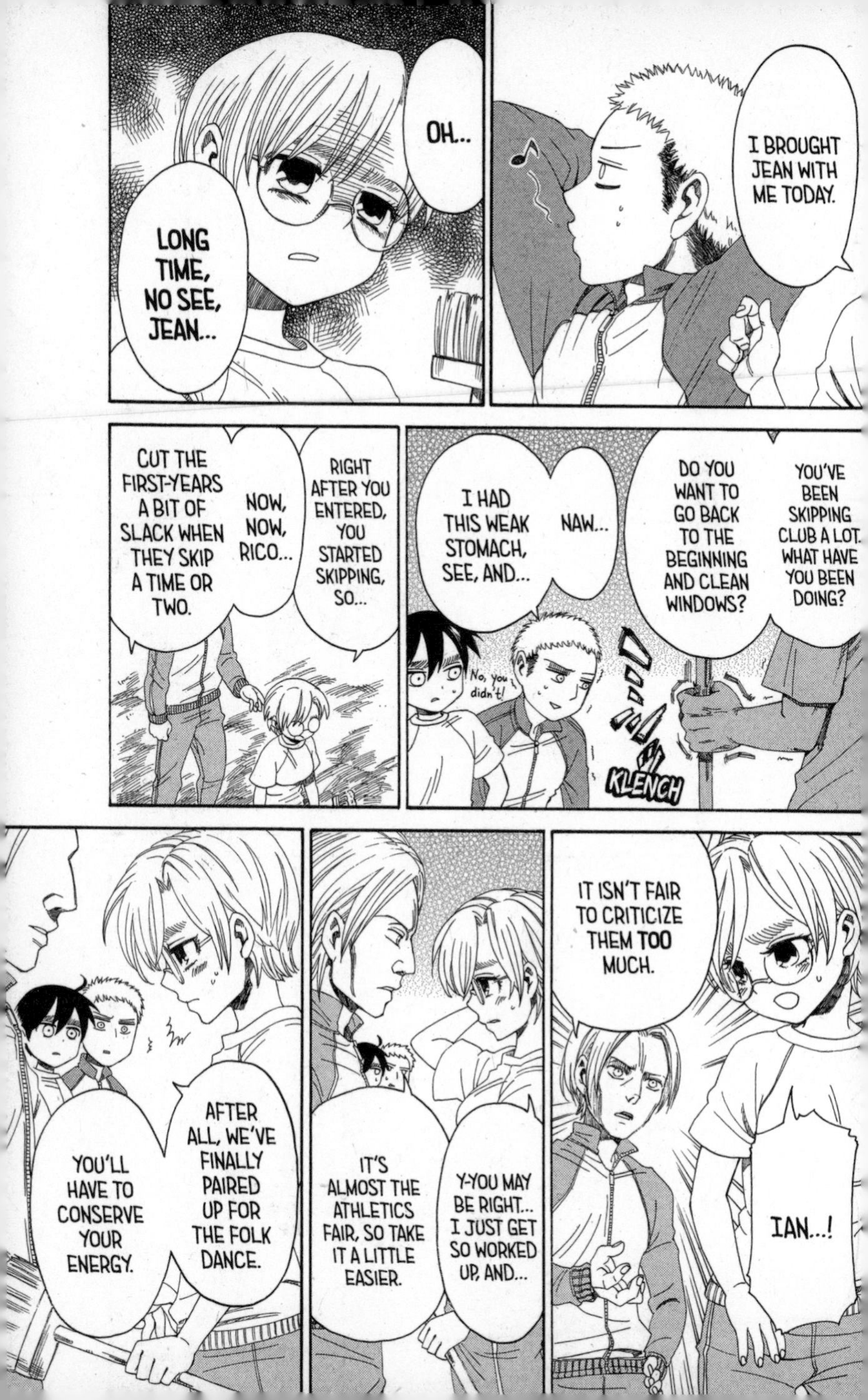
I BROUGHT JEAN WITH ME TODAY.
OH...
LONG TIME, NO SEE, JEAN...
YOU'VE BEEN SKIPPING CLUB A LOT. WHAT HAVE YOU BEEN DOING?
DO YOU WANT TO GO BACK TO THE BEGINNING AND CLEAN WINDOWS?
KLENCH
NAW...
I HAD THIS WEAK STOMACH, SEE, AND...
No, you didn't!
RIGHT AFTER YOU ENTERED, YOU STARTED SKIPPING, SO...
NOW, NOW, RICO...
CUT THE FIRST-YEARS A BIT OF SLACK WHEN THEY SKIP A TIME OR TWO.
IT ISN'T FAIR TO CRITICIZE THEM TOO MUCH.
IAN...!
Y-YOU MAY BE RIGHT... I JUST GET SO WORKED UP, AND...
IT'S ALMOST THE ATHLETICS FAIR, SO TAKE IT A LITTLE EASIER.
AFTER ALL, WE'VE FINALLY PAIRED UP FOR THE FOLK DANCE.
YOU'LL HAVE TO CONSERVE YOUR ENERGY.

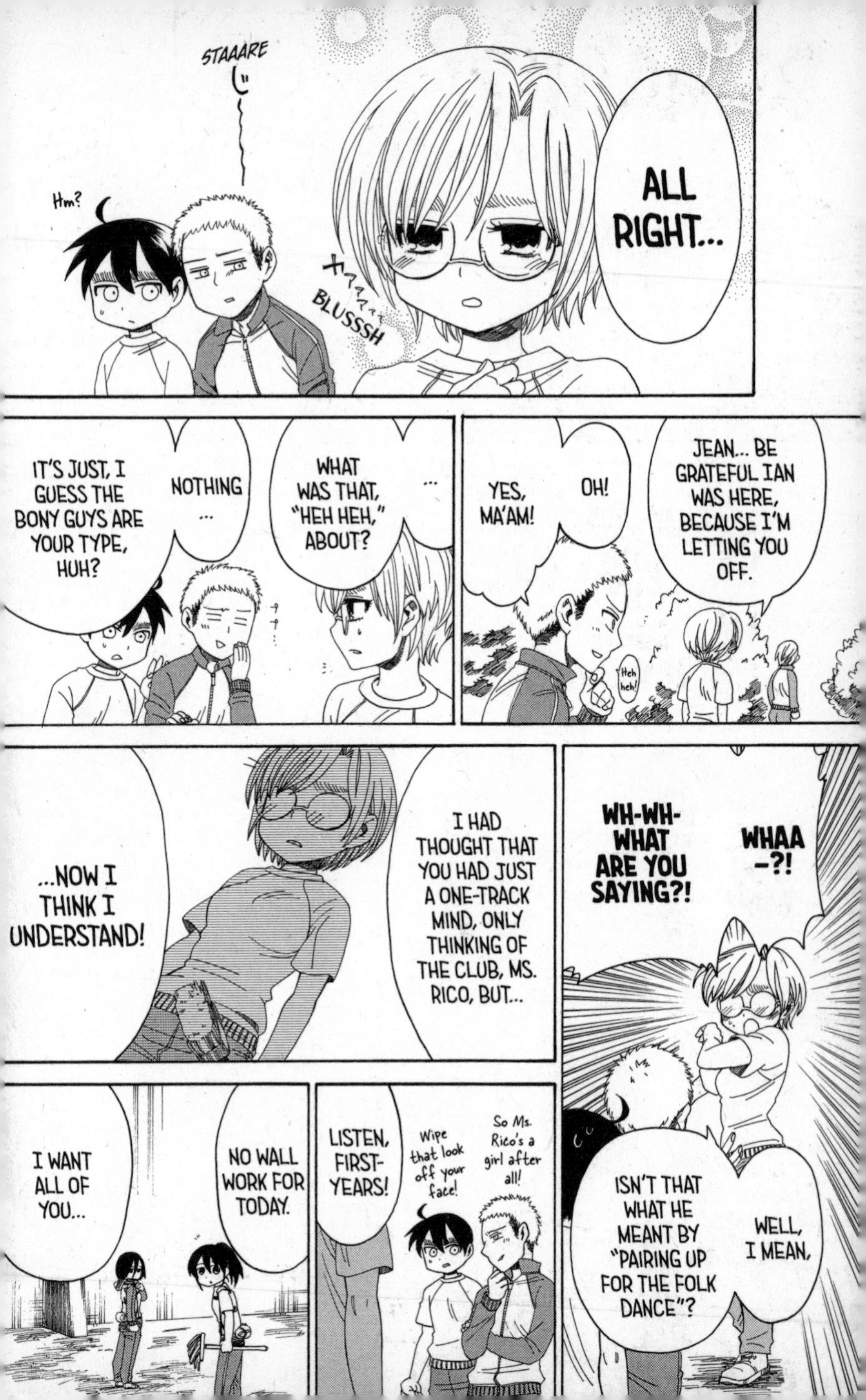
ALL RIGHT...
BLUSSSH
STAAARE
Hm?
JEAN... BE GRATEFUL IAN WAS HERE, BECAUSE I'M LETTING YOU OFF.
OH!
YES, MA'AM!
Heh heh!
...
WHAT WAS THAT, "HEH HEH," ABOUT?
NOTHING ...
IT'S JUST, I GUESS THE BONY GUYS ARE YOUR TYPE, HUH?
WHAA—?!
WH-WH-WHAT ARE YOU SAYING?!
WELL, I MEAN,
ISN'T THAT WHAT HE MEANT BY "PAIRING UP FOR THE FOLK DANCE"?
I HAD THOUGHT THAT YOU HAD JUST A ONE-TRACK MIND, ONLY THINKING OF THE CLUB, MS. RICO, BUT...
...NOW I THINK I UNDERSTAND!
So Ms. Rico's a girl after all!
Wipe that look off your face!
LISTEN, FIRST-YEARS!
NO WALL WORK FOR TODAY.
I WANT ALL OF YOU...

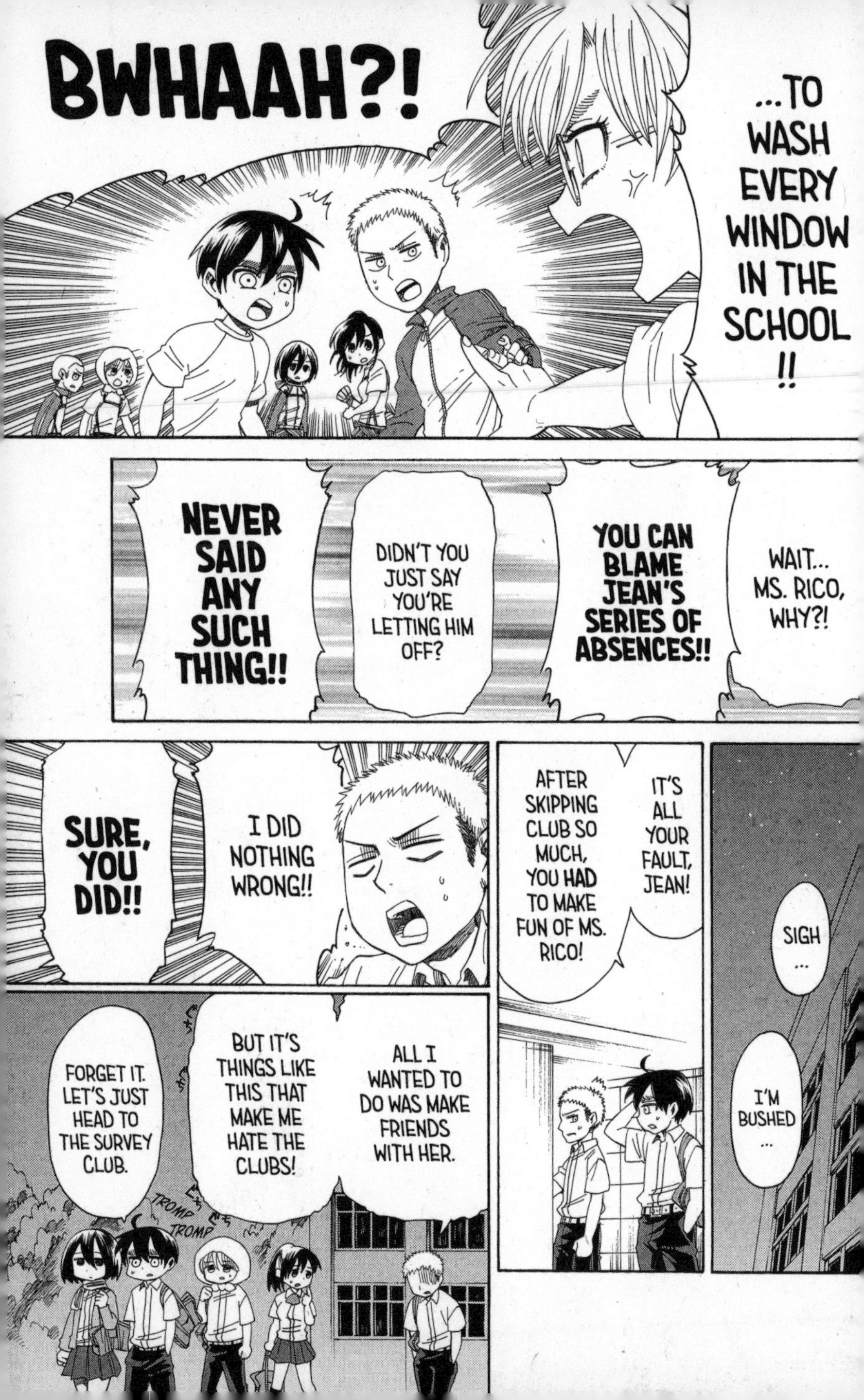
...TO WASH EVERY WINDOW IN THE SCHOOL!!
BWHAAH?!
WAIT... MS. RICO, WHY?!
YOU CAN BLAME JEAN'S SERIES OF ABSENCES!!
DIDN'T YOU JUST SAY YOU'RE LETTING HIM OFF?
NEVER SAID ANY SUCH THING!!
SIGH...
I'M BUSHED...
IT'S ALL YOUR FAULT, JEAN!
AFTER SKIPPING CLUB SO MUCH, YOU HAD TO MAKE FUN OF MS. RICO!
I DID NOTHING WRONG!!
SURE, YOU DID!!
ALL I WANTED TO DO WAS MAKE FRIENDS WITH HER.
BUT IT'S THINGS LIKE THIS THAT MAKE ME HATE THE CLUBS!
FORGET IT. LET'S JUST HEAD TO THE SURVEY CLUB.
TROMP
TROMP

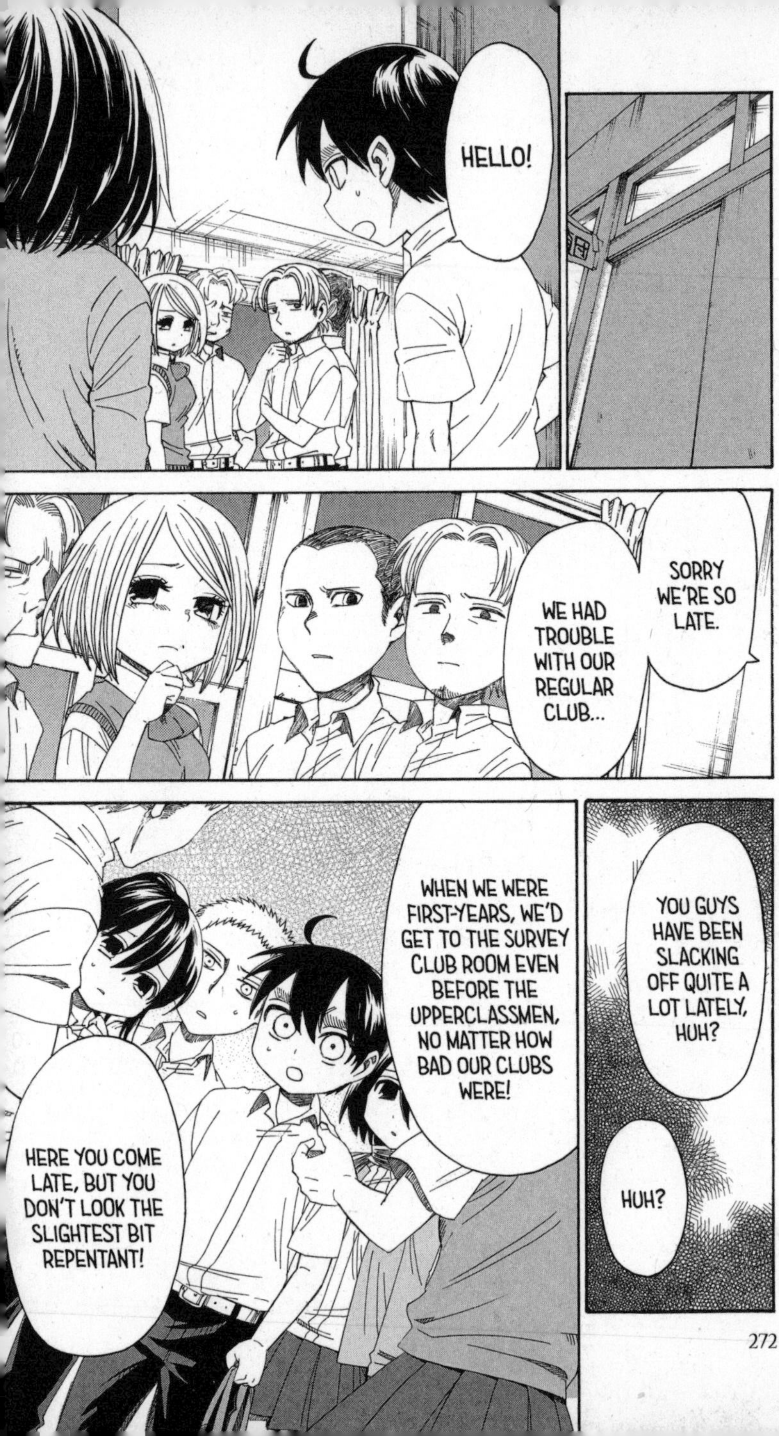
HELLO!
SORRY WE'RE SO LATE.
WE HAD TROUBLE WITH OUR REGULAR CLUB...
YOU GUYS HAVE BEEN SLACKING OFF QUITE A LOT LATELY, HUH?
HUH?
WHEN WE WERE FIRST-YEARS, WE'D GET TO THE SURVEY CLUB ROOM EVEN BEFORE THE UPPERCLASSMEN, NO MATTER HOW BAD OUR CLUBS WERE!
HERE YOU COME LATE, BUT YOU DON'T LOOK THE SLIGHTEST BIT REPENTANT!

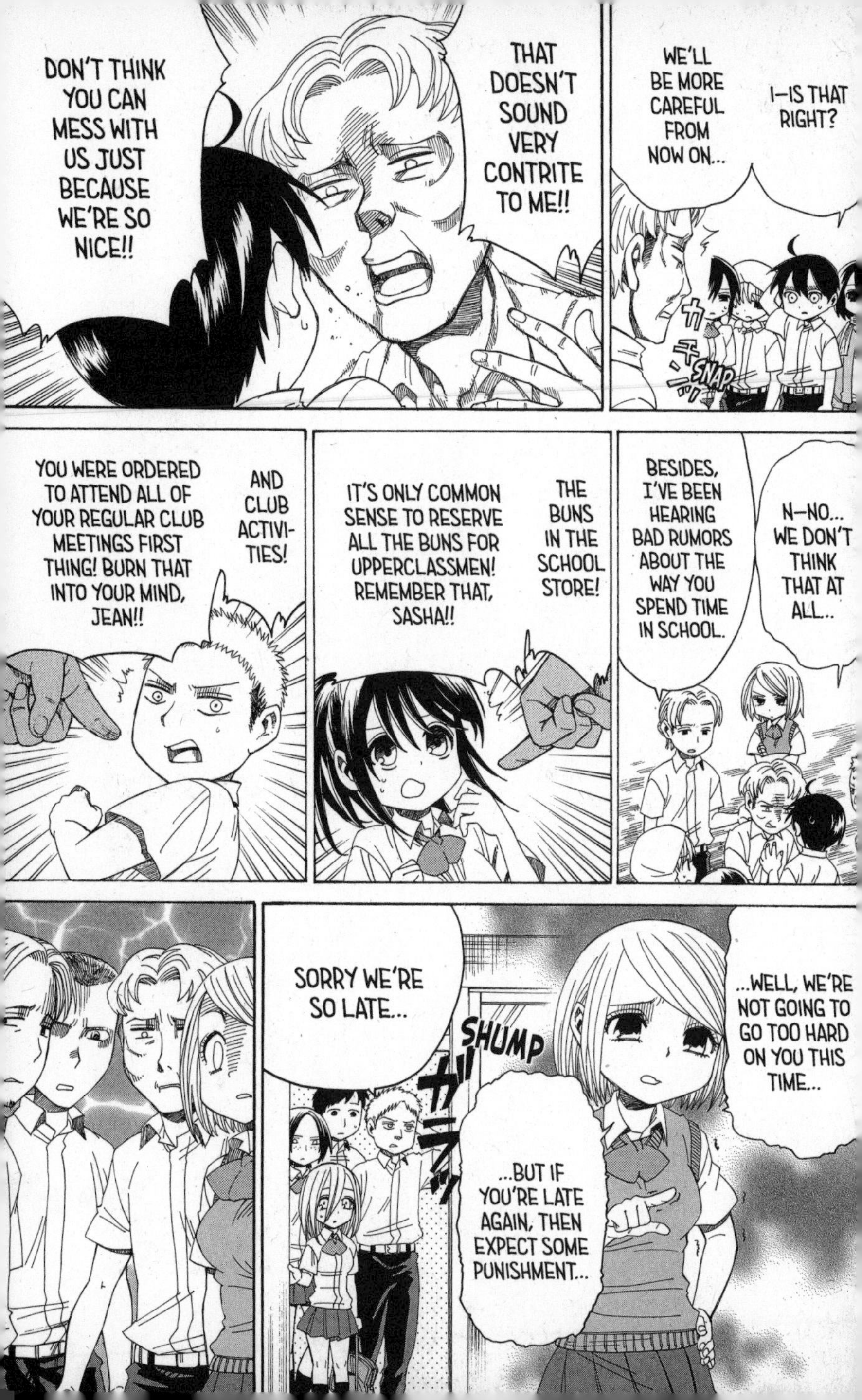
I—IS THAT RIGHT?
WE'LL BE MORE CAREFUL FROM NOW ON...
SNAP
THAT DOESN'T SOUND VERY CONTRITE TO ME!!
DON'T THINK YOU CAN MESS WITH US JUST BECAUSE WE'RE SO NICE!!
N—NO... WE DON'T THINK THAT AT ALL...
BESIDES, I'VE BEEN HEARING BAD RUMORS ABOUT THE WAY YOU SPEND TIME IN SCHOOL.
THE BUNS IN THE SCHOOL STORE!
IT'S ONLY COMMON SENSE TO RESERVE ALL THE BUNS FOR UPPERCLASSMEN! REMEMBER THAT, SASHA!!
AND CLUB ACTIVI-TIES!
YOU WERE ORDERED TO ATTEND ALL OF YOUR REGULAR CLUB MEETINGS FIRST THING! BURN THAT INTO YOUR MIND, JEAN!!
...WELL, WE'RE NOT GOING TO GO TOO HARD ON YOU THIS TIME...
...BUT IF YOU'RE LATE AGAIN, THEN EXPECT SOME PUNISHMENT...
SHUMP
SORRY WE'RE SO LATE...

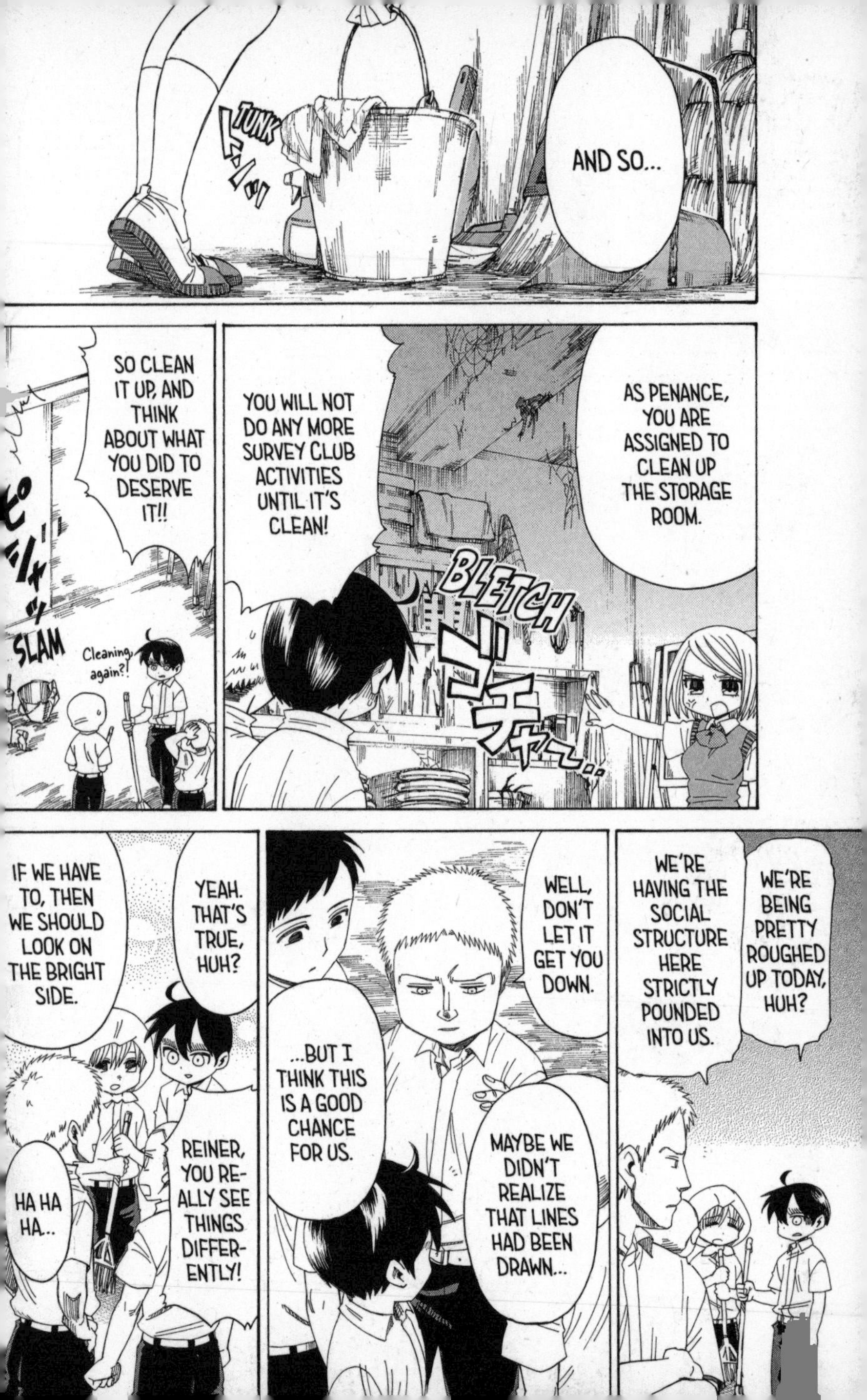

TUNK
AND SO...
AS PENANCE, YOU ARE ASSIGNED TO CLEAN UP THE STORAGE ROOM.
BLETCH
YOU WILL NOT DO ANY MORE SURVEY CLUB ACTIVITIES UNTIL IT'S CLEAN!
SO CLEAN IT UP, AND THINK ABOUT WHAT YOU DID TO DESERVE IT!!
SLAM
Cleaning, again?!
WE'RE BEING PRETTY ROUGHED UP TODAY, HUH?
WE'RE HAVING THE SOCIAL STRUCTURE HERE STRICTLY POUNDED INTO US.
WELL, DON'T LET IT GET YOU DOWN.
...BUT I THINK THIS IS A GOOD CHANCE FOR US.
MAYBE WE DIDN'T REALIZE THAT LINES HAD BEEN DRAWN...
YEAH. THAT'S TRUE, HUH?
IF WE HAVE TO, THEN WE SHOULD LOOK ON THE BRIGHT SIDE.
REINER, YOU REALLY SEE THINGS DIFFERENTLY!
HA HA HA...

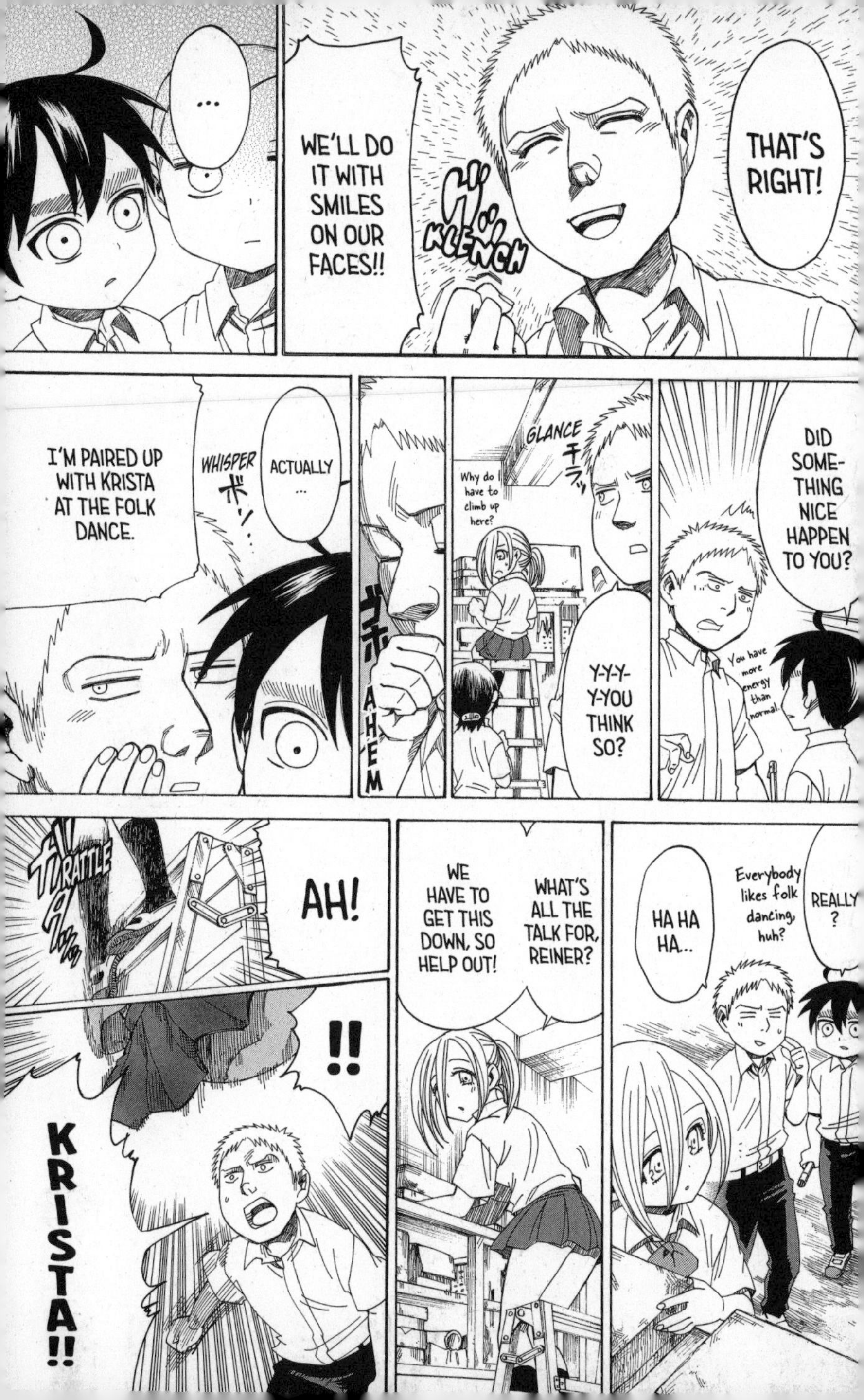
THAT'S RIGHT!
KLENCH
WE'LL DO IT WITH SMILES ON OUR FACES!!
...
DID SOMETHING NICE HAPPEN TO YOU?
You have more energy than normal.
GLANCE
Why do I have to climb up here?
Y-Y-Y-Y-YOU THINK SO?
AHEM
ACTUALLY ...
WHISPER
I'M PAIRED UP WITH KRISTA AT THE FOLK DANCE.
REALLY?
Everybody likes folk dancing, huh?
HA HA HA..
WHAT'S ALL THE TALK FOR, REINER?
WE HAVE TO GET THIS DOWN, SO HELP OUT!
RATTLE
AH!
!!
KRISTA!!

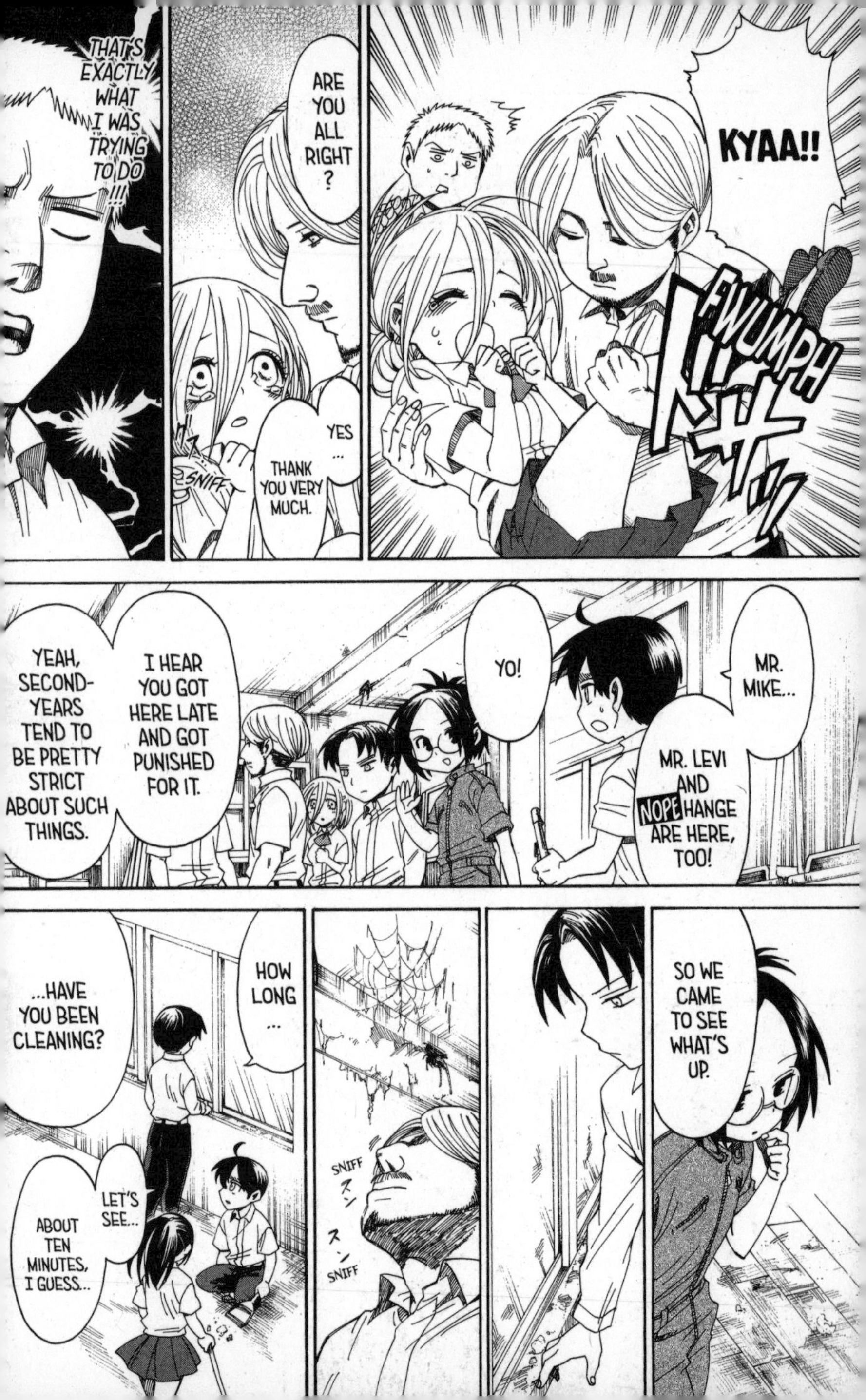
KYAA!!
FWUMPH
ARE YOU ALL RIGHT?
YES... THANK YOU VERY MUCH.
SNIFF
THAT'S EXACTLY WHAT I WAS TRYING TO DO!!!
MR. MIKE...
MR. LEVI AND NOPE HANGE ARE HERE, TOO!
YO!
I HEAR YOU GOT HERE LATE AND GOT PUNISHED FOR IT.
YEAH, SECOND-YEARS TEND TO BE PRETTY STRICT ABOUT SUCH THINGS.
SO WE CAME TO SEE WHAT'S UP.
SNIFF
スン
スン
SNIFF
HOW LONG ...
...HAVE YOU BEEN CLEANING?
LET'S SEE...
ABOUT TEN MINUTES, I GUESS...

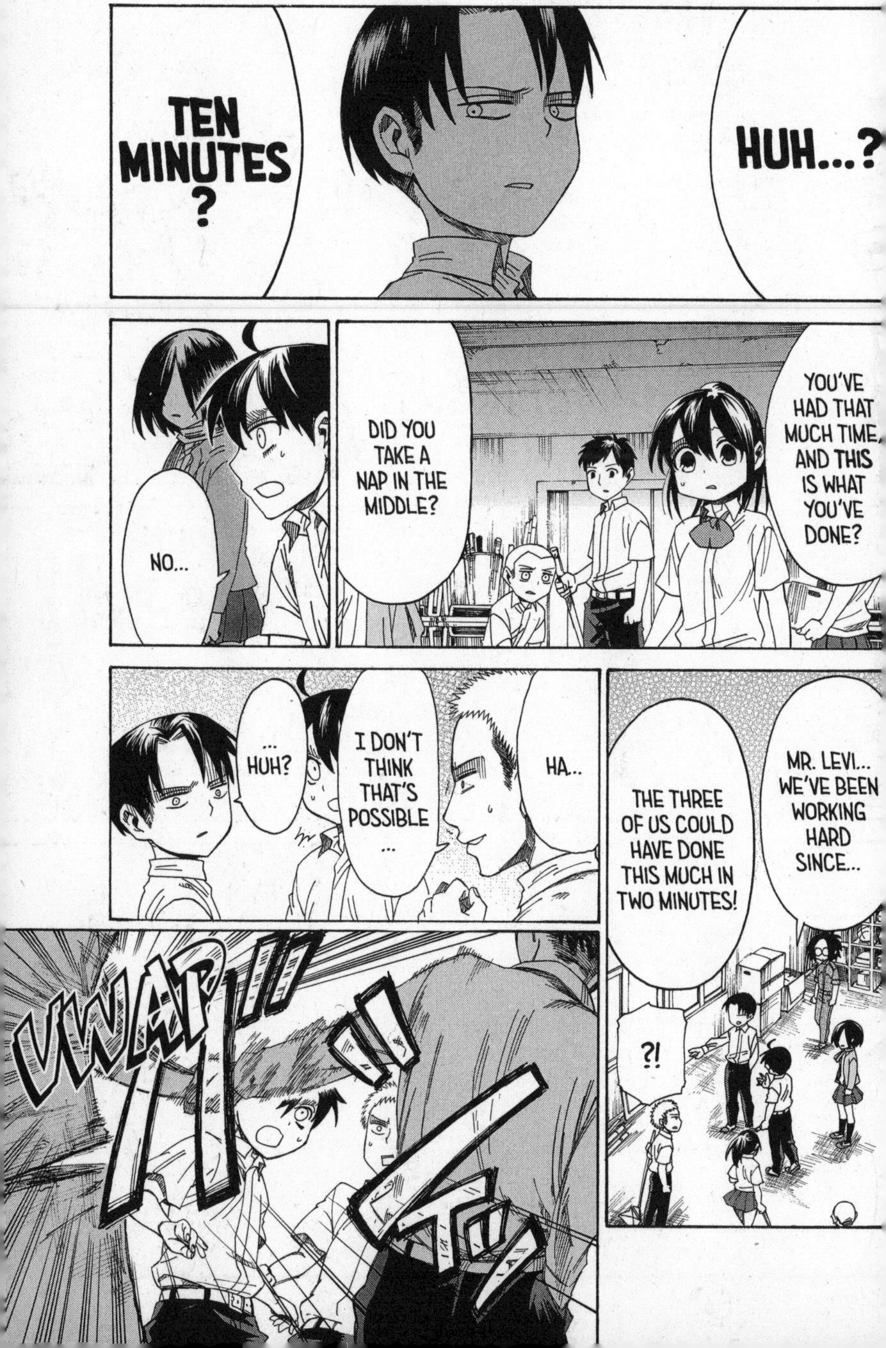
HUH...?
TEN MINUTES ?
YOU'VE HAD THAT MUCH TIME, AND THIS IS WHAT YOU'VE DONE?
DID YOU TAKE A NAP IN THE MIDDLE?
NO...
MR. LEVI... WE'VE BEEN WORKING HARD SINCE...
THE THREE OF US COULD HAVE DONE THIS MUCH IN TWO MINUTES!
?!
HA...
I DON'T THINK THAT'S POSSIBLE ...
... HUH?
WAP!!

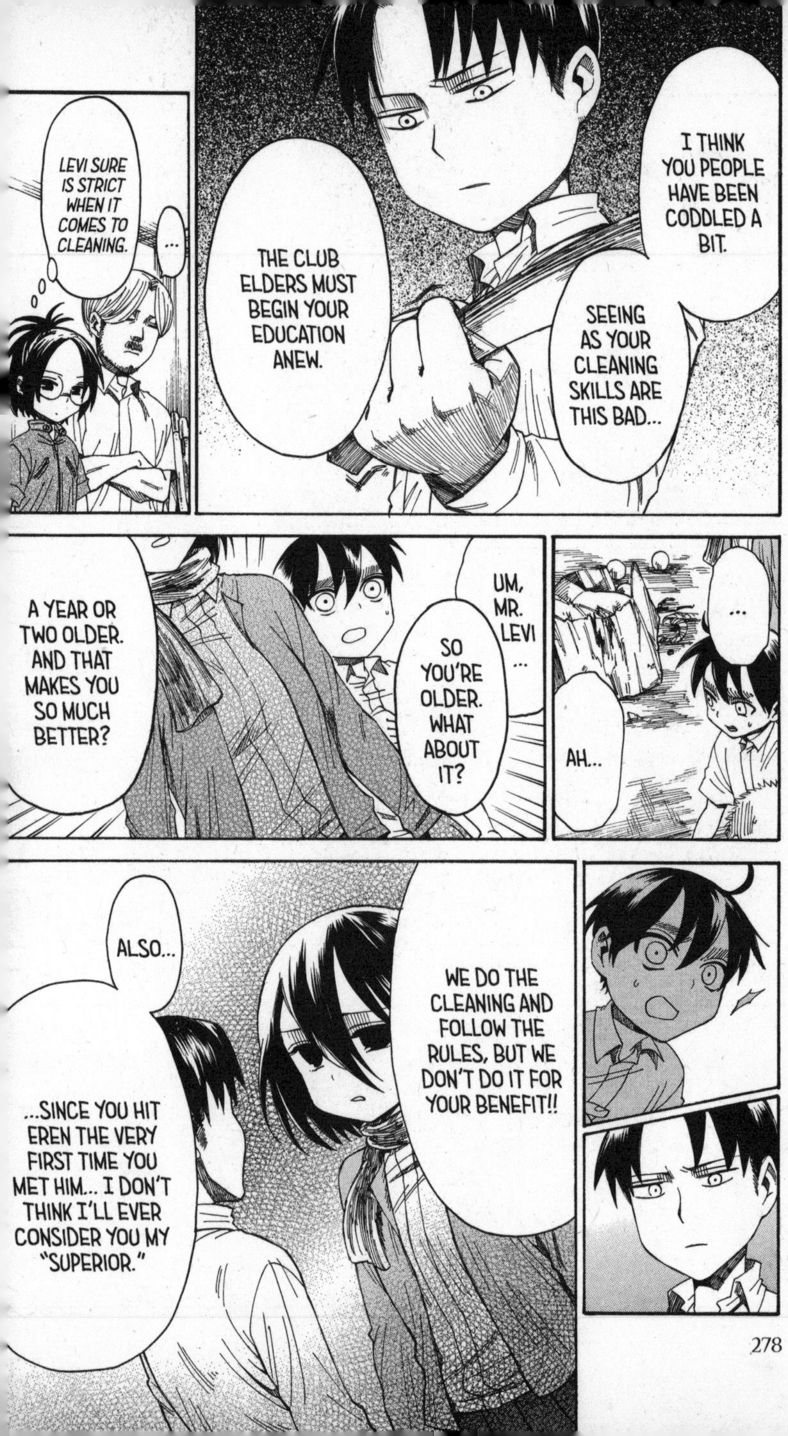

I THINK YOU PEOPLE HAVE BEEN CODDLED A BIT.
SEEING AS YOUR CLEANING SKILLS ARE THIS BAD...
THE CLUB ELDERS MUST BEGIN YOUR EDUCATION ANEW.
...
LEVI SURE IS STRICT WHEN IT COMES TO CLEANING.
...
AH...
UM, MR. LEVI ...
SO YOU'RE OLDER. WHAT ABOUT IT?
A YEAR OR TWO OLDER. AND THAT MAKES YOU SO MUCH BETTER?
WE DO THE CLEANING AND FOLLOW THE RULES, BUT WE DON'T DO IT FOR YOUR BENEFIT!!
ALSO...
...SINCE YOU HIT EREN THE VERY FIRST TIME YOU MET HIM... I DON'T THINK I'LL EVER CONSIDER YOU MY "SUPERIOR."

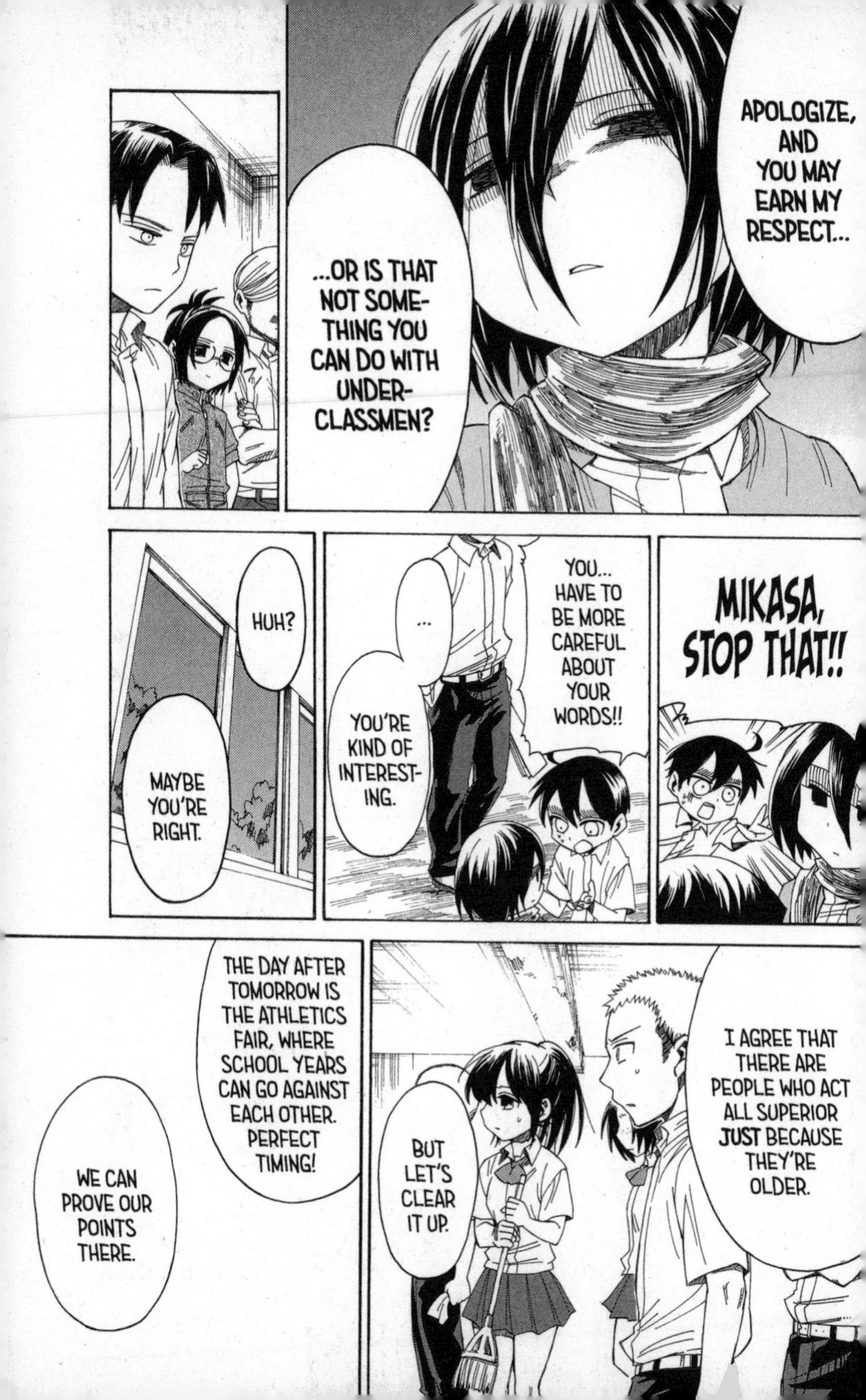
APOLOGIZE, AND YOU MAY EARN MY RESPECT...
...OR IS THAT NOT SOME-THING YOU CAN DO WITH UNDER-CLASSMEN?
MIKASA, STOP THAT!!
YOU... HAVE TO BE MORE CAREFUL ABOUT YOUR WORDS!!
...
YOU'RE KIND OF INTEREST-ING.
HUH?
MAYBE YOU'RE RIGHT.
I AGREE THAT THERE ARE PEOPLE WHO ACT ALL SUPERIOR **JUST** BECAUSE THEY'RE OLDER.
BUT LET'S CLEAR IT UP.
THE DAY AFTER TOMORROW IS THE ATHLETICS FAIR, WHERE SCHOOL YEARS CAN GO AGAINST EACH OTHER. PERFECT TIMING!
WE CAN PROVE OUR POINTS THERE.

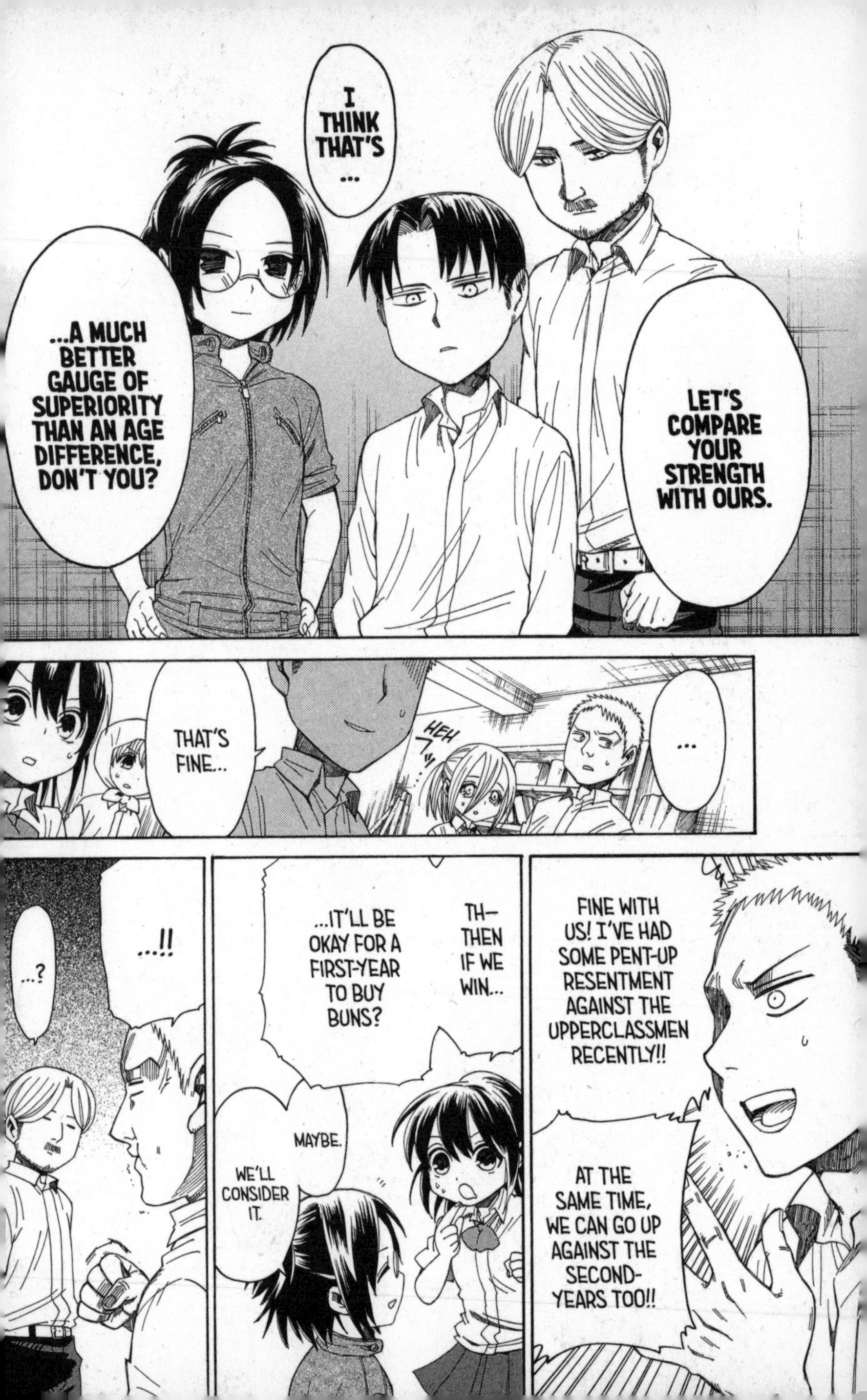
LET'S COMPARE YOUR STRENGTH WITH OURS.
I THINK THAT'S ...
...A MUCH BETTER GAUGE OF SUPERIORITY THAN AN AGE DIFFERENCE, DON'T YOU?
...
HEH
THAT'S FINE...
FINE WITH US! I'VE HAD SOME PENT-UP RESENTMENT AGAINST THE UPPERCLASSMEN RECENTLY!!
AT THE SAME TIME, WE CAN GO UP AGAINST THE SECOND-YEARS TOO!!
TH— THEN IF WE WIN...
...IT'LL BE OKAY FOR A FIRST-YEAR TO BUY BUNS?
MAYBE.
WE'LL CONSIDER IT.
...!!
...?

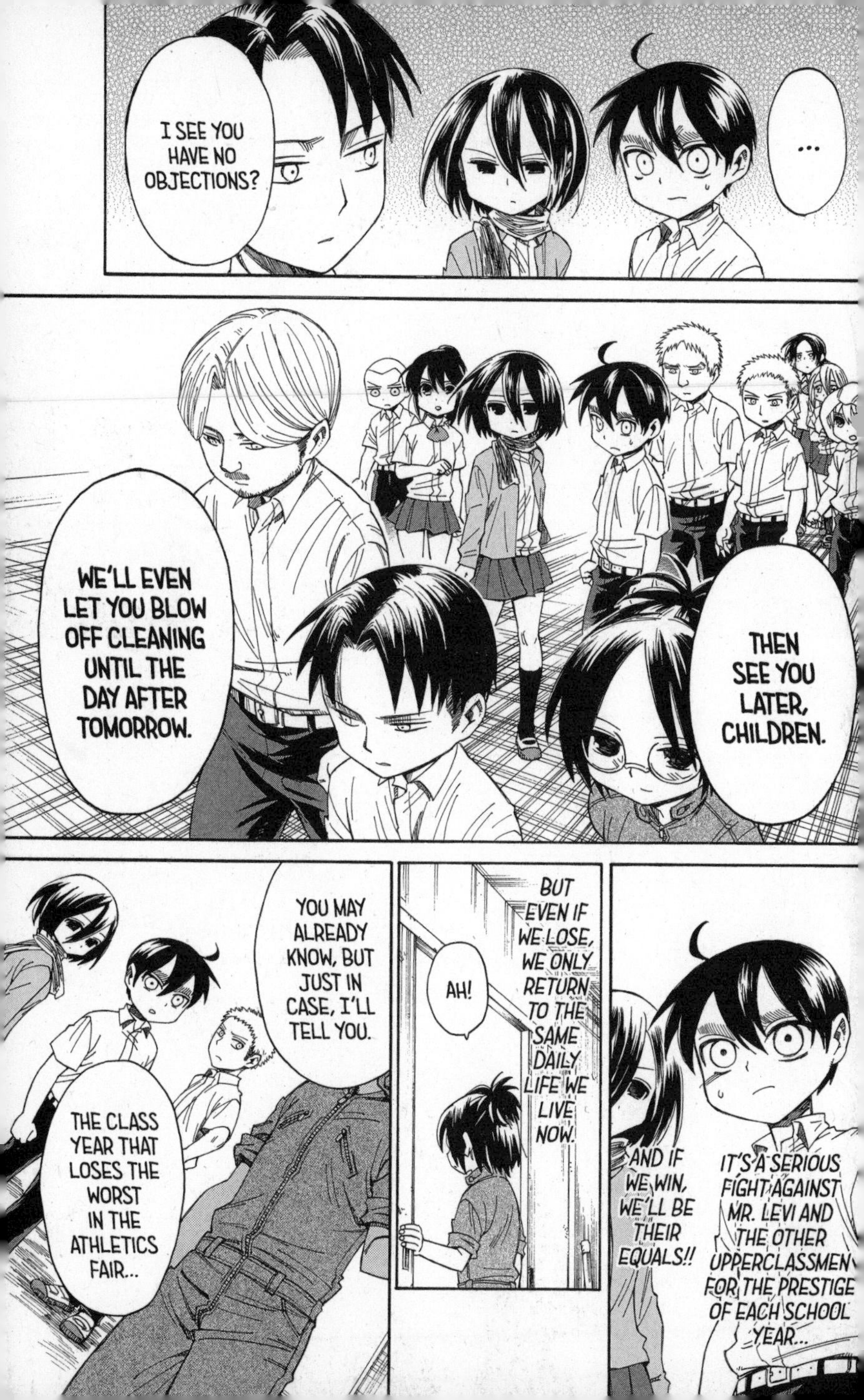
...
I SEE YOU HAVE NO OBJECTIONS?
THEN SEE YOU LATER, CHILDREN.
WE'LL EVEN LET YOU BLOW OFF CLEANING UNTIL THE DAY AFTER TOMORROW.
IT'S A SERIOUS FIGHT AGAINST MR. LEVI AND THE OTHER UPPERCLASSMEN FOR THE PRESTIGE OF EACH SCHOOL YEAR...
AND IF WE WIN, WE'LL BE THEIR EQUALS!!
BUT EVEN IF WE LOSE, WE ONLY RETURN TO THE SAME DAILY LIFE WE LIVE NOW.
AH!
YOU MAY ALREADY KNOW, BUT JUST IN CASE, I'LL TELL YOU.
THE CLASS YEAR THAT LOSES THE WORST IN THE ATHLETICS FAIR...

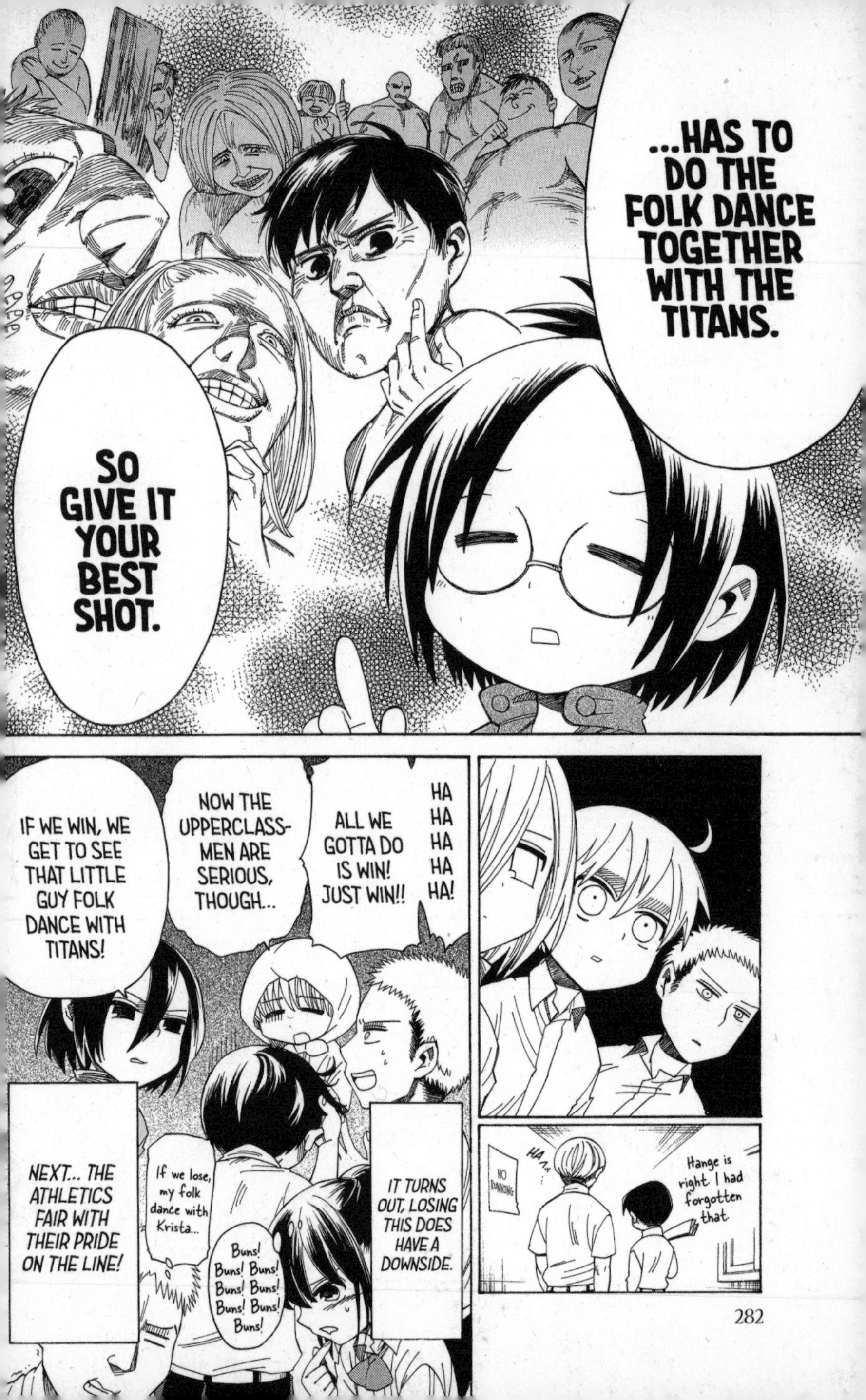
...HAS TO DO THE FOLK DANCE TOGETHER WITH THE TITANS.
SO GIVE IT YOUR BEST SHOT.
NO RUNNING
HA...
Hange is right. I had forgotten that.
HA HA HA HA HA!
ALL WE GOTTA DO IS WIN! JUST WIN!!
NOW THE UPPERCLASSMEN ARE SERIOUS, THOUGH...
IF WE WIN, WE GET TO SEE THAT LITTLE GUY FOLK DANCE WITH TITANS!
IT TURNS OUT, LOSING THIS DOES HAVE A DOWNSIDE.
Buns! Buns! Buns! Buns! Buns! Buns! Buns! Buns!
If we lose, my folk dance with Krista...
NEXT... THE ATHLETICS FAIR WITH THEIR PRIDE ON THE LINE!

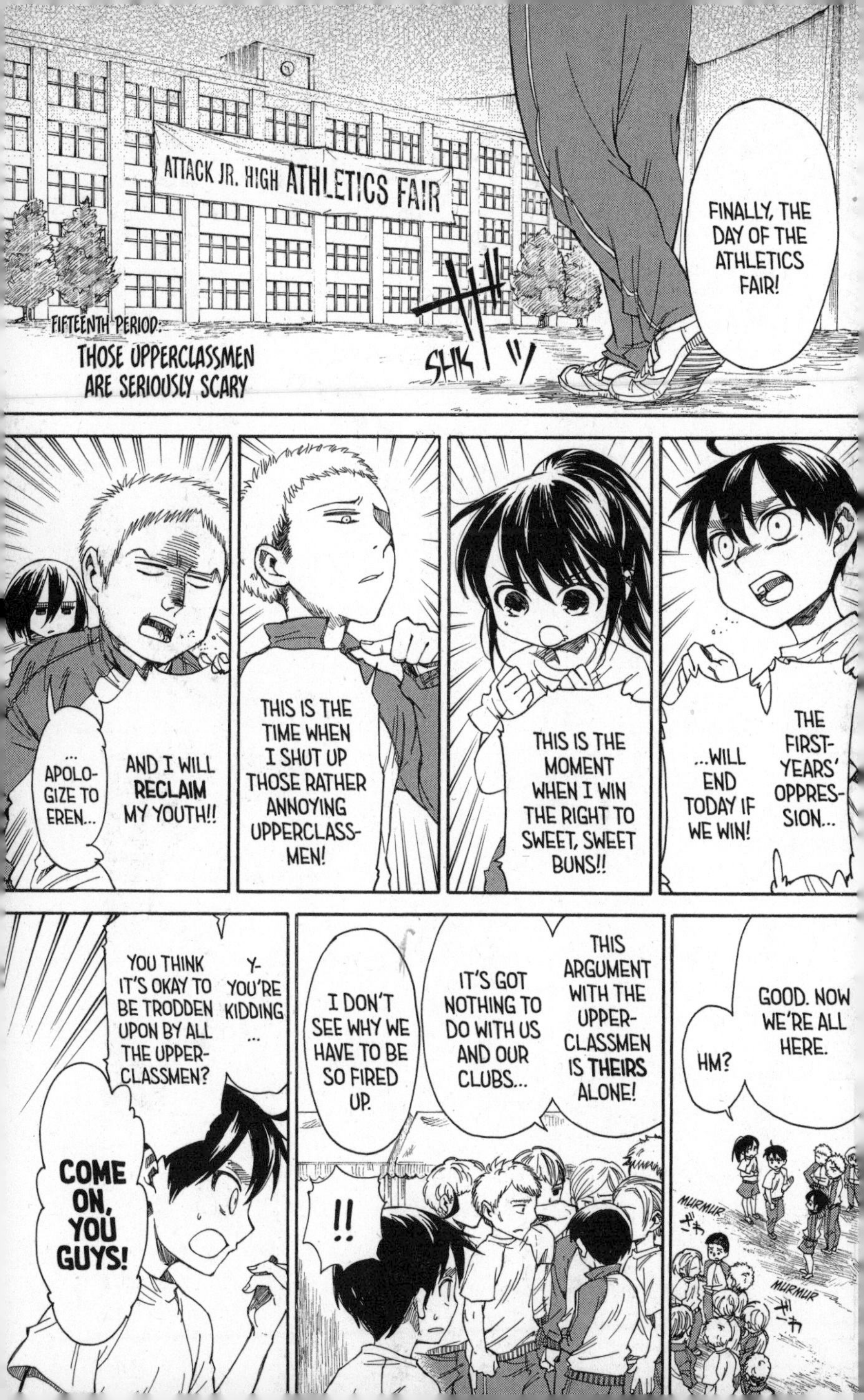

FINALLY, THE DAY OF THE ATHLETICS FAIR!
ATTACK JR. HIGH ATHLETICS FAIR
SHK
FIFTEENTH PERIOD:
THOSE UPPERCLASSMEN ARE SERIOUSLY SCARY
THE FIRST-YEARS' OPPRESSION...
...WILL END TODAY IF WE WIN!
THIS IS THE MOMENT WHEN I WIN THE RIGHT TO SWEET, SWEET BUNS!!
THIS IS THE TIME WHEN I SHUT UP THOSE RATHER ANNOYING UPPERCLASSMEN!
AND I WILL RECLAIM MY YOUTH!!
...APOLOGIZE TO EREN...
GOOD. NOW WE'RE ALL HERE.
HM?
MURMUR ざわ
MURMUR ざわ
THIS ARGUMENT WITH THE UPPERCLASSMEN IS THEIRS ALONE!
IT'S GOT NOTHING TO DO WITH US AND OUR CLUBS...
I DON'T SEE WHY WE HAVE TO BE SO FIRED UP.
!!
Y-YOU'RE KIDDING...
YOU THINK IT'S OKAY TO BE TRODDEN UPON BY ALL THE UPPER-CLASSMEN?
COME ON, YOU GUYS!

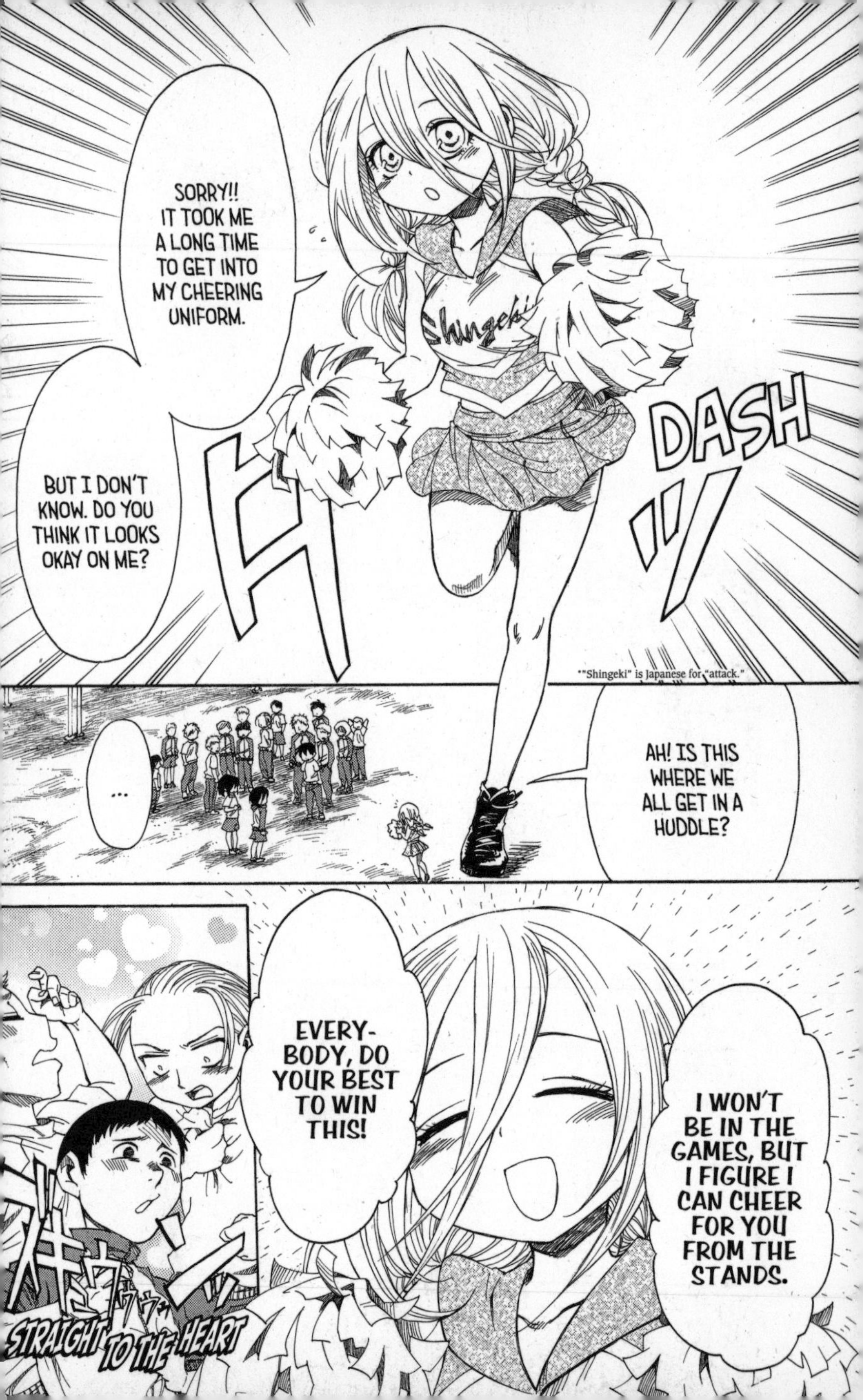
DASH
Shingeki
SORRY!! IT TOOK ME A LONG TIME TO GET INTO MY CHEERING UNIFORM.
BUT I DON'T KNOW. DO YOU THINK IT LOOKS OKAY ON ME?
AH! IS THIS WHERE WE ALL GET IN A HUDDLE?
...
I WON'T BE IN THE GAMES, BUT I FIGURE I CAN CHEER FOR YOU FROM THE STANDS.
EVERY-BODY, DO YOUR BEST TO WIN THIS!
STRAIGHT TO THE HEART

*"Shingeki" is Japanese for "attack."

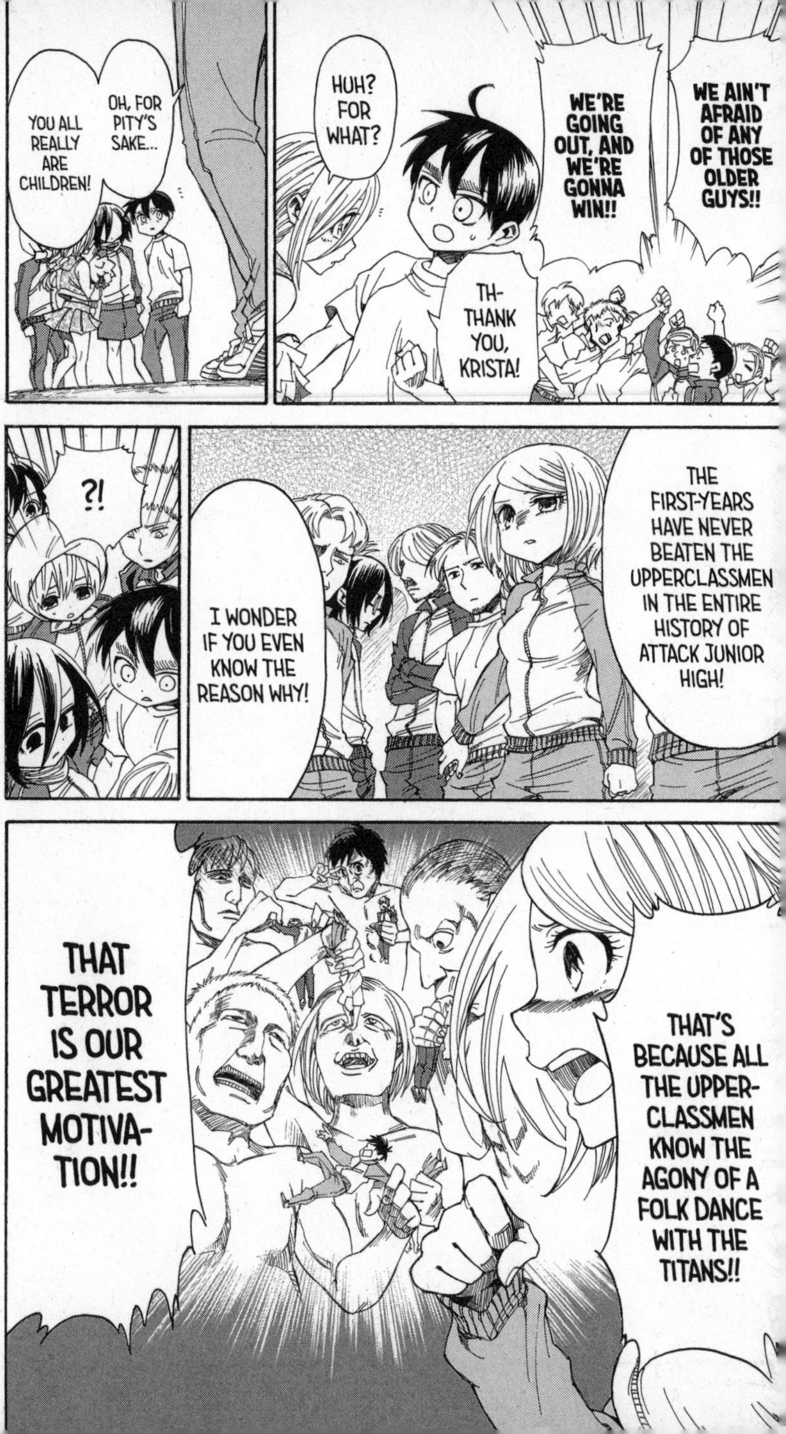
WE AIN'T AFRAID OF ANY OF THOSE OLDER GUYS!!
WE'RE GOING OUT, AND WE'RE GONNA WIN!!
HUH? FOR WHAT?
TH-THANK YOU, KRISTA!
OH, FOR PITY'S SAKE...
YOU ALL REALLY ARE CHILDREN!
THE FIRST-YEARS HAVE NEVER BEATEN THE UPPERCLASSMEN IN THE ENTIRE HISTORY OF ATTACK JUNIOR HIGH!
I WONDER IF YOU EVEN KNOW THE REASON WHY!
?!
THAT'S BECAUSE ALL THE UPPER-CLASSMEN KNOW THE AGONY OF A FOLK DANCE WITH THE TITANS!!
THAT TERROR IS OUR GREATEST MOTIVA-TION!!

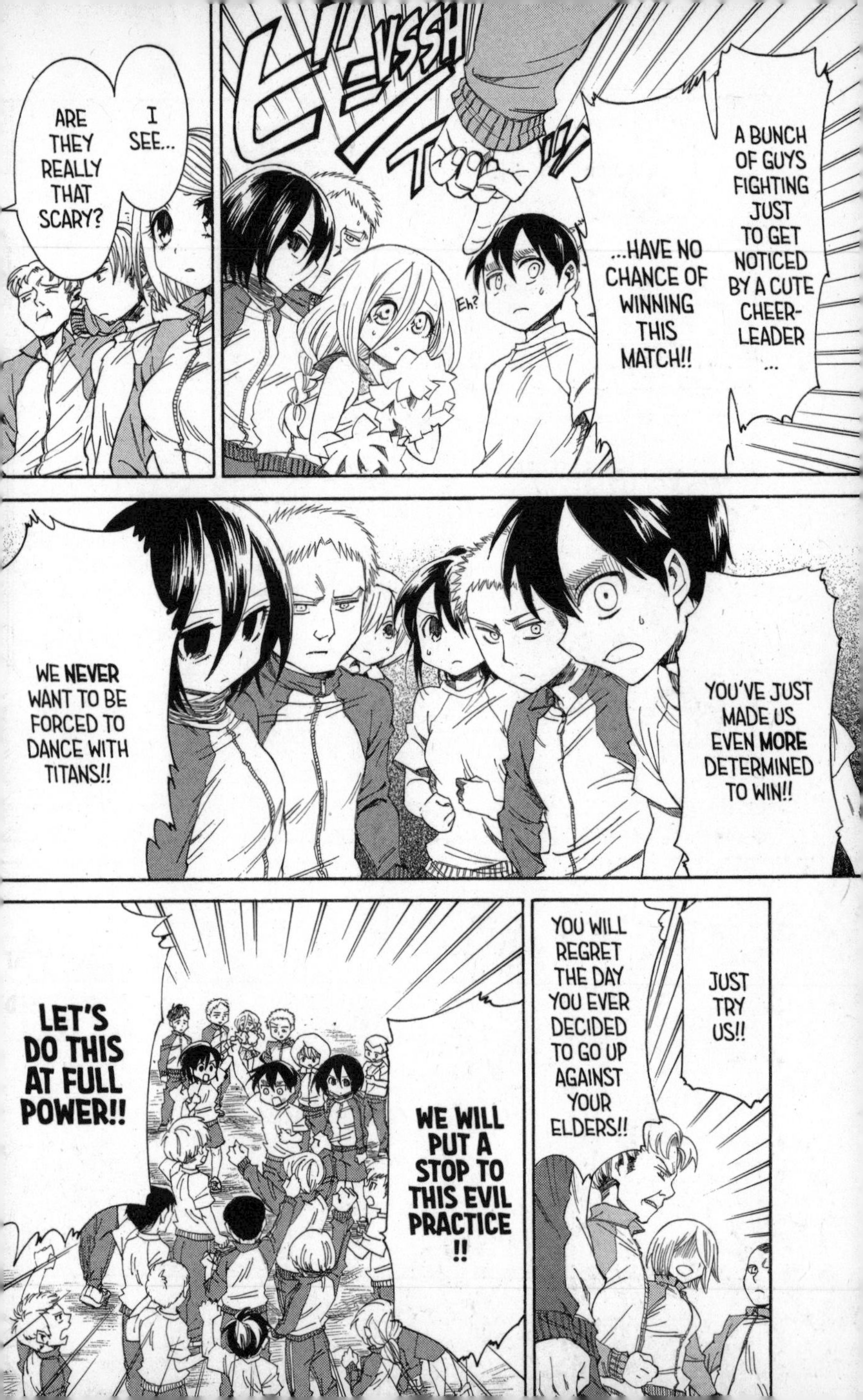
VSSH
A BUNCH OF GUYS FIGHTING JUST TO GET NOTICED BY A CUTE CHEER-LEADER...
...HAVE NO CHANCE OF WINNING THIS MATCH!!
Eh?
I SEE...
ARE THEY REALLY THAT SCARY?
YOU'VE JUST MADE US EVEN MORE DETERMINED TO WIN!!
WE NEVER WANT TO BE FORCED TO DANCE WITH TITANS!!
JUST TRY US!!
YOU WILL REGRET THE DAY YOU EVER DECIDED TO GO UP AGAINST YOUR ELDERS!!
WE WILL PUT A STOP TO THIS EVIL PRACTICE!!
LET'S DO THIS AT FULL POWER!!

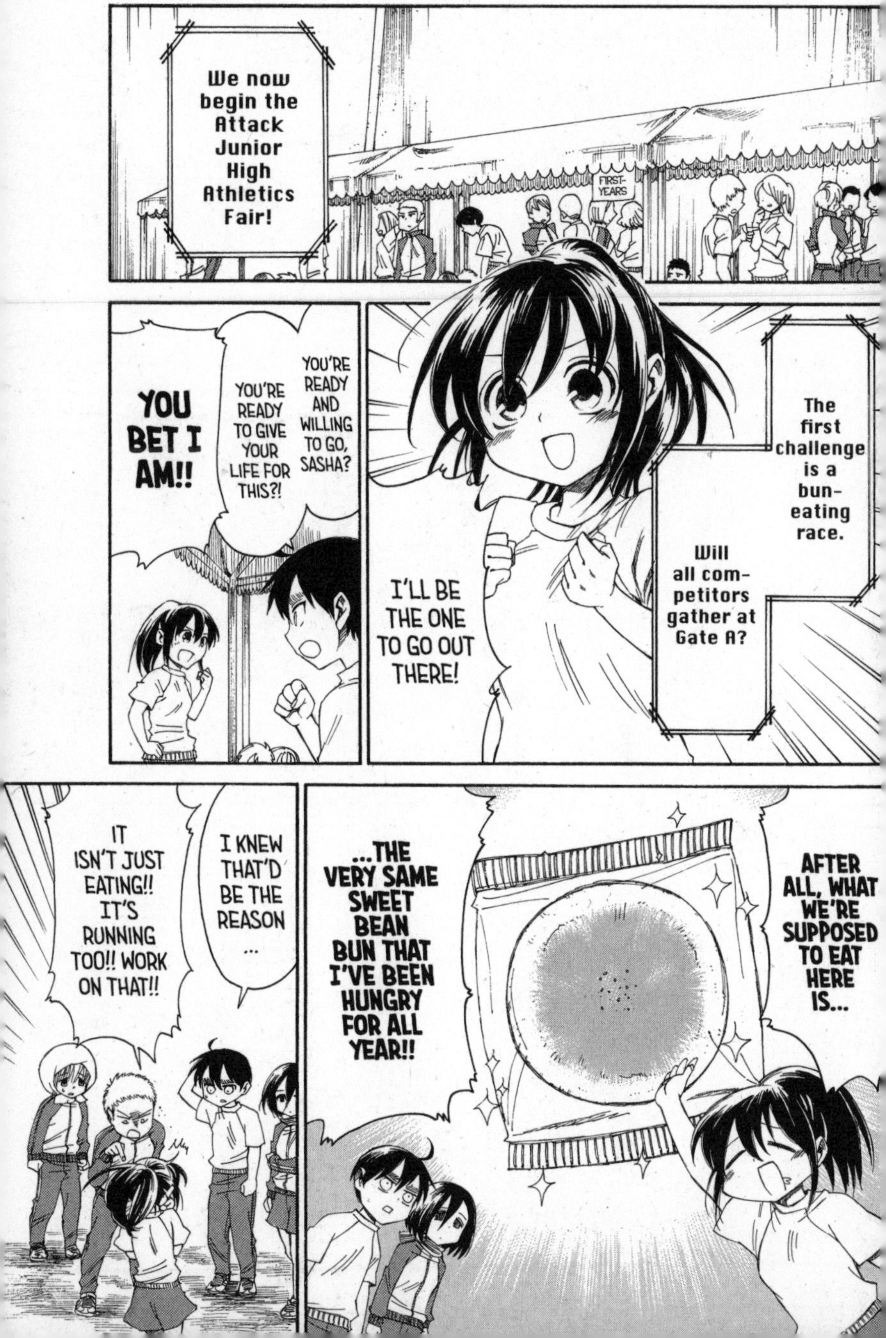
We now begin the Attack Junior High Athletics Fair!
FIRST-YEARS
The first challenge is a bun-eating race.
Will all competitors gather at Gate A?
I'LL BE THE ONE TO GO OUT THERE!
YOU'RE READY AND WILLING TO GO, SASHA? YOU'RE READY TO GIVE YOUR LIFE FOR THIS?!
YOU BET I AM!!
AFTER ALL, WHAT WE'RE SUPPOSED TO EAT HERE IS...
...THE VERY SAME SWEET BEAN BUN THAT I'VE BEEN HUNGRY FOR ALL YEAR!!
I KNEW THAT'D BE THE REASON ...
IT ISN'T JUST EATING!! IT'S RUNNING TOO!! WORK ON THAT!!

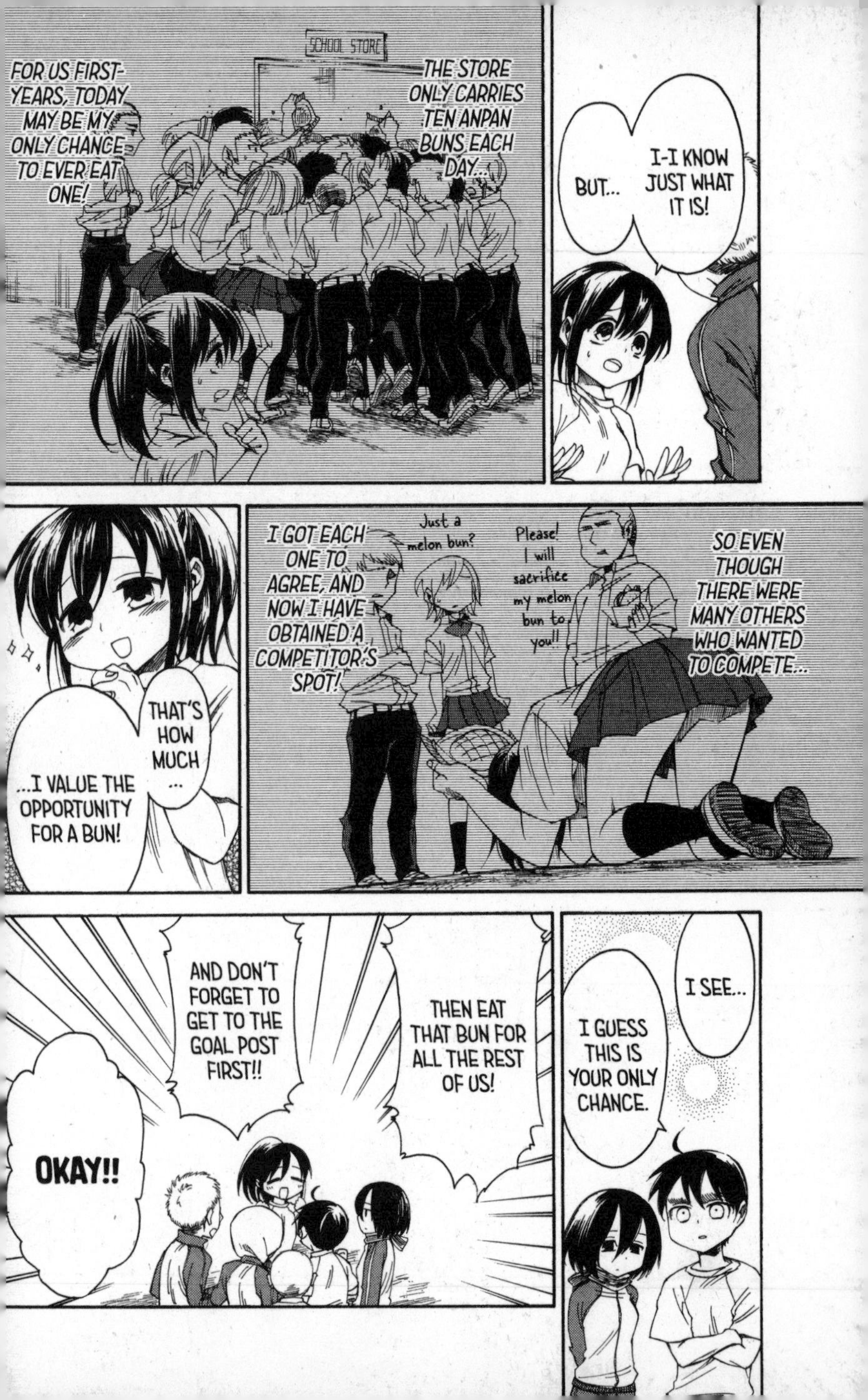
I-I KNOW JUST WHAT IT IS!
BUT...
SCHOOL STORE
THE STORE ONLY CARRIES TEN ANPAN BUNS EACH DAY...
FOR US FIRST-YEARS, TODAY MAY BE MY ONLY CHANCE TO EVER EAT ONE!
SO EVEN THOUGH THERE WERE MANY OTHERS WHO WANTED TO COMPETE...
Please! I will sacrifice my melon bun to you!
Just a melon bun?
I GOT EACH ONE TO AGREE, AND NOW I HAVE OBTAINED A COMPETITOR'S SPOT!
THAT'S HOW MUCH ...
...I VALUE THE OPPORTUNITY FOR A BUN!
I SEE...
I GUESS THIS IS YOUR ONLY CHANCE.
THEN EAT THAT BUN FOR ALL THE REST OF US!
AND DON'T FORGET TO GET TO THE GOAL POST FIRST!!
OKAY!!

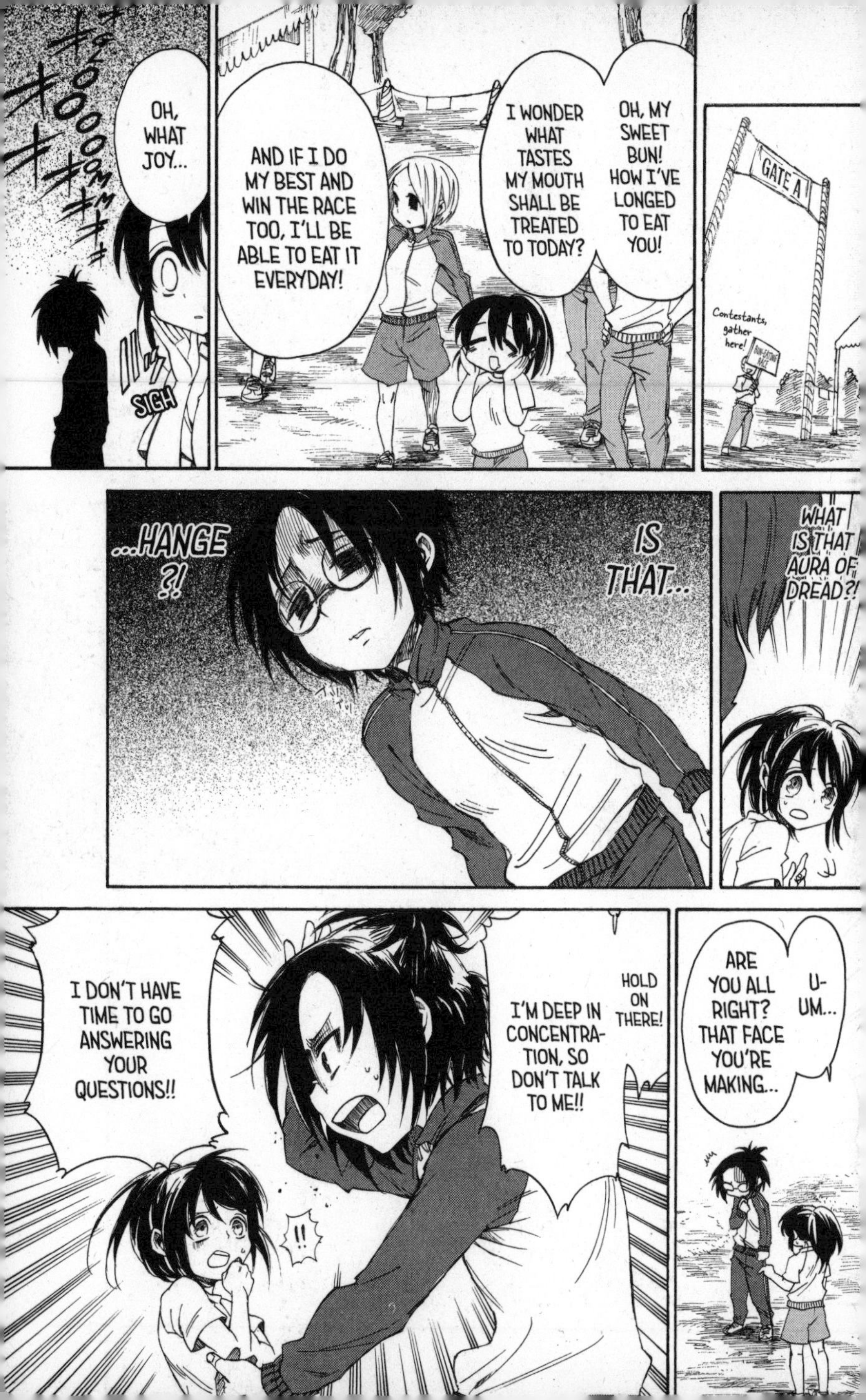
GATE A
Contestants, gather here!
BUN-EATING RACE
OH, MY SWEET BUN! HOW I'VE LONGED TO EAT YOU!
I WONDER WHAT TASTES MY MOUTH SHALL BE TREATED TO TODAY?
AND IF I DO MY BEST AND WIN THE RACE TOO, I'LL BE ABLE TO EAT IT EVERYDAY!
OH, WHAT JOY...
SIGH
WHAT IS THAT AURA OF DREAD?!
IS THAT...
...HANGE?!
U-UM...
ARE YOU ALL RIGHT? THAT FACE YOU'RE MAKING...
HOLD ON THERE!
I'M DEEP IN CONCENTRATION, SO DON'T TALK TO ME!!
I DON'T HAVE TIME TO GO ANSWERING YOUR QUESTIONS!!
!!

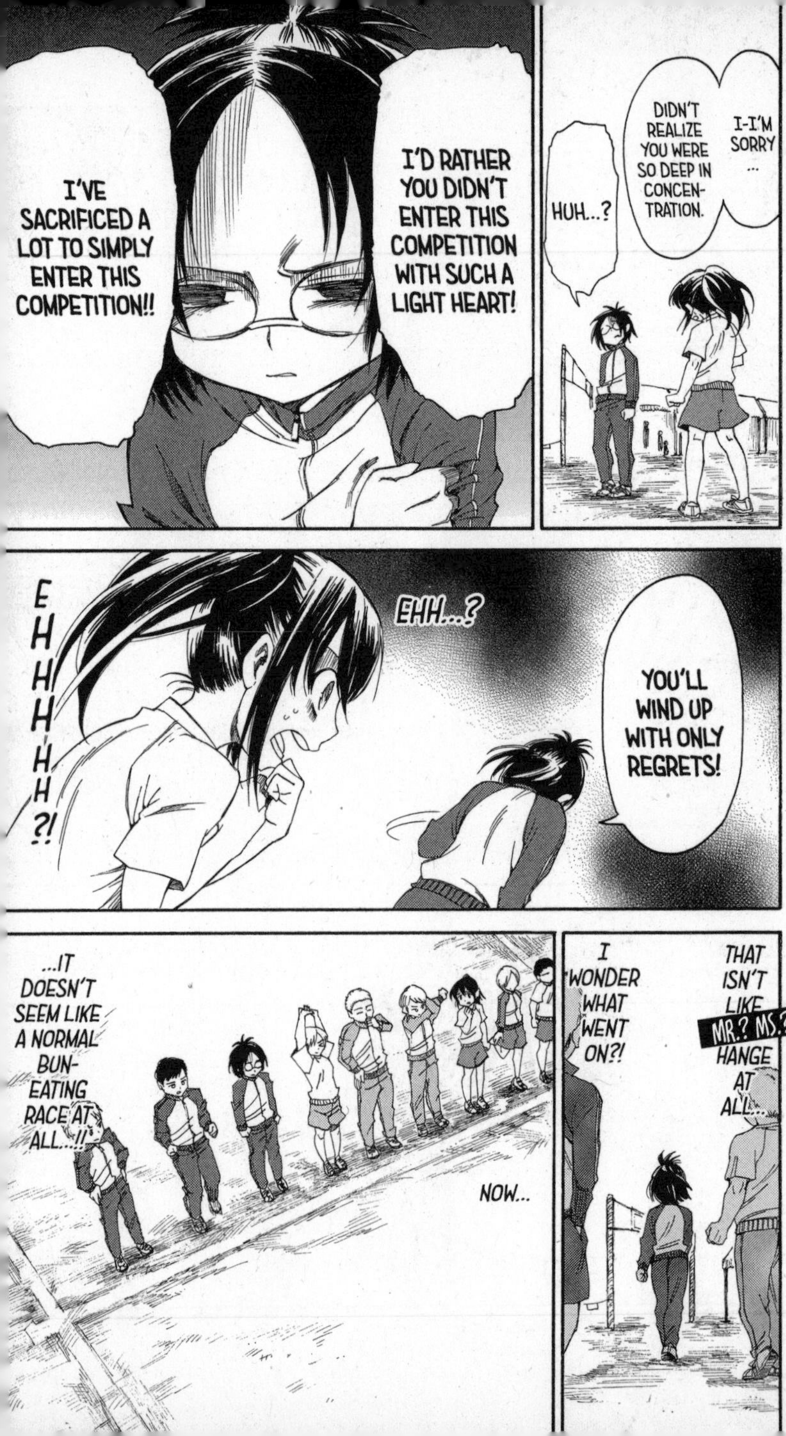
I-I'M SORRY ...
DIDN'T REALIZE YOU WERE SO DEEP IN CONCENTRATION.
HUH...?
I'D RATHER YOU DIDN'T ENTER THIS COMPETITION WITH SUCH A LIGHT HEART!
I'VE SACRIFICED A LOT TO SIMPLY ENTER THIS COMPETITION!!
YOU'LL WIND UP WITH ONLY REGRETS!
EHH...?
EHHHHH?!
THAT ISN'T LIKE MR.? MS.? HANGE AT ALL...
I WONDER WHAT WENT ON?!
NOW...
...IT DOESN'T SEEM LIKE A NORMAL BUN-EATING RACE AT ALL...!!

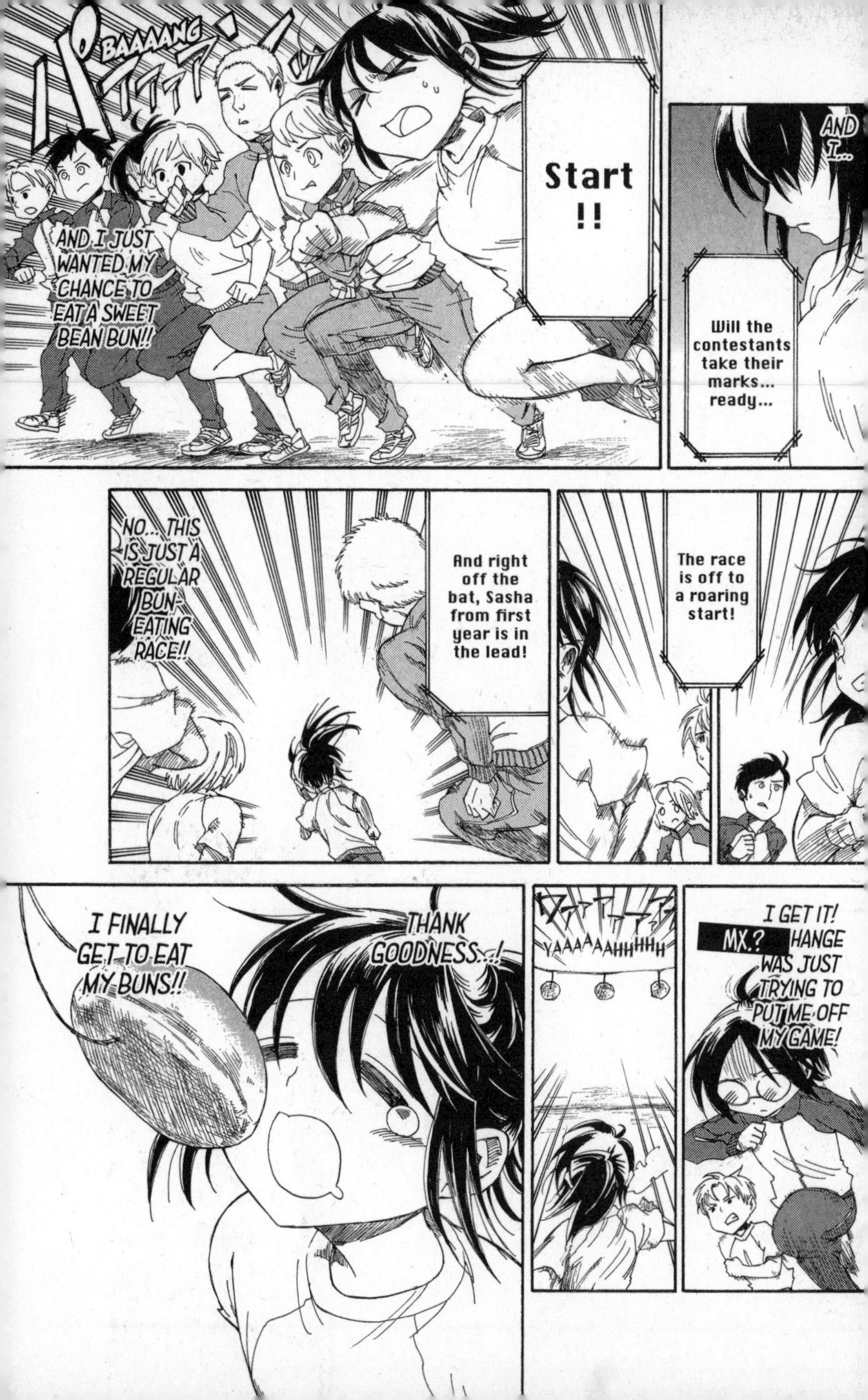
AND I...
Will the contestants take their marks... ready...
Start!!
BAAAANG
AND I JUST WANTED MY CHANCE TO EAT A SWEET BEAN BUN!!
The race is off to a roaring start!
And right off the bat, Sasha from first year is in the lead!
NO... THIS IS JUST A REGULAR BUN-EATING RACE!!
I GET IT! MX.? HANGE WAS JUST TRYING TO PUT ME OFF MY GAME!
YAAAAAAHHHHHH
THANK GOODNESS...!
I FINALLY GET TO EAT MY BUNS!!

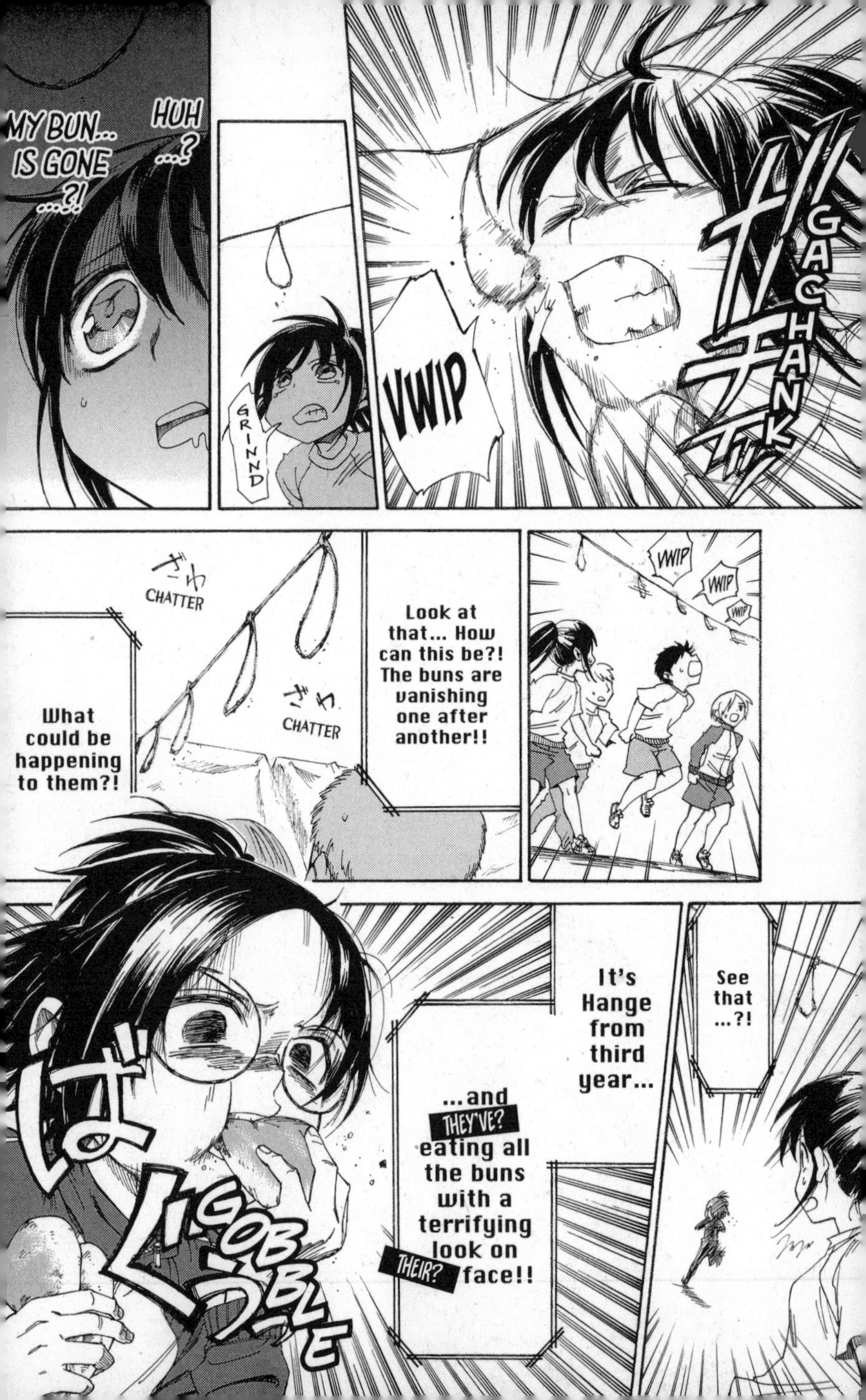
GACHANK
VWIP
GRINND
HUH ...?
MY BUN... IS GONE ...?!
VWIP
VWIP
VWIP
Look at that... How can this be?! The buns are vanishing one after another!!
ざわ
CHATTER
ざわ
CHATTER
What could be happening to them?!
See that ...?!
It's Hange from third year...
...and THEY'VE? eating all the buns with a terrifying look on THEIR? face!!
GOBBLE

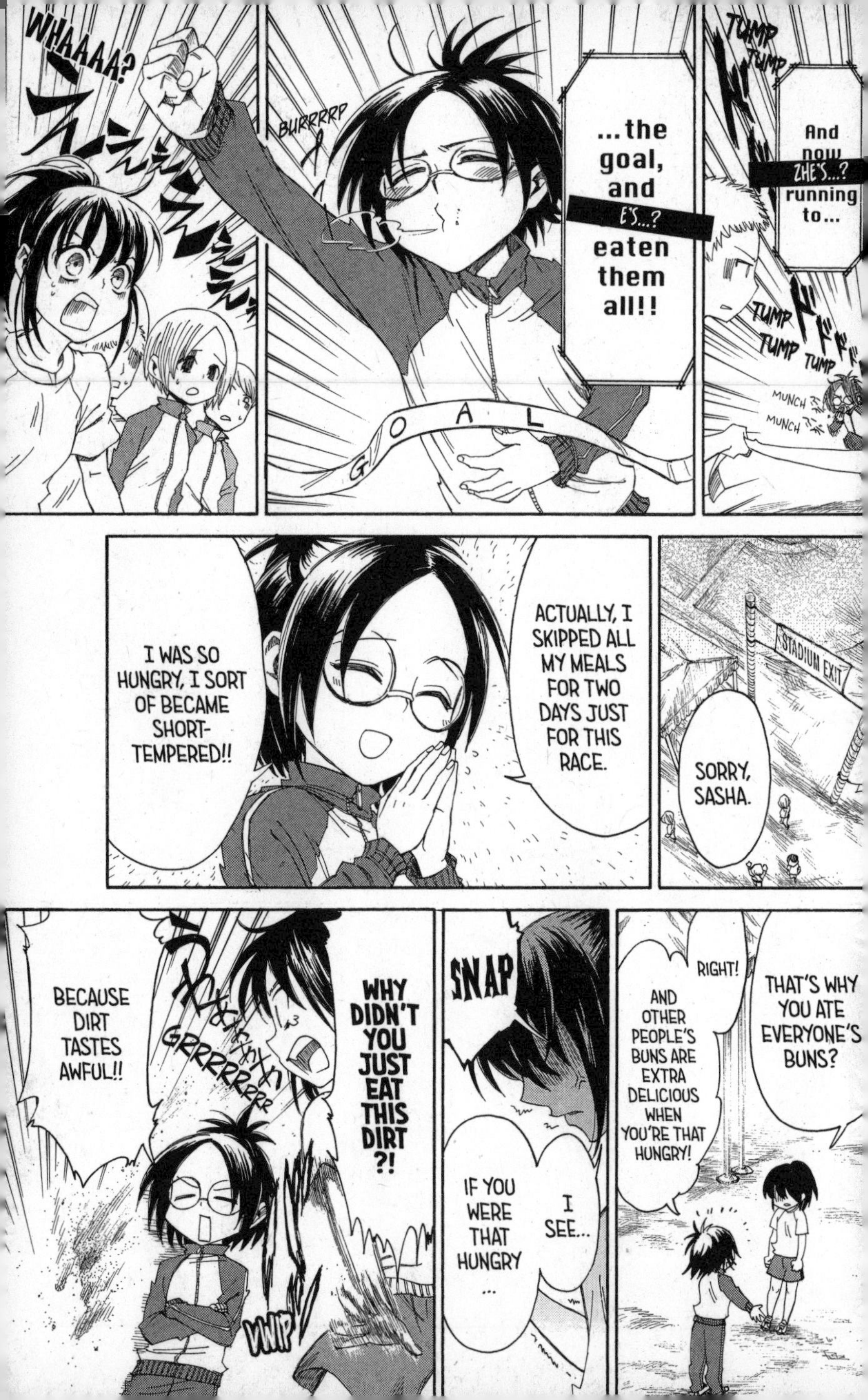
TUMP
TUMP
And now ZHE'S...? running to...
TUMP
TUMP
TUMP
MUNCH
MUNCH
BURRRRP
...the goal, and E'S...? eaten them all!!
GOAL
WHAAAAA?
STADIUM EXIT
SORRY, SASHA.
ACTUALLY, I SKIPPED ALL MY MEALS FOR TWO DAYS JUST FOR THIS RACE.
I WAS SO HUNGRY, I SORT OF BECAME SHORT-TEMPERED!!
THAT'S WHY YOU ATE EVERYONE'S BUNS?
RIGHT!
AND OTHER PEOPLE'S BUNS ARE EXTRA DELICIOUS WHEN YOU'RE THAT HUNGRY!
SNAP
I SEE...
IF YOU WERE THAT HUNGRY ...
WHY DIDN'T YOU JUST EAT THIS DIRT?!
GRRRRRRRR
BECAUSE DIRT TASTES AWFUL!!
VWIP

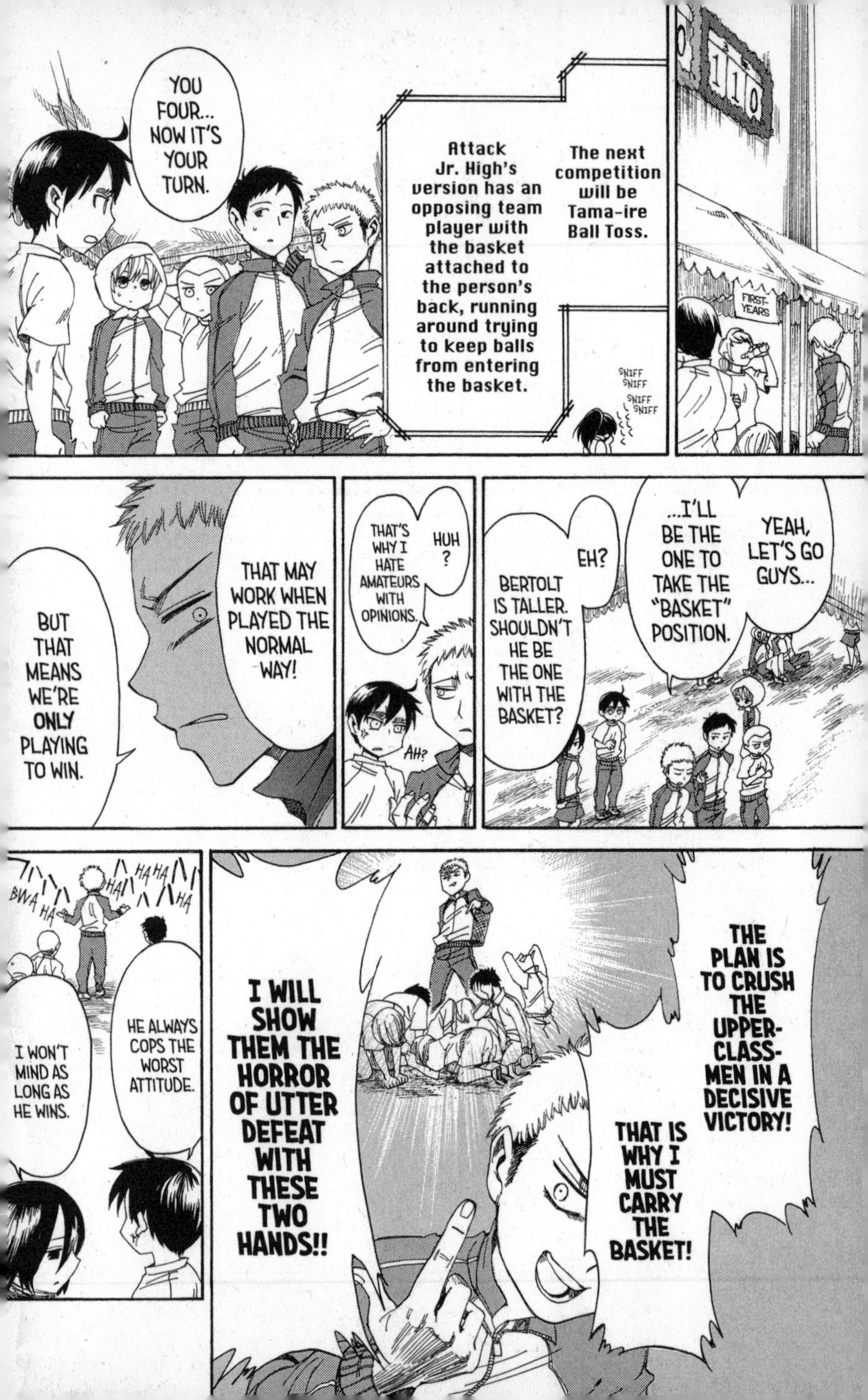
The next competition will be Tama-ire Ball Toss.
Attack Jr. High's version has an opposing team player with the basket attached to the person's back, running around trying to keep balls from entering the basket.
SNIFF SNIFF SNIFF SNIFF
YOU FOUR... NOW IT'S YOUR TURN.
YEAH, LET'S GO GUYS...
...I'LL BE THE ONE TO TAKE THE "BASKET" POSITION.
EH?
BERTOLT IS TALLER. SHOULDN'T HE BE THE ONE WITH THE BASKET?
HUH?
AH?
THAT'S WHY I HATE AMATEURS WITH OPINIONS.
THAT MAY WORK WHEN PLAYED THE NORMAL WAY!
BUT THAT MEANS WE'RE ONLY PLAYING TO WIN.
THE PLAN IS TO CRUSH THE UPPER-CLASS-MEN IN A DECISIVE VICTORY!
THAT IS WHY I MUST CARRY THE BASKET!
I WILL SHOW THEM THE HORROR OF UTTER DEFEAT WITH THESE TWO HANDS!!
BWA HA HA HA HA HA HA
HE ALWAYS COPS THE WORST ATTITUDE.
I WON'T MIND AS LONG AS HE WINS.

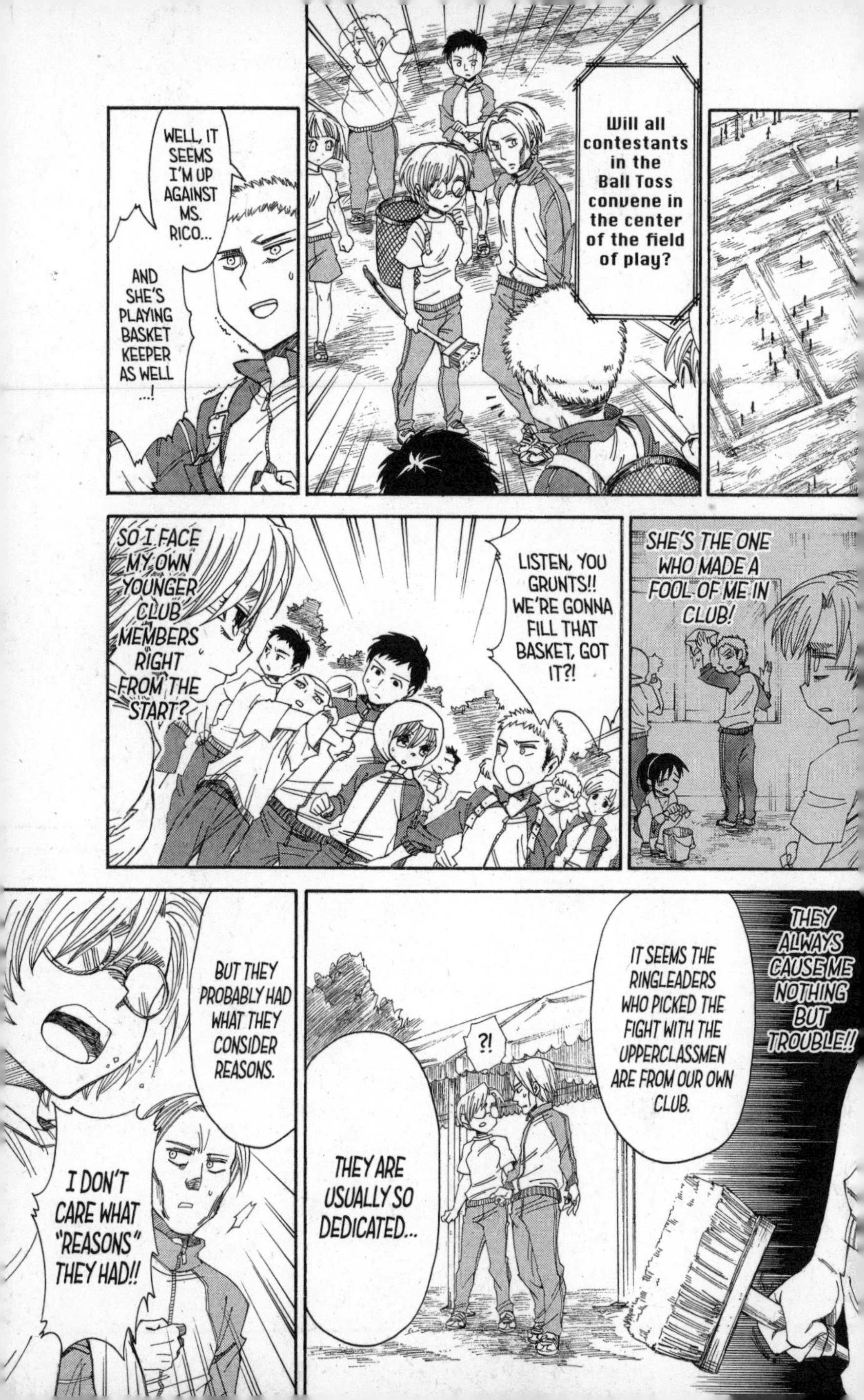
Will all contestants in the Ball Toss convene in the center of the field of play?
WELL, IT SEEMS I'M UP AGAINST MS. RICO...
AND SHE'S PLAYING BASKET KEEPER AS WELL ...!
SHE'S THE ONE WHO MADE A FOOL OF ME IN CLUB!
LISTEN, YOU GRUNTS!! WE'RE GONNA FILL THAT BASKET, GOT IT?!
SO I FACE MY OWN YOUNGER CLUB MEMBERS RIGHT FROM THE START?
THEY ALWAYS CAUSE ME NOTHING BUT TROUBLE!!
IT SEEMS THE RINGLEADERS WHO PICKED THE FIGHT WITH THE UPPERCLASSMEN ARE FROM OUR OWN CLUB.
?!
THEY ARE USUALLY SO DEDICATED...
BUT THEY PROBABLY HAD WHAT THEY CONSIDER REASONS.
I DON'T CARE WHAT "REASONS" THEY HAD!!

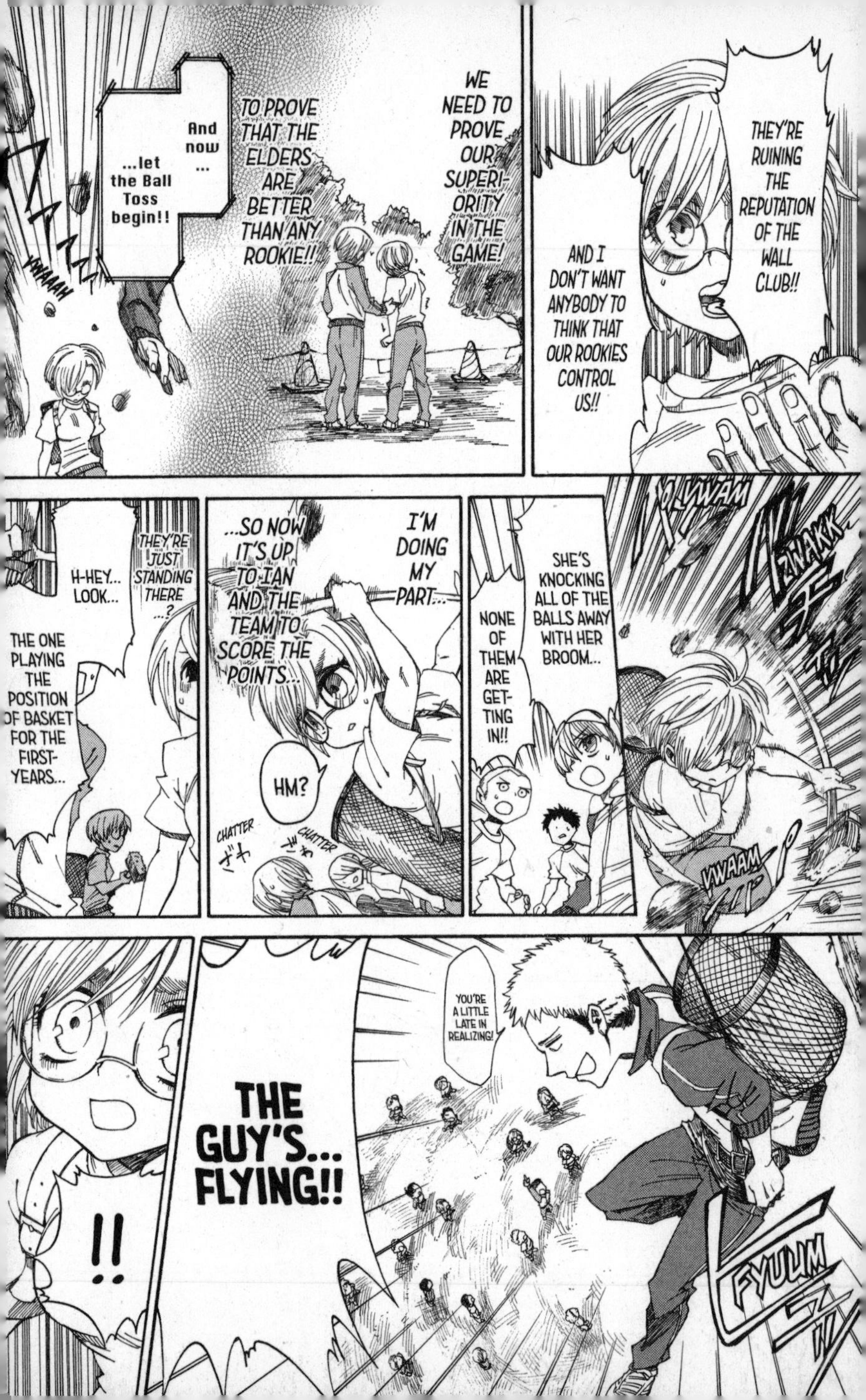

THEY'RE RUINING THE REPUTATION OF THE WALL CLUB!!
AND I DON'T WANT ANYBODY TO THINK THAT OUR ROOKIES CONTROL US!!
WE NEED TO PROVE OUR SUPERIORITY IN THE GAME!
TO PROVE THAT THE ELDERS ARE BETTER THAN ANY ROOKIE!!
And now ... ...let the Ball Toss begin!!
VWAAAH
VWAM
ZWAKK
VWAAM
SHE'S KNOCKING ALL OF THE BALLS AWAY WITH HER BROOM...
NONE OF THEM ARE GETTING IN!!
I'M DOING MY PART...
...SO NOW IT'S UP TO IAN AND THE TEAM TO SCORE THE POINTS...
HM?
CHATTER
CHATTER
THEY'RE JUST STANDING THERE ...?
H-HEY... LOOK...
THE ONE PLAYING THE POSITION OF BASKET FOR THE FIRST-YEARS...
YOU'RE A LITTLE LATE IN REALIZING!
FYUUM
THE GUY'S... FLYING!!
!!

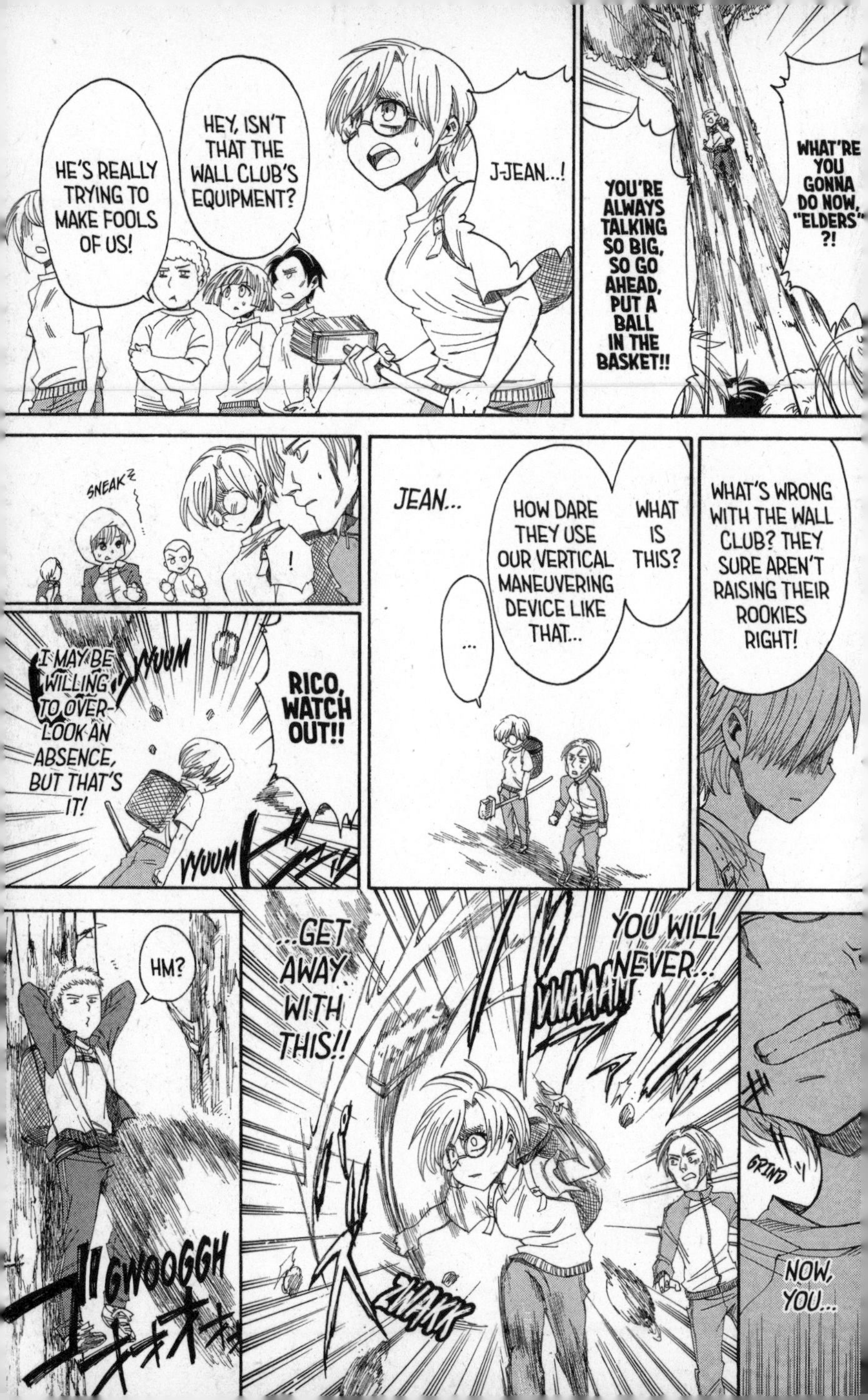
WHAT'RE YOU GONNA DO NOW, "ELDERS"?!
YOU'RE ALWAYS TALKING SO BIG, SO GO AHEAD, PUT A BALL IN THE BASKET!!
J-JEAN...!
HEY, ISN'T THAT THE WALL CLUB'S EQUIPMENT?
HE'S REALLY TRYING TO MAKE FOOLS OF US!
WHAT'S WRONG WITH THE WALL CLUB? THEY SURE AREN'T RAISING THEIR ROOKIES RIGHT!
WHAT IS THIS?
HOW DARE THEY USE OUR VERTICAL MANEUVERING DEVICE LIKE THAT...
JEAN...
...
SNEAK
!
RICO, WATCH OUT!!
VYUUM
I MAY BE WILLING TO OVER-LOOK AN ABSENCE, BUT THAT'S IT!
VYUUM
NOW, YOU...
GRIND
YOU WILL NEVER...
...GET AWAY WITH THIS!!
ZWAKK
HM?
GWOOGGH

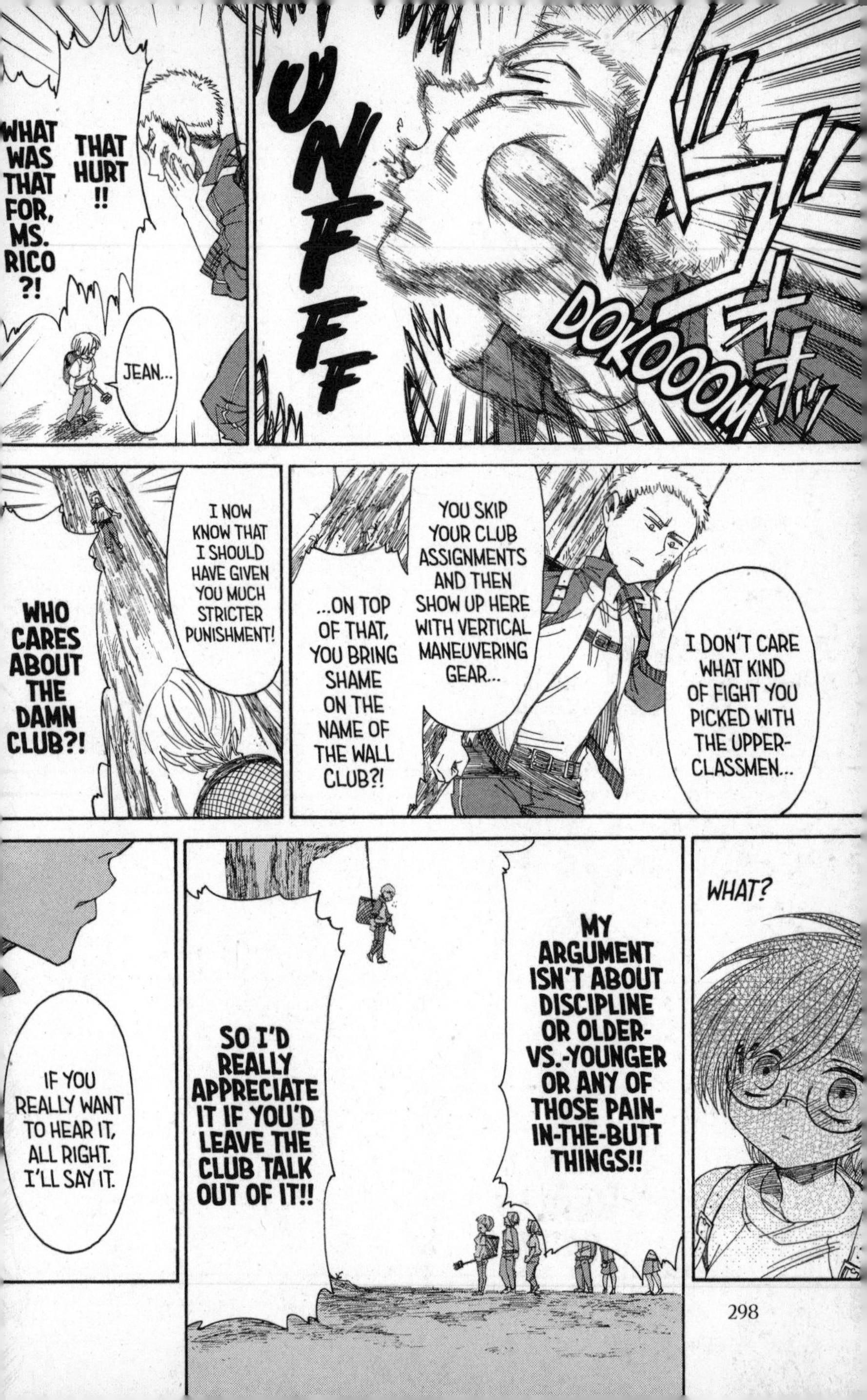
DOKOOOM
UNFFF
THAT HURT!!
WHAT WAS THAT FOR, MS. RICO?!
JEAN...
I DON'T CARE WHAT KIND OF FIGHT YOU PICKED WITH THE UPPER-CLASSMEN...
YOU SKIP YOUR CLUB ASSIGNMENTS AND THEN SHOW UP HERE WITH VERTICAL MANEUVERING GEAR...
...ON TOP OF THAT, YOU BRING SHAME ON THE NAME OF THE WALL CLUB?!
I NOW KNOW THAT I SHOULD HAVE GIVEN YOU MUCH STRICTER PUNISHMENT!
WHO CARES ABOUT THE DAMN CLUB?!
WHAT?
MY ARGUMENT ISN'T ABOUT DISCIPLINE OR OLDER-VS.-YOUNGER OR ANY OF THOSE PAIN-IN-THE-BUTT THINGS!!
SO I'D REALLY APPRECIATE IT IF YOU'D LEAVE THE CLUB TALK OUT OF IT!!
IF YOU REALLY WANT TO HEAR IT, ALL RIGHT. I'LL SAY IT.

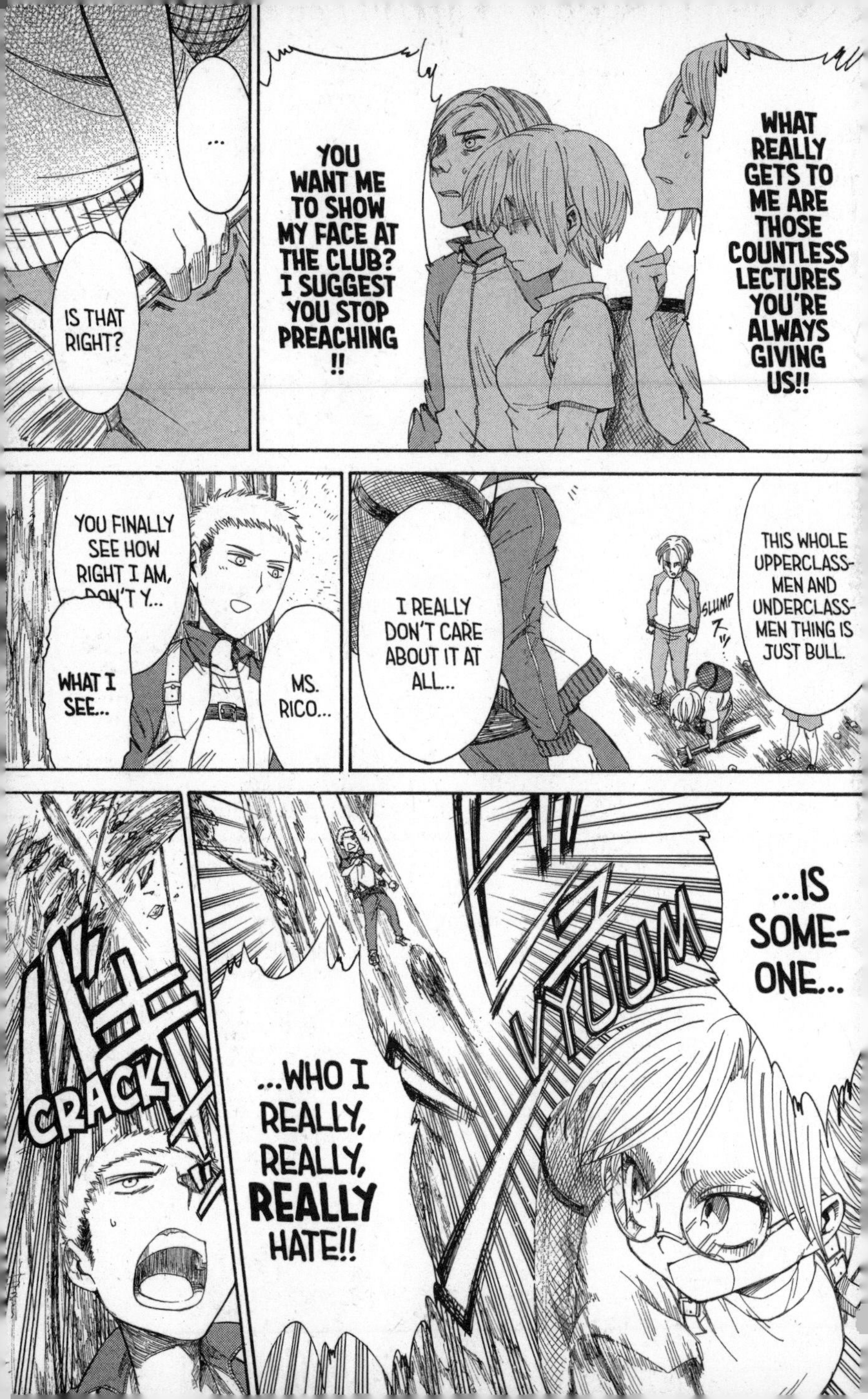
WHAT REALLY GETS TO ME ARE THOSE COUNTLESS LECTURES YOU'RE ALWAYS GIVING US!!
YOU WANT ME TO SHOW MY FACE AT THE CLUB? I SUGGEST YOU STOP PREACHING!!
...
IS THAT RIGHT?
THIS WHOLE UPPERCLASSMEN AND UNDERCLASSMEN THING IS JUST BULL.
SLUMP
I REALLY DON'T CARE ABOUT IT AT ALL...
MS. RICO...
YOU FINALLY SEE HOW RIGHT I AM, DON'T Y...
WHAT I SEE...
...IS SOME-ONE...
VYUUM
...WHO I REALLY, REALLY, REALLY HATE!!
CRACK

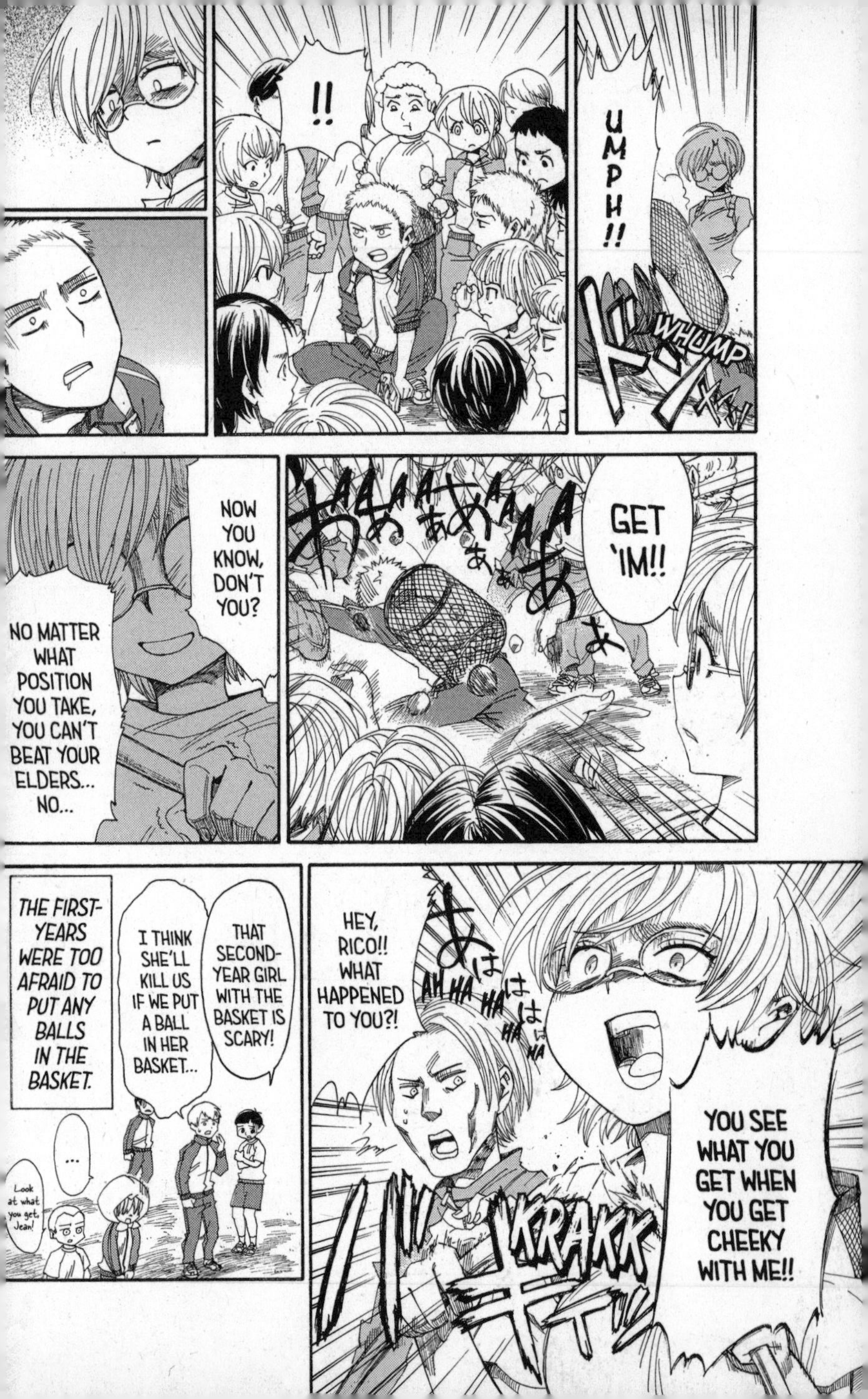
UMPH!!
WHUMP
!!
GET 'IM!!
AAAAAAAAA
NOW YOU KNOW, DON'T YOU?
NO MATTER WHAT POSITION YOU TAKE, YOU CAN'T BEAT YOUR ELDERS... NO...
HEY, RICO!! WHAT HAPPENED TO YOU?!
AH HA HA HA HA HA
YOU SEE WHAT YOU GET WHEN YOU GET CHEEKY WITH ME!!
KRAKK
THAT SECOND-YEAR GIRL WITH THE BASKET IS SCARY!
I THINK SHE'LL KILL US IF WE PUT A BALL IN HER BASKET...
...
Look at what you get, Jean!
THE FIRST-YEARS WERE TOO AFRAID TO PUT ANY BALLS IN THE BASKET.

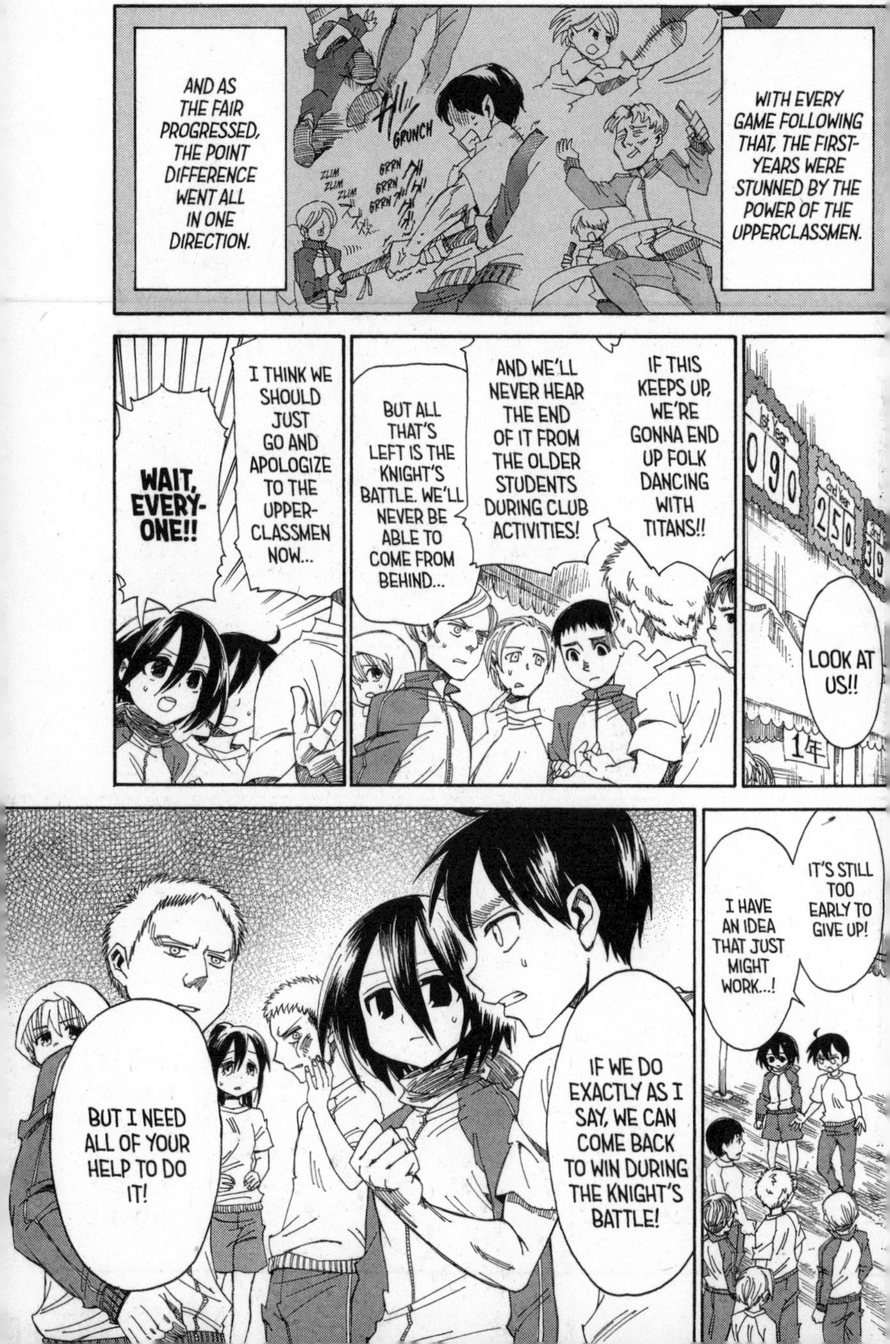
WITH EVERY GAME FOLLOWING THAT, THE FIRST-YEARS WERE STUNNED BY THE POWER OF THE UPPERCLASSMEN.
GRUNCH
GRRN GRRN GRRN
ZLIM ZLIM ZLIM
AND AS THE FAIR PROGRESSED, THE POINT DIFFERENCE WENT ALL IN ONE DIRECTION.
1st Year
0 9 0
2nd Year
2 5 0
LOOK AT US!!
1年
IF THIS KEEPS UP, WE'RE GONNA END UP FOLK DANCING WITH TITANS!!
AND WE'LL NEVER HEAR THE END OF IT FROM THE OLDER STUDENTS DURING CLUB ACTIVITIES!
BUT ALL THAT'S LEFT IS THE KNIGHT'S BATTLE. WE'LL NEVER BE ABLE TO COME FROM BEHIND...
I THINK WE SHOULD JUST GO AND APOLOGIZE TO THE UPPER-CLASSMEN NOW...
WAIT, EVERY-ONE!!
IT'S STILL TOO EARLY TO GIVE UP!
I HAVE AN IDEA THAT JUST MIGHT WORK...!
IF WE DO EXACTLY AS I SAY, WE CAN COME BACK TO WIN DURING THE KNIGHT'S BATTLE!
BUT I NEED ALL OF YOUR HELP TO DO IT!

IT CONTINUES
BONUS MANGA

WANDERING ANNIE

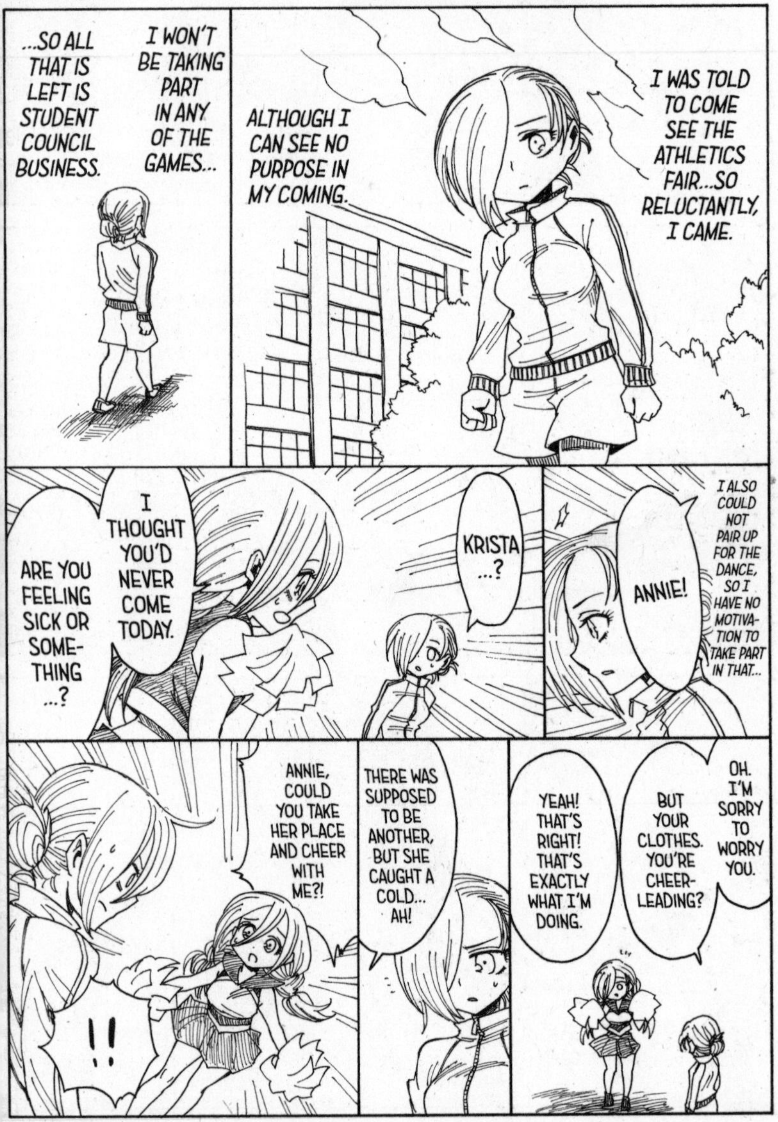
I WAS TOLD TO COME SEE THE ATHLETICS FAIR...SO RELUCTANTLY, I CAME.
ALTHOUGH I CAN SEE NO PURPOSE IN MY COMING.
I WON'T BE TAKING PART IN ANY OF THE GAMES...
...SO ALL THAT IS LEFT IS STUDENT COUNCIL BUSINESS.
I ALSO COULD NOT PAIR UP FOR THE DANCE, SO I HAVE NO MOTIVATION TO TAKE PART IN THAT...
ANNIE!
KRISTA...?
I THOUGHT YOU'D NEVER COME TODAY.
ARE YOU FEELING SICK OR SOMETHING...?
OH. I'M SORRY TO WORRY YOU.
BUT YOUR CLOTHES. YOU'RE CHEERLEADING?
YEAH! THAT'S RIGHT! THAT'S EXACTLY WHAT I'M DOING.
THERE WAS SUPPOSED TO BE ANOTHER, BUT SHE CAUGHT A COLD... AH!
ANNIE, COULD YOU TAKE HER PLACE AND CHEER WITH ME?!
!!

TO BE CONTINUED...

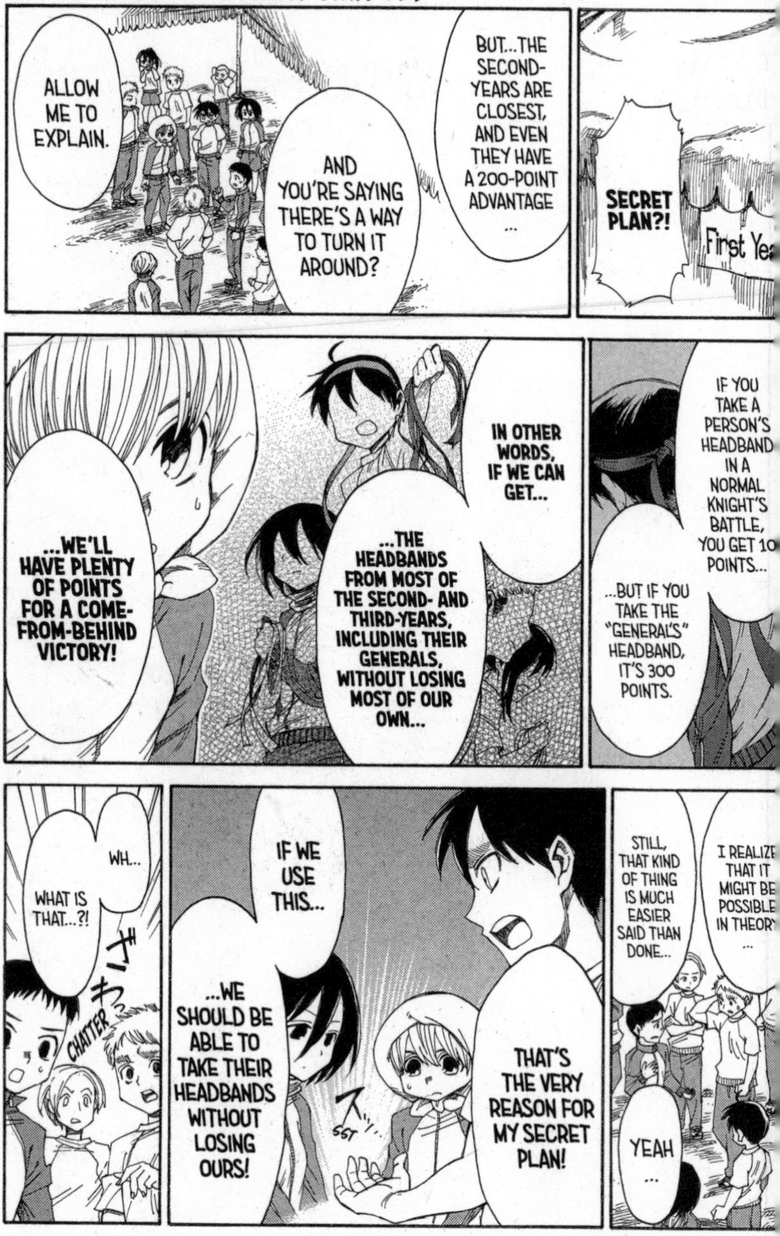
SECRET PLAN?!
First Ye
BUT...THE SECOND-YEARS ARE CLOSEST, AND EVEN THEY HAVE A 200-POINT ADVANTAGE...
AND YOU'RE SAYING THERE'S A WAY TO TURN IT AROUND?
ALLOW ME TO EXPLAIN.
IF YOU TAKE A PERSON'S HEADBAND IN A NORMAL KNIGHT'S BATTLE, YOU GET 10 POINTS...
...BUT IF YOU TAKE THE "GENERAL'S" HEADBAND, IT'S 300 POINTS.
IN OTHER WORDS, IF WE CAN GET...
...THE HEADBANDS FROM MOST OF THE SECOND- AND THIRD-YEARS, INCLUDING THEIR GENERALS, WITHOUT LOSING MOST OF OUR OWN...
...WE'LL HAVE PLENTY OF POINTS FOR A COME-FROM-BEHIND VICTORY!
I REALIZE THAT IT MIGHT BE POSSIBLE IN THEORY...
STILL, THAT KIND OF THING IS MUCH EASIER SAID THAN DONE...
YEAH...
THAT'S THE VERY REASON FOR MY SECRET PLAN!
SST
IF WE USE THIS...
...WE SHOULD BE ABLE TO TAKE THEIR HEADBANDS WITHOUT LOSING OURS!
WH...
WHAT IS THAT...?!
CHATTER

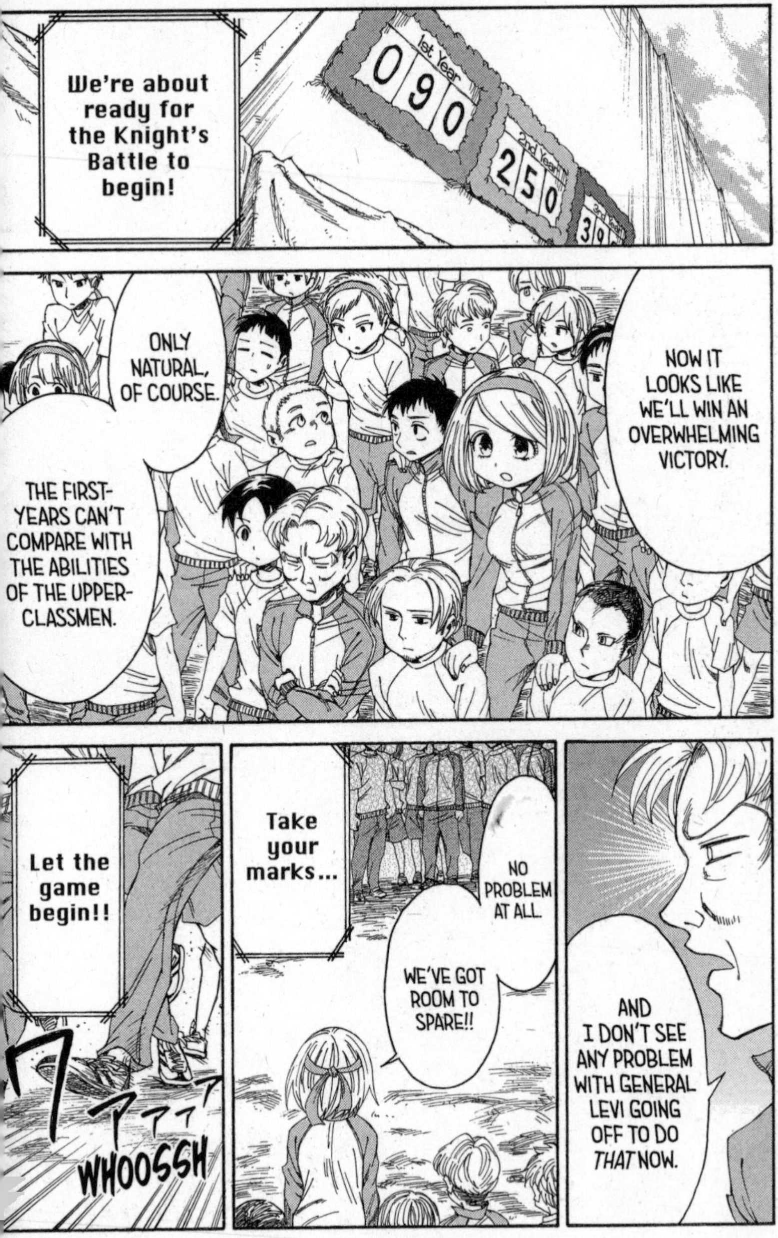
We're about ready for the Knight's Battle to begin!
1st Year
090
2nd Year
250
NOW IT LOOKS LIKE WE'LL WIN AN OVERWHELMING VICTORY.
ONLY NATURAL, OF COURSE.
THE FIRST-YEARS CAN'T COMPARE WITH THE ABILITIES OF THE UPPER-CLASSMEN.
AND I DON'T SEE ANY PROBLEM WITH GENERAL LEVI GOING OFF TO DO *THAT* NOW.
NO PROBLEM AT ALL.
Take your marks...
WE'VE GOT ROOM TO SPARE!!
Let the game begin!!
ワアァァ
WHOOSSH

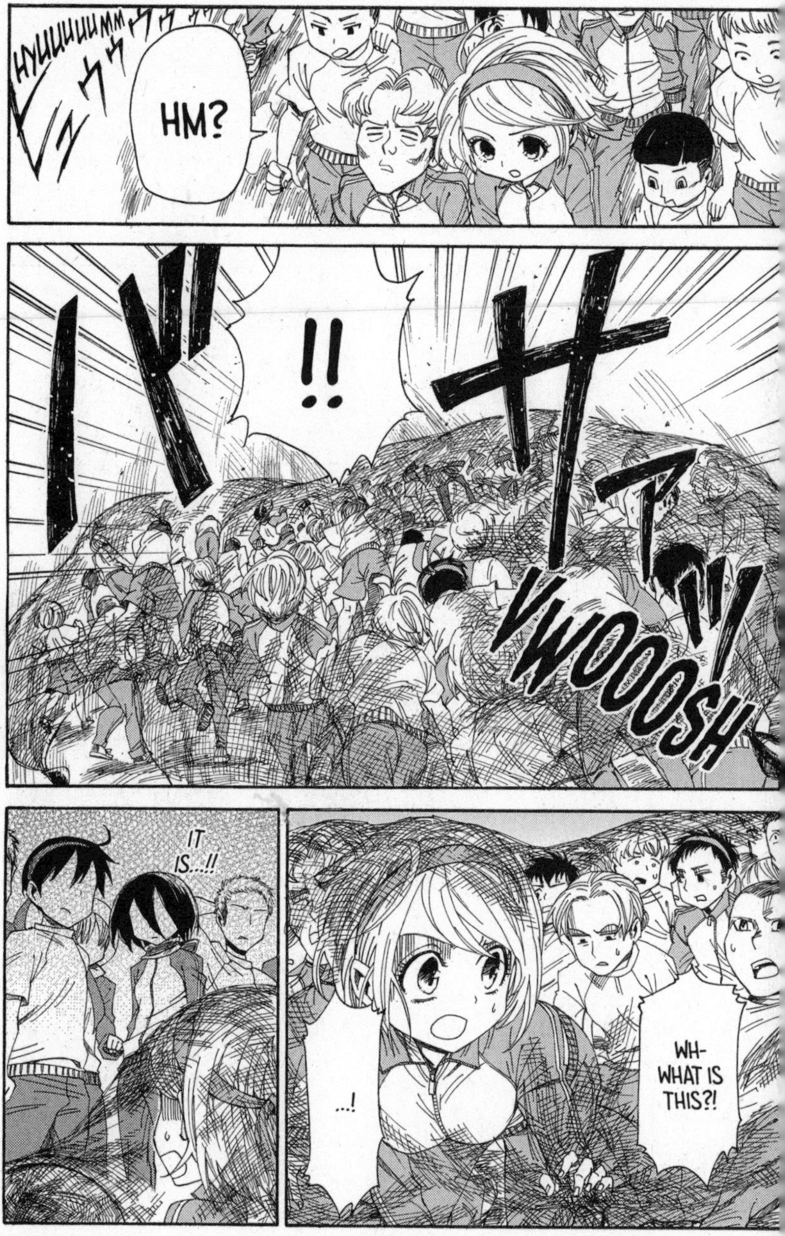
HYUUUUUMM
HM?
!!
VWOOOSH
WH- WHAT IS THIS?!
...!
IT IS...!!

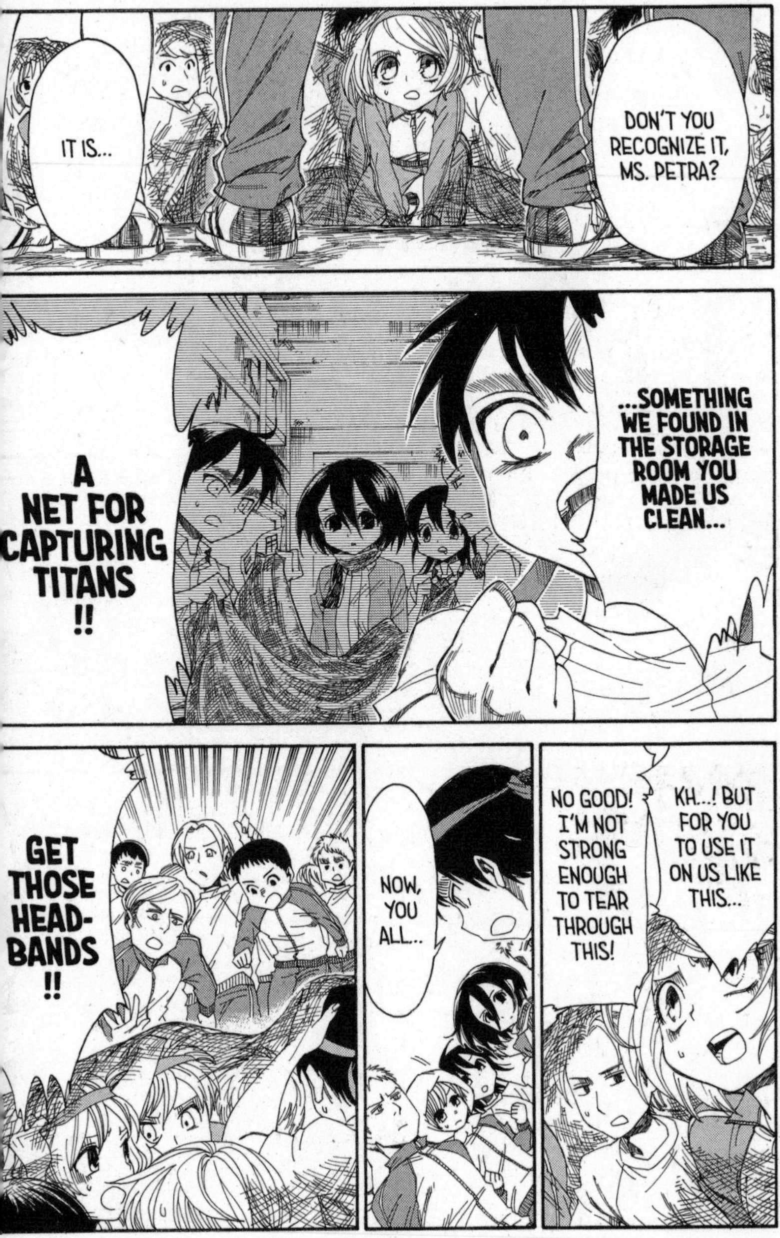
DON'T YOU RECOGNIZE IT, MS. PETRA?
IT IS...
...SOMETHING WE FOUND IN THE STORAGE ROOM YOU MADE US CLEAN...
A NET FOR CAPTURING TITANS !!
KH...! BUT FOR YOU TO USE IT ON US LIKE THIS...
NO GOOD! I'M NOT STRONG ENOUGH TO TEAR THROUGH THIS!
NOW, YOU ALL...
GET THOSE HEAD-BANDS !!

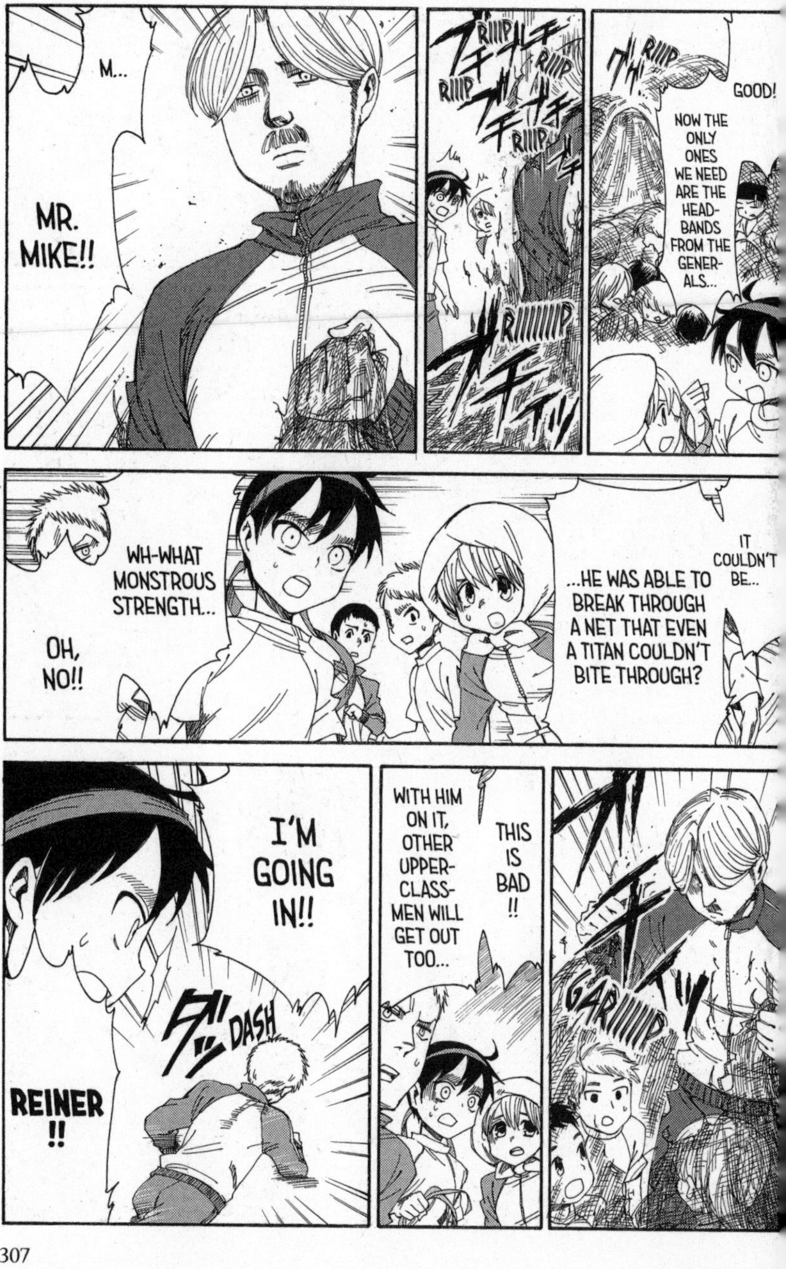
RIIIP
GOOD!
NOW THE ONLY ONES WE NEED ARE THE HEAD-BANDS FROM THE GENER-ALS...
RIIIP
RIIIP
RIIIP
RIIIP
RIIIIIIIP
M...
MR. MIKE!!
IT COULDN'T BE...
...HE WAS ABLE TO BREAK THROUGH A NET THAT EVEN A TITAN COULDN'T BITE THROUGH?
WH-WHAT MONSTROUS STRENGTH...
OH, NO!!
GARIIIIP
THIS IS BAD!!
WITH HIM ON IT, OTHER UPPER-CLASS-MEN WILL GET OUT TOO...
I'M GOING IN!!
DASH
REINER!!

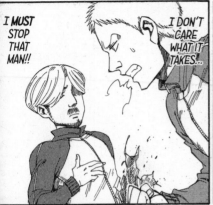

IF WE LOSE HERE, I WON'T BE ABLE TO DANCE WITH KRISTA!!
You mean I won't be able to dance with Reiner?
SHKK
I REFUSE TO BOW TO THAT FATE!!
I DON'T CARE WHAT IT TAKES...
I MUST STOP THAT MAN!!
...
COME AT ME!
HYAAAAAHH!!
DOOM
HE'S GOING FOR THE TACKLE!!
GO FOR IT, REINER!!
BOOM
BOOM
BOOM
BOOM
BOOM
BOOM
SLIP
BOOM
BOOM
BOOM
BOOM
BOOM
WHUMMMMPH
OHHHHHHHH

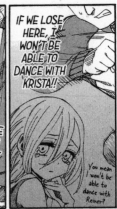

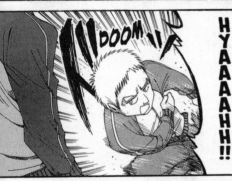

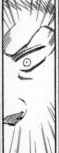

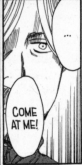

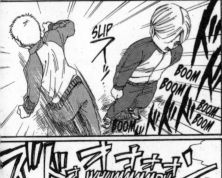

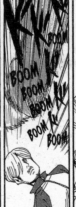

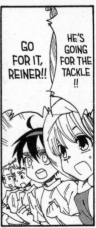

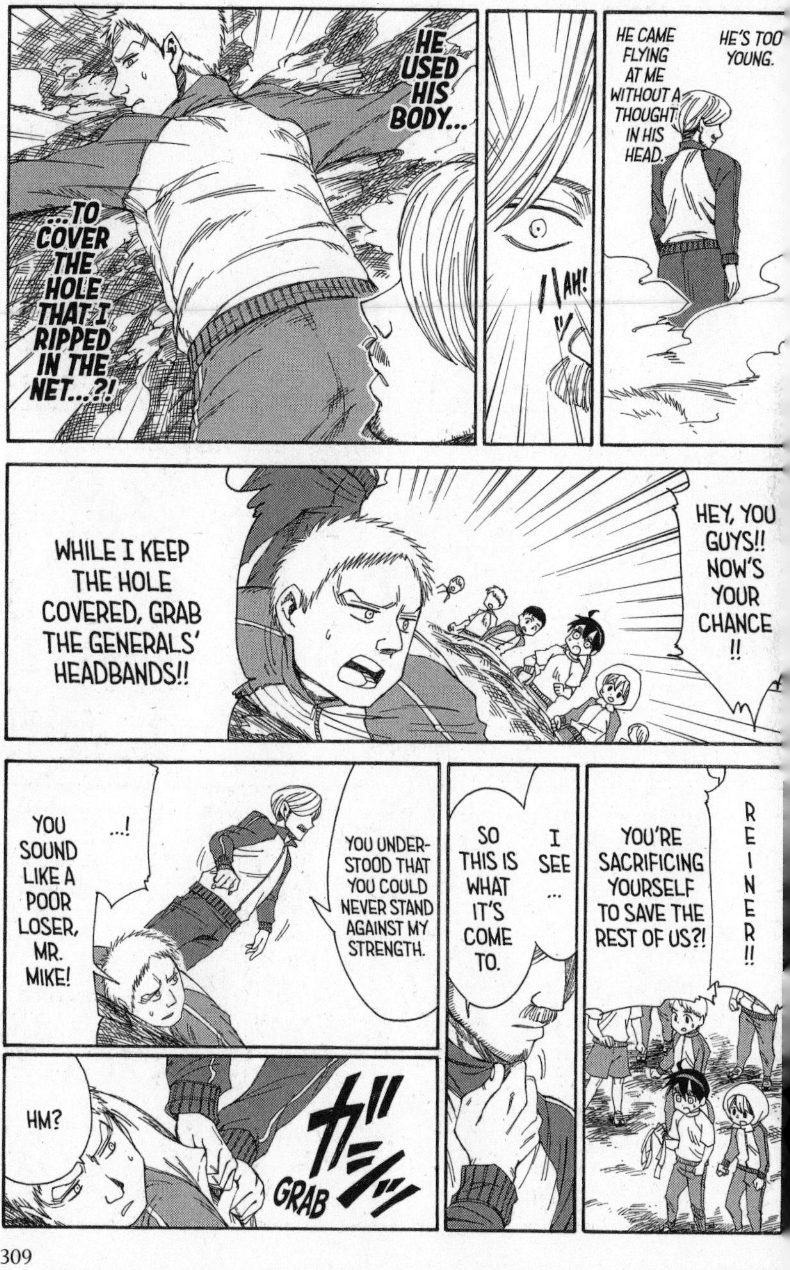
HE'S TOO YOUNG.
HE CAME FLYING AT ME WITHOUT A THOUGHT IN HIS HEAD.
AH!
HE USED HIS BODY...
...TO COVER THE HOLE THAT I RIPPED IN THE NET...?!
HEY, YOU GUYS!! NOW'S YOUR CHANCE!!
WHILE I KEEP THE HOLE COVERED, GRAB THE GENERALS' HEADBANDS!!
REINER!!
YOU'RE SACRIFICING YOURSELF TO SAVE THE REST OF US?!
I SEE...
SO THIS IS WHAT IT'S COME TO.
YOU UNDERSTOOD THAT YOU COULD NEVER STAND AGAINST MY STRENGTH.
...!
YOU SOUND LIKE A POOR LOSER, MR. MIKE!
ガシッ
GRAB
HM?

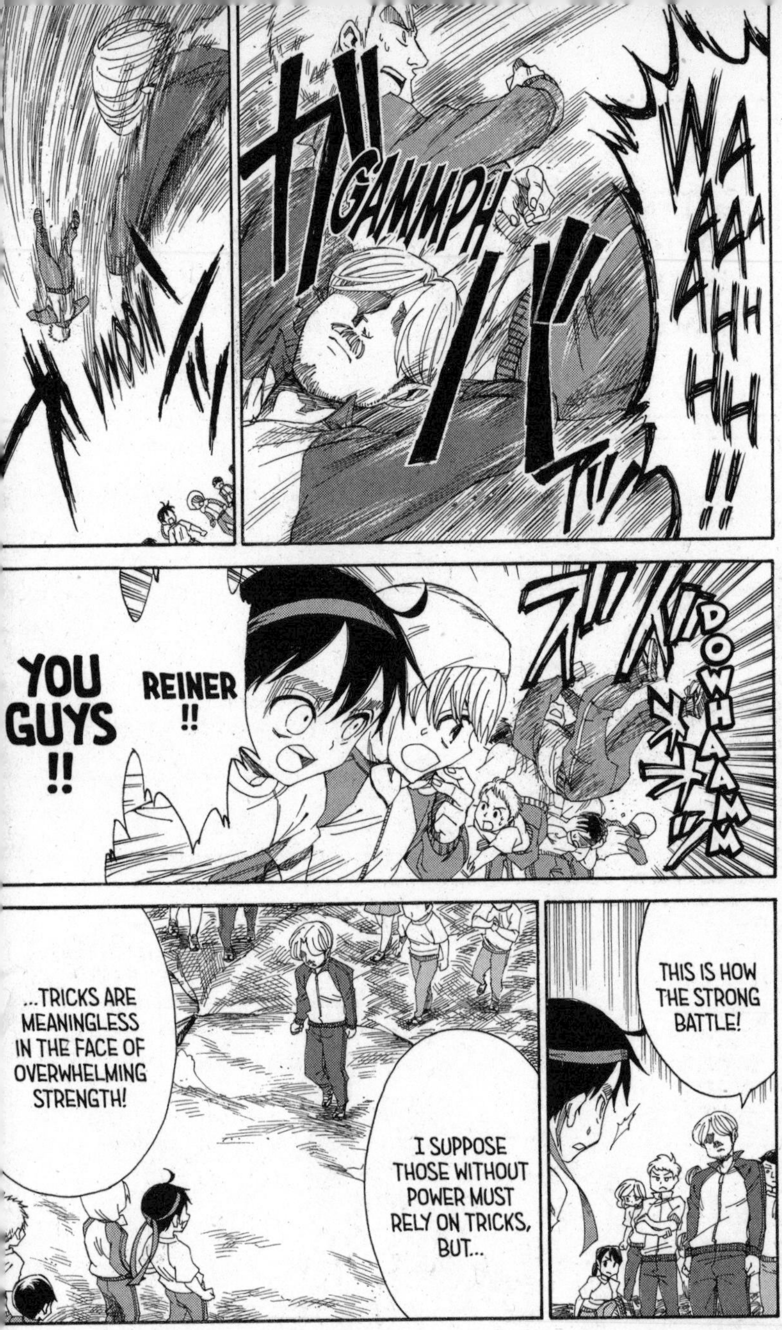
GAMMPH
WAAAAAHHHHH!!
WOOM
DOWHAAMM
REINER!!
YOU GUYS!!
THIS IS HOW THE STRONG BATTLE!
I SUPPOSE THOSE WITHOUT POWER MUST RELY ON TRICKS, BUT...
...TRICKS ARE MEANINGLESS IN THE FACE OF OVERWHELMING STRENGTH!

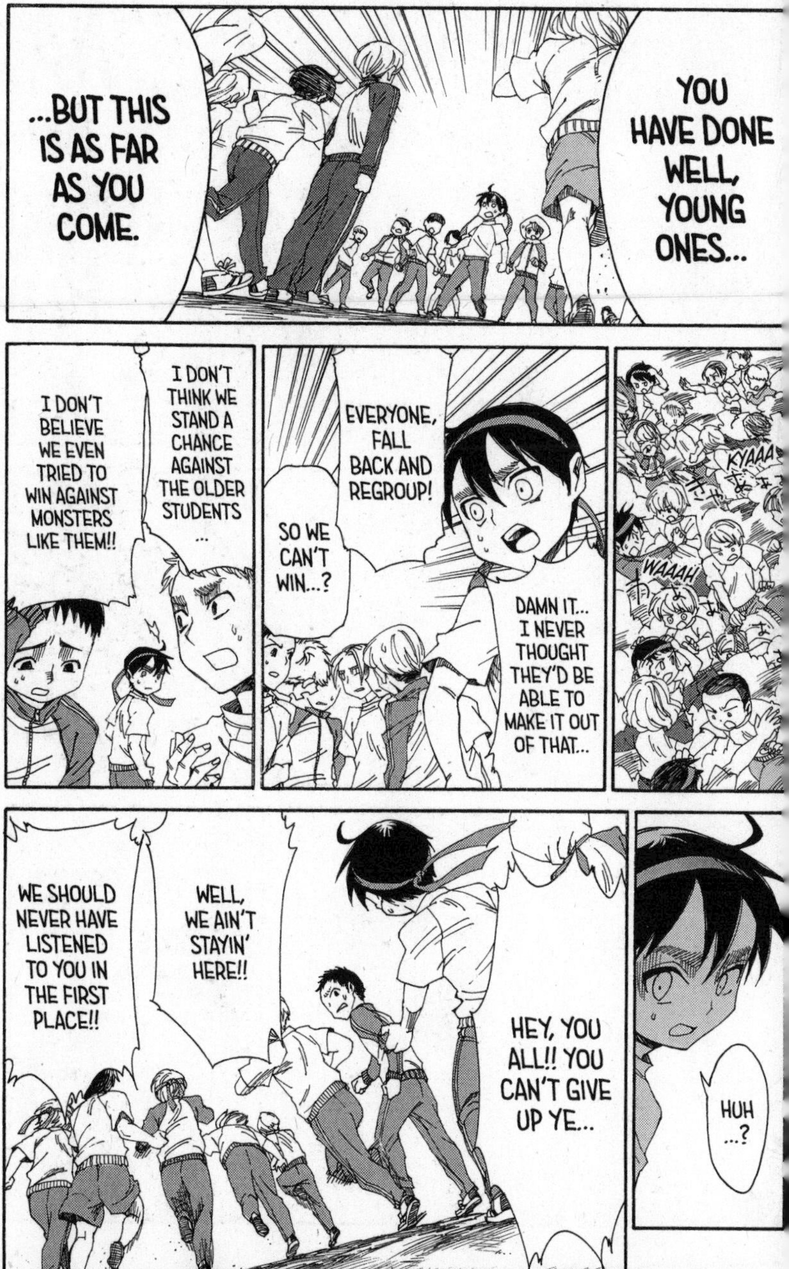
YOU HAVE DONE WELL, YOUNG ONES...
...BUT THIS IS AS FAR AS YOU COME.
KYAAA
WAAAH
EVERYONE, FALL BACK AND REGROUP!
DAMN IT... I NEVER THOUGHT THEY'D BE ABLE TO MAKE IT OUT OF THAT...
SO WE CAN'T WIN...?
I DON'T THINK WE STAND A CHANCE AGAINST THE OLDER STUDENTS ...
I DON'T BELIEVE WE EVEN TRIED TO WIN AGAINST MONSTERS LIKE THEM!!
HUH ...?
HEY, YOU ALL!! YOU CAN'T GIVE UP YE...
WELL, WE AIN'T STAYIN' HERE!!
WE SHOULD NEVER HAVE LISTENED TO YOU IN THE FIRST PLACE!!

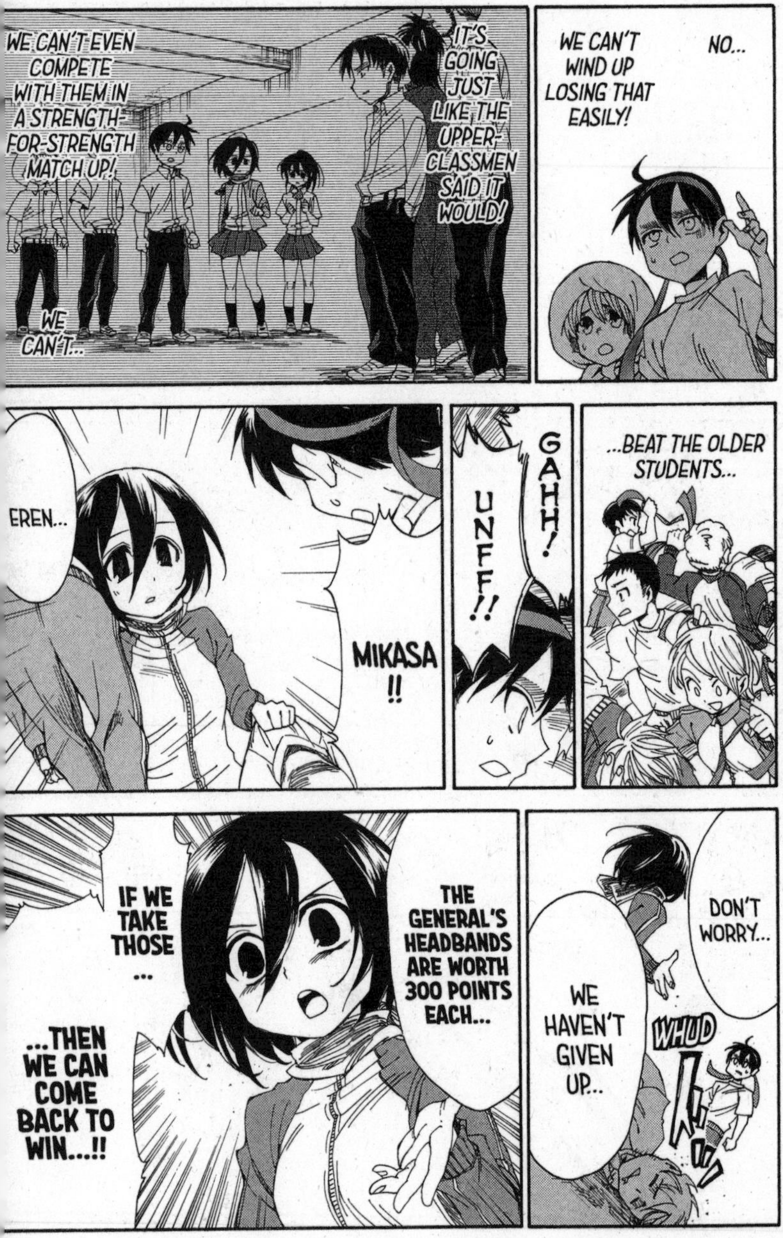
NO...
WE CAN'T WIND UP LOSING THAT EASILY!
IT'S GOING JUST LIKE THE UPPER-CLASSMEN SAID IT WOULD!
WE CAN'T EVEN COMPETE WITH THEM IN A STRENGTH-FOR-STRENGTH MATCH UP!
WE CAN'T...
...BEAT THE OLDER STUDENTS...
GAHH!
UNFF!!
MIKASA!!
EREN...
DON'T WORRY...
WE HAVEN'T GIVEN UP...
WHUD
THE GENERAL'S HEADBANDS ARE WORTH 300 POINTS EACH...
IF WE TAKE THOSE ...
...THEN WE CAN COME BACK TO WIN...!!

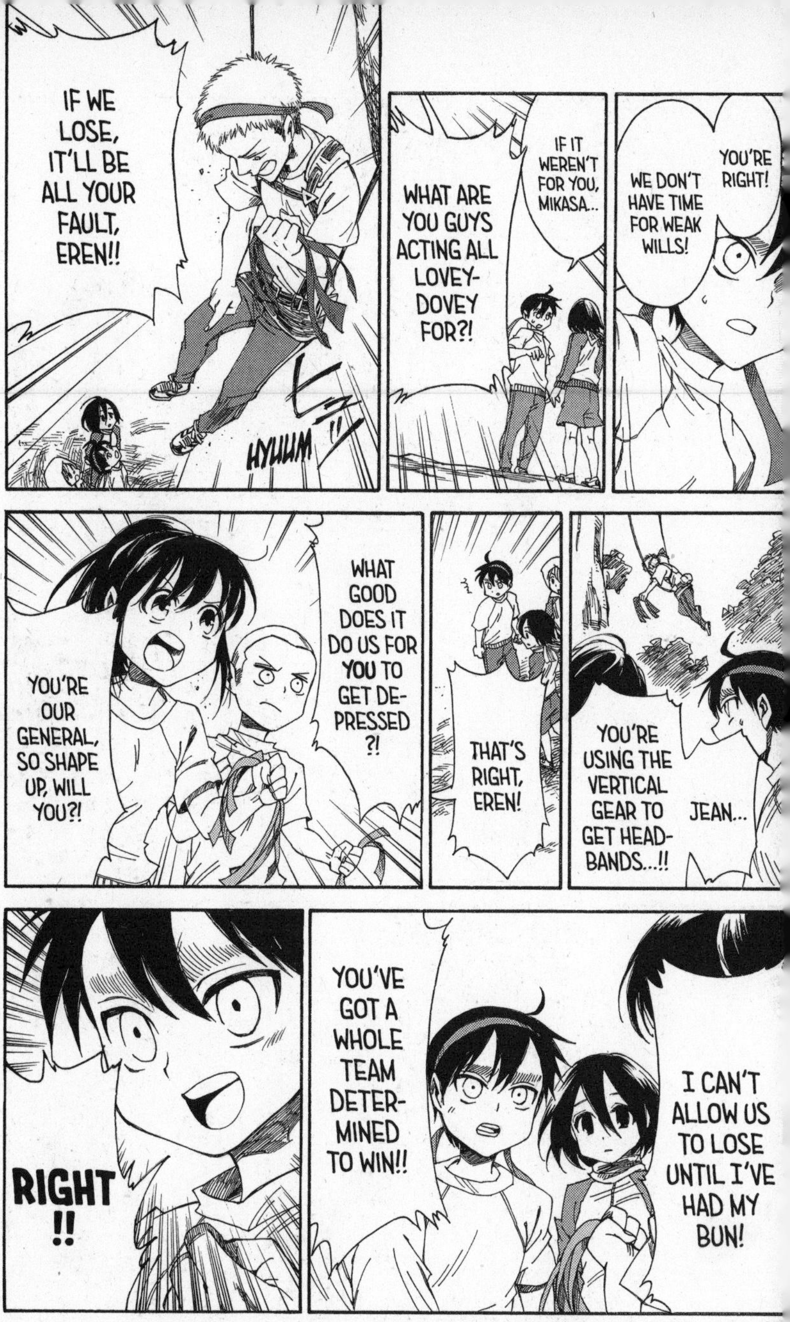
YOU'RE RIGHT!
WE DON'T HAVE TIME FOR WEAK WILLS!
IF IT WEREN'T FOR YOU, MIKASA...
WHAT ARE YOU GUYS ACTING ALL LOVEY-DOVEY FOR?!
IF WE LOSE, IT'LL BE ALL YOUR FAULT, EREN!!
HYUUM
JEAN...
YOU'RE USING THE VERTICAL GEAR TO GET HEAD-BANDS...!!
THAT'S RIGHT, EREN!
WHAT GOOD DOES IT DO US FOR YOU TO GET DE-PRESSED?!
YOU'RE OUR GENERAL, SO SHAPE UP, WILL YOU?!
I CAN'T ALLOW US TO LOSE UNTIL I'VE HAD MY BUN!
YOU'VE GOT A WHOLE TEAM DETER-MINED TO WIN!!
RIGHT!!

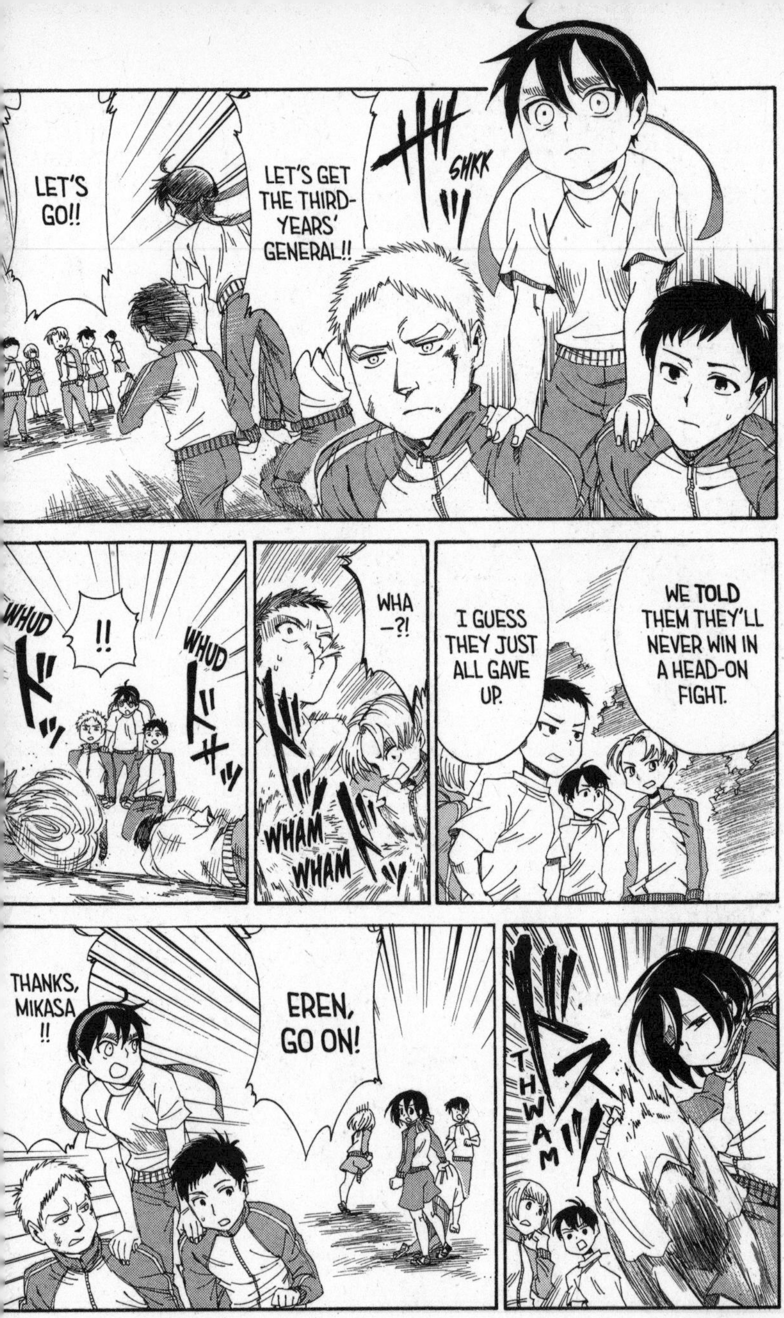
SHKK
LET'S GET THE THIRD-YEARS' GENERAL!!
LET'S GO!!
WE TOLD THEM THEY'LL NEVER WIN IN A HEAD-ON FIGHT.
I GUESS THEY JUST ALL GAVE UP.
WHA—?!
WHAM
WHAM
WHUD
!!
WHUD
THWAM
EREN, GO ON!
THANKS, MIKASA!!

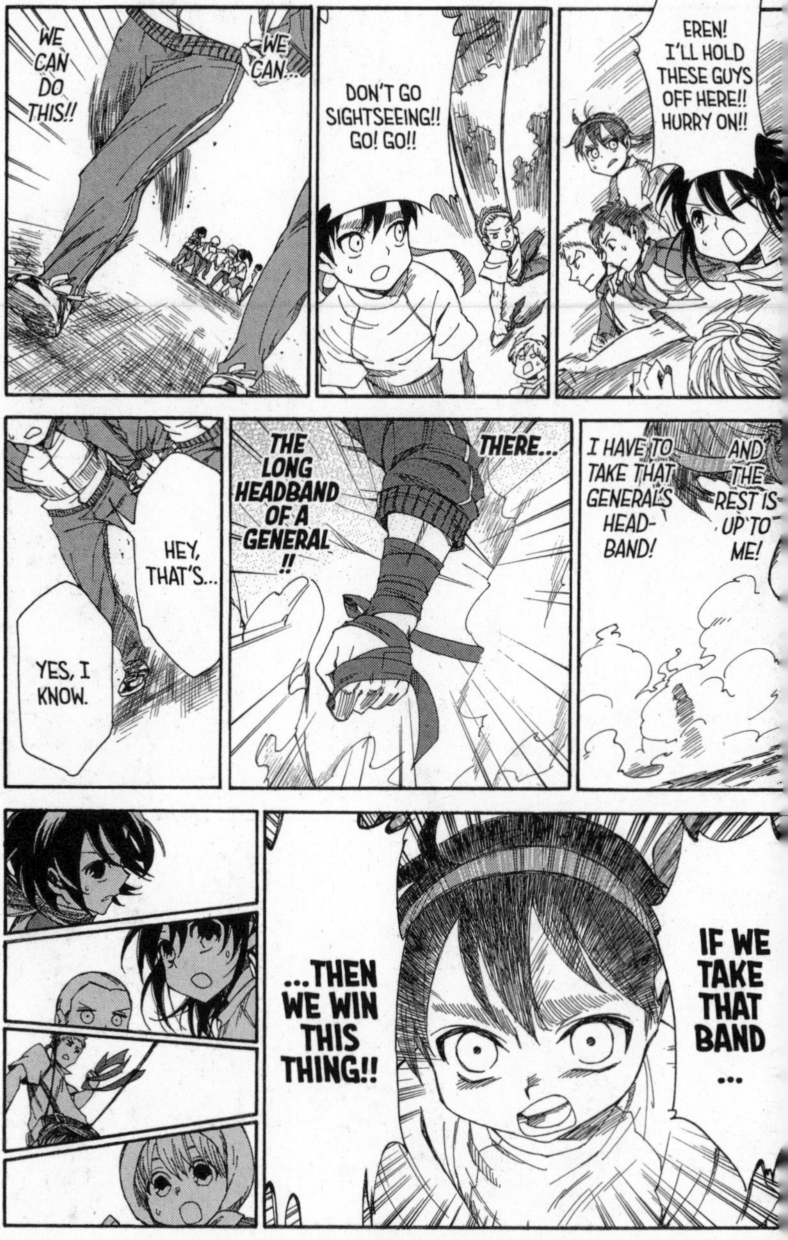
EREN! I'LL HOLD THESE GUYS OFF HERE!! HURRY ON!!
DON'T GO SIGHTSEEING!! GO! GO!!
WE CAN...
WE CAN DO THIS!!
AND THE REST IS UP TO ME!
I HAVE TO TAKE THAT GENERAL'S HEAD-BAND!
THERE...
THE LONG HEADBAND OF A GENERAL!!
HEY, THAT'S...
YES, I KNOW.
IF WE TAKE THAT BAND...
...THEN WE WIN THIS THING!!

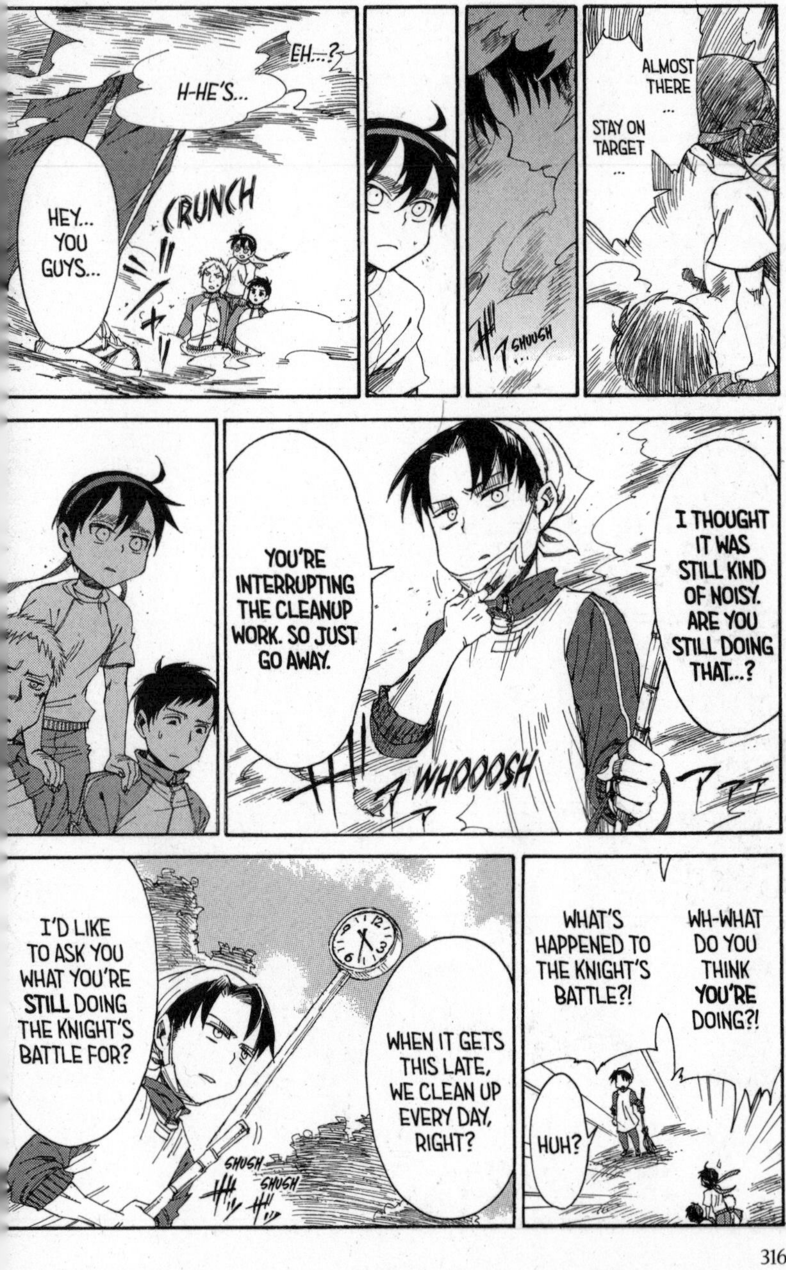
ALMOST THERE ...
STAY ON TARGET ...
SHUUSH ...
EH...?
H-HE'S...
CRUNCH
HEY... YOU GUYS...
I THOUGHT IT WAS STILL KIND OF NOISY. ARE YOU STILL DOING THAT...?
YOU'RE INTERRUPTING THE CLEANUP WORK. SO JUST GO AWAY.
WHOOOSH
WH-WHAT DO YOU THINK **YOU'RE** DOING?!
WHAT'S HAPPENED TO THE KNIGHT'S BATTLE?!
HUH?
WHEN IT GETS THIS LATE, WE CLEAN UP EVERY DAY, RIGHT?
I'D LIKE TO ASK YOU WHAT YOU'RE **STILL** DOING THE KNIGHT'S BATTLE FOR?
SHUSH
SHUSH

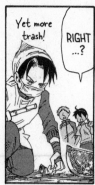

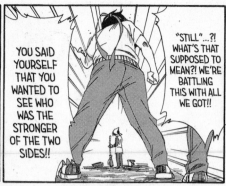

...
"STILL"...?! WHAT'S THAT SUPPOSED TO MEAN?! WE'RE BATTLING THIS WITH ALL WE GOT!!
YOU SAID YOURSELF THAT YOU WANTED TO SEE WHO WAS THE STRONGER OF THE TWO SIDES!!
RIGHT ...?
Yet more trash!
YOU'RE KIDDING ...
WELL, IF YOU DON'T FEEL LIKE FIGHTING, THEN...
...
ZWOOSH
ZWOOSH
...GO AHEAD AND CLEAN ALL YOU LIKE!!
WE'LL JUST TAKE THAT HEADBAND OFF YOUR HANDS!!
DASH
SHK
SHK
SHK
WELL, THAT WAS...
... THEN AND THIS ...
THAT IS MIIIIINE !!
GRAB
!!

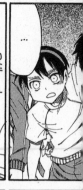

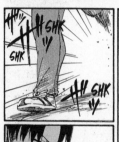

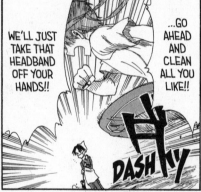

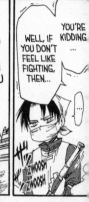

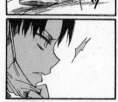

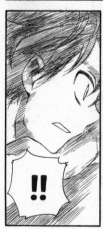

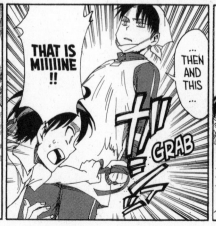

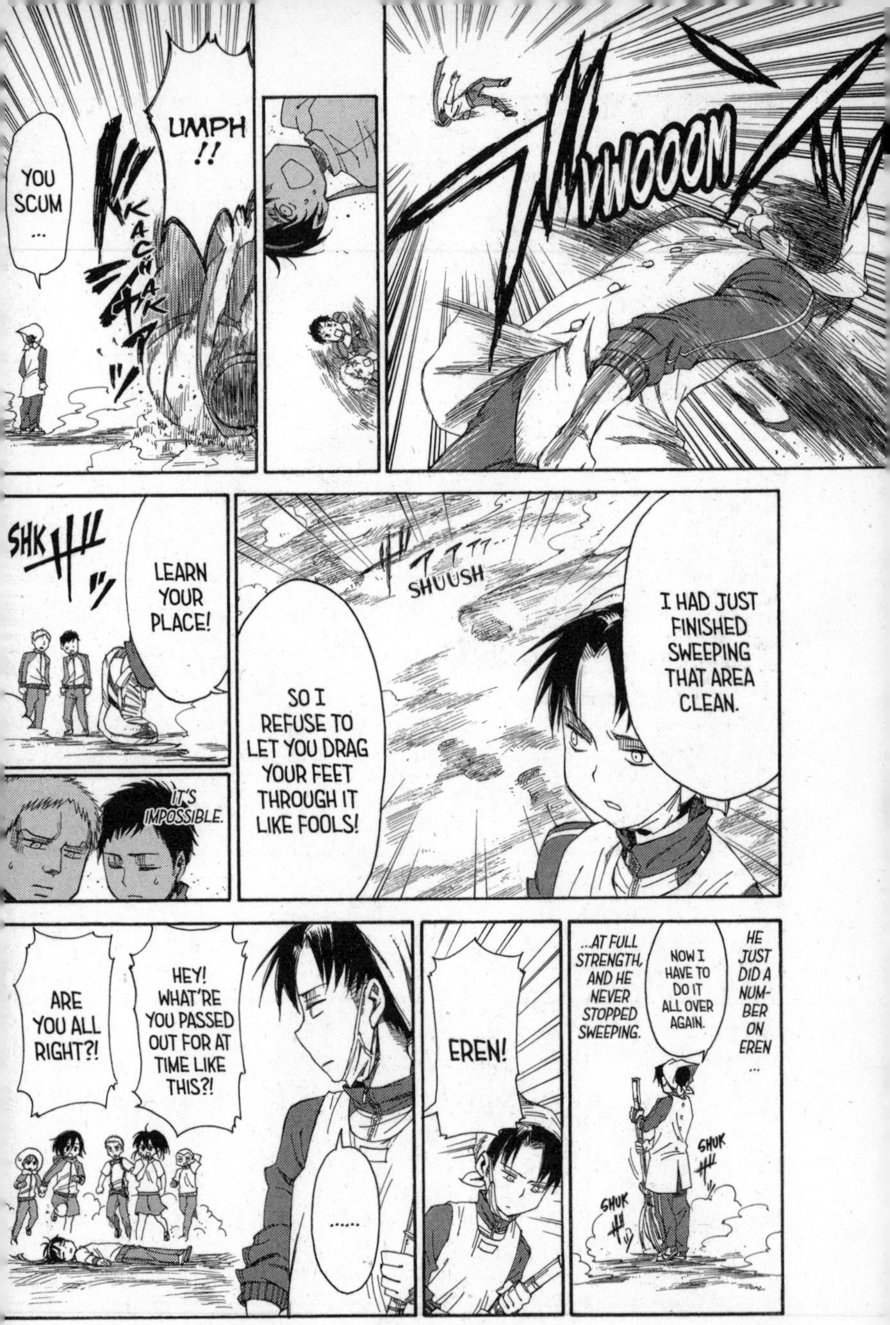
VWOOOM
UMPH !!
KACHAK
YOU SCUM ...
SHUUSH
I HAD JUST FINISHED SWEEPING THAT AREA CLEAN.
SO I REFUSE TO LET YOU DRAG YOUR FEET THROUGH IT LIKE FOOLS!
LEARN YOUR PLACE!
SHK
IT'S IMPOSSIBLE.
HE JUST DID A NUMBER ON EREN ...
NOW I HAVE TO DO IT ALL OVER AGAIN.
...AT FULL STRENGTH, AND HE NEVER STOPPED SWEEPING.
SHUK
SHUK
EREN!
......
HEY! WHAT'RE YOU PASSED OUT FOR AT TIME LIKE THIS?!
ARE YOU ALL RIGHT?!

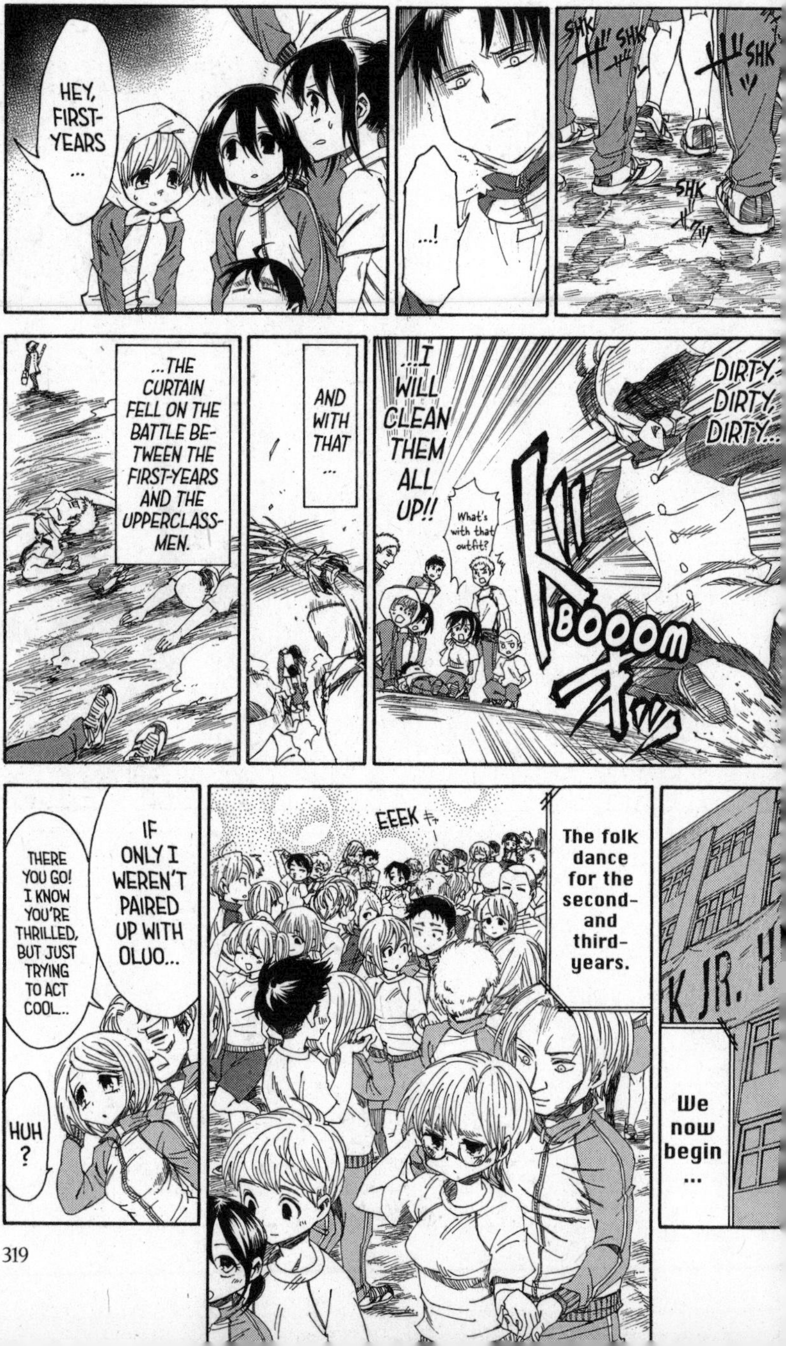
SHK SHK
SHK
SHK
...!
HEY, FIRST-YEARS ...
DIRTY, DIRTY, DIRTY...
BOOOM
...I WILL CLEAN THEM ALL UP!!
What's with that outfit?
AND WITH THAT ...
...THE CURTAIN FELL ON THE BATTLE BETWEEN THE FIRST-YEARS AND THE UPPERCLASSMEN.
K JR. H
We now begin ...
The folk dance for the second- and third-years.
EEEK
IF ONLY I WEREN'T PAIRED UP WITH OLUO...
THERE YOU GO! I KNOW YOU'RE THRILLED, BUT JUST TRYING TO ACT COOL...
HUH ?

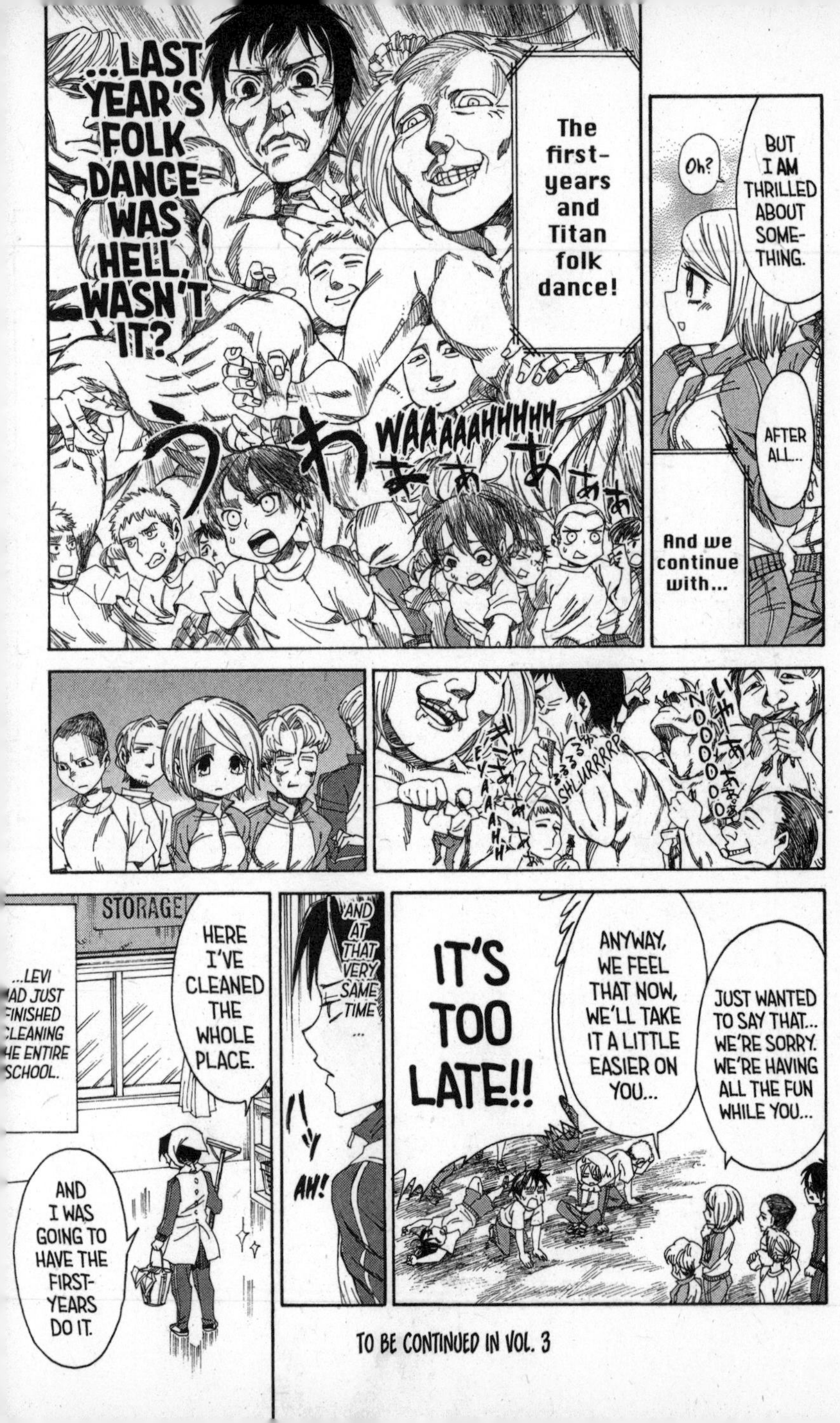
Oh?
BUT I AM THRILLED ABOUT SOME-THING.
AFTER ALL...
And we continue with...
The first-years and Titan folk dance!
...LAST YEAR'S FOLK DANCE WAS HELL, WASN'T IT?
WAAAAAHHHHH
うわあああ
NOOOOOOOO
SHLURRRRP
EYAAAAHHH
JUST WANTED TO SAY THAT... WE'RE SORRY. WE'RE HAVING ALL THE FUN WHILE YOU...
ANYWAY, WE FEEL THAT NOW, WE'LL TAKE IT A LITTLE EASIER ON YOU...
IT'S TOO LATE!!
AND AT THAT VERY SAME TIME...
AH!
...LEVI AD JUST INISHED LEANING HE ENTIRE SCHOOL.
STORAGE
HERE I'VE CLEANED THE WHOLE PLACE.
AND I WAS GOING TO HAVE THE FIRST-YEARS DO IT.
TO BE CONTINUED IN VOL. 3

WANDERING ANNIE CONTINUED

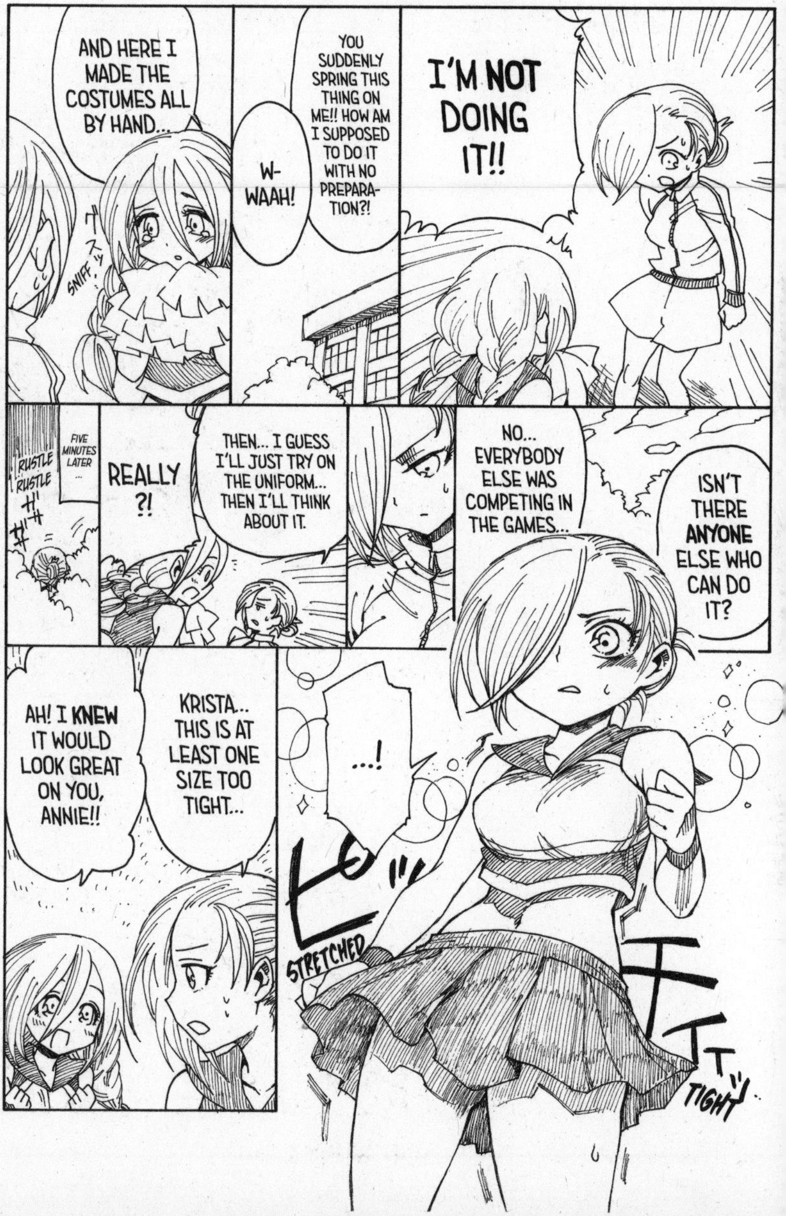
I'M NOT DOING IT!!
YOU SUDDENLY SPRING THIS THING ON ME!! HOW AM I SUPPOSED TO DO IT WITH NO PREPARATION?!
W-WAAH!
AND HERE I MADE THE COSTUMES ALL BY HAND...
SNIFF
ISN'T THERE ANYONE ELSE WHO CAN DO IT?
NO... EVERYBODY ELSE WAS COMPETING IN THE GAMES...
THEN... I GUESS I'LL JUST TRY ON THE UNIFORM... THEN I'LL THINK ABOUT IT.
REALLY?!
FIVE MINUTES LATER ...
RUSTLE RUSTLE
...!
STRETCHED
TIGHT
KRISTA... THIS IS AT LEAST ONE SIZE TOO TIGHT...
AH! I KNEW IT WOULD LOOK GREAT ON YOU, ANNIE!!

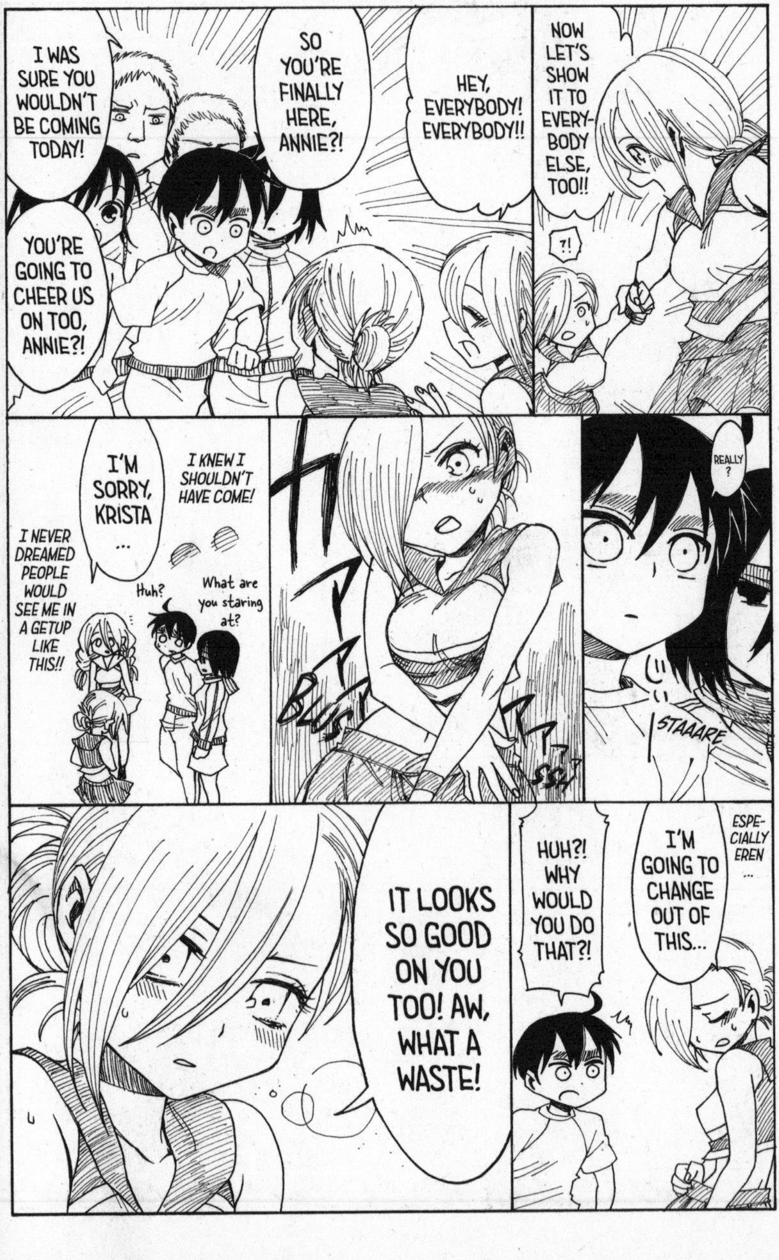
NOW LET'S SHOW IT TO EVERY-BODY ELSE, TOO!!
?!
HEY, EVERYBODY! EVERYBODY!!
SO YOU'RE FINALLY HERE, ANNIE?!
I WAS SURE YOU WOULDN'T BE COMING TODAY!
YOU'RE GOING TO CHEER US ON TOO, ANNIE?!
REALLY?
STAAARE
BLUSH
I KNEW I SHOULDN'T HAVE COME!
I'M SORRY, KRISTA ...
I NEVER DREAMED PEOPLE WOULD SEE ME IN A GETUP LIKE THIS!!
What are you staring at?
Huh?
ESPE-CIALLY EREN ...
I'M GOING TO CHANGE OUT OF THIS...
HUH?! WHY WOULD YOU DO THAT?!
IT LOOKS SO GOOD ON YOU TOO! AW, WHAT A WASTE!

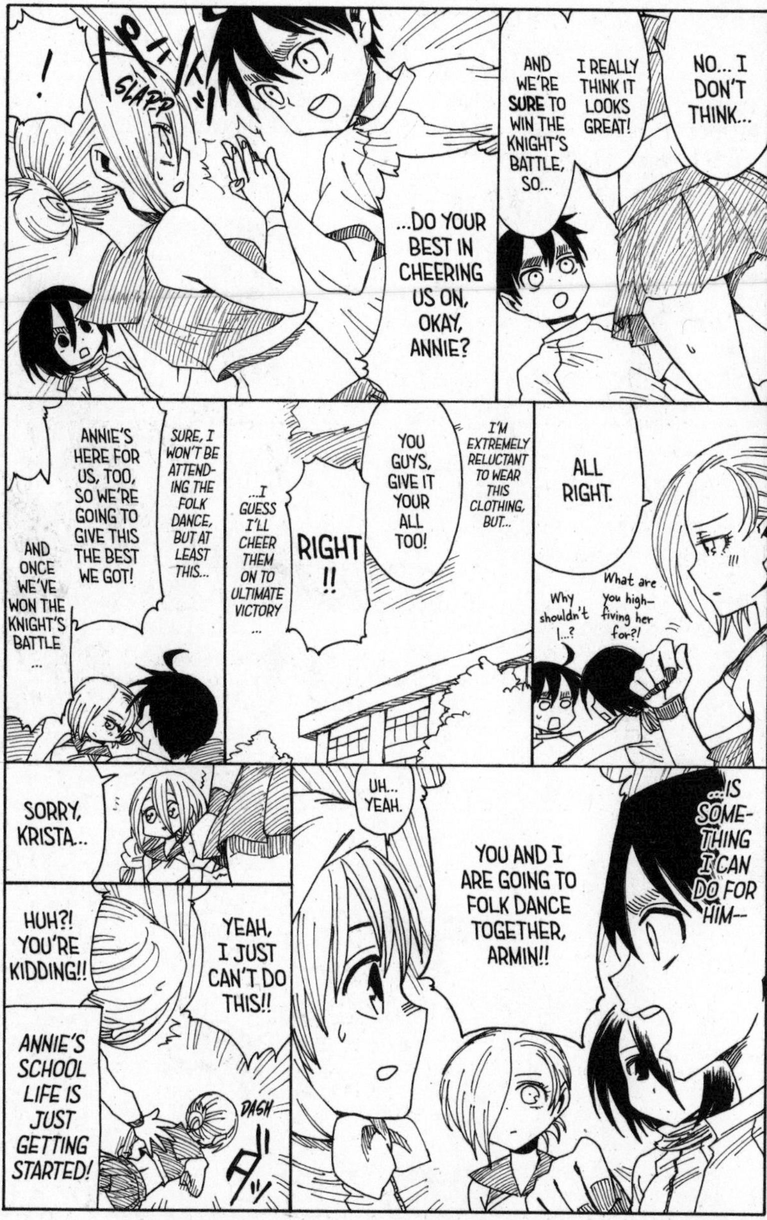
NO... I DON'T THINK...
I REALLY THINK IT LOOKS GREAT!
AND WE'RE **SURE** TO WIN THE KNIGHT'S BATTLE, SO...
...DO YOUR BEST IN CHEERING US ON, OKAY, ANNIE?
!
SLAPP
ALL RIGHT.
What are you high-fiving her for?!
Why shouldn't I...?
I'M EXTREMELY RELUCTANT TO WEAR THIS CLOTHING, BUT...
YOU GUYS, GIVE IT YOUR ALL TOO!
RIGHT!!
...I GUESS I'LL CHEER THEM ON TO ULTIMATE VICTORY...
SURE, I WON'T BE ATTENDING THE FOLK DANCE, BUT AT LEAST THIS...
ANNIE'S HERE FOR US, TOO, SO WE'RE GOING TO GIVE THIS THE BEST WE GOT!
AND ONCE WE'VE WON THE KNIGHT'S BATTLE...
...IS SOMETHING I CAN DO FOR HIM--
YOU AND I ARE GOING TO FOLK DANCE TOGETHER, ARMIN!!
UH... YEAH.
SORRY, KRISTA...
YEAH, I JUST CAN'T DO THIS!!
HUH?! YOU'RE KIDDING!!
ANNIE'S SCHOOL LIFE IS JUST GETTING STARTED!
DASH

Translation Notes:

Japanese is a tricky language for most Westerners, and translation is often more art than science. For your edification and reading pleasure, here are notes on some of the places where we could have gone in a different direction with our translation of the work, or where a Japanese cultural reference is used.

Page 24, Cheese meatloaf

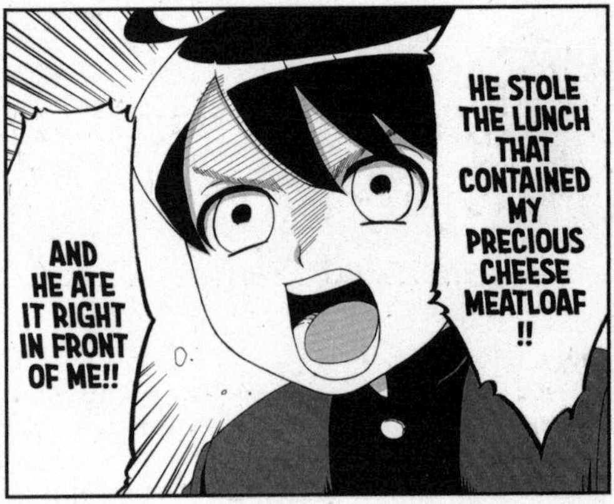
HE STOLE THE LUNCH THAT CONTAINED MY PRECIOUS CHEESE MEATLOAF !!
AND HE ATE IT RIGHT IN FRONT OF ME!!

The words Eren used in Japanese are "cheese hamburg" (the English words). In Japanese, *hamubaagu* (hamburg) is ground beef (usually, although other ground meats or tofu can be used) mixed with onions, spices and other flavorings, bread crumbs for volume, and in many cases other ingredients are added, also. Then they are shaped—usually in a patty shape, but not exclusively. This is rather similar to Western meatloaf. The cheese hamburg generally has cheese in a pocket in the center of the patty.

Page 30, New Year's cards

The New Year's cards *(nengajou)* are a huge tradition in Japan. About three or four weeks prior to the new year, most Japanese people buy a particular type of postcard, and send them to nearly everyone they know to arrive on New Year's Day. Like Jean, people tend to measure their popularity by how many New Year's cards they receive each year. Twelve would not be considered a very large number.

Page 55, Back attackers (Japanese dodgeball)

There are a few rules to Japanese dodgeball that I never encountered when playing dodgeball in the West. The basics are the same. Catch a ball, and your opponent is out. If a ball hits you and is not caught before it hits the ground, you are out. But in Japanese dodgeball, once you are out, you go to the out-of-bounds area behind the opposing team's play area and hope that a ball can come to you. If it does, you can pick it up and throw it at an opposing player from behind. If you can get that opposing player out, you are allowed back onto the playing field yourself. The "out" members trying to get back into the game are called "back attackers."

Page 70, Yakisoba

Yakisoba is a Japanese fried noodle dish. The noodles are fried up in a brown sauce along with cabbage, carrots and other veggies; as well as pork, squid, and other kinds of meat. Yakisoba is a very popular dish at festivals, at beach food stands, and at other fun places. Although it is better eaten hot, Sasha did not really have to buy it just before the game. Yakisoba can be quickly fixed all throughout the event.

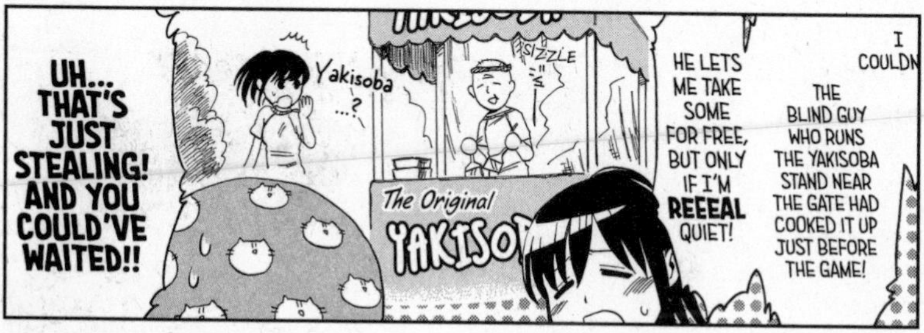
I COULDN
THE BLIND GUY WHO RUNS THE YAKISOBA STAND NEAR THE GATE HAD COOKED IT UP JUST BEFORE THE GAME!
HE LETS ME TAKE SOME FOR FREE, BUT ONLY IF I'M REEEAL QUIET!
SIZZLE
The Original
YAKISO
Yakisoba ...?
UH... THAT'S JUST STEALING! AND YOU COULD'VE WAITED!!

Page 81 Mozuku

Mozuku is a kind of viscous edible seaweed that probably was first introduced to Japan through the southern island of Okinawa, but is not popular all throughout Japan. It is considered a healthy food, especially for those with ulcers or tummy trouble, as it is thought to be very easy on the stomach.

Page 113, High school entrance exams

Entrance exams are found at all levels of the Japanese school system from preschool all the way through graduate schools. They are pass/fail exams that determine whether you have the knowledge and aptitude to enter the school. At the lower levels (up through junior high) they are rather rare, but at high school level, they are much more common, and they are present in just about every college. For many, their junior high is determined by where they live, but since one can get into any high school, competition for good high schools (with high educational standards that will lead to good colleges) is fierce, so many students spend their final year of junior high in intense study for the exam. Still, the group Eren and his friends see are first-year students who have a full three years before their exams. To see first-year students study so hard is unusual.

Page 139, Harisen

A harisen is a folded heavy paper (or in rare cases, metal) fan that was commonly used in the past for punishing indolent students, apprentices, disciples, new military recruits, servants, and other lower-level indoctrinates. The folded nature of the fan lessens the impact, so a hit by a harisen will not break any bones or do permanent injury, but a slap by one can still hurt.

Page 147 Nose election club

In Japanese, the "nose election" club is the *kitaku kurabu* or "go-home club." It's what people who can't be bothered with joining a school club call their "club" when asked. All it really means is to leave when school is out and not do any club activities. That's why Connie can't put it on his application.

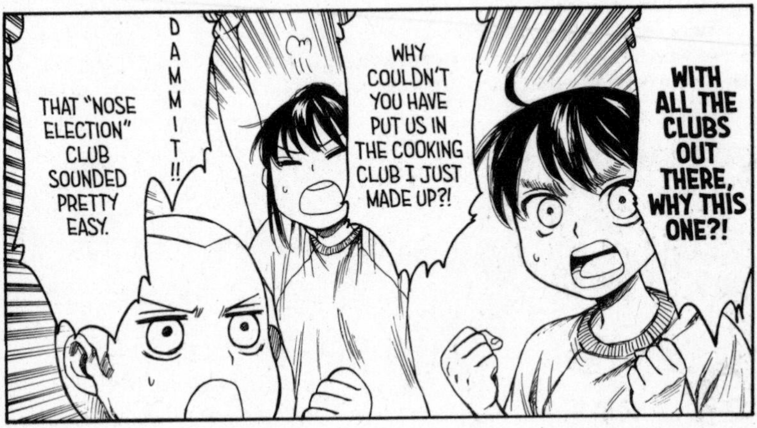
WITH ALL THE CLUBS OUT THERE, WHY THIS ONE?!
WHY COULDN'T YOU HAVE PUT US IN THE COOKING CLUB I JUST MADE UP?!
DAMMIT!!
THAT "NOSE ELECTION" CLUB SOUNDED PRETTY EASY.

Page 175, Win a free snack

Some snacks, most famously the popsicle-style snack, Garigari-kun, have a way of doing a kind of lottery with every snack you buy. In the case of Garigari-kun, the lottery aspect is found low on the popsicle stick covered by the edible part. If you "win," you can take it to a retailer for another snack of the same type for free.

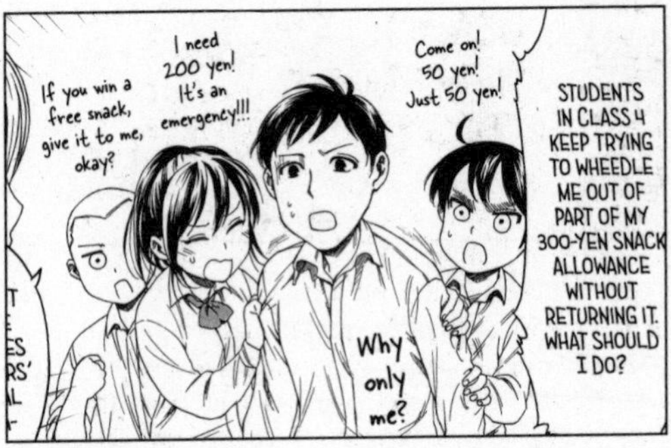
STUDENTS IN CLASS 4 KEEP TRYING TO WHEEDLE ME OUT OF PART OF MY 300-YEN SNACK ALLOWANCE WITHOUT RETURNING IT. WHAT SHOULD I DO?
Come on! 50 yen! Just 50 yen!
I need 200 yen! It's an emergency!!!
If you win a free snack, give it to me, okay?
Why only me?

Page 185, Helmet and harisen rock, paper, scissors

There is a variation on the rock, paper, scissors game called *Tataite Kabutte Jankenpon* (Hit and Cover Paper Scissors Rock) where the winner grabs an attack object (for example one of those soft plastic hammers that squeak) and tries to hit the loser over the head with it. At the same time, the loser grabs a helmet or some other head covering also on the table, and tries to cover his or her head before the attacker can hit him or her. If the loser can cover his or her head in time, the game is considered a "draw," and they start over, throwing paper, scissors, or rock. If the winner can hit the loser on the head before the loser can cover his or her head, then the winner wins the round. This helmet and harisen version is not normal.

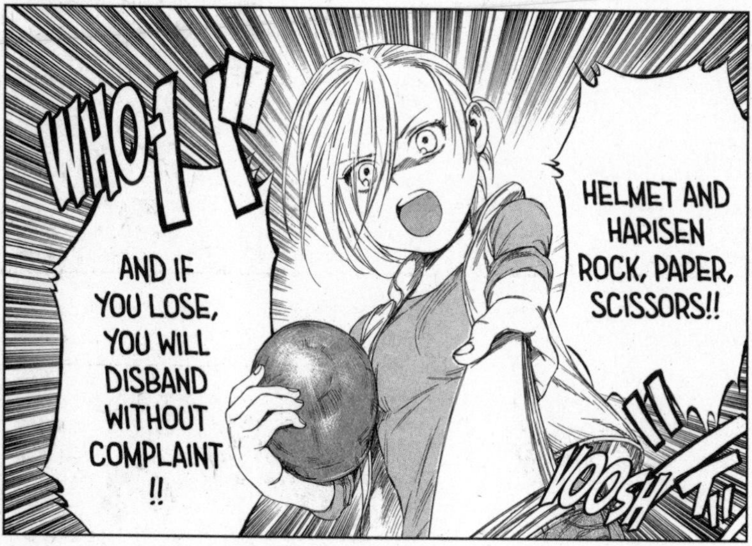
WHO-I-!!
HELMET AND HARISEN ROCK, PAPER, SCISSORS!!
AND IF YOU LOSE, YOU WILL DISBAND WITHOUT COMPLAINT !!
VOOSH!!

Page 203, Time to eat!

This is the standard phrase, *itadakimasu,* which is said before each meal (and in some cases, even snacks). It is a way of thanking God, the gods, or the fates (depending on one's religion) for the food.

Page 220, Bean buns

Anpan (sweet bean buns) are shaped like a jam-filled doughnut, but baked instead of fried, and instead of jam, they're filled with a paste made from red sweet beans. They are very popular, and anpan buns can be found in every bakery, grocery store, or convenience store in Japan.

Page 287, Bun-eating race

There are many different kinds of games that are held at athletics fairs throughout Japan every year. One of them is a bun-eating race *(pangui-kyôsô)* where in preparation, buns (or other self-contained foods) are strung from strings at just above mouth height. The contestants line up at a start line, then they race to grab the bun with their mouths (no hands allowed), and once they've secured the bun, they race to the goal. It is like an obstacle race but with a single obstacle.

Page 288, Melon bun

Melon-*pan* (melon bread) is only called that because the cuts made in the dough along the top make the final very large, round bun of sweetbread look like a melon. Some have cream (and a few even have melon-flavored cream), but most are just a large bun of sweetbread.

Page 301, Knight's Battle

The standard way a Knight's Battle is played is for each team to divide up into squads of four people. Three people link arms in a triangular formation in such a way as to create footholds for the fourth. The fourth stands where the three people's arms intersect and acts as the "rider" to the other three's "horse." The "rider" has a headband which other "knights" try to take. If one's headband is taken, one's 4-person team is out of the competition. The game normally continues until all knights of the opposing team (or teams) are eliminated.

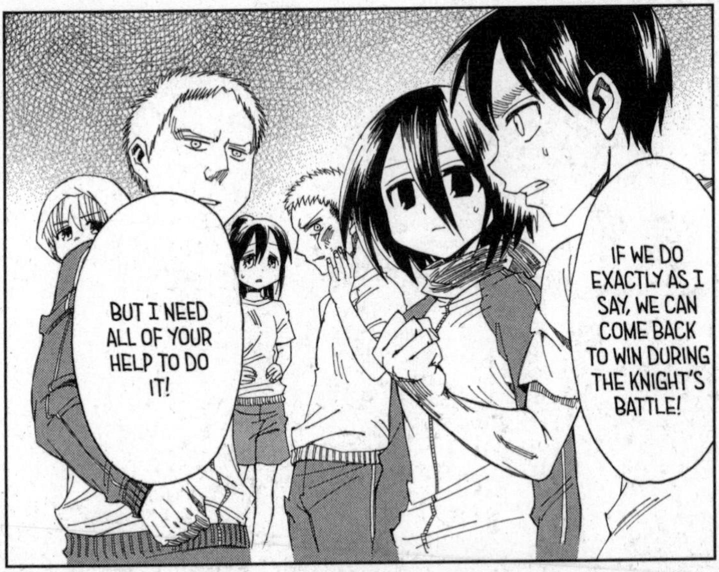
IF WE DO EXACTLY AS I SAY, WE CAN COME BACK TO WIN DURING THE KNIGHT'S BATTLE!
BUT I NEED ALL OF YOUR HELP TO DO IT!

WANT MORE TITAN?

The following pages contain a preview of "Attack on Titan: Before the Fall," a new manga spin-off set 70 years before "Attack on Titan," when the human race had no way to fight back against these gigantic monsters.

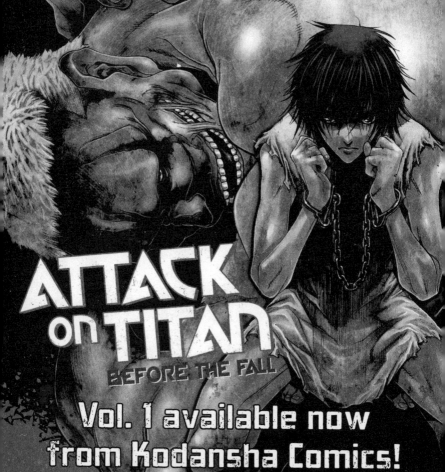

ATTACK on TITAN
BEFORE THE FALL

Vol. 1 available now from Kodansha Comics!

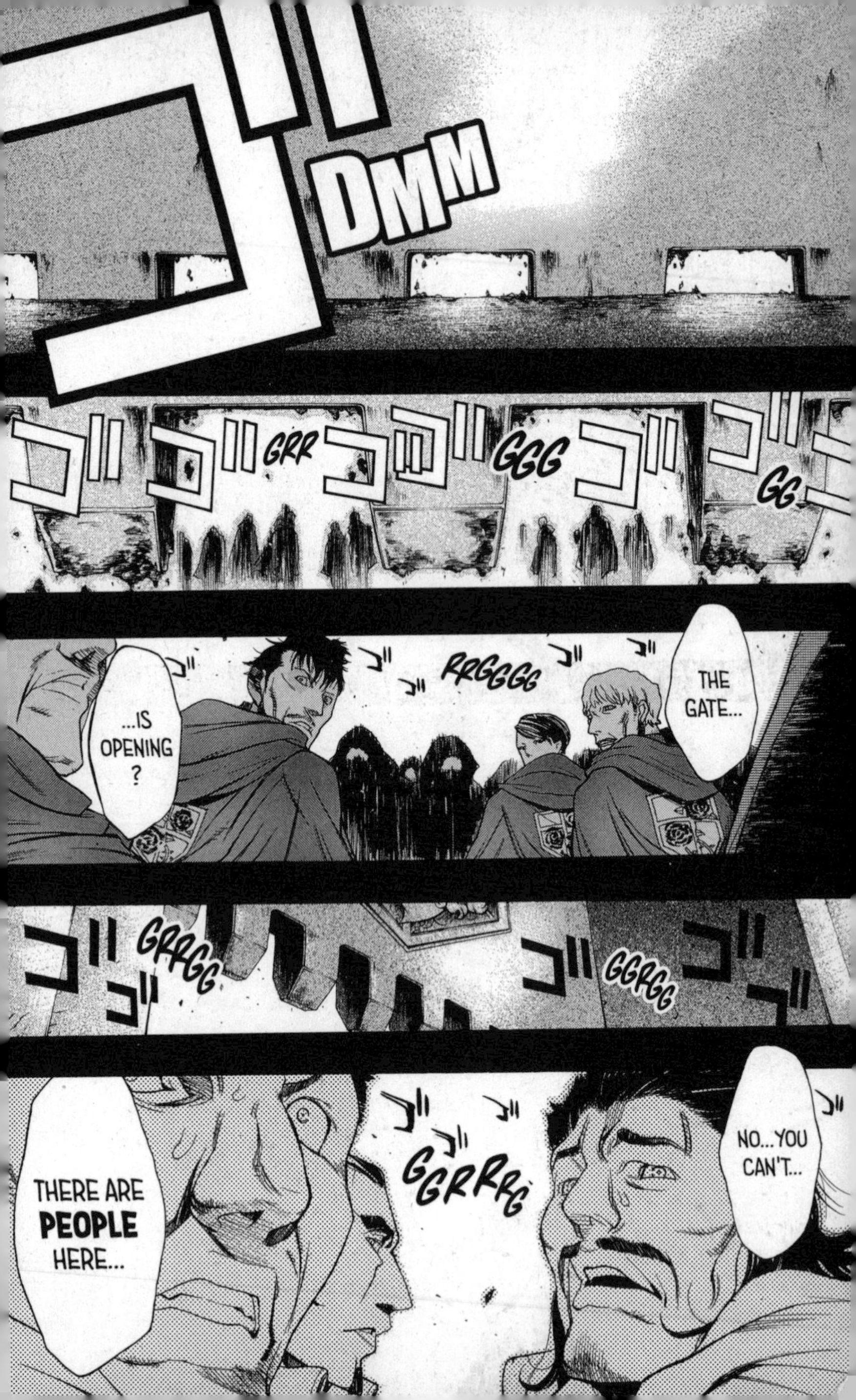
DMM
GG
GGG
GRR
THE GATE...
RRGGGG
...IS OPENING ?
GGRGG
GRRGG
NO...YOU CAN'T...
GGRRRG
THERE ARE **PEOPLE** HERE...

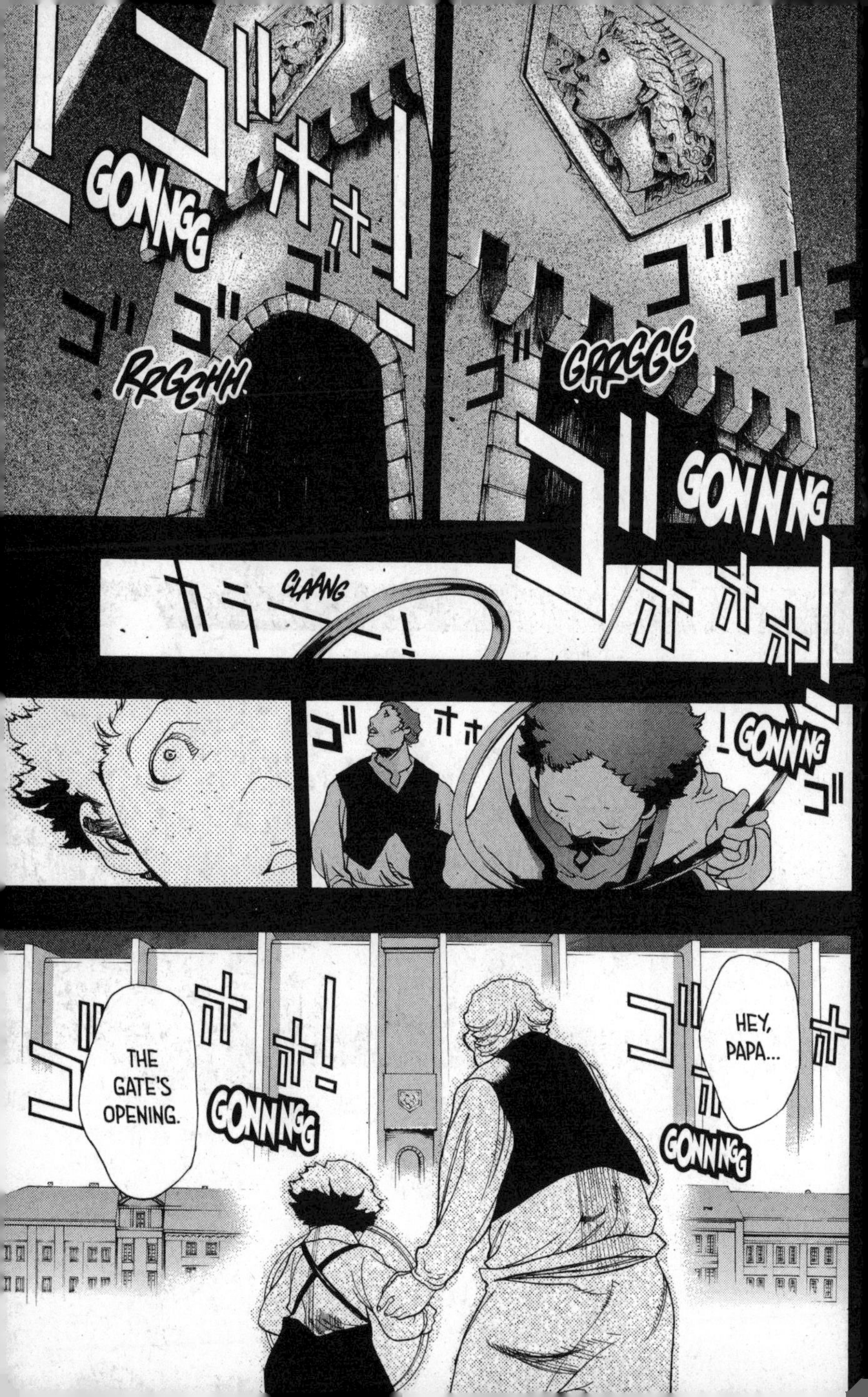
GRRGGG
GONNNG
GONNGG
RRGGHH
CLAANG
GONNNG
HEY, PAPA...
GONNNGG
THE GATE'S OPENING.
GONNNGG

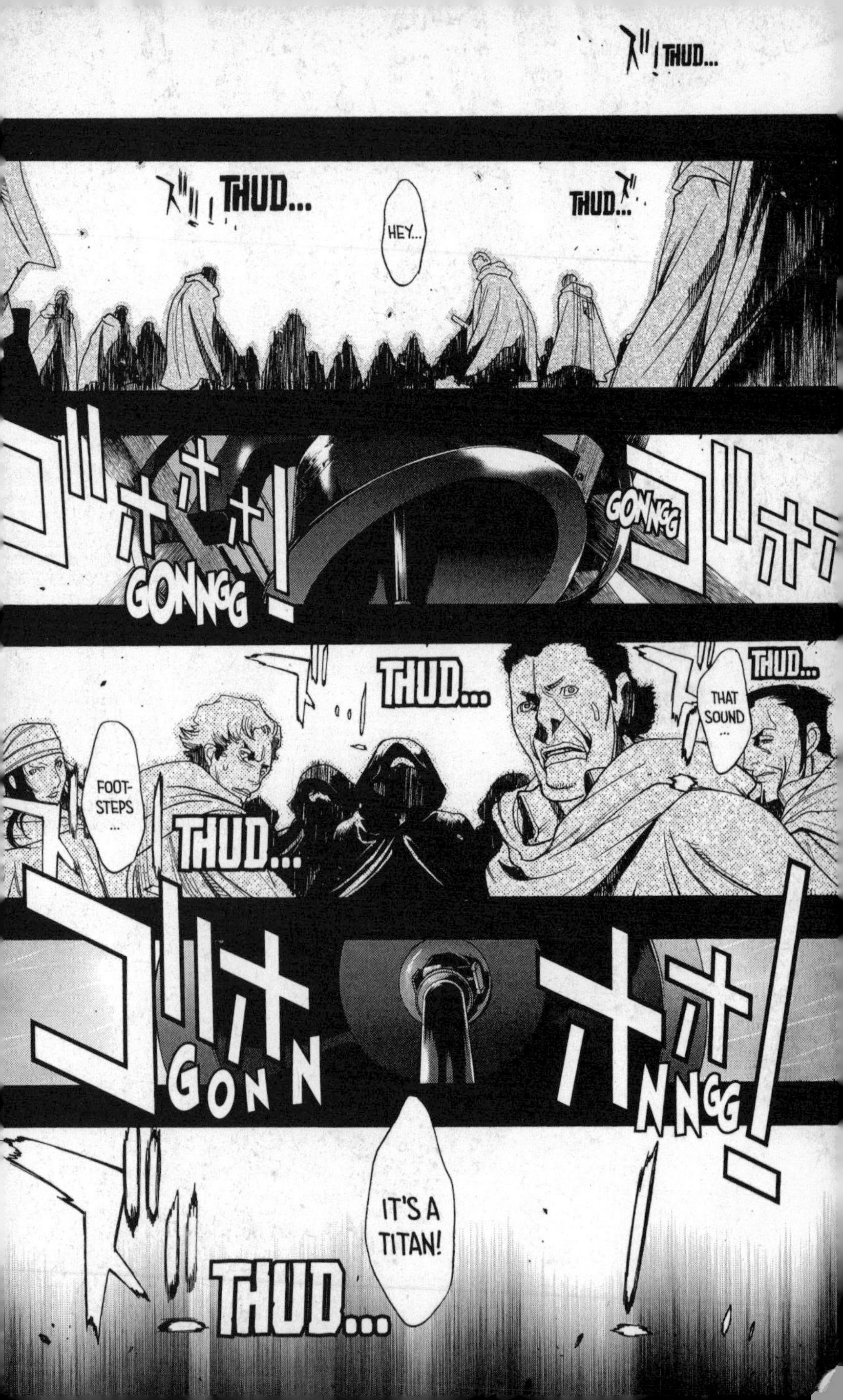
THUD...
THUD...
HEY...
THUD...
GONNGG
GONNGG
THUD...
THAT SOUND...
THUD...
FOOT-STEPS...
THUD...
GONN
NNGG
IT'S A TITAN!
THUD...

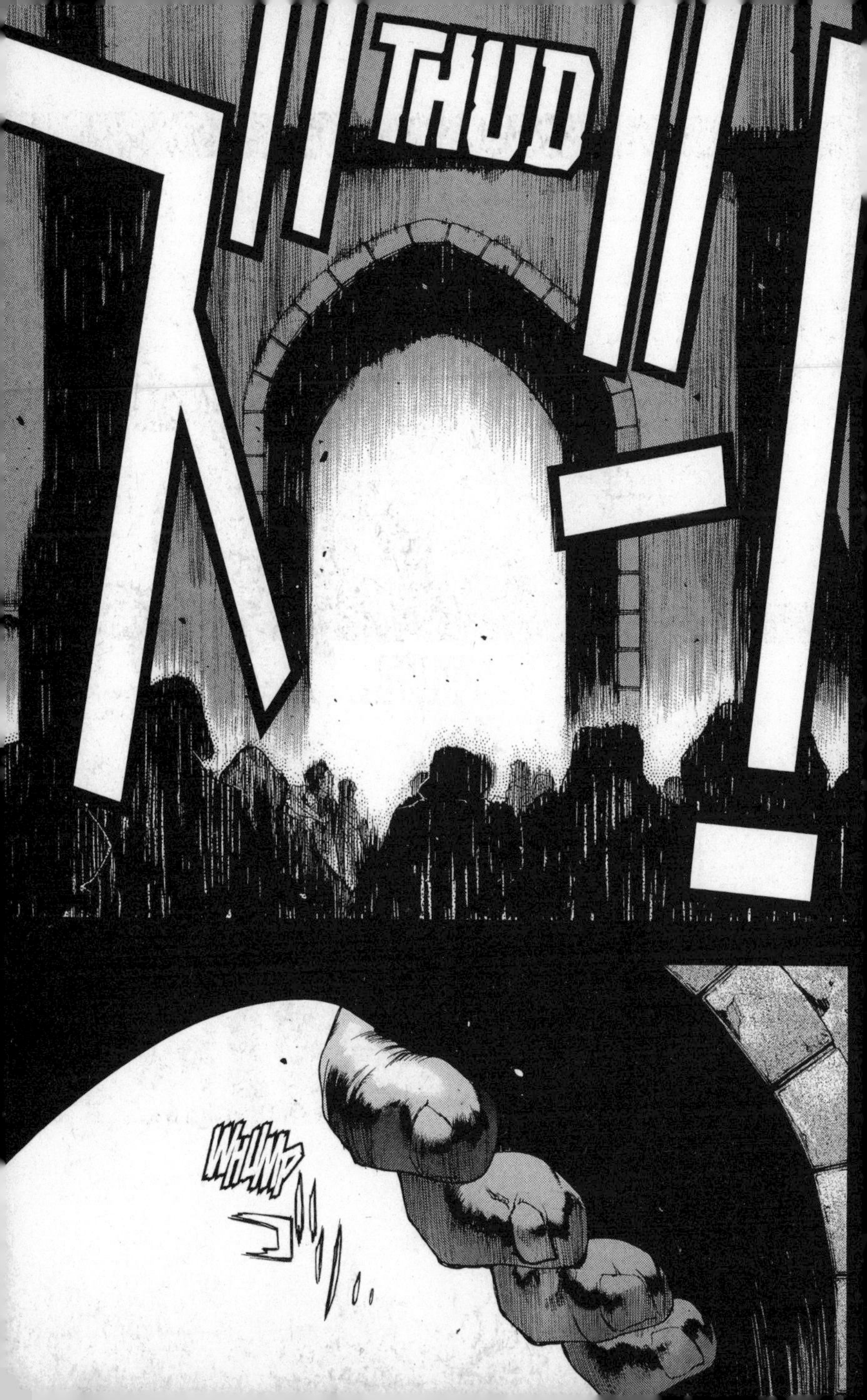
THUD
WHUMP

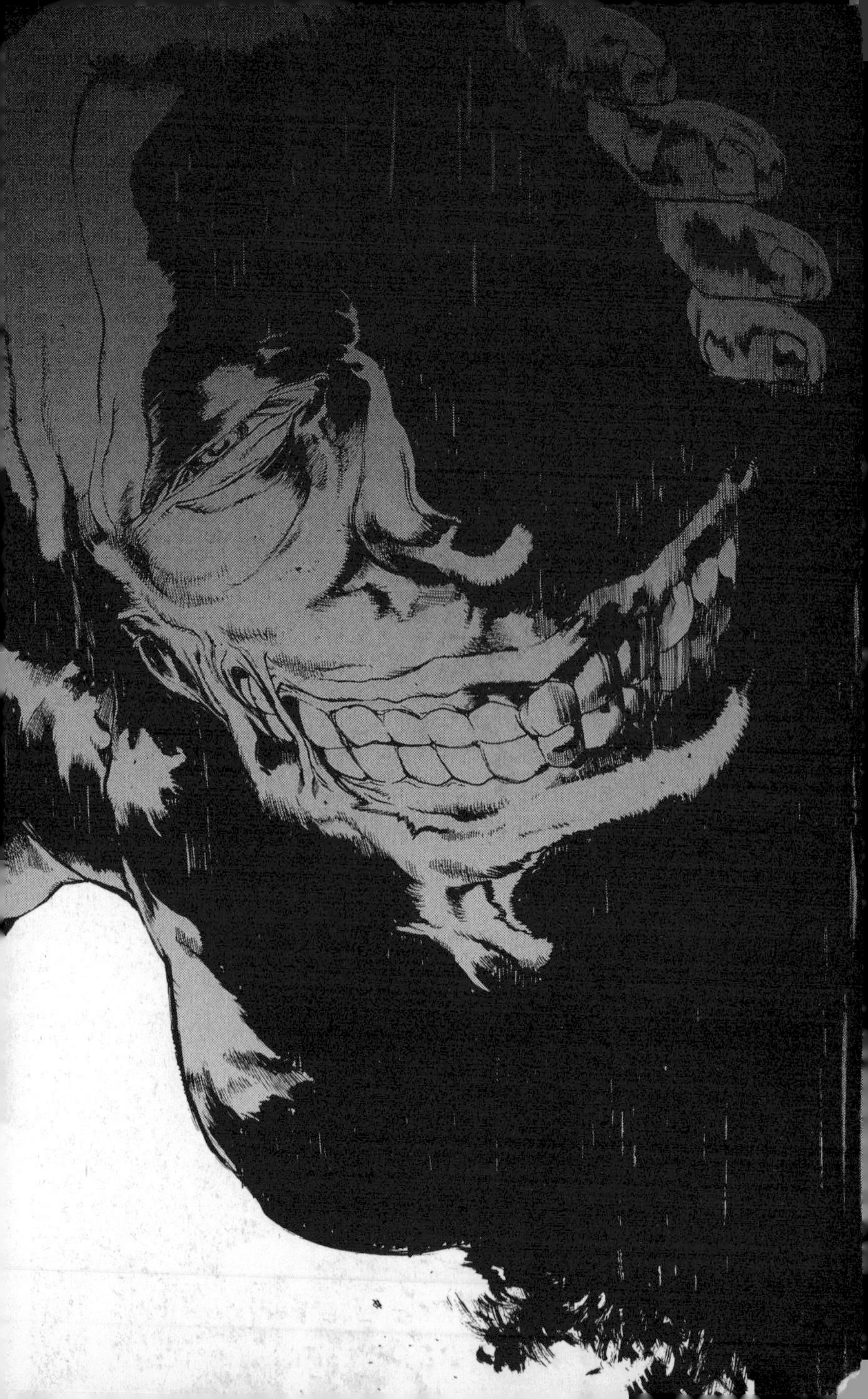

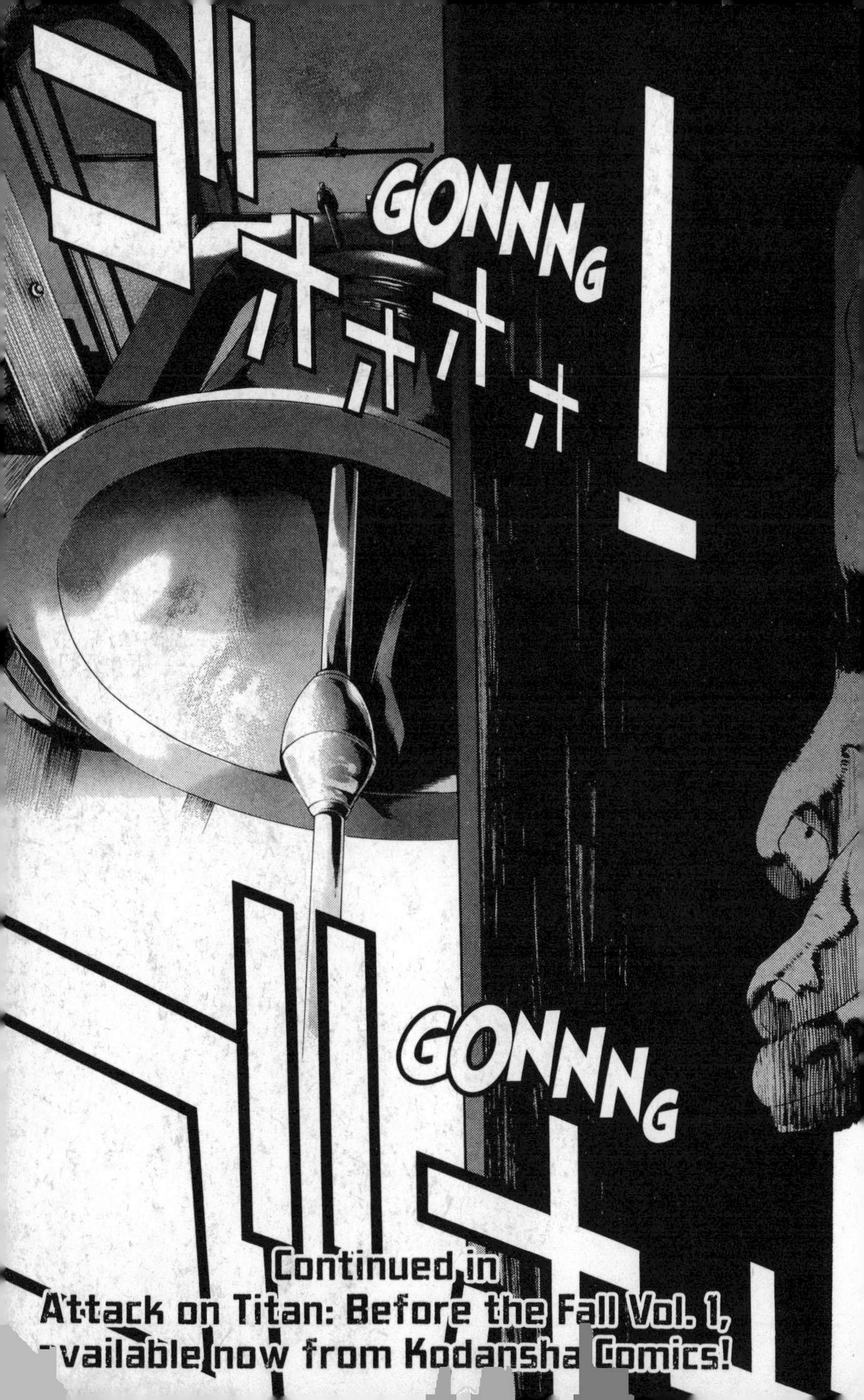
ゴオォオォー
GONNNG
GONNNG

Continued in
Attack on Titan: Before the Fall Vol. 1,
available now from Kodansha Comics!

Attack on Titan: Junior High volume 1 is a work of fiction. Names, characters, places, and incidents are the products of the author's imagination or are used fictitiously. Any resemblance to actual events, locales, or persons, living or dead, is entirely coincidental.

A Kodansha Comics Trade Paperback Original

Published in the United States by Kodansha Comics, an imprint of Kodansha USA Publishing, LLC, New York.

Publication rights for this English edition arranged through Kodansha Ltd, Tokyo.

First published in Japan in 2013 by Kodansha Ltd., Tokyo as *Shingeki! Kyojin chûgakkô*, volumes 1 and 2.

ISBN 978-1-61262-916-2

Original cover design by Takashi Shimoyama/Saya Takagi (Red Rooster)

Printed in the United States of America.

www.kodanshacomics.com

9 8 7 6 5 4 3 2
Translation: William Flanagan
Lettering: AndWorld Design
Editing: Ben Applegate